Explorations in
CORE MATH

for Common Core
Geometry

HOUGHTON MIFFLIN HARCOURT

Contents

COMMON
CORE

© Houghton Mifflin Harcourt Publishing Company

▶ Chapter 3 Parallel and Perpendicular Lines

▶ Chapter 4 Triangle Congruence

▶ Chapter 5 Properties and Attributes of Triangles

Chapter 9 Extending Transformational Geometry

Chapter 10 Extending Perimeter, Circumference, and Area

Chapter 11 Spatial Reasoning

▶ Chapter 12 Circles

▶ Chapter 13 Probability

Learning the Standards for Mathematical Practice

The Common Core State Standards include eight Standards for Mathematical Practice. Here's how *Explorations in Core Math Geometry* helps students learn those standards as they master the Standards for Mathematical Content.

① Make sense of problems and persevere in solving them.

In *Explorations in Core Math Geometry*, students will work through Explores and Examples that present a solution pathway for them to follow. They will be asked questions along the way so that they gain an understanding of the solution process, and then they will apply what they've learned in the Practice for the lesson.

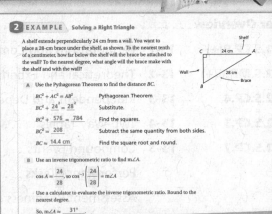

2 EXAMPLE Solving a Right Triangle

A shelf extends perpendicularly 24 cm from a wall. You want to place a 28-cm brace under the shelf, as shown. To the nearest tenth of a centimeter, how far below the shelf will the brace be attached to the wall? To the nearest degree, what angle will the brace make with the shelf and with the wall?

A Use the Pythagorean Theorem to find the distance BC.

$BC^2 + AC^2 = AB^2$ Pythagorean Theorem
$BC^2 + \underline{24}^2 = \underline{28}^2$ Substitute.
$BC^2 + \underline{576} = \underline{784}$ Find the squares.
$BC^2 = \underline{208}$ Subtract the same quantity from both sides.
$BC \approx \underline{14.4 \text{ cm}}$ Find the square root and round.

B Use an inverse trigonometric ratio to find $m\angle A$.

$\cos A = \dfrac{24}{28}$, so $\cos^{-1}\left(\dfrac{24}{28}\right) = m\angle A$

Use a calculator to evaluate the inverse trigonometric ratio. Round to the nearest degree.

So, $m\angle A \approx \underline{31}°$.

② Reason abstractly and quantitatively.

When students solve a real-world problem in *Explorations in Core Math Geometry*, they will learn to represent the situation symbolically by translating the problem into a mathematical expression or equation. Students will use these mathematical models to solve the problem and then state their answers in terms of the problem context. They will reflect on the solution process in order to check their answers for reasonableness and to draw conclusions.

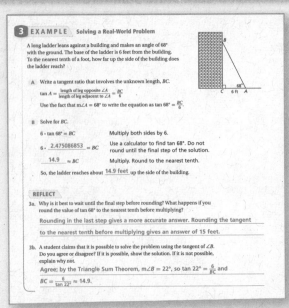

3 EXAMPLE Solving a Real-World Problem

A long ladder leans against a building and makes an angle of 68° with the ground. The base of the ladder is 6 feet from the building. To the nearest tenth of a foot, how far up the side of the building does the ladder reach?

A Write a tangent ratio that involves the unknown length, BC.

$\tan A = \dfrac{\text{length of leg opposite } \angle A}{\text{length of leg adjacent to } \angle A} = \dfrac{BC}{6}$

Use the fact that $m\angle A = 68°$ to write the equation as $\tan 68° = \dfrac{BC}{6}$.

B Solve for BC.

$6 \cdot \tan 68° = BC$ Multiply both sides by 6.
$6 \cdot \underline{2.475086853} = BC$ Use a calculator to find tan 68°. Do not round until the final step of the solution.
$\underline{14.9} \approx BC$ Multiply. Round to the nearest tenth.

So, the ladder reaches about $\underline{14.9 \text{ feet}}$ up the side of the building.

REFLECT

3a. Why is it best to wait until the final step before rounding? What happens if you round the value of tan 68° to the nearest tenth before multiplying?

Rounding in the last step gives a more accurate answer. Rounding the tangent

to the nearest tenth before multiplying gives an answer of 15 feet.

3b. A student claims that it is possible to solve the problem using the tangent of $\angle B$. Do you agree or disagree? If it is possible, show the solution. If it is not possible, explain why not.

Agree; by the Triangle Sum Theorem, $m\angle B = 22°$, so $\tan 22° = \dfrac{6}{BC}$ and

$BC = \dfrac{6}{\tan 22°} \approx 14.9$.

③ Construct viable arguments and critique the reasoning of others.

Throughout *Explorations in Core Math Geometry*, students will be asked to make conjectures, construct a mathematical argument, explain their reasoning, and justify their conclusions. Reflect questions offer opportunities for cooperative learning and class discussion. Students will have additional opportunities to critique reasoning in Error Analysis problems.

REFLECT

2a. Given that $\triangle PQR \cong \triangle STU$, $PQ = 2.7$ ft, and $PR = 3.4$ ft, is it possible to determine the length of $\overline{TU}$? If so, find the length. If not, explain why not.

No; the side of $\triangle PQR$ that corresponds to $\overline{TU}$ is $\overline{QR}$, and the length of this side is not known.

2b. A student claims that any two congruent triangles must have the same perimeter. Do you agree or disagree? Why?

Agree; since the corresponding sides are congruent, the sum of the side lengths (perimeter) must be the same for both triangles.

3. Error Analysis A student who is 72 inches tall wants to find the height of a flagpole. He measures the length of the flagpole's shadow and the length of his own shadow at the same time of day, as shown in his sketch below. Explain the error in the student's work.

> The triangles are similar by the AA Similarity Criterion, so corresponding sides are proportional.
> $\frac{x}{72} = \frac{48}{128}$
> $x = 72 \cdot \frac{48}{128}$, so $x = 27$ in.

The proportion is incorrect because the ratios do not compare the triangles in the same order. It should be $\frac{x}{72} = \frac{128}{48}$ and $x = 192$ in.

④ Model with mathematics.

Explorations in Core Math Geometry presents problems in a variety of contexts such as science, business, and everyday life. Students will use models such as equations, tables, diagrams, and graphs to represent the information in the problem and to solve the problem. Then they will interpret their results in context.

④ EXAMPLE Solving a Real-World Problem

Police want to set up a camera to identify drivers who run the red light at point C on Mason Street. The camera must be mounted on a fence that intersects Mason Street at a $40°$ angle, as shown, and the camera should ideally be 120 feet from point C. What points along the fence, if any, are suitable locations for the camera?

A Because the side opposite $\angle A$ is shorter than $\overline{AC}$, it may be possible to form two triangles. Use the Law of Sines to find possible values for $m\angle B$.

$\frac{\sin A}{a} = \frac{\sin B}{b}$ Law of Sines

$\frac{\sin 40°}{120} = \frac{\sin B}{170}$ Substitute.

$\frac{170 \sin 40°}{120} = \sin B$ Solve for sin B.

$0.9106 \approx \sin B$ Use a calculator. Round to 4 decimal places.

There is an acute angle and an obtuse angle that have this value as their sine. To find the acute angle, use a calculator and round to the nearest tenth.

$\sin^{-1}(0.9106) \approx 65.6°$

To find the obtuse angle, note that $\angle 1$ and $\angle 2$ have the same sine, $\frac{y}{\sqrt{x^2+y^2}}$, and notice that these angles are supplementary. Thus, the obtuse angle is supplementary to the acute angle you found above.

So, $m\angle B \approx 65.6°$ or $114.4°$.

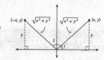

REFLECT

4a. How you can check your answers?
Possible answer: Use the calculated values to check that $\frac{\sin A}{a} = \frac{\sin B}{b} = \frac{\sin C}{c}$.

4b. Suppose the camera needs to be *at most* 120 feet from point C. In this case, where should the camera be mounted along the fence?
The camera should be mounted more than 80.7 ft from point A but less than 179.8 ft from point A.

4c. What is the minimum distance at which the camera can be located from point C if it is to be mounted on the fence? Explain your answer.
About 109.3 ft. The minimum distance occurs when $\angle B$ is a right angle. In this case, $\sin 40° = \frac{CB}{170}$, so $CB \approx 109.3$.

⑤ Use appropriate tools strategically.

Students will use a variety of tools in *Explorations in Core Math Geometry*, including manipulatives, paper and pencil, and technology. They might use manipulatives to develop concepts, paper and pencil to practice skills, and technology (such as graphing calculators, spreadsheets, or geometry software) to investigate more complicated mathematical ideas.

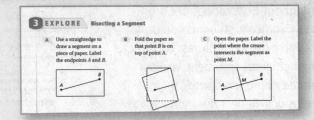

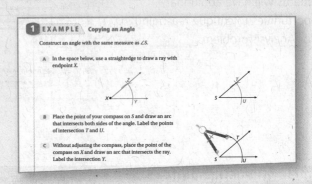

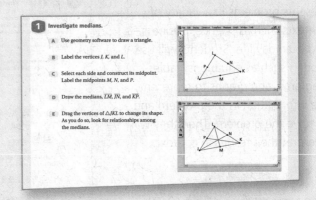

⑥ Attend to precision.

Precision refers not only to the correctness of arithmetic calculations, algebraic manipulations, and geometric reasoning but also to the proper use of mathematical language, symbols, and units to communicate mathematical ideas. Throughout *Explorations in Core Math Geometry* students will demonstrate their skills in these areas when they are asked to calculate, describe, show, explain, prove, and predict.

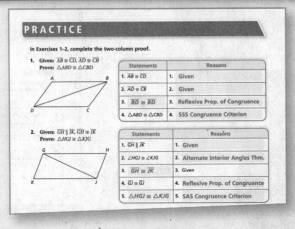

⑦ Look for and make use of structure.

In *Explorations in Core Math Geometry*, students will look for patterns or regularity in mathematical structures such as expressions, equations, geometric figures, and graphs. Becoming familiar with underlying structures will help students build their understanding of more complicated mathematical ideas.

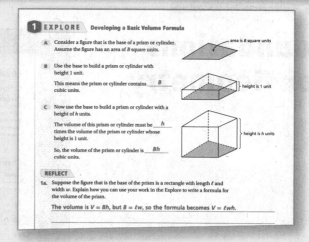

⑧ Look for and express regularity in repeated reasoning.

In *Explorations in Core Math Geometry*, students will have the opportunity to explore and reflect on mathematical processes in order to come up with general methods for performing calculations and solving problems.

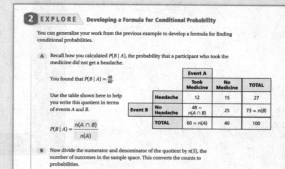

Foundations for Geometry

Foundations for Geometry

Chapter Focus

This unit introduces the building blocks of geometry. You will learn how definitions of essential geometric terms, such as *line segment* and *angle*, are built from more basic terms. You will also learn to use a variety of tools and techniques to construct geometric figures. Finally, you will begin to transform geometric figures in the coordinate plane and use coordinates to determine midpoints and lengths of edges.

Chapter at a Glance

COMMON CORE

CHAPTER 1

Chapter 1   1   Foundations for Geometry

© Houghton Mifflin Harcourt Publishing Company

COMMON CORE PROFESSIONAL DEVELOPMENT

CC.9-12.G.CO.1

Students begin their study of formal geometry in earnest in this chapter. Much of the content is known as Euclidean geometry as it is based on the work of the ancient Greek mathematician Euclid. Euclidean geometry is built on 5 essential axioms upon which an entire system of rules is developed through logical proofs and constructions. Encourage students to research Euclid and his most famous work, the *Elements*. The basic definitions and theorems presented in this chapter are critical to student success because they lay the foundation for the remainder of the theorems and postulates that students will study.

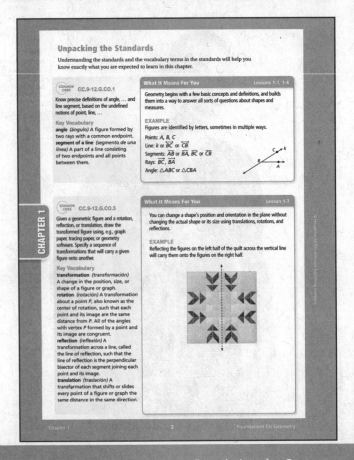

Unpacking the Standards

Understanding the standards and the vocabulary terms in the standards will help you know exactly what you are expected to learn in this chapter.

COMMON CORE   **CC.9-12.G.CO.1**

Know precise definitions of angle, ... and line segment, based on the undefined notions of point, line, ...

Key Vocabulary

angle *(ángulo)* A figure formed by two rays with a common endpoint.
segment of a line *(segmento de una línea)* A part of a line consisting of two endpoints and all points between them.

What It Means For You   Lessons 1-1, 1-4

Geometry begins with a few basic concepts and definitions, and builds them into a way to answer all sorts of questions about shapes and measures.

EXAMPLE
Figures are identified by letters, sometimes in multiple ways.

Points: A, B, C
Line: k or $\overleftrightarrow{BC}$ or $\overleftrightarrow{CB}$
Segments: $\overline{AB}$ or $\overline{BA}$, $\overline{BC}$ or $\overline{CB}$
Rays: $\overrightarrow{BC}$, $\overrightarrow{BA}$
Angle: $\triangle ABC$ or $\triangle CBA$

COMMON CORE   **CC.9-12.G.CO.5**

Given a geometric figure and a rotation, reflection, or translation, draw the transformed figure using, e.g., graph paper, tracing paper, or geometry software. Specify a sequence of transformations that will carry a given figure onto another.

Key Vocabulary

transformation *(transformación)* A change in the position, size, or shape of a figure or graph.
rotation *(rotación)* A transformation about a point P, also known as the center of rotation, such that each point and its image are the same distance from P. All of the angles with vertex P formed by a point and its image are congruent.
reflection *(reflexión)* A transformation across a line, called the line of reflection, such that the line of reflection is the perpendicular bisector of each segment joining each point and its image.
translation *(traslación)* A transformation that shifts or slides every point of a figure or graph the same distance in the same direction.

What It Means For You   Lesson 1-7

You can change a shape's position and orientation in the plane without changing the actual shape or its size using translations, rotations, and reflections.

EXAMPLE
Reflecting the figures on the left half of the quilt across the vertical line will carry them onto the figures on the right half.

CHAPTER 1

Chapter 1   2   Foundations for Geometry

© Houghton Mifflin Harcourt Publishing Company

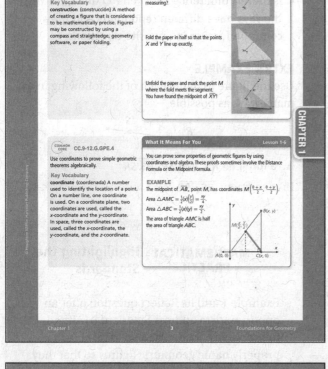

CC.9-12.G.CO.12

Make formal geometric constructions with a variety of tools and methods (compass and straightedge, string, reflective devices, paper folding, dynamic geometric software, etc.).

Key Vocabulary

construction (construcción) A method of creating a figure that is considered to be mathematically precise. Figures may be constructed by using a compass and straightedge, geometry software, or paper folding.

What It Means For You — Lessons 1-2, 1-3

Construction methods give you precise ways to create or copy geometric figures without having to measure and/or estimate.

EXAMPLE

How can you divide $\overline{XY}$ in half without measuring?

Fold the paper in half so that the points X and Y line up exactly.

Unfold the paper and mark the point M where the fold meets the segment. You have found the midpoint of $\overline{XY}$!

CC.9-12.G.GPE.4

Use coordinates to prove simple geometric theorems algebraically.

Key Vocabulary

coordinate (coordenada) A number used to identify the location of a point. On a number line, one coordinate is used. On a coordinate plane, two coordinates are used, called the x-coordinate and the y-coordinate. In space, three coordinates are used, called the x-coordinate, the y-coordinate, and the z-coordinate.

What It Means For You — Lesson 1-6

You can prove some properties of geometric figures by using coordinates and algebra. These proofs sometimes involve the Distance Formula or the Midpoint Formula.

EXAMPLE

The midpoint of $\overline{AB}$, point M, has coordinates $M\left(\frac{0+x}{2}, \frac{0+y}{2}\right)$.

Area $\triangle AMC = \frac{1}{2}(x)\left(\frac{y}{2}\right) = \frac{xy}{4}$.

Area $\triangle ABC = \frac{1}{2}(x)(y) = \frac{xy}{2}$.

The area of triangle AMC is half the area of triangle ABC.

COMMON CORE PROFESSIONAL DEVELOPMENT

CC.9-12.G.CO.12
CC.9-12.G.GPE.4

Constructions and coordinate proofs give students two excellent tools to demonstrate and prove geometric concepts. Both of these methods can help students develop a strong concrete understanding of basic geometric principles before moving into formal, logical proofs. By constructing figures, students can "see for themselves" that what they are learning is true and can be applied in real-world contexts. Similarly, coordinate proofs allow students to apply previously learned algebra skills to develop and understand new concepts.

CHAPTER 1

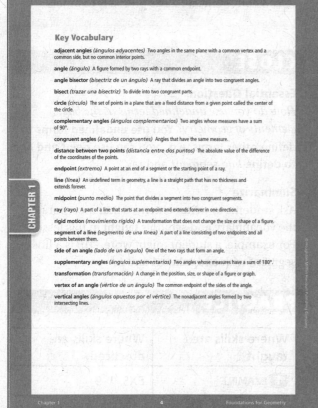

Key Vocabulary

adjacent angles (ángulos adyacentes) Two angles in the same plane with a common vertex and a common side, but no common interior points.

angle (ángulo) A figure formed by two rays with a common endpoint.

angle bisector (bisectriz de un ángulo) A ray that divides an angle into two congruent angles.

bisect (trazar una bisectriz) To divide into two congruent parts.

circle (círculo) The set of points in a plane that are a fixed distance from a given point called the center of the circle.

complementary angles (ángulos complementarios) Two angles whose measures have a sum of 90°.

congruent angles (ángulos congruentes) Angles that have the same measure.

distance between two points (distancia entre dos puntos) The absolute value of the difference of the coordinates of the points.

endpoint (extremo) A point at an end of a segment or the starting point of a ray.

line (línea) An undefined term in geometry, a line is a straight path that has no thickness and extends forever.

midpoint (punto medio) The point that divides a segment into two congruent segments.

ray (rayo) A part of a line that starts at an endpoint and extends forever in one direction.

rigid motion (movimiento rígido) A transformation that does not change the size or shape of a figure.

segment of a line (segmento de una línea) A part of a line consisting of two endpoints and all points between them.

side of an angle (lado de un ángulo) One of the two rays that form an angle.

supplementary angles (ángulos suplementarios) Two angles whose measures have a sum of 180°.

transformation (transformación) A change in the position, size, or shape of a figure or graph.

vertex of an angle (vértice de un ángulo) The common endpoint of the sides of the angle.

vertical angles (ángulos opuestos por el vértice) The nonadjacent angles formed by two intersecting lines.

CHAPTER 1

Understanding Points, Lines, and Planes
Going Deeper

Essential question: *How do you use undefined terms as the basic elements of geometry?*

COMMON **Standards for**
CORE **Mathematical Content**

CC.9-12.G.CO.1 Know precise definitions of ... line segment, based on the undefined notions of point, line, ...

Vocabulary
point, line, plane, line segment, ray, endpoint

Prerequisites
None

Math Background
Students have worked with points, lines, angles, triangles, and other geometric figures since the elementary grades. This course revisits many ideas that may be familiar to students, but does so in a systematic way in order to build a deductive system. The first step in this process is to decide which terms will be assumed to be understood (undefined terms) and to give definitions of basic vocabulary words using these undefined terms.

INTRODUCE

You may wish to begin by having students look up an adjective in the dictionary, such as *furious*. The definition of *furious* may include the word *angry*. Have students look up the word *angry*. Its definition may include the word *enraged*. Have students look up the word *enraged*. Its definition may include the word *furious*. This sort of circular logic can help students understand that in mathematics it is not possible to define every word in terms of more basic words. Certain words must be taken as undefined terms.

TEACH

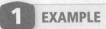

Questioning Strategies
- What are the endpoints of the segment? *P* and *Q*
- Is there a difference between $\overrightarrow{PQ}$ and $\overrightarrow{QP}$? No; they name the same line.

- Is there a difference between $\overrightarrow{PQ}$ and $\overrightarrow{QP}$? Yes; the rays have different endpoints and they continue forever in opposite directions.

EXTRA EXAMPLE
Use the figure to name each of the following in as many ways as possible.

A. a line   line *RS*, line *SR*, $\overleftrightarrow{RS}$ $\overleftrightarrow{SR}$
B. a segment $\overline{RS}$, $\overline{SR}$

MATHEMATICAL PRACTICE   **Highlighting the Standards**

Example 1 and its Reflect question offer an opportunity to address Standard 8 (Attend to precision). Students need to be able to properly name geometric figures so that they can communicate ideas precisely to others.

CLOSE

Essential Question
How do you use undefined terms as the basic elements of geometry? You use undefined terms to define other terms, e.g., you can use *point* and *line* to define *line segment* and *ray*.

Summarize
Ask students to write sentences that incorporate the vocabulary and symbols taught in this lesson. For example, a student might write, "$\overline{AB}$ is a line segment with endpoints *A* and *B*."

PRACTICE

Where skills are taught	Where skills are practiced
1 EXAMPLE	EXS. 1–9

© Houghton Mifflin Harcourt Publishing Company

Name_____ Class_____ Date_____

1-1

Understanding Points, Lines, and Planes
Going Deeper

Video Tutor

Essential question: *How do you use undefined terms as the basic elements of geometry?*

In geometry, the terms *point*, *line*, and *plane* are undefined terms. Although these terms do not have formal definitions, the table shows how mathematicians use these words.

Term	Geometric Figure	Ways to Reference the Figure
A **point** is a specific location. It has no dimension and is represented by a dot.	• *P*	Point *P*
A **line** is a connected straight path. It has no thickness and it continues forever in both directions.	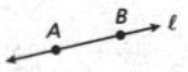 *A B ℓ*	Line ℓ, line *AB*, line *BA*, $\overleftrightarrow{AB}$, or $\overleftrightarrow{BA}$
A **plane** is a flat surface that has no thickness and extends forever.	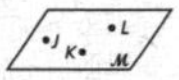 *J L K M*	A script capital letter, or three points on the plane that do not all lie on a line. plane M, or plane *JKL*

As shown in the following table, other terms can be defined using the above terms as building blocks.

Term	Geometric Figure	Ways to Reference the Figure
A **line segment** (or *segment*) is a portion of a line consisting of two points and all points between them.	 *C D*	Line segment *CD*, line segment *DC*, $\overline{CD}$, or $\overline{DC}$
A **ray** is a portion of a line that starts at a point and continues forever in one direction.	 *G H*	Ray *GH* or $\overrightarrow{GH}$

An **endpoint** is a point at either end of a line segment or the starting point of a ray. In the above examples, *C* and *D* are the endpoints of $\overline{CD}$, and point *G* is the endpoint of $\overrightarrow{GH}$.

CC 9-12.G.CO.1

1 EXAMPLE Naming Geometric Figures

Use the figure at the right in Parts A and B.

P Q m

A One name for the line shown in the figure is $\overleftrightarrow{PQ}$.

Other names for $\overleftrightarrow{PQ}$ are **line m, line PQ, line QP, and $\overleftrightarrow{QP}$.**

B $\overline{PQ}$ is a line segment because it is a portion of a line consisting of two points and all the points between them.

Other names for $\overline{PQ}$ are **line segment PQ, line segment QP, and $\overline{QP}$.**

© Houghton Mifflin Harcourt Publishing Company

REFLECT

1a. Why does the order in which you name the points when you name a ray matter? Use points *P* and *Q* in your answer.

$\overrightarrow{PQ}$ and $\overrightarrow{QP}$ are not the same ray. $\overrightarrow{PQ}$ has endpoint P, but $\overrightarrow{QP}$ has endpoint

Q. The rays point in opposite directions.

PRACTICE

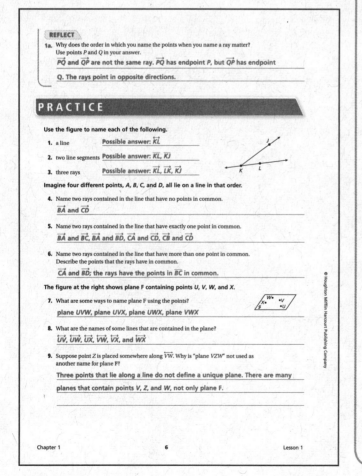

Use the figure to name each of the following.

1. a line   Possible answer: $\overleftrightarrow{KL}$

2. two line segments   Possible answer: $\overline{KL}$, $\overline{KJ}$

3. three rays   Possible answer: $\overrightarrow{KL}$, $\overrightarrow{LK}$, $\overrightarrow{KJ}$

Imagine four different points, *A, B, C,* and *D,* all lie on a line in that order.

4. Name two rays contained in the line that have no points in common.

$\overrightarrow{BA}$ and $\overrightarrow{CD}$

5. Name two rays contained in the line that have exactly one point in common.

$\overrightarrow{BA}$ and $\overrightarrow{BC}$, $\overrightarrow{BA}$ and $\overrightarrow{BD}$, $\overrightarrow{CA}$ and $\overrightarrow{CD}$, $\overrightarrow{CB}$ and $\overrightarrow{CD}$

6. Name two rays contained in the line that have more than one point in common. Describe the points that the rays have in common.

$\overrightarrow{CA}$ and $\overrightarrow{BD}$; the rays have the points in $\overline{BC}$ in common.

The figure at the right shows plane F containing points *U, V, W,* and *X*.

W V X U

7. What are some ways to name plane F using the points?

plane *UVW*, plane *UVX*, plane *UWX*, plane *VWX*

8. What are the names of some lines that are contained in the plane?

$\overleftrightarrow{UV}$, $\overleftrightarrow{UW}$, $\overleftrightarrow{UX}$, $\overleftrightarrow{VW}$, $\overleftrightarrow{VX}$, and $\overleftrightarrow{WX}$

9. Suppose point *Z* is placed somewhere along $\overleftrightarrow{VW}$. Why is "plane *VZW*" not used as another name for plane F?

Three points that lie along a line do not define a unique plane. There are many

planes that contain points V, Z, and W, not only plane F.

© Houghton Mifflin Harcourt Publishing Company

Assign these pages to help your students practice
and apply important lesson concepts. For
additional exercises, see the Student Edition.

Answers

Additional Practice

1. Possible answers: plane *BCD*; plane *BED*

2. $\overline{BD}$, $\overline{BC}$, $\overline{BE}$, or $\overline{CE}$

3. Possible answers: $\overleftrightarrow{EC}$; $\overleftrightarrow{BC}$; $\overleftrightarrow{BE}$

4. Points *B*, *C*, and *E*

5. Possible answers: points *B*, *C*, and *D* or point *B*, *E*, and *D*

6. point *B*   7. $\overrightarrow{BC}$ and $\overrightarrow{BE}$

8. points *X*, *Y*, and *Z*   9. point *Z*

10. $\overleftrightarrow{XZ}$ and $\overleftrightarrow{YZ}$ 11. $\overleftrightarrow{XY}$

12. 
L———————M

13.  ray
L———————M———→

14. 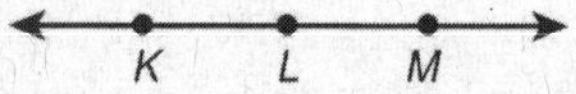 ←———K———L———M———→

Problem Solving

1. Point *D*; E. Travis St. and Navarro St.

2. Point *A* does not lie on the line that contains $\overline{BE}$.

3. Sample answer: $\overleftrightarrow{UV}$ intersects plane P.

4. 0 times; if two lines intersect, then they intersect in exactly one point.

5. B   6. J

7. C

© Houghton Mifflin Harcourt Publishing Company

Name_____ Class_____ Date_____ **1-1**

Additional Practice

Use the figure for Exercises 1–7.

1. Name a plane. _____

2. Name a segment. _____

3. Name a line. _____

4. Name three collinear points.

_____

5. Name three noncollinear points.

_____

6. Name the intersection of a line and a segment not on the line. _____

7. Name a pair of opposite rays. _____

Use the figure for Exercises 8–11.

8. Name the points that determine plane R.

_____

9. Name the point at which line *m* intersects

plane R. _____

10. Name two lines in plane R that intersect line *m*.

_____

11. Name a line in plane R that does not intersect

line *m*. _____

Draw your answers in the space provided.

Michelle Kwan won a bronze medal in figure skating at the 2002 Salt Lake City Winter Olympic Games.

12. Michelle skates straight ahead from point *L* and stops at point *M*. Draw her path.

13. Michelle skates straight ahead from point *L* and continues through point *M*. Name a figure that represents her path. Draw her path.

14. Michelle and her friend Alexei start back to back at point *L* and skate in opposite directions. Michelle skates through point *M*, and Alexei skates through point *K*. Draw their paths.

Chapter 1   7   Lesson 1

© Houghton Mifflin Harcourt Publishing Company

Problem Solving

Use the map of part of San Antonio for Exercises 1 and 2.

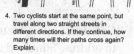

1. Name a point that appears to be collinear with $\overline{EF}$. Which streets intersect at this point?

_____

_____

2. Explain why point *A* is NOT collinear with $\overline{BE}$.

_____

_____

3. Suppose $\overline{UV}$ represents the pencil that you are using to do your homework and plane *P* represents the paper that you are writing on. Describe the relationship between $\overline{UV}$ and plane P.

_____

_____

4. Two cyclists start at the same point, but travel along two straight streets in different directions. If they continue, how many times will their paths cross again? Explain.

_____

_____

Choose the best answer.

5. In a building, planes W, X, and Y represent each of the three floors; planes Q and R represent the front and back of the building; planes S and T represent the sides. Which is a true statement?

  A Planes W and Y intersect in a line.

  B Planes Q and X intersect in a line.

  C Planes W, X, and T intersect in a point.

  D Planes Q, R, and S intersect in a point.

6. Suppose point *G* represents a duck flying over a lake, points *H* and *J* represent two ducks swimming on the lake, and plane L represents the lake. Which is a true statement?

  F There are two lines through *G* and *J*.

  G The line containing *G* and *H* lies in plane L.

  H *G*, *H*, and *J* are noncoplanar.

  J There is exactly one plane containing points *G*, *H*, and *J*.

Use the figure for Exercise 7.

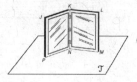

7. A frame holding two pictures sits on a table. Which is NOT a true statement?

  A $\overline{PN}$ and $\overline{NM}$ lie in plane T.

  B $\overline{PN}$ and $\overline{NM}$ intersect in a point.

  C $\overline{LM}$ and N intersect in a line.

  D P and $\overline{NM}$ are coplanar.

Chapter 1   8   Lesson 1

© Houghton Mifflin Harcourt Publishing Company

Measuring and Constructing Segments
Going Deeper

Essential question: *What tools and methods can you use to copy a segment, bisect a segment, and construct a circle?*

COMMON CORE Standards for Mathematical Content

CC.9-12.G.CO.1 Know precise definitions of ... circle, ... and line segment, based on the undefined notions of point, line, distance along a line, ...

CC.9-12.G.CO.12 Make formal geometric constructions with a variety of tools and methods (compass and straightedge, string, reflective devices, paper folding, dynamic geometric software, etc.).

Vocabulary

distance along a line   circle

length   center

midpoint   radius

bisect

Prerequisites

Basic geometric terms

Math Background

Classical constructions in geometry involve the use of a straightedge and compass only. The straightedge allows you to draw straight lines. The compass allows you to draw circular arcs, with all points on an arc the same distance from the point of the compass. Although neither of these tools allows you to take measurements as a ruler would, you can still transfer lengths by opening the compass to match a given length. This allows you to copy a segment, construct a circle with a given radius, and even construct triangles with given side lengths.

INTRODUCE

You may want to begin by challenging students to copy a given line segment using only the edge of a book, a piece of string, and a pencil. Students should realize that they can use the book's edge to draw a line segment that is too long, and then use the string to "measure" the length of the given segment and transfer that length to the new segment. This is essentially what happens when you use a straightedge in place of the book's edge and a compass in place of the string.

TEACH

1 EXAMPLE

Questioning Strategies

• Does it matter if endpoint *C* is on the right side of the line segment that you construct? Why or why not? **It does not matter, as long as $\overline{CD}$ has the same length as $\overline{AB}$.**

• How can you check your construction with a ruler? **Measure $\overline{AB}$ and $\overline{CD}$ to check that they have the same length.**

EXTRA EXAMPLE

Construct a segment with the same length as $\overline{JK}$.

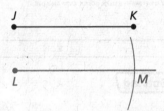

MATHEMATICAL PRACTICE
Highlighting the Standards

Constructions offer an excellent opportunity to address Standard 6 (Attend to precision). In this lesson, students use a compass and straightedge to copy a segment. In order to reproduce the segment accurately, students must work carefully to set the opening of their compass to the correct length. They must also follow directions attentively as they label the segment they construct. Have students work with a partner to check each other's attention to detail.

Name_____ Class_____ Date_____

1-2

Measuring and Constructing Segments
Going Deeper

Essential question: *What tools and methods can you use to copy a segment, bisect a segment, and construct a circle?*

The **distance along a line** is undefined until a unit distance, such as 1 inch or 1 centimeter, is chosen. By placing a ruler alongside the line, you can associate a number from the ruler with each of two points on the line and then take the absolute value of the difference of the numbers to find the distance between the points. This distance is the **length** of the segment determined by the points.

In the figure, the length of $\overline{RS}$, written RS, is the distance between R and S. $RS = |4-1| = |3| = 3$ cm.

A *construction* is a geometric drawing that uses only a compass and a straightedge. You can construct a line segment whose length is equal to that of a given segment by using only these tools.

CC.9-12.G.CO.12

1 EXAMPLE   Copying a Segment

Construct a segment with the same length as $\overline{AB}$.

A   In the space below, draw a line segment that is longer than $\overline{AB}$. Choose an endpoint of the segment and label it C.

B   Set the opening of your compass to the distance AB, as shown.

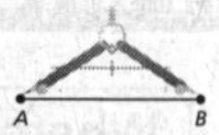

C   Place the point of the compass on C. Make a small arc that intersects your line segment. Label the point D where the arc intersects the segment. $\overline{CD}$ is the required line segment.

REFLECT

1a. Why does this construction result in a line segment with the same length as $\overline{AB}$?

The compass opening matches the length of $\overline{AB}$ and reproduces this length on

the new segment.

1b. What must you assume about the compass for this construction to work?

The size of the compass opening does not change when the compass is moved

to a new location.

Chapter 1   9   Lesson 2

The **midpoint** of a line segment is the point that divides the segment into two segments that have the same length. The midpoint is said to **bisect** the segment. In the figure, the tick marks show that $PM = MQ$. Therefore, M is the midpoint of $\overline{PQ}$ and M bisects $\overline{PQ}$.

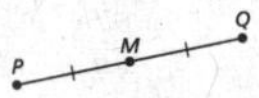

CC.9-12.G.CO.12

2 EXPLORE   Bisecting a Segment

A   Use a straightedge to draw a segment on a piece of paper. Label the endpoints A and B.

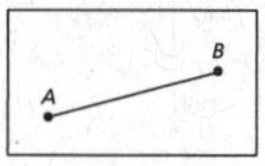

B   Fold the paper so that point B is on top of point A.

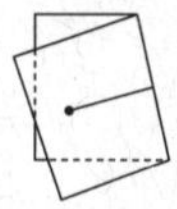

C   Open the paper. Label the point where the crease intersects the segment as point M.

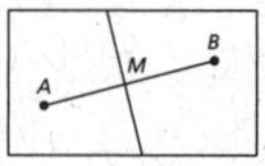

REFLECT

2a. How can you use a ruler to check the construction?

Measure the length of $\overline{AM}$ and $\overline{MB}$ to check that $AM = MB$.

2b. Fold your paper along the segment. What happens to the crease that bisects the segment? What can you say about the four angles formed at point M?

The crease that bisects the segment folds onto itself.

The four angles formed at point M appear to be right angles.

2c. Explain how you could use paper folding to divide a line segment into four segments of equal length.

Construct the midpoint of the segment. Then construct the midpoint of each

of the new segments.

Chapter 1   10   Lesson 2

Materials: straightedge, tracing paper (optional)

Questioning Strategies

- Why do you fold the paper so that point *B* is on top of point *A*? **Matching the endpoints in this way ensures that the fold divides the segment in half.**

Teaching Strategies

If possible, have students use tracing paper for this activity. This will make it easier to see the original segment once the paper is folded. Restaurant supply stores sell small squares of paper that are used to separate hamburger patties. These thin sheets of "patty paper" are inexpensive and work especially well in all paper-folding investigations.

3 EXAMPLE

Questioning Strategies

- Why do you set the opening of the compass to the distance *AB*? **This ensures that the radius of the circle equals the length of the segment.**

- How can you name the circle you constructed? **Circle C**

EXTRA EXAMPLE

Construct a circle with radius *MN*.

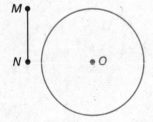

CLOSE

Essential Question

What tools and methods can you use to copy a segment, bisect a segment, and construct a circle? **You can use a compass and straightedge to copy a segment, paper folding to bisect a segment, and a compass to construct a circle.**

Summarize

Have students write step-by-step instructions for copying a segment, bisecting a segment, and constructing a circle with a given radius.

PRACTICE

Where skills are taught	Where skills are practiced
1 EXAMPLE	EXS. 1, 4–7
3 EXAMPLE	EX. 2

Exercise 3: Students use reasoning to consider what it would mean to construct the midpoint of a ray.

© Houghton Mifflin Harcourt Publishing Company

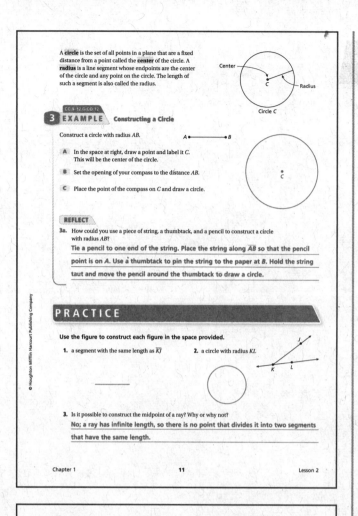

A **circle** is the set of all points in a plane that are a fixed distance from a point called the **center** of the circle. A **radius** is a line segment whose endpoints are the center of the circle and any point on the circle. The length of such a segment is also called the radius.

Center

Radius

Circle C

3 EXAMPLE Constructing a Circle

Construct a circle with radius AB.

A • ——— • B

A In the space at right, draw a point and label it C. This will be the center of the circle.

B Set the opening of your compass to the distance AB.

C Place the point of the compass on C and draw a circle.

• C

REFLECT

3a. How could you use a piece of string, a thumbtack, and a pencil to construct a circle with radius $\overline{AB}$?

Tie a pencil to one end of the string. Place the string along $\overline{AB}$ so that the pencil

point is on A. Use a thumbtack to pin the string to the paper at B. Hold the string

taut and move the pencil around the thumbtack to draw a circle.

PRACTICE

Use the figure to construct each figure in the space provided.

1. a segment with the same length as $\overline{KJ}$

2. a circle with radius KL

J
K   L

3. Is it possible to construct the midpoint of a ray? Why or why not?

No; a ray has infinite length, so there is no point that divides it into two segments

that have the same length.

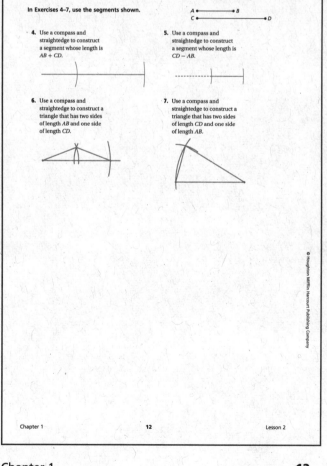

In Exercises 4–7, use the segments shown.

A • ——— • B
C • ——— • D

4. Use a compass and straightedge to construct a segment whose length is AB + CD.

5. Use a compass and straightedge to construct a segment whose length is CD − AB.

6. Use a compass and straightedge to construct a triangle that has two sides of length AB and one side of length CD.

7. Use a compass and straightedge to construct a triangle that has two sides of length CD and one side of length AB.

© Houghton Mifflin Harcourt Publishing Company

ADDITIONAL PRACTICE AND PROBLEM SOLVING

Assign these pages to help your students practice and apply important lesson concepts. For additional exercises, see the Student Edition.

Answers

Additional Practice

1–4. Check students' constructions.

Problem Solving

1. Check students' constructions.
2. Extend $\overline{ST}$ through the center of the circle to a point on the other side of the circle to divide the circle into two half circles. Check students' constructions.
3. Check students' constructions. The length of the third side is less than 2 • *MN*.
4. B
5. J

Additional Practice

For Exercises 1–4, use the segment shown below. Draw your answers in the space provided.

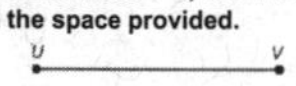

U •————————• V

1. Use a compass and straightedge to construct $\overline{XY}$ with the same length as $\overline{UV}$.

2. Use a compass and straightedge to construct a segment whose length is 2 • UV.

3. Use a compass and straightedge to construct a triangle with sides of length UV.

4. Copy $\overline{UV}$. Then bisect $\overline{UV}$ and label the midpoint M. Construct a circle with center M and radius MU. Construct a second circle with center V and radius MU.

Problem Solving

For Exercises 1–3, use the circle shown.

1. Copy the circle.

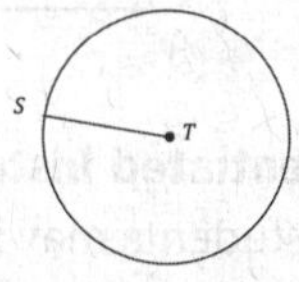

2. Explain how you can use your construction from Exercise 1 to construct two half circles with radius ST. Then construct the two half circles.

_____
_____

3. Construct a segment MN that is the same length as $\overline{ST}$. Then construct a triangle that has exactly two sides with length MN. How does the length of the third side compare with 2 • MN?

Choose the best answer.

4. Julia drew $\overline{PQ}$ on a piece of paper. She folded the paper so that point P was on top of point Q, forming a crease through $\overline{PQ}$. She labeled the intersection of this crease and $\overline{PQ}$ point S. If PQ = 2.4 centimeters, then what is the length of $\overline{QS}$?

   A 0.6 cm   C 2.4 cm
   B 1.2 cm   D 4.8 cm

5. Points J, K, and L lie on the same line, and point K is between J and L. Todd constructs $\overline{SV}$ with the same length as $\overline{JL}$. Then he draws point T on $\overline{SV}$ so that $\overline{ST}$ is the same length as $\overline{JK}$. Which statement is not true?

   F JK = ST
   G ST = SV − TV
   H SV = JK + KL
   J TV = ST + KL

© Houghton Mifflin Harcourt Publishing Company

Measuring and Constructing Angles
Going Deeper

Essential question: *What tools and methods can you use to copy an angle and bisect an angle?*

COMMON CORE Standards for Mathematical Content

CC.9-12.G.CO.1 Know precise definitions of angle, ...

CC.9-12.G.CO.12 Make formal geometric constructions with a variety of tools and methods (compass and straightedge, string, reflective devices, paper folding, dynamic geometric software, etc.).

Vocabulary

angle

vertex

sides

angle bisector

Prerequisites

Basic geometric terms and constructions

Math Background

Compass and straightedge constructions date to ancient Greece. In fact, one of the classic problems of ancient Greek mathematics was the trisection of the angle. That is, using a compass and straightedge is it possible to construct an angle whose measure is one-third that of an arbitrary given angle? It was not until 1837 that this construction was proven to be impossible. On the other hand, it is straightforward to bisect any angle, and students learn this fundamental construction in this lesson.

INTRODUCE

You may want to start with a brief brainstorming session in which students share their prior knowledge about angles. List students' ideas on the board, perhaps in the form of an idea web or other graphic organizer. Prior knowledge may include vocabulary related to angles and/or facts about angles in geometric figures. Tell the class that this lesson introduces two constructions related to angles.

TEACH

1 EXAMPLE

Questioning Strategies

- Do the rays of the angle you construct need to be the same length as the rays of the given angle? Why or why not? No; the measure of the angle is determined only by the size of the opening between the rays, not by the lengths of the rays.

- When you draw the initial arc that intersects the sides of ∠S, does it matter how wide you open the compass? No, as long as the arc intersects both sides of the angle.

EXTRA EXAMPLE

Construct an angle with the same measure as ∠A.

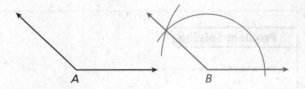

Differentiated Instruction

Some students may have difficulty visualizing two angles that have the same measure, especially if the sides of the angles are shown with rays of different lengths. You want to have students construct their copy of ∠S on a piece of tracing paper. Then students can place the copy on the top of the original angle to check that the measures are the same.

Name_____ Class_____ Date_____

1-3

Measuring and Constructing Angles
Going Deeper

Essential question: *What tools and methods can you use to copy an angle and bisect an angle?*

An **angle** is a figure formed by two rays with the same endpoint. The common endpoint is the **vertex** of the angle. The rays are the **sides** of the angle.

Angles may be measured in degrees (°). There are 360° in a circle, so an angle that measures 1° is $\frac{1}{360}$ of a circle. You write m∠A for the measure of ∠A.

Angles may be classified by their measures.

Acute Angle	Right Angle	Obtuse Angle	Straight Angle
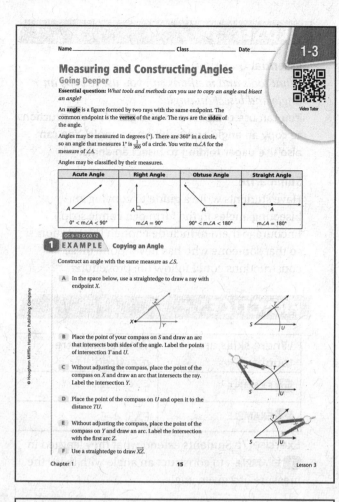			
0° < m∠A < 90°	m∠A = 90°	90° < m∠A < 180°	m∠A = 180°

CC.9-12.G.CO.12

1 EXAMPLE Copying an Angle

Construct an angle with the same measure as ∠S.

A. In the space below, use a straightedge to draw a ray with endpoint X.

B. Place the point of your compass on S and draw an arc that intersects both sides of the angle. Label the points of intersection T and U.

C. Without adjusting the compass, place the point of the compass on X and draw an arc that intersects the ray. Label the intersection Y.

D. Place the point of the compass on U and open it to the distance TU.

E. Without adjusting the compass, place the point of the compass on Y and draw an arc. Label the intersection with the first arc Z.

F. Use a straightedge to draw $\overrightarrow{XZ}$.

Chapter 1   15   Lesson 3

REFLECT

1a. How can you use a protractor to check your construction?

Check that m∠S = m∠X.

1b. If you draw ∠X so that its sides appear to be longer than the sides shown for ∠S, can the two angles have the same measure? Explain.

Yes; the measure of an angle depends only upon the portion of a circle that the angle encompasses, not upon the apparent length of its sides.

An **angle bisector** is a ray that divides an angle into two angles that both have the same measure. In the figure, $\overrightarrow{BD}$ bisects ∠ABC, so m∠ABD = m∠DBC. The arcs in the figure show equal angle measures.

The following example shows how you can use a compass and straightedge to bisect an angle.

CC.9-12.G.CO.12

2 EXAMPLE Constructing the Bisector of an Angle

Construct the bisector of ∠M. Work directly on the angle at right.

A. Place the point of your compass on point M. Draw an arc that intersects both sides of the angle. Label the points of intersection P and Q.

B. Place the point of the compass on P and draw an arc in the interior of the angle.

C. Without adjusting the compass, place the point of the compass on Q and draw an arc that intersects the arc from Step B. Label the intersection of the arcs R.

D. Use a straightedge to draw $\overrightarrow{MR}$.

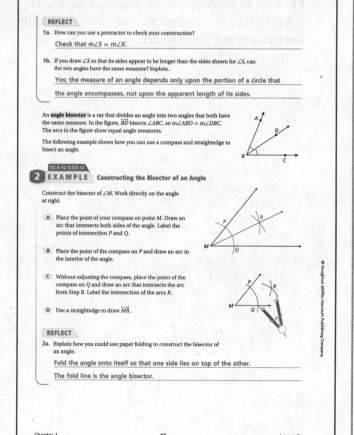

REFLECT

2a. Explain how you could use paper folding to construct the bisector of an angle.

Fold the angle onto itself so that one side lies on top of the other.

The fold line is the angle bisector.

Chapter 1   16   Lesson 3

© Houghton Mifflin Harcourt Publishing Company

Highlighting the Standards

Discuss Standard 5 (Use appropriate tools strategically) as students work on Example 2. In particular, ask students whether they think a compass and straightedge create an angle bisector more or less accurately than paper folding or measuring with a protractor. Have students justify their responses and state any assumptions they may be making about these tools.

2 EXAMPLE

Questioning Strategies

- How can you use a protractor to check your construction? **Measure each of the smaller angles created by the bisector. Their measure should be half that of the original angle.**

- How is the bisector of an angle similar to the bisector of a line segment? **The bisector of an angle divides it into two angles with the same measure; the bisector of a line segment divides it into two line segments with the same length.**

EXTRA EXAMPLE

Construct the bisector of ∠J.

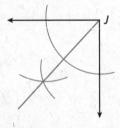

Avoid Common Errors

Remind students not to change the compass setting when they draw the intersecting arcs from points P and Q. In order to help students see why this is important, you may want to have them do a construction in which they change the compass setting between arcs. Students will see that the resulting ray does not bisect the angle.

CLOSE

Essential Question

What tools and methods can you use to copy an angle and bisect an angle?
You can use compass-and-straightedge constructions to copy an angle and to bisect an angle. You can also use paper folding to bisect an angle.

Summarize

Have students write a guide to copying and bisecting angles in the form of a comic strip. Encourage them to include enough information so that someone who has never done these constructions could follow the procedure.

PRACTICE

Where skills are taught	Where skills are practiced
1 EXAMPLE	EXS. 1–3
2 EXAMPLE	EXS. 4–6

Exercise 7: Students extend what they learned in **1** EXAMPLE to construct an angle with twice the measure of a given angle.

Exercise 8: Students extend what they learned in **2** EXAMPLE to construct an angle with one-fourth the measure of a given angle.

PRACTICE

Construct an angle with the same measure as the given angle.

1.

2.

3.

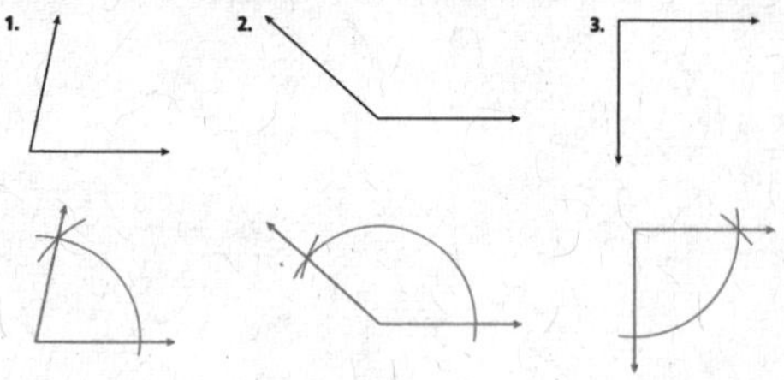

Construct the bisector of the angle.

4.

5.

6.

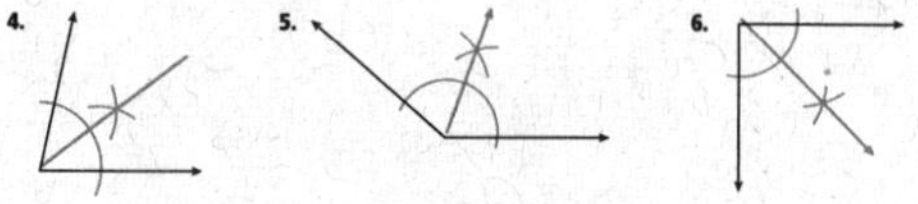

7. Explain how you can use a compass and straightedge to construct an angle that has twice the measure of ∠A. Then do the construction in the space provided.

A

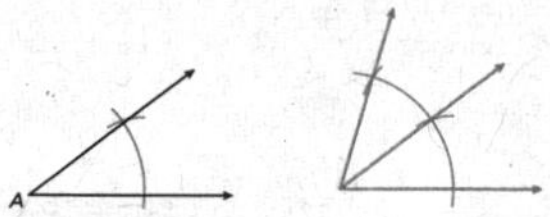

Copy ∠A. Then make another copy of ∠A that shares a side with the first

copy. The large angle that is formed has twice the measure of ∠A.

© Houghton Mifflin Harcourt Publishing Company

8. Explain how you can use a compass and straightedge to construct an angle that has $\frac{1}{4}$ the measure of ∠B. Then do the construction in the space provided.

B

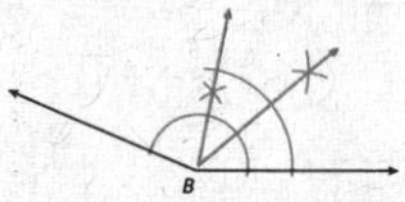

Bisect ∠B. Then construct the bisector of one of the small angles formed by

the first bisector. The resulting angles will have $\frac{1}{4}$ the measure of ∠B.

© Houghton Mifflin Harcourt Publishing Company

© Houghton Mifflin Harcourt Publishing Company

Assign these pages to help your students practice and apply important lesson concepts. For additional exercises, see the Student Edition.

Answers

Additional Practice

1.

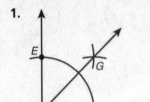

$m\angle EDG = 45°$

2. Check students' constructions. Students should construct $\angle XYZ$ congruent to $\angle EDG$ in Exercise 1.

3. Check students' constructions. Students should draw an acute angle, copy the angle, and then bisect the copy of the angle.

4. Check students' constructions. Students should draw an obtuse angle, copy the angle, and then bisect the copy of the angle.

Problem Solving

1. Check students' constructions. Students should construct the angle bisectors of the triangle.

2. The bisectors intersect at a point inside the triangle.

3. Check students' constructions. Students should construct an angle whose measure is 4 times the measure of the given angle.

4. B   5. H

Additional Practice

For Exercises 1 and 2, use the figure shown.

1. Use a compass and straightedge to construct angle bisector $\overrightarrow{DG}$. Given that m∠EDF = 90°, find m∠EDG.

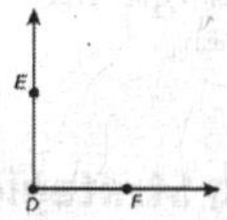

   m∠EDG = _____

2. Use your construction of ∠EDG from Exercise 1. Construct ∠XYZ with the same measure as ∠EDG.

3. Use a straightedge to draw an acute angle. Use a compass and straightedge to copy the angle. Then bisect the copy of the angle.

4. Use a straightedge to draw an obtuse angle. Use a compass and straightedge to copy the angle. Then bisect the copy of the angle.

Problem Solving

For Exercises 1–2, use the figure shown.

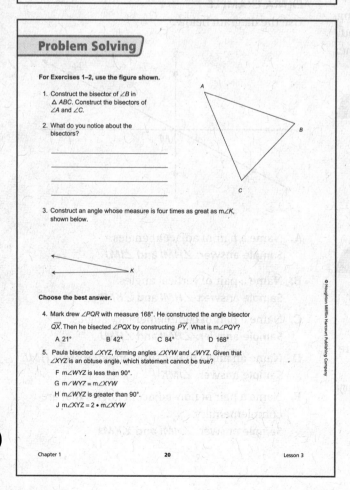

1. Construct the bisector of ∠B in △ ABC. Construct the bisectors of ∠A and ∠C.

2. What do you notice about the bisectors?

   _____

   _____

   _____

3. Construct an angle whose measure is four times as great as m∠K, shown below.

Choose the best answer.

4. Mark drew ∠PQR with measure 168°. He constructed the angle bisector $\overrightarrow{QX}$. Then he bisected ∠PQX by constructing $\overrightarrow{PY}$. What is m∠PQY?

   A 21°   B 42°   C 84°   D 168°

5. Paula bisected ∠XYZ, forming angles ∠XYW and ∠WYZ. Given that ∠XYZ is an obtuse angle, which statement cannot be true?

   F m∠WYZ is less than 90°.

   G m∠WYZ = m∠XYW

   H m∠WYZ is greater than 90°.

   J m∠XYZ = 2 • m∠XYW

Pairs of Angles
Going Deeper

Essential question: *How can you use angle pairs to solve problems?*

COMMON CORE **Standards for Mathematical Content**

CC.9-12.A.CED.1 Create equations ... in one variable and use them to solve problems.*

CC.9-12.G.CO.9 Prove theorems about lines and angles.

Vocabulary

congruent angles   adjacent angles

supplementary angles   vertical angles

complementary angles

Prerequisites

Measuring angles

Math Background

Students will work with special angles. Congruent angles have the same measure. A pair of angles is supplementary if they have a sum of 180°. A pair of angles is complementary if they have a sum of 90°. Adjacent angles share one side without overlapping. Vertical angles are the non-adjacent angles formed by intersecting lines. They lie opposite of each other at the point of intersection.

INTRODUCE

Connect to previous learning by reviewing angle measurement. Have students use their protractors to draw angles of 43°, 125°, and 180°. Then have students draw three angles with three different measures. Have students switch drawings and then measure each other's angles with their protractors.

TEACH

 EXPLORE

Questioning Strategies

• Which pair of angles are congruent in the picture of intersecting lines? **opposite angles**

• How would you describe a pair of supplementary angles in the picture of intersecting lines? **any side-by-side pair of angles**

Teaching Strategies

To help students remember the definitions of *complementary* and *supplementary*, explain that the letter *c* for complementary comes before *s* for *supplementary* just as 90° comes before 180°.

2 **EXAMPLE**

Questioning Strategies

• How do you name an angle using the three points on the angle? **You name an angle with the names of the three points. Start with a point on one side of the angle; then the vertex is always in the middle; and the point on the other side of the angle is last.**

• How do you identify vertical angles? **They are opposite angles formed by intersecting lines.**

• Are angles *BFD* and *EFA* vertical angles? **yes**

EXTRA EXAMPLE

Use the diagram below.

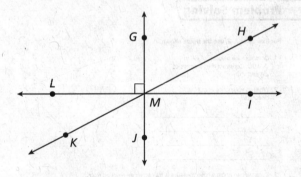

A. Name a pair of adjacent angles.
Sample answer: ∠HMI and ∠IMJ

B. Name a pair of vertical angles.
Sample answer: ∠HMI and ∠KML

C. Name a pair of complementary angles.
Sample answer: ∠HMI and ∠HMJ

D. Name an angle that is supplementary to ∠HMI.
Sample answer: ∠IMK

E. Name a pair of non-adjacent angles that are complementary.
Sample answer: ∠HMI and ∠KMJ

Name_____ Class_____ Date_____

1-4

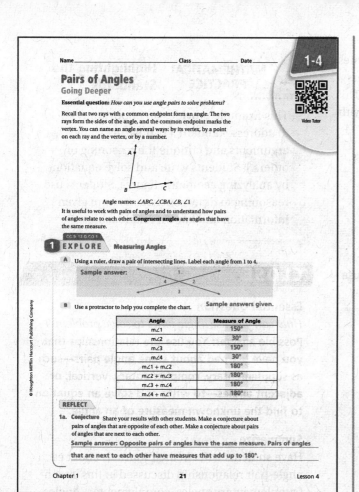

Pairs of Angles
Going Deeper

Essential question: *How can you use angle pairs to solve problems?*

Recall that two rays with a common endpoint form an angle. The two rays form the sides of the angle, and the common endpoint marks the vertex. You can name an angle several ways: by its vertex, by a point on each ray and the vertex, or by a number.

Angle names: $\angle ABC$, $\angle CBA$, $\angle B$, $\angle 1$

It is useful to work with pairs of angles and to understand how pairs of angles relate to each other. **Congruent angles** are angles that have the same measure.

1 EXPLORE   Measuring Angles

A Using a ruler, draw a pair of intersecting lines. Label each angle from 1 to 4.

Sample answer:

B Use a protractor to help you complete the chart.   **Sample answers given.**

Angle	Measure of Angle
m∠1	150°
m∠2	30°
m∠3	150°
m∠4	30°
m∠1 + m∠2	180°
m∠2 + m∠3	180°
m∠3 + m∠4	180°
m∠4 + m∠1	180°

REFLECT

1a. Conjecture Share your results with other students. Make a conjecture about pairs of angles that are opposite of each other. Make a conjecture about pairs of angles that are next to each other.

Sample answer: Opposite pairs of angles have the same measure. Pairs of angles that are next to each other have measures that add up to 180°.

Vertical angles are the opposite angles formed by two intersecting lines. Vertical angles are congruent because the angles have the same measure. **Adjacent angles** are pairs of angles that share a vertex and one side but do not overlap.

Complementary angles are two angles whose measures have a sum of 90°. **Supplementary angles** are two angles whose measures have a sum of 180°. You have discovered in Explore 1 that adjacent angles formed by two intersecting lines are supplementary.

2 EXAMPLE   Identifying Angles and Angle Pairs

Use the diagram below.

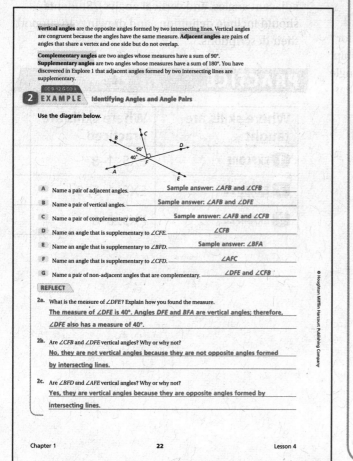

A Name a pair of adjacent angles. _____ Sample answer: ∠AFB and ∠CFB

B Name a pair of vertical angles. _____ Sample answer: ∠AFB and ∠DFE

C Name a pair of complementary angles. _____ Sample answer: ∠AFB and ∠CFB

D Name an angle that is supplementary to ∠CFE. _____ ∠CFB

E Name an angle that is supplementary to ∠BFD. _____ Sample answer: ∠BFA

F Name an angle that is supplementary to ∠CFD. _____ ∠AFC

G Name a pair of non-adjacent angles that are complementary. _____ ∠DFE and ∠CFB

REFLECT

2a. What is the measure of ∠DFE? Explain how you found the measure.

The measure of ∠DFE is 40°. Angles DFE and BFA are vertical angles; therefore, ∠DFE also has a measure of 40°.

2b. Are ∠CFB and ∠DFE vertical angles? Why or why not?

No, they are not vertical angles because they are not opposite angles formed by intersecting lines.

2c. Are ∠BFD and ∠AFE vertical angles? Why or why not?

Yes, they are vertical angles because they are opposite angles formed by intersecting lines.

Teaching Strategies

As students answer the questions with angle names, encourage them to trace the angle along its letters and say the angle's name aloud as they write it. This will help students get used to naming an angle with three letters.

3 EXAMPLE

Questioning Strategies

- What fact about angles do you use to find the angle measure in part A? **The two angles are supplementary.**

- Do you need to solve for x in part B? **No, because the measure of angle *EHF* equals 2*x*, not *x*.**

EXTRA EXAMPLE

Find the value of x and m$\angle JML$.

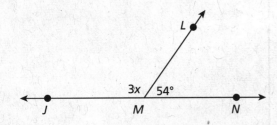

42; 126°

Teaching Strategies

Encourage students to write an equation to solve for the measure of an angle in an angle pair relationship. Students will write an equation to represent the angle pair relationship and substitute the information that they are given to solve for the unknown.

CLOSE

Essential Question

How can you use angle pairs to solve problems?
Possible answer: You use the relationships that you have learned about some angle pairs—such as supplementary, complementary, vertical, or adjacent angles—to write and solve an equation to find the unknown measure of an angle.

Summarize

Have students write in their journals about each angle-pair relationship discussed in this lesson (supplementary angles, complementary angles, adjacent angles, and vertical angles). Students should include definitions and drawings to support their descriptions.

PRACTICE

Where skills are taught	Where skills are practiced
1 EXPLORE	EXS. 1–8
2 EXAMPLE	EXS. 1–5, 9
3 EXAMPLE	EXS. 6–8

3 EXAMPLE CC.9.12.A.CED.1 **Finding Angle Measures**

Find the measure of each angle.

A ∠BDC

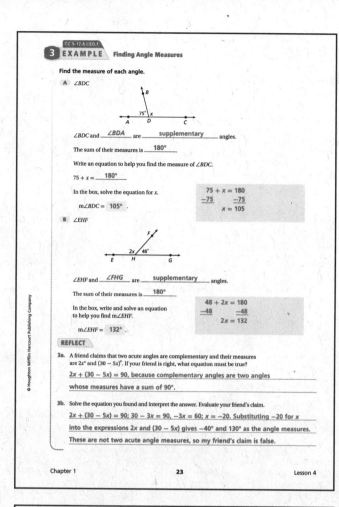

∠BDC and ___∠BDA___ are ___supplementary___ angles.

The sum of their measures is ___180°___.

Write an equation to help you find the measure of ∠BDC.

$75 + x =$ ___180°___

In the box, solve the equation for x.

m∠BDC = ___105°___.

$$75 + x = 180$$
$$\underline{-75 \qquad -75}$$
$$x = 105$$

B ∠EHF

∠EHF and ___∠FHG___ are ___supplementary___ angles.

The sum of their measures is ___180°___.

In the box, write and solve an equation to help you find m∠EHF.

m∠EHF = ___132°___.

$$48 + 2x = 180$$
$$\underline{-48 \qquad -48}$$
$$2x = 132$$

REFLECT

3a. A friend claims that two acute angles are complementary and their measures are $2x°$ and $(30 - 5x)°$. If your friend is right, what equation must be true?

___$2x + (30 - 5x) = 90$, because complementary angles are two angles___
___whose measures have a sum of 90°.___

3b. Solve the equation you found and interpret the answer. Evaluate your friend's claim.

___$2x + (30 - 5x) = 90$; $30 - 3x = 90$, $-3x = 60$; $x = -20$. Substituting -20 for x___
___into the expressions $2x$ and $(30 - 5x)$ gives $-40°$ and $130°$ as the angle measures.___
___These are not two acute angle measures, so my friend's claim is false.___

Chapter 1   23   Lesson 4

PRACTICE

Use the figure for Exercises 1–5.

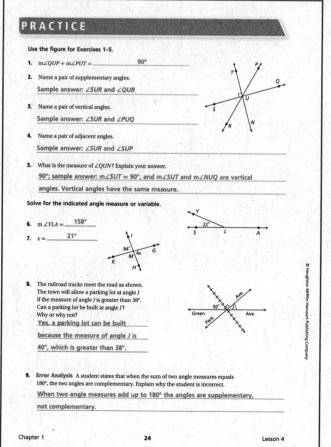

1. m∠QUP + m∠PUT = ___90°___

2. Name a pair of supplementary angles.

Sample answer: ∠SUR and ∠QUR

3. Name a pair of vertical angles.

Sample answer: ∠SUR and ∠PUQ

4. Name a pair of adjacent angles.

Sample answer: ∠SUR and ∠SUP

5. What is the measure of ∠QUN? Explain your answer.

90°; sample answer: m∠SUT = 90°, and m∠SUT and m∠NUQ are vertical

angles. Vertical angles have the same measure.

Solve for the indicated angle measure or variable.

6. m ∠YLA = ___158°___

7. x = ___21°___

8. The railroad tracks meet the road as shown. The town will allow a parking lot at angle J if the measure of angle J is greater than 38°. Can a parking lot be built at angle J? Why or why not?

Yes, a parking lot can be built

because the measure of angle J is

40°, which is greater than 38°.

9. Error Analysis A student states that when the sum of two angle measures equals 180°, the two angles are complementary. Explain why the student is incorrect.

When two angle measures add up to 180° the angles are supplementary,

not complementary.

Chapter 1   24   Lesson 4

ADDITIONAL PRACTICE AND PROBLEM SOLVING

Assign these pages to help your students practice and apply important lesson concepts. For additional exercises, see the Student Edition.

Answers

Additional Practice

1. 180°
2. $\overrightarrow{QR}$
3. 137.9°
4. $(110 - 8x)°$
5. 132°
6. 135°
7. $m\angle DEF = 29°$; $m\angle FEG = 61°$
8. $m\angle DEF = 91°$; $m\angle FEG = 89°$
9. Possible answers: ∠1 and ∠3 or ∠2 and ∠4
10. Possible answers: ∠1 and ∠2; ∠2 and ∠3; ∠3 and ∠4; or ∠1 and ∠4
11. right
12. 45°; 45°

Problem Solving

1. Sample answer: ∠*ALB* and ∠*BLC*
2. Sample answer: ∠*AML* and ∠*YML*
3. 45°; they are vertical angles.
4. 45°; the angles are supplementary.
5. Sample answer: ∠*ABM*, ∠*MBK*, and ∠*KBC*
6. C
7. G
8. A

Name_____ Class_____ Date_____

1-4

Additional Practice

1. ∠PQR and ∠SQR form a linear pair. Find the sum of their measures. _____

2. Name the ray that ∠PQR and ∠SQR share. _____

Use the figures for Exercises 3 and 4.

3. supplement of ∠Z _____

4. complement of ∠Y _____

(8x − 20)° Y

Z 42.1°

5. An angle measures 12 degrees less than three times its supplement. Find the measure of the angle. _____

6. An angle is its own complement. Find the measure of a supplement to this angle.

_____

7. ∠DEF and ∠FEG are complementary. m∠DEF = (3x − 4)°, and m∠FEG = (5x + 6)°.

Find the measures of both angles. _____

8. ∠DEF and ∠FEG are supplementary. m∠DEF = (9x + 1)°, and m∠FEG = (8x + 9)°.

Find the measures of both angles. _____

Use the figure for Exercises 9 and 10.

In 2004, several nickels were minted to commemorate the Louisiana Purchase and Lewis and Clark's expedition into the American West. One nickel shows a pipe and a hatchet crossed to symbolize peace between the American government and Native American tribes.

9. Name a pair of vertical angles.

_____
_____

10. Name a linear pair of angles.

_____

11. ∠ABC and ∠CBD form a linear pair and have equal measures. Tell if ∠ABC is acute, right, or obtuse.

_____

12. ∠KLM and ∠MLN are complementary. $\overline{LM}$ bisects ∠KLN. Find the measures of ∠KLM and ∠MLN.

_____

Problem Solving

Use the drawing of part of the Eiffel Tower for Exercises 1–5.

1. Name a pair of angles that appear to be complementary.

_____

2. Name a pair of supplementary angles.

_____

3. If m∠CSW = 45°, what is m∠JST? How do you know?

_____
_____

4. If m∠FKB = 135°, what is m∠BKL? How do you know?

_____
_____

5. Name three angles whose measures sum to 180°.

_____
_____

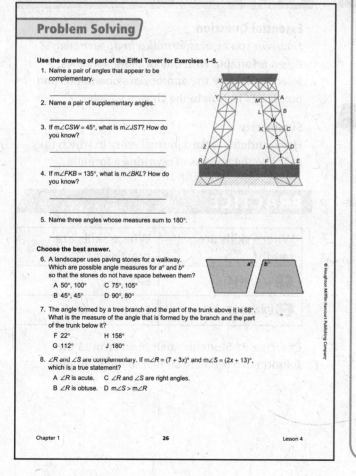

Choose the best answer.

6. A landscaper uses paving stones for a walkway. Which are possible angle measures for a° and b° so that the stones do not have space between them?

A 50°, 100°   C 75°, 105°
B 45°, 45°   D 90°, 80°

7. The angle formed by a tree branch and the part of the trunk above it is 68°. What is the measure of the angle that is formed by the branch and the part of the trunk below it?

F 22°   H 158°
G 112°   J 180°

8. ∠R and ∠S are complementary. If m∠R = (7 + 3x)° and m∠S = (2x + 13)°, which is a true statement?

A ∠R is acute.   C ∠R and ∠S are right angles.
B ∠R is obtuse.   D m∠S > m∠R

Using Formulas In Geometry
Extension: Rewriting Formulas

Essential question: *How can you express formulas in different ways?*

CC.9-12.A.CED.4 Rearrange formulas to highlight a quantity of interest, using the same reasoning as in solving equations.*

Prerequisites
Solving Equations in One Variable
Perimeter

Math Background
Skills used to solve equations in one variable with numerical coefficients can be applied to rewriting formulas in order to isolate a different variable of interest. For example, an area formula such as $A = bh$ can be rewritten so that the height is written as a function of the area and the base length.

INTRODUCE

Review the formula for the area of a triangle. Remind students that it is a formula that requires base and height, two input measurements, and gives area, one output measurement.

TEACH

1 EXAMPLE

Questioning Strategies
- What is the variable you need to solve for? What does it represent? *h; height*
- Explain another way you could find the height. **Possible answers: You could substitute first then solve the equation.**

EXTRA EXAMPLE
The circumference C of a circle with radius r is given by the formula $C = 2\pi r$. A circle has circumference 36π. Solve the formula for r and then find the radius.

$r = \frac{C}{2\pi}; r = 18$

2 EXAMPLE

Questioning Strategies
- The diagram does not show all side lengths. How should the sides be labeled? **The long sides all have length 5 and the short sides have length x.**

EXTRA EXAMPLE
Three congruent triangles are arranged along three sides of a square region as shown. Write an expression for the perimeter P of the figure. Then solve for s.

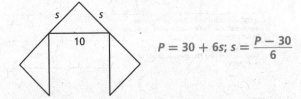

$P = 30 + 6s; s = \frac{P - 30}{6}$

CLOSE

Essential Question
How can you express formulas in different ways?
Given a formula with one or more variables, select and apply the appropriate operations and properties to isolate the chosen variable.

Summarize
Have students write a journal entry in which they describe the process of rewriting a formula.

PRACTICE

Where skills are taught	Where skills are practiced
1 EXAMPLE	EXS. 1–2
2 EXAMPLE	EX. 2

Exercise 3: Students analyze an error in the solution of a problem similar to the Examples.

Name_____ Class_____ Date_____

1-5

Using Formulas in Geometry
Extension: Rewriting Formulas

Essential question: *How can you express formulas in different ways?*

If you solve a formula for an unknown variable, you can substitute the known quantities into the rewritten formula to find the unknown value directly.

CC.9-12.A.CED.4

1 EXAMPLE Solving Formulas for Specified Variables

A triangle with area 24 square inches has a base of 3 inches. What is its height?

A The area A of a triangle with base b and height h is given by the formula $A = \frac{1}{2}bh$. Solve the formula for h. Explain your steps.

$A = \frac{1}{2}bh$ Write the original formula.

$2A = bh$ Multiply each side by ___2___.

$\frac{2A}{b} = h$ Divide each side by ___b___.

B Use the rewritten formula to solve the problem.

$h = \frac{2A}{b}$ Write the rewritten formula.

$h = \frac{2(\boxed{24})}{\boxed{3}}$ Substitute given values.

$h = \boxed{16}$ Evaluate.

REFLECT

1a. Suppose a problem gives you the area and the height of a triangle and asks for the base. What might you do?

Write a new formula for b in terms of A and h. The formula is $b = \frac{2A}{h}$. Substitute values for A and h, and then evaluate. Or, make the substitutions first to get an equation for b, and then solve the equation for b.

1b. Show how to use the original formula to solve the problem in the example without rewriting the formula.

Write $24 = \frac{1}{2}(3)h$ and then solve for h: $2(24) = 3h$; $48 = 3h$; $h = 16$.

© Houghton Mifflin Harcourt Publishing Company

CC.9-12.A.CED.4

2 EXAMPLE Rewriting Formulas to Solve Problems

Four congruent rectangles are arranged around a central rectangle as shown. Write an expression for the perimeter P of the figure. Then solve for x.

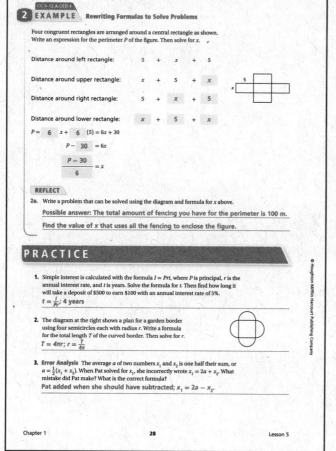

Distance around left rectangle: 5   + x +   5

Distance around upper rectangle: x +   5   + x

Distance around right rectangle: 5   + x +   5

Distance around lower rectangle: x +   5   + x

$P = \boxed{6}\;x + \boxed{6}\;(5) = 6x + 30$

$P - \boxed{30} = 6x$

$\frac{P - \boxed{30}}{6} = x$

REFLECT

2a. Write a problem that can be solved using the diagram and formula for x above.

Possible answer: The total amount of fencing you have for the perimeter is 100 m. Find the value of x that uses all the fencing to enclose the figure.

PRACTICE

1. Simple interest is calculated with the formula $I = Prt$, where P is principal, r is the annual interest rate, and t is years. Solve the formula for t. Then find how long it will take a deposit of $500 to earn $100 with an annual interest rate of 5%.

$t = \frac{I}{Pr}$; 4 years

2. The diagram at the right shows a plan for a garden border using four semicircles each with radius r. Write a formula for the total length T of the curved border. Then solve for r.

$T = 4\pi r$; $r = \frac{T}{4\pi}$

3. **Error Analysis** The average a of two numbers x_1 and x_2 is one half their sum, or $a = \frac{1}{2}(x_1 + x_2)$. When Pat solved for x_1, she incorrectly wrote $x_1 = 2a + x_2$. What mistake did Pat make? What is the correct formula?

Pat added when she should have subtracted; $x_1 = 2a - x_2$.

© Houghton Mifflin Harcourt Publishing Company

Assign these pages to help your students practice and apply important lesson concepts. For additional exercises, see the Student Edition.

Answers

Additional Practice

1. Check students' work.

$$w = \frac{P - 2\ell}{2}$$

2. 6 ft

3. $d = \frac{c}{\pi}$; $d = 6$ in

4. $r = \frac{c}{2\pi}$; $r = 4.5$ in

5. $r = \sqrt{\frac{A}{\pi}}$; $r = 6$ cm

6. $2(3) + 9 + 2(3.5) + 2x + y = 39$; $x = \dfrac{17 - y}{2}$

7. $y = 2$ ft; $x = 7.5$ ft

Problem Solving

1. $w = \frac{A}{\ell}$; $w = 100$ yd

2. $P = 2(w + \ell)$; $P = 320$ yd

3. $r = \sqrt{\frac{2A}{\pi}}$; $r = 16$ yd

4. $A = 6000 - 2(401.92) = 5196.16$ square yards

5. A   6. G

Additional Practice

The perimeter of a rectangle is given by the formula $A = 2\ell + 2w$, where ℓ is the length of the rectangle and w is the width of the rectangle. Use this formula for Exercises 1 and 2.

1. Solve the formula for w, the width of the rectangle. Show your work.

_____

_____

2. The perimeter of a rectangle is 24.5 feet, and its length is 6.25 feet. Use your formula from Exercise 1 to find the width of the rectangle.

_____

For Exercises 3–5, write and solve a formula to find each value. Use 3.14 for π.

3. The circumference of a circle is 18.84 inches. Find the diameter of the circle.

_____

4. The circumference of a circle is 28.26 inches. Find the radius of the circle.

_____

5. The area of a circle is 113.04 cm². Find the radius of the circle.

_____

Use the figure for Exercises 6 and 7.

Lucas has a 39-foot-long rope. He uses all the rope to outline this T-shape in his backyard. All the angles in the figure are right angles.

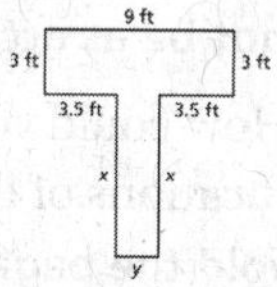

6. Write a formula for the perimeter of the T-shape in terms of x and y. Solve the formula for x.

_____

7. Find the value of y and use that value in your formula from Exercise 6 to find x.

_____

Problem Solving

Use the diagram of a hockey field for Exercises 1–4.

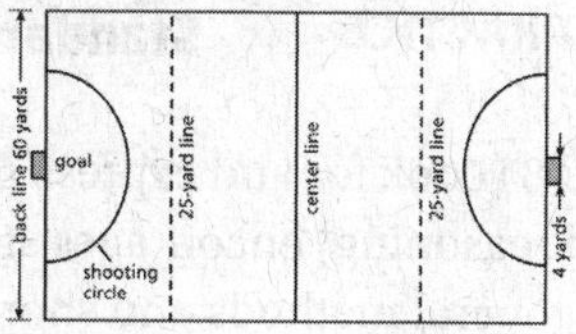

1. The area of the field is 6000 square yards. Write and solve a formula to find the width of the field.

_____

_____

2. Write and solve a formula to find the perimeter of the field.

_____

_____

3. The area enclosed by one shooting circle is 401.92 square yards. Write and solve a formula to find the radius of the shooting circle. Use 3.14 for π.

_____

_____

4. Write and solve a formula to find the area of the field excluding the two shooting circles.

_____

_____

Choose the best answer.

5. A rectangular counter 3 feet wide and 5 feet long has a circle cut out of it in order to have a sink installed. The circle has a diameter of 18 inches. What is the approximate area of the remaining countertop surface? Use 3.14 for π.

    A 13.2 ft²   C 18.9 ft²

    B 15.0 ft²   D 29.5 ft²

6. The base of a triangular garden measures 5.5 feet. It takes 33 pounds of mulch to cover the garden. If 4 pounds of mulch are needed to cover a square foot, what is the height of the garden?

    F 1.5 ft   H 4 ft

    G 3 ft   J 6.6 ft

© Houghton Mifflin Harcourt Publishing Company

Midpoint and Distance in the Coordinate Plane
Going Deeper

Essential question: *How can you find midpoints of segments and distances in the coordinate plane?*

COMMON CORE Standards for Mathematical Content

CC.9-12.G.GPE.4 Use coordinates to prove simple geometric theorems algebraically.

CC.9-12.G.GPE.6 Find the point on a directed line segment between two given points that partitions the segment in a given ratio.

Prerequisites
The Pythagorean Theorem

Math Background
The midpoint and distance formulas are two of the key tools of coordinate geometry. Students will write coordinate proofs later in this course and they will find that these two formulas, along with facts about the slopes of parallel and perpendicular lines, are enough to prove a wide range of theorems.

The distance formula is a direct consequence of the Pythagorean Theorem. Note that the distance formula reduces to a simpler version in the case of points that lie on a horizontal or vertical line. For example, if two points lie on a vertical line, then they have the same x-coordinates and the distance between the points is $\sqrt{(x_2 - x_1)^2 + (y_2 - y_1)^2} = \sqrt{(y_2 - y_1)^2} = |y_2 - y_1|$. Similarly, the distance between two points that lie on a horizontal line is $|x_2 - x_1|$.

INTRODUCE

Remind students that they have already worked with midpoints. In particular, students learned to use paper folding to find the midpoint of a segment. Explain that in this lesson, students will harness the power of coordinate geometry to find the exact coordinates of the midpoint of a given line segment.

Begin by briefly reviewing the Pythagorean Theorem. Explain that the Pythagorean Theorem can be used to find the distance between two points in a coordinate plane.

TEACH

1 EXPLORE

Materials: ruler

Questioning Strategies

- In Step A, what would happen if you measured to the nearest centimeter instead of the nearest millimeter? **The location of the midpoint would not be as accurate.**

- How could you use paper folding to check the locations of the midpoints? **For each segment, fold the page so that the endpoints lie on top of each other. The crease intersects the segment at the midpoint.**

- How could you use the distance formula to check the locations of the midpoints? **Check that the distance from one endpoint to the midpoint equals the distance from the other endpoint to the midpoint.**

MATHEMATICAL PRACTICE   Highlighting the Standards

Standard 8 (Look for and express regularity in repeated reasoning) encourages students to look for general methods and shortcuts. The Explore gives students a chance to find midpoints by measuring, then discover the "shortcut" known as the midpoint formula.

2 EXAMPLE

Questioning Strategies

- What do you know about points that lie in Quadrant III? **The x- and y-coordinates are both negative.**

EXTRA EXAMPLE

$\overline{JK}$ has endpoints $J(5, 1)$ and $K(-3, -3)$. Prove that the midpoint M of $\overline{JK}$ lies in Quadrant IV.

The midpoint of $\overline{JK}$ is $M(1, -1)$. Since the x-coordinate is positive and the y-coordinate is negative, M lies in Quadrant IV.

© Houghton Mifflin Harcourt Publishing Company

Name_____ Class_____ Date_____

1-6

Midpoint and Distance in the Coordinate Plane

Going Deeper

Essential question: *How can you find midpoints of segments and distances in the coordinate plane?*

Video Tutor

CC.9-12.G.GPE.6

1 EXPLORE   Finding Midpoints of Line Segments

Follow the steps below for each of the given line segments.

A   Use a ruler to measure the length of the line segment to the nearest millimeter.

B   Find half the length of the segment. Measure this distance from one endpoint to locate the midpoint of the segment. Plot a point at the midpoint.

C   Record the coordinates of the segment's endpoints and the coordinates of the segment's midpoint in the table below.

D   In each row of the table, compare the *x*-coordinates of the endpoints to the *x*-coordinate of the midpoint. Then compare the *y*-coordinates of the endpoints to the *y*-coordinate of the midpoint. Look for patterns.

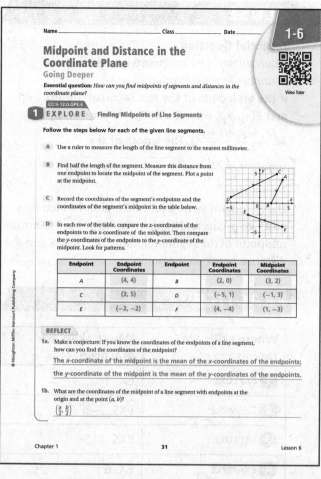

Endpoint	Endpoint Coordinates	Endpoint	Endpoint Coordinates	Midpoint Coordinates
A	(4, 4)	B	(2, 0)	(3, 2)
C	(3, 5)	D	(−5, 1)	(−1, 3)
E	(−2, −2)	F	(4, −4)	(1, −3)

REFLECT

1a. Make a conjecture: If you know the coordinates of the endpoints of a line segment, how can you find the coordinates of the midpoint?

The *x*-coordinate of the midpoint is the mean of the *x*-coordinates of the endpoints; the *y*-coordinate of the midpoint is the mean of the *y*-coordinates of the endpoints.

1b. What are the coordinates of the midpoint of a line segment with endpoints at the origin and at the point (*a, b*)?

$\left(\frac{a}{2}, \frac{b}{2}\right)$

Chapter 1   31   Lesson 6

© Houghton Mifflin Harcourt Publishing Company

The patterns you observed can be generalized to give a formula for the coordinates of the midpoint of any line segment in the coordinate plane.

The Midpoint Formula

The midpoint M of $\overline{AB}$ with endpoints $A(x_1, y_1)$ and $B(x_2, y_2)$ is given by $M\left(\frac{x_1 + x_2}{2}, \frac{y_1 + y_2}{2}\right)$.

CC.9-12.G.GPE.4

2 EXAMPLE   Using the Midpoint Formula

$\overline{PQ}$ has endpoints $P(-4, 1)$ and $Q(2, -3)$. Prove that the midpoint M of $\overline{PQ}$ lies in Quadrant III.

A   Use the given endpoints to identify $x_1, x_2, y_1,$ and y_2.

$x_1 = -4, x_2 = 2, y_1 = $ __1__ , $y_2 = $ __−3__

B   By the midpoint formula, the *x*-coordinate of M is $\frac{x_1 + x_2}{2} = \frac{-4 + 2}{2} = \frac{-2}{2} = -1$.

The *y*-coordinate of M is $\frac{y_1 + y_2}{2} = \frac{1 + -3}{2} = \frac{-2}{2} = -1$.

M lies in Quadrant III because its *x*- and *y*-coordinates are both negative.

REFLECT

2a. What must be true about PM and QM? Show that this is the case.

$PM = PQ$; by the distance formula $PM = PQ = \sqrt{13}$.

CC.9-12.G.GPE.4

3 EXPLORE   Finding a Distance in the Coordinate Plane

You can use the Pythagorean Theorem to help you find the distance between the points $A(2, 5)$ and $B(-4, -3)$.

A   Plot the points A and B in the coordinate plane at right.

B   Draw $\overline{AB}$.

C   Draw a vertical line through point A and a horizontal line through point B to create a right triangle. Label the intersection of the vertical line and the horizontal line as point C.

D   Each small grid square is 1 unit by 1 unit. Use this fact to find the lengths AC and BC.

$AC = $ __8__ $BC = $ __6__

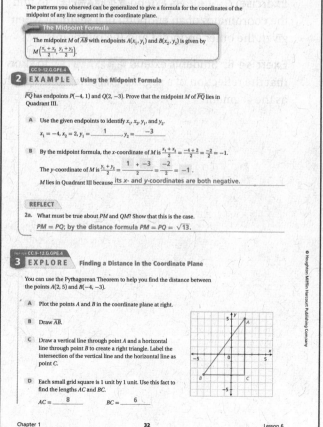

Chapter 1   32   Lesson 6

© Houghton Mifflin Harcourt Publishing Company

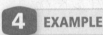

3 EXPLORE

Questioning Strategies

- Can you apply the Pythagorean Theorem to any triangle? **No; it applies only to right triangles.**

- What does the Pythagorean Theorem say? **The sum of the squares of the lengths of the legs of a right triangle is equal to the square of the length of the hypotenuse.**

4 EXAMPLE

Questioning Strategies

- How do you know that $\sqrt{41} > \sqrt{37}$? **41 > 37, and the inequality is preserved when you take the positive square root of both numbers.**

EXTRA EXAMPLE

Prove that $\overline{ST}$ is longer than $\overline{UV}$.

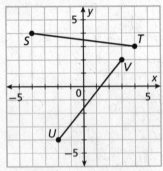

$ST = \sqrt{65}$, $UV = \sqrt{61}$ and $\sqrt{65} > \sqrt{61}$.

MATHEMATICAL PRACTICE **Highlighting the Standards**

Example 4 and its Reflect question address Standard 7 (Look for and make use of structure). In particular, as students work with the distance formula, help them to recognize that $(x_2 - x_1)^2 = (x_1 - x_2)^2$. This means that you can subtract the coordinates in either order when you use the formula.

CLOSE

Essential Question

How can you find midpoints of segments and distances in the coordinate plane?
If the endpoints of the line segment are $A(x_1, y_1)$ and $B(x_2, y_2)$, then the midpoint is given by $M\left(\frac{x_1 + x_2}{2}, \frac{y_1 + y_2}{2}\right)$. The length of the segment is $AB = \sqrt{(x_2 - x_1)^2 + (y_2 - y_1)^2}$.

Summarize

Have students write a journal entry in which they plot two points and explain the steps for finding the midpoint of the segment joining the points and the distance between the points.

PRACTICE

Where skills are taught	Where skills are practiced
1 EXPLORE	EX. 1
2 EXAMPLE	EXS. 2–3
3 EXPLORE	EXS. 4–5
4 EXAMPLE	EX. 6

Exercise 7: Students extend 2 EXAMPLE to find the coordinates of an endpoint of a segment when given the other endpoint and the midpoint.

Exercise 8: Students extend 4 EXAMPLE to show that the reflection of a segment has the same length as the segment.

E By the Pythagorean Theorem, $AB^2 = AC^2 + BC^2$.
Complete the following using the lengths from Step D.

$$AB^2 = \boxed{8}^2 + \boxed{6}^2$$

F Simplify the right side of the equation. Then solve for AB.

$$AB^2 = \underline{100}, \ AB = \underline{10}$$

REFLECT

3a. Explain how you solved for AB in Step F.

I took the positive square root of both sides of the equation $AB^2 = 100$.

3b. Can you use the above method to find the distance between any two points in the coordinate plane? Explain.

Yes; if the two points lie on the same vertical or horizontal line, then the method

does not create a triangle but the equation still works.

The process of using the Pythagorean Theorem can be generalized to give a formula for finding the distance between two points in the coordinate plane.

The Distance Formula

The distance between two points (x_1, y_1) and (x_2, y_2) in the coordinate plane is

$$\sqrt{(x_2 - x_1)^2 + (y_2 - y_1)^2}.$$

4 EXAMPLE CC.9-12.G.GPE.4 Using the Distance Formula

Prove that $\overline{CD}$ is longer than $\overline{AB}$.

A Write the coordinates of A, B, C, and D.

$A(-2, 3)$, $B \underline{(4, 2)}$, $C \underline{(2, 0)}$, $D \underline{(-3, -4)}$

B Use the distance formula to find AB and CD.

$$AB = \sqrt{[4 - (-2)]^2 + (2 - 3)^2} = \sqrt{6^2 + (-1)^2} = \sqrt{36 + 1} = \sqrt{37}$$

$$CD = \sqrt{(-3 - \boxed{2})^2 + (-4 - \boxed{0})^2} = \sqrt{(-5)^2 + (-4)^2} = \sqrt{41}$$

So, $\overline{CD}$ is longer than $\overline{AB}$ because $\underline{\sqrt{41} > \sqrt{37}.}$

REFLECT

4a. When you use the distance formula, does the order in which you subtract the x-coordinates and the y-coordinates matter? Explain.

No; $(x_2 - x_1)^2 = (x_1 - x_2)^2$ and $(y_2 - y_1)^2 = (y_1 - y_2)^2$.

Chapter 1   33   Lesson 6

© Houghton Mifflin Harcourt Publishing Company

PRACTICE

1. Find the coordinates of the midpoint of $\overline{AB}$ with endpoints $A(-10, 3)$ and $B(2, -2)$. $\left(\frac{-10 + 2}{2}, \frac{3 + (-2)}{2}\right) = \left(-4, \frac{1}{2}\right)$

2. $\overline{RS}$ has endpoints $R(3, 5)$ and $S(-3, -1)$. Prove that the midpoint M of $\overline{RS}$ lies on the y-axis.

By the midpoint formula, M has coordinates $(0, 2)$. M lies on the y-axis because its

x-coordinate is 0.

3. $\overline{CD}$ has endpoints $C(1, 4)$ and $D(5, 0)$. $\overline{EF}$ has endpoints $E(4, 5)$ and $F(2, -1)$. Prove that the segments have the same midpoint.

The midpoint of $\overline{CD}$ is $(3, 2)$. The midpoint of $\overline{EF}$ is $(3, 2)$. So, the midpoints of the

segments are the same point.

Use the figure for Exercises 4–6.

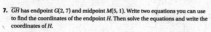

4. Find the distance between J and L. $\underline{\sqrt{26}}$

5. Find the length of $\overline{LM}$. $\underline{\sqrt{40}}$

6. Prove that $JK = KL$.

By the distance formula, $JK = \sqrt{13}$ and $KL = \sqrt{13}$,

so $JK = KL$.

7. $\overline{GH}$ has endpoint $G(2, 7)$ and midpoint $M(5, 1)$. Write two equations you can use to find the coordinates of the endpoint H. Then solve the equations and write the coordinates of H.

$\frac{2 + x_2}{2} = 5$ and $\frac{7 + y_2}{2} = 1$ are the two equations. Solving for x: $2 + x_2 = 10$,

so $x_2 = 8$. Solving for y: $7 + y_2 = 2$, so $y_2 = -5$. The other endpoint is $H(8, -5)$.

8. A segment $\overline{AB}$ has endpoints $A(x_1, y_1)$ and $B(x_2, y_2)$. The segment is reflected across the x-axis. Find the coordinates of the reflected segment. Then show the length of the reflected segment is the same as the length of the original segment. Explain your reasoning.

The image of $A(x_1, y_1)$ is $A'(x_1, -y_1)$. The image of $B(x_2, y_2)$ is $B'(x_2, -y_2)$.

Using the distance formula, $AB = \sqrt{(x_2 - x_1)^2 + (y_2 - y_1)^2}$ and

$A'B' = \sqrt{(x_2 - x_1)^2 + [-y_2 - (-y_1)]^2} = \sqrt{(x_2 - x_1)^2 + (y_1 - y_2)^2}$. Because $(y_2 - y_1)$

and $(y_1 - y_2)$ are opposites, their squares are the same. This means $AB = A'B'$.

© Houghton Mifflin Harcourt Publishing Company

Chapter 1   34   Lesson 6

© Houghton Mifflin Harcourt Publishing Company

ADDITIONAL PRACTICE AND PROBLEM SOLVING

Assign these pages to help your students practice and apply important lesson concepts. For additional exercises, see the Student Edition.

Answers

Additional Practice

1. (3, −3)
2. $\left(\frac{x}{2}, \frac{y-3}{2}\right)$
3. (−4, −2)
4. $\sqrt{26}$ units
5. $\sqrt{26}$ units
6. $4\sqrt{2}$ units
7. $\overline{AB}$ and $\overline{BC}$
8. 6.4 units
9. 11.4 units
10. 13.4 ft
11. 101.8 in.

Problem Solving

1. 82.5 ft
2. 85.9 ft
3. 47.4 m
4. 18.4 m
5. B
6. H
7. C

Name_____ Class_____ Date_____ **1-6**

Additional Practice

Find the coordinates of the midpoint of each segment.

1. $\overline{TU}$ with endpoints $T(5, -1)$ and $U(1, -5)$ _____

2. $\overline{VW}$ with endpoints $V(-2, -6)$ and $W(x + 2, y + 3)$ _____

3. Y is the midpoint of $\overline{XZ}$. X has coordinates $(2, 4)$, and Y has coordinates $(-1, 1)$. Find the coordinates of Z.   _____

Use the figure for Exercises 4–7.

4. Find AB. _____

5. Find BC. _____

6. Find CA. _____

7. Name a pair of congruent segments. _____

Find the distances.

8. Use the Distance Formula to find the distance, to the nearest tenth, between $K(-7, -4)$ and $L(-2, 0)$.   _____

9. Use the Pythagorean Theorem to find the distance, to the nearest tenth, between $F(9, 5)$ and $G(-2, 2)$.   _____

Use the figure for Exercises 10 and 11.

Snooker is a kind of pool or billiards played on a 6-foot-by-12-foot table. The side pockets are halfway down the rails (long sides).

10. Find the distance, to the nearest tenth of a foot, diagonally across the table from corner pocket to corner pocket.

    _____

11. Find the distance, to the nearest tenth of an inch, diagonally across the table from corner pocket to side pocket.

6 ft

12 ft

side pocket

corner pocket

Chapter 1   35   Lesson 6

© Houghton Mifflin Harcourt Publishing Company

Problem Solving

For Exercises 1 and 2, use the diagram of a tennis court.

1. A singles tennis court is a rectangle 27 feet wide and 78 feet long. Suppose a player at corner A hits the ball to her opponent in the diagonally opposite corner B. Approximately how far does the ball travel, to the nearest tenth of a foot?

   _____

2. A doubles tennis court is a rectangle 36 feet wide and 78 feet long. If two players are standing in diagonally opposite corners, about how far apart are they, to the nearest tenth of a foot?

   _____

36 ft

27 ft

78 ft

A map of an amusement park is shown on a coordinate plane, where each square of the grid represents 1 square meter. The water ride is at $(-17, 12)$, the roller coaster is at $(26, -8)$, and the Ferris wheel is at $(2, 20)$. Find each distance to the nearest tenth of a meter.

3. What is the distance between the water ride and the roller coaster?

   _____

4. A caricature artist is at the midpoint between the roller coaster and the Ferris wheel. What is the distance from the artist to the Ferris wheel?

   _____

Use the map of the Sacramento Zoo on a coordinate plane for Exercises 5–7. Choose the best answer.

5. To the nearest tenth of a unit, how far is it from the tigers to the hyenas?

   A 5.1 units   C 9.9 units

   B 7.1 units   D 50.0 units

6. Between which of these exhibits is the distance the least?

   F tigers and primates

   G hyenas and gibbons

   H otters and gibbons

   J tigers and otters

7. Suppose you walk straight from the jaguars to the tigers and then to the otters. What is the total distance to the nearest tenth of a unit?

   A 11.4 units   C 13.9 units

   B 13.0 units   D 14.2 units

Sacramento Zoo

Otters   Hyenas

Gibbons

Tigers

Jaguars

Primates

Chapter 1   36   Lesson 6

© Houghton Mifflin Harcourt Publishing Company

1-7 Transformations in the Coordinate Plane
Extension: Properties of Rigid Motions

Essential question: *How do you identify transformations that are rigid motions?*

COMMON CORE Standards for Mathematical Content

CC.9-12.G.CO.2 ... Compare transformations that preserve distance and angle to those that do not (e.g., translation versus horizontal stretch).

CC.9-12.G.CO.5 Given a geometric figure and a rotation, reflection, or translation, draw the transformed figure ...

CC.9-12.G.CO.6 Use geometric descriptions of rigid motions ...

Vocabulary

transformation

pre-image

image

rigid motion (isometry)

Prerequisites

None

Math Background

This book takes a transformations-based approach to much of geometry. For example, both congruence and similarity will be defined in terms of transformations. Because transformations play such a central role in the course, this introductory lesson is especially important. In addition to providing definitions of key terms, the lesson introduces transformations as functions and gives students a chance to explore a wide range of transformations before focusing on specific transformations in upcoming lessons.

INTRODUCE

Students have seen transformations in earlier grades, but in a more informal way. Begin this lesson by asking them to define *transformation* in their own words. Then have students give examples of transformations. If no one suggests it, remind students that they have already worked with flips, turns, and slides in earlier grades. Tell students that they will greatly enhance their knowledge of these transformations in this course.

TEACH

1 ENGAGE

Questioning Strategies

• How is the notation $T(A) = A'$ similar to the more familiar function notation $y = f(x)$? **The object inside the parentheses is the input. The object on the other side of the equal sign is the output. The letter in front of the parentheses gives the name of the function or transformation.**

• What does the "prime" symbol mean in A'? **It tells you that the point A' is the image of point A.**

• In the coordinate notation $(x, y) \rightarrow (x + 2, y - 3)$, what does the arrow tell you? **It tells you that the point (x, y) is mapped to the point $(x + 2, y + 3)$.**

Teaching Strategies

You may want to give students verbal descriptions of a variety of transformations. For example, the simplest transformation is the transformation that maps every point to itself. This is known as the identity transformation. Another transformation is the transformation that maps every point to the origin. Giving students examples of these "extreme" transformations will help them realize that not every transformation is a flip, turn, or slide.

2 EXPLORE

Questioning Strategies

• What do all of the transformations have in common? **They all map a right triangle to a right triangle.**

• Which of these transformations would you use if you wanted to make an enlargement of the given triangle? **D**

© Houghton Mifflin Harcourt Publishing Company

Name_____ Class_____ Date_____

1-7

Transformations in the Coordinate Plane

Extension: Properties of Rigid Motions

Essential question: *How do you identify transformations that are rigid motions?*

Video Tutor

CC.9-12.G.CO.2

1 ENGAGE   Introducing Transformations

A **transformation** is a function that changes the position, shape, and/or size of a figure. The inputs for the function are points in the plane; the outputs are other points in the plane. A figure that is used as the input of a transformation is the **pre-image**. The output is the **image**.

For example, the transformation T moves point A to point A'. Point A is the pre-image, and A' is the image. You can use function notation to write $T(A) = A'$. Note that a transformation is sometimes called a *mapping*. Transformation T maps point A to point A'.

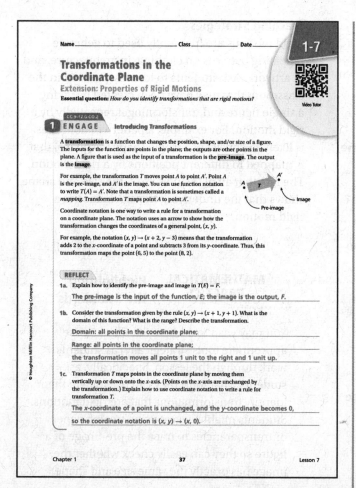

Coordinate notation is one way to write a rule for a transformation on a coordinate plane. The notation uses an arrow to show how the transformation changes the coordinates of a general point, (x, y).

For example, the notation $(x, y) \rightarrow (x + 2, y - 3)$ means that the transformation adds 2 to the x-coordinate of a point and subtracts 3 from its y-coordinate. Thus, this transformation maps the point $(6, 5)$ to the point $(8, 2)$.

REFLECT

1a. Explain how to identify the pre-image and image in $T(E) = F$.

The pre-image is the input of the function, E; the image is the output, F.

1b. Consider the transformation given by the rule $(x, y) \rightarrow (x + 1, y + 1)$. What is the domain of this function? What is the range? Describe the transformation.

Domain: all points in the coordinate plane;

Range: all points in the coordinate plane;

the transformation moves all points 1 unit to the right and 1 unit up.

1c. Transformation T maps points in the coordinate plane by moving them vertically up or down onto the x-axis. (Points on the x-axis are unchanged by the transformation.) Explain how to use coordinate notation to write a rule for transformation T.

The x-coordinate of a point is unchanged, and the y-coordinate becomes 0,

so the coordinate notation is $(x, y) \rightarrow (x, 0)$.

Chapter 1   37   Lesson 7

CC.9-12.G.CO.5

2 EXPLORE   Classifying Transformations

Investigate the effects of various transformations on the given right triangle.

- Use coordinate notation to help you find the image of each vertex of the triangle.
- Plot the images of the vertices.
- Connect the images of the vertices to draw the image of the triangle.

A $(x, y) \rightarrow (x - 4, y + 3)$ B $(x, y) \rightarrow (-x, y)$ C $(x, y) \rightarrow (-y, x)$

D $(x, y) \rightarrow (2x, 2y)$ E $(x, y) \rightarrow (2x, y)$ F $(x, y) \rightarrow (x, \frac{1}{2}y)$

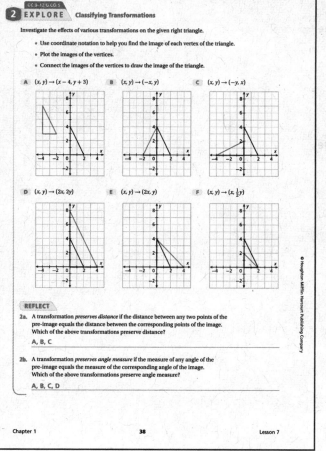

REFLECT

2a. A transformation *preserves distance* if the distance between any two points of the pre-image equals the distance between the corresponding points of the image. Which of the above transformations preserve distance?

A, B, C

2b. A transformation *preserves angle measure* if the measure of any angle of the pre-image equals the measure of the corresponding angle of the image. Which of the above transformations preserve angle measure?

A, B, C, D

Chapter 1   38   Lesson 7

Questioning Strategies

- How can you describe a rigid motion in your own words? **A rigid motion moves a figure without changing its size or shape.**

- What must be true about the pre-image and image under a rigid motion? **They have the same size and shape.**

EXTRA EXAMPLE

The figures show the pre-image (△*MNP*) and image (△*M′N′P′*) under a transformation. Determine whether the transformation appears to be a rigid motion. Explain.

A.

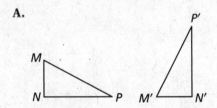

Rigid motion; the transformation does not change the size or shape of the figure.

B.

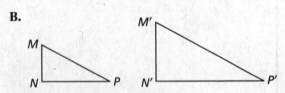

Not a rigid motion; the transformation changes the size of the figure.

C.

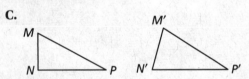

Not a rigid motion; the transformation changes the shape of the figure.

Teaching Strategies

Rigid motions are frequently used to generate repeating patterns on clothing, in architecture, and in artwork. Ask students to identify patterns in the classroom that may have been created by taking a single figure and transforming it repeatedly by a rigid motion. For example, a pattern of floor tiles is likely to consist of a single shape (a square) that is mapped to different positions by a rigid motion. The fact that all of the tiles are same size and shape shows that the underlying transformation is a rigid motion.

MATHEMATICAL PRACTICE — Highlighting the Standards

You may wish to address Standard 5 (Use appropriate tools strategically) as students work through the lesson. Specifically, ask students what tools they can use to help them identify transformations that are rigid motions. Students might suggest using tracing paper or transparencies to trace the pre-image of a figure so they can easily check whether the image has exactly the same size and shape.

A **rigid motion** (or *isometry*) is a transformation that changes the position of a figure without changing the size or shape of the figure.

3 EXAMPLE   Identifying Rigid Motions

The figures show the pre-image ($\triangle ABC$) and image ($\triangle A'B'C'$) under a transformation. Determine whether the transformation appears to be a rigid motion. Explain.

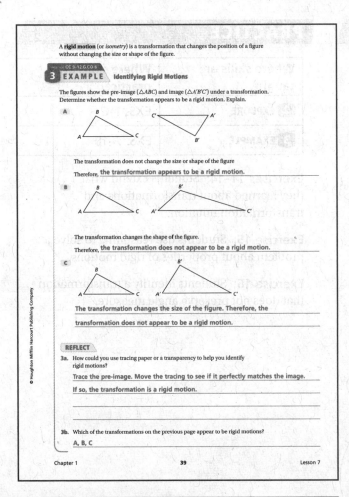

A

The transformation does not change the size or shape of the figure

Therefore, **the transformation appears to be a rigid motion.**

B

The transformation changes the shape of the figure.

Therefore, **the transformation does not appear to be a rigid motion.**

C

The transformation changes the size of the figure. Therefore, the

transformation does not appear to be a rigid motion.

REFLECT

3a. How could you use tracing paper or a transparency to help you identify rigid motions?

Trace the pre-image. Move the tracing to see if it perfectly matches the image.

If so, the transformation is a rigid motion.

3b. Which of the transformations on the previous page appear to be rigid motions?

A, B, C

© Houghton Mifflin Harcourt Publishing Company

Rigid motions have some important properties. These are summarized below.

> **Properties of Rigid Motions (Isometries)**
> - Rigid motions preserve distance.
> - Rigid motions preserve angle measure.
> - Rigid motions preserve betweenness.
> - Rigid motions preserve collinearity.

Reflections, rotations, and translations are all rigid motions. So, they all preserve distance, angle measure, betweenness, and collinearity.

The above properties ensure that if a figure is determined by certain points, then its image after a rigid motion is also determined by those points. For example, $\triangle ABC$ is determined by its vertices, points A, B, and C. The image of $\triangle ABC$ after a rigid motion is the triangle determined by A', B', and C'.

PRACTICE

Draw the image of the triangle under the given transformation. Then tell whether the transformation appears to be a rigid motion.

1. $(x, y) \rightarrow (x + 3, y)$

rigid motion

2. $(x, y) \rightarrow (3x, 3y)$

not a rigid motion

3. $(x, y) \rightarrow (x, -y)$

rigid motion

4. $(x, y) \rightarrow (-x, -y)$

rigid motion

5. $(x, y) \rightarrow (x, 3y)$

not a rigid motion

6. $(x, y) \rightarrow (x - 4, y - 4)$

rigid motion

© Houghton Mifflin Harcourt Publishing Company

© Houghton Mifflin Harcourt Publishing Company

Essential Question

How do you identify transformations that are rigid motions?

Rigid motions are those transformations that change the position of a figure without changing the figure's size or shape.

Summarize

Have students make a graphic organizer to summarize what they know so far about transformations and rigid motions. An example is shown below.

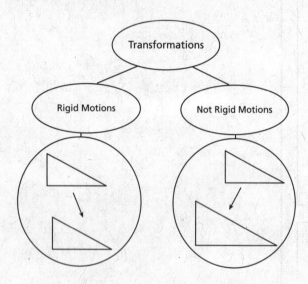

Where skills are taught	Where skills are practiced
2 EXPLORE	EXS. 1–6
3 EXAMPLE	EXS. 7–10

Exercises 11–14: Students extend what they learned about transformations and transformation notation.

Exercise 15: Students use reasoning to solve a problem about properties of rigid motions.

Exercise 16: Students identify a transformation that does not preserve angle measure.

The figures show the pre-image (*ABCD*) and image (*A'B'C'D'*) under a transformation. Determine whether the transformation appears to be a rigid motion. Explain.

7.

No; the transformation changes the shape of the figure.

8.

Yes; the transformation does not change the shape or size of the figure.

9.

Yes; the transformation does not change the shape or size of the figure.

10.

No; the transformation changes the size of the figure.

In Exercises 11–14, consider a transformation *T* that maps △*XYZ* to △*X'Y'Z'*.

11. What is the image of $\overline{XY}$? $\overline{X'Y'}$

12. What is $T(Z)$? Z'

13. What is the pre-image of ∠*Y'*?   ∠*Y*

14. Can you conclude that $XY = X'Y'$? Why or why not?

No; you do not know if the transformation is a rigid motion.

15. Point *M* is the midpoint of $\overline{AB}$. After a rigid motion, can you conclude that *M'* is the midpoint of $\overline{A'B'}$? Why or why not?

Yes; a rigid motion preserves distance, betweenness, and collinearity, so *M'* will be equidistant from *A'* and *B'* and also on $\overline{A'B'}$, so it is the midpoint of $\overline{A'B'}$.

16. Error Analysis A student claims that all of the transformations in Exercises 1–6 preserve angle measure. However, the student made an error. Which of the exercises shows a transformation that *does not* preserve angle measure? Use a protractor to estimate the measures of the angles in the pre-image triangle and image triangle to justify your answer.

Exercise 5 shows a transformation, a vertical stretch, that does not preserve angle measure. The angle measures of the pre-image triangle are about 14°, 14°, and 152°. The angle measures of the image triangle are about 37°, 37°, and 106°. So, angle measure is not preserved in the stretch.

Assign these pages to help your students practice
and apply important lesson concepts. For
additional exercises, see the Student Edition.

Answers

Additional Practice

1. 2

2. 1

3. 3

4. rotation

5. $G'(-2.5, 4)$, $H'(-3.5, 2)$, $I'(-4, 4)$, $J'(-5, 6)$

6. $(x, y) \rightarrow (x - 7, y + 5)$

7.

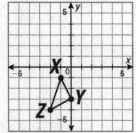

Problem Solving

1. player 3: $(x, y) \rightarrow (x + 4.5, y - 1)$;
player 4: $(x, y) \rightarrow (x - 4, y + 1)$

2. player 3: $(-5.5, -2)$; player 4: $(4, -1.5)$

3. $(-5, 9)$, $\left(\frac{1}{2}, 9\right)$, $(-1, 6)$, $\left(-3\frac{1}{2}, 6\right)$

4. reflection across the y-axis

5. $A'(6, 17)$, $C'(10, 14)$, $D'\left(-7\frac{1}{2}, 14\right)$

6. C

7. J

Name_____ Class_____ Date_____

Additional Practice

Use the figure for Exercises 1–3.

The figure in the plane at right shows the preimage in the transformation $ABCD \rightarrow A'B'C'D'$. Match the number of the image (below) with the name of the correct transformation.

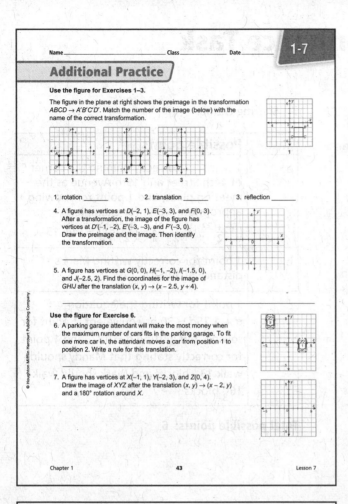

1. rotation _____   2. translation _____   3. reflection _____

4. A figure has vertices at $D(-2, 1)$, $E(-3, 3)$, and $F(0, 3)$. After a transformation, the image of the figure has vertices at $D'(-1, -2)$, $E'(-3, -3)$, and $F'(-3, 0)$. Draw the preimage and the image. Then identify the transformation.

5. A figure has vertices at $G(0, 0)$, $H(-1, 2)$, $I(-1.5, 0)$, and $J(-2.5, 2)$. Find the coordinates for the image of $GHIJ$ after the translation $(x, y) \rightarrow (x - 2.5, y + 4)$.

Use the figure for Exercise 6.

6. A parking garage attendant will make the most money when the maximum number of cars fits in the parking garage. To fit one more car in, the attendant moves a car from position 1 to position 2. Write a rule for this translation.

7. A figure has vertices at $X(-1, 1)$, $Y(-2, 3)$, and $Z(0, 4)$. Draw the image of XYZ after the translation $(x, y) \rightarrow (x - 2, y)$ and a 180° rotation around X.

Problem Solving

Use the diagram of the starting positions of five basketball players for Exercises 1 and 2.

1. After the first step of a play, player 3 is at $(-1.5, 0)$ and player 4 is at $(1, 0.5)$. Write a rule to describe the translations of players 3 and 4 from their starting positions to their new positions.

2. For the second step of the play, player 3 is to move to a position described by the rule $(x, y) \rightarrow (x - 4, y - 2)$ and player 4 is to move to a position described by the rule $(x, y) \rightarrow (x + 3, y - 2)$. What are the positions of these two players after this step of the play?

Use the diagram for Exercises 3–5.

3. Find the coordinates of the image of $ABCD$ after it is moved 6 units left and 2 units up.

4. The original image is moved so that its new coordinates are $A'(-1, 7)$, $B'(-6\frac{1}{2}, 7)$, $C'(-5, 4)$, and $D'(-2\frac{1}{2}, 4)$. Identify the transformation.

5. The original image is translated so that the coordinates of B' are $(11\frac{1}{2}, 17)$. What are the coordinates of the other three vertices of the image after this translation?

6. Triangle HJK has vertices $H(0, -9)$, $J(-1, -5)$, and $K(7, 8)$. What are the coordinates of the vertices after the translation $(x, y) \rightarrow (x - 1, y - 3)$?

  A $H'(-1, 12)$, $J'(-2, 8)$, $K'(6, -5)$ C $H'(-1, -12)$, $J'(-2, -8)$, $K'(6, 5)$
  B $H'(1, -12)$, $J'(2, -8)$, $K'(-6, 5)$ D $H'(1, 12)$, $J'(2, 8)$, $K'(-6, -5)$

7. A segment has endpoints at $S(2, 3)$ and $T(-2, 8)$. After a transformation, the image has endpoints at $S'(2, 3)$ and $T'(6, 8)$. Which best describes the transformation?

  F reflection across the y-axis   H rotation about the origin
  G translation $(x, y) \rightarrow (x + 8, y)$ J rotation about the point $(2, 3)$

This page provides students with the opportunity to apply concepts from the Common Core in real-world problem situations. There are three different levels of performance tasks:

⭐**Novice:** These are short word problems that require students to apply the math they have learned in straightforward, real-world situations.

⭐⭐**Apprentice:** These are more involved problems that guide students step-by-step through more complex tasks. These exercises include more complicated reasoning, writing, and open-ended elements.

⭐⭐⭐**Expert:** These are open-ended, non-routine problems that, instead of stepping the students through, ask them to choose their own methods for solving and justify their answers and reasoning.

Sample answers

1. Possible answer: They are rotations of the first place setting with the center of rotation in the center of the table, clockwise or counterclockwise. The second setting is a rotation of 90 degrees, the third is 180 degrees, and the fourth is 270 degrees.

2. Possible answer: Draw a line segment. Starting at one of the first segment's endpoints, draw a second segment that is congruent and perpendicular to the first. Repeat this process starting with the second segment, and then one more time starting with the third segment.

3. Scoring Guide:

Task	Possible points
a	1 point for correctly naming the corner of 44th Street and 15th Avenue as the meeting place, and 1 point for showing appropriate work, for example: $\left(\frac{56+32}{2}, \frac{12+18}{2}\right) = \left(\frac{88}{2}, \frac{30}{2}\right) = (44, 15)$
b	1 point for correctly writing Mark's distance as $1.25d$
c	1 point for writing the equation $d + 1.25d = 30$ or equivalent, 1 point for solving and getting $d = 13\frac{1}{3}$, and 1 point for correctly stating that Mandy should walk $13\frac{1}{3}$ blocks and Mark should walk $16\frac{2}{3}$ blocks

Total possible points: 6

Performance Tasks

COMMON
CORE
CC.9-12.A.SSE.1
CC.9-12.G.CO.1
CC.9-12.G.CO.5

⭐ **1.** A square table is set with four identical place settings, one on each side of the table. Each setting consists of a plate and spoon, with the spoon always to the right of the plate. If you start with one setting, what transformation describes the location of each of the other three? Express your answer in terms of degrees, lines of reflection, or directions from the original place setting.

⭐ **2.** Without using the word "square," how would you explain how to draw one to a classmate on the telephone?

⭐ **3.** The east-west streets and north-south avenues of a certain city are numbered consecutively from south to north and east to west. All blocks are squares with the same side lengths. Mandy is standing on the corner of 56th Street and 12th Avenue. Mark is standing on the corner of 32nd Street and 18th Avenue. Mark calls Mandy and asks her to meet him at a spot halfway between their current locations.

   a. Use the Midpoint Formula to find out where Mark wants to meet. Show your work.

   b. Mandy says that Mark walks faster than she does, so he should have to walk farther. Assume that Mark walks 1.25 times as fast as Mandy. If Mandy's distance walked in a given time period is d, what is the distance Mark can walk in the same time period?

   c. Use your results in part **b** to write and solve an equation to find the distances Mark and Mandy should each walk.

continued

⭐⭐⭐ **4.** Tanya is using the tile design shown at right to tile her bathroom floor. Each tile has the pattern on only one side.

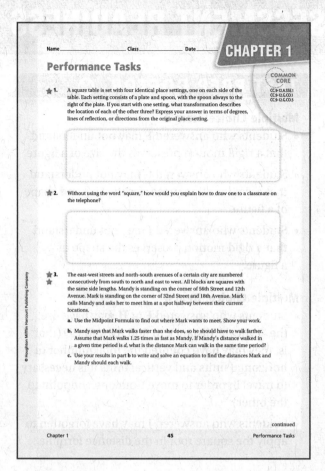

   a. Tanya wants to make a pattern by creating 2-by-2 squares using the tile. Draw an example of a 2-by-2 square she could create and explain what transformations she could use to make the square.

   b. Tanya wants to make the 2-by-2 square shown at right. What transformation would she need to use to make it? Why is this not physically possible?

4. Scoring Guide:

Task	Possible points
a	1 point for each design, and 1 point for each description, for a total of 4 points, for example: Tanya can create this pattern by starting with the upper-left tile, then translating it three times and rotating two of them by 180°.
b	1 point for identifying that a reflection would be needed to make the pattern shown, and 1 point for explaining that Tanya would not be able to get a reflection image of a physical tile

Total possible points: 6

© Houghton Mifflin Harcourt Publishing Company

COMMON CORE CORRELATION

Standard	Items
CC.9-12.G.CO.1	1, 6
CC.9-12.G.CO.2	2
CC.9-12.G.CO.5	9
CC.9-12.G.CO.9	7
CC.9-12.G.CO.12	3, 5
CC.9-12.GPE.4	4, 8
CC.9-12.GPE.6	7

TEST PREP DOCTOR ✚

Multiple Choice: Item 2
- Students who answered **F** may not understand that a rigid motion preserves the size of a figure.
- Students who answered **G** may not understand that a rigid motion preserves the size and shape of a figure.
- Students who answered **J** may not understand that a rigid motion preserves the shape of a figure.

Multiple Choice: Item 4
- Students who answered **F** or **H** may have use the "taxicab" distance to find *AB* and *CD* (that is, they may have counted the total number of horizontal units and vertical units it is necessary to travel in order to move from one endpoint to the other).
- Students who answered **J** may have forgotten to apply the square root in the distance formula.

CHAPTER 1 COMMON CORE ASSESSMENT READINESS

Name _____ Class _____ Date _____

MULTIPLE CHOICE

1. Which term has the following definition?

It is a portion of a line consisting of two points and all points between them.

A. angle   **C.** line segment

B. endpoint   D. ray

2. Each figure shows the pre-image ($\triangle JKL$) and image ($\triangle J'K'L'$) under a transformation. Which transformation appears to be a rigid motion?

F.

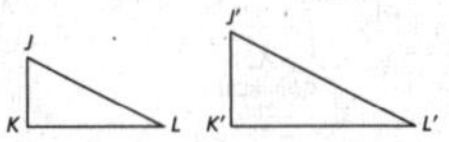

G.

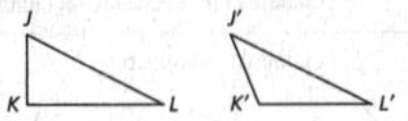

H.

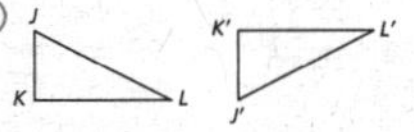

J.

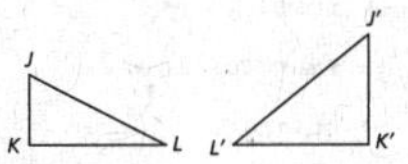

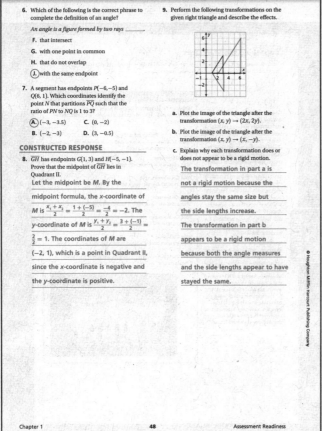

3. Lisa wants to use a compass and straightedge to copy $\overline{XY}$. She uses the straightedge to draw a line segment, and she labels one endpoint Q. What should she do next?

A. Open the compass to distance XY.

B. Open the compass to distance XQ.

C. Use a ruler to measure $\overline{XY}$.

D. Use the straightedge to draw $\overline{XQ}$.

4. You want to prove that $\overline{AB}$ is longer than $\overline{CD}$. To do so, you use the distance formula to find the lengths of the segments. Which of the following are the correct lengths?

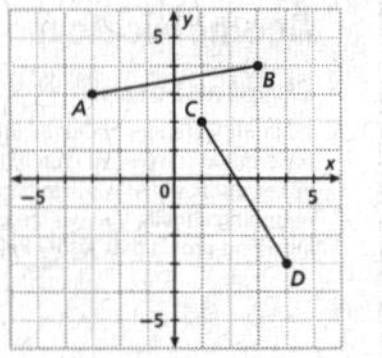

F. $AB = 7$, $CD = 8$

G. $AB = \sqrt{37}$, $CD = \sqrt{34}$

H. $AB = \sqrt{49}$, $CD = \sqrt{64}$

J. $AB = 37$, $CD = 34$

5. Kendrick is using a compass and straightedge to copy $\angle Q$. The figure shows the portion of the construction that he has already completed. Where should Kendrick place the point of the compass to do the next step of the construction?

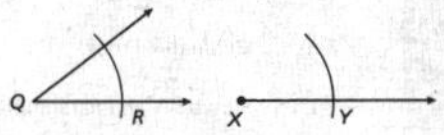

A. point Q

B. point R

C. point X

D. point Y

---

6. Which of the following is the correct phrase to complete the definition of an angle?

An angle is a figure formed by two rays _____.

F. that intersect

G. with one point in common

H. that do not overlap

J. with the same endpoint

7. A segment has endpoints $P(-6, -5)$ and $Q(6, 1)$. Which coordinates identify the point N that partitions $\overline{PQ}$ such that the ratio of PN to NQ is 1 to 3?

A. $(-3, -3.5)$ C. $(0, -2)$

B. $(-2, -3)$ D. $(3, -0.5)$

CONSTRUCTED RESPONSE

8. $\overline{GH}$ has endpoints $G(1, 3)$ and $H(-5, -1)$. Prove that the midpoint of $\overline{GH}$ lies in Quadrant II.

Let the midpoint be M. By the

midpoint formula, the x-coordinate of

M is $\frac{x_1 + x_2}{2} = \frac{1 + (-5)}{2} = \frac{-4}{2} = -2$. The

y-coordinate of M is $\frac{y_1 + y_2}{2} = \frac{3 + (-1)}{2} =$

$\frac{2}{2} = 1$. The coordinates of M are

$(-2, 1)$, which is a point in Quadrant II,

since the x-coordinate is negative and

the y-coordinate is positive.

9. Perform the following transformations on the given right triangle and describe the effects.

a. Plot the image of the triangle after the transformation $(x, y) \rightarrow (2x, 2y)$.

b. Plot the image of the triangle after the transformation $(x, y) \rightarrow (x, -y)$.

c. Explain why each transformation does or does not appear to be a rigid motion.

The transformation in part a is

not a rigid motion because the

angles stay the same size but

the side lengths increase.

The transformation in part b

appears to be a rigid motion

because both the angle measures

and the side lengths appear to have

stayed the same.

CHAPTER 2

Geometric Reasoning

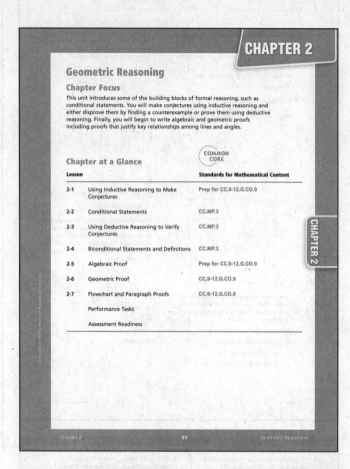

CHAPTER 2

Geometric Reasoning

Chapter Focus

This unit introduces some of the building blocks of formal reasoning, such as conditional statements. You will make conjectures using inductive reasoning and either disprove them by finding a counterexample or prove them using deductive reasoning. Finally, you will begin to write algebraic and geometric proofs including proofs that justify key relationships among lines and angles.

Chapter at a Glance

Lesson		Standards for Mathematical Content
2-1	Using Inductive Reasoning to Make Conjectures	Prep for CC.9-12.G.CO.9
2-2	Conditional Statements	CC.MP.3
2-3	Using Deductive Reasoning to Verify Conjectures	CC.MP.3
2-4	Biconditional Statements and Definitions	CC.MP.3
2-5	Algebraic Proof	Prep for CC.9-12.G.CO.9
2-6	Geometric Proof	CC.9-12.G.CO.9
2-7	Flowchart and Paragraph Proofs	CC.9-12.G.CO.9
	Performance Tasks	
	Assessment Readiness	

Chapter 2 49 Geometric Reasoning

COMMON CORE PROFESSIONAL DEVELOPMENT **CC.MP.3**

Throughout the program and this course, in lab activities and explorations, students have made conjectures and justified their reasoning. In this chapter, students will begin a formal study of logic and reasoning, which opens doors to new explorations into geometric concepts. It is important for students to understand that by inductive reasoning, many mathematical principles are discovered. However, it is also very important for students to realize that making a conjecture based on the observation of many trials can never constitute a proof. Students will learn that deductive reasoning, the process of using logic to draw conclusions from established facts, can be used to prove conjectures and theorems.

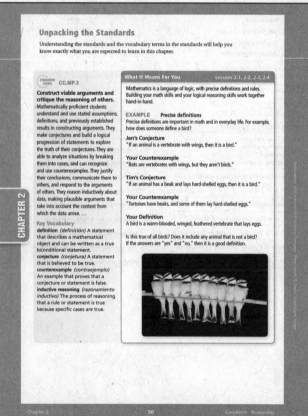

Unpacking the Standards

Understanding the standards and the vocabulary terms in the standards will help you know exactly what you are expected to learn in this chapter.

COMMON CORE CC.MP.3

Construct viable arguments and critique the reasoning of others. Mathematically proficient students understand and use stated assumptions, definitions, and previously established results in constructing arguments. They make conjectures and build a logical progression of statements to explore the truth of their conjectures. They are able to analyze situations by breaking them into cases, and can recognize and use counterexamples. They justify their conclusions, communicate them to others, and respond to the arguments of others. They reason inductively about data, making plausible arguments that take into account the context from which the data arose. ...

Key Vocabulary

definition *(definición)* A statement that describes a mathematical object and can be written as a true biconditional statement.
conjecture *(conjetura)* A statement that is believed to be true.
counterexample *(contraejemplo)* An example that proves that a conjecture or statement is false.
inductive reasoning *(razonamiento inductivo)* The process of reasoning that a rule or statement is true because specific cases are true.

What It Means For You Lessons 2-1, 2-2, 2-3, 2-4

Mathematics is a language of logic, with precise definitions and rules. Building your math skills and your logical reasoning skills work together hand-in-hand.

EXAMPLE Precise definitions
Precise definitions are important in math and in everyday life. For example, how does someone define a bird?

Jen's Conjecture
"If an animal is a vertebrate with wings, then it is a bird."

Your Counterexample
"Bats are vertebrates with wings, but they aren't birds."

Tim's Conjecture
"If an animal has a beak and lays hard-shelled eggs, then it is a bird."

Your Counterexample
"Tortoises have beaks, and some of them lay hard-shelled eggs."

Your Definition
A bird is a warm-blooded, winged, feathered vertebrate that lays eggs.

Is this true of all birds? Does it include any animal that is not a bird? If the answers are "yes" and "no," then it is a good definition.

Chapter 2 50 Geometric Reasoning

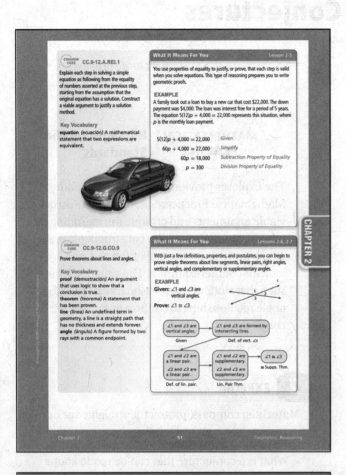

Students have previously used deductive reasoning when solving equations by applying a property of equality to each step of the solution. In this chapter, students begin writing formal two-column proofs by using the familiar concept of solving equations, and then they move into formal geometric proofs of basic concepts and theorems. Point out to students that, although some simple statements do not appear to need proof, students need to use these cases to learn how to make logically sound and well-structured arguments. They also will learn the various forms of geometric proof that may be used (e.g., two-column proofs, flowchart proofs, and paragraph proofs).

CHAPTER 2

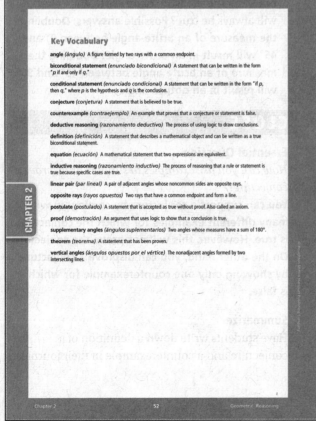

Using Inductive Reasoning to Make Conjectures
Going Deeper

Essential question: How can you use examples to support or disprove a conjecture?

COMMON CORE Standards for Mathematical Content

CC.9-12.G.CO.12 Make formal geometric constructions with a variety of tools ...

Prep for CC.9-12.G.CO.9 Prove theorems about lines and angles.

Prerequisites
Measuring and Constructing Angles
Classifying Angles

Math Background
Mathematical reasoning can take two directions. Deductive reasoning steps logically from definite premises to a definite general conclusion. Inductive reasoning makes a conjecture about what is true in general by examining several cases. You can sometimes prove a conjecture using deductive reasoning, or disprove it by finding a counterexample.

INTRODUCE

Ask students if they know what a conjecture and a counterexample are. Tell them that they will use inductive reasoning to make conjectures about angle measures that result from geometric constructions.

TEACH

1 EXPLORE

Materials: compass, protractor, straightedge or ruler

Questioning Strategies
- Describe what you see in the diagram. **Possible answer: obtuse angle *ABC*, congruent acute angles *ABD* and *DBC***
- Without measuring, how can you be sure that an angle you draw is obtuse? **Possible answer: It forms an angle bigger than the corner of a textbook but not as big as a straight line.**
- What do all the angles formed by the bisectors and the rays of the original angles have in common? **They are all acute.**

MATHEMATICAL PRACTICE — Highlighting the Standards

The Explores provide opportunities to address Mathematical Practices Standard 3 (Construct viable arguments and critique the reasoning of others). Students perform constructions, make conjectures about the angles formed, and look for counterexamples. The situations are such that students can reasonably deduce the angle relationships to confirm or refute their conjectures.

2 EXPLORE

Materials: compass, protractor, straightedge or ruler

Questioning Strategies
- What is a conjecture that can be made about doubling the measure of an acute angle that will always be true? **Possible answers: Doubling the measure of an acute angle between 0° and 45° will result in an acute angle. Doubling the measure of an acute angle between 45° and 90° will result in an obtuse angle.**

CLOSE

Essential Question
How can you use examples to support or disprove a conjecture?
You can support a conjecture by coming up with many different examples for which the conjecture is true. However, this will not prove the conjecture. On the other hand, you can disprove a conjecture by showing only one counterexample for which it is false.

Summarize
Have students write down a definition of a conjecture and a counterexample in their journals.

Name_____ Class_____ Date_____

2-1

Using Inductive Reasoning to Make Conjectures
Going Deeper

Essential question: How can you use examples to support or disprove a conjecture?

Video Tutor

PREP FOR CC.9-12.G.CO.9

1 **E X P L O R E**   Making Conjectures about Bisectors of Obtuse Angles

A   Draw several obtuse angles. Recall that an obtuse angle is an angle whose measure is between 90° and 180°. One such angle, ∠*ABC*, is shown in the diagram. Ray *BD* shows the angle bisector of ∠*ABC*.

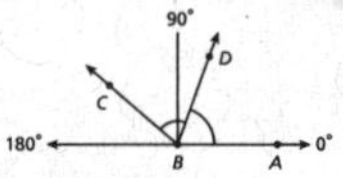

B   Using a protractor, measure each angle. Record each measure for each drawing.

C   Construct the angle bisector of each angle you drew. Record the measures of the two angles determined by the bisectors on your drawings.

D   Fill in the table to record your work. Angle 1 is an example for you.

Angle	1	2	3	4	5	6
Measure	140°					
Measures of Angles Formed by Bisector	70°					
	70°					

REFLECT

1a. Based on your table, make a conjecture about the classification of the angles formed when you bisect an obtuse angle.

Conjecture: The two congruent angles formed by an angle bisector in the interior of an obtuse angle are acute.

1b. Write a range of angle measures for each of the two angles formed by the angle bisector in each of your diagrams. Justify your range.

The original angles have measures between 90° and 180°. Each angle formed by a bisector has a measure between half of 90° and half of 180°. So, the measures of the bisected angles range from 45° to 90°.

PREP FOR CC.9-12.G.CO.9

2 **E X P L O R E**   Making Conjectures about Double Angles of Acute Angles

A   Draw several acute angles. Recall that an acute angle measures between 0° and 90°. One such angle, ∠*ABC*, is shown in the diagram. Be sure to draw 30° and 60° angles as examples.

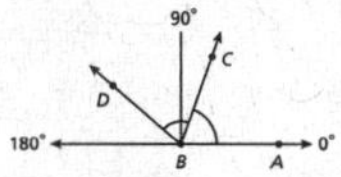

B   Using a protractor, measure each angle. Record each measure on each angle drawing.

C   Using angle construction, draw an adjacent angle for each original angle. In the diagram above, ∠*CBD* is the congruent adjacent angle. Record the measures of the original angles and the double angles on your drawings.

D   Fill in the table to record your work. Angle 1 is an example for you.

Angle	1	2	3	4	5	6
Measure	70°					
Double Angle Measure	140°					

REFLECT

2a. Comment on the following conjecture: When an acute angle is copied so that the new angle is adjacent to the original angle, the resulting double angle is always obtuse.

This statement is not always true. It is true for a 60° angle but is not true for a 30° angle.

2b. How many angles must you test in order to determine that the conjecture above is not always true?

One counterexample is enough to disprove a conjecture. A 30° angle is a counterexample that proves the conjecture is not always true.

2c. For what angle measure will an angle along with its adjacent copy form neither an acute nor an obtuse angle? Explain.

A 45° angle; such an angle along with its adjacent copy will form a right angle. Right angles are neither acute nor obtuse.

© Houghton Mifflin Harcourt Publishing Company

Assign these pages to help your students practice and apply important lesson concepts. For additional exercises, see the Student Edition.

Answers

Additional Practice

1.

Figure	A	B	C	D
Number of sides	4	5	6	7
Number of triangles formed	2	3	4	5

2. $n - 2$ triangles

3. positive   4. $n - 3$

5. Possible answers: zero, any negative number

6.

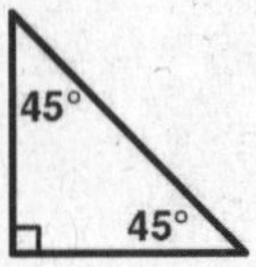

7. One-third of the bills were counterfeit.

Problem Solving

1. D: $6 + 8 = 14$, $6 + 10 = 16$, $8 + 10 = 18$;
   E: $9 + 6 = 15$, $9 + 5 = 14$, $6 + 5 = 11$;
   F: $5 + 7 = 12$, $5 + 5 = 10$, $7 + 5 = 12$;
   G: $10 + 15 = 25$; $10 + 9 = 19$; $15 + 9 = 24$.
   For all four triangles, the sum of the lengths of any two sides is greater than the length of the third side. Conjecture: The lengths of any two sides of a triangle is greater than the length of the third side.

2. Match 7 lasted 1 hour 3 minutes.

3. Match 4 was 18 minutes long.

4. A   5. H

© Houghton Mifflin Harcourt Publishing Company

2-1

Name_____ Class_____ Date_____

Additional Practice

In each figure, all possible diagonals are drawn from a single vertex.
Use the figures in Exercises 1 and 2.

A   B   C   D

1. Fill in the table.

Figure	A	B	C	D
Number of sides				
Number of triangles formed				

2. Use inductive reasoning to make a conjecture about the number of triangles formed when all possible diagonals are drawn from one vertex of a polygon with n sides.

_____

Complete each conjecture.

3. The square of any negative number is _____.

4. The number of segments determined by n points is _____.

Show that each conjecture is false by finding a counterexample.

5. For any integer n, $n^3 > 0$.

_____

6. Each angle in a right triangle has a different measure.

_____

7. For many years in the United States, each bank printed its own currency. The variety of different bills led to widespread counterfeiting. By the time of the Civil War, a significant fraction of the currency in circulation was counterfeit. If one Civil War soldier had 48 bills, 16 of which were counterfeit, and another soldier had 39 bills, 13 of which were counterfeit, make a conjecture about what fraction of bills were counterfeit at the time of the Civil War.

Chapter 2   55   Lesson 1

© Houghton Mifflin Harcourt Publishing Company

Problem Solving

1. Residents of an apartment complex were given use of plots of land in a community garden. Some of the plots were shaped like triangles. The lengths (in feet) of the three sides a, b, and c of some of the triangular plots are shown in the table. For each triangular plot, compare the sum of the lengths of any two sides to the length of the third side. Then use inductive reasoning to make a conjecture comparing the sum of the lengths of any two sides of a triangle to the length of the third side.

Triangle	a	b	c
D	6	8	10
E	9	6	5
F	5	7	5
G	10	15	9

_____
_____
_____

The times for the first eight matches of the Santa Barbara Open women's volleyball tournament are shown. Show that each conjecture is false by finding a counterexample.

Match	1	2	3	4	5	6	7	8
Time	0:31	0:56	0:51	0:18	0:50	0:34	1:03	0:36

2. Every one of the first eight matches lasted less than 1 hour.

3. These matches were all longer than a half hour.

For each of the tiles shown, all of the angles have the same measure. Use a protractor to find the measure of the angles for each tile. Select the best answer.

A   B   C

4. Which expressions could you use in the given order to complete the following statement: Figure ▢ has ▢ sides and the sum of the angle measures is ▢ × 180°.

A B; 5; 3   C C; 6; 3
B A; 4; 4   D A; 4; 3

5. Which is a reasonable conjecture?

F The sum of the angle measures of a polygon with n sides is $(4n)°$.

G The sum of the angle measures of a polygon with n sides is $n(360°)$.

H The sum of the angle measures of a polygon with n sides is $(n-2)(180°)$.

J The sum of the angle measures of a polygon with n sides is $(n-2)(360°)$.

Chapter 2   56   Lesson 1

© Houghton Mifflin Harcourt Publishing Company

Conditional Statements
Extension: Inference Using Venn Diagrams

Essential question: How can you use a Venn diagram to interpret conditional statements?

© Houghton Mifflin Harcourt Publishing Company

COMMON CORE **Standards for Mathematical Content**

CC.MP.3 Construct viable arguments and critique the reasoning of others.

Prerequisites
Drawing Venn Diagrams
Conditional Statements

Math Background
The conditional statement is the backbone of mathematical logic and reasoning. Many theorems and definitions are given in conditional-statement form, indicated by *If/Then*. It is important for students to understand that a statement and its contrapositive are logically equivalent but that a statement and its converse or inverse are equivalent only under certain conditions.

INTRODUCE

Review or introduce the concepts of set and subset. Point out that a subset is a set completely contained in another set. Remind students that they can use Venn diagrams to illustrate set relationships.

TEACH

MATHEMATICAL PRACTICE **Highlighting the Standards**

The lesson provides opportunities to address Mathematical Practices Standard 4 (Model with mathematics). Students use Venn diagrams to visually represent an hypothesis and a conclusion in order to analyze the abstract concept of a conditional statement.

1 EXPLORE

Questioning Strategies
- In the diagram in Part A, which set is the subset of the other set? **The set of dogs is a subset of the set of animals.**

- If you shade inside a circle to show membership, *p*, how do you indicate that something is not a member? **Shade outside the circle, ~*p*.**
- If a point is in the circle for animals, is it in the circle for dogs? **Not necessarily. It could be inside the large circle and outside the small circle.**
- Suppose a point is outside the circle for animals. Look at the diagram in Part D. Can the point represent a dog? **No. If the point is outside the large circle, then it is also outside the small circle.**
- Suppose that you know an object is a cat. Where would you place a point to represent this? **Place the point inside the circle representing animals but outside the circle representing dogs.**

CLOSE

Essential Question
How can you use a Venn diagram to interpret conditional statements?
Sketch a rectangle with a pair of nesting circles inside. Represent the hypothesis of the conditional statement by a letter in the inner circle and the conclusion by a letter in the outer circle.

Summarize
Have students draw a blank Venn diagram like the one below in their journals, write a conditional statement, and label the circles accordingly.

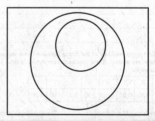

PRACTICE

Where skills are taught	Where skills are practiced
1 EXPLORE	EXS. 1–5

Exercise 6: Students visually examine the case when a statement and its converse are both true.

Exercise 7: Students visually examine logical statements that relate three conditions.

Name_____ Class_____ Date_____

2-2

Conditional Statements
Extension: Inference Using Venn Diagrams

Essential question: *How can you use a Venn diagram to interpret conditional statements?*

A conditional statement is one that has the form *If p, then q,* denoted *p → q*. The notation ~*p* is used to denote "not *p*." You can use Venn diagrams to study conditionals.

CC MP3

1 EXPLORE Using Venn Diagrams to Analyze Conditional Statements

Shade the region in the Venn diagram that represents each statement. Part A is already filled in as an example.

All dogs are animals. If an object is a dog, then it is an animal.
               p   *q*

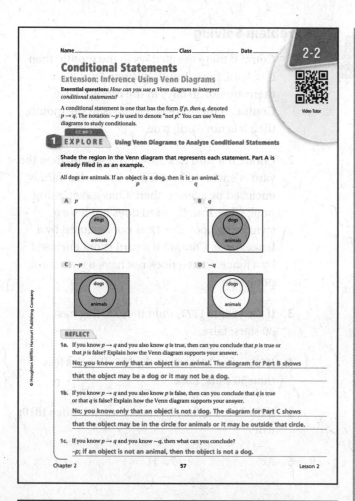

A *p*

B *q*

C ~*p*

D ~*q*

REFLECT

1a. If you know *p → q* and you also know *q* is true, then can you conclude that *p* is true or that *p* is false? Explain how the Venn diagram supports your answer.

No; you know only that an object is an animal. The diagram for Part B shows that the object may be a dog or it may not be a dog.

1b. If you know *p → q* and you also know *p* is false, then can you conclude that *q* is true or that *q* is false? Explain how the Venn diagram supports your answer.

No; you know only that an object is not a dog. The diagram for Part C shows that the object may be in the circle for animals or it may be outside that circle.

1c. If you know *p → q* and you know ~*q*, then what can you conclude?

~*p*; if an object is not an animal, then the object is not a dog.

Chapter 2   57   Lesson 2

PRACTICE

Four Venn diagrams related to *q → p* are shown. Shade the region that represents each statement.

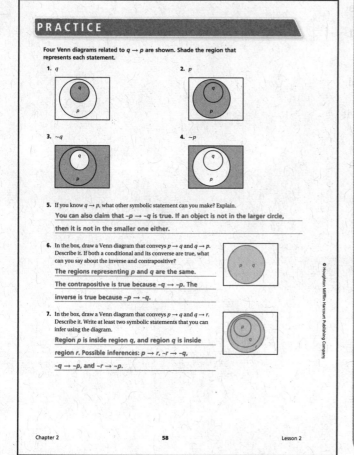

1. *q*

2. *p*

3. ~*q*

4. ~*p*

5. If you know *q → p*, what other symbolic statement can you make? Explain.

You can also claim that ~*p → ~q* is true. If an object is not in the larger circle, then it is not in the smaller one either.

6. In the box, draw a Venn diagram that conveys *p → q* and *q → p*. Describe it. If both a conditional and its converse are true, what can you say about the inverse and contrapositive?

The regions representing *p* and *q* are the same.

The contrapositive is true because ~*q → ~p*. The inverse is true because ~*p → ~q*.

7. In the box, draw a Venn diagram that conveys *p → q* and *q → r*. Describe it. Write at least two symbolic statements that you can infer using the diagram.

Region *p* is inside region *q*, and region *q* is inside region *r*. Possible inferences: *p → r*, ~*r → ~q*, ~*q → ~p*, and ~*r → ~p*.

Chapter 2   58   Lesson 2

Assign these pages to help your students practice and apply important lesson concepts. For additional exercises, see the Student Edition.

Answers

Additional Practice

1. Hypothesis: You can see the stars. Conclusion: It is night.

2. Hypothesis: A pencil is sharp. Conclusion: The pencil writes well.

3. If three points are noncollinear, then they determine a plane.

4. If a food is a kumquat, then it is a fruit.

5. true   6. true

7. false; sample answer: a frog

8. Converse: If GH is 3, then G is at 4; false

   Inverse: If G is not at 4, then GH is not 3; false

   Contrapositive: If GH is not 3, then G is not at 4; true

9. If an animal is a primate, then it is a mammal.

10. Sample answer: If an animal is a lemur, then it is not a rodent.

11. Sample answer: If an animal is a rodent, then it is not an ape.

12. If an animal is an ape, then it is a mammal.

Problem Solving

1. Conv.: If there are 30 days in the month, then it is April; false. Inv.: If it is not April, then there are not 30 days in the month; false. Contra.: If there are not 30 days in the month, then it is not April; true.

2. Cond.: If a yard has a swimming pool, then the yard is enclosed by a fence. Conv.: If a yard is enclosed by a fence, then it has a swimming pool; false. Inv.: If a yard does not have a swimming pool, then it is not enclosed by a fence; false. Contra.: If a yard is not enclosed by a fence, then it does not have a swimming pool; true.

3. If the year is 1777, then the U.S. flag has 30 stars; false.

4. If it is after 1818, then the U.S. flag has less than 50 stars; false.

5. If the U.S. flag has 30 stars, then it is after 1818; true.

6. A   7. H

Additional Practice

Identify the hypothesis and conclusion of each conditional.

1. If you can see the stars, then it is night.

   Hypothesis: _____

   Conclusion: _____

2. A pencil writes well if it is sharp.

   Hypothesis: _____

   Conclusion: _____

Write a conditional statement from each of the following.

3. Three noncollinear points determine a plane.

   _____

4.

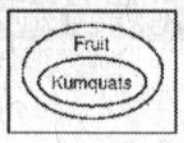

   Fruit
   Kumquats

   _____

   _____

   _____

Determine if each conditional is true. If false, give a counterexample.

5. If two points are noncollinear, then a right triangle contains one obtuse angle.

   _____

6. If a liquid is water, then it is composed of hydrogen and oxygen.

   _____

7. If a living thing is green, then it is a plant.

   _____

8. "If G is at 4, then GH is 3." Write the converse, inverse, and contrapositive of this statement. Find the truth value of each.

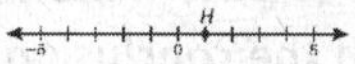

   Converse: _____

   Inverse: _____

   Contrapositive: _____

This chart shows a small part of the *Mammalia* class of animals, the mammals. Write a conditional to describe the relationship between each given pair.

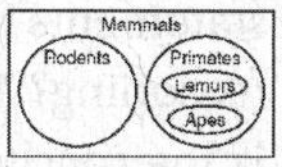

Mammals
Rodents   Primates
Lemurs
Apes

9. primates and mammals_____

10. lemurs and rodents_____

11. rodents and apes_____

12. apes and mammals_____

Problem Solving

1. Write the converse, inverse, and contrapositive of the conditional statement. Find the truth value of each.

   If it is April, then there are 30 days in the month.

   _____

   _____

   _____

2. Write a conditional statement from the diagram. Then write the converse, inverse, and contrapositive. Find the truth value of each.

   Yard
   Enclosed by a fence
   Has swimming pool

   _____

   _____

   _____

   _____

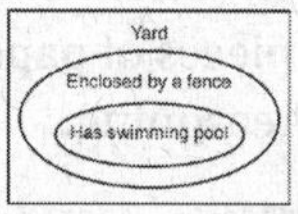

Use the table and the statements listed. Write each conditional and find its truth value.

p: 1777   *q*: 30 stars   *r*: after 1818   *s*: less than 50 stars

U.S. Flag	
Year	Number of Stars
1777	13
1818	20
1848	30
1959	50

3. $p \rightarrow q$_____

   _____

4. $r \rightarrow s$_____

5. $q \rightarrow s$_____

Choose the best answer.

6. What is the converse of "If you saw the movie, then you know how it ends"?

   A If you know how the movie ends, then you saw the movie.

   B If you did not see the movie, then you do not know how it ends.

   C If you do not know how the movie ends, then you did not see the movie.

   D If you do not know how the movie ends, then you saw the movie.

7. What is the inverse of "If you received a text message, then you have a cell phone"?

   F If you have a cell phone, then you received a text message.

   G If you do not have a cell phone, then you did not receive a text message.

   H If you did not receive a text message, then you do not have a cell phone.

   J If you received a text message, then you do not have a cell phone.

Notes

Using Deductive Reasoning to Verify Conjectures
Going Deeper

Essential question: *How can you connect statements to visualize a chain of reasoning?*

COMMON CORE **Standards for Mathematical Content**

CC.MP.3 Construct viable arguments and critique the reasoning of others.

Prerequisites

Conditional Statements

Math Background

Deductive reasoning is a thought process used throughout geometry. Students may take different paths to reach a conclusion, but if deductive reasoning is used, the conclusion is valid. Success in deductive reasoning relies on the order used to present statements of an argument or proof. Students should be familiar with the importance of order in conditional statements. These statements can be written using symbolic notation, where an implication arrow ($\rightarrow$) is used to connect the conclusion that follows from the hypothesis. By introducing symbolic notation, students can clearly see the structure of deductive reasoning. Understanding this structure is a precursor to writing geometric proofs.

INTRODUCE

Review the Law of Detachment. Then present each of the following statements in its own rectangle: p, $p \rightarrow q$, q. State the Law of Detachment again and draw arrows from one rectangle to the next to show the reasoning used in the law. Discuss how the arrows from one rectangle to the next show the structure of the reasoning used. A similar presentation can be done for the Law of Syllogism, but place the rectangles out of order and ask the students to help draw the arrows from one rectangle to the next.

TEACH

 EXAMPLE

Questioning Strategies

• Suppose no arrows are given in Parts A and B. Is it possible to draw all of the arrows to prove the statement? Explain. **Yes; the statements can be used to determine the chain of reasoning used to reach the conclusion.**

• How do you determine whether one of the statements in a box will be used in the chain of reasoning? **The statement will be used if its given is the conclusion of a previous statement, and its conclusion is the given of a following statement.**

• Why are there two separate chains of reasoning in Part B? **Two conditions must be true (q and b) in order for z to be true. So there is a separate chain of reasoning for each condition.**

Differentiated Instruction

To assist students in forming a chain of reasoning, each statement can be written on a piece of paper (or sticky note) and arranged to form the chain of reasoning. Then the arrangement can be used to draw the missing arrows. This can be made into an interactive activity by having students hold the pieces of paper and form a line to show the chain of reasoning.

2 **EXAMPLE**

Questioning Strategies

• In Example 2, is it possible to complete the chain of reasoning without using the statement with missing information? Explain. **No; the statement that contains the conclusion, $m \rightarrow b$, must be used, and the statement with the missing information is the only statement that can precede the statement $m \rightarrow b$.**

© Houghton Mifflin Harcourt Publishing Company

continued

Name_____ Class_____ Date_____

2-3

Using Deductive Reasoning to Verify Conjectures

Going Deeper

Essential question: *How can you connect statements to visualize a chain of reasoning?*

Deductive reasoning connects true statements to form a valid conclusion. This process can be represented visually by using arrows to show how one true statement follows from a previous true statement. Such a diagram shows the sequence used to link given statements to a final conclusion.

Video Tutor

1 EXAMPLE   Showing Logical Reasoning

Draw arrows to show the logical reasoning used to prove the statement. Some arrows are already drawn to help you.

A Given: m, and the conditional statements in the boxes

Prove: c

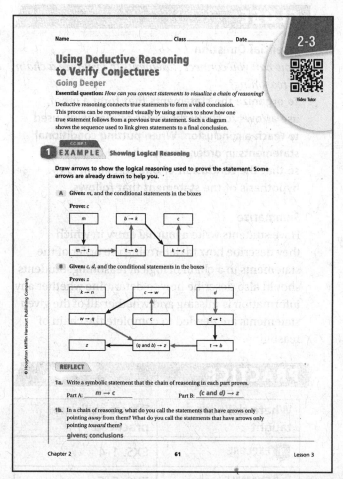

B Given: c, d, and the conditional statements in the boxes

Prove: z

REFLECT

1a. Write a symbolic statement that the chain of reasoning in each part proves.

Part A: $m \rightarrow c$ Part B: $(c \text{ and } d) \rightarrow z$

1b. In a chain of reasoning, what do you call the statements that have arrows only pointing *away* from them? What do you call the statements that have arrows only pointing *toward* them?

givens; conclusions

1c. Are there any statements in Part B that are not used in the chain of reasoning? Explain.

Yes; $k \rightarrow n$ is not used in the reasoning. The statement is not needed.

1d. In the space below, arrange the statements from Part B and draw arrows connecting them in a way that makes the order of the reasoning clearer.

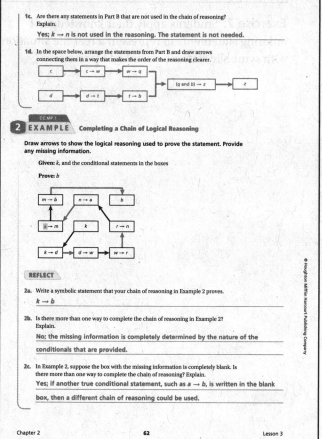

2 EXAMPLE   Completing a Chain of Logical Reasoning

Draw arrows to show the logical reasoning used to prove the statement. Provide any missing information.

Given: k, and the conditional statements in the boxes

Prove: b

REFLECT

2a. Write a symbolic statement that your chain of reasoning in Example 2 proves.

$k \rightarrow b$

2b. Is there more than one way to complete the chain of reasoning in Example 2? Explain.

No; the missing information is completely determined by the nature of the conditionals that are provided.

2c. In Example 2, suppose the box with the missing information is completely blank. Is there more than one way to complete the chain of reasoning? Explain.

Yes; if another true conditional statement, such as $a \rightarrow b$, is written in the blank box, then a different chain of reasoning could be used.

© Houghton Mifflin Harcourt Publishing Company

2 EXAMPLE continued

- Explain how to find missing information in one of the statements of a chain of logical reasoning. Start the chain of logical reasoning from the given statement until no more statements can be connected. Then work backwards from the conclusion until no more statements can be connected. Fill in the missing information to complete the chain of reasoning.

EXTRA EXAMPLE

Reorder the statements below to show the logical reasoning used to prove the statement. Provide any missing information.

$$t, k \rightarrow n, d \rightarrow y, n \rightarrow s, ? \rightarrow d, y \rightarrow q,$$
$$s \rightarrow a, t \rightarrow k, q$$

Given: t, and the conditional statements

Prove: q

$$t, t \rightarrow k, k \rightarrow n, n \rightarrow s, s \rightarrow a, a \rightarrow d,$$
$$d \rightarrow y, y \rightarrow q, q$$

Teaching Strategy

To assist students in finding missing information, give them three of the letters as possible answers. Ask students to try forming a chain of reasoning with each letter.

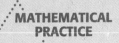

MATHEMATICAL PRACTICE — **Highlighting the Standards**

This lesson provides opportunities to address Mathematical Practices Standard 3 (Construct viable arguments and critique the reasoning of others). Explain to students that they are constructing arguments by using arrows to complete the diagrams. Understanding the importance of the order of statements in an argument will help students when they write more formal arguments later in the course.

© Houghton Mifflin Harcourt Publishing Company

CLOSE

Essential Question

How can you connect statements to visualize a chain of reasoning?

To organize the statements that form a proof, use arrows to show the order of reasoning used to reach a conclusion. When putting conditional statements in order, arrows should be placed so that the conclusion of one statement is the hypothesis of the statement that follows.

Summarize

Have students write a journal entry in which they describe how to determine the order of the statements in a chain of logical reasoning. Students should also describe how to determine whether any information is missing and whether all of the given statements are needed to complete the chain of reasoning.

PRACTICE

Where skills are taught	Where skills are practiced
1 EXPLORE	EXS. 1–4
2 EXAMPLE	EXS. 5, 6

Exercise 7: Students apply their knowledge of ordering statements to represent a real-life situation with symbolic statements linked by arrows.

PRACTICE

Draw arrows to show the logical reasoning used to prove the statement.

1. Given: z, and statements in boxes

Prove: c

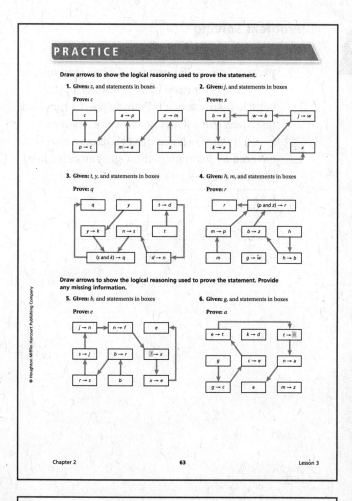

2. Given: j, and statements in boxes

Prove: x

3. Given: t, y, and statements in boxes

Prove: q

4. Given: h, m, and statements in boxes

Prove: r

Draw arrows to show the logical reasoning used to prove the statement. Provide any missing information.

5. Given: b, and statements in boxes

Prove: e

6. Given: g, and statements in boxes

Prove: a

---

7. Write a symbolic statement for each conditional statement. Then represent the chain of reasoning using symbolic statements linked by arrows.

Band members must stay after school on Wednesday.	s
If the marching band performs at halftime, then the band practices on Wednesday.	h → w
If the band practices on Wednesday, then band members must stay after school on Wednesday.	w → s
If there is a football game on Friday, then the marching band performs at halftime.	f → h
There is a football game on Friday.	f

Possible answer:

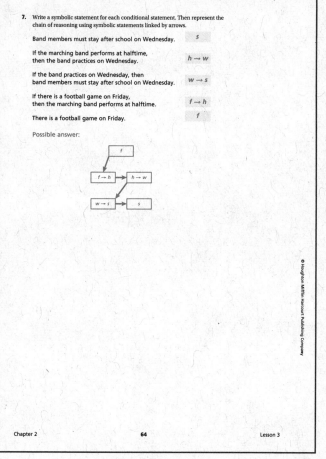

ADDITIONAL PRACTICE AND PROBLEM SOLVING

Assign these pages to help your students practice and apply important lesson concepts. For additional exercises, see the Student Edition.

Answers

Additional Practice

1.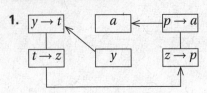

2.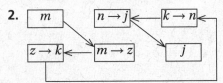

3.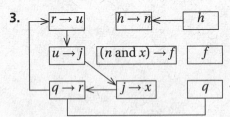

4.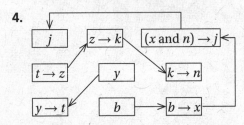

5. Possible answer:

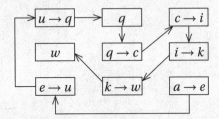

6. Possible answer:

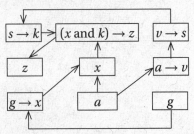

Problem Solving

1. Possible answers: Paloma can drive her parents' car: d; Paloma passes her road test: r; Paloma is covered by her parents' motor vehicle insurance: i; If Paloma passes her road test, then she will get her driver's license: $r \rightarrow l$; If Paloma has a driver's license and is covered by insurance, then she can drive her parents' car: $l + i \rightarrow d$.

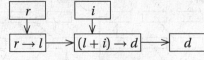

2. A   3. H

4. B

Name_____ Class_____ Date_____ **2-3**

Additional Practice

Draw arrows to show the logical reasoning used to prove the statement.

1. **Given:** *y*, and statements in boxes.
   Prove: *a*

$y \to t$	a	$p \to a$
$t \to z$	y	$z \to p$

2. **Given:** *m*, and statements in boxes.
   Prove: *j*

m	$n \to j$	$k \to n$
$z \to k$	$m \to z$	j

3. **Given:** *h*, *q*, and statements in boxes.
   Prove: *f*

$r \to u$	$h \to n$	h
$u \to j$	$(n \text{ and } x) \to f$	f
$q \to r$	$j \to x$	q

4. **Given:** *b*, *y*, and statements in boxes.
   Prove: *j*

j	$z \to k$	$(x \text{ and } n) \to j$
$t \to z$	y	$k \to n$
$y \to t$	b	$b \to x$

Draw arrows to show the logical reasoning used to prove the statement. Provide any missing information.

5. **Given:** *a*, and statements in boxes.
   Prove: *w*

$u \to q$	q	$c \to i$
w	$\blacksquare \to c$	$i \to k$
$e \to u$	$k \to w$	$a \to e$

6. **Given:** *a*, and statements in boxes.
   Prove: *z*

$s \to k$	$(x \text{ and } k) \to z$	$v \to s$
z	x	$a \to \blacksquare$
$g \to x$	a	g

Problem Solving

Write a symbolic statement for each conditional statement. Then represent the chain of reasoning using symbolic statements linked by arrows.

1. Paloma can drive her parents' car.   _____

   Paloma passes her road test.   _____

   Paloma is covered by her parents' motor vehicle insurance.   _____

   If Paloma passes her road test, then she will get her driver's license.   _____

   If Paloma has a driver's license and is covered by insurance, then she can drive her parents car.   _____

Given *t* and *z*, and the conditional statements in the boxes shown, Jeremy drew arrows to complete the chain of reasoning. Select the best answer.

2. Which statement can you *not* assume to be true from the chain of reasoning?

   A $t \to w$

   B $t \to n$

   C $z \to y$

   D $(n \text{ and } y) \to w$

t	→	$t \to n$
$t \to s$	$z \to y$	$(n \text{ and } y) \to w$
z		w

3. Which symbolic statement did Jeremy prove?

   F $t \to n \to w$

   G $z \to (y \text{ and } w)$

   H $(t \text{ and } z) \to w$

   J $(n \text{ and } y) \to w$

4. Which statement is *not* necessary in the chain of reasoning?

   A $t \to n$

   B $t \to s$

   C z

   D $z \to y$

Biconditional Statements and Definitions
Going Deeper

Essential question: *How can you analyze the truth of a biconditional statement?*

COMMON CORE Standards for Mathematical Content

CC.MP.3 Construct viable arguments and critique the reasoning of others.

Prerequisites

Using Inductive Reasoning to Make Conjectures

Conditional Statements

Using Deductive Reasoning to Verify Conjectures

Math Background

A mathematical system is based on certain assumptions (postulates or axioms) and definitions. A *good definition* is biconditional. That is, the hypothesis implies the conclusion and the conclusion implies the hypothesis.

INTRODUCE

Review the meaning of conditional statement, converse, and the connective "and." Have students try to think of a true statement that has a true converse. For example, if a number is even, then it is divisible by two.

TEACH

1 **EXAMPLE**

Questioning Strategies

- Does the student's definition of square include all squares and exclude polygons that are not squares? No. Squares are included but rectangles whose lengths and widths are unequal are not excluded.

- How do Parts A, B, and C help you evaluate a proposed definition? They follow a process where you write the proposed definition as a pair of conditional statements and then determine whether both statements are true.

EXTRA EXAMPLE

A student defined *circle* this way:

A circle is the set of all points the same distance from a fixed point.

A. Write the biconditional as a pair of conditional statements.
If a geometric figure is a circle, then it is the set of all points the same distance from a fixed point. If a set of points is all the points the same distance from a fixed point, then it is a circle.

B. Analyze each part and tell whether it is true or false. If false, give a counterexample. Explain your thinking.
Every point on a circle is the same distance from the center. However, not all sets of points the same distance from a fixed point form a circle. For instance, a sphere is the set of all points equidistant from a fixed point, but a sphere is not a circle.

C. Tell whether the student's definition of circle is a good one. Explain.
The definition is not good. The phrase "in a plane" should be inserted after "points." Then spheres are excluded and the definition is good.

CLOSE

Essential Question
How can you analyze the truth of a biconditional statement?
Check to see if both conditionals are true.

Summarize
In their journals, have students write a faulty definition of triangle, point out the flaw, and correct the definition.

PRACTICE

Where skills are taught	Where skills are practiced
EXAMPLE	EXS. 1–3

Name_____ Class_____ Date_____

2-4

[QR code]
Video Tutor

Biconditional Statements and Definitions
Going Deeper
Essential question: *How can you analyze the truth of a biconditional statement?*

You have seen *If p, then q* and the notation $p \rightarrow q$. The notation **iff** is shorthand for *if and only if* and means a pair of statements.

$$p \text{ iff } q$$

p if q	and	q if p
$q \rightarrow p$	and	$p \rightarrow q$

The conjunction of these two statements is a biconditional statement. It is true only if both parts are true. It is false if either part is false.

1 EXAMPLE CC.MP.3 **Analyzing Biconditionals and Definitions**

A student defined *square* this way:

A polygon is a square if and only if it has four right angles.

A Write the biconditional as a pair of conditional statements.

If a polygon ___is a square___, then the polygon has four right angles.

If a polygon ___has four right angles___, then the polygon is a square.

B Analyze each part and tell whether it is true or false. If false, give a counterexample. Explain your thinking.

square → four right angles

Every square has four right angles. This statement is true.

four right angles → square

All rectangles have four right angles. However, not all rectangles are squares.

C Tell whether the student's definition of square is a good one. Explain.

The definition does not adequately distinguish a square from other geometric figures such as the rectangle. The biconditional is false, because there is a counterexample for one of its parts.

© Houghton Mifflin Harcourt Publishing Company

REFLECT

1a. Why is it necessary to prove only one of the two parts of a biconditional is false to conclude that the biconditional is false?

A biconditional is a conjunction. The conjunction is false if either part is false.

1b. Revise the student's definition of a square so that it is a good one.

Possible answers: A polygon is a square if and only if it has four congruent sides and one right angle. A polygon is a square if and only if it is a rectangle and it has four congruent sides.

PRACTICE

1. A student defined a scalene triangle as follows: A triangle is scalene if and only if it is a right triangle. Is the biconditional true or false? Justify your claim.

Neither part of the biconditional is true. Many scalene triangles are not right triangles. Many right triangles are not scalene triangles; for example, isosceles right triangles are right but not scalene.

2. A student defined a rectangle as a parallelogram with opposite sides the same length. Describe what is wrong with this definition. Then write a correct definition of a rectangle.

Possible answer: All parallelograms have opposite sides the same length. A rectangle is a parallelogram with opposite sides the same length and a right angle.

3. An acute triangle is a triangle whose angles are acute. Find the error in the following statement.

A triangle is acute if and only if it has one or more acute angles.

One direction of the biconditional is false: If a triangle has one or more acute angles, then it is an acute triangle. A triangle with angle measures 20°, 20°, and 140° has one or more acute angles, but it is an obtuse triangle, because it has an obtuse angle.

© Houghton Mifflin Harcourt Publishing Company

Assign these pages to help your students practice and apply important lesson concepts. For additional exercises, see the Student Edition.

Answers

Additional Practice

1. Conditional: If the tea kettle is whistling, then the water is boiling.
   Converse: If the water is boiling, then the tea kettle is whistling.

2. Conditional: If a biconditional is true, then the conditional and converse are both true.
   Converse: If the conditional and converse are both true, then the biconditional is true.

3. Converse: If $n - 1$ is divisible by 2, then n is an odd number.
   Biconditional: n is an odd number if and only if $n - 1$ is divisible by 2.

4. Converse: If an angle measures between 90° and 180°, then the angle is obtuse.
   Biconditional: An angle is obtuse if and only if it measures between 90° and 180°.

5. No; sample answer: The switch could be off.

6. No; possible answer: Leap years have a Feb. 29th.

7. A figure is a cube if and only if it is a three-dimensional solid with six square faces.

8. A person is a doofus if and only if the person is Tanya's younger brother.

Problem Solving

1. No; marathon races are also massstarted, so the conditional is false.

2. No; time is also a factor in freeride races, so the converse is false.

3. Yes; a mountain bike race covers 250 kilometers if and only if it is a marathon race.

4. No; a downhill race does not contain cliffs, drops, and ramps, so the converse is false.

5. C   6. G

Additional Practice

Write the conditional statement and converse within each biconditional.

1. The tea kettle is whistling if and only if the water is boiling.

   Conditional: _____

   Converse: _____

2. A biconditional is true if and only if the conditional and converse are both true.

   Conditional: _____

   Converse: _____

For each conditional, write the converse and a biconditional statement.

3. Conditional: If n is an odd number, then $n - 1$ is divisible by 2.

   Converse: _____

   Biconditional: _____

4. Conditional: An angle is obtuse when it measures between 90° and 180°.

   Converse: _____

   Biconditional: _____

Determine whether a true biconditional can be written from each conditional statement. If not, give a counterexample.

5. If the lamp is unplugged, then the bulb does not shine.

   _____

6. The date can be the 29th if and only if it is not February.

   _____

Write each definition as a biconditional.

7. A cube is a three-dimensional solid with six square faces.

   _____

   _____

8. Tanya claims that the definition of *doofus* is "her younger brother."

   _____

   _____

   _____

Problem Solving

Use the table for Exercises 1–4. Determine if a true biconditional statement can be written from each conditional. If so, then write a biconditional. If not, then explain why not.

Mountain Bike Races	Characteristics
Cross-country	A massed-start race. Riders must carry their own tools to make repairs.
Downhill	Riders start at intervals. The rider with the lowest time wins.
Freeride	Courses contain cliffs, drops, and ramps. Scoring depends on the style and the time.
Marathon	A massed-start race that covers more than 250 kilometers.

1. If a mountain bike race is mass-started, then it is a cross-country race.

   _____

   _____

2. If a mountain bike race is downhill, then time is a factor in who wins.

   _____

   _____

3. If a mountain bike race covers more than 250 kilometers, then it is a marathon race.

   _____

   _____

4. If a race course contains cliffs, drops, and ramps, then it is not a marathon race.

   _____

   _____

Choose the best answer.

5. The cat is the only species that can hold its tail vertically while it walks.

   A The converse of this statement is false.

   B The biconditional of this statement is false.

   C The biconditional of this statement is true.

   D This statement cannot be written as a biconditional.

6. Which conditional statement can be used to write a true biconditional?

   F If you travel 2 miles in 4 minutes, then distance is a function of time.

   G If the distance depends on the time, then distance is a function of time.

   H If y increases as x increases, then y is a function of x.

   J If y is not a function of x, then y does not increase as x increases.

Algebraic Proof
Going Deeper

Essential question: *What kinds of justifications can you use in writing algebraic and geometric proofs?*

Standards for Mathematical Content

Prep for CC.9-12.G.CO.9 Prove theorems about lines and angles.

Vocabulary
proof
theorem
postulate

Prerequisites
Properties of equality

Math Background
In an algebra course, students might have been asked to provide a justification for each step taken when solving an equation. The justifications would have included the properties of equality reviewed in this lesson. Such algebraic properties, together with a postulate about segment addition, allow students in this lesson to write simple proofs involving the lengths of line segments.

INTRODUCE

Ask students to provide the missing reasons for steps in solving the equation $2x + 5 = 11$:

Equation	Reason
$2x + 5 = 11$	Given
$2x = 6$	?
$x = 3$	?

Although students may respond with "Subtract 5 from both sides" and "Divide both sides by 2," they should recognize that these are specific instances of the Subtraction Property of Equality and the Division Property of Equality.

TEACH

Questioning Strategies
- Which property do you use when you solve the equation $x + 2 = 16$? Why? **Subtraction Property of Equality; you subtract 2 from both sides of the equation.**
- What is an example of the Transitive Property of Equality? **If $3 + 1 = 4$ and $4 = 6 - 2$, then $3 + 1 = 6 - 2$.**

> **MATHEMATICAL PRACTICE** **Highlighting the Standards**
>
> This lesson is an ideal opportunity to discuss Standard 7 (Look for and make use of structure). In earlier courses, students may have used the Addition Property of Equality without much thought about the underlying principle. Now, as students begin to write proofs, they must "slow down" their thinking and recognize when such properties are at work.

CLOSE

Essential Question
What kinds of justifications can you use in writing algebraic and geometric proofs?
Justifications can be given information, a definition, a previously proved theorem, or a mathematical property (such as the properties of equality or geometric postulates).

PRACTICE

Exercises 1–2: Students practice what they learned in the lesson by writing short proofs about line segments.

Name _____ Class _____ Date _____

2-5

Algebraic Proof
Going Deeper
Essential question: *What kinds of justifications can you use in writing algebraic and geometric proofs?*

Video Tutor

CC.9-12.G.CO.9

1 ENGAGE   Introducing Proofs

In mathematics, a **proof** is a logical argument that uses a sequence of statements to prove a conjecture. Once the conjecture is proved, it is called a **theorem**.

Each statement in a proof must follow logically from what has come before and must have a reason to support it. The reason may be a piece of given information, a definition, a previously proven theorem, or a mathematical property.

The table states some properties of equality that you have seen in earlier courses. You have used these properties to solve algebraic equations and you will often use these properties as reasons in a proof.

Properties of Equality	
Addition Property of Equality	If $a = b$, then $a + c = b + c$.
Subtraction Property of Equality	If $a = b$, then $a - c = b - c$.
Multiplication Property of Equality	If $a = b$, then $ac = bc$.
Division Property of Equality	If $a = b$ and $c \neq 0$, then $\frac{a}{c} = \frac{b}{c}$.
Reflexive Property of Equality	$a = a$
Symmetric Property of Equality	If $a = b$, then $b = a$.
Transitive Property of Equality	If $a = b$ and $b = c$, then $a = c$.
Substitution Property of Equality	If $a = b$, then b can be substituted for a in any expression.

REFLECT

1a. Given the equation $3 = x - 2$, you quickly write the solution as $x = 5$. Which property or properties of equality are you using? Explain.

You use the Addition Property of Equality when you add 2 to both sides of the

equation and the Symmetric Property of Equality when you write 5 = x as x = 5.

1b. Give an example of an equation that you can solve using the Division Property of Equality. Explain how you would use this property to solve the equation.

Possible answer: 3x = 18. You would use the Division Property of Equality

to divide both sides of the equation by 3.

A **postulate** (or *axiom*) is a statement that is accepted as true without proof. Like undefined terms, postulates are basic building blocks of geometry. The following postulate states that the lengths of segments "add up" in a natural way.

Segment Addition Postulate

If B is between A and C, then
$AB + BC = AC$.

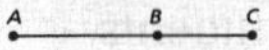

The Angle Addition Postulate is similar to the Segment Addition Postulate.

Angle Addition Postulate

If D is in the interior of $\angle ABC$, then
$m\angle ABD + m\angle DBC = m\angle ABC$.

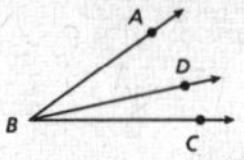

Properties of equality and postulates can be used as reasons in proofs. Note how the proof shown below in Exercise 1 is arranged in a two-column format so that it is easy to see the logical sequence of the statements and their corresponding reasons.

PRACTICE

1. If A, B, C, and D are collinear, as shown in the figure, with $AC = BD$, then $AB = CD$. Complete the proof by writing the missing statements or reasons.

Given: $AC = BD$
Prove: $AB = CD$

Statements	Reasons
1. $AC = BD$	1. Given
2. $AC = AB + BC$; $BD = BC + CD$	2. Segment Addition Postulate
3. $AB + BC = BC + CD$	3. Substitution Property of Equality
4. $AB = CD$	4. Subtraction Property of Equality

2. In the figure, X is the midpoint of $\overline{WY}$, and Y is the midpoint of $\overline{XZ}$. Explain how to prove $WX = YZ$.

By the definition of midpoint, $WX = XY$ and $XY = YZ$. By the Substitution

Property of Equality, $WX = YZ$.

Assign these pages to help your students practice and apply important lesson concepts. For additional exercises, see the Student Edition.

Answers

Additional Practice

1.

$5\left[\frac{1}{5}(a+10)\right] = 5(-3)$	(Mult. Prop. of =)
$a + 10 = -15$	(Simplify.)
$a + 10 - 10 = -15 - 10$	(Subtr. Prop. of =)
$a = -25$	(Simplify.)

2.

$t + 6.5 - t = 3t - 1.3 - t$	(Subtr. Prop. of =)
$6.5 = 2t - 1.3$	(Simplify.)
$6.5 + 1.3 = 2t - 1.3 + 1.3$	(Add. Prop. of =)
$7.8 = 2t$	(Simplify.)
$\frac{7.8}{2} = \frac{2t}{2}$	(Div. Prop. of =)
$3.9 = t$	(Simplify.)
$t = 3.9$	(Symmetric Prop. of =)

3.

$P = 2(\ell + w)$	(Given)
$9\frac{1}{2} = 2\left(\ell + 1\frac{1}{4}\right)$	(Subst. Prop. of =)
$9\frac{1}{2} = 2\ell + 2\frac{1}{2}$	(Distrib. Prop.)
$9\frac{1}{2} - 2\frac{1}{2} = 2\ell + 2\frac{1}{2} - 2\frac{1}{2}$	(Subtr. Prop. of =)
$7 = 2\ell$	(Simplify.)
$7 = \frac{2\ell}{2}$	(Div. Prop. of =)
$3\frac{1}{2} = \ell$	(Simplify.)
$\ell = 3\frac{1}{2}$	(Symmetric Prop. of =)

4. Seg. Add. Post.
   Subst. Prop. of =
   Simplify.
   Add. Prop. of =
   Subtr. Prop. of =
   Div. Prop. of =

5. Symmetric Prop. of =

6. Reflexive Prop. of $\cong$

7. Reflexive Prop. of $\cong$

8. Transitive Prop. of = or Subst.

Problem Solving

1.

$n(p + t) = 3298.75$	Given equation
$1015(p + 1.39) = 3298.75$	Subst. Prop. of =
$p + 1.39 = 3.25$	Div. Prop. of =
$p = \$1.86$	Subtr. Prop. of =

2.

$C = 7.25s + 15.95a$	Given equation
$298.70 = 7.25s + 15.95(6)$	Subst. Prop. of =
$298.70 = 7.25s + 95.7$	Simplify.
$203 = 7.25s$	Subtr. Prop. of =
$28 = s$	Div. Prop. of =
$s = 28$ students	Sym. Prop. of =

3. B

4. F

Additional Practice

Solve each equation. Show all your steps and write a justification for each step.

1. $\frac{1}{5}(a + 10) = -3$

2. $t + 6.5 = 3t - 1.3$

3. The formula for the perimeter P of a rectangle with length ℓ and width w is $P = 2(\ell + w)$. Find the length of the rectangle shown here if the perimeter is $9\frac{1}{2}$ feet. Solve the equation for ℓ and justify each step.

Write a justification for each step.

4.

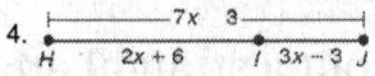

$HJ = HI + IJ$ _____

$7x - 3 = (2x + 6) + (3x - 3)$ _____

$7x - 3 = 5x + 3$ _____

$7x = 5x + 6$ _____

$2x = 6$ _____

$x = 3$ _____

Identify the property that justifies each statement.

5. $m = n$, so $n = m$.

_____

6. $\angle ABC \cong \angle ABC$

_____

7. $\overline{KL} \cong \overline{LK}$

_____

8. $p = q$ and $q = -1$, so $p = -1$.

_____

Problem Solving

1. Because of a recent computer glitch, an airline mistakenly sold tickets for round-trip flights at a discounted price. The equation $n(p + t) = 3298.75$ relates the number of discounted tickets sold n, the price of each ticket p, and the tax per ticket t. What was the discounted price of each ticket if 1015 tickets were sold and the tax per ticket was $1.39? Solve the equation for p. Justify each step.

2. The equation $C = 7.25s + 15.95a$ describes the total cost of admission C to the aquarium. How many student tickets were sold if the total cost for the entire class and 6 adults was $298.70? Solve the equation for s. Justify each step.

s = number of student tickets
a = number of adult tickets
C = total cost of admission

Refer to the figure. Choose the best answer.

3. Which could be used to find the value of x?
   A Segment Addition Postulate
   B Angle Addition Postulate
   C Transitive Property of Congruence
   D Definition of supplementary angles

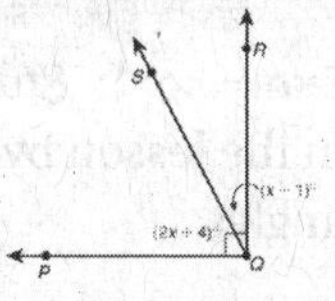

4. What is $m\angle SQR$?
   F 28°
   G 29°
   H 61°
   J 62°

Notes

Geometric Proof
Going Deeper

Essential question: *How can you organize the deductive reasoning of a geometric proof?*

© Houghton Mifflin Harcourt Publishing Company

CC.9-12.G.CO.9 Prove theorems about ... angles.

Vocabulary

opposite rays

linear pair

Prerequisites

Justifications for proofs

Math Background

Proof is a central focus of geometry. It takes time for students to understand the difference between a proof, a convincing argument, and an "off-the-cuff" explanation. In this lesson, students are introduced to proofs and the two-column format for writing proofs. In later lessons, students will write flow proofs and paragraph proofs. At this early stage, however, two-column proofs are usually best because they emphasize the fact that every statement must be justified with a supporting reason.

INTRODUCE

Ask students what it means to prove something. Have students give examples from everyday life or from literature and movies. For example, students may be familiar with mystery novels in which a detective proves that a suspect is guilty or innocent of a crime. Be sure students understand that a key aspect of such novels is a logical sequence of ideas (alibis, clues, etc.) that leads to a conclusion. In the same way, a proof in geometry is a logical sequence of statements and reasons that demonstrates the truth of a theorem.

TEACH

1 PROOF

Questioning Strategies

• What does it mean for two angles to be a linear pair? The angles are adjacent angles whose noncommon sides are opposite rays.

• What do you need to do in order to show that two angles are supplementary? You must show that the sum of the angle measures is 180°.

• What must be true about opposite rays? The rays form a straight angle.

• What can you conclude about a straight angle? Its measure is 180°.

MATHEMATICAL
PRACTICE
Highlighting the Standards

This lesson is an opportunity to discuss Standard 3 (Construct viable arguments and critique the reasoning of others). This lesson presents mostly-complete two-column proofs and asks students to supply missing statements or reasons. When given a statement, students need to ask themselves, "What reason justifies this statement?" And when given a reason, students need to ask themselves, "What statement is a consequence of this reason?"

CLOSE

Essential Question

How can you organize the deductive reasoning of a geometric proof?

A geometric proof is organized into statements and the reasons justifying those statements. The proof typically starts with given information and proceeds, in a sequence of logical steps, to the statement being proved.

PRACTICE

Exercise 1: Students practice what they learned in the lesson by proving a theorem about vertical angles.

Name_____ Class_____ Date_____

2-6

Geometric Proof
Going Deeper

Essential question: *How can you organize the deductive reasoning of a geometric proof?*

You will use the Angle Addition Postulate and the following definitions to prove an important theorem about angles.

Opposite rays are two rays that have a common endpoint and form a straight line. A **linear pair** of angles is a pair of adjacent angles whose noncommon sides are opposite rays.

In the figure, $\vec{JK}$ and $\vec{JL}$ are opposite rays; $\angle MJK$ and $\angle MJL$ are a linear pair of angles.

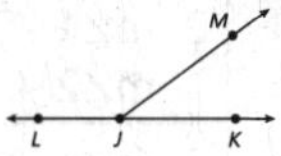

Recall that two angles are *complementary* if the sum of their measures is 90°. Two angles are *supplementary* if the sum of their measures is 180°. The following theorem ties together some of the preceding ideas.

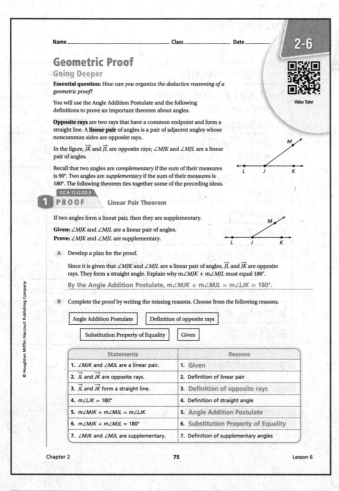

1 PROOF   Linear Pair Theorem

CC.9-12.G.CO.9

If two angles form a linear pair, then they are supplementary.

Given: $\angle MJK$ and $\angle MJL$ are a linear pair of angles.
Prove: $\angle MJK$ and $\angle MJL$ are supplementary.

A Develop a plan for the proof.

Since it is given that $\angle MJK$ and $\angle MJL$ are a linear pair of angles, $\vec{JL}$ and $\vec{JK}$ are opposite rays. They form a straight angle. Explain why $m\angle MJK + m\angle MJL$ must equal 180°.

By the Angle Addition Postulate, $m\angle MJK + m\angle MJL = m\angle LJK = 180°$.

B Complete the proof by writing the missing reasons. Choose from the following reasons.

| Angle Addition Postulate | Definition of opposite rays |
| Substitution Property of Equality | Given |

Statements	Reasons
1. $\angle MJK$ and $\angle MJL$ are a linear pair.	1. Given
2. $\vec{JL}$ and $\vec{JK}$ are opposite rays.	2. Definition of linear pair
3. $\vec{JL}$ and $\vec{JK}$ form a straight line.	3. Definition of opposite rays
4. $m\angle LJK = 180°$	4. Definition of straight angle
5. $m\angle MJK + m\angle MJL = m\angle LJK$	5. Angle Addition Postulate
6. $m\angle MJK + m\angle MJL = 180°$	6. Substitution Property of Equality
7. $\angle MJK$ and $\angle MJL$ are supplementary.	7. Definition of supplementary angles

REFLECT

1a. Is it possible to prove the theorem by measuring $\angle MJK$ and $\angle MJL$ in the figure and showing that the sum of the angle measures is 180°? Explain.

No; you must prove the theorem in general and not just for the specific angles in the figure.

1b. The proof shows that if two angles form a linear pair, then they are supplementary. Is this statement true in the other direction? That is, if two angles are supplementary, must they be a linear pair? Why or why not?

No; two angles can be supplementary without being adjacent angles, and if they are not adjacent angles, they cannot be a linear pair.

PRACTICE

1. You can use the Linear Pair Theorem to prove a result about vertical angles. Complete the proof by writing the missing statements or reasons.

Given: $\angle VXW$ and $\angle ZXY$ are vertical angles, as shown.
Prove: $m\angle VXW = m\angle ZXY$

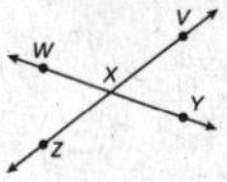

Statements	Reasons
1. $\angle VXW$ and $\angle ZXY$ are vertical angles.	1. Given
2. $\angle VXW$ and $\angle ZXY$ are formed by intersecting lines.	2. Definition of vertical angles
3. $\angle VXW$ and $\angle WXZ$ are a linear pair. $\angle WXZ$ and $\angle ZXY$ are a linear pair.	3. Definition of linear pair
4. $\angle VXW$ and $\angle WXZ$ are supplementary.	4. Linear Pair Theorem
5. $m\angle VXW + m\angle WXZ = 180°$	5. Def. of supplementary angles
6. $\angle WXZ$ and $\angle ZXY$ are supplementary.	6. Linear Pair Theorem
7. $m\angle WXZ + m\angle ZXY = 180°$	7. Definition of supplementary angles
8. $m\angle VXW + m\angle WXZ = m\angle WXZ + m\angle ZXY$	8. Transitive Property of Equality
9. $m\angle VXW = m\angle ZXY$	9. Subtraction Property of Equality

© Houghton Mifflin Harcourt Publishing Company

ADDITIONAL PRACTICE AND PROBLEM SOLVING

Assign these pages to help your students practice and apply important lesson concepts. For additional exercises, see the Student Edition.

Answers

Additional Practice

1. Given

2. Def. of mdpt.

3. Def. of ≅ segments

4. Seg. Add. Post.

5. Subst.

6. Given

7. Mult. Prop. of =

8. Subst. Prop. of =

9. Def. of ≅ segments

10.

Statements	Reasons
1. a. ∠*HKJ* is a straight angle.	1. Given
2. m∠*HKJ* = 180°	2. b. Def. of straight ∠
3. c. $\overrightarrow{KI}$ bisects ∠*HKJ*	3. Given
4. ∠*IKJ* ≅ ∠*IKH*	4. Def. of ∠ bisector
5. m∠*IKJ* = m∠*IKH*	5. Def. of ≅ ∠s
6. d. m∠*IKJ* + m∠*IKH* = m∠*HKJ*	6. ∠ Add. Post.
7. 2m∠*IKJ* = 180°	7. e. Subst. (Steps 2, 5, 6)
8. m∠*IKJ* = 90°	8. Div. Prop. of =
9. ∠*IKJ* is a right angle.	9. f. Def. of right ∠

Problem Solving

1.

Statements	Reasons
1. ∠1 and ∠3 are supplementary. ∠2 and ∠4 are supplementary.	1. Given
2. m∠1 + m∠3 = 180° m∠2 + m∠4 = 180°	2. Def. of supp. ∠s
3. m∠1 + m∠3 = m∠2 + m∠4	3. Subst. Prop. of ≅
4. ∠3 ≅ ∠4	4. Given
5. m∠3 = m∠4	5. Def. of ≅ ∠s
6. m∠1 + m∠4 = m∠2 + m∠4	6. Subst. Prop. of =
7. m∠4 + m∠4	7. Reflex. Prop. of =
8. m∠1 + m∠2	8. Subtr. Prop. of =
9. ∠1 ≅ ∠2	9. Def. of ≅ ∠s

2. ∠1≅ ∠4

3. ∠3 ≅ ∠5

Name________________________ Class__________ Date__________

2-6

Additional Practice

Write a justification for each step.

Given: $AB = EF$, B is the midpoint of $\overline{AC}$, and E is the midpoint of $\overline{DF}$.

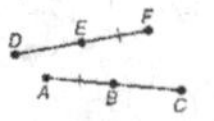

1. B is the midpoint of $\overline{AC}$, and E is the midpoint of $\overline{DF}$. ______________
2. $\overline{AB} \cong \overline{BC}$, and $\overline{DE} \cong \overline{EF}$. ______________
3. $AB = BC$, and $DE = EF$. ______________
4. $AB + BC = AC$, and $DE + EF = DF$. ______________
5. $2AB = AC$, and $2EF = DF$. ______________
6. $AB = EF$ ______________
7. $2AB = 2EF$ ______________
8. $AC = DF$ ______________
9. $\overline{AC} \cong \overline{DF}$ ______________

Fill in the blanks to complete the two-column proof.

10. **Given:** $\angle HKJ$ is a straight angle. $\overrightarrow{KI}$ bisects $\angle HKJ$.
Prove: $\angle IKJ$ is a right angle.
Proof:

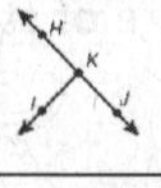

Statements	Reasons
1. a. ______________	1. Given
2. $m\angle HKJ = 180°$	2. b. ______________
3. c. ______________	3. Given
4. $\angle IKJ \cong \angle IKH$	4. Def. of $\angle$ bisector
5. $m\angle IKJ = m\angle IKH$	5. Def. of $\cong$ $\angle$
6. d. ______________	6. $\angle$ Add. Post.
7. $2m\angle IKJ = 180°$	7. e. Subst. (Steps ______)
8. $m\angle IKJ = 90°$	8. Div. Prop. of =
9. $\angle IKJ$ is a right angle.	9. f. ______________

Problem Solving

1. Refer to the diagram of the stained-glass window and use the given plan to write a two-column proof.
Given: $\angle 1$ and $\angle 3$ are supplementary.
$\angle 2$ and $\angle 4$ are supplementary.
$\angle 3 \cong \angle 4$
Prove: $\angle 1 \cong \angle 2$
Plan: Use the definition of supplementary angles to write the given information in terms of angle measures. Then use the Substitution Property of Equality and the Subtraction Property of Equality to conclude that $\angle 1 \cong \angle 2$.

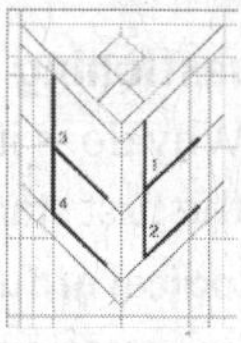

The position of a sprinter at the starting blocks is shown in the diagram. Which statement can be proved using the given information? Choose the best answer.

2. **Given:** $\angle 1$ and $\angle 4$ are right angles.
A $\angle 3 \cong \angle 5$
C $m\angle 1 + m\angle 4 = 90°$
B $\angle 1 \cong \angle 4$
D $m\angle 3 + m\angle 5 = 180°$
3. **Given:** $\angle 2$ and $\angle 3$ are supplementary.
$\angle 2$ and $\angle 5$ are supplementary.
F $\angle 3 \cong \angle 5$
H $\angle 3$ and $\angle 5$ are complementary.
G $\angle 2 \cong \angle 5$
J $\angle 1$ and $\angle 2$ are supplementary.

© Houghton Mifflin Harcourt Publishing Company

Notes

© Houghton Mifflin Harcourt Publishing Company

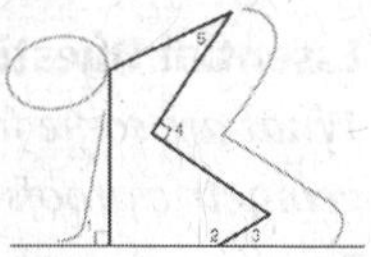

Flowchart and Paragraph Proofs
Going Deeper

Essential question: *What are some formats you can use to organize geometric proofs?*

COMMON CORE **Standards for Mathematical Content**

CC.9-12.G.CO.9 Prove theorems about lines and angles.

Prerequisites
Writing two-column proofs

Math Background
As students will see in this lesson, there are a variety of ways to write a proof. A two-column format is best suited for proofs where each statement depends only on the preceding statement. A flowchart format, on the other hand, is best suited for proofs where some statements are a consequence of two or more preceding statements. A paragraph format has a less formal structure than a two-column or flowchart format and is more of a narrative, a style that may appeal to students.

INTRODUCE

Ask students to discuss the two-column proof of the Vertical Angles Theorem they completed in Practice Exercise 1 in Lesson 2-6. Students may notice that the proof involves a parallel use of definitions, theorems, and properties for two pairs of angles, angles 1 and 2 and angles 2 and 3. In this lesson, they will see a proof that makes that parallel development more apparent.

TEACH

1 PROOF

Questioning Strategies
• How can you describe vertical angles in your own words? When two lines intersect to form an X, vertical angles are the angles on opposite sides of the X.
• When two lines intersect, how many pairs of vertical angles are formed? Two pairs of vertical angles are formed.

• What is the difference between the plan for the proof and the actual proof? The plan just outlines the main steps and does not provide reasons for every statement. The proof has a complete sequence of statements and reasons.

MATHEMATICAL PRACTICE | **Highlighting the Standards**

This proof is an opportunity to discuss Standard 7 (Look for and make use of structure). Students should recognize that they can link ∠1 and ∠3 using ∠2. Point out the parallel structure in the middle third of the proof. Once students obtain two equations where 180° appears on one side of each, they can combine the equations into a single equation that leads to the desired conclusion.

2 PROOF

Questioning Strategies
• Why does it make sense that the reason for the first statement in the proof is "Given"? The logical argument must begin with the specific information that is assumed to be true.
• What should the last statement in any two-column proof be? It should be the conclusion that you are trying to prove.

Teaching Strategies
You may wish to have students write the given reasons on sticky notes that they can rearrange as needed to put the reasons in the correct order.

CLOSE

Essential Question
What are some formats you can use to organize geometric proofs?
Besides a two-column format, you can use a flowchart format or a paragraph format.

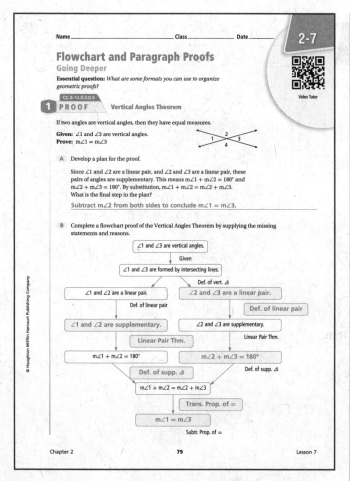

Name _____ **Class** _____ **Date** _____

2-7

Flowchart and Paragraph Proofs
Going Deeper

Essential question: *What are some formats you can use to organize geometric proofs?*

CC.9-12.G.CO.9

1 PROOF   Vertical Angles Theorem

If two angles are vertical angles, then they have equal measures.

Given: ∠1 and ∠3 are vertical angles.
Prove: m∠1 = m∠3

A Develop a plan for the proof.

Since ∠1 and ∠2 are a linear pair, and ∠2 and ∠3 are a linear pair, these pairs of angles are supplementary. This means m∠1 + m∠2 = 180° and m∠2 + m∠3 = 180°. By substitution, m∠1 + m∠2 = m∠2 + m∠3. What is the final step in the plan?

Subtract m∠2 from both sides to conclude m∠1 = m∠3.

B Complete a flowchart proof of the Vertical Angles Theorem by supplying the missing statements and reasons.

∠1 and ∠3 are vertical angles.	
Given	
∠1 and ∠3 are formed by intersecting lines.	
Def. of vert. ∠	
∠1 and ∠2 are a linear pair.	∠2 and ∠3 are a linear pair.
Def. of linear pair	Def. of linear pair
∠1 and ∠2 are supplementary.	∠2 and ∠3 are supplementary.
Linear Pair Thm.	Linear Pair Thm.
m∠1 + m∠2 = 180°	m∠2 + m∠3 = 180°
Def. of supp. ∠	Def. of supp. ∠
m∠1 + m∠2 = m∠2 + m∠3	
Trans. Prop. of =	
m∠1 = m∠3	
Subtr. Prop. of =	

Chapter 2   79   Lesson 7

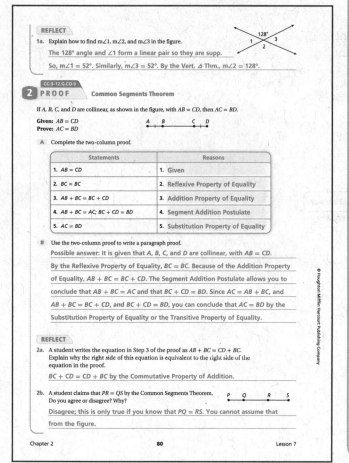

REFLECT

1a. Explain how to find m∠1, m∠2, and m∠3 in the figure.

The 128° angle and ∠1 form a linear pair so they are supp.

So, m∠1 = 52°. Similarly, m∠3 = 52°. By the Vert. ∠ Thm., m∠2 = 128°.

CC.9-12.G.CO.9

2 PROOF   Common Segments Theorem

If A, B, C, and D are collinear, as shown in the figure, with AB = CD, then AC = BD.

Given: AB = CD
Prove: AC = BD

A Complete the two-column proof.

Statements	Reasons
1. AB = CD	1. Given
2. BC = BC	2. Reflexive Property of Equality
3. AB + BC = BC + CD	3. Addition Property of Equality
4. AB + BC = AC; BC + CD = BD	4. Segment Addition Postulate
5. AC = BD	5. Substitution Property of Equality

B Use the two-column proof to write a paragraph proof.

Possible answer: It is given that A, B, C, and D are collinear, with AB = CD.

By the Reflexive Property of Equality, BC = BC. Because of the Addition Property

of Equality, AB + BC = BC + CD. The Segment Addition Postulate allows you to

conclude that AB + BC = AC and that BC + CD = BD. Since AC = AB + BC, and

AB + BC = BC + CD, and BC + CD = BD, you can conclude that AC = BD by the

Substitution Property of Equality or the Transitive Property of Equality.

REFLECT

2a. A student writes the equation in Step 3 of the proof as AB + BC = CD + BC. Explain why the right side of this equation is equivalent to the right side of the equation in the proof.

BC + CD = CD + BC by the Commutative Property of Addition.

2b. A student claims that PR = QS by the Common Segments Theorem. Do you agree or disagree? Why?

Disagree; this is only true if you know that PQ = RS. You cannot assume that

from the figure.

Chapter 2   80   Lesson 7

ADDITIONAL PRACTICE
AND PROBLEM SOLVING

Assign these pages to help your students practice
and apply important lesson concepts. For
additional exercises, see the Student Edition.

Answers

Additional Practice

1.

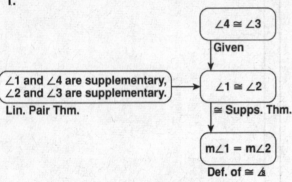

2. It is given that $AB = CD$ and $BC = DE$,
so by the Addition Property of Equality,
$AB + BC = CD + DE$. But by the
Segment Addition Postulate, $AB + BC = AC$
and $CD + DE = CE$. Therefore substitution
yields $AC = CE$. By the definition of congruent
segments, $\overline{AC} \cong \overline{CE}$ and thus C is the midpoint
of $\overline{AE}$ by the definition of midpoint.

Problem Solving

1.

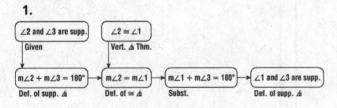

2. A

© Houghton Mifflin Harcourt Publishing Company

Name_____ Class_____ Date_____

2-7

Additional Practice

1. Use the given two-column proof to write a flowchart proof.

   Given: $\angle 4 \cong \angle 3$

   Prove: $m\angle 1 = m\angle 2$

Statements	Reasons
1. $\angle 1$ and $\angle 4$ are supplementary, $\angle 2$ and $\angle 3$ are supplementary.	1. Linear Pair Thm.
2. $\angle 4 \cong \angle 3$	2. Given
3. $\angle 1 \cong \angle 2$	3. $\cong$ Supps. Thm.
4. $m\angle 1 = m\angle 2$	4. Def. of $\cong \angle$

2. Use the given two-column proof to write a paragraph proof.

   Given: $AB = CD$, $BC = DE$

   Prove: C is the midpoint of $\overline{AE}$.

Statements	Reasons
1. $AB = CD$, $BC = DE$	1. Given
2. $AB + BC = CD + DE$	2. Add. Prop. of =
3. $AB + BC = AC$, $CD + DE = CE$	3. Seg. Add. Post.
4. $AC = CE$	4. Subst.
5. $\overline{AC} \cong \overline{CE}$	5. Def. of $\cong$ segs.
6. C is the midpoint of $\overline{AE}$.	6. Def. of mdpt.

_____

_____

_____

_____

_____

Problem Solving

The diagram shows the second-floor glass railing at a mall.

1. Use the given two-column proof to write a flowchart proof.

   Given: $\angle 2$ and $\angle 3$ are supplementary.

   Prove: $\angle 1$ and $\angle 3$ are supplementary.

   Two-Column Proof:

Statements	Reasons
1. $\angle 2$ and $\angle 3$ are supplementary.	1. Given
2. $m\angle 2 + m\angle 3 = 180°$	2. Def. of supp. $\angle$
3. $\angle 2 \cong \angle 1$	3. Vert. $\angle$ Thm.
4. $m\angle 2 = m\angle 1$	4. Def. of $\cong \angle$
5. $m\angle 1 + m\angle 3 = 180°$	5. Subst.
6. $\angle 1$ and $\angle 3$ are supplementary.	6. Def. of supp. $\angle$

Choose the best answer.

2. Which would NOT be included in a paragraph proof of the two-column proof above?

   A Since $\angle 2$ and $\angle 3$ are supplementary, $m\angle 2 = m\angle 3$.

   B $\angle 2 \cong \angle 1$ by the Vertical Angles Theorem.

   C Using substitution, $m\angle 1 + m\angle 3 = 180°$.

   D $m\angle 2 = m\angle 1$ by the definition of congruent angles.

CHAPTER 2 Performance Task

This page provides students with the opportunity to apply concepts from the Common Core in real-world problem situations. There are three different levels of performance tasks:

★ **Novice:** These are short word problems that require students to apply the math they have learned in straightforward, real-world situations.

★★ **Apprentice:** These are more involved problems that guide students step-by-step through more complex tasks. These exercises include more complicated reasoning, writing, and open-ended elements.

★★★ **Expert:** These are open-ended, non-routine problems that, instead of stepping the students through, ask them to choose their own methods for solving and justify their answers and reasoning.

Sample answers

1. 1. $\overleftrightarrow{PQ}$ bisects $\angle RST$; 2. $\angle RSQ \cong \angle TSQ$; 3. $\angle RSQ$ and $\angle RSP$ are supplementary; 4. $\angle TSQ$ and $\angle TSP$ are supplementary (statements 3 and 4 can be reversed). 5. $\angle RSP \cong \angle TSP$.

2. 1. Given; 2. Given; 3. Vertical angles are ≅; 4) Substitution.

3. Scoring Guide:

Task	Possible points
a	2 points for correctly drawing the figure 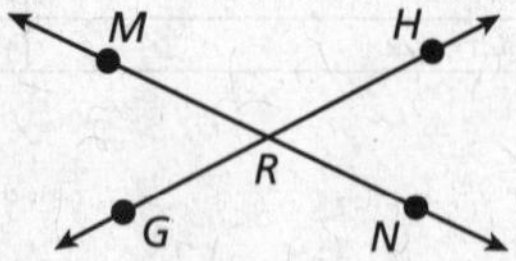
b	2 points for correctly stating that, since the lines are not perpendicular, the angles cannot measure 90°. Since the angle measures of each linear pair must total 180°, one of the two angles must be less than 90° (acute) and the other must be greater than 90° (obtuse).
c	2 points for correctly stating that, since vertical angles are congruent, the obtuse angles must be congruent to each other and the acute angles must be congruent to each other

Total possible points: 6

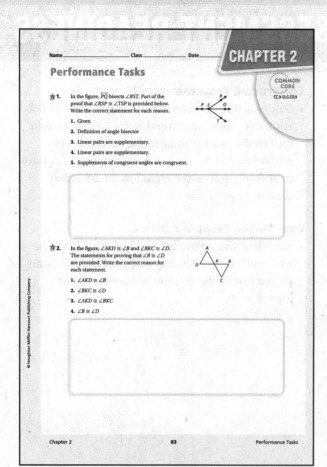

Name_____ Class_____ Date_____

Performance Tasks

COMMON CORE CC.9-12.G.CO.9

⭐ 1. In the figure, $\overrightarrow{PQ}$ bisects $\angle RST$. Part of the proof that $\angle RSP \cong \angle TSP$ is provided below. Write the correct statement for each reason.

1. Given
2. Definition of angle bisector
3. Linear pairs are supplementary.
4. Linear pairs are supplementary.
5. Supplements of congruent angles are congruent.

⭐ 2. In the figure, $\angle AKD \cong \angle B$ and $\angle BKC \cong \angle D$. The statements for proving that $\angle B \cong \angle D$ are provided. Write the correct reason for each statement.

1. $\angle AKD \cong \angle B$
2. $\angle BKC \cong \angle D$
3. $\angle AKD \cong \angle BKC$
4. $\angle B \cong \angle D$

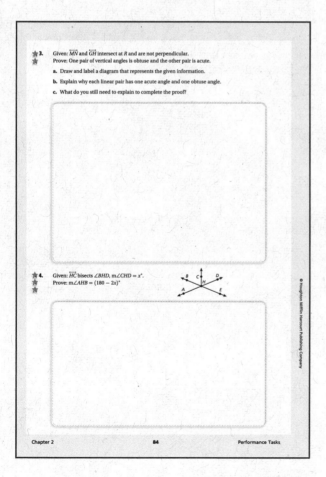

⭐ 3. Given: $\overline{MN}$ and $\overline{GH}$ intersect at R and are not perpendicular.

⭐ Prove: One pair of vertical angles is obtuse and the other pair is acute.

a. Draw and label a diagram that represents the given information.

b. Explain why each linear pair has one acute angle and one obtuse angle.

c. What do you still need to explain to complete the proof?

⭐ 4. Given: $\overrightarrow{HC}$ bisects $\angle BHD$, $m\angle CHD = x°$.

⭐ Prove: $m\angle AHB = (180 - 2x)°$

⭐

---

4. Scoring Guide:

Task	Possible points
a	6 points for correctly proving $m\angle AHB = (180 - 2x)°$. Possible answer: 1. $\overrightarrow{HC}$ bisects $\angle BHD$ and $m\angle CHD = x°$ (Given); 2. $m\angle BHD = 2x°$ (Add. Post); 3. $\angle BHD$ and $\angle AHB$ are a linear pair (Def. linear pair); 4. $\angle BHD$ and $\angle AHB$ are supp. (Linear pairs are supp.); 5. $m\angle AHB + m\angle BHD = 180°$ (Def. of supp. $\angle$s); 6. $m\angle AHB + 2x° = 180°$ (Substitution postulate); 7. $m\angle AHB = (180 - 2x)°$ (Subtr. Prop. of =)

Total possible points: 6

© Houghton Mifflin Harcourt Publishing Company

COMMON CORE CORRELATION

Standard	Items
CC.MP.3	1, 2, 3
CC.9-12.A.REI.1	4, 5, 7, 8
CC.9-12.G.CO.9	5, 6, 8
CC.9-12.G.MG.3*	7

TEST PREP DOCTOR ⊕

Multiple Choice: Item 1

- Students who answered **G** or **J** may not understand what deductive reasoning is.

- Students who answered **H** may not understand what inductive reasoning is.

Multiple Choice: Item 3

- Students who answered **B** may not know the definition of *prime number*.

- Students who answered **C** may have considered that 7 is not a perfect square, when they should have been considering that $7^2 - 16(7) + 64 = 1$ *is* a perfect square and is less than 4, so 7 is *not* a counterexample.

- Students who answered **D** may not realize that $0 = 0 \cdot 0$ is a perfect square, and because $0 < 1$, 0 is not a counterexample.

Multiple Choice: Item 5

- Students who answered **A** may have assumed that the Substitution Property of Equality was used to substitute $EF + FG$ and $FG + GH$ for EG and FH respectively, without realizing that the Substitution Property requires that the expressions being substituted are equal, which is a result of the Segment Addition Postulate.

- Students who answered **B** may have assumed that since expressions are being added, the Addition Property of Equality was involved.

- Students who answered **D** may have confused the Angle Addition and Segment Addition Postulates.

Constructed Response: Item 7

- Students who answered that the garden is 19.5 ft wide may have substituted 15 for 2ℓ rather than for ℓ in the perimeter formula. Students who answered that the garden is 24 feet long may have mistakenly solved the equation for $2w$ rather than w.

Constructed Response: Item 8

- Students who answered $x = 7$ or $x = 23$ may have assumed incorrectly that $\overrightarrow{KM}$ bisects $\angle JKL$, and solved one of the equations $6x + 8 = 50$ or $2x + 4 = 50$.

CHAPTER 2 COMMON CORE ASSESSMENT READINESS

Name _____ Class _____ Date _____

MULTIPLE CHOICE

1. Show that the conjecture is false by finding a counterexample.

Conjecture: If $a > b$, then $\frac{a}{b} > 0$.

A. $a = 11, b = -3$
B. $a = 11, b = 3$
C. $a = 3, b = 11$
D. $a = -11, b = 3$

2. There is a myth that a duck's quack does not echo. A group of scientists observed a duck in a special room, and they found that the quack does echo. Therefore, the myth is false.

Is the conclusion a result of inductive or deductive reasoning?

F. Since the conclusion is based on a pattern of observation, it is a result of inductive reasoning.

G. Since the conclusion is based on a pattern of observation, it is a result of deductive reasoning.

H. Since the conclusion is based on logical reasoning from scientific research, it is a result of inductive reasoning.

J. Since the conclusion is based on logical reasoning from scientific research, it is a result of deductive reasoning.

3. Let x be an integer from 1 to 6. Make a table of values for the rule $x^2 - 16x + 64$. Make a conjecture about the type of number generated by the rule. Continue your table. What value of x generates a counterexample?

A. The pattern appears to be a decreasing set of perfect squares.

$x = 9$ generates a counterexample.

B. The pattern appears to be a decreasing set of prime numbers.

$x = 8$ generates a counterexample.

C. The pattern appears to be a decreasing set of perfect squares.

$x = 7$ generates a counterexample.

D. The pattern appears to be an increasing set of perfect squares.

$x = 8$ generates a counterexample.

4. What are the missing reasons that justify the solution of the equation $4x - 6 = 34$?

$4x - 6 = 34$	Given equation
$\underline{+6 \quad +6}$	[1]
$4x = 40$	Simplify.
$\frac{4x}{4} = \frac{40}{4}$	[2]
$x = 10$	Simplify.

F. [1] Substitution Property of Equality;
[2] Division Property of Equality

G. [1] Addition Property of Equality;
[2] Division Property of Equality

H. [1] Division Property of Equality;
[2] Subtraction Property of Equality

J. [1] Addition Property of Equality;
[2] Reflexive Property of Equality

© Houghton Mifflin Harcourt Publishing Company

Chapter 2   85   Assessment Readiness

---

5. Steps 2 and 3 can be justified with the same reason. What is that reason?

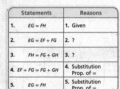

Statements	Reasons
1. $EG = FH$	1. Given
2. $EG = EF + FG$	2. ?
3. $FH = FG + GH$	3. ?
4. $EF + FG = FG + GH$	4. Substitution Prop. of =
5. $EG = FH$	5. Substitution Prop. of =

A. Substitution Property of Equality
B. Addition Property of Equality
C. Segment Addition Postulate
D. Angle Addition Postulate

6. Alberto is proving that vertical angles have the same measure. He begins as shown below. Which reason should he use for Step 3?

Given: $\angle 1$ and $\angle 2$ are vertical angles.
Prove: $m\angle 1 = m\angle 2$

Statements	Reasons
1. $\angle 1$ and $\angle 2$ are vertical angles.	1. Given
2. $\angle 1$ and $\angle 3$ are a linear pair.	2. Definition of linear pair
3. $\angle 1$ and $\angle 3$ are supplementary.	3. ?

F. Definition of supplementary angles
G. Definition of vertical angles
H. Vertical Angles Theorem
J. Linear Pair Theorem

CONSTRUCTED RESPONSE

7. A gardener has 54 feet of fencing for a garden. To find the width of the rectangular garden, the gardener uses the formula $P = 2l + 2w$, where P is the perimeter, l is the length, and w is the width of the rectangle. The gardener wants to fence a garden that is 15 feet long. How wide is the garden? Solve the equation for w, and justify each step.

The garden is 12 ft wide.

$P = 2l + 3w$	Given
$54 = 2(15) + 2w$	Subst. Prop. of =
$54 = 30 + 2w$	Simplify.
$\underline{-30 \quad -30}$	Subtr. Prop. of =
$24 = 2w$	Simplify.
$\frac{24}{2} = \frac{2w}{2}$	Div. Prop. of =
$12 = w$	Simplify.
$w = 12$	Sym. Prop. of =

8. Find the value of x and justify each step, given that $m\angle JKL = 100°$.

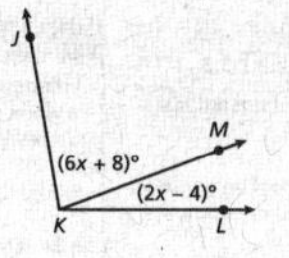

$m\angle JKL = m\angle JKM + m\angle MKL$

(Angle Addition Postulate)

$100° = (6x + 8)° + (2x - 4)°$

(Substitution Property of Equality)

$100 = 8x + 4$ (Simplify.)

$96 = 8x$ (Subtraction Property of =)

$12 = x$ (Division Property of =)

$x = 12$ (Symmetric Property of =)

© Houghton Mifflin Harcourt Publishing Company

Chapter 2   86   Assessment Readiness

Chapter 2   86   Assessment Readiness

Notes

CHAPTER 3

Parallel and Perpendicular Lines

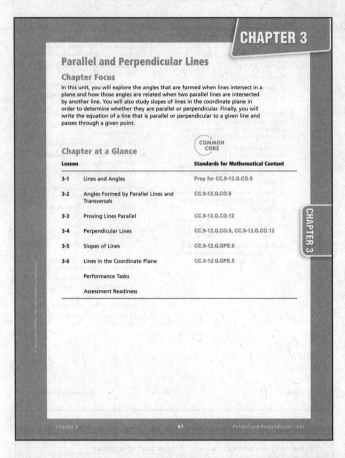

Parallel and Perpendicular Lines

Chapter Focus

In this unit, you will explore the angles that are formed when lines intersect in a plane and how those angles are related when two parallel lines are intersected by another line. You will also study slopes of lines in the coordinate plane in order to determine whether they are parallel or perpendicular. Finally, you will write the equation of a line that is parallel or perpendicular to a given line and passes through a given point.

Chapter at a Glance

Lesson		Standards for Mathematical Content
3-1	Lines and Angles	Prep for CC.9-12.G.CO.9
3-2	Angles Formed by Parallel Lines and Transversals	CC.9-12.G.CO.9
3-3	Proving Lines Parallel	CC.9-12.G.CO.12
3-4	Perpendicular Lines	CC.9-12.G.CO.9, CC.9-12.G.CO.12
3-5	Slopes of Lines	CC.9-12.G.GPE.6
3-6	Lines in the Coordinate Plane	CC.9-12.G.GPE.5
	Performance Tasks	
	Assessment Readiness	

COMMON CORE PROFESSIONAL DEVELOPMENT

CC.9-12.G.CO.1
CC.9-12.G.CO.9

In this chapter, students extend their knowledge involving lines and angles into the arena of proof to develop more concepts and logically organize them. Students learn the precise definitions of parallel and perpendicular lines based on fundamental concepts, such as point and line. It is critical that students develop a solid understanding and fluency with reasoning about properties and relationships of lines and angles, as it will lay the foundation upon which they are able to succeed with proofs to come.

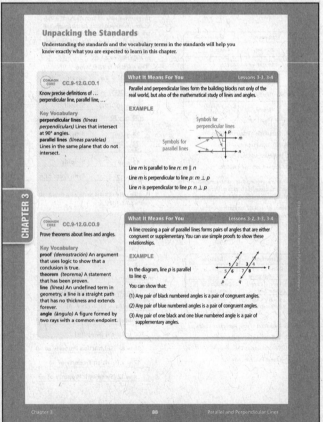

Unpacking the Standards

Understanding the standards and the vocabulary terms in the standards will help you know exactly what you are expected to learn in this chapter.

CC.9-12.G.CO.1

Know precise definitions of ... perpendicular line, parallel line, ...

Key Vocabulary
perpendicular lines *(líneas perpendiculares)* Lines that intersect at 90° angles.
parallel lines *(líneas paralelas)* Lines in the same plane that do not intersect.

What It Means For You   Lessons 3-3, 3-4

Parallel and perpendicular lines form the building blocks not only of the real world, but also of the mathematical study of lines and angles.

EXAMPLE

Line m is parallel to line n: m ∥ n
Line m is perpendicular to line p: m ⊥ p
Line n is perpendicular to line p: n ⊥ p

CC.9-12.G.CO.9

Prove theorems about lines and angles.

Key Vocabulary
proof *(demostración)* An argument that uses logic to show that a conclusion is true.
theorem *(teorema)* A statement that has been proven.
line *(línea)* An undefined term in geometry, a line is a straight path that has no thickness and extends forever.
angle *(ángulo)* A figure formed by two rays with a common endpoint.

What It Means For You   Lessons 3-2, 3-3, 3-4

A line crossing a pair of parallel lines forms pairs of angles that are either congruent or supplementary. You can use simple proofs to show these relationships.

EXAMPLE

In the diagram, line p is parallel to line q.

You can show that:

(1) Any pair of black numbered angles is a pair of congruent angles.

(2) Any pair of blue numbered angles is a pair of congruent angles.

(3) Any pair of one black and one blue numbered angle is a pair of supplementary angles.

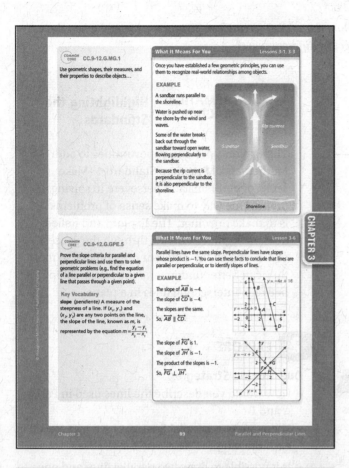

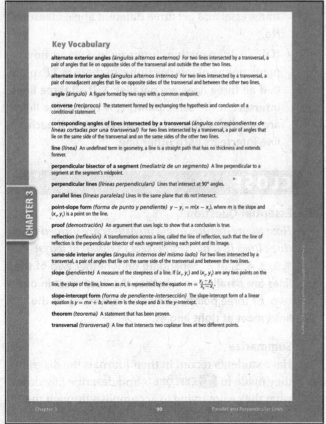

COMMON CORE
PROFESSIONAL
DEVELOPMENT
CC.9-12.G.GPE.5
CC.9-12.G.CO.9

In this chapter, students expand their previous work with coordinate proofs. Students have used the slope criteria to state that lines in the coordinate plane are parallel or perpendicular, but in this chapter they will learn to formally prove that the criteria they have been using are valid. This functional intermingling of algebra and geometry concepts provides great opportunities for students to make significant connections in mathematics. Connections between geometry and algebra concepts and skills continue to surface and merge as students grow in their studies of mathematics. Take these opportunities to review previously learned topics and connect them to newer concepts to build a strong mathematical foundation.

3-1

Lines and Angles
Going Deeper

Essential question: *How many distinct angle measures are formed when three lines in a plane intersect in different ways?*

COMMON CORE Standards for Mathematical Content

Prep for CC.9-12.G.CO.9 Prove theorems about lines and angles.

Vocabulary
transversal

Prerequisites
Drawing and Measuring Angles

Math Background
Experimentation with various drawings to gain insight into a problem is an integral part of the discovery method used in mathematics. Students should be encouraged to make drawings that represent all possibilities.

INTRODUCE

Review the possible relationships between two lines in a plane. You might want to include some real-world examples.

TEACH

1 EXPLORE

Materials: protractor, ruler

Questioning Strategies
- How can you check to see if your drawings and angle measures satisfy the stated requirement?
  Measure every angle.
- What is true about the side lengths of the triangle where there are only three angle measures? only two angle measures?
  When there are only three angle measures, the triangle has two congruent sides. When there are only two angle measures, the triangle has three congruent sides.
- What is the least number of different angle measures you can get? two
- What is the greatest number of different angle measures you can get? six

MATHEMATICAL PRACTICE Highlighting the Standards

The Explores provide opportunities to address Mathematical Practices Standard 1 (Make sense of problems and persevere in solving them). One way to make sense of problems is to make drawings. The Explore and Reflect questions guide students through the process of drawing all the different possibilities so that they can better understand the relationships between intersecting lines in a plane.

2 EXPLORE

Questioning Strategies
- How would you describe the lines used in Parts A and B?
  There are two parallel lines cut by a transversal in each drawing.
- Is it possible to draw two parallel lines and one transversal and get three different angle measures?
  No.
- If three different lines intersect in a plane, how many points of intersection can there be? Explain.
  0, if all three lines are parallel; 1, if all three lines intersect in the same point; 2, if two of the lines are parallel and one is a transversal; 3, if each line intersects each other line.

CLOSE

Essential Question
How many distinct angle measures are formed when three lines in a plane intersect in different ways?
1, 2, 3, 4, 5, or 6, depending on whether two of the lines are parallel, on whether the lines meet in one, two, or three points, and on whether any of the lines meet at right angles.

Summarize
Have students record in their journals the diagrams they made in **1 EXPLORE** and describe in words what they were trying to accomplish through the drawings.

© Houghton Mifflin Harcourt Publishing Company

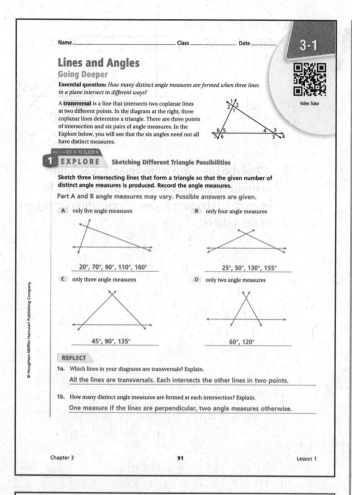

Name_____ Class_____ Date_____

Lines and Angles
Going Deeper

Essential question: *How many distinct angle measures are formed when three lines in a plane intersect in different ways?*

A **transversal** is a line that intersects two coplanar lines at two different points. In the diagram at the right, three coplanar lines determine a triangle. There are three points of intersection and six pairs of angle measures. In the Explore below, you will see that the six angles need not all have distinct measures.

Video Tutor

CC.9-12.G.CO.9

1 EXPLORE   Sketching Different Triangle Possibilities

Sketch three intersecting lines that form a triangle so that the given number of distinct angle measures is produced. Record the angle measures.

Part A and B angle measures may vary. Possible answers are given.

A only five angle measures

20°, 70°, 90°, 110°, 160°

B only four angle measures

25°, 50°, 130°, 155°

C only three angle measures

45°, 90°, 135°

D only two angle measures

60°, 120°

REFLECT

1a. Which lines in your diagrams are transversals? Explain.

All the lines are transversals. Each intersects the other lines in two points.

1b. How many distinct angle measures are formed at each intersection? Explain.

One measure if the lines are perpendicular, two angle measures otherwise.

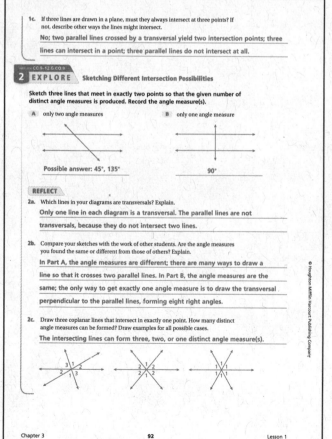

1c. If three lines are drawn in a plane, must they always intersect at three points? If not, describe other ways the lines might intersect.

No; two parallel lines crossed by a transversal yield two intersection points; three lines can intersect in a point; three parallel lines do not intersect at all.

CC.9-12.G.CO.9

2 EXPLORE   Sketching Different Intersection Possibilities

Sketch three lines that meet in exactly two points so that the given number of distinct angle measures is produced. Record the angle measure(s).

A only two angle measures

Possible answer: 45°, 135°

B only one angle measure

90°

REFLECT

2a. Which lines in your diagrams are transversals? Explain.

Only one line in each diagram is a transversal. The parallel lines are not transversals, because they do not intersect two lines.

2b. Compare your sketches with the work of other students. Are the angle measures you found the same or different from those of others? Explain.

In Part A, the angle measures are different; there are many ways to draw a line so that it crosses two parallel lines. In Part B, the angle measures are the same; the only way to get exactly one angle measure is to draw the transversal perpendicular to the parallel lines, forming eight right angles.

2c. Draw three coplanar lines that intersect in exactly one point. How many distinct angle measures can be formed? Draw examples for all possible cases.

The intersecting lines can form three, two, or one distinct angle measure(s).

© Houghton Mifflin Harcourt Publishing Company

Assign these pages to help your students practice
and apply important lesson concepts. For
additional exercises, see the Student Edition.

Answers

Additional Practice

1. The measures are the same. The angles are
   vertical angles, so they are congruent by the
   Vertical Angles Theorem.

2. 180°. The angles form a linear pair, so by
   the Linear Pairs Theorem, the angles are
   supplementary, that is, the sum of their
   measures is 180°.

3. $\angle 1$ and $\angle 2$, $\angle 3$ and $\angle 4$

4. line z

5. $\angle 1$ and $\angle 7$, $\angle 2$ and $\angle 8$, $\angle 3$ and $\angle 5$, $\angle 4$ and $\angle 6$

6. $m\angle 2 = m\angle 4 = m\angle 6 = m\angle 8 = 50°$,
   $m\angle 1 = m\angle 3 = m\angle 5 = m\angle 7 = 130°$

7. $\angle 2$ and $\angle 3$ are supplementary. $\angle 2$ and $\angle 3$
   are congruent, and $\angle 3$ and $\angle 4$ are
   supplementary. Because $m\angle 3 + m\angle 4 = 180°$,
   and $m\angle 2 = m\angle 3$, $m\angle 2 + m\angle 4 = 180°$ by
   the Substitution Property of Equality. So,
   $\angle 2$ and $\angle 3$ are supplementary.

Problem Solving

1. The tension wire and the utility pole are
   transversals because each intersects two lines,
   the electrical line and the telephone line.

2. $\angle 1$ and $\angle 4$ are congruent by the Vertical
   Angles Theorem. The electrical line and the
   the telephone line are perpendicular to the
   utility pole, so $\angle 2$, $\angle 3$, $\angle 5$, and $\angle 6$ all have
   measure 90°, so they are all congruent.

3. Drawings may vary, but the quadrilateral
   must be a rectangle, so the angle measure
   must be 90°.

4. Possible answer:
   90°, 45°, 135°

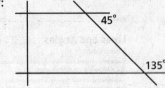

5. All of the lines are transversals. Each line
   actually intersects all three of the other lines,
   even though each *segment* only intersects two
   of the others.

Name_____ Class_____ Date_____ **3-1**

Additional Practice

For Exercises 1–3, refer to the figure from the lesson, shown at the right.

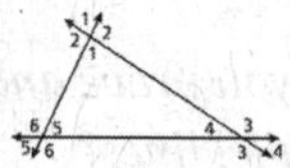

1. What is true of the measures of any two angles labeled with the same number? Explain how you know.

_____

_____

2. What is the sum of the measures of the angles labeled 5 and 6? Explain how you know.

_____

_____

3. Identify any other angle pairs in the figure for which the sum of the angle measures is the same as for the pair in Exercise 2.

_____

_____

For Exercises 4–7, refer to the figure, in which x and y are parallel lines.

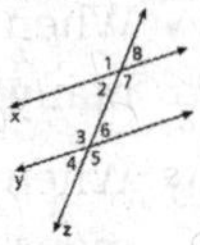

4. Identify a transversal. _____

5. Identify all pairs of vertical angles. _____

6. Suppose you know that m∠2 = m∠4 = 50°. Find the measure of each numbered angle.

_____

7. Given that m∠2 = m∠4, what do you know about ∠2 and ∠3? Explain your reasoning.

_____

_____

_____

Problem Solving

For Exercises 1 and 2, refer to the figure, which shows a utility pole with an electrical line and a telephone line. The angled wire is a tension wire. Assume that the electrical line and the telephone line are perpendicular to the utility pole. (For these exercises, you may think of the utility pole as a line.)

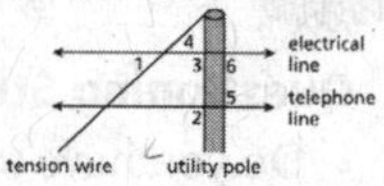

1. Identify any transversals in the figure. Explain your reasoning.

_____

2. Identify any congruent angles. Explain your reasoning.

_____

For Exercises 3–5, refer to the figure, which shows four intersecting segments that form a quadrilateral with eight pairs of angle measures. Sketch four intersecting segments that form a quadrilateral so that the given number of distinct angle measures is produced. Record the angle measures.

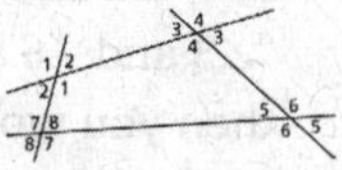

3. only one angle measure

4. only three angle measures

5. Each of the segments in the figure shown above is contained in a line. How many of those lines are transversals? Explain your reasoning.

_____

_____

Angles Formed by Parallel Lines and Transversals
Going Deeper

Essential question: *How can you prove and use theorems about angles formed by transversals that intersect parallel lines?*

COMMON CORE Standards for Mathematical Content

CC.9-12.G.CO.9 Prove theorems about lines and angles.

Vocabulary
converse

Prerequisites
Linear Pair Theorem and Vertical Angles Theorem

Math Background
When two parallel lines are cut by a transversal, alternate interior angles have the same measure, corresponding angles have the same measure, and same-side interior angles are supplementary. One of these three facts must be taken as a postulate and then the other two may be proved. In this book, the statement about same-side interior angles is taken as the postulate. This is closely related to one of the postulates stated in Euclid's *Elements*: "If a straight line falling on two straight lines make the interior angles on the same side less than two right angles, the two straight lines, if produced indefinitely, meet on that side on which are the angles less than the two right angles."

INTRODUCE

Draw a pair of parallel lines on the board and then draw a transversal that intersects them. Ask students which of the angles in the figure appear to have the same measure. Ask them if they think the relationships hold only for this figure or if they hold for any pair of parallel lines that are cut by a transversal. Have students draw their own sets of parallel lines that are cut by a transversal so they can test their conjectures. Tell them they will investigate and prove some of these conjectures in this lesson.

TEACH

1 ENGAGE

Questioning Strategies
- When two lines are cut by a transversal, how many pairs of corresponding angles are formed? **4**
- When two lines are cut by a transversal, how many pairs of same-side interior angles are formed? **2**
- In the figure where $p \parallel q$, what does the Same-Side Interior Angles Postulate tell you about m∠3 and m∠6? **The sum of these measures is 180°.**

Differentiated Instruction
Have visual learners use highlighters to color-code the different angle pairs. For example, students can use a yellow highlighter to highlight the term *corresponding angles* and then use the same highlighter to mark ∠1 and ∠5.

2 PROOF

Questioning Strategies
- Do you have to write separate proof for every pair of alternate interior angles in the figure? Why or why not? **No; you can write the proof for any pair of alternate interior angles. The same reasoning applies to all the pairs.**

- For the second statement in the proof, could you use "∠4 and ∠5 are supplementary" rather than "∠3 and ∠6 are supplementary"? Explain. **Yes, but then you would need to rewrite the subsequent steps accordingly to arrive at the conclusion that m∠3 = m∠5.**

© Houghton Mifflin Harcourt Publishing Company

Name_____ Class_____ Date_____

3-2

Angles Formed by Parallel Lines and Transversals
Going Deeper

Essential question: *How can you prove and use theorems about angles formed by transversals that intersect parallel lines?*

CC.9-12.G.CO.9

Video Tutor

1 ENGAGE   Introducing Transversals

Recall that a *transversal* is a line that intersects two coplanar lines at two different points. In the figure, line *t* is a transversal. The table summarizes the names of angle pairs formed by a transversal.

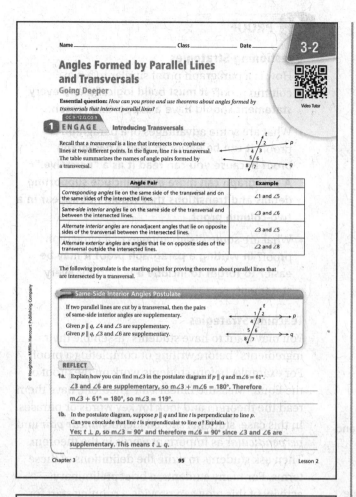

Angle Pair	Example
Corresponding angles lie on the same side of the transversal and on the same sides of the intersected lines.	∠1 and ∠5
Same-side interior angles lie on the same side of the transversal and between the intersected lines.	∠3 and ∠6
Alternate interior angles are nonadjacent angles that lie on opposite sides of the transversal between the intersected lines.	∠3 and ∠5
Alternate exterior angles are angles that lie on opposite sides of the transversal outside the intersected lines.	∠2 and ∠8

The following postulate is the starting point for proving theorems about parallel lines that are intersected by a transversal.

Same-Side Interior Angles Postulate

If two parallel lines are cut by a transversal, then the pairs of same-side interior angles are supplementary.

Given $p \parallel q$, ∠4 and ∠5 are supplementary.
Given $p \parallel q$, ∠3 and ∠6 are supplementary.

REFLECT

1a. Explain how you can find m∠3 in the postulate diagram if $p \parallel q$ and m∠6 = 61°.

∠3 and ∠6 are supplementary, so m∠3 + m∠6 = 180°. Therefore

m∠3 + 61° = 180°, so m∠3 = 119°.

1b. In the postulate diagram, suppose $p \parallel q$ and line *t* is perpendicular to line *p*. Can you conclude that line *t* is perpendicular to line *q*? Explain.

Yes; $t \perp p$, so m∠3 = 90° and therefore m∠6 = 90° since ∠3 and ∠6 are

supplementary. This means $t \perp q$.

© Houghton Mifflin Harcourt Publishing Company

CC.9-12.G.CO.9

2 PROOF   Alternate Interior Angles Theorem

If two parallel lines are cut by a transversal, then the pairs of alternate interior angles have the same measure.

Given: $p \parallel q$
Prove: m∠3 = m∠5

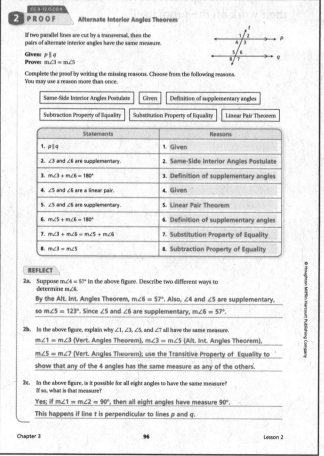

Complete the proof by writing the missing reasons. Choose from the following reasons. You may use a reason more than once.

Same-Side Interior Angles Postulate	Given	Definition of supplementary angles
Subtraction Property of Equality	Substitution Property of Equality	Linear Pair Theorem

Statements	Reasons
1. $p \parallel q$	1. Given
2. ∠3 and ∠6 are supplementary.	2. Same-Side Interior Angles Postulate
3. m∠3 + m∠6 = 180°	3. Definition of supplementary angles
4. ∠5 and ∠6 are a linear pair.	4. Given
5. ∠5 and ∠6 are supplementary.	5. Linear Pair Theorem
6. m∠5 + m∠6 = 180°	6. Definition of supplementary angles
7. m∠3 + m∠6 = m∠5 + m∠6	7. Substitution Property of Equality
8. m∠3 = m∠5	8. Subtraction Property of Equality

REFLECT

2a. Suppose m∠4 = 57° in the above figure. Describe two different ways to determine m∠6.

By the Alt. Int. Angles Theorem, m∠6 = 57°. Also, ∠4 and ∠5 are supplementary,

so m∠5 = 123°. Since ∠5 and ∠6 are supplementary, m∠6 = 57°.

2b. In the above figure, explain why ∠1, ∠3, ∠5, and ∠7 all have the same measure.

m∠1 = m∠3 (Vert. Angles Theorem), m∠3 = m∠5 (Alt. Int. Angles Theorem),

m∠5 = m∠7 (Vert. Angles Theorem); use the Transitive Property of Equality to

show that any of the 4 angles has the same measure as any of the others.

2c. In the above figure, is it possible for all eight angles to have the same measure? If so, what is that measure?

Yes; if m∠1 = m∠2 = 90°, then all eight angles have measure 90°.

This happens if line *t* is perpendicular to lines *p* and *q*.

© Houghton Mifflin Harcourt Publishing Company

© Houghton Mifflin Harcourt Publishing Company

Highlighting the Standards

Standard 3 (Construct viable arguments and critique the reasoning of others) is at the heart of this proof-based lesson. You may wish to have students pair up with a "proof buddy." Students can exchange their work with this partner and check that their partner's logical arguments make sense. This is a good way to get students in the habit of constructively critiquing other students' reasoning.

3 PROOF

Questioning Strategies

- What can you use as reasons in a proof? **Given information, properties, postulates, previously-proven theorems**

- How can you check that the first and last statements in a two-column proof are correct? **The first statement should match the "Given" and the last statement should match the "Prove."**

Teaching Strategy

Before introducing the converses of the Same-Side Interior Angles Postulate, the Alternate Interior Angles Theorem, and the Corresponding Angles Theorem, you may want to spend a few minutes talking about statements and their converses. Have students give the converse for statements based on everyday situations such as, "If you live in Cleveland, then you live in Ohio." Forming the converses of such statements can help students see that the converse of a true statement may or may not be true.

4 PROOF

Questioning Strategies

- How is a paragraph proof similar to a two-column proof? **It must build logically, and every statement should have a supporting reason.**

- What are some advantages of a paragraph proof? **It can be easier to read a paragraph proof because you can read it as a "narrative." A paragraph can more easily include supporting details and transitions that would not appear in a two-column proof.**

- What are some disadvantages of a paragraph proof? **In writing a paragraph proof it may be easier to forget to include a reason for every statement.**

Teaching Strategies

You may want to have students "assemble their ingredients" before writing or completing a proof. For example, before students work on the proof of the Equal-Measure Linear Pair Theorem, have them read the theorem and look for key words or phrases. In this case, students should identify *linear pair* and *perpendicular* as important words in the theorem. Then ask students to write the definitions of these terms. For many students, a brief preliminary activity of this type can provide a running start for their work on the proof itself.

© Houghton Mifflin Harcourt Publishing Company

3 PROOF — Corresponding Angles Theorem

CC.9-12.G.CO.9

If two parallel lines are cut by a transversal, then the
pairs of corresponding angles have the same measure.

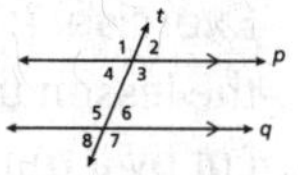

Given: $p \parallel q$
Prove: $m\angle 1 = m\angle 5$

Complete the proof by writing the missing reasons.

Statements	Reasons
1. $p \parallel q$	1. Given
2. $m\angle 3 = m\angle 5$	2. Alternate Interior Angles Theorem
3. $m\angle 1 = m\angle 3$	3. Vertical Angles Theorem
4. $m\angle 1 = m\angle 5$	4. Substitution Property of Equality

REFLECT

3a. Explain how you can you prove the Corresponding Angles Theorem using the
Same-Side Interior Angles Postulate and a linear pair of angles.

By the Same-Side Int. Angles Thm., $m\angle 4 + m\angle 5 = 180°$. As a linear pair,

$m\angle 4 + m\angle 1 = 180°$. Therefore, $m\angle 4 + m\angle 1 = m\angle 4 + m\angle 5$, so

$m\angle 1 = m\angle 5$.

Many postulates and theorems are written in the form "If p, then q." The **converse** of
such a statement has the form "If q, then p." The converse of a postulate or theorem may
or may not be true. The converse of the Same-Side Interior Angles Postulate is accepted
as true, and this makes it possible to prove that the converses of the previous theorems
are true.

Converse of the Same-Side Interior Angles Postulate
If two lines are cut by a transversal so that a pair of same-side interior
angles are supplementary, then the lines are parallel.

Converse of the Alternate Interior Angles Theorem
If two lines are cut by a transversal so that a pair of alternate interior
angles have the same measure, then the lines are parallel.

Converse of the Corresponding Angles Theorem
If two lines are cut by a transversal so that a pair of corresponding
angles have the same measure, then the lines are parallel.

A *paragraph proof* is another way of presenting a mathematical argument. As in a
two-column proof, the argument must flow logically and every statement should
have a reason.

4 PROOF — Equal-Measure Linear Pair Theorem

CC.9-12.G.CO.9

If two intersecting lines form a linear pair of angles
with equal measures, then the lines are perpendicular.

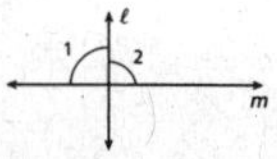

Given: $m\angle 1 = m\angle 2$
Prove: $\ell \perp m$

Complete the following paragraph proof.

It is given that $\angle 1$ and $\angle 2$ form a linear pair. Therefore, $\angle 1$ and $\angle 2$ are supplementary

by the___Linear Pair Theorem___. By the definition of supplementary angles,

$m\angle 1 + m\angle 2 = 180°$. It is also given that $m\angle 1 = m\angle 2$. So, $m\angle 1 + m\angle 1 = 180°$ by the

Substitution Property of Equality . Simplifying gives $2m\angle 1 = 180°$ and $m\angle 1 = 90°$

by the Division Property of Equality. Therefore, $\angle 1$ is a right angle and $\ell \perp m$ by the

definition of perpendicular .

REFLECT

4a. State the converse of the Equal-Measure Linear Pair Theorem shown above.
Is the converse true?

If two intersecting lines are perpendicular, then they form a linear pair of angles

with equal measures; yes.

PRACTICE

In Exercises 1–2, complete each proof by writing the missing statements or reasons.

1. If two parallel lines are cut by a transversal, then the
pairs of alternate exterior angles have the same measure.

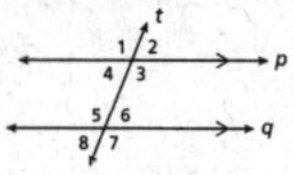

Given: $p \parallel q$
Prove: $m\angle 1 = m\angle 7$

Statements	Reasons
1. $p \parallel q$	1. Given
2. $m\angle 1 = m\angle 5$	2. Corresponding Angles Theorem
3. $m\angle 5 = m\angle 7$	3. Vertical Angles Theorem
4. $m\angle 1 = m\angle 7$	4. Substitution Property of Equality

© Houghton Mifflin Harcourt Publishing Company

Essential Question

How can you prove and use theorems about angles formed by transversals that intersect parallel lines?
Start by establishing a postulate about certain pairs of angles, such as same-side interior angles. The postulate allows you to prove a theorem about other pairs of angles, such as alternate interior angles. You can then use the postulate and the theorem to prove other theorems about other pairs of angles, such as corresponding angles.

Summarize

Have students write a journal entry in which they summarize the key postulates and theorems of this lesson. Encourage them to include a labeled figure with each posulate or theorem.

Exercise 1: Students practice what they learned in the lesson to prove that when two parallel lines are cut by a transversal, the pairs of alternate exterior angles have the same measure.

Exercise 2: Students practice what they learned in the lesson to prove the Converse of the Alternate Interior Angles Theorem.

Exercise 3: Students use theorems from the lesson to complete a paragraph proof.

Exercise 4: Students use theorems from the lesson to justify a construction.

Exercise 5: Students extend their knowledge to solve a problem about angle measures.

2. Prove the Converse of the Alternate Interior Angles Theorem.

Given: $m\angle 3 = m\angle 5$
Prove: $p \parallel q$

Statements	Reasons
1. $m\angle 3 = m\angle 5$	1. Given
2. $\angle 5$ and $\angle 6$ are a linear pair.	2. Definition of linear pair
3. $\angle 5$ and $\angle 6$ are supplementary.	3. Linear Pair Theorem
4. $m\angle 5 + m\angle 6 = 180°$	4. Definition of supplementary angles
5. $m\angle 3 + m\angle 6 = 180°$	5. Substitution Property of Equality
6. $\angle 3$ and $\angle 6$ are supplementary.	6. Definition of supplementary angles
7. $p \parallel q$	7. Conv. of Same-Side Int. Angles Post.

3. Complete the paragraph proof.

Given: $\ell \parallel m$ and $p \parallel q$
Prove: $m\angle 1 = m\angle 2$

It is given that $p \parallel q$, so $m\angle 1 = m\angle 3$ by the <u>Corresponding Angles Theorem</u>

It is also given that $\ell \parallel m$, so $m\angle 3 = m\angle 2$ by the <u>Alt. Int. Angles Theorem</u>

Therefore, $m\angle 1 = m\angle 2$ by the <u>Transitive Property of Equality</u>.

4. The figure shows a given line m, a given point P, and the construction of a line ℓ that is parallel to line m. Explain why line ℓ is parallel to line m.

<u>The construction creates a pair of corresponding angles with the same</u>

<u>measure, so the lines are parallel by the Converse of the Corresponding</u>

<u>Angles Theorem.</u>

5. Can you use the information in the figure to conclude that $p \parallel q$? Why or why not?

<u>Yes; $m\angle 3 = 71°$ (Vert. Angles Thm.) and $71° + 109° = 180°$, so same-side interior</u>

<u>angles are supplementary, and by the Converse of the Same-Side Interior Angles</u>

<u>Postulate, $p \parallel q$.</u>

ADDITIONAL PRACTICE AND PROBLEM SOLVING

Assign these pages to help your students practice and apply important lesson concepts. For additional exercises, see the Student Edition.

Answers

Additional Practice

1. 47° **2.** 119°

3. 97° **4.** 62°

5.

Statements	Reasons
1. $p \parallel q$	1. Given
2. a. m∠2 + m∠3 = 180°	2. Lin. Pair Thm.
3. ∠1 ≅ ∠2	3. b. Corr. ∠s Post.
4. c. m∠1 = m∠2	4. Def. of ≅ ∠s
5. d. m∠1 + m∠3 = 180°	5. e. Subst.

6. 15; 40

Problem Solving

1. 17; Alt. Int. ∠s Thm.

2. 102°; Alt. Ext. ∠s Thm.

3. $x = 10$; $y = 3$; $(12x + 2y)° = 126°$ by the Corr. ∠s Post. and $(3x + 2y)° = 36°$ by the Alt. Int. ∠s Thm.

4. D **5.** H

Name_____ Class_____ Date_____ **3-2**

Additional Practice

Find each angle measure.

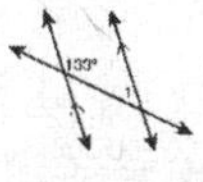

1. m∠1 _____

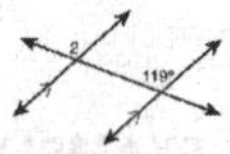

2. m∠2 _____

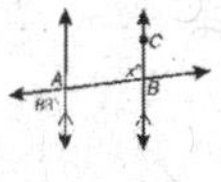

3. m∠ABC _____

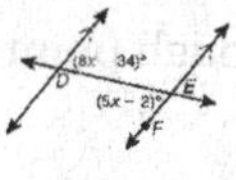

4. m∠DEF _____

Complete the two-column proof to show that same-side exterior angles are supplementary.

5. **Given:** $p \parallel q$

   Prove: m∠1 + m∠3 = 180°

   Proof:

Statements	Reasons
1. $p \parallel q$	1. Given
2. a. _____	2. Lin. Pair Thm.
3. ∠1 ≅ ∠2	3. b. _____
4. c. _____	4. Def. of ≅ ∡
5. d. _____	5. e. _____

6. Ocean waves move in parallel lines toward the shore. The figure shows Sandy Beaches windsurfing across several waves. For this exercise, think of Sandy's wake as a line. m∠1 = (2x + 2y)° and m∠2 = (2x + y)°. Find x and y.

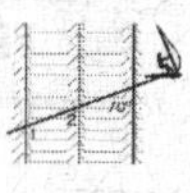

   x = _____

   y = _____

Chapter 3   101   Lesson 2

Problem Solving

Find each value. Name the postulate or theorem that you used to find the values.

1. In the diagram of movie theater seats, the incline of the floor, f, is parallel to the seats, s.

   If m∠1 = 68°, what is x?

   _____

2. In the diagram, roads a and b are parallel.

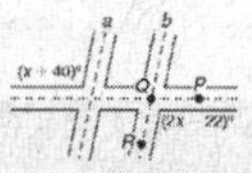

   What is the measure of ∠PQR?

   _____

3. In the diagram of the gate, the horizontal bars are parallel and the vertical bars are parallel. Find x and y.

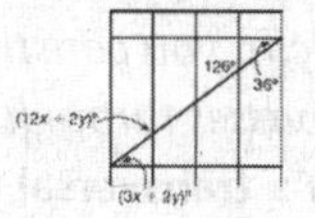

   _____

   _____

   _____

Use the diagram of a staircase railing for Exercises 4 and 5. $\overline{AG} \parallel \overline{CJ}$ and $\overline{AD} \parallel \overline{FJ}$. Choose the best answer.

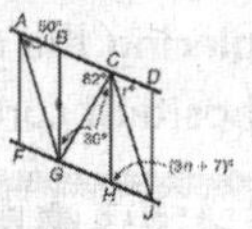

4. Which is a true statement about the measure of ∠DCJ?

   A It equals 30°, by the Alternate Interior Angles Theorem.

   B It equals 30°, by the Corresponding Angles Postulate.

   C It equals 50°, by the Alternate Interior Angles Theorem.

   D It equals 50°, by the Corresponding Angles Postulate.

5. Which is a true statement about the value of n?

   F It equals 25°, by the Alternate Interior Angles Theorem.

   G It equals 25°, by the Same-Side Interior Angles Theorem.

   H It equals 35°, by the Alternate Interior Angles Theorem.

   J It equals 35°, by the Same-Side Interior Angles Theorem.

Chapter 3   102   Lesson 2

Proving Lines Parallel
Connection: Constructing Parallel Lines

Essential question: *How can you construct a line parallel to another line that passes through a given point?*

© Houghton Mifflin Harcourt Publishing Company

COMMON CORE Standards for Mathematical Content

CC.9-12.G.CO.1 Know precise definitions of ... parallel line ...

CC.9-12.G.CO.12 Make formal geometric constructions with a variety of tools and methods (compass and straightedge, string, reflective devices, paper folding, dynamic geometric software, etc.).
Also: **CC.9-12.G.GPE.6**

Vocabulary
parallel lines

Prerequisites
Basic constructions

Math Background
The construction of a line parallel to a given line through a given point is justified by the Converse of the Corresponding Angles Theorem. In the construction, an angle formed by the given line and a transversal that passes through the given point is copied. The copy of the angle is constructed with its vertex at the given point and with its position corresponding to the position of the original angle.

INTRODUCE

Ask students to give examples of parallel lines in everyday situations. Students might mention railroad tracks or the stripes on a shirt.

TEACH

1 EXAMPLE

Questioning Strategies
• What construction is this construction based on?
  copying an angle

• What is the role of point *R* in the construction?
  It makes it possible to name ∠PQR.

EXTRA EXAMPLE
Construct a line parallel to line *n* that passes through point *A*.

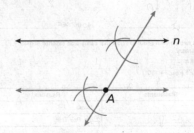

MATHEMATICAL PRACTICE — Highlighting the Standards

Example 1 provides an opportunity to address Standard 5 (Use appropriate tools strategically). Ask students whether the construction can be done another way using compass and straightedge. It can; for instance, use alternate interior angles rather than corresponding angles as the basis for the construction. Also ask students how to draw parallel lines using a straightedge and protractor instead. Measure ∠PQR and then draw an angle with that measure at point *P*.

CLOSE

Essential Question
How can you construct a line parallel to another line that passes through a given point?
Draw a transversal that passes through the given point and intersects the given line. Then copy the angle formed by the transversal and the given line, placing the copy's vertex at the given point and in a position corresponding to the original angle.

PRACTICE

Where skills are taught	Where skills are practiced
1 EXAMPLE	EXS. 1–2

Exercise 3: Students extend their knowledge of constructions by constructing parallel lines that divide a line segment into three equal parts.

3-3

Proving Lines Parallel
Connection: Constructing Parallel Lines

Essential question: *How can you construct a line parallel to another line that passes through a given point?*

Video Tutor

Parallel lines lie in the same plane and do not intersect. In the figure, line ℓ is parallel to line m and you write $\ell \parallel m$. The arrows on the lines also indicate that the lines are parallel.

CC.9-12.G.CO.12

1 EXAMPLE   Constructing Parallel Lines

Construct a line parallel to line m that passes through point P. Work directly on the figure below.

A Choose points Q and R on line m.

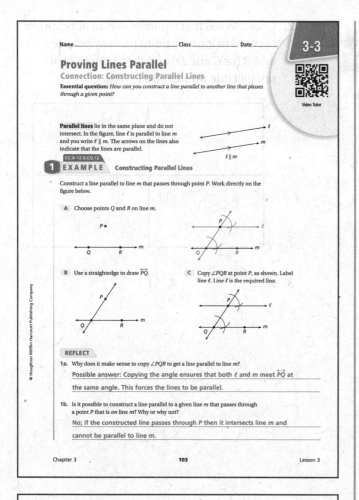

B Use a straightedge to draw $\overleftrightarrow{PQ}$.

C Copy $\angle PQR$ at point P, as shown. Label line ℓ. Line ℓ is the required line.

REFLECT

1a. Why does it make sense to copy $\angle PQR$ to get a line parallel to line m?

Possible answer: Copying the angle ensures that both ℓ and m meet $\overleftrightarrow{PQ}$ at the same angle. This forces the lines to be parallel.

1b. Is it possible to construct a line parallel to a given line m that passes through a point P that is *on* line m? Why or why not?

No; if the constructed line passes through P then it intersects line m and cannot be parallel to line m.

Chapter 3   103   Lesson 3

1c. Write an if-then statement that justifies the method used in the construction of parallel lines.

If two lines are cut by a transversal so that a pair of corresponding angles have the same measure, then the lines are parallel.

PRACTICE

Construct a line parallel to line m that passes through point P.

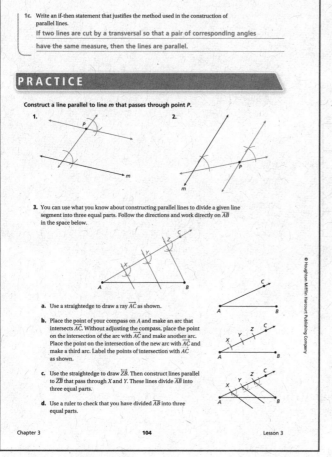

1.

2.

3. You can use what you know about constructing parallel lines to divide a given line segment into three equal parts. Follow the directions and work directly on $\overline{AB}$ in the space below.

a. Use a straightedge to draw a ray $\overrightarrow{AC}$ as shown.

b. Place the point of your compass on A and make an arc that intersects $\overrightarrow{AC}$. Without adjusting the compass, place the point on the intersection of the arc with $\overrightarrow{AC}$ and make another arc. Place the point on the intersection of the new arc with $\overrightarrow{AC}$ and make a third arc. Label the points of intersection with $\overrightarrow{AC}$ as shown.

c. Use the straightedge to draw $\overleftrightarrow{ZB}$. Then construct lines parallel to $\overleftrightarrow{ZB}$ that pass through X and Y. These lines divide $\overline{AB}$ into three equal parts.

d. Use a ruler to check that you have divided $\overline{AB}$ into three equal parts.

Chapter 3   104   Lesson 3

© Houghton Mifflin Harcourt Publishing Company

Assign these pages to help your students practice
and apply important lesson concepts. For
additional exercises, see the Student Edition.

Answers

Additional Practice

1–2. Check students' constructions.

3.

4.

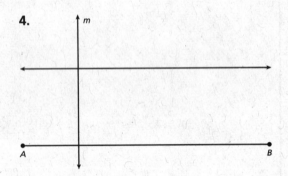

Problem Solving

1.

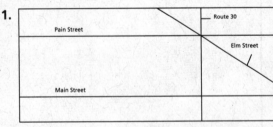

2. Check to see that students use an appropriate
method to locate a point halfway between *A*
and *B* (or *C* and *D*) and then constructed a
parallel line through that point.

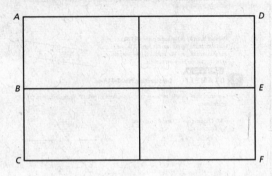

3. B   **4.** H

Name_____ Class_____ Date_____

Additional Practice

Construct a line parallel to line *r* that passes through point *P*.

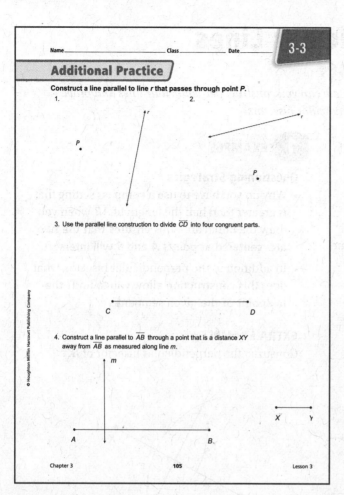

1.

2.

3. Use the parallel line construction to divide $\overline{CD}$ into four congruent parts.

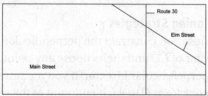

C ————————————— D

4. Construct a line parallel to $\overline{AB}$ through a point that is a distance *XY* away from $\overline{AB}$ as measured along line *m*.

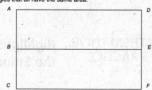

Problem Solving

1. A cartographer is creating a map of the city center, as shown below. Pine Street is parallel to Main Street and passes through the intersection of Elm Street and Route 30. Construct a line to represent Pine Street.

Route 30

Elm Street

Main Street

2. A graphic designer is drawing a logo, as shown below. In the logo, *AB = BC = DE = EF*. Construct another line so that the logo is divided into four rectangles that all have the same area.

A ——————————— D

B ——————————— E

C ——————————— F

Select the best answer.

3. Which of the following facts do you use when constructing parallel lines?

A   A transversal that intersects two parallel lines is parallel to both.

B   Corresponding angles formed by two parallel lines and a transversal are congruent.

C   Corresponding angles formed by two parallel lines are supplementary.

D   All right angles are congruent.

4. When given a line *m* and a point *P* not on *m*, what is the first step in constructing a line parallel to *m*?

F   Construct a circle with center *P*.

G   Measure the distance between *m* and *P*.

H   Draw a line that intersects *m* and contains *P*.

J   Draw a triangle with one side on *m* and a vertex at *P*.

Perpendicular Lines
Going Deeper

Essential question: *How can you construct perpendicular lines and prove theorems about perpendicular bisectors?*

COMMON CORE Standards for Mathematical Content

CC.9-12.G.CO.1 Know precise definitions of ... perpendicular line, ...

CC.9-12.G.CO.2 ... describe transformations as functions that take points in the plane as inputs and give other points as outputs. ...

CC.9-12.G.CO.4 Develop definitions of ... reflections ... in terms of ... perpendicular lines ... and line segments.

CC.9-12.G.CO.9 Prove theorems about lines and angles.

CC.9-12.G.CO.12 Make formal geometric constructions with a variety of tools and methods (compass and straightedge, string, reflective devices, paper folding, dynamic geometric software, etc.).

Vocabulary
perpendicular lines
perpendicular bisector
reflection

Prerequisites
The Pythagorean Theorem

Math Background
Perpendicular bisectors play an important role in geometry. In this lesson, students learn to construct the perpendicular bisector of a line segment. Students also learn that points on the perpendicular bisector of a segment are exactly those points that are equidistant from the endpoints of the segment. Later, students will use this property as they prove congruence criteria for triangles.

INTRODUCE

Ask students to give examples of perpendicular lines in everyday situations. Students might suggest the corner of a window frame or the lines in a plus sign.

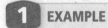

1 EXAMPLE

Questioning Strategies
- Why do you have to use a compass setting that is greater than half the length of $\overline{AB}$ when you draw the initial arc? **This ensures that the two arcs centered at points A and B will intersect.**

- In addition to the perpendicular bisector, what does this construction allow you to find? **the midpoint of the given segment**

EXTRA EXAMPLE
Construct the perpendicular bisector of $\overline{JK}$.

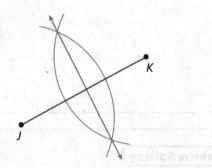

2 PROOF

Questioning Strategies
- Suppose you construct the perpendicular bisector of $\overline{CD}$ and then choose any point Q on the perpendicular bisector. If you measure the distance from Q to each endpoint of the segment, what do you expect to find? **QC = QD**

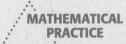

MATHEMATICAL PRACTICE — **Highlighting the Standards**

As students answer the Reflect questions following the proof of the Perpendicular Bisector Theorem, ask them to share their answers with classmates and have them constructively critique each other's reasoning. Doing so addresses a key aspect of Standard 3 (Construct viable arguments and critique the reasoning of others).

3-4

Name_____ Class_____ Date_____

Perpendicular Lines
Going Deeper

Essential question: *How can you construct perpendicular lines and prove theorems about perpendicular bisectors?*

Perpendicular lines are lines that intersect at right angles. In the figure, line ℓ is perpendicular to line *m* and you write ℓ ⊥ *m*. The right angle mark in the figure indicates that the lines are perpendicular.

The **perpendicular bisector** of a line segment is a line perpendicular to the segment at the segment's midpoint.

Video Tutor

CC.9-12.G.CO.12

1 EXAMPLE   Constructing a Perpendicular Bisector

Construct the perpendicular bisector of $\overline{AB}$. Work directly on the figure below.

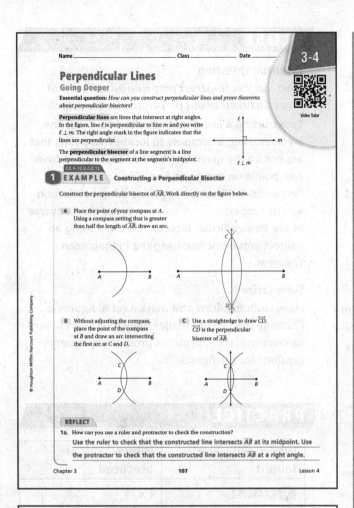

A Place the point of your compass at *A*. Using a compass setting that is greater than half the length of $\overline{AB}$, draw an arc.

B Without adjusting the compass, place the point of the compass at *B* and draw an arc intersecting the first arc at *C* and *D*.

C Use a straightedge to draw $\overleftrightarrow{CD}$. $\overleftrightarrow{CD}$ is the perpendicular bisector of $\overline{AB}$.

REFLECT

1a. How can you use a ruler and protractor to check the construction?

Use the ruler to check that the constructed line intersects $\overline{AB}$ at its midpoint. Use
the protractor to check that the constructed line intersects $\overline{AB}$ at a right angle.

You can use reflections and their properties to prove a theorem about perpendicular bisectors. Refer to the diagram in the Proof below as you read this definition of reflection.

A **reflection** across line *m* maps a point *A* to its image *B* as follows.

- Line *m* is the perpendicular bisector of $\overline{AB}$ if and only if *A* is not on line *m*.
- The image of *P* is *P* if and only if *P* is on line *m*.

The notation $r_m(A) = B$ means that the image of point *A* after a reflection across line *m* is point *B*. The notation $r_m(P) = P$ means that the image of point *P* is point *P*, which implies that *P* is on line *m*.

CC.9-12.G.CO.9

2 PROOF   Perpendicular Bisector Theorem

If a point is on the perpendicular bisector of a segment, then it is equidistant from the endpoints of the segment.

Given: *P* is on the perpendicular bisector *m* of $\overline{AB}$.

Prove: *PA* = *PB*

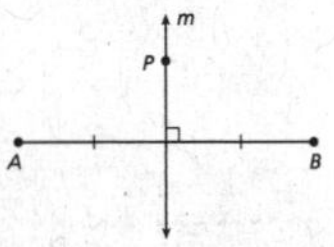

Complete the following proof.

Consider the reflection across line *m*. Then $r_m(P) = P$ because
point P lies on line m, which is the line of reflection.

Also, $r_m(A) = B$ by the definition of reflection.

Therefore, *PA* = *PB* because   reflections preserve distance.

REFLECT

2a. Suppose you use a compass and straightedge to construct the perpendicular bisector of a segment, $\overline{AB}$. If you choose a point *P* on the perpendicular bisector, how can you use your compass to check that *P* is equidistant from *A* and *B*?

Place the point of the compass on P and open the compass to the distance PA.

Draw an arc passing through A and check that the arc also passes through B.

If so, PA = PB.

2b. What conclusion can you make about △*KLJ* in the figure? Explain.

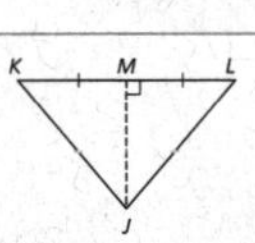

The triangle is isosceles; JK = JL because point J

lies on the perpendicular bisector of $\overline{KL}$.

2c. Describe the point on the perpendicular bisector of a segment that is closest to the endpoints of the segment.

The midpoint of the segment is the point on the perpendicular bisector that is

closest to the endpoints of the segment.

© Houghton Mifflin Harcourt Publishing Company

3 PROOF

Questioning Strategies

- How can you tell that this is an indirect proof? In the first step, you assume that what you are trying to prove is false.

- Near the end of the proof, you know that $AQ^2 = BQ^2$ and you conclude that $AQ = BQ$. How do you justify this step? Take the square root of both sides and use the fact that distance is non-negative.

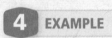

Questioning Strategies

- When you draw the arc in Step A, does the size of the compass opening matter? No, as long as it is large enough so that the arc intersects line m in two points.

- How can you use a protractor to check the construction? Measure the angle formed by the perpendicular to make sure it measures 90°.

EXTRA EXAMPLE

Construct a line perpendicular to line n that passes through point Q.

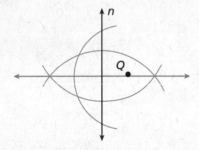

Differentiated Instruction

Kinesthetic learners may benefit from constructing perpendicular bisectors by paper folding. To do so, have students fold the given line upon itself so that the fold passes through the given point. When the paper is unfolded, the crease will be the perpendicular bisector.

CLOSE

Essential Question

How can you construct perpendicular lines and prove theorems about perpendicular bisectors? Constructing a line perpendicular to a given line involves using a compass to locate two points that are not on the given line but are equidistant from two points on the given line. You can prove the Perpendicular Bisector Theorem using a reflection and its properties, and you can prove the Converse of the Perpendicular Bisector Theorem using an indirect argument involving the Pythagorean Theorem.

Summarize

Have students draw and mark a set of figures to illustrate the Perpendicular Bisector Theorem and its converse. Have students provide explanatory captions for the figures.

PRACTICE

Where skills are taught	Where skills are practiced
1 EXAMPLE	EX. 1
4 EXAMPLE	EX. 2

The converse of the Perpendicular Bisector Theorem is also true. In order to prove the converse, you will use the Pythagorean Theorem.

Recall that the Pythagorean Theorem states that in a right triangle with legs of length a and b and hypotenuse of length c, $a^2 + b^2 = c^2$.

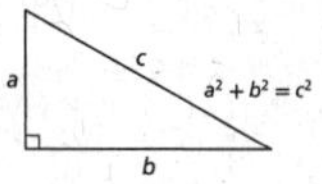

$a^2 + b^2 = c^2$

CC.9-12.G.CO.9

3 PROOF   Converse of the Perpendicular Bisector Theorem

If a point is equidistant from the endpoints of a segment, then it lies on the perpendicular bisector of the segment.

Given: $PA = PB$

Prove: P is on the perpendicular bisector m of $\overline{AB}$.

A Use the method of *indirect proof*. Assume the *opposite* of what you want to prove and show this leads to a contradiction.

Assume that point P is *not* on the perpendicular bisector m of $\overline{AB}$. Then when you draw a perpendicular from P to the line containing A and B, the perpendicular intersects this line at a point Q, which is not the midpoint of $\overline{AB}$.

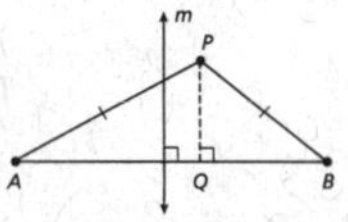

B Complete the following to show that this assumption leads to a contradiction.

$\overline{PQ}$ forms two right triangles, $\triangle AQP$ and $\triangle BQP$.

$AQ^2 + QP^2 = PA^2$ and $BQ^2 + QP^2 = PB^2$ by ___the Pythagorean Theorem.___

Subtract these equations:
$$AQ^2 + QP^2 = PA^2$$
$$BQ^2 + QP^2 = PB^2$$
$$\overline{AQ^2 - BQ^2 = PA^2 - PB^2}$$

However, $PA^2 - PB^2 = 0$ because ___$PA = PB$.___

Therefore, $AQ^2 - BQ^2 = 0$. This means $AQ^2 = BQ^2$ and $AQ = BQ$. This contradicts the fact that Q is not the midpoint of $\overline{AB}$. Thus, the initial assumption must be incorrect, and P must lie on the perpendicular bisector of $\overline{AB}$.

> REFLECT

3a. In the proof, once you know $AQ^2 = BQ^2$, why can you conclude $AQ = BQ$?

   Take the square root of both sides. Since distances are nonnegative, $AQ = BQ$.

3b. Explain how the converse of the Perpendicular Bisector Theorem justifies the compass-and-straightedge construction of the perpendicular bisector of a segment.

   The construction involves making two arcs that intersect in two points. Each of

   these two intersection points is equidistant from the endpoints of the segment,

   because the arcs use the same radius. So, both of the intersection points are on

   the perpendicular bisector of the segment.

The perpendicular bisector construction can be used as part of the method for drawing the perpendicular to a line through a given point not on the line.

CC.9-12.G.CO.12

4 EXAMPLE   Constructing a Perpendicular to a Line

Construct a line perpendicular to line m that passes through point P. Work directly on the figure at right.

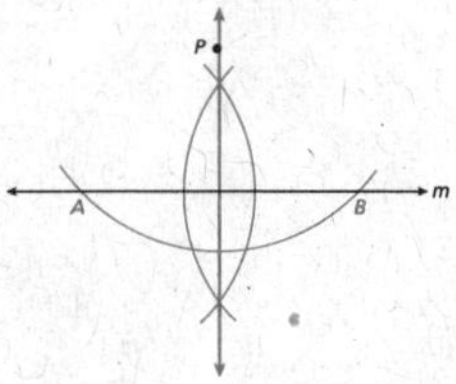

A Place the point of your compass at P. Draw an arc that intersects line m at two points, A and B.

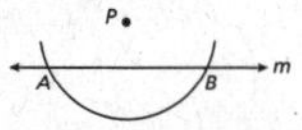

B Construct the perpendicular bisector of $\overline{AB}$. This line will pass through P and be perpendicular to line m.

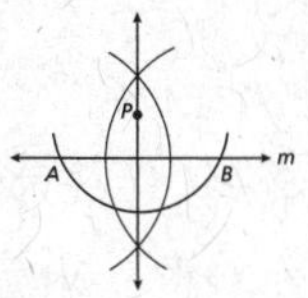

> REFLECT

4a. Does the construction still work if point P is on line m? Why or why not?

   Yes; in the first step, it is still possible to draw an arc centered at P that

   intersects the line at two points.

PRACTICE

1. Construct the perpendicular bisector of the segment shown below.

2. Construct a line perpendicular to line m that passes through point P.

© Houghton Mifflin Harcourt Publishing Company

Assign these pages to help your students practice
and apply important lesson concepts. For
additional exercises, see the Student Edition.

Answers

Additional Practice

1–2. Check students' constructions.

3. Check to see that student properly constructed
a perpendicular and correctly copied the
given segment.

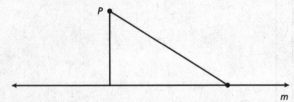

Problem Solving

1. Check that student properly constructed the
perpendicular bisectors of both segments and
found their intersection.

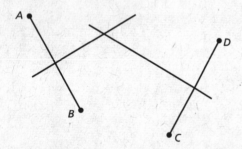

2. No; possible explanation: If I construct the
perpendicular bisectors to both segments, that
means both bisectors are perpendicular to the
same line. The perpendicular bisectors will
therefore be parallel and never intersect.

3. B

Name _____ Class _____ Date _____

Additional Practice

1. Construct a line perpendicular to line *r*.

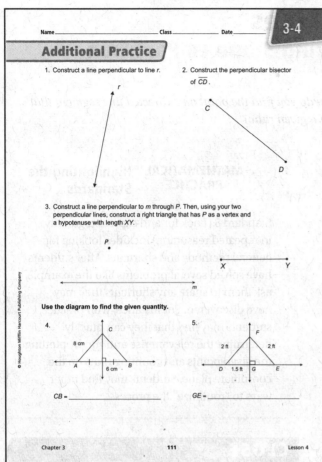

2. Construct the perpendicular bisector of $\overline{CD}$.

3. Construct a line perpendicular to *m* through *P*. Then, using your two perpendicular lines, construct a right triangle that has *P* as a vertex and a hypotenuse with length *XY*.

Use the diagram to find the given quantity.

4.

8 cm

CB = _____

5.

2 ft   2 ft

1.5 ft

GE = _____

Problem Solving

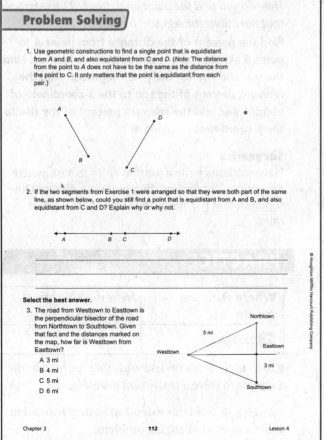

1. Use geometric constructions to find a single point that is equidistant from *A* and *B*, and also equidistant from *C* and *D*. (*Note*: The distance from the point to *A* does not have to be the same as the distance from the point to *C*. It only matters that the point is equidistant from each pair.)

2. If the two segments from Exercise 1 were arranged so that they were both part of the same line, as shown below, could you still find a point that is equidistant from A and B, and also equidistant from C and D? Explain why or why not.

A   B   C   D

_____
_____
_____

Select the best answer.

3. The road from Westtown to Easttown is the perpendicular bisector of the road from Northtown to Southtown. Given that fact and the distances marked on the map, how far is Westtown from Easttown?

   A 3 mi
   B 4 mi
   C 5 mi
   D 6 mi

Northtown

5 mi

Easttown

Westtown

3 mi

Southtown

Slopes of Lines
Extension: Using Slope to Partition Segments

Essential question: How do you find the point on a directed line segment that partitions the segment in a given ratio?

COMMON CORE **Standards for Mathematical Content**

CC.9-12.G.GPE.6 Find the point on a directed line segment between two given points that partitions the segment in a given ratio.

Prerequisites
Slope

Math Background
Students studied slope in Algebra 1 and learned to find the slope of a line. They also used slope to write the equation of a line, either in slope-intercept form ($y = mx + b$) or in point-slope form ($y - y_1 = m(x - x_1)$). In this lesson, students use the definition of slope (i.e., the ratio of the rise to the run) to help them find a point that divides a given line segment in a given ratio.

INTRODUCE

Draw the figure shown below on the board. Tell students that point P divides $\overline{AB}$ in the ratio 3 to 1. Ask students to explain what this means. Encourage students to give as many equivalent explanations as possible. For example, AP is 3 times PB; $\overline{AP}$ is 3 units long, while $\overline{PB}$ is 1 unit long; $\frac{AP}{BP} = 3$; and so on.

TEACH

Questioning Strategies
• Do you expect point P to be closer to A or closer to B? Why? Closer to B; P is located 60% of the way from A to B and 60% is greater than 50%.
• How does the slope of $\overline{AP}$ compare with the slope of $\overline{AB}$? Why? The slopes are the same since P is on $\overline{AB}$.

EXTRA EXAMPLE
Find the coordinates of the point P that lies along the directed line segment from $A(1, 1)$ to $B(7, 3)$ and partitions the segment in the ratio 1 to 4. (2.2, 1.4)

MATHEMATICAL PRACTICE | **Highlighting the Standards**

Standard 8 (Look for and express regularity in repeated reasoning) includes looking for general methods and shortcuts. After students have solved several problems like the example, ask them to share any shortcuts they may have discovered. For instance, with practice, students may find that they can quickly determine the relevant rise and run by plotting the given points and counting units on the coordinate plane. Students may find other ways to "routinize" the process.

CLOSE

Essential Question
How do you find the point on a directed line segment that partitions the segment in a given ratio?
Find the percent of the distance from point A to point B at which the required point is located. Find the run and rise for the given segment. Add the relevant percent of the run to the x-coordinate of point A and add the relevant percent of the rise to the y-coordinate of point A.

Summarize
Have students write a journal entry to summarize the process for finding the point on a directed line segment that partitions the segment in a given ratio.

PRACTICE

Where skills are taught	Where skills are practiced
1 EXAMPLE	EXS. 1–4

Exercise 5: Students use what they learned in the example to solve a real-world problem.

Exercise 6: Students extend what they learned to solve a more challenging problem.

Name_____ Class_____ Date_____

Slopes of Lines
Extension: Using Slope to Partition Segments

Essential question: *How do you find the point on a directed line segment that partitions the segment in a given ratio?*

Recall that the *slope* of a straight line in a coordinate plane is the ratio of the *rise* to the *run*.

In the figure, the slope of $\overline{AB}$ is $\frac{\text{rise}}{\text{run}} = \frac{4}{8} = \frac{1}{2}$.

In the next several lessons, you will see how to use slope to solve geometry problems and to prove geometry theorems.

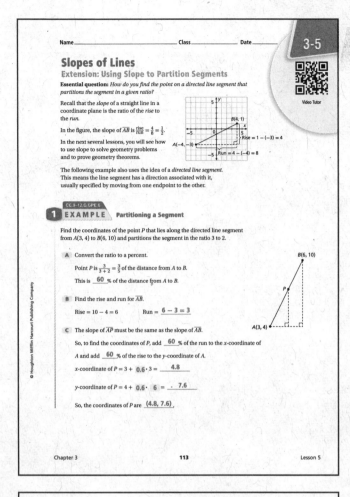

The following example also uses the idea of a *directed line segment*. This means the line segment has a direction associated with it, usually specified by moving from one endpoint to the other.

CC.9-12.G.GPE.6

1 EXAMPLE   Partitioning a Segment

Find the coordinates of the point P that lies along the directed line segment from $A(3, 4)$ to $B(6, 10)$ and partitions the segment in the ratio 3 to 2.

A Convert the ratio to a percent.

Point P is $\frac{3}{3+2} = \frac{3}{5}$ of the distance from A to B.

This is __60__% of the distance from A to B.

B Find the rise and run for $\overline{AB}$.

Rise = $10 - 4 = 6$ Run = __$6 - 3 = 3$__

C The slope of $\overline{AP}$ must be the same as the slope of $\overline{AB}$.

So, to find the coordinates of P, add __60__% of the run to the x-coordinate of A and add __60__% of the rise to the y-coordinate of A.

x-coordinate of $P = 3 + 0.6 \cdot 3 =$ __4.8__

y-coordinate of $P = 4 + 0.6 \cdot 6 =$ __7.6__

So, the coordinates of P are __(4.8, 7.6)__.

Chapter 3   113   Lesson 5

REFLECT

1a. Explain how you can check that the slope of $\overline{AP}$ equals the slope of $\overline{AB}$.

Slope of $\overline{AP} = \frac{\text{rise}}{\text{run}} = \frac{7.6 - 4}{4.8 - 3} = \frac{3.6}{1.8} = 2$; slope of $\overline{AB} = \frac{\text{rise}}{\text{run}} = \frac{10 - 4}{6 - 3} = \frac{6}{3} = 2$

1b. Explain how you can use the distance formula to check that P partitions $\overline{AB}$ in the ratio 3 to 2.

By the distance formula $AP \approx 4.025$ and $PB \approx 2.683$, and $\frac{AP}{PB} \approx 1.5$, which is 3 to 2.

PRACTICE

1. Find the coordinates of the point P that lies along the directed segment from $C(-3, -2)$ to $D(6, 1)$ and partitions the segment in the ratio 2 to 1.

(3, 0)

2. Find the coordinates of the point P that lies along the directed segment from $R(-3, -4)$ to $S(5, 0)$ and partitions the segment in the ratio 2 to 3.

(0.2, −2.4)

3. Find the coordinates of the point P that lies along the directed segment from $J(-2, 5)$ to $K(2, -3)$ and partitions the segment in the ratio 4 to 1.

(1.2, −1.4)

4. Find the coordinates of the point P that lies along the directed segment from $M(5, -2)$ to $N(-5, 3)$ and partitions the segment in the ratio 1 to 3.

(2.5, −0.75)

5. The map shows a straight highway between two towns. Highway planners want to build two new rest stops between the towns so that the two rest stops divide the highway into three equal parts. Find the coordinates of the points at which the rest stops should be built.

$\left(-1, -\frac{1}{3}\right)$ and $\left(1, 1\frac{1}{3}\right)$

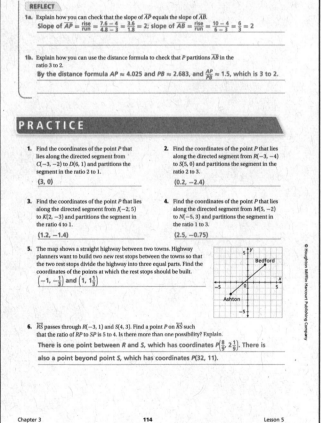

6. $\overline{RS}$ passes through $R(-3, 1)$ and $S(4, 3)$. Find a point P on $\overleftrightarrow{RS}$ such that the ratio of RP to SP is 5 to 4. Is there more than one possibility? Explain.

There is one point between R and S, which has coordinates $P\left(\frac{8}{9}, 2\frac{1}{9}\right)$. There is

also a point beyond point S, which has coordinates $P(32, 11)$.

Chapter 3   114   Lesson 5

© Houghton Mifflin Harcourt Publishing Company

ADDITIONAL PRACTICE AND PROBLEM SOLVING

Assign these pages to help your students practice and apply important lesson concepts. For additional exercises, see the Student Edition.

Answers

Additional Practice

1. zero **2.** $-\frac{2}{3}$

3. 2 **4.** undefined

5. (5, 5)

6. (−1.4, −1.2)

7. (−3.6, 2.2)

8. (2.75, 1)

Problem Solving

1. Yes; the station would be located at (36, 42), which is south of Highway 10.

2. $(3, 1\frac{2}{3}), (5, 2\frac{1}{3})$

3. B **4.** G **5.** D

Additional Practice

Use the slope formula to determine the slope of each line.

1. $\overline{AB}$ _____

2. $\overline{CD}$ _____

3. $\overline{EF}$ _____

4. $\overline{GH}$ _____

5. Find the coordinates of the point P that lies along the directed line segment from $A(3, 1)$ to $B(6, 7)$ and partitions the segment in the ratio 2 to 1.

_____

6. Find the coordinates of the point P that lies along the directed line segment from $C(-3, -2)$ to $D(5, 2)$ and partitions the segment in the ratio 1 to 4.

_____

7. Find the coordinates of the point P that lies along the directed line segment from $E(-5, 5)$ to $F(-2, -2)$ and partitions the segment in the ratio 1 to 1.5.

_____

8. Find the coordinates of the point P that lies along the directed line segment from $G(1, 1)$ to $H(8, 1)$ and partitions the segment in the ratio 1 to 3.

_____

Problem Solving

1. The map shows a highway between Acton and Beauville and its intersection with Highway 10. A power station needs to be built along the highway between Acton and Beauville. The station must be located so that the ratio of its distance to Acton to its distance to Beauville is 2 to 3, but the builders also want to locate it south of Highway 10. Can this be achieved? Explain why or why not.

_____

_____

_____

2. The segment represented by endpoints $C(1, 1)$ and $D(7, 3)$ is *not* directed. What two points would partition the segment such that the ratio of the lengths is 1 to 2?

_____

Select the best answer.

3. Which point partitions the directed segment from $A(-3, -2)$ to $B(5, -1)$ in a ratio of 2 to 3?

A $\left(1\frac{1}{5}, -1\frac{2}{5}\right)$

B $\left(\frac{1}{5}, -1\frac{3}{5}\right)$

C $\left(2\frac{1}{3}, -1\frac{2}{3}\right)$

D $\left(-\frac{1}{3}, -1\frac{1}{3}\right)$

4. The directed line segment from $C(-2, -1)$ to $D(4, 2)$ is partitioned by $P(2, 1)$. What is the ratio of CP to DP?

F 1:1   H 1:2

G 2:1   J 2:3

5. A directed line segment from $E(-3, 3.6)$ to $F(5.3, 3.0)$ is partitioned by point P in the ratio 2:7. What is the y-coordinate of P?

A 0.3

B 1.15

C 1.35

D 3.6

Lines in the Coordinate Plane
Going Deeper

Essential question: *How can you use slope to write equations of lines that are parallel or perpendicular?*

© Houghton Mifflin Harcourt Publishing Company

COMMON CORE Standards for Mathematical Content

CC.9-12.G.GPE.5 ... use [the slope criteria for parallel and perpendicular lines] to solve geometric problems (e.g., find the equation of a line parallel or perpendicular to a given line that passes through a given point).

Prerequisites

Slope

Forms of linear equations

Math Background

Students learned in a previous algebra course that equations of non-vertical lines can be written in various forms, including standard form ($Ax + By = C$), slope-intercept form ($y = mx + b$), and point-slope form ($y - y_1 = m(x - x_1)$). While students are most comfortable using slope-intercept form, they will find that point-slope form is more useful in this lesson.

INTRODUCE

Have students draw the three lines determined by the pairs of points given in the table.

	Point 1	Point 2
Line 1	$(-1, 3)$	$(5, 0)$
Line 2	$(-2, 4)$	$(10, -2)$
Line 3	$(-2, 4)$	$(0, 8)$

Ask students to determine which lines are parallel and which are perpendicular and to explain how they know. **Lines 1 and 2 are parallel because their slopes are the same. Lines 1 and 3 as well as lines 2 and 3 are perpendicular because the product of their slopes in each case is −1.**

1 EXAMPLE

Questioning Strategies

- In Part A, how do you know that the given line is in slope-intercept form? **It is in the form $y = mx + b$.**

- In Part A, the given line has a negative slope. What does this tell you about the given line and the required line? **Both lines slope downward as you move from left to right.**

- How can you use graphing to check your answer in Part A? **Graph the given line and the line you find as your answer. The two lines should be parallel, and the line you find as your answer should pass through the point (1, −4).**

EXTRA EXAMPLE

Write the equation of each line in slope-intercept form.

A. a line that is parallel to $y = -x - 3$ and passes through $(-1, 3)$

$y = -x + 2$

B. The line that passes through $(4, 2)$ and is parallel to the line through $(1, 5)$ and $(-3, -3)$

$y = 2x - 6$

Avoid Common Errors

Remind students that the x-coefficient gives the slope of a line only when the equation of the line is written in slope-intercept form. For example, some students might say that the slope of the line represented by the equation $y - 2x = 4$ is -2. However, the equation is not in slope-intercept form. Rewriting the equation in this form gives $y = 2x + 4$, which shows that the correct slope is 2.

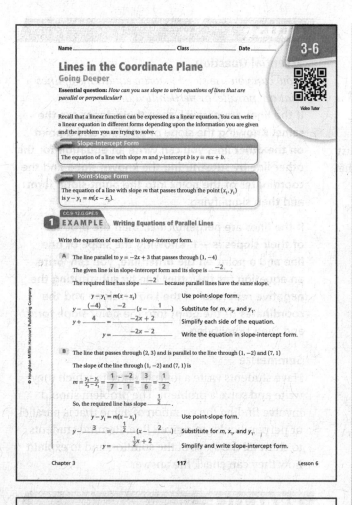

Name_____ Class_____ Date_____

3-6

Video Tutor

Lines in the Coordinate Plane
Going Deeper

Essential question: *How can you use slope to write equations of lines that are parallel or perpendicular?*

Recall that a linear function can be expressed as a linear equation. You can write a linear equation in different forms depending upon the information you are given and the problem you are trying to solve.

Slope-Intercept Form

The equation of a line with slope m and y-intercept b is $y = mx + b$.

Point-Slope Form

The equation of a line with slope m that passes through the point (x_1, y_1) is $y - y_1 = m(x - x_1)$.

CC.9-12.G.GPE.5
1 EXAMPLE Writing Equations of Parallel Lines

Write the equation of each line in slope-intercept form.

A The line parallel to $y = -2x + 3$ that passes through $(1, -4)$

The given line is in slope-intercept form and its slope is ___−2___.

The required line has slope ___−2___ because parallel lines have the same slope.

$y - y_1 = m(x - x_1)$ Use point-slope form.

$y - \underline{(-4)} = \underline{-2}(x - \underline{1})$ Substitute for m, x_1, and y_1.

$y + \underline{4} = \underline{-2x + 2}$ Simplify each side of the equation.

$y = \underline{-2x - 2}$ Write the equation in slope-intercept form.

B The line that passes through $(2, 3)$ and is parallel to the line through $(1, -2)$ and $(7, 1)$

The slope of the line through $(1, -2)$ and $(7, 1)$ is

$m = \dfrac{y_2 - y_1}{x_2 - x_1} = \dfrac{1 - \underline{-2}}{7 - \underline{1}} = \dfrac{3}{6} = \dfrac{1}{2}$

So, the required line has slope ___$\frac{1}{2}$___.

$y - y_1 = m(x - x_1)$ Use point-slope form.

$y - \underline{3} = \underline{\frac{1}{2}}(x - \underline{2})$ Substitute for m, x_1, and y_1.

$y = \underline{\frac{1}{2}x + 2}$ Simplify and write slope-intercept form.

Chapter 3   117   Lesson 6

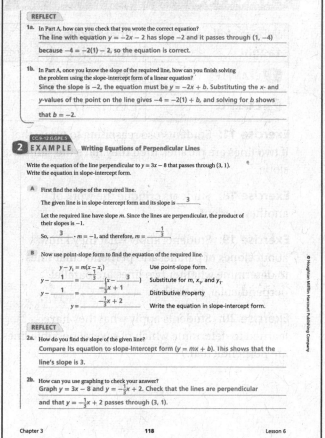

REFLECT

1a. In Part A, how can you check that you wrote the correct equation?

The line with equation $y = -2x - 2$ has slope −2 and it passes through $(1, -4)$

because $-4 = -2(1) - 2$, so the equation is correct.

1b. In Part A, once you know the slope of the required line, how can you finish solving the problem using the slope-intercept form of a linear equation?

Since the slope is −2, the equation must be $y = -2x + b$. Substituting the x- and

y-values of the point on the line gives $-4 = -2(1) + b$, and solving for b shows

that $b = -2$.

CC.9-12.G.GPE.5
2 EXAMPLE Writing Equations of Perpendicular Lines

Write the equation of the line perpendicular to $y = 3x - 8$ that passes through $(3, 1)$. Write the equation in slope-intercept form.

A First find the slope of the required line.

The given line is in slope-intercept form and its slope is ___3___.

Let the required line have slope m. Since the lines are perpendicular, the product of their slopes is −1.

So, $\underline{3} \cdot m = -1$, and therefore, $m = \underline{-\frac{1}{3}}$.

B Now use point-slope form to find the equation of the required line.

$y - y_1 = m(x - x_1)$ Use point-slope form.

$y - \underline{1} = \underline{-\frac{1}{3}}(x - \underline{3})$ Substitute for m, x_1, and y_1.

$y - \underline{1} = \underline{-\frac{1}{3}x + 1}$ Distributive Property

$y = \underline{-\frac{1}{3}x + 2}$ Write the equation in slope-intercept form.

REFLECT

2a. How do you find the slope of the given line?

Compare its equation to slope-intercept form ($y = mx + b$). This shows that the

line's slope is 3.

2b. How can you use graphing to check your answer?

Graph $y = 3x - 8$ and $y = -\frac{1}{3}x + 2$. Check that the lines are perpendicular

and that $y = -\frac{1}{3}x + 2$ passes through $(3, 1)$.

Chapter 3   118   Lesson 6

© Houghton Mifflin Harcourt Publishing Company

Questioning Strategies

- What is the y-intercept of the given line? How do you know? **The equation is in slope-intercept form, so the y-intercept must be −8.**

- The given line has a positive slope. What does this tell you about the required line? Why? **It must have a negative slope because the product of the slopes is −1.**

- How can you check your answer? **Check that the product of the slopes is −1 ($-\frac{1}{3} \cdot 3 = -1$) and that (3, 1) is a solution of the equation of the required line, ($1 = -\frac{1}{3}(3) + 2$).**

EXTRA EXAMPLE

Write the equation of the line perpendicular to $y = 2x + 1$ that passes through (5, 1). Write the equation in slope-intercept form.

$$y = -\frac{1}{2}x + \frac{7}{2}$$

Technology

Students can use their graphing calculators to check that two equations represent perpendicular lines. However, students should be aware that perpendicular lines may or may not appear to be perpendicular on a graphing calculator, depending upon the viewing window that is used. To ensure that perpendicular lines appear to be perpendicular, students should go to the ZOOM menu and choose **5:ZSquare**.

CLOSE

Essential Question

How can you use slope to write equations of lines that are parallel or perpendicular?

If the lines are parallel, then their slopes are the same. Knowing the slope of one line and a point on the other line, you can write an equation for the other line by substituting the known slope and the coordinates of the point into the point-slope form and then simplifying.

If the lines are perpendicular, then the product of their slopes is −1. Knowing the slope of one line and a point on the other line, you can write an equation for the other line by substituting the negative reciprocal of the known slope and the coordinates of the point into the point-slope form and then simplifying.

Summarize

Have students write a journal entry in which they write and solve a problem. The problem should involve finding the equation of a line that is parallel or perpendicular to a given line. Remind students to show all the steps of the solution and to explain how they can check the answer.

PRACTICE

Where skills are taught	Where skills are practiced
1 EXAMPLE	EXS. 1–10
2 EXAMPLE	EXS. 12–17

Exercise 11: Students use reasoning to prove that if two lines are parallel, then they have the same slope.

Exercise 18: Students critique the work of another student.

Exercise 19: Students apply what they know about slopes of parallel and perpendicular lines to determine whether two lines are parallel, perpendicular, or neither.

Exercise 20: Students apply what they have learned to determine which of several possible lines are perpendicular.

2c. Confirm your answer by graphing on the grid below.

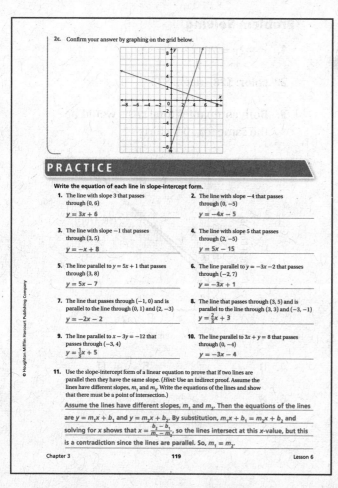

PRACTICE

Write the equation of each line in slope-intercept form.

1. The line with slope 3 that passes through $(0, 6)$

$y = 3x + 6$

2. The line with slope -4 that passes through $(0, -5)$

$y = -4x - 5$

3. The line with slope -1 that passes through $(3, 5)$

$y = -x + 8$

4. The line with slope 5 that passes through $(2, -5)$

$y = 5x - 15$

5. The line parallel to $y = 5x + 1$ that passes through $(3, 8)$

$y = 5x - 7$

6. The line parallel to $y = -3x - 2$ that passes through $(-2, 7)$

$y = -3x + 1$

7. The line that passes through $(-1, 0)$ and is parallel to the line through $(0, 1)$ and $(2, -3)$

$y = -2x - 2$

8. The line that passes through $(3, 5)$ and is parallel to the line through $(3, 3)$ and $(-3, -1)$

$y = \frac{2}{3}x + 3$

9. The line parallel to $x - 3y = -12$ that passes through $(-3, 4)$

$y = \frac{1}{3}x + 5$

10. The line parallel to $3x + y = 8$ that passes through $(0, -4)$

$y = -3x - 4$

11. Use the slope-intercept form of a linear equation to prove that if two lines are parallel then they have the same slope. (*Hint:* Use an indirect proof. Assume the lines have different slopes, m_1 and m_2. Write the equations of the lines and show that there must be a point of intersection.)

Assume the lines have different slopes, m_1 and m_2. Then the equations of the lines are $y = m_1x + b_1$ and $y = m_2x + b_2$. By substitution, $m_1x + b_1 = m_2x + b_2$ and solving for x shows that $x = \frac{b_2 - b_1}{m_1 - m_2}$, so the lines intersect at this x-value, but this is a contradiction since the lines are parallel. So, $m_1 = m_2$.

© Houghton Mifflin Harcourt Publishing Company

Write the equation of each line in slope-intercept form.

12. The line perpendicular to $y = \frac{1}{2}x + 1$ that passes through $(1, 4)$

$y = -2x + 6$

13. The line perpendicular to $y = -x + 2$ that passes through $(-1, -7)$

$y = x - 6$

14. The line that passes through $(1, 2)$ and is perpendicular to the line through $(3, -2)$ and $(-3, 0)$

$y = 3x - 1$

15. The line that passes through $(-2, 3)$ and is perpendicular to the line through $(0, 1)$ and $(-3, -1)$

$y = -\frac{3}{2}x$

16. The line perpendicular to $2y = x + 5$ that passes through $(2, 1)$

$y = -2x + 5$

17. The line perpendicular to $3x + y = 8$ that passes through $(0, -2)$

$y = \frac{1}{3}x - 2$

18. **Error Analysis** A student was asked to find the equation of the line perpendicular to $y - 2x = 1$ that passes through the point $(4, 3)$. The student's work is shown at right. Explain the error and give the correct equation.

The given equation is not in slope-intercept form. The slope of the given line is 2, so the required line has slope $-\frac{1}{2}$. The required line's equation is $y = -\frac{1}{2}x + 5$.

The given line has slope -2, so the required line has slope $\frac{1}{2}$.	
$y - y_1 = m(x - x_1)$	*Use point-slope form.*
$y - 3 = \frac{1}{2}(x - 4)$	*Substitute for m, x_1, y_1.*
$y - 3 = \frac{1}{2}x - 2$	*Distributive Property*
$y = \frac{1}{2}x + 1$	*Add 3 to both sides.*

19. Are the lines given by the equations $-4x + y = 5$ and $-x + 4y = 12$ parallel, perpendicular, or neither? Why?

Neither; the slopes are 4 and $\frac{1}{4}$. Since the slopes are not equal and their product is not -1, the lines are neither parallel nor perpendicular.

20. Consider the points $A(-7, 10)$, $B(12, 7)$, $C(10, -24)$, and $D(-8, -3)$. Which two lines determined by these points are perpendicular? Explain.

$\overrightarrow{AC} \perp \overrightarrow{BD}$ since the slope of $\overrightarrow{AC}$ is -2, the slope of $\overrightarrow{BD}$ is $\frac{1}{2}$, and the product of the slopes is -1.

© Houghton Mifflin Harcourt Publishing Company

Assign these pages to help your students practice and apply important lesson concepts. For additional exercises, see the Student Edition.

Answers

Additional Practice

1. $y - 7 = 0$

2. $y + 5 = -\dfrac{8}{5}(x - 1)$

3. $y = 7x$ **4.** $y = -\dfrac{1}{2}x - 1$

5.
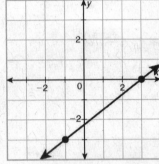

6.
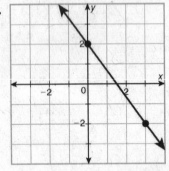

7. coincide   **8.** parallel

9. intersect

10. RS: $y = -52x + 4500$; AS: $y = -8x + 3000$; 34 days

Problem Solving

1. $x + 2y = 78$, $x + y = 53$

2. color: $28, black: $25

3. Both companies total costs would be the same for 10 T-shirts.

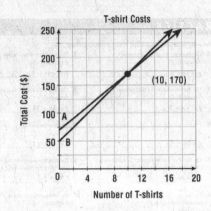

4. B   **5.** H

6. B

Additional Practice

Write the equation of each line in the given form.

1. the horizontal line through (3, 7) in point-slope form

2. the line with slope $-\frac{8}{5}$ through (1, −5) in point-slope form

3. the line through $\left(-\frac{1}{2}, -\frac{7}{2}\right)$ and (2, 14) in slope-intercept form

4. the line with x-intercept −2 and y-intercept −1 in slope-intercept form

Graph each line.

5. $y + 3 = \frac{3}{4}(x + 1)$

6. $y = -\frac{4}{3}x + 2$

Determine whether the lines are parallel, intersect, or coincide.

7. $x - 5y = 0,\ y + 1 = \frac{1}{5}(x + 5)$ _____

8. $2y + 2 = x,\ \frac{1}{2}x = -1 + y$ _____

9. $y = 4(x - 3),\ \frac{3}{4} + 4y = -\frac{1}{4}x$ _____

An *aquifer* is an underground storehouse of water. The water is in tiny crevices and pockets in the rock or sand, but because aquifers underlay large areas of land, the amount of water in an aquifer can be vast. Wells and springs draw water from aquifers.

10. Two relatively small aquifers are the Rush Springs (RS) aquifer and the Arbuckle-Simpson (AS) aquifer, both in Oklahoma. Suppose that starting on a certain day in 1985, 52 million gallons of water per day were taken from the RS aquifer, and 8 million gallons of water per day were taken from the AS aquifer. If the RS aquifer began with 4500 million gallons of water and the AS aquifer began with 3000 million gallons of water and no rain fell, write a slope-intercept equation for each aquifer and find how many days passed until both aquifers held the same amount of water. (Round to the nearest day.)

Problem Solving

Use the following information for Exercises 1 and 2. Josh can order 1 color ink cartridge and 2 black ink cartridges for his printer for $78. He can also order 1 color ink cartridge and 1 black ink cartridge for $53.

1. Let x equal the cost of a color ink cartridge and y equal the cost of a black ink cartridge. Write a system of equations to represent this situation.

2. What is the cost of each cartridge?

3. Ms. Williams is planning to buy T-shirts for the cheerleading camp that she is running. Both companies' total costs would be the same after buying how many T-shirts? Use a graph to find your solution.

	Art Creation Fee	Cost per T-shirt
Company A	$70	$10
Company B	$50	$12

Choose the best answer.

4. Two floats begin a parade at different times, but travel at the same speeds. Which is a true statement about the lines that represent the distance traveled by each float at a given time?

   A The lines intersect.

   B The lines are parallel.

   C The lines are the same.

   D The lines have a negative slope.

5. A piano teacher charges $20 for each half hour lesson, plus an initial fee of $50. Another teacher charges $40 per hour, plus a fee of $50. Which is a true statement about the lines that represent the total cost by each piano teacher?

   F The lines intersect.

   G The lines are parallel.

   H The lines are the same.

   J The lines have a negative slope.

6. Serina is trying to decide between two similar packages for starting her own Web site. Which is a true statement?

   A Both packages cost $235.50 for 5 months.

   B Both packages cost $295 for 10 months.

   C Both packages cost $355 for 15 months.

   D The packages will never have the same cost.

	Design and Setup	Monthly Fee to Host
Package A	$150.00	$14.50
Package B	$175.00	$12.00

This page provides students with the opportunity to apply concepts from the Common Core in real-world problem situations. There are three different levels of performance tasks:

⭐ **Novice:** These are short word problems that require students to apply the math they have learned in straightforward, real-world situations.

⭐⭐ **Apprentice:** These are more involved problems that guide students step-by-step through more complex tasks. These exercises include more complicated reasoning, writing, and open-ended elements.

⭐⭐⭐ **Expert:** These are open-ended, non-routine problems that, instead of stepping the students through, ask them to choose their own methods for solving and justify their answers and reasoning.

Sample answers

1. $\frac{1}{4}$ rotation and $\frac{3}{4}$ rotation; 90° and 270°

2. AG is less than 6 ft because $\overline{AG}$ is perpendicular to $\overline{BC}$, and the shortest distance from a point to a line is along the perpendicular. AB is greater than AG, but since you only know that AG is less than 6 ft, you cannot tell whether AB is less than or greater than 6 ft.

3. Scoring Guide:

Task	Possible points
a	3 points for any workable method, for example: measure alternate interior angles, where the wall is one line, a stripe is another line, and the edge of the square is the transversal; if the angles are congruent, the lines are parallel by the Converse of the Alternate Interior Angles Theorem .
b	1 point for any plausible measurements for the method in part **a**, for example: the angle between the side and the wall is 50°, and the alternate interior angle between the side and a stripe is 55°, and 2 points for a correct rotation: in the sample case, the tile would need to be rotated counterclockwise.

Total possible points: 6

CHAPTER 3

Performance Tasks

COMMON CORE
CC.9-12.G.CO.1
CC.9-12.G.CO.9
CC.9-12.G.GPE.5
CC.9-12.G.MG.1

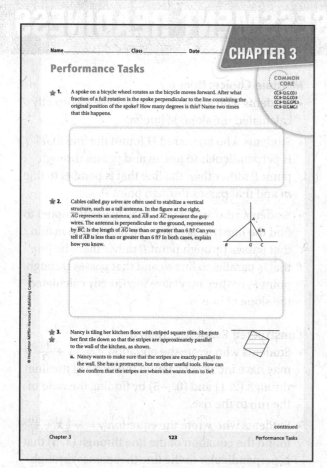

★ 1. A spoke on a bicycle wheel rotates as the bicycle moves forward. After what fraction of a full rotation is the spoke perpendicular to the line containing the original position of the spoke? How many degrees is this? Name two times that this happens.

★ 2. Cables called *guy wires* are often used to stabilize a vertical structure, such as a tall antenna. In the figure at the right, $\overline{AG}$ represents an antenna, and $\overline{AB}$ and $\overline{AC}$ represent the guy wires. The antenna is perpendicular to the ground, represented by $\overline{BC}$. Is the length of $\overline{AG}$ less than or greater than 6 ft? Can you tell if $\overline{AB}$ is less than or greater than 6 ft? In both cases, explain how you know.

★ 3. Nancy is tiling her kitchen floor with striped square tiles. She puts
★ her first tile down so that the stripes are approximately parallel to the wall of the kitchen, as shown.

   a. Nancy wants to make sure that the stripes are exactly parallel to the wall. She has a protractor, but no other useful tools. How can she confirm that the stripes are where she wants them to be?

continued

   b. Nancy uses the protractor and finds that the stripes aren't quite parallel to the wall. What angle measures could she have found that tell her this? Given your measurements, which way should she turn the tile to fix the situation, clockwise or counterclockwise?

★ 4. A segment has endpoints (a, b) and (c, d). The segment is translated so that its image is
★ 6 units up and 3 units left of the preimage. Are the two segments parallel, perpendicular, or
★ neither? Prove your answer.

---

4. Scoring Guide:

Task	Possible points
a	1 point for identifying the segments as parallel, and 5 points for correctly proving it. The proof should contain slopes for both of the line segments, comparing them to find they are equal, and using that statement to conclude they are parallel, for example: The slope of the preimage is $\frac{d-b}{c-a}$. The slope of the image is $\frac{(d+6)-(b+6)}{(c-3)-(a-3)}$, which simplifies to $\frac{d-b}{c-a}$ by combining like terms. Since the slopes are the same, the segments are parallel.

Total possible points: 6

© Houghton Mifflin Harcourt Publishing Company

COMMON CORE CORRELATION

Standard	Items
CC.9-12.G.CO.9	1, 7
CC.9-12.G.CO.12	2, 10, 11, 12
CC.9-12.GPE.5	3, 5, 6, 8, 9
CC.9-12.GPE.6	4

TEST PREP DOCTOR ✚

Multiple Choice: Item 1

- Students who answered **A** may have incorrectly assumed that any statement that uses the term *supplementary* must have *Definition of supplementary angles* as its reason.
- Students who answered **C** may not understand that ∠4 and ∠5 are not a linear pair.
- Students who answered **D** may not understand the definition of vertical angles.

Multiple Choice: Item 4

- Students who answered **F** may have found the correct percent of the run and the rise but added these values to the *x*- and *y*-coordinates of point *M* in the wrong order.
- Students who answered **H** found the point that partitions the segment in the ratio 1 to 3.
- Students who answered **J** found the correct percent of the run and the rise, but forgot to add these values to the *x*- and *y*-coordinates of point *M*.

Multiple Choice: Item 6

- Students who answered **F** may have incorrectly calculated the slope of line *m*.
- Students who answered **H** found the line that is perpendicular to line *m* and passes through point *P* rather than the line that is parallel to line *m* and that passes through point *P*.
- Students who answered **J** may have attempted to find the line that is perpendicular to line *m* and that passes through point *P* rather than the line that is parallel to line *m* and that passes through point *P*, or they may have incorrectly calculated the slope of line *m*.

Constructed Response: Item 8

- Students who wrote the equation $y = \frac{1}{3}x + \frac{14}{3}$ may have incorrectly found the slope of the line through (2, 1) and (0, −5) by finding the ratio of the run to the rise.
- Students who wrote the equation $y = -\frac{1}{3}x + \frac{16}{3}$ found the equation of the line through (1, 5) that is perpendicular to the line that passes through (2, 1) and (0, −5).
- Students who wrote the equation $y = 3x + b$ for any value of *b* other than 2 may have had difficulty substituting the coordinates of the given point and simplifying to find *b*.

Constructed Response: Item 11

- Students who failed to draw any perpendicular bisector may have had trouble because they drew arcs from points *J* and *K* that did not intersect. Remind students to set their compass opening to more than half the length of $\overline{JK}$.
- Students who drew a perpendicular that does not intersect $\overline{JK}$ at its midpoint may have changed the compass setting after drawing the arc from one of the endpoints.

Name _____ Class _____ Date _____

MULTIPLE CHOICE

1. Keiko is writing the proof shown below. Which reason should she use for Step 2?

Given: $\ell \parallel m$
Prove: $m\angle 4 = m\angle 6$

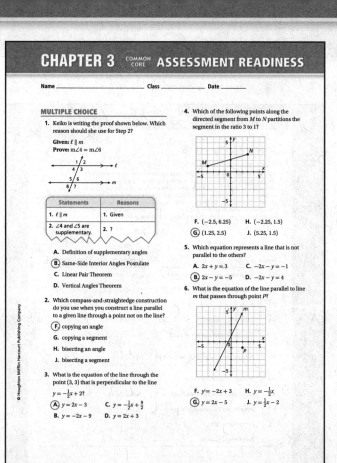

Statements	Reasons
1. $\ell \parallel m$	1. Given
2. $\angle 4$ and $\angle 5$ are supplementary.	2. ?

   A. Definition of supplementary angles

   B. Same-Side Interior Angles Postulate

   C. Linear Pair Theorem

   D. Vertical Angles Theorem

2. Which compass-and-straightedge construction do you use when you construct a line parallel to a given line through a point not on the line?

   F. copying an angle

   G. copying a segment

   H. bisecting an angle

   J. bisecting a segment

3. What is the equation of the line through the point (3, 3) that is perpendicular to the line $y = -\frac{1}{2}x + 2$?

   A. $y = 2x - 3$ **C.** $y = -\frac{1}{2}x + \frac{9}{2}$

   B. $y = -2x - 9$ **D.** $y = 2x + 3$

4. Which of the following points along the directed segment from M to N partitions the segment in the ratio 3 to 1?

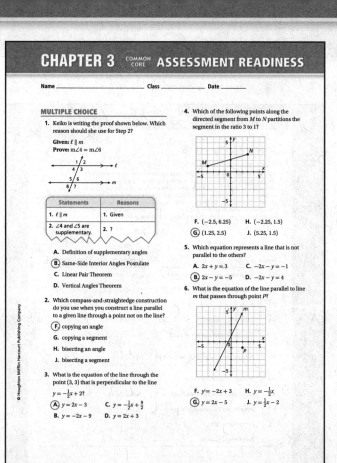

   F. $(-2.5, 6.25)$ **H.** $(-2.25, 1.5)$

   G. $(1.25, 2.5)$ **J.** $(5.25, 1.5)$

5. Which equation represents a line that is not parallel to the others?

   A. $2x + y = 3$ **C.** $-2x - y = -1$

   B. $2x - y = -5$ **D.** $-2x - y = 4$

6. What is the equation of the line parallel to m that passes through point P?

   F. $y = -2x + 3$ **H.** $y = -\frac{1}{2}x$

   G. $y = 2x - 5$ **J.** $y = \frac{1}{2}x - 2$

---

7. Which lines can be proven parallel given the following diagram?

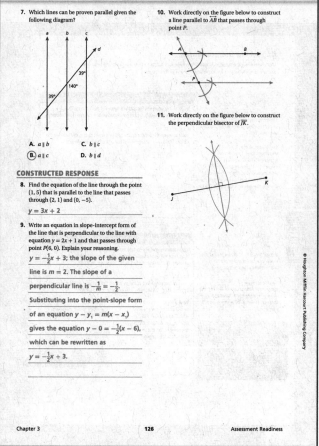

   A. $a \parallel b$ **C.** $b \parallel c$

   B. $a \parallel c$ **D.** $b \parallel d$

CONSTRUCTED RESPONSE

8. Find the equation of the line through the point (1, 5) that is parallel to the line that passes through (2, 1) and (0, −5).

$y = 3x + 2$

9. Write an equation in slope-intercept form of the line that is perpendicular to the line with equation $y = 2x + 1$ and that passes through point $P(6, 0)$. Explain your reasoning.

$y = -\frac{1}{2}x + 3$; the slope of the given

line is $m = 2$. The slope of a

perpendicular line is $-\frac{1}{m} = -\frac{1}{2}$.

Substituting into the point-slope form

of an equation $y - y_1 = m(x - x_1)$

gives the equation $y - 0 = -\frac{1}{2}(x - 6)$,

which can be rewritten as

$y = -\frac{1}{2}x + 3$.

10. Work directly on the figure below to construct a line parallel to $\overleftrightarrow{AB}$ that passes through point P.

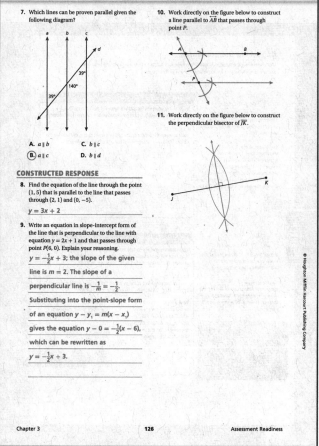

11. Work directly on the figure below to construct the perpendicular bisector of $\overline{JK}$.

Triangle Congruence

Triangle Congruence

Chapter Focus

You have already learned that rigid motions preserve the size and shape of a figure. In this unit, you will learn that two figures are congruent (have the same size and shape) if and only if one figure can be mapped to the other by a sequence of rigid motions. You will also learn that there are some shortcuts for showing that triangles are congruent. Once you know these shortcuts, which are called congruence criteria, you will use them to prove facts about triangles. Along the way, you will also learn to write coordinate proofs.

Chapter at a Glance

Lesson		COMMON CORE Standards for Mathematical Content
4-1	Congruence and Transformations	CC.9-12.G.CO.5, CC.9-12.G.CO.6
4-2	Classifying Triangles	CC.9-12.G.GPE.4, CC.9-12.G.GPE 7
4-3	Angle Relationships in Triangles	CC.9-12.G.CO.10
4-4	Congruent Triangles	CC.9-12.G.CO.7
4-5	Triangle Congruence: SSS and SAS	CC.9-12.G.CO.8, CC.9-12.G.CO.9, CC.9-12.G.SRT.5
4-6	Triangle Congruence: ASA, AAS, and HL	CC.9-12.G.CO.8, CC.9-12.G.CO.10, CC.9-12.G.SRT.5
4-7	Triangle Congruence: CPCTC	CC.9-12.G.GPE.5
4-8	Introduction to Coordinate Proof	CC.9-12.G.GPE.4
4-9	Isosceles and Equilateral Triangles	CC.9-12.G.CO.10
	Performance Tasks	
	Assessment Readiness	

COMMON CORE PROFESSIONAL DEVELOPMENT — CC.9-12.G.CO.6

Transformations are a prominent topic in geometry, and there are different types of transformations. One way to classify transformations and sequences of transformations is by the resulting effects on the figures on which they are performed. Transformations that preserve size and shape of a figure, resulting in a congruent figure, are called rigid transformations. Applying rigid transformations in many different ways often helps students understand the concept of congruence. By seeing a given shape from many perspectives, students can focus on the elements that actually define congruence rather than getting distracted by the different orientations of figures.

Unpacking the Standards

Understanding the standards and the vocabulary terms in the standards will help you know exactly what you are expected to learn in this chapter.

COMMON CORE CC.9-12.G.CO.6

Use geometric descriptions of rigid motions to transform figures and to predict the effect of a given rigid motion on a given figure; ...

Key Vocabulary
transformation *(transformación)* A change in the position, size, or shape of a figure or graph.
rigid motion *(movimiento rígido)* A transformation that does not change the size or shape of a figure.

What It Means For You — Lesson 4-1

In geometry, when you reposition a figure but don't change its size or shape in the process, you have performed what is called a *rigid motion*.

EXAMPLE
You can create the pattern on the grid by a series of rigid motions—in this case reflections and rotations—of one of the blue crescent shapes.

COMMON CORE CC.9-12.G.SRT.5

Use congruence ... criteria for triangles to solve problems and to prove relationships in geometric figures.

Key Vocabulary
congruent *(congruente)* Having the same size and shape, denoted by ≅.
triangle *(triángulo)* A three-sided polygon.

What It Means For You — Lessons 4-5, 4-6

When two triangles are *congruent*, it means that matching sides have the same measure and matching angles have the same measure. You can use this fact to help you solve problems.

EXAMPLE
You can use congruent triangles to find the distance across a canyon by measuring distances on only one side of the canyon.

Walk from *D* perpendicular to *BD* until you are in line with *C* and *A*. Call this point *E*. The distance *DE* is the same as the distance *AB* across the canyon.

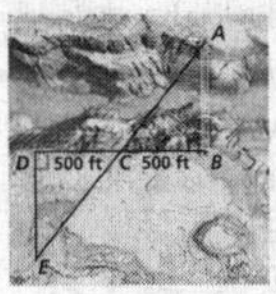

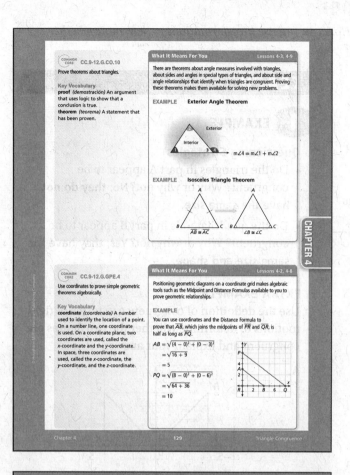

CC.9-12.G.SRT.5

In this chapter, students examine pairs of congruent triangles and note various characteristics that they share. Through exploration and construction, students form conjectures about the minimum information required to construct the triangle and prove that two triangles are congruent. Finally students are guided through some proofs of their conjectures so they have the necessary criteria to prove when triangles are congruent. With triangle congruence criteria in their toolbox, students can apply the properties of congruent triangles in real-world scenarios.

CC.9-12.G.CO.10

Prove theorems about triangles.

Key Vocabulary
proof (*demostración*) An argument that uses logic to show that a conclusion is true.
theorem (*teorema*) A statement that has been proven.

What It Means For You
Lessons 4-3, 4-9

There are theorems about angle measures involved with triangles, about sides and angles in special types of triangles, and about side and angle relationships that identify when triangles are congruent. Proving these theorems makes them available for solving new problems.

EXAMPLE   Exterior Angle Theorem

Exterior

Interior

$m\angle 4 = m\angle 1 + m\angle 2$

EXAMPLE   Isosceles Triangle Theorem

$\overline{AB} \cong \overline{AC}$

$\angle B \cong \angle C$

CC.9-12.G.GPE.4

Use coordinates to prove simple geometric theorems algebraically.

Key Vocabulary
coordinate (*coordenada*) A number used to identify the location of a point. On a number line, one coordinate is used. On a coordinate plane, two coordinates are used, called the x-coordinate and the y-coordinate. In space, three coordinates are used, called the x-coordinate, the y-coordinate, and the z-coordinate.

What It Means For You
Lessons 4-2, 4-8

Positioning geometric diagrams on a coordinate grid makes algebraic tools such as the Midpoint and Distance Formulas available to you to prove geometric relationships.

EXAMPLE
You can use coordinates and the Distance Formula to prove that $\overline{AB}$, which joins the midpoints of $\overline{PR}$ and $\overline{QR}$, is half as long as $\overline{PQ}$.

$AB = \sqrt{(4-0)^2 + (0-3)^2}$

$= \sqrt{16 + 9}$

$= 5$

$PQ = \sqrt{(8-0)^2 + (0-6)^2}$

$= \sqrt{64 + 36}$

$= 10$

CHAPTER 4

Key Vocabulary

acute triangle (*triángulo acutángulo*) A triangle with three acute angles.

base of an isosceles triangle (*base de un triángulo isósceles*) The side opposite the vertex angle.

base angle of an isosceles triangle (*ángulo base de un triángulo isósceles*) One of the two angles that have the base of the triangle as a side.

congruent (*congruente*) Having the same size and shape, denoted by ≅.

coordinate (*coordenada*) A number used to identify the location of a point. On a number line, one coordinate is used. On a coordinate plane, two coordinates are used, called the x-coordinate and the y-coordinate. In space, three coordinates are used, called the x-coordinate, the y-coordinate, and the z-coordinate.

corollary (*corolario*) A theorem whose proof follows directly from another theorem.

equilateral triangle (*triángulo equilátero*) A triangle with three congruent sides.

exterior angle of a polygon (*ángulo externo de un polígono*) An angle formed by one side of a polygon and the extension of an adjacent side.

indirect proof (*demostración indirecta*) A proof in which the statement to be proved is assumed to be false and a contradiction is shown.

interior angle (*ángulo interno*) An angle formed by two sides of a polygon with a common vertex.

isosceles triangle (*triángulo isósceles*) A triangle with at least two congruent sides.

leg of an isosceles triangle (*cateto de un triángulo isósceles*) One of the two congruent sides of the isosceles triangle.

obtuse triangle (*triángulo obtusángulo*) A triangle with one obtuse angle.

remote interior angle (*ángulo interno remoto*) An interior angle of a polygon that is not adjacent to the exterior angle.

right triangle (*triángulo rectángulo*) A triangle with one right angle.

rigid motion (*movimiento rígido*) A transformation that does not change the size or shape of a figure.

scalene triangle (*triángulo escaleno*) A triangle with no congruent sides.

transformation (*transformación*) A change in the position, size, or shape of a figure or graph.

triangle (*triángulo*) A three-sided polygon.

vertex angle of an isosceles triangle (*ángulo del vértice de un triángulo isósceles*) The angle formed by the legs of an isosceles triangle.

CHAPTER 4

Congruence and Transformations
Going Deeper

Essential question: *How can you use transformations to determine whether figures are congruent?*

COMMON **Standards for**
CORE **Mathematical Content**

CC.9-12.G.CO.5 ... Specify a sequence of transformations that will carry a given figure onto another.

CC.9-12.G.CO.6 ... given two figures, use the definition of congruence in terms of rigid motions to decide if they are congruent.

Vocabulary
congruent

Prerequisites
Transformations that are rigid motions

Math Background
The definition of congruence given in this book is different from the definition that is presented in many traditional geometry texts. In those texts, two figures are defined to be congruent if they have the same size and shape. Here, two figures are defined to be congruent if there is a sequence of rigid motions that maps one to the other. From this definition it follows that the two figures have the same size and shape. Over the next few lessons, this transformations-based definition will be used to develop the standard congruence criteria for triangles (SSS, SAS, and ASA).

INTRODUCE

Define *congruence*. Ask students to give examples of congruent figures in the classroom. Students might mention floor tiles that have the same size and shape, or desktops that are all rectangles with the same size and shape. Tell students that "the same size and shape" is an informal way of deciding whether two figures may be congruent, but that a more formal mathematical definition of congruence is based on rigid motions.

TEACH

1 EXAMPLE

Questioning Strategies
- Do the triangles in part A appear to be congruent? Why or why not? No; they do not have the same size.
- Do the quadrilaterals in part B appear to be congruent? Why or why not? Yes; they have the same size and shape.

EXTRA EXAMPLE
Use the definition of congruence in terms of rigid motions to determine whether the two figures are congruent and explain your answer.

A.

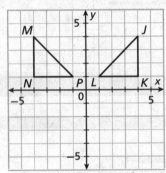

Congruent; a rigid motion (reflection across the y-axis) maps △JKL to △MNP.

B.

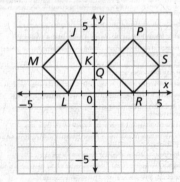

Not congruent; there is no sequence of rigid motions that maps *JKLM* to *PQRS*.

Name_____ Class_____ Date_____

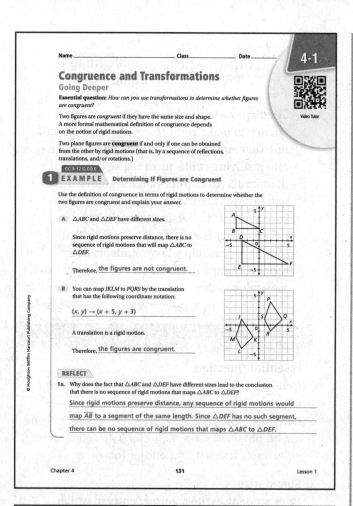

Congruence and Transformations
Going Deeper

Essential question: *How can you use transformations to determine whether figures are congruent?*

Two figures are *congruent* if they have the same size and shape. A more formal mathematical definition of congruence depends on the notion of rigid motions.

Two plane figures are **congruent** if and only if one can be obtained from the other by rigid motions (that is, by a sequence of reflections, translations, and/or rotations.)

CC.9-12.G.CO.6

1 EXAMPLE   Determining If Figures are Congruent

Use the definition of congruence in terms of rigid motions to determine whether the two figures are congruent and explain your answer.

A   △ABC and △DEF have different sizes.

Since rigid motions preserve distance, there is no sequence of rigid motions that will map △ABC to △DEF.

Therefore, the figures are not congruent.

B   You can map JKLM to PQRS by the translation that has the following coordinate notation:

$(x, y) \rightarrow (x + 5, y + 3)$

A translation is a rigid motion.

Therefore, the figures are congruent.

REFLECT

1a. Why does the fact that △ABC and △DEF have different sizes lead to the conclusion that there is no sequence of rigid motions that maps △ABC to △DEF?

Since rigid motions preserve distance, any sequence of rigid motions would map $\overline{AB}$ to a segment of the same length. Since △DEF has no such segment, there can be no sequence of rigid motions that maps △ABC to △DEF.

Chapter 4   131   Lesson 1

The definition of congruence tells you that when two figures are known to be congruent, there must be some sequence of rigid motions that maps one to the other. You will investigate this idea in the next example.

CC.9-12.G.CO.5

2 EXAMPLE   Finding a Sequence of Rigid Motions

For each pair of congruent figures, find a sequence of rigid motions that maps one figure to the other.

Possible answers are given.

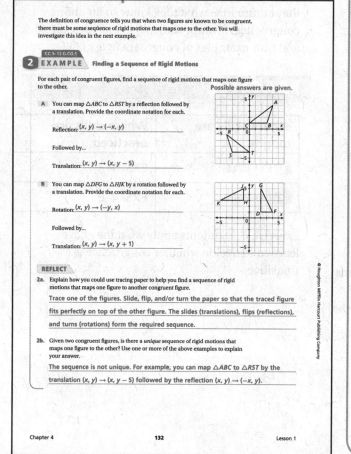

A   You can map △ABC to △RST by a reflection followed by a translation. Provide the coordinate notation for each.

Reflection: $(x, y) \rightarrow (-x, y)$

Followed by...

Translation: $(x, y) \rightarrow (x, y - 5)$

B   You can map △DFG to △HJK by a rotation followed by a translation. Provide the coordinate notation for each.

Rotation: $(x, y) \rightarrow (-y, x)$

Followed by...

Translation: $(x, y) \rightarrow (x, y + 1)$

REFLECT

2a. Explain how you could use tracing paper to help you find a sequence of rigid motions that maps one figure to another congruent figure.

Trace one of the figures. Slide, flip, and/or turn the paper so that the traced figure fits perfectly on top of the other figure. The slides (translations), flips (reflections), and turns (rotations) form the required sequence.

2b. Given two congruent figures, is there a *unique* sequence of rigid motions that maps one figure to the other? Use one or more of the above examples to explain your answer.

The sequence is not unique. For example, you can map △ABC to △RST by the translation $(x, y) \rightarrow (x, y - 5)$ followed by the reflection $(x, y) \rightarrow (-x, y)$.

Chapter 4   132   Lesson 1

2 EXAMPLE

Questioning Strategies

- For each pair of figures, how do you know that a sequence of rigid motions that maps one figure to the other must exist? **The figures are known to be congruent. By definition, there is a sequence of rigid motions that maps one to the other.**

EXTRA EXAMPLE

For each pair of congruent figures, find a sequence of rigid motions that maps one figure to the other.

A.

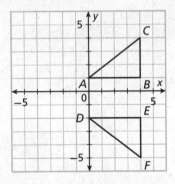

Reflection across the x-axis, $(x, y) \rightarrow (x, -y)$, followed by the translation $(x, y) \rightarrow (x, y - 1)$.

B.

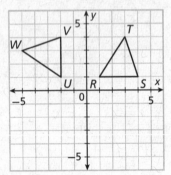

Rotation of 90°, $(x, y) \rightarrow (-y, x)$, followed by the translation $(x, y) \rightarrow (x - 1, y)$.

3 EXPLORE

Materials: ruler, protractor

Questioning Strategies

- If there is a sequence of flips, slides, and/or turns that maps one figure to another, what can you conclude? Why? **The figures are congruent by the definition of congruence.**

<table>
<tr><td>MATHEMATICAL PRACTICE</td><td>**Highlighting the Standards**</td></tr>
</table>

The Explore in this lesson gives students a chance to make conjectures about congruent line segments and congruent angles. Making and justifying conjectures is a key part of Standard 3 (Construct viable arguments and critique the reasoning of others). Be sure students understand that the type of reasoning used in the Explore is called inductive reasoning. Have students describe other instances in which they used inductive reasoning to develop a conjecture.

CLOSE

Essential Question

How can you use transformations to determine whether figures are congruent?

Two plane figures are congruent if and only if one can be obtained from the other by a sequence of reflections, translations, and/or rotations.

Summarize

Have students write a journal entry in which they summarize what they know so far about congruence. Prompt students to include examples and non-examples of congruent figures.

PRACTICE

Where skills are taught	Where skills are practiced
1 EXAMPLE	EXS. 1–3
2 EXAMPLE	EXS. 4–6

Exercise 7: Students apply what they have learned to decide whether congruence is transitive.

© Houghton Mifflin Harcourt Publishing Company

3 EXPLORE Investigating Congruent Segments and Angles

A Use a straightedge to trace $\overline{AB}$ on a piece of tracing paper. Then slide, flip, and/or turn the tracing paper to determine if there is a sequence of rigid motions that maps $\overline{AB}$ to one of the other line segments.

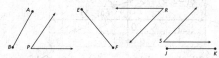

B Repeat the process with the other line segments and the angles in order to determine which pairs of line segments and which pairs of angles, if any, are congruent.

Congruent line segments: $\overline{EF}$ and $\overline{JK}$

Congruent angles: $\angle R$ and $\angle S$

C Use a ruler to measure the congruent line segments. Use a protractor to measure the congruent angles.

REFLECT

3a. Make a conjecture about congruent line segments.

Congruent line segments have the same length.

3b. Make a conjecture about congruent angles.

Congruent angles have the same measure.

The symbol of congruence is $\cong$. You read the statement $\overline{UV} \cong \overline{XY}$ as "Line segment UV is congruent to line segment XY."

Congruent line segments have the same length, so $\overline{UV} \cong \overline{XY}$ implies $UV = XY$ and vice versa. Congruent angles have the same measure, so $\angle C \cong \angle D$ implies $m\angle C = m\angle D$ and vice versa. Because of this, there are properties of congruence that resemble the properties of equality, and you can use these properties as reasons in proofs.

Properties of Congruence	
Reflexive Property of Congruence	$\overline{AB} \cong \overline{AB}$
Symmetric Property of Congruence	If $\overline{AB} \cong \overline{CD}$, then $\overline{CD} \cong \overline{AB}$.
Transitive Property of Congruence	If $\overline{AB} \cong \overline{CD}$ and $\overline{CD} \cong \overline{EF}$, then $\overline{AB} \cong \overline{EF}$.

PRACTICE

Use the definition of congruence in terms of rigid motions to determine whether the two figures are congruent and explain your answer.

1.

Congruent; a rigid motion (reflection across y-axis) maps $\triangle ABC$ to $\triangle DEF$.

2.

Not congruent; there is no sequence of rigid motions that maps $JKLM$ to $PQRS$.

3.

Congruent; a rigid motion (rotation by 180°) maps $\triangle TUV$ to $\triangle XYZ$.

For each pair of congruent figures, find a sequence of rigid motions that maps one figure to the other. Give coordinate notation for the transformations you use. Possible answers are given.

4.

Reflect $\triangle CDE$ across x-axis, $(x, y) \rightarrow (x, -y)$, then use the translation $(x, y) \rightarrow (x + 5, y)$.

5.

Rotate $JKLM$ 180°, $(x, y) \rightarrow (-x, -y)$, then use the translation $(x, y) \rightarrow (x - 1, y + 1)$.

6.

Reflect $\triangle ABC$ across y-axis, $(x, y) \rightarrow (-x, y)$, then use the translation $(x, y) \rightarrow (x, y - 2)$.

7. $\triangle ABC \cong \triangle DEF$ and $\triangle DEF \cong \triangle GHJ$. Can you conclude $\triangle ABC \cong \triangle GHJ$? Explain.

Yes; extend the sequence of rigid motions that maps $\triangle ABC$ to $\triangle DEF$ by the sequence that maps $\triangle DEF$ to $\triangle GHJ$ to make a sequence that maps $\triangle ABC$ to $\triangle GHJ$.

ADDITIONAL PRACTICE AND PROBLEM SOLVING

Assign these pages to help your students practice and apply important lesson concepts. For additional exercises, see the Student Edition.

Answers

Additional Practice

1.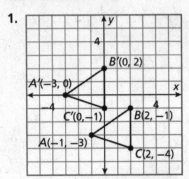

   translation 2 units left and 3 units up

2.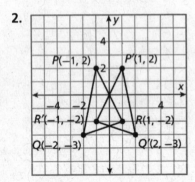

   reflection in the y-axis

3.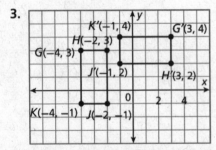

   rotation about (0, 0), 90° clockwise

4.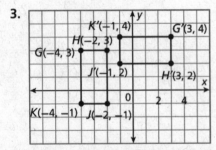

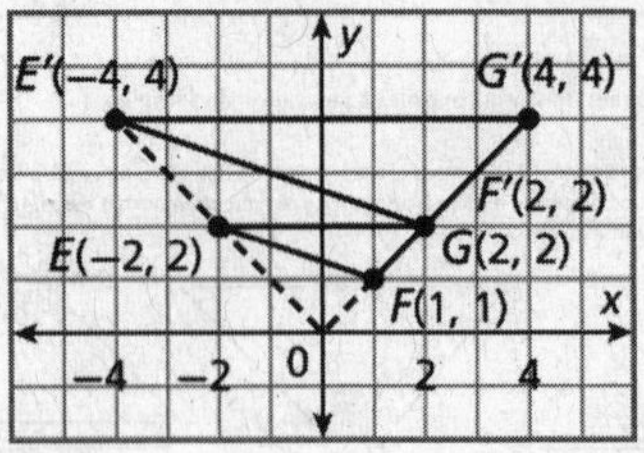

   dilation with scale factor 2 and center (0, 0)

5. Yes, the pentagons are congruent because pentagon *ABCDE* can be mapped to pentagon *PQRST* by a translation: $(x, y) \rightarrow (x + 6, y + 2)$.

6. No, the triangles are not congruent because triangle *JKL* can be mapped to triangle *PQR* by a dilation with scale factor 2 and a center of (0, 0).

Problem Solving

1. rotation 90° clockwise

2. repeated translations

3. reflection in the *y*-axis

4. translation followed by a reflection

5. A

6. H

Name_____ Class_____ Date_____

4-1

Additional Practice

Apply the transformation *M* to the polygon with the given vertices. Identify and describe the transformation.

1. $M: (x, y) \rightarrow (x - 2, y + 3)$
   $A(-1, -3), B(2, -1), C(2, -4)$

2. $M: (x, y) \rightarrow (-x, y)$
   $P(-1, 2), Q(-2, -3), R(1, -2)$

3. $M: (x, y) \rightarrow (y, -x)$
   $G(-4, 3), H(-2, 3), J(-2, -1), K(-4, -1)$

4. $M: (x, y) \rightarrow (2x, 2y)$
   $E(-2, 2), F(1, 1), G(2, 2)$

Determine whether the polygons with the given vertices are congruent.

5. $A(-4, 4), B(-2, 4), C(-2, 2), D(-3, 1), E(-4, 2); P(2, 6), Q(4, 6), R(4, 4), S(3, 3), T(2, 4)$

6. $P(4, 4), Q(-4, 2), R(-2, 6); J(2, 2), K(-2, 1), L(-1, 3)$

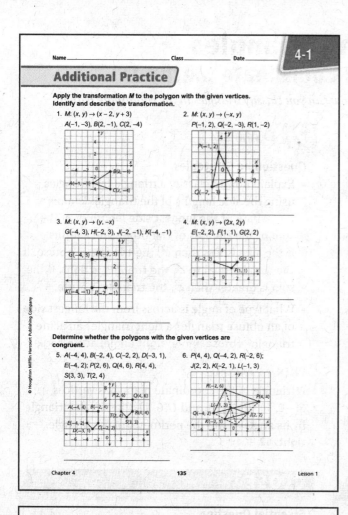

© Houghton Mifflin Harcourt Publishing Company

Chapter 4   135   Lesson 1

Problem Solving

1. Irena is designing a quilt. She made this diagram to follow when making her quilt. What transformation(s) are used on the triangles to create the pattern in the quilt design?

2. An architect used this design for a stained glass window. What frieze transformation(s) is used to create the pattern in the window?

3. A graphic artist incorporated the universal symbol for radiation for one of his designs. Describe the transformation(s) he used.

4. Richard developed a tessellating shape for floor tile. Describe the series of transformations he used to create the design.

Choose the best answer.

5. A team flag is made using a fabric with the design shown. What transformation is used?

   A translation
   B reflection
   C rotation
   D dilation

6. An art student used transformations in all her art. What transformation did she use for her design shown?

   F translation
   G reflection
   H rotation
   J dilation

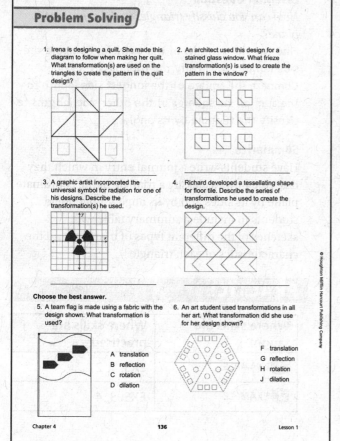

© Houghton Mifflin Harcourt Publishing Company

Chapter 4   136   Lesson 1

Classifying Triangles
Connection: Coordinate Methods

Essential question: *How can you classify triangles in the coordinate plane?*

© Houghton Mifflin Harcourt Publishing Company

COMMON CORE Standards for Mathematical Content

CC.9-12.G.GPE.4 Use coordinates to prove simple theorems algebraically.

CC.9-12.G.GPE.7 Use coordinates to compute perimeters ... of polygons... e.g., using the distance formula.*

Prerequisites
The Distance Formula

Perimeter

Math Background
Students can use their knowledge of the distance formula to find the side lengths of a triangle given the coordinates of the vertices. The side lengths can be used to classify the triangle. These skills will be helpful when students are asked to complete coordinate proofs later in this course.

INTRODUCE

Review scalene, isosceles, and equilateral triangles. Then draw a triangle in a coordinate plane. (The triangle should not be obviously scalene or isosceles.) Ask students if they can easily classify the triangle by its sides just by looking at it. If not, then ask how they can be certain about their classification.

TEACH

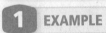 **EXAMPLE**

Questioning Strategies
- What do you need to know about a triangle in order to classify it by its sides? whether any of the sides are congruent

- How could you estimate the perimeter of the triangle to check your answer? Draw the triangle and estimate the lengths of sides $\overline{PQ}$ and $\overline{QR}$ in comparison to the length 6 of side $\overline{PR}$. Add the three side lengths.

EXTRA EXAMPLE
A triangle in the coordinate plane has vertices $L(-2, 3)$, $M(4, 4)$, and $N(0, 0)$. Classify the triangle by its sides. Find the perimeter of the triangle.
scalene; $\sqrt{37} + 4\sqrt{2} + \sqrt{13}$

2 EXAMPLE

Questioning Strategies
- Explain how to classify a triangle by its angles using the side lengths of the triangle. Compare the square of the longest side length c^2 to the sum of the squares of the other side lengths. If the sum is less than c^2, the triangle is obtuse. If the sum is equal to c^2, the triangle is right. If the sum is greater than c^2, the triangle is acute.

- What type of angle is across from the longest side of an obtuse triangle? a right triangle? an acute triangle? obtuse angle; right angle; acute angle

EXTRA EXAMPLE
A triangle in the coordinate plane has vertices $S(-2, 1)$, $T(-2, 5)$, and $U(6, 1)$. Classify the triangle by its angles. Find the perimeter of the triangle.
right; $12 + 4\sqrt{5}$

CLOSE

Essential Question
How can you classify triangles in the coordinate plane?
Find the side lengths of the triangle. Compare the side lengths to classify the triangle by its sides. Compare the square of the longest side length to the sum of the squares of the other side lengths to classify the triangle by its angles.

Summarize
Have students write a journal entry in which they describe how to classify a triangle in the coordinate plane by its sides and by its angles. Encourage students to include a summary table with sketches of the different types of triangles and the characteristics of each triangle.

PRACTICE

Where skills are taught	Where skills are practiced
1 EXAMPLE	EXS. 1, 2
2 EXAMPLE	EXS. 3, 4

Name_____ Class_____ Date_____

Classifying Triangles
Connection: Coordinate Methods

Essential question: *How can you classify triangles in the coordinate plane?*

Recall that triangles can be classified by their side lengths. A *scalene* triangle has no congruent sides, an *isosceles* triangle has at least two congruent sides, and an *equilateral* triangle has three congruent sides.

Video Tutor

CC.9-12.G.GPE.4

1 EXAMPLE   Classifying Triangles by Side Lengths

A triangle in the coordinate plane has vertices $P(4, 0)$, $Q(-3, 3)$, and $R(4, 6)$. Classify the triangle by its sides. Then write an expression for the perimeter of the triangle.

A Find the side lengths of the triangle using the distance formula.

$PQ = \sqrt{(x_2 - x_1)^2 + (y_2 - y_1)^2} = \sqrt{(-3 - 4)^2 + (3 - 0)^2} = \sqrt{58}$

$QR = \sqrt{(x_2 - x_1)^2 + (y_2 - y_1)^2} = \sqrt{(4 - (-3))^2 + (6 - 3)^2} = \sqrt{58}$

$RP = \sqrt{(x_2 - x_1)^2 + (y_2 - y_1)^2} = \sqrt{(4 - 4)^2 + (0 - 6)^2} = 6$

B Use the side lengths to classify the triangle.

$\triangle PQR$ is ___isosceles___ because ___sides PQ and QR have the same length.___

C Use the side lengths to write an expression for the perimeter of the triangle.

Perimeter $= PQ + QR + RP =$ $\sqrt{58} + \sqrt{58} + 6 = 6 + 2\sqrt{58}$

REFLECT

1a. Explain how you know that $\triangle PQR$ is not equilateral.

The sides of the triangle are not all the same length.

1b. The points $T(0, 0)$, $U(a, b)$, and $V(b, a)$ form a triangle. Explain why the triangle can be classified as isosceles.

Two of the side lengths are $TU = \sqrt{a^2 + b^2}$ and $TV = \sqrt{b^2 + a^2}$.

Because at least two sides have the same length, the triangle is isosceles.

You can use the side lengths of a triangle to classify a triangle as *obtuse*, *acute*, or *right* as shown below. Test the longest side c to classify the largest angle C.

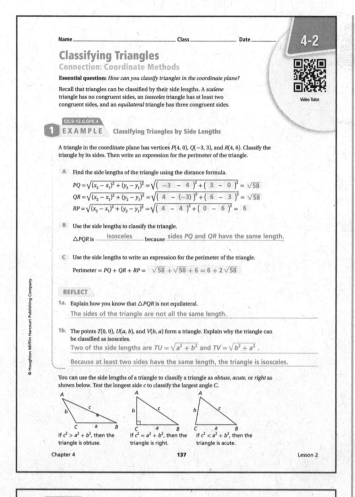

If $c^2 > a^2 + b^2$, then the triangle is obtuse.

If $c^2 = a^2 + b^2$, then the triangle is right.

If $c^2 < a^2 + b^2$, then the triangle is acute.

Chapter 4   137   Lesson 2

CC.9-12.G.GPE.7

2 EXAMPLE   Classifying Triangles by Angles Using Side Lengths

A triangle in the coordinate plane has vertices $J(-1, 0)$, $K(2, 4)$, and $M(7, 1)$. Classify the triangle by its angles. Then write an expression for the perimeter of the triangle.

A Find the side lengths of the triangle using the distance formula.

$JK = \sqrt{(2 - (-1))^2 + (4 - 0)^2} = 5$

$KM = \sqrt{(7 - 2)^2 + (1 - 4)^2} = \sqrt{34}$

$MJ = \sqrt{(-1 - 7)^2 + (0 - 1)^2} = \sqrt{65}$

B Use the side lengths to classify the triangle. The largest angle is opposite the longest side length.

$c^2 = a^2 + b^2$ Compare c^2 to $a^2 + b^2$.

$(\sqrt{65})^2 \overset{?}{=} 5^2 + (\sqrt{34})^2$ Substitute the longest side length for c.

$65 \overset{?}{=} 25 + 34$ Simplify.

$65 > 59$ Add and compare.

Since $c^2 > a^2 + b^2$, the angle opposite the longest side is ___obtuse___ and the triangle is ___obtuse___.

C Write an expression for the perimeter: Perimeter $= 5 + \sqrt{34} + \sqrt{65}$

REFLECT

2a. Explain why the points $A(0, 0)$, $B(k, k)$, and $C(2k, 0)$ are vertices of a right triangle.

$AC^2 = 4k^2$, $AB^2 = 2k^2$, and $BC^2 = 2k^2$. Because $4k^2 = 2k^2 + 2k^2$,

$AC^2 = AB^2 + BC^2$, so the angle at B is right and the triangle is right.

PRACTICE

A triangle has the given vertices. Classify the triangle by its sides. Then write an expression for the perimeter of the triangle.

1. $L(-2, -2)$, $M(1, 3)$, $N(3, 0)$
scalene; $\sqrt{13} + \sqrt{29} + \sqrt{34}$

2. $F(1, -1)$, $G(3, 5)$, $H(5, -1)$
isosceles; $4 + 4\sqrt{10}$

A triangle has the given vertices. Classify the triangle by its sides. Then write an expression for the perimeter of the triangle.

3. $D(5, 5)$, $E(-1, 1)$, $F(-1, 5)$
right; $10 + 2\sqrt{13}$

4. $X(-3, 1)$, $Y(4, 6)$, $Z(2, 2)$
obtuse; $2\sqrt{5} + \sqrt{74} + \sqrt{26}$

Chapter 4   138   Lesson 2

ADDITIONAL PRACTICE AND PROBLEM SOLVING

Assign these pages to help your students practice and apply important lesson concepts. For additional exercises, see the Student Edition.

Answers

Additional Practice

1. obtuse

2. right

3. acute

4. scalene

5. equilateral; isosceles

6. isosceles

7. $PR = RQ = 2.3; PQ = 1$

8. $ST = SU = TU = 5\frac{1}{4}$

9. 22 pieces of pita bread

10. scalene, right

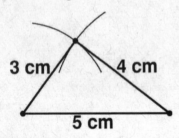

Problem Solving

1. 3 frames

2. $4\frac{3}{8}$ ft; $4\frac{3}{8}$ ft; $5\frac{1}{4}$ ft

3. Santa Fe and El Paso, 427 km; El Paso and Phoenix, 561 km; Phoenix and Santa Fe, 609 km

4. scalene

5. B

6. J

Name_____ Class_____ Date_____ **4-2**

Additional Practice

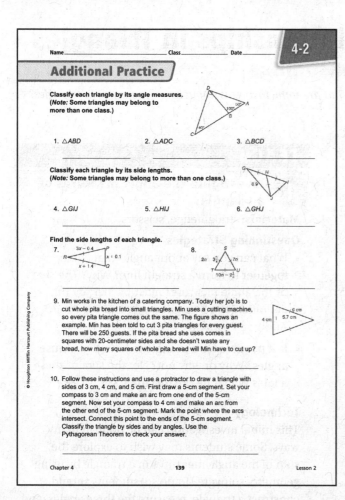

Classify each triangle by its angle measures.
(*Note:* Some triangles may belong to
more than one class.)

1. △ABD _____

2. △ADC _____

3. △BCD _____

Classify each triangle by its side lengths.
(*Note:* Some triangles may belong to more than one class.)

4. △GIJ _____

5. △HIJ _____

6. △GHJ _____

Find the side lengths of each triangle.

7. _____

8. _____

9. Min works in the kitchen of a catering company. Today her job is to cut whole pita bread into small triangles. Min uses a cutting machine, so every pita triangle comes out the same. The figure shows an example. Min has been told to cut 3 pita triangles for every guest. There will be 250 guests. If the pita bread she uses comes in squares with 20-centimeter sides and she doesn't waste any bread, how many squares of whole pita bread will Min have to cut up?

_____

10. Follow these instructions and use a protractor to draw a triangle with sides of 3 cm, 4 cm, and 5 cm. First draw a 5-cm segment. Set your compass to 3 cm and make an arc from one end of the 5-cm segment. Now set your compass to 4 cm and make an arc from the other end of the 5-cm segment. Mark the point where the arcs intersect. Connect this point to the ends of the 5-cm segment. Classify the triangle by sides and by angles. Use the Pythagorean Theorem to check your answer.

_____

Chapter 4   139   Lesson 2

Problem Solving

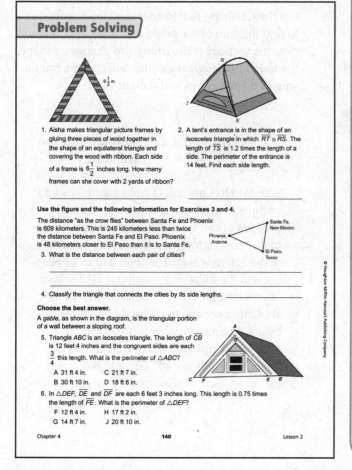

1. Aisha makes triangular picture frames by gluing three pieces of wood together in the shape of an equilateral triangle and covering the wood with ribbon. Each side of a frame is $6\frac{1}{2}$ inches long. How many frames can she cover with 2 yards of ribbon?

_____

2. A tent's entrance is in the shape of an isosceles triangle in which $\overline{RT} \cong \overline{RS}$. The length of $\overline{TS}$ is 1.2 times the length of a side. The perimeter of the entrance is 14 feet. Find each side length.

_____

Use the figure and the following information for Exercises 3 and 4.

The distance "as the crow flies" between Santa Fe and Phoenix is 609 kilometers. This is 245 kilometers less than twice the distance between Santa Fe and El Paso. Phoenix is 48 kilometers closer to El Paso than it is to Santa Fe.

Santa Fe, New Mexico
Phoenix, Arizona
El Paso, Texas

3. What is the distance between each pair of cities?

_____

4. Classify the triangle that connects the cities by its side lengths. _____

Choose the best answer.

A *gable*, as shown in the diagram, is the triangular portion of a wall between a sloping roof.

5. Triangle ABC is an isosceles triangle. The length of $\overline{CB}$ is 12 feet 4 inches and the congruent sides are each $\frac{3}{4}$ this length. What is the perimeter of △ABC?

  A 31 ft 4 in.   C 21 ft 7 in.

  B 30 ft 10 in.   D 18 ft 6 in.

6. In △DEF, $\overline{DE}$ and $\overline{DF}$ are each 6 feet 3 inches long. This length is 0.75 times the length of $\overline{FE}$. What is the perimeter of △DEF?

  F 12 ft 4 in.   H 17 ft 2 in.

  G 14 ft 7 in.   J 20 ft 10 in.

Chapter 4   140   Lesson 2

Angle Relationships in Triangles
Focus on Reasoning

Essential question: *What are some theorems about angle measures in triangles?*

© Houghton Mifflin Harcourt Publishing Company

COMMON CORE Standards for Mathematical Content

CC.9-12.G.CO.10 Prove theorems about triangles.

Vocabulary
corollary

interior angle

exterior angle

remote interior angle

Prerequisites
Parallel lines and transversals

Math Background
This is the first of several Focus on Reasoning lessons in this book. These lessons all include a hands-on investigation that gives students a chance to use inductive reasoning to make a conjecture. This is followed by a proof in which students use deductive reasoning to justify their conjecture. Although the inductive/deductive format is the central organizing feature of Focus on Reasoning lessons, these lessons may also include examples, real-world applications, and/or additional proofs.

INTRODUCE

Begin by asking students to state properties that hold for every triangle. Students might mention that every triangle has three sides or that every triangle has three angles. Tell students that they will be learning some additional properties that can be added to the list. You may want to record the properties on a large sheet of paper and add to the list as students learn new properties.

TEACH

1 Investigate the angle measures of a triangle.

Materials: straightedge, scissors

Questioning Strategies
- What can you say about angles that come together to form a straight line? Why? **The sum of the angle measures must be 180° by the definition of a straight angle and the Angle Addition Postulate.**

- Is it possible for a triangle to have two obtuse angles? Why or why not? **No; the sum of these angles would be greater than 180°.**

Technology
This initial investigation can be done in many ways. Some students may wish to explore the sum of the angle measures in a triangle by using geometry software. To do so, students should construct a triangle, measure the three angles, and use the Calculate tool (under the Measure menu) to find the sum of the angle measures. As students drag the vertices of the triangle to change its shape, the individual angle measures will change, but the sum of the measures will remain 180°.

MATHEMATICAL PRACTICE — Highlighting the Standards

Standard 3 (Construct viable arguments and critique the reasoning of others) includes the idea of counterexamples. You may wish to discuss counterexamples in the context of the Triangle Sum Theorem. For example, present the following statement to the class: "Every triangle has an obtuse angle." Give students a chance to refute this statement by asking them to provide a specific counterexample, such as a triangle whose angle measures are 40°, 60°, and 80°.

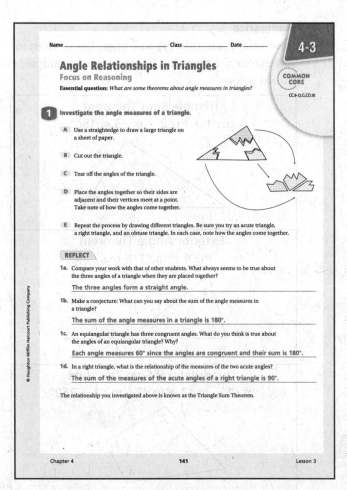

Name _____ Class _____ Date _____

4-3

Angle Relationships in Triangles
Focus on Reasoning

Essential question: *What are some theorems about angle measures in triangles?*

COMMON CORE
CC.9-12.G.CO.10

1 Investigate the angle measures of a triangle.

A Use a straightedge to draw a large triangle on a sheet of paper.

B Cut out the triangle.

C Tear off the angles of the triangle.

D Place the angles together so their sides are adjacent and their vertices meet at a point. Take note of how the angles come together.

E Repeat the process by drawing different triangles. Be sure you try an acute triangle, a right triangle, and an obtuse triangle. In each case, note how the angles come together.

REFLECT

1a. Compare your work with that of other students. What always seems to be true about the three angles of a triangle when they are placed together?

The three angles form a straight angle.

1b. Make a conjecture: What can you say about the sum of the angle measures in a triangle?

The sum of the angle measures in a triangle is 180°.

1c. An equiangular triangle has three congruent angles. What do you think is true about the angles of an equiangular triangle? Why?

Each angle measures 60° since the angles are congruent and their sum is 180°.

1d. In a right triangle, what is the relationship of the measures of the two acute angles?

The sum of the measures of the acute angles of a right triangle is 90°.

The relationship you investigated above is known as the Triangle Sum Theorem.

Chapter 4   141   Lesson 3

© Houghton Mifflin Harcourt Publishing Company

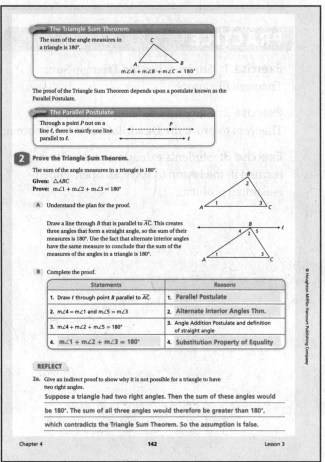

The Triangle Sum Theorem

The sum of the angle measures in a triangle is 180°.

$$m\angle A + m\angle B + m\angle C = 180°$$

The proof of the Triangle Sum Theorem depends upon a postulate known as the Parallel Postulate.

The Parallel Postulate

Through a point P not on a line ℓ, there is exactly one line parallel to ℓ.

2 Prove the Triangle Sum Theorem.

The sum of the angle measures in a triangle is 180°.

Given: $\triangle ABC$
Prove: $m\angle 1 + m\angle 2 + m\angle 3 = 180°$

A Understand the plan for the proof.

Draw a line through B that is parallel to $\overline{AC}$. This creates three angles that form a straight angle, so the sum of their measures is 180°. Use the fact that alternate interior angles have the same measure to conclude that the sum of the measures of the angles in a triangle is 180°.

B Complete the proof.

Statements	Reasons
1. Draw ℓ through point B parallel to $\overline{AC}$.	1. Parallel Postulate
2. $m\angle 4 = m\angle 1$ and $m\angle 5 = m\angle 3$	2. Alternate Interior Angles Thm.
3. $m\angle 4 + m\angle 2 + m\angle 5 = 180°$	3. Angle Addition Postulate and definition of straight angle
4. $m\angle 1 + m\angle 2 + m\angle 3 = 180°$	4. Substitution Property of Equality

REFLECT

2a. Give an indirect proof to show why it is not possible for a triangle to have two right angles.

Suppose a triangle had two right angles. Then the sum of these angles would

be 180°. The sum of all three angles would therefore be greater than 180°,

which contradicts the Triangle Sum Theorem. So the assumption is false.

Chapter 4   142   Lesson 3

© Houghton Mifflin Harcourt Publishing Company

2 **Prove the Triangle Sum Theorem.**

Questioning Strategies
- What type of reasoning did you use to make your conjecture? inductive reasoning
- What type of reasoning are you using in this proof? deductive reasoning
- Is it possible to draw more than one line through point B that is parallel to $\overline{AC}$? Explain. No; according to the Parallel Postulate, there is exactly one such line.

3 **Prove the Exterior Angle Theorem.**

Questioning Strategies
- Why is the Exterior Angle Theorem sometimes called a corollary of the Triangle Sum Theorem? The Exterior Angle Theorem can be proved easily once you know the Triangle Sum Theorem.
- In the figure, if ∠4 is a right angle, what can you say about ∠1 and ∠2? ∠1 and ∠2 are complementary.

CLOSE

Essential Question
What are some theorems about angle measures in triangles?
Two theorems about angle measures in triangles state the sum of the measures of the interior angles is 180° (Triangle Sum Theorem) and the measure of an exterior angle is the sum of the measures of its remote interior angles (Exterior Angle Theorem).

Summarize
Have students make a graphic organizer or chart to summarize the theorems in this lesson. A sample is shown below.

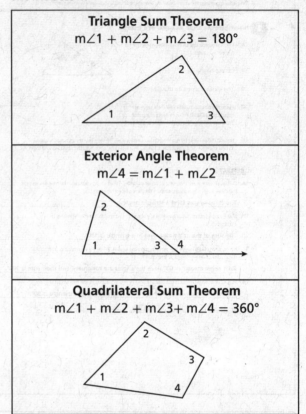

| **Triangle Sum Theorem** |
| m∠1 + m∠2 + m∠3 = 180° |

| **Exterior Angle Theorem** |
| m∠4 = m∠1 + m∠2 |

| **Quadrilateral Sum Theorem** |
| m∠1 + m∠2 + m∠3 + m∠4 = 360° |

PRACTICE

Exercise 1: Students use the Triangle Sum Theorem in a proof.

Exercise 2: Students use the Triangle Sum Theorem to prove the Quadrilateral Sum Theorem.

Exercise 3: Students extend what they have learned in the lesson to solve an open-ended reasoning problem.

A **corollary** to a theorem is a statement that can be proved easily by using the theorem. A useful corollary to the Triangle Sum Theorem involves exterior angles of a triangle.

When you extend the sides of a polygon, the original angles may be called **interior angles** and the angles that form linear pairs with the interior angles are the **exterior angles**.

Each exterior angle of a triangle has two remote interior angles. A **remote interior angle** is an interior angle that is not adjacent to the exterior angle.

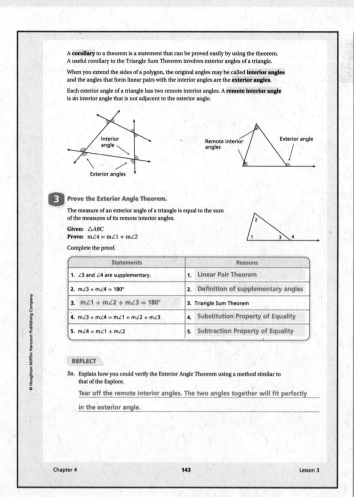

Interior angle

Exterior angles

Remote interior angles

Exterior angle

3 Prove the Exterior Angle Theorem.

The measure of an exterior angle of a triangle is equal to the sum of the measures of its remote interior angles.

Given: $\triangle ABC$
Prove: $m\angle 4 = m\angle 1 + m\angle 2$

Complete the proof.

Statements	Reasons
1. $\angle 3$ and $\angle 4$ are supplementary.	1. Linear Pair Theorem
2. $m\angle 3 + m\angle 4 = 180°$	2. Definition of supplementary angles
3. $m\angle 1 + m\angle 2 + m\angle 3 = 180°$	3. Triangle Sum Theorem
4. $m\angle 3 + m\angle 4 = m\angle 1 + m\angle 2 + m\angle 3$	4. Substitution Property of Equality
5. $m\angle 4 = m\angle 1 + m\angle 2$	5. Subtraction Property of Equality

REFLECT

3a. Explain how you could verify the Exterior Angle Theorem using a method similar to that of the Explore.

Tear off the remote interior angles. The two angles together will fit perfectly

in the exterior angle.

© Houghton Mifflin Harcourt Publishing Company

Another important corollary of the Triangle Sum Theorem is the Quadrilateral Sum Theorem. You will prove the theorem as an exercise.

Quadrilateral Sum Theorem

The sum of the angle measures in a quadrilateral is 360°.

PRACTICE

1. Complete the proof that the acute angles of a right triangle are complementary.

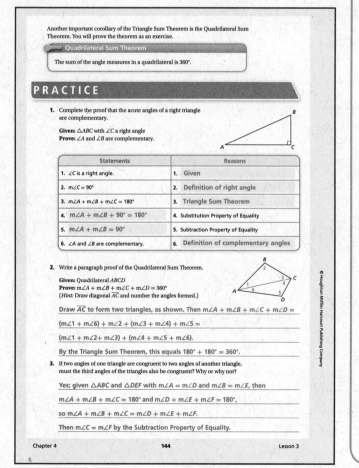

Given: $\triangle ABC$ with $\angle C$ a right angle
Prove: $\angle A$ and $\angle B$ are complementary.

Statements	Reasons
1. $\angle C$ is a right angle.	1. Given
2. $m\angle C = 90°$	2. Definition of right angle
3. $m\angle A + m\angle B + m\angle C = 180°$	3. Triangle Sum Theorem
4. $m\angle A + m\angle B + 90° = 180°$	4. Substitution Property of Equality
5. $m\angle A + m\angle B = 90°$	5. Subtraction Property of Equality
6. $\angle A$ and $\angle B$ are complementary.	6. Definition of complementary angles

2. Write a paragraph proof of the Quadrilateral Sum Theorem.

Given: Quadrilateral $ABCD$
Prove: $m\angle A + m\angle B + m\angle C + m\angle D = 360°$
(*Hint:* Draw diagonal $\overline{AC}$ and number the angles formed.)

Draw $\overline{AC}$ to form two triangles, as shown. Then $m\angle A + m\angle B + m\angle C + m\angle D =$

$(m\angle 1 + m\angle 6) + m\angle 2 + (m\angle 3 + m\angle 4) + m\angle 5 =$

$(m\angle 1 + m\angle 2 + m\angle 3) + (m\angle 4 + m\angle 5 + m\angle 6).$

By the Triangle Sum Theorem, this equals $180° + 180° = 360°$.

3. If two angles of one triangle are congruent to two angles of another triangle, must the third angles of the triangles also be congruent? Why or why not?

Yes; given $\triangle ABC$ and $\triangle DEF$ with $m\angle A = m\angle D$ and $m\angle B = m\angle E$, then

$m\angle A + m\angle B + m\angle C = 180°$ and $m\angle D + m\angle E + m\angle F = 180°$,

so $m\angle A + m\angle B + m\angle C = m\angle D + m\angle E + m\angle F.$

Then $m\angle C = m\angle F$ by the Subtraction Property of Equality.

© Houghton Mifflin Harcourt Publishing Company

© Houghton Mifflin Harcourt Publishing Company

ADDITIONAL PRACTICE AND PROBLEM SOLVING

Assign these pages to help your students practice and apply important lesson concepts. For additional exercises, see the Student Edition.

Answers

Additional Practice

1. 101.1°	**2.** 45°
3. 45.1°	**4.** z°
5. 89.7°	**6.** 60°
7. 47°	**8.** 33°; 66°; 81°
9. 44°; 44°	**10.** 108°; 108°
11. 55°	**12.** 54°; 72°; 54°

Problem Solving

1. 121°	**2.** 59°
3. $n = 12$	**4.** 76°, 76°, 28°
5. 32°	**6.** 113°
7. B	**8.** H
9. B	

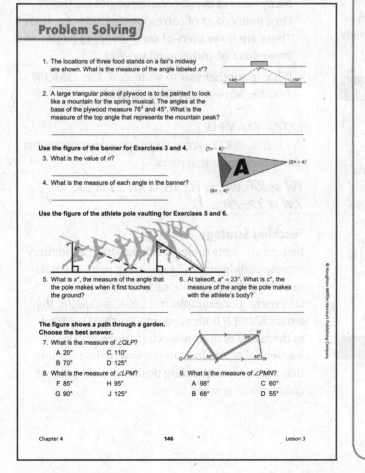

Name _____ Class _____ Date _____

Additional Practice

1. An area in central North Carolina is known as the Research Triangle because of the relatively large number of high-tech companies and research universities located there. Duke University, the University of North Carolina at Chapel Hill, and North Carolina State University are all within this area. The Research Triangle is roughly bounded by the cities of Chapel Hill, Durham, and Raleigh. From Chapel Hill, the angle between Durham and Raleigh measures 54.8°. From Raleigh, the angle between Chapel Hill and Durham measures 24.1°. Find the angle between Chapel Hill and Raleigh from Durham.   _____

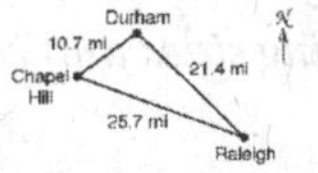

2. The acute angles of right triangle *ABC* are congruent. Find their measures.   _____

The measure of one of the acute angles in a right triangle is given. Find the measure of the other acute angle.

3. 44.9° _____   4. $(90 - z)°$ _____   5. 0.3° _____

Find each angle measure.

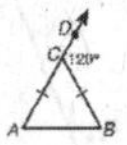

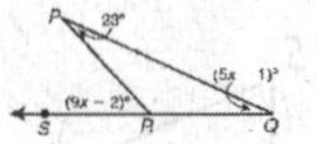

6. m∠B _____   7. m∠PRS _____

8. In △LMN, the measure of an exterior angle at N measures 99°.
   $m∠L = \frac{1}{3}x°$ and $m∠M = \frac{2}{3}x°$. Find m∠L, m∠M, and m∠LNM.   _____

9. m∠E and m∠G _____   10. m∠T and m∠V _____

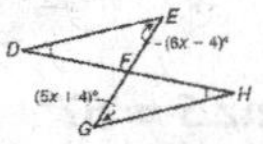

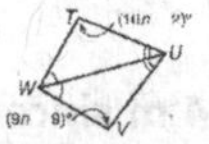

11. In △ABC and △DEF, m∠A = m∠D and m∠B = m∠E. Find m∠F if an exterior angle at A measures 107°, m∠B = (5x + 2)°, and m∠C = (5x + 5)°.   _____

12. The angle measures of a triangle are in the ratio 3 : 4 : 3. Find the angle measures of the triangle.   _____

Chapter 4   145   Lesson 3

Problem Solving

1. The locations of three food stands on a fair's midway are shown. What is the measure of the angle labeled x°?

2. A large triangular piece of plywood is to be painted to look like a mountain for the spring musical. The angles at the base of the plywood measure 76° and 45°. What is the measure of the top angle that represents the mountain peak?

   _____

Use the figure of the banner for Exercises 3 and 4.

3. What is the value of *n*?

   _____

4. What is the measure of each angle in the banner?

   _____

Use the figure of the athlete pole vaulting for Exercises 5 and 6.

5. What is x°, the measure of the angle that the pole makes when it first touches the ground?

   _____

6. At takeoff, a° = 23°. What is c°, the measure of the angle the pole makes with the athlete's body?

   _____

The figure shows a path through a garden. Choose the best answer.

7. What is the measure of ∠QLP?
   A 20°   C 110°
   B 70°   D 125°

8. What is the measure of ∠LPM?
   F 85°   H 95°
   G 90°   J 125°

9. What is the measure of ∠PMN?
   A 98°   C 60°
   B 68°   D 55°

Chapter 4   146   Lesson 3

4-4 Congruent Triangles
Connection: Using Rigid Motions

Essential question: *How can you use properties of rigid motions to draw conclusions about corresponding sides and corresponding angles in congruent triangles?*

COMMON CORE Standards for Mathematical Content

CC.9-12.G.CO.7 Use the definition of congruence in terms of rigid motions to show that two triangles are congruent if and only if corresponding pairs of sides and corresponding pairs of angles are congruent.

Vocabulary
corresponding parts

Prerequisites
Congruence

Math Background
In this lesson, students learn that if two triangles are congruent then corresponding pairs of sides and corresponding pairs of angles are congruent. This follows readily from the rigid-motion definition of congruence. In the next lesson, students prove the converse. That is, they will show that if corresponding pairs of sides and corresponding pairs of angles are congruent, then the triangles are congruent.

INTRODUCE

Ask students to imagine two cars that are congruent. That is, have them consider two cars that have exactly the same size and shape. Ask students what they can conclude about specific parts of the cars. For example, students might mention that the cars' steering wheels must also be congruent (same size and same shape). Similarly, the cars' dashboards must be congruent (same size and same shape). These types of observations should seem natural in the familiar context of identical cars. Tell students that in this lesson they will apply this type of reasoning to congruent triangles.

TEACH

1 EXAMPLE

Questioning Strategies
- What is the pre-image of $\overline{DE}$? $\overline{AB}$
- What is the image of $\angle B$? $\angle E$

EXTRA EXAMPLE
$\triangle RST \cong \triangle UVW$. Find UW and m$\angle S$. Explain your reasoning.

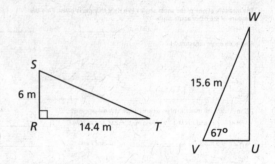

$UW = 14.4$ m since $\overline{UW} \cong \overline{RT}$; m$\angle S = 67°$ since $\angle S \cong \angle V$.

2 EXAMPLE

Questioning Strategies
- When you are given two congruent triangles, how many pairs of corresponding angles are there? How many pairs of corresponding sides are there? **There are three pairs of corresponding angles and three pairs of corresponding sides.**
- What is another way to write $\triangle RGK \cong \triangle MQB$? **Possible answer: $\triangle GKR \cong \triangle QBM$**

EXTRA EXAMPLE
$\triangle TWH \cong \triangle KPL$. Write six congruence statements about corresponding parts.

$\overline{TW} \cong \overline{KP}$; $\overline{WH} \cong \overline{PL}$; $\overline{TH} \cong \overline{KL}$; $\angle T \cong \angle K$; $\angle W \cong \angle P$; $\angle H \cong \angle L$

Teaching Strategy
Be sure students understand that they can identify corresponding angles by choosing pairs of letters in corresponding positions in a congruence statement. For example, in $\triangle RGK \cong \triangle MQB$, the letters K and B both appear in the third position in the name of their respective triangles. This means $\angle K \cong \angle B$. In a similar way, pairs of letters that are in corresponding positions yield pairs of corresponding sides.

© Houghton Mifflin Harcourt Publishing Company

Name_____ Class_____ Date_____

Congruent Triangles
Connection: Using Rigid Motions

Essential question: *How can you use properties of rigid motions to draw conclusions about corresponding sides and corresponding angles in congruent triangles?*

When you know that two triangles are congruent, you can make conclusions about the sides and angles of the triangles.

CC.9-12.G.CO.7

1 EXAMPLE Finding an Unknown Dimension

$\triangle ABC \cong \triangle DEF$. Find DE and m$\angle B$. Explain your reasoning.

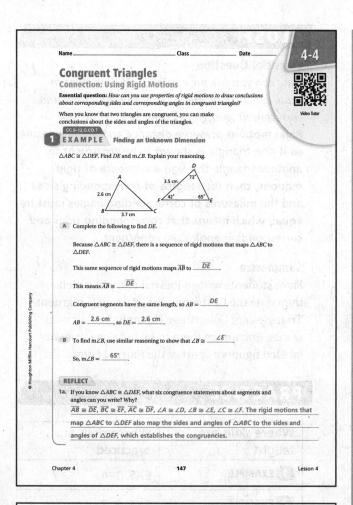

A Complete the following to find DE.

Because $\triangle ABC \cong \triangle DEF$, there is a sequence of rigid motions that maps $\triangle ABC$ to $\triangle DEF$.

This same sequence of rigid motions maps $\overline{AB}$ to _____$\overline{DE}$_____.

This means $\overline{AB} \cong$ _____$\overline{DE}$_____

Congruent segments have the same length, so $AB =$ _____DE_____

$AB =$ ___2.6 cm___, so $DE =$ ___2.6 cm___

B To find m$\angle B$, use similar reasoning to show that $\angle B \cong$ ___$\angle E$___

So, m$\angle B =$ ___65°___

REFLECT

1a. If you know $\triangle ABC \cong \triangle DEF$, what six congruence statements about segments and angles can you write? Why?

$\overline{AB} \cong \overline{DE}$, $\overline{BC} \cong \overline{EF}$, $\overline{AC} \cong \overline{DF}$, $\angle A \cong \angle D$, $\angle B \cong \angle E$, $\angle C \cong \angle F$. The rigid motions that map $\triangle ABC$ to $\triangle DEF$ also map the sides and angles of $\triangle ABC$ to the sides and angles of $\triangle DEF$, which establishes the congruencies.

Chapter 4   147   Lesson 4

© Houghton Mifflin Harcourt Publishing Company

When two triangles are congruent, the **corresponding parts** are the sides and angles that are images of each other. You write a congruence statement for two figures by matching the corresponding parts. In other words, the statement $\triangle ABC \cong \triangle DEF$ contains the information that $\overline{AB}$ corresponds to $\overline{DE}$ (and $\overline{AB} \cong \overline{DE}$), $\angle A$ corresponds to $\angle D$ (and $\angle A \cong \angle D$), and so on.

The following theorem is often abbreviated CPCTC. The proof of the theorem is similar to the argument presented in the previous example.

> **Corresponding Parts of Congruent Triangles are Congruent Theorem (CPCTC)**
>
> If two triangles are congruent, then corresponding sides are congruent and corresponding angles are congruent.

The converse of CPCTC is also true. That is, if you are given two triangles and you know that the six pairs of corresponding sides and corresponding angles are congruent, then you can conclude that the triangles are congruent. In the next lesson, you will see that you need only three pairs of congruent corresponding parts in order to conclude that the triangles are congruent, provided they are chosen in the right way.

CC.9-12.G.CO.7

2 EXAMPLE Using CPCTC

$\triangle RGK \cong \triangle MQB$. Write six congruence statements about corresponding parts.

A Identify corresponding sides.

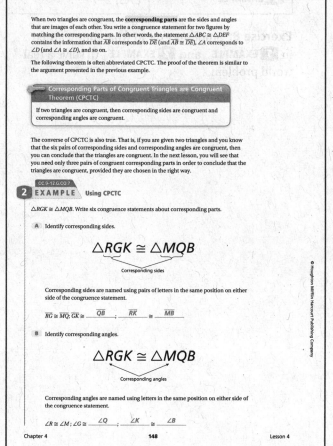

Corresponding sides are named using pairs of letters in the same position on either side of the congruence statement.

$\overline{RG} \cong \overline{MQ}$; $\overline{GK} \cong$ ___$\overline{QB}$___ ; ___$\overline{RK}$___ $\cong$ ___$\overline{MB}$___

B Identify corresponding angles.

$$\triangle RGK \cong \triangle MQB$$

Corresponding angles

Corresponding angles are named using letters in the same position on either side of the congruence statement.

$\angle R \cong \angle M$; $\angle G \cong$ ___$\angle Q$___ ; $\angle K \cong$ ___$\angle B$___

Chapter 4   148   Lesson 4

© Houghton Mifflin Harcourt Publishing Company

MATHEMATICAL PRACTICE

Highlighting the Standards

This lesson provides an interesting connection to Standard 6 (Attend to precision). Specifically, students must be careful when they write congruence statements. A statement like $\triangle ABC \cong \triangle DEF$ contains the information that the triangles are congruent, as well as information about the corresponding sides and angles. In other words, students should recognize that the above congruence statement contains the same information as $\triangle BCA \cong \triangle EFD$, but different information from the statement $\triangle ABC \cong \triangle DFE$.

Essential Question

How can you use properties of rigid motions to draw conclusions about corresponding sides and corresponding angles in congruent triangles?
Rigid motions preserve distance and angle measure, so if one triangle is shown to be congruent to another triangle through a sequence of rigid motions, then the lengths of corresponding sides and the measures of corresponding angles must be equal, which means that corresponding sides and corresponding angles are congruent.

Summarize

Have students write a journal entry in which they state the Corresponding Parts of Congruent Triangles are Congruent Theorem in their own words. Encourage them to include one or more labeled figures as part of the journal entry.

PRACTICE

Where skills are taught	Where skills are practiced
1 EXAMPLE	EXS. 1–4
2 EXAMPLE	EXS. 5–7

Exercise 8: Students extend what they learned in **1** EXAMPLE and **2** EXAMPLE to solve a real-world problem.

REFLECT

2a. Given that △PQR ≅ △STU, PQ = 2.7 ft, and PR = 3.4 ft, is it possible to determine the length of $\overline{TU}$? If so, find the length. If not, explain why not.

No; the side of △PQR that corresponds to $\overline{TU}$ is $\overline{QR}$, and the length of this

side is not known.

2b. A student claims that any two congruent triangles must have the same perimeter. Do you agree or disagree? Why?

Agree; since the corresponding sides are congruent, the sum of the side

lengths (perimeter) must be the same for both triangles.

PRACTICE

1. △ABC ≅ △DEF. Find AB and m∠E.

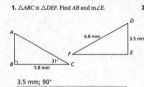

6.8 mm
3.5 mm
31°
5.8 mm

3.5 mm; 90°

2. △MNP ≅ △QRS. Find NP and m∠P.

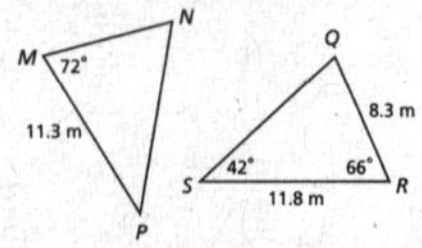

72°
11.3 m
8.3 m
42° 66°
11.8 m

11.8 m; 42°

3. △JKL ≅ △LMJ. Find JK and m∠JLM.

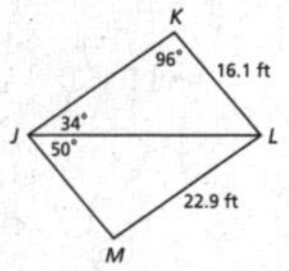

96° 16.1 ft
34°
50°
22.9 ft

22.9 ft; 34°

4. △ABC ≅ △DEF. Find DF and m∠EDC.

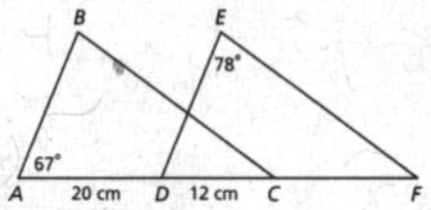

78°
67°
20 cm 12 cm

32 cm; 67°

For each given congruence statement, write six congruence statements about corresponding parts.

5. △JWT ≅ △GKH

$\overline{JW} \cong \overline{GK}$, $\overline{WT} \cong \overline{KH}$,

$\overline{JT} \cong \overline{GH}$, ∠J ≅ ∠G,

∠W ≅ ∠K, ∠T ≅ ∠H

6. △PQL ≅ △KYU

$\overline{PQ} \cong \overline{KY}$, $\overline{QL} \cong \overline{YU}$,

$\overline{PL} \cong \overline{KU}$, ∠P ≅ ∠K,

∠Q ≅ ∠Y, ∠L ≅ ∠U

7. △HTJ ≅ △NRZ

$\overline{HT} \cong \overline{NR}$, $\overline{TJ} \cong \overline{RZ}$,

$\overline{HJ} \cong \overline{NZ}$, ∠H ≅ ∠N,

∠T ≅ ∠R, ∠J ≅ ∠Z

8. The figure shows a portion of the truss of a bridge. △ABG ≅ △BCH ≅ △HGB.

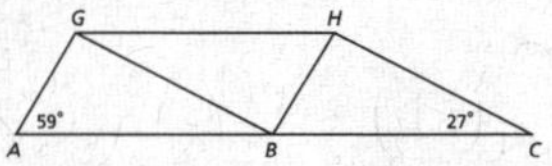

G   H
59°   27°
A   B   C

a. Is it possible to determine m∠GBH? If so, how? If not, why not?

Yes; by CPCTC, m∠ABG = 27° and m∠HBC = 59°, so m∠GBH = 94°

by the Angle Addition Postulate and the fact that m∠ABC = 180°.

b. A student claims that B is the midpoint of $\overline{AC}$. Do you agree? Explain.

Yes; by CPCTC, $\overline{AB} \cong \overline{BC}$, and B is between A and C, so B is the midpoint of $\overline{AC}$.

ADDITIONAL PRACTICE AND PROBLEM SOLVING

Assign these pages to help your students practice and apply important lesson concepts. For additional exercises, see the Student Edition.

Answers

Additional Practice

1. $\angle D$ **2.** $\angle Q$

3. $\overline{TP}$ **4.** $\angle T$

5. $\overline{AB}$ **6.** $\overline{ED}$

7. $40°$ **8.** 37.3

9. Possible answer:

Statements	Reasons
1. $\angle U \cong \angle UWV \cong \angle ZXY \cong \angle Z$	1. Given
2. $\angle V \cong \angle Y$	2. Third $\angle$ Thm.
3. $\overline{UV} \cong \overline{WV}$, $\overline{XY} \cong \overline{ZY}$	3. Given
4. $\overline{UX} \cong \overline{WZ}$	4. Given
5. $UX = WZ$, $WX = WX$	5. Def. of $\cong$ segs. Reflexive Prop. of =
6. $UX = UW + WX$, $WZ = XZ + WX$	6. Seg. Add. Post.
7. $UW + WX = XZ + WX$	7. Subst.
8. $UW = XZ$	8. Subtr. Prop. of =
9. $\triangle UVW \cong \triangle XYZ$	9. Def. of $\cong \triangle$s

10. $x = \frac{3}{2}$; $DE = 13\frac{1}{2}$

11. $y = 26$; $m\angle D = 131°$

Problem Solving

1. $x = 15.5$ **2.** 8 ft

3. $x = 19$ **4.** $72°$

5. B   **6.** J

7. C

Additional Practice

In baseball, home plate is a pentagon. Pentagon *ABCDE* is a diagram of a regulation home plate. The baseball rules are very specific about the exact dimensions of this pentagon so that every home plate is congruent to every other home plate. If pentagon *PQRST* is another home plate, identify each congruent corresponding part.

1. $\angle S \cong$ _____
2. $\angle B \cong$ _____
3. $\overline{EA} \cong$ _____
4. $\angle E \cong$ _____
5. $\overline{PQ} \cong$ _____
6. $\overline{TS} \cong$ _____

Given: $\triangle DEF \cong \triangle LMN$. Find each value.

7. $m\angle L =$ _____
8. $EF =$ _____
9. Write a two-column proof.

Given: $\angle U \cong \angle UWV \cong \angle ZXY \cong \angle Z$, $\overline{UV} \cong \overline{WV}, \overline{XY} \cong \overline{ZY}, \overline{UX} \cong \overline{WZ}$

Prove: $\triangle UVW \cong \triangle XYZ$

Proof:

10. Given: $\triangle CDE \cong \triangle HIJ$, $DE = 9x$, and $IJ = 7x + 3$. Find x and DE.

_____

11. Given: $\triangle CDE \cong \triangle HIJ$, $m\angle D = (5y + 1)°$, and $m\angle I = (6y - 25)°$. Find y and $m\angle D$.

_____

Problem Solving

Use the diagram of the fence for Exercises 1 and 2.

$\triangle RQW \cong \triangle TVW$

1. If $m\angle RWQ = 36°$ and $m\angle TWV = (2x + 5)°$, what is the value of x?

_____

2. If $RW = (3y - 1)$ feet and $TW = (y + 5)$ feet, what is the length of $\overline{RW}$?

_____

Use the diagram of a section of the Bank of China Tower for Exercises 3 and 4.

$\triangle JKL \cong \triangle LHJ$

3. What is the value of x?

_____

4. Find $m\angle JHL$.

_____

Choose the best answer.

5. Chairs with triangular seats were popular in the Middle Ages. Suppose a chair has a seat that is an isosceles triangle and the congruent sides measure $1\frac{1}{2}$ feet. A second chair has a triangular seat with a perimeter of $5\frac{1}{10}$ feet, and it is congruent to the first seat. What is a side length of the second seat?

A $1\frac{4}{5}$ ft   C 3 ft

B $2\frac{1}{10}$ ft   D $3\frac{3}{5}$ ft

Use the diagram for Exercises 6 and 7.

6. C is the midpoint of $\overline{EB}$ and $\overline{AD}$. What additional information would allow you to prove $\triangle ABC \cong \triangle DEC$ by the definition of congruent triangles?

F $\overline{EB} \cong \overline{AD}$ H $\angle ECD \cong \angle ACB$

G $\overline{DE} \cong \overline{AB}$ J $\angle A \cong \angle D, \angle B \cong \angle E$

7. If $\triangle ABC \cong \triangle DEC$, $ED = 4y + 2$, and $AB = 6y - 4$, what is the length of $\overline{AB}$?

A 3   C 14

B 12   D 18

Triangle Congruence: SSS and SAS
Going Deeper

Essential question: *How can you establish the SSS and SAS triangle congruence criteria using properties of rigid motions?*

COMMON CORE Standards for Mathematical Content

CC.9-12.G.CO.7 Use the definition of congruence in terms of rigid motions to show that two triangles are congruent if and only if corresponding pairs of sides and corresponding pairs of angles are congruent.

CC.9-12.G.CO.8 Explain how the criteria for triangle congruence (ASA, SAS, and SSS) follow from the definition of congruence in terms of rigid motions.

CC.9-12.G.CO.9 Prove theorems about lines and angles.

CC.9-12.G.SRT.5 Use congruence ... criteria for triangles to solve problems and to prove relationships in geometric figures.

Prerequisites

Congruence and triangles

Perpendicular Bisector Theorem

Reflections and notation for reflections

Math Background

This lesson establishes the SSS and SAS Congruence Criteria, each of which is a converse of the CPCTC Theorem. The proof of the SSS Congruency Criterion relies upon the Perpendicular Bisector Theorem, which was proved in an earlier lesson. The proof of the SAS Congruence Criterion, however, relies on the Reflected Points on an Angle Theorem, which in turn relies on the Angle Bisection Theorem. The proofs of these two theorems are presented in this lesson (between the proofs of the SSS and SAS Congruence Criteria).

INTRODUCE

Introduce the word *criterion* and its plural, *criteria*. Ask students if they can define *criterion* and give an example of its use. If no one suggests it, you might discuss a college's criteria for deciding which students they will accept (a completed application, a minimum grade-point average, a minimum SAT score, and so on.) Tell students that they will develop criteria for determining when two triangles are congruent.

TEACH

1 PROOF

Questioning Strategies

- What do you need to do in order to prove that two triangles are congruent? **You must show that there is a sequence of rigid motions that maps one triangle to the other.**

- What is the sequence of rigid motions that maps $\triangle ABC$ to $\triangle DEF$? **It is the initial sequence of rigid motions that maps $\overline{AB}$ to $\overline{DE}$ as in Step A, followed by the reflection across $\overline{DE}$.**

Differentiated Instruction

Some students may have difficulty following the reasoning behind this proof. These students may profit from a brief hands-on investigation of the proof. Have the students trace the triangles in the figure that accompanies the "given" and "prove" statements. Then have them cut out the triangles. Ask students to find a sequence of rigid motions that maps one triangle onto the other. Students should keep track of the flips, turns, and slides they use. Tell students that the proof is a more formal written description of this sequence of rigid motions.

2 PROOF

Questioning Strategies

- What are you trying to prove? **The image of $\overrightarrow{BA}$ under a reflection across line *m* is $\overrightarrow{BC}$.**

- How can you write a statement that says that this is false? **The image of $\overrightarrow{BA}$ under a reflection across line *m* is not $\overrightarrow{BC}$.**

- The proof shows that the image of $\overrightarrow{BA}$ under a reflection across line *m* is $\overrightarrow{BC}$. Do you also need to prove that the image of $\overrightarrow{BC}$ under a reflection across line *m* is $\overrightarrow{BA}$? Why or why not? **No; the names of the rays are arbitrary, so the same argument shows that the image of $\overrightarrow{BC}$ under a reflection across line *m* is $\overrightarrow{BA}$.**

Name_____ Class_____ Date_____

4-5

Triangle Congruence: SSS and SAS
Going Deeper

Essential question: *How can you establish the SSS and SAS triangle congruence criteria using properties of rigid motions?*

You have seen that when two triangles are congruent, the corresponding sides and corresponding angles are congruent. Conversely, if all six pairs of corresponding sides and corresponding angles of two triangles are congruent, then the triangles are congruent.

The proofs of the SSS and SAS congruence criteria that follow serve as proof of this converse. In each case, the proof demonstrates a "shortcut," in which only three pairs of congruent corresponding parts are needed in order to conclude that the triangles are congruent.

1 PROOF CC.9-12.G.CO.8 **SSS Congruence Criterion**

If three sides of one triangle are congruent to three sides of another triangle, then the triangles are congruent.

Given: $\overline{AB} \cong \overline{DE}$, $\overline{BC} \cong \overline{EF}$, and $\overline{AC} \cong \overline{DF}$.

Prove: $\triangle ABC \cong \triangle DEF$

To prove the triangles are congruent, you will find a sequence of rigid motions that maps $\triangle ABC$ to $\triangle DEF$. Complete the following steps of the proof.

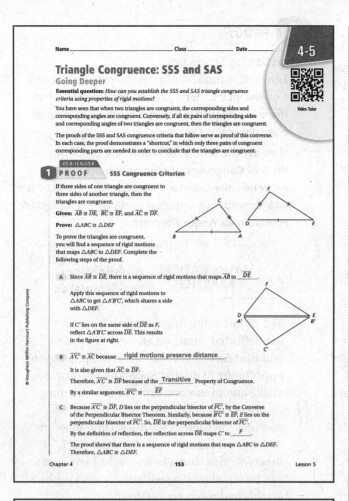

A Since $\overline{AB} \cong \overline{DE}$, there is a sequence of rigid motions that maps $\overline{AB}$ to __$\overline{DE}$__.

Apply this sequence of rigid motions to $\triangle ABC$ to get $\triangle A'B'C'$, which shares a side with $\triangle DEF$.

If C' lies on the same side of $\overline{DE}$ as F, reflect $\triangle A'B'C'$ across $\overline{DE}$. This results in the figure at right.

B $\overline{A'C'} \cong \overline{AC}$ because __rigid motions preserve distance__.

It is also given that $\overline{AC} \cong \overline{DF}$.

Therefore, $\overline{A'C'} \cong \overline{DF}$ because of the __Transitive__ Property of Congruence.

By a similar argument, $\overline{B'C'} \cong$ __$\overline{EF}$__.

C Because $\overline{A'C'} \cong \overline{DF}$, D lies on the perpendicular bisector of $\overline{FC'}$, by the Converse of the Perpendicular Bisector Theorem. Similarly, because $\overline{B'C'} \cong \overline{EF}$, E lies on the perpendicular bisector of $\overline{FC'}$. So, $\overline{DE}$ is the perpendicular bisector of $\overline{FC'}$.

By the definition of reflection, the reflection across $\overline{DE}$ maps C' to __F__.

The proof shows that there is a sequence of rigid motions that maps $\triangle ABC$ to $\triangle DEF$. Therefore, $\triangle ABC \cong \triangle DEF$.

REFLECT

1a. The proof uses the fact that congruence is transitive. That is, if you know figure $A \cong$ figure B, and figure $B \cong$ figure C, you can conclude that figure $A \cong$ figure C. Why is this true?

__You can extend the sequence of rigid motions that maps figure A to figure B__

__by the sequence that maps figure B to figure C to make a sequence that maps__

__figure A to figure C. This shows that figure $A \cong$ figure C.__

You can use reflections and their properties to prove theorems about angle bisectors. These theorems will be very useful in proofs later on.

The first proof is an indirect proof (or a *proof by contradiction*). To write such a proof, you assume that what you are trying to prove is false and you show that this assumption leads to a contradiction.

2 PROOF CC.9-12.G.CO.9 **Angle Bisection Theorem**

If a line bisects an angle, then each side of the angle is the image of the other under a reflection across the line.

Given: Line m is the bisector of $\angle ABC$.

Prove: The image of $\overrightarrow{BA}$ under a reflection across line m is $\overrightarrow{BC}$.

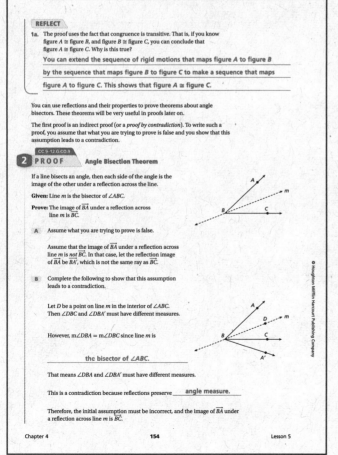

A Assume what you are trying to prove is false.

Assume that the image of $\overrightarrow{BA}$ under a reflection across line m is *not* $\overrightarrow{BC}$. In that case, let the reflection image of $\overrightarrow{BA}$ be $\overrightarrow{BA'}$, which is not the same ray as $\overrightarrow{BC}$.

B Complete the following to show that this assumption leads to a contradiction.

Let D be a point on line m in the interior of $\angle ABC$. Then $\angle DBC$ and $\angle DBA'$ must have different measures.

However, $m\angle DBA = m\angle DBC$ since line m is

__the bisector of $\angle ABC$.__

That means $\angle DBA$ and $\angle DBA'$ must have different measures.

This is a contradiction because reflections preserve __angle measure.__

Therefore, the initial assumption must be incorrect, and the image of $\overrightarrow{BA}$ under a reflection across line m is $\overrightarrow{BC}$.

Questioning Strategies

- What does $r_m(A) = A'$ mean? Point A' is the image of point A under a reflection across line m.

- Why do you think the Reflected Points on an Angle Theorem is the last of the three theorems presented in this lesson? The proof of this theorem depends upon the Angle Bisection Theorem, so that theorem must be proved first.

Differentiated Instruction

Some students may have difficulty visualizing the Reflected Points on an Angle Theorem. You may want to have students do a brief hands-on activity to explore the theorem. To do so, have students draw an angle on a sheet of tracing paper. Then have them use a ruler to plot points on each side of the angle that are the same distance from the vertex. Students can fold the paper to find the angle bisector and note that the two points they plotted are images of each other under the reflection across the bisector.

Questioning Strategies

- How is this proof similar to the proof of the SSS Congruence Criterion? Both proofs show that there is a sequence of rigid motions that maps one triangle to the other.

- How are the proofs different? The proof of the SSS Congruence Criterion requires the Perpendicular Bisector Theorem. The proof of the SAS Congruence Criterion requires the Reflected Points on an Angle Theorem.

MATHEMATICAL PRACTICE **Highlighting the Standards**

The proofs of the Angle Bisection Theorem, the Reflected Points on an Angle Theorem, and the SAS Congruence Criterion provide an opportunity to discuss Standard 3 (Construct viable arguments and critique the reasoning of others). Point out how the first theorem provides the support for the second theorem, which provides the support for the third theorem. This shows how a logical argument can be built up by systematically stacking one established result on another.

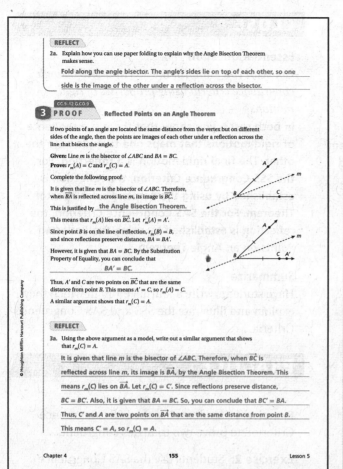

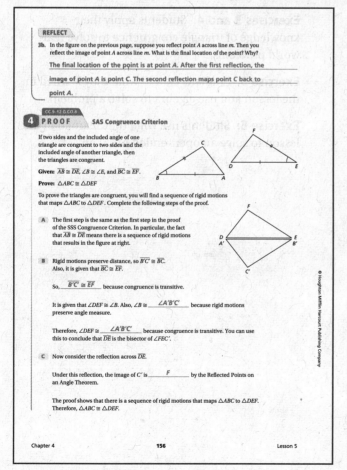

REFLECT

2a. Explain how you can use paper folding to explain why the Angle Bisection Theorem makes sense.

Fold along the angle bisector. The angle's sides lie on top of each other, so one

side is the image of the other under a reflection across the bisector.

CC.9-12.G.CO.9

3 PROOF Reflected Points on an Angle Theorem

If two points of an angle are located the same distance from the vertex but on different sides of the angle, then the points are images of each other under a reflection across the line that bisects the angle.

Given: Line m is the bisector of $\angle ABC$ and $BA = BC$.

Prove: $r_m(A) = C$ and $r_m(C) = A$.

Complete the following proof.

It is given that line m is the bisector of $\angle ABC$. Therefore, when $\overrightarrow{BA}$ is reflected across line m, its image is $\overrightarrow{BC}$.

This is justified by ___the Angle Bisection Theorem.___

This means that $r_m(A)$ lies on $\overrightarrow{BC}$. Let $r_m(A) = A'$.

Since point B is on the line of reflection, $r_m(B) = B$, and since reflections preserve distance, $BA = BA'$.

However, it is given that $BA = BC$. By the Substitution Property of Equality, you can conclude that

$$BA' = BC.$$

Thus, A' and C are two points on $\overrightarrow{BC}$ that are the same distance from point B. This means $A' = C$, so $r_m(A) = C$.

A similar argument shows that $r_m(C) = A$.

REFLECT

3a. Using the above argument as a model, write out a similar argument that shows that $r_m(C) = A$.

It is given that line m is the bisector of $\angle ABC$. Therefore, when $\overrightarrow{BC}$ is

reflected across line m, its image is $\overrightarrow{BA}$, by the Angle Bisection Theorem. This

means $r_m(C)$ lies on $\overrightarrow{BA}$. Let $r_m(C) = C'$. Since reflections preserve distance,

$BC = BC'$. Also, it is given that $BA = BC$. So, you can conclude that $BC' = BA$.

Thus, C' and A are two points on $\overrightarrow{BA}$ that are the same distance from point B.

This means $C' = A$, so $r_m(C) = A$.

REFLECT

3b. In the figure on the previous page, suppose you reflect point A across line m. Then you reflect the image of point A across line m. What is the final location of the point? Why?

The final location of the point is at point A. After the first reflection, the

image of point A is point C. The second reflection maps point C back to

point A.

CC.9-12.G.CO.8

4 PROOF SAS Congruence Criterion

If two sides and the included angle of one triangle are congruent to two sides and the included angle of another triangle, then the triangles are congruent.

Given: $\overline{AB} \cong \overline{DE}$, $\angle B \cong \angle E$, and $\overline{BC} \cong \overline{EF}$.

Prove: $\triangle ABC \cong \triangle DEF$.

To prove the triangles are congruent, you will find a sequence of rigid motions that maps $\triangle ABC$ to $\triangle DEF$. Complete the following steps of the proof.

A The first step is the same as the first step in the proof of the SSS Congruence Criterion. In particular, the fact that $\overline{AB} \cong \overline{DE}$ means there is a sequence of rigid motions that results in the figure at right.

B Rigid motions preserve distance, so $\overline{B'C'} \cong \overline{BC}$. Also, it is given that $\overline{BC} \cong \overline{EF}$.

So, ___$B'C' \cong EF$___ because congruence is transitive.

It is given that $\angle DEF \cong \angle B$. Also, $\angle B \cong$ ___$\angle A'B'C'$___ because rigid motions preserve angle measure.

Therefore, $\angle DEF \cong$ ___$\angle A'B'C'$___ because congruence is transitive. You can use this to conclude that $\overline{DE}$ is the bisector of $\angle FEC'$.

C Now consider the reflection across $\overline{DE}$.

Under this reflection, the image of C' is ___F___ by the Reflected Points on an Angle Theorem.

The proof shows that there is a sequence of rigid motions that maps $\triangle ABC$ to $\triangle DEF$. Therefore, $\triangle ABC \cong \triangle DEF$.

© Houghton Mifflin Harcourt Publishing Company

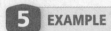

5 **EXAMPLE**

Questioning Strategies

- What are some advantages of a flowchart proof? The flowchart proof makes it easy to see how one statement of a proof leads to another.

- Would it be possible to write this proof in two-column format? Explain. Yes; each statement in the flowchart proof has a reason, so it would be possible to reorganize the proof into a two-column table.

- Why does it make sense that there are three arrows pointing to the last cell of the proof? It takes three pieces of information to use the SSS Congruence Criterion.

EXTRA EXAMPLE
Complete the flowchart proof.

Given: D is the midpoint of $\overline{EF}$; $\overline{EC} \cong \overline{FC}$

Prove: $\triangle EDC \cong \triangle FDC$

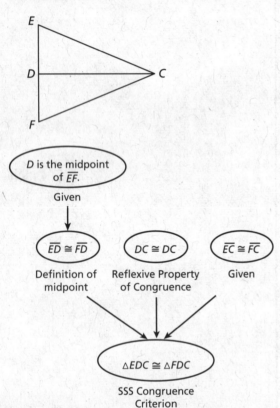

Avoid Common Errors
Remind students that they should not assume information from a figure unless it is marked or stated in the given information. For example, some students may assume that $\angle RSM \cong \angle TSM$ because these angles appear to be congruent in the figure. Although these angles can be proven to be congruent using CPCTC, students should not assume this in proving that $\triangle RSM \cong \triangle TSM$.

CLOSE

Essential Question
How can you establish the SSS and SAS triangle congruence criteria using properties of rigid motions?
In both cases, you show that there is a sequence of rigid motions that maps one triangle onto the other. The final rigid motion is a reflection. For the SSS Congruence Criterion, the reflection is established by using the Perpendicular Bisector Theorem. For the SAS Congruence Criterion, the reflection is established by using the Reflected Points on an Angle Theorem.

Summarize
Have students write a journal entry in which they explain and illustrate the SSS and SAS Congruence Criteria.

PRACTICE

Exercise 1: Students use the SSS Congruence Criterion to prove two triangles congruent.

Exercise 2: Students use the SAS Congruence Criterion to prove two triangles congruent.

Exercises 3 and 4: Students apply their knowledge of triangle congruence to solve real-world problems.

Exercise 5: Students extend what they learned in the lesson and use algebra to solve a problem.

Exercise 6: Students use what they learned in the lesson to solve an open-ended problem.

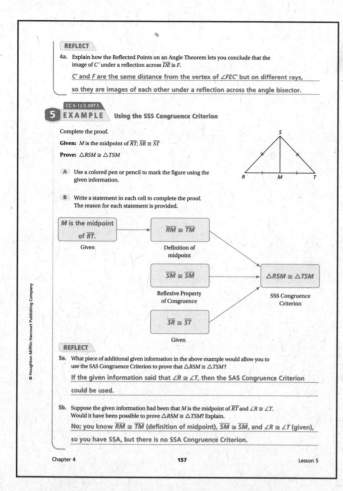

REFLECT

4a. Explain how the Reflected Points on an Angle Theorem lets you conclude that the image of C' under a reflection across $\overline{DE}$ is F.

C' and F are the same distance from the vertex of ∠FEC' but on different rays,

so they are images of each other under a reflection across the angle bisector.

CC.9-12.G.SRT.5
5 EXAMPLE Using the SSS Congruence Criterion

Complete the proof.

Given: M is the midpoint of $\overline{RT}$; $\overline{SR} \cong \overline{ST}$

Prove: △RSM ≅ △TSM

A Use a colored pen or pencil to mark the figure using the given information.

B Write a statement in each cell to complete the proof. The reason for each statement is provided.

| M is the midpoint of $\overline{RT}$. | → | $\overline{RM} \cong \overline{TM}$ | |
| Given | | Definition of midpoint | |

| | | $\overline{SM} \cong \overline{SM}$ | → | △RSM ≅ △TSM |
| | | Reflexive Property of Congruence | | SSS Congruence Criterion |

| | | $\overline{SR} \cong \overline{ST}$ | |
| | | Given | |

REFLECT

5a. What piece of additional given information in the above example would allow you to use the SAS Congruence Criterion to prove that △RSM ≅ △TSM?

If the given information said that ∠R ≅ ∠T, then the SAS Congruence Criterion

could be used.

5b. Suppose the given information had been that M is the midpoint of $\overline{RT}$ and ∠R ≅ ∠T. Would it have been possible to prove △RSM ≅ △TSM? Explain.

No; you know $\overline{RM} \cong \overline{TM}$ (definition of midpoint), $\overline{SM} \cong \overline{SM}$, and ∠R ≅ ∠T (given),

so you have SSA, but there is no SSA Congruence Criterion.

Chapter 4   157   Lesson 5

PRACTICE

Complete the two-column proof.

1. **Given:** $\overline{AB} \cong \overline{CD}$, $\overline{AD} \cong \overline{CB}$
Prove: △ABD ≅ △CBD

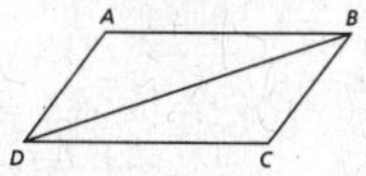

Statements	Reasons
1. $\overline{AB} \cong \overline{CD}$	1. Given
2. $\overline{AD} \cong \overline{CB}$	2. Given
3. $\overline{BD} \cong \overline{BD}$	3. Reflexive Prop. of Congruence
4. △ABD ≅ △CBD	4. SSS Congruence Criterion

2. **Given:** $\overline{GH} \parallel \overline{JK}$, $\overline{GH} \cong \overline{JK}$
Prove: △HGJ ≅ △KJG

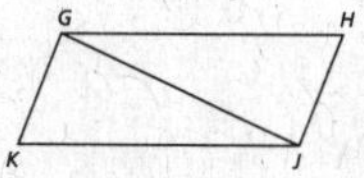

Statements	Reasons
1. $\overline{GH} \parallel \overline{JK}$	1. Given
2. ∠HGJ ≅ ∠KJG	2. Alternate Interior Angles Thm.
3. $\overline{GH} \cong \overline{JK}$	3. Given
4. $\overline{GJ} \cong \overline{GJ}$	4. Reflexive Prop. of Congruence
5. △HGJ ≅ △KJG	5. SAS Congruence Criterion

3. To find the distance JK across a large rock formation, you locate points as shown in the figure. Explain how to use this information to find JK.

△LNM ≅ △KNJ by the SAS Congruence Criterion;

$\overline{JK} \cong \overline{ML}$ by CPCTC; JK = 160 ft

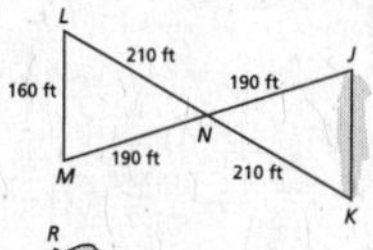

4. To find the distance RS across a lake, you locate points as shown in the figure. Can you use this information to find RS? Explain.

No; there is not enough information to conclude that

the triangles are congruent, so you cannot use CPCTC.

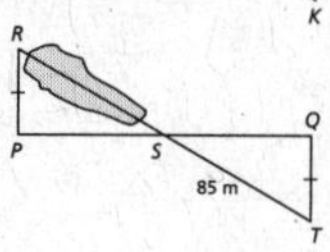

5. △DEF ≅ △GHJ, DF = 3x + 2, GJ = 6x − 13, and HJ = 5x. Find HJ.

HJ = 25

6. In the figure, $\overline{MC}$ is the perpendicular bisector of $\overline{AB}$. Is it possible to prove that △AMC ≅ △BMC? Why or why not?

Yes; $\overline{AM} \cong \overline{MB}$, ∠AMC ≅ ∠BMC since both are right

angles, and $\overline{MC} \cong \overline{MC}$, so △AMC ≅ △BMC by SAS.

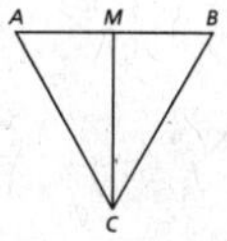

Chapter 4   158   Lesson 5

© Houghton Mifflin Harcourt Publishing Company

ADDITIONAL PRACTICE AND PROBLEM SOLVING

Assign these pages to help your students practice and apply important lesson concepts. For additional exercises, see the Student Edition.

Answers

Additional Practice

1. neither
2. SAS
3. neither
4. SAS
5. 1.8
6. 17
7. Possible answer:

Statements	Reasons
1. C is the midpoint of $\overline{AD}$ and $\overline{BE}$.	1. Given
2. $AC = CD$, $BC = CE$	2. Def. of mdpt.
3. $\overline{AC} \cong \overline{CD}$, $\overline{BC} \cong \overline{CE}$	3. Def. of $\cong$ segs.
4. $\angle ACB \cong \angle DCE$	4. Vert. $\angle$s Thm.
5. $\triangle ABC \cong \triangle DEC$	5. SAS

Problem Solving

1. We know that $\overline{AB} \cong \overline{DC}$. $\angle ADC$ and $\angle DAB$ are right angles, so $\angle ADC \cong \angle DAB$ by Rt. $\angle \cong$ Thm. $\overline{AD} \cong \overline{DA}$ by Reflex. Prop. of $\cong$. So $\triangle ABD \cong \triangle DCA$ by SAS.

2. We know that $\overline{AK} \cong \overline{BK}$. Since J is the midpoint of $\overline{AB}$, $\overline{AJ} \cong \overline{BJ}$ by def. of midpoint. $\overline{JK} \cong \overline{JK}$ by Reflex. Prop. of $\cong$. So $\triangle AKJ \cong \triangle BKJ$ by SSS.

3. By the $\triangle$ Sum Thm., $m\angle H = 54°$. For $x = 6$, $WY = FH = 10$ in., $m\angle Y = m\angle H = 54°$, and $XY = HG = 12$ in. So $\triangle WXY \cong \triangle FHG$ by SAS.

4. A
5. G

4-5

Additional Practice

Write whether SSS or SAS, if either, can be used to prove the triangles congruent. If no triangles can be proved congruent, write *neither*.

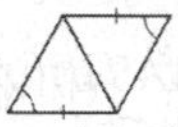

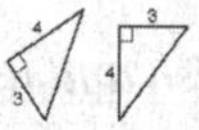

1. _____   2. _____

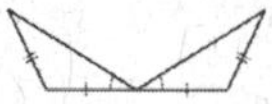

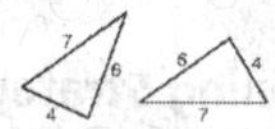

3. _____   4. _____

Find the value of x so that the triangles are congruent.

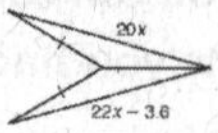

5. $x =$ _____   6. $x =$ _____

The Hatfield and McCoy families are feuding over some land. Neither family will be satisfied unless the two triangular fields are exactly the same size. You know that C is the midpoint of each of the intersecting segments. Write a two-column proof that will settle the dispute.

7. **Given:** C is the midpoint of $\overline{AD}$ and $\overline{BE}$.

   Prove: $\triangle ABC \cong \triangle DEC$

   Proof:

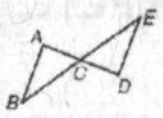

Problem Solving

Use the diagram for Exercises 1 and 2.

A shed door appears to be divided into congruent right triangles.

1. Suppose $\overline{AB} \cong \overline{CD}$. Use SAS to show $\triangle ABD \cong \triangle DCA$.

   _____

   _____

   _____

2. J is the midpoint of AB and $\overline{AK} \cong \overline{BK}$. Use SSS to explain why $\triangle AKJ \cong \triangle BKJ$.

   _____

   _____

3. A *balalaika* is a Russian stringed instrument. Show that the triangular parts of the two balalaikas are congruent for x = 6.

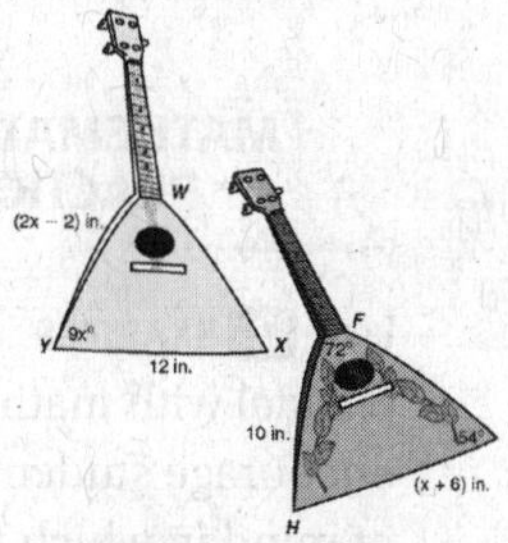

   _____

   _____

   _____

A quilt pattern of a dog is shown. Choose the best answer.

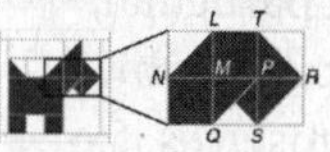

4. ML = MP = MN = MQ = 1 inch. Which statement is correct?

   A $\triangle LMN \cong \triangle QMP$ by SAS.

   B $\triangle LMN \cong \triangle QMP$ by SSS.

   C $\triangle LMN \cong \triangle MQP$ by SAS.

   D $\triangle LMN \cong \triangle MQP$ by SSS.

5. P is the midpoint of $\overline{TS}$ and TR = SR = 1.4 inches. What can you conclude about $\triangle TRP$ and $\triangle SRP$?

   F $\triangle TRP \cong \triangle SRP$ by SAS.

   G $\triangle TRP \cong \triangle SRP$ by SSS.

   H $\triangle TRP \cong \triangle SPR$ by SAS.

   J $\triangle TRP \cong \triangle SPR$ by SSS.

Notes

Triangle Congruence: ASA, AAS, and HL
Going Deeper

Essential question: *How can you establish and use the ASA and AAS triangle congruence criteria?*

© Houghton Mifflin Harcourt Publishing Company

COMMON CORE Standards for Mathematical Content

CC.9-12.G.CO.8 Explain how the criteria for triangle congruence (ASA, SAS, and SSS) follow from the definition of congruence in terms of rigid motions.

CC.9-12.G.CO.10 Prove theorems about triangles.

CC.9-12.G.SRT.5 Use congruence ... criteria for triangles to solve problems and to prove relationships in geometric figures.

Prerequisites
Angle Bisection Theorem

Math Background
This lesson establishes the ASA and AAS Congruence Criteria, each of which is a converse of the CPCTC Theorem. The proof of the ASA Congruency Criterion relies upon the Angle Bisection Theorem, which was proved in the previous lesson. The proof of the AAS Congruency Criterion is a direct consequence of the ASA Congruency Criterion when coupled with the Triangle Sum Theorem.

INTRODUCE

Begin by reviewing the SSS and SAS Congruence Criteria. Point out that other congruence criteria can also be established for two triangles when two pairs of corresponding angles and one pair of corresponding sides are known to be congruent.

TEACH

1 PROOF

Questioning Strategies
- Which earlier theorem plays a key role in this proof? **The Angle Bisection Theorem**
- How is this proof similar to the proofs of the SSS and SAS Congruence Criteria? **They all begin the same way: You use the pair of congruent sides to state that there is a sequence of rigid motions that results in the figure that accompanies step A of each proof.**

2 EXAMPLE

Questioning Strategies
- In order to solve the problem, why do you first show that $\triangle ABC \cong \triangle EDC$? **Once you know these triangles are congruent, you can conclude that $\overline{AB} \cong \overline{ED}$ by CPCTC. This lets you find the length of $\overline{AB}$.**
- What other lengths can you find in the figure? Explain. **You can find EC using the Pythagorean Theorem ($EC \approx 1328.8$ ft) and then you can find AC using CPCTC.**

EXTRA EXAMPLE
To find the distance PQ across a pond, you locate points as shown in the figure. Explain how to use this information to find PQ.

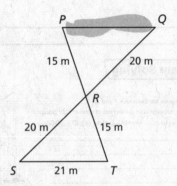

$\triangle PQR \cong \triangle TSR$ by the SAS Congruence Criterion. $\overline{TS} \cong \overline{PQ}$ by CPCTC, so $PQ = 21$ m.

MATHEMATICAL PRACTICE — Highlighting the Standards

Use **2 EXAMPLE** to discuss Standard 4 (Model with mathematics). In particular, encourage students to develop the habit of mind in which they ask themselves if the answer to a modeling problem seems reasonable. Prompt students to understand that an answer of 875 feet seems reasonable as the distance across a river. Had the answer been 3 feet or 125,000 feet, a review of the solution for errors would have been indicated.

Name _____ Class _____ Date _____

4-6

Video Tutor

Triangle Congruence: ASA, AAS, and HL
Going Deeper

Essential question: *How can you establish and use the ASA and AAS triangle congruence criteria?*

CC.9-12.G.CO.8

1 PROOF   ASA Congruence Criterion

If two angles and the included side of one triangle are congruent to two angles and the included side of another triangle, then the triangles are congruent.

Given: $\overline{AB} \cong \overline{DE}$, $\angle A \cong \angle D$, and $\angle B \cong \angle E$.

Prove: $\triangle ABC \cong \triangle DEF$

To prove the triangles are congruent, you will find a sequence of rigid motions that maps $\triangle ABC$ to $\triangle DEF$. Complete the following steps of the proof.

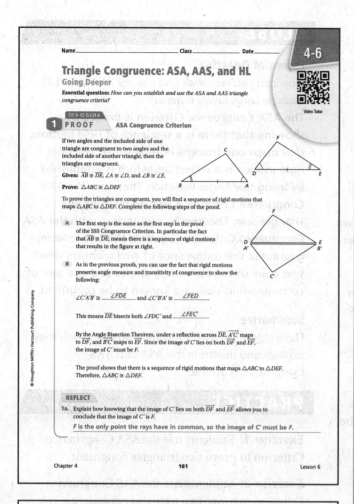

A   The first step is the same as the first step in the proof of the SSS Congruence Criterion. In particular the fact that $\overline{AB} \cong \overline{DE}$, means there is a sequence of rigid motions that results in the figure at right.

B   As in the previous proofs, you can use the fact that rigid motions preserve angle measure and transitivity of congruence to show the following:

$\angle C'A'B' \cong$ ___∠FDE___ and $\angle C'B'A' \cong$ ___∠FED___.

This means $\overline{DE}$ bisects both $\angle FDC$ and $\angle FEC'$.

By the Angle Bisection Theorem, under a reflection across $\overline{DE}$, $\overrightarrow{A'C'}$ maps to $\overrightarrow{DF}$, and $\overrightarrow{B'C'}$ maps to $\overline{EF}$. Since the image of C' lies on both $\overline{DF}$ and $\overline{EF}$, the image of C' must be F.

The proof shows that there is a sequence of rigid motions that maps $\triangle ABC$ to $\triangle DEF$. Therefore, $\triangle ABC \cong \triangle DEF$.

REFLECT

1a. Explain how knowing that the image of C' lies on both $\overrightarrow{DF}$ and $\overrightarrow{EF}$ allows you to conclude that the image of C' is F.

___F is the only point the rays have in common, so the image of C' must be F.___

Chapter 4   161   Lesson 6

Once you have shown that two triangles are congruent, you can use the fact that corresponding parts of congruent triangles are congruent (CPCTC) to draw conclusions about side lengths and angle measures.

CC.9-12.G.SRT.5

2 EXAMPLE   Using the ASA Congruence Criterion

Solve the following problem.

You want to find the distance across a river. In order to find the distance AB, you locate points as described below. Explain how to use this information and the figure to find AB.

1. Identify a landmark, such as a tree, at A. Place a marker (B) directly across the river from A.

2. At B, turn 90° away from A and walk 1000 feet in a straight line. Place a marker (C) at this location.

3. Continue walking another 1000 feet. Place a marker (D) at this location.

4. Turn 90° away from the river and walk until the marker C aligns with A. Place a marker (E) at this location. Measure $\overline{DE}$.

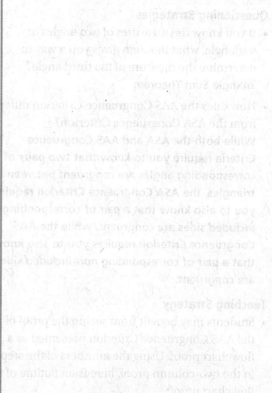

A   Show $\triangle ABC \cong \triangle EDC$.

- Based on the information marked in the figure, which pairs of sides or pairs of angles do you know to be congruent?

  ___$\angle B \cong \angle D$, $\overline{BC} \cong \overline{DC}$___

- What additional pair of sides or pair of angles do you know to be congruent? Why?

  ___$\angle BCA \cong \angle DCE$ by the Vertical Angles Theorem.___

- How can you conclude that $\triangle ABC \cong \triangle EDC$?

  ___ASA Congruence Criterion___

B   Use corresponding parts of congruent triangles.

- Which side of $\triangle EDC$ corresponds to $\overline{AB}$?   ___$\overline{ED}$___

- What is the length of $\overline{AB}$? Why?

  ___875 feet; $\overline{AB} \cong \overline{ED}$ by CPCTC___

REFLECT

2a. Suppose you had walked 500 feet from B to C and then walked another 500 feet from C to D. Would that have changed the distance ED? Explain.

___No; you would still have $ED = AB$ by CPCTC. Since the distance across the river___

___does not change, ED does not change.___

Chapter 4   162   Lesson 6

Questioning Strategies

- If you know the measures of two angles of a triangle, what theorem gives you a way to determine the measure of the third angle? **Triangle Sum Theorem**

- How does the AAS Congruence Criterion differ from the ASA Congruence Criterion? **While both the ASA and AAS Congruence Criteria require you to know that two pairs of corresponding angles are congruent between two triangles, the ASA Congruence Criterion requires you to also know that a pair of corresponding *included* sides are congruent, while the AAS Congruence Criterion requires you to also know that a pair of corresponding *non-included* sides are congruent.**

Teaching Strategy

- Students may benefit from seeing the proof of the AAS Congruence Criterion presented as a flowchart proof. Using the numbers of the steps in the two-column proof, here is an outline of the flowchart proof:

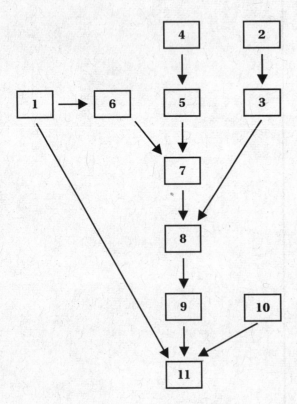

CLOSE

Essential Question

How can you establish and use the ASA and AAS triangle congruence criteria?
The ASA Congruence Criterion is proved by showing that there is a sequence of rigid motions that maps one triangle onto another. The final rigid motion is a reflection, which is established by using the Angle Bisection Theorem. The AAS Congruence Criterion is proved by using the Triangle Sum Theorem in conjunction with the ASA Congruence Criterion. Together, the two criteria guarantee the congruence of two triangles when two pairs of corresponding angles and one pair of corresponding sides are known to be congruent.

Summarize

Have students write a journal entry in which they explain and illustrate the ASA and AAS Congruence Criteria.

PRACTICE

Exercise 1: Students use the ASA Congruence Criterion to prove two triangles congruent.

Exercise 2: Students use the AAS Congruence Criterion to prove two triangles congruent.

You have already used three triangle congruence criteria: SSS, SAS, and ASA. There is another criterion that is useful in proofs, the AAS Congruence Criterion.

AAS Congruence Criterion

If two angles and a non-included side of one triangle are congruent to two angles and the corresponding non-included side of another triangle, then the triangles are congruent.

CC.9-12.G.CO.10

3 PROOF   ASA Congruence Criterion

Given: $\angle B \cong \angle E$, $\angle C \cong \angle F$, $\overline{AC} \cong \overline{DF}$

Prove: $\triangle ABC \cong \triangle DEF$

To prove the triangles are congruent, you can use the Triangle Sum Theorem and reasoning about the angles of the triangles to show that $\angle A \cong \angle D$. Then you can show the triangles are congruent by using ASA.

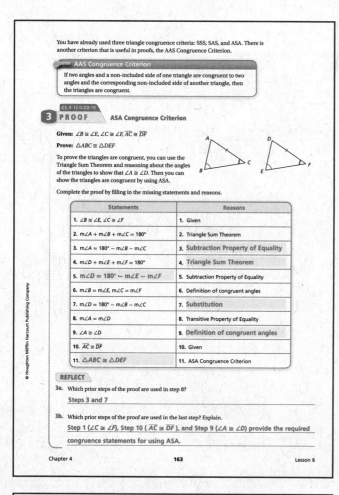

Complete the proof by filling in the missing statements and reasons.

Statements	Reasons
1. $\angle B \cong \angle E$, $\angle C \cong \angle F$	1. Given
2. $m\angle A + m\angle B + m\angle C = 180°$	2. Triangle Sum Theorem
3. $m\angle A = 180° - m\angle B - m\angle C$	3. **Subtraction Property of Equality**
4. $m\angle D + m\angle E + m\angle F = 180°$	4. **Triangle Sum Theorem**
5. $m\angle D = 180° - m\angle E - m\angle F$	5. Subtraction Property of Equality
6. $m\angle B = m\angle E$, $m\angle C = m\angle F$	6. Definition of congruent angles
7. $m\angle D = 180° - m\angle B - m\angle C$	7. **Substitution**
8. $m\angle A = m\angle D$	8. Transitive Property of Equality
9. $\angle A \cong \angle D$	9. **Definition of congruent angles**
10. $\overline{AC} \cong \overline{DF}$	10. Given
11. $\triangle ABC \cong \triangle DEF$	11. ASA Congruence Criterion

REFLECT

3a. Which prior steps of the proof are used in step 8?

Steps 3 and 7

3b. Which prior steps of the proof are used in the last step? Explain.

Step 1 ($\angle C \cong \angle F$), Step 10 ($\overline{AC} \cong \overline{DF}$), and Step 9 ($\angle A \cong \angle D$) provide the required congruence statements for using ASA.

PRACTICE

1. Complete the proof.
Given: $\overline{GE}$ bisects $\angle DGF$ and $\angle DEF$.
Prove: $\triangle GDE \cong \triangle GFE$

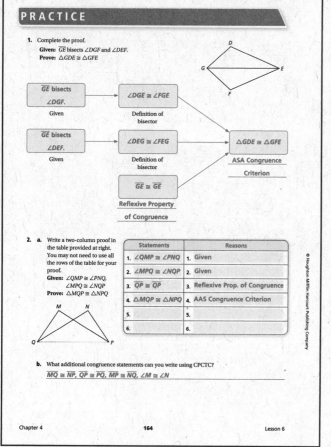

2. a. Write a two-column proof in the table provided at right. You may not need to use all the rows of the table for your proof.
Given: $\angle QMP \cong \angle PNQ$, $\angle MPQ \cong \angle NQP$
Prove: $\triangle MQP \cong \triangle NPQ$

Statements	Reasons
1. $\angle QMP \cong \angle PNQ$	1. Given
2. $\angle MPQ \cong \angle NQP$	2. Given
3. $\overline{QP} \cong \overline{QP}$	3. Reflexive Prop. of Congruence
4. $\triangle MQP \cong \triangle NPQ$	4. AAS Congruence Criterion
5.	5.
6.	6.

b. What additional congruence statements can you write using CPCTC?

$\overline{MQ} \cong \overline{NP}$, $\overline{QP} \cong \overline{PQ}$, $\overline{MP} \cong \overline{NQ}$, $\angle M \cong \angle N$

Notes

ADDITIONAL PRACTICE AND PROBLEM SOLVING

Assign these pages to help your students practice and apply important lesson concepts. For additional exercises, see the Student Edition.

Answers

Additional Practice

1. No; you need to know that $\overline{AB} \cong \overline{CB}$.

2. Yes

3. Yes, if you use Third ∡ Thm. first.

4. HL 5. ASA or AAS

4. none 5. AAS or ASA

8. Possible answer: All right angles are congruent, so $\angle QUR \cong \angle SUR$. $\angle RQU$ and $\angle PQU$ are supplementary and $\angle RSU$ and $\angle TSU$ are supplementary by the Linear Pair Theorem. But it is given that $\angle PQU \cong \angle TSU$, so by the Congruent Supplements Theorem, $\angle RQU \cong \angle RSU$. $\overline{RU} \cong \overline{RU}$ by the Reflexive Property of ≅, so $\Delta RUQ \cong \Delta RUS$ by *AAS*.

Problem Solving

1. Possible drawing:

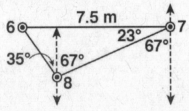

2. Yes; the Δ is uniquely determined by *AAS*.

3. No; you need to know that $\angle KJN$ and $\angle LMN$ are rt. ∡.

4. C 5. J

4-6

Additional Practice

Students in Mrs. Marquez's class are watching a film on the uses of geometry in architecture. The film projector casts the image on a flat screen as shown in the figure. The dotted line is the bisector of $\angle ABC$. Tell whether you can use each congruence theorem to prove that $\triangle ABD \cong \triangle CBD$. If not, tell what else you need to know.

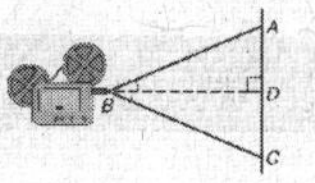

1. Hypotenuse-Leg

_____

2. Angle-Side-Angle

_____

3. Angle-Angle-Side

_____

Write which postulate, if any, can be used to prove the pair of triangles congruent.

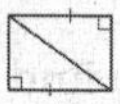

4.

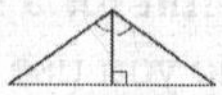

5.

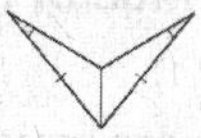

6.

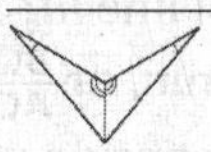

7.

Write a paragraph proof.

8. **Given:** $\angle PQU \cong \angle TSU$,
   $\angle QUR$ and $\angle SUR$ are right angles.

   Prove: $\triangle RUQ \cong \triangle RUS$

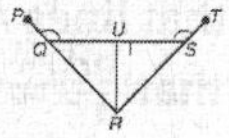

Problem Solving

Use the following information for Exercises 1 and 2.

Melanie is at hole 6 on a miniature golf course. She walks east 7.5 meters to hole 7. She then faces south, turns 67° west, and walks to hole 8. From hole 8, she faces north, turns 35° west, and walks to hole 6.

1. Draw the section of the golf course described. Label the measures of the angles in the triangle.

2. Is there enough information given to determine the location of holes 6, 7, and 8? Explain.

_____

3. A section of the front of an English Tudor home is shown in the diagram. If you know that $\overline{KN} \cong \overline{LN}$ and $\overline{JN} \cong \overline{MN}$, can you use HL to conclude that $\triangle JKN \cong \triangle MLN$? Explain.

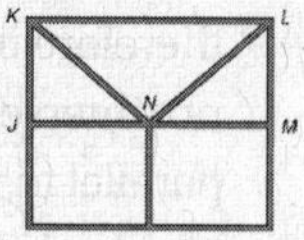

_____

Use the diagram of a kite for Exercises 4 and 5.

$\overline{AE}$ is the angle bisector of $\angle DAF$ and $\angle DEF$.

4. What can you conclude about $\triangle DEA$ and $\triangle FEA$?

   A $\triangle DEA \cong \triangle FEA$ by HL.

   B $\triangle DEA \cong \triangle FEA$ by AAA.

   C $\triangle DEA \cong \triangle FEA$ by ASA.

   D $\triangle DEA \cong \triangle FEA$ by SAS.

5. Based on the diagram, what can you conclude about $\triangle BCA$ and $\triangle HGA$?

   F $\triangle BCA \cong \triangle HGA$ by HL.

   G $\triangle BCA \cong \triangle HGA$ by AAS.

   H $\triangle BCA \cong \triangle HGA$ by ASA.

   J It cannot be shown using the given information that $\triangle BCA \cong \triangle HGA$.

Notes

Triangle Congruence: CPCTC
Connection: Proving Slope Criteria

Essential question: How can CPCTC be used in proving slope criteria for parallel and perpendicular lines?

COMMON CORE Standards for Mathematical Content

CC.9-12.G.GPE.5 Prove the slope criteria for parallel and perpendicular lines ...

Prerequisites
Triangle congruence criteria
Slope

Math Background
In this lesson, students prove the slope criterion for parallel lines as well as the slope criterion for perpendicular lines. Note that the proofs given here assume that the lines are not vertical. It the lines are vertical, the criterion does not apply, since slope is not defined for vertical lines.

INTRODUCE

Introduce the Slope Criterion for Parallel Lines. You may want to spend a moment discussing the biconditional nature of the criterion. Because it is an *if and only if* statement, the criterion can be used in either direction. That is, if you know that two lines are parallel, you can conclude that they have the same slope. Conversely, if you know that two lines have the same slope, you can conclude that they are parallel. You can draw a simple graphic organizer on the board to illustrate this.

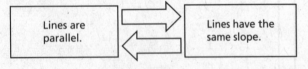

Be sure students understand that each direction of the criterion has its own proof.

You can have a similar discussion with students about the biconditional nature of the Slope Criterion for Perpendicular Lines.

TEACH

 PROOF

Questioning Strategies
- What is a "slope triangle"? **It is a right triangle that you can use to calculate the ratio of the rise to the run for a straight line.**
- How do you use the slope triangle to find the slope of line *m*? **The slope is the ratio of the rise to the run, or $\frac{BC}{AC}$.**
- What ratios do you need to show are equal to prove that lines *m* and *n* have the same slope? **Show that $\frac{BC}{AC} = \frac{EF}{DF}$.**

MATHEMATICAL PRACTICE   Highlighting the Standards

You can address Standard 6 (Attend to precision) by discussing some of the finer points of the proof with students. For example, the proof that parallel lines have the same slope begins by drawing a "slope triangle" for line *m* and extending the horizontal side $\overline{AC}$ to intersect line *n*. Ask students how they know this horizontal line must eventually intersect line *n*. Help students understand that line *n* continues in both directions and, assuming that line *n* is not itself horizontal, it must therefore intersect any horizontal line. (If it did not intersect the horizontal line, it would be parallel to the horizontal line, meaning line *n* is also horizontal, which is a contradiction.)

2 **PROOF**

Questioning Strategies
- How is this proof similar to the proof that parallel lines have the same slope? **In both proofs, you start by drawing slope triangles.**
- When you extend $\overline{AC}$, why do you do it in such a way that $DF = AC$? **Doing so eventually lets you conclude that $\triangle BAC \cong \triangle EDF$.**

Name _____ Class _____ Date _____

4-7

Triangle Congruence: CPCTC
Connection: Proving Slope Criteria

Essential question: *How can CPCTC be used in proving slope criteria for parallel and perpendicular lines?*

Slope is useful for determining whether two lines are parallel.

Slope Criterion for Parallel Lines

Two non-vertical lines are parallel if and only if they have the same slope.

Because the theorem is stated as a biconditional (*if and only if*), the proof has two parts, one for each "direction" of the theorem.

CC.9-12.G.GPE.5

1 PROOF   Parallel Lines Have the Same Slope

Given: Non-vertical lines *m* and *n*, *m* ∥ *n*

Prove: Line *m* and line *n* have the same slope.

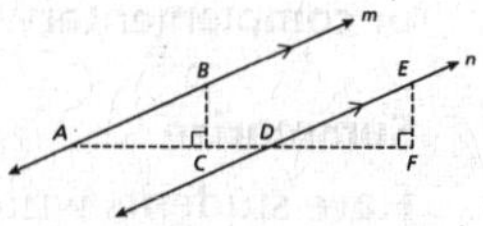

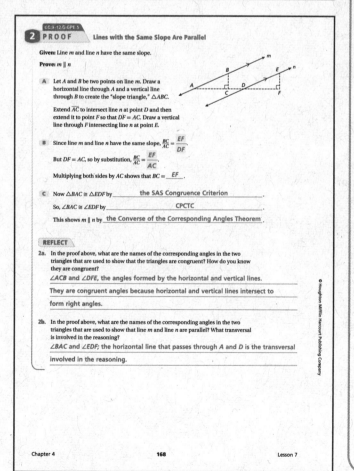

A Let *A* and *B* be two points on line *m*. Draw a horizontal line through *A* and a vertical line through *B* to create the "slope triangle," △*ABC*.

Extend $\overline{AC}$ to intersect line *n* at point *D* and then extend it to point *F* so that *AC* = *DF*. Draw a vertical line through *F* intersecting line *n* at point *E*.

B Since *m* ∥ *n*, ∠*BAC* ≅ ∠*EDF* by ____the Corresponding Angles Theorem____.

△*BAC* ≅ △*EDF* by ____the ASA Congruence Criterion____

So, $\overline{BC}$ ≅ $\overline{EF}$ by ____CPCTC____

This means *BC* = *EF*, so $\frac{BC}{AC} = \frac{EF}{DF}$ by ____the Division Property of Equality____.

This shows that the slope of *m* equals the slope of *n* by the definition of slope.

REFLECT

1a. Does the above proof work if the lines are horizontal? If not, does the theorem still hold? Explain.

The proof does not work in the case of horizontal lines, but the theorem still

holds because both slopes are 0 in this case.

1b. How can you estimate the slope of lines *m* and *n* in the above figure?

$\overline{BC}$ appears to be about half as long as $\overline{AC}$, so the slope is about $\frac{1}{2}$.

CC.9-12.G.GPE.5

2 PROOF   Lines with the Same Slope Are Parallel

Given: Line *m* and line *n* have the same slope.

Prove: *m* ∥ *n*

A Let *A* and *B* be two points on line *m*. Draw a horizontal line through *A* and a vertical line through *B* to create the "slope triangle," △*ABC*.

Extend $\overline{AC}$ to intersect line *n* at point *D* and then extend it to point *F* so that *DF* = *AC*. Draw a vertical line through *F* intersecting line *n* at point *E*.

B Since line *m* and line *n* have the same slope, $\frac{BC}{AC} = \frac{EF}{DF}$.

But *DF* = *AC*, so by substitution, $\frac{BC}{AC} = \frac{EF}{AC}$.

Multiplying both sides by *AC* shows that *BC* = ____*EF*____.

C Now △*BAC* ≅ △*EDF* by ____the SAS Congruence Criterion____

So, ∠*BAC* ≅ ∠*EDF* by ____CPCTC____

This shows *m* ∥ *n* by ____the Converse of the Corresponding Angles Theorem____.

REFLECT

2a. In the proof above, what are the names of the corresponding angles in the two triangles that are used to show that the triangles are congruent? How do you know they are congruent?

∠*ACB* and ∠*DFE*, the angles formed by the horizontal and vertical lines.

They are congruent angles because horizontal and vertical lines intersect to

form right angles.

2b. In the proof above, what are the names of the corresponding angles in the two triangles that are used to show that line *m* and line *n* are parallel? What transversal is involved in the reasoning?

∠*BAC* and ∠*EDF*; the horizontal line that passes through *A* and *D* is the transversal

involved in the reasoning.

Questioning Strategies

- Can either of the lines be horizontal? Why or why not? **No; it is specified that neither line is vertical. Since the lines are perpendicular, if one line were horizontal, the other would be vertical.**

- How do you find the slope of line m? **The slope is the ratio of the rise to the run in the slope triangle, $\triangle PQR$. This ratio is $\frac{QR}{PR}$, or $\frac{a}{b}$.**

MATHEMATICAL PRACTICE

Highlighting the Standards

You can address Standard 7 (Look for and make use of structure) by discussing what it means for two numbers to have a product of -1. For example, if the product of a and b is -1, then $ab = -1$, and solving for a shows that $a = -\frac{1}{b}$. This is equivalent to saying that a and b are opposite reciprocals of each other. You may want to have students give examples of pairs of numbers that are opposite reciprocals of each other. Possibilities include 1 and -1, $\frac{2}{3}$ and $-\frac{3}{2}$, and $\frac{1}{7}$ and -7. Students can check that the product of the numbers in each pair is -1.

---

4 PROOF

Questioning Strategies

- How do you know one line has a positive slope and one line has a negative slope? **The product of the slopes is -1, so one slope must be positive and one must be negative.**

- In Step C, how do you know $\angle 2$ and $\angle 3$ are complementary? **They are adjacent angles that form a right angle.**

CLOSE

Essential Question

How can CPCTC be used in proving slope criteria for parallel and perpendicular lines?

By drawing "slope triangles," you can show that the triangles are congruent. You can then use CPCTC to show that slopes are equal or negative reciprocals from ratios of corresponding side lengths or show that certain angles are congruent or complementary.

Summarize

Have students write a journal entry where they state the slope criteria for parallel and perpendicular lines and illustrate each with a drawing that includes "slope triangles."

© Houghton Mifflin Harcourt Publishing Company

Slope is useful for determining whether two lines are perpendicular.

Slope Criterion for Perpendicular Lines

Two non-vertical lines are perpendicular if and only if the product of their slopes is −1.

Like the Slope Criterion for Parallel Lines, the theorem is stated as a biconditional. Therefore, the proof has two parts, one for each "direction" of the theorem.

3 **PROOF**   CC.9-12.G.GPE.5   Perpendicular Lines Have Slopes Whose Product Is −1

Given: Non-vertical lines m and n, $m \perp n$

Prove: The product of the slope of line m and the slope of line n is −1.

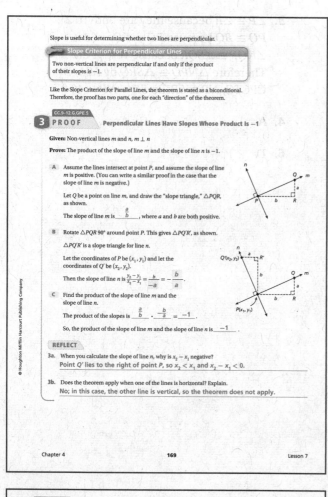

A   Assume the lines intersect at point P, and assume the slope of line m is positive. (You can write a similar proof in the case that the slope of line m is negative.)

Let Q be a point on line m, and draw the "slope triangle," $\triangle PQR$, as shown.

The slope of line m is $\dfrac{a}{b}$, where a and b are both positive.

B   Rotate $\triangle PQR$ 90° around point P. This gives $\triangle PQ'R'$, as shown.

$\triangle PQ'R'$ is a slope triangle for line n.

Let the coordinates of P be (x_1, y_1) and let the coordinates of Q' be (x_2, y_2).

Then the slope of line n is $\dfrac{y_2 - y_1}{x_2 - x_1} = \dfrac{b}{-a} = -\dfrac{b}{a}$.

C   Find the product of the slope of line m and the slope of line n.

The product of the slopes is $\dfrac{a}{b} \cdot -\dfrac{b}{a} = \underline{-1}$.

So, the product of the slope of line m and the slope of line n is $\underline{-1}$.

REFLECT

3a.   When you calculate the slope of line n, why is $x_2 - x_1$ negative?

Point Q' lies to the right of point P, so $x_2 < x_1$ and $x_2 - x_1 < 0$.

3b.   Does the theorem apply when one of the lines is horizontal? Explain.

No; in this case, the other line is vertical, so the theorem does not apply.

© Houghton Mifflin Harcourt Publishing Company

Chapter 4   169   Lesson 7

---

4 **PROOF**   CC.9-12.G.GPE.5   Lines with Slopes Whose Product Is −1 Are Perpendicular

Given: The product of the slope of line m and the slope of line n is −1.

Prove: $m \perp n$

A   Let line m have positive slope $\dfrac{a}{b}$, where a and b are both positive.

Let line n have slope z. It is given that $z \cdot \dfrac{a}{b} = -1$.

Solving for z shows that the slope of line n is $\underline{-\dfrac{b}{a}}$.

B   Assume the lines intersect at point P. Set up slope triangles for lines m and n as shown.

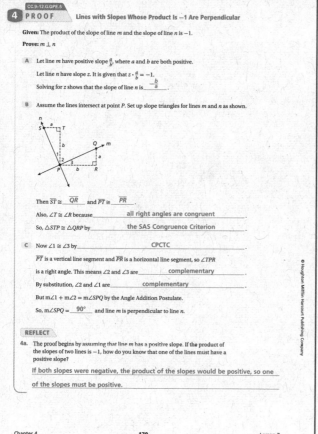

Then $\overline{ST} \cong \underline{\overline{QR}}$ and $\overline{PT} \cong \underline{\overline{PR}}$.

Also, $\angle T \cong \angle R$ because ___all right angles are congruent___.

So, $\triangle STP \cong \triangle QRP$ by ___the SAS Congruence Criterion___.

C   Now $\angle 1 \cong \angle 3$ by ___CPCTC___.

$\overline{PT}$ is a vertical line segment and $\overline{PR}$ is a horizontal line segment, so $\angle TPR$ is a right angle. This means $\angle 2$ and $\angle 3$ are ___complementary___.

By substitution, $\angle 2$ and $\angle 1$ are ___complementary___.

But $m\angle 1 + m\angle 2 = m\angle SPQ$ by the Angle Addition Postulate.

So, $m\angle SPQ = \underline{90°}$ and line m is perpendicular to line n.

REFLECT

4a.   The proof begins by assuming that line m has a positive slope. If the product of the slopes of two lines is −1, how do you know that one of the lines must have a positive slope?

If both slopes were negative, the product of the slopes would be positive, so one of the slopes must be positive.

© Houghton Mifflin Harcourt Publishing Company

Chapter 4   170   Lesson 7

© Houghton Mifflin Harcourt Publishing Company

ADDITIONAL PRACTICE AND PROBLEM SOLVING

Assign these pages to help your students practice and apply important lesson concepts. For additional exercises, see the Student Edition.

Answers

Additional Practice

1. Possible answer: Because $\angle DCE \cong \angle BCA$ by the Vertical ∠s Thm. the triangles are congruent by ASA, and each side in $\triangle ABC$ has the same length as its corresponding side in $\triangle EDC$. Heike could jump about 23 ft. The distance along path *BA* is 20 ft because *BA* corresponds with *DE*, so Heike could have jumped this distance. The distance along path *CA* is 25 ft because *CA* corresponds with *CE*, so Heike could not have jumped this distance.

2.

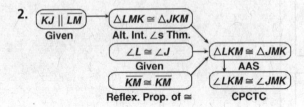

3.

Statements	Reasons
1. *FGHI* is a rectangle.	1. Given
2. $\overline{FI} \cong \overline{GH}$, $\angle FIH$ and $\angle GHI$ are right angles.	2. Def. of rectangle
3. $\angle FIH \cong \angle GHI$	3. Rt. ∠ ≅ Thm.
4. $\overline{IH} \cong \overline{IH}$	4. Reflex. Prop. of ≅
5. $\triangle FIH \cong \triangle GHI$	5. SAS
6. $\overline{FH} \cong \overline{GI}$	6. CPCTC
7. $FH = GI$	7. Def. of ≅ segs.

Problem Solving

1. 60 in^2; Since the triangles are ≅, they have the same measures. So, the triangles also have the same areas.

2. 82 m; $\triangle UVW \cong \triangle XYW$ by SAS, so $\overline{UV} \cong \overline{XY}$ by CPCTC. Therefore $UV = XY = 82$ m.

3. $\angle P \cong \angle R$ because they are both rt. ∠s. $PQ \cong RQ$ because $PQ = RQ = 65$ ft. $\angle NQP \cong \angle SQR$ because vert. ∠s are ≅. Therefore $\triangle NPQ \cong \triangle SRQ$ by ASA. By CPCTC, $NP \cong SR$. So $SR = NP = 40$ ft.

4. A

5. G

6. D

Additional Practice

1. Heike Dreschler set the Woman's World Junior Record for the long jump in 1983. She jumped about 23.4 feet. The diagram shows two triangles and a pond. Explain whether Heike could have jumped the pond along path *BA* or along path *CA*.

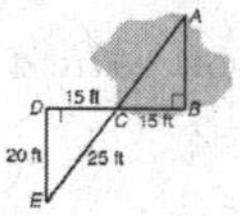

_____

_____

_____

Write a flowchart proof.

2. **Given:** $\angle L \cong \angle J$, $\overline{KJ} \parallel \overline{LM}$

   Prove: $\angle LKM \cong \angle JMK$

Write a two-column proof.

3. **Given:** *FGHI* is a rectangle.

   Prove: The diagonals of a rectangle have equal lengths.

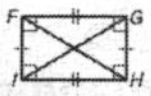

Problem Solving

1. Two triangular plates are congruent. The area of one of the plates is 60 square inches. What is the area of the other plate? Explain.

_____

2. An archaeologist draws the triangles to find the distance *XY* across a ravine. What is *XY*? Explain.

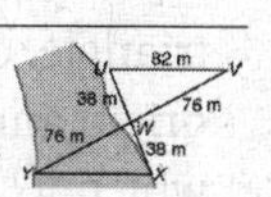

_____

3. A city planner sets up the triangles to find the distance *RS* across a river. Describe the steps that she can use to find *RS*.

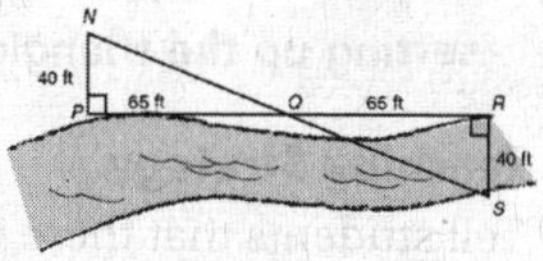

_____

_____

_____

Choose the best answer.

4. A lighthouse and the range of its shining light are shown. What can you conclude?

   A $x = y$ by CPCTC   C $\angle AED \cong \angle ADE$ by CPCTC

   B $x = 2y$ D $\angle AED \cong \angle ACB$

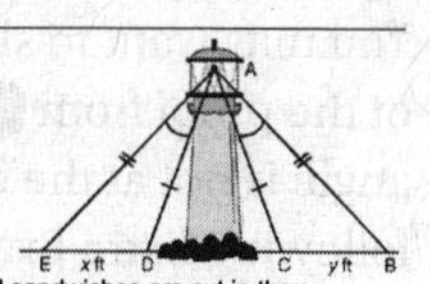

5. A rectangular piece of cloth 15 centimeters long is cut along a diagonal to form two triangles. One of the triangles has a side length of 9 centimeters. Which is a true statement?

   F The second triangle has an angle measure of 15° by CPCTC.

   G The second triangle has a side length of 9 centimeters by CPCTC.

   H You cannot make a conclusion about the side length of the second triangle.

   J The triangles are not congruent.

6. Small sandwiches are cut in the shape of right triangles. The longest sides of all the sandwiches are 3 inches. One sandwich has a side length of 2 inches. Which is a true statement?

   A All the sandwiches have a side length of 2 inches by CPCTC.

   B All the sandwiches are isosceles triangles with side lengths of 2 inches.

   C None of the other sandwiches have side lengths of 2 inches.

   D You cannot make a conclusion using CPCTC.

© Houghton Mifflin Harcourt Publishing Company

COMMON Standards for
CORE Mathematical Content

CC.9-12.G.CO.10 Prove theorems about triangles.

CC.9-12.G.GPE.4 Use coordinates to prove simple geometric theorems algebraically.

Prerequisites

The Distance Formula

The Midpoint Formula

Math Background

Analytic geometry is the study of geometry using a coordinate system. Although certain aspects of the subject date to ancient times, the French mathematician René Descartes (1596–1650) is traditionally considered the father of analytic geometry. The strength of analytic geometry lies in its use of tools from algebra to solve geometry problems. In particular, this lesson shows how it is possible to use a Cartesian coordinate system, the distance formula, and the midpoint formula to prove results about geometric figures.

INTRODUCE

Begin with a brief review of the distance formula and the midpoint formula. Explain to students that they will be using these tools, as well as other ideas from algebra, to prove geometry theorems. Emphasize that coordinate proofs, like all other proofs that students have written up until now, require a logical sequence of ideas and supporting reasons for each statement in the proof.

TEACH

EXAMPLE

Questioning Strategies

• What must you do in order to show that the triangle is or is not isosceles? **You must show that there are (or are not) two congruent sides.**

• Do you need to plot the vertices and draw the triangle in order to write the proof? **No; drawing the triangle makes the proof clearer, but the proof does not depend upon the drawing.**

EXTRA EXAMPLE

Prove or disprove that the triangle with vertices $R(-3, 1)$, $S(1, 5)$, and $T(3, -1)$ is an isosceles triangle.

By the distance formula,

$$RS = \sqrt{(1 - (-3))^2 + (5 - 1)^2} = \sqrt{4^2 + 4^2} = \sqrt{32},$$

$$ST = \sqrt{(3 - 1)^2 + (-1 - 5)^2} = \sqrt{2^2 + (-6)^2} = \sqrt{40},$$

$$RT = \sqrt{(3 - (-3))^2 + (-1 - 1)^2} = \sqrt{6^2 + (-2)^2} = \sqrt{40}.$$

Since $\overline{ST} \cong \overline{RT}$, the triangle is isosceles.

2 EXAMPLE

Questioning Strategies

• Once the coordinates are assigned as shown, what do you need to do to write the proof? **You must use the distance formula to show that $MA = MB = MC$.**

• Why are you allowed to place two sides of $\triangle ABC$ along the axes of the coordinate plane? Can you do this with any triangle when you write a coordinate proof? **You can do this because $\triangle ABC$ has a right angle. You can only do this in coordinate proofs that involve right triangles.**

• When you write a coordinate proof about a triangle, can you always place one vertex at the origin and one side along the x-axis? Why or why not? **Yes; you do not lose any generality by setting up the triangle in this way.**

Teaching Strategy

Tell students that there is often more than one correct way to set up a figure for a coordinate proof. You may want to show students an alternate version of the proof from **2 EXAMPLE** in which the right angle is not at the origin. This is outlined in the following Extra Example.

Introduction to Coordinate Proof
Going Deeper

Essential question: *How do you write a coordinate proof?*

You have already seen a wide range of purely geometric proofs. These proofs used postulates and theorems to build logical arguments. Now you will learn how to write coordinate proofs. These proofs also use logic, but they apply ideas from algebra to help demonstrate geometric relationships.

CC.9-12.G.GPE.4

1 EXAMPLE   Proving or Disproving a Statement

Prove or disprove that the triangle with vertices $A(4, 2)$, $B(-1, 4)$, and $C(2, -3)$ is an isosceles triangle.

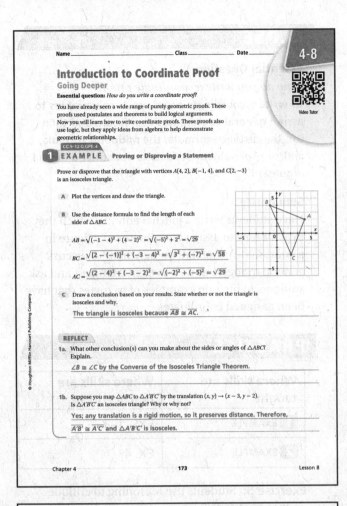

A   Plot the vertices and draw the triangle.

B   Use the distance formula to find the length of each side of $\triangle ABC$.

$$AB = \sqrt{(-1-4)^2 + (4-2)^2} = \sqrt{(-5)^2 + 2^2} = \sqrt{29}$$

$$BC = \sqrt{(2-(-1))^2 + (-3-4)^2} = \sqrt{3^2 + (-7)^2} = \sqrt{58}$$

$$AC = \sqrt{(2-4)^2 + (-3-2)^2} = \sqrt{(-2)^2 + (-5)^2} = \sqrt{29}$$

C   Draw a conclusion based on your results. State whether or not the triangle is isosceles and why.

The triangle is isosceles because $\overline{AB} \cong \overline{AC}$.

REFLECT

1a. What other conclusion(s) can you make about the sides or angles of $\triangle ABC$? Explain.

$\angle B \cong \angle C$ by the Converse of the Isosceles Triangle Theorem.

1b. Suppose you map $\triangle ABC$ to $\triangle A'B'C'$ by the translation $(x, y) \rightarrow (x - 3, y - 2)$. Is $\triangle A'B'C'$ an isosceles triangle? Why or why not?

Yes; any translation is a rigid motion, so it preserves distance. Therefore,

$\overline{A'B'} \cong \overline{A'C'}$ and $\triangle A'B'C'$ is isosceles.

You can write a coordinate proof to prove general facts about geometric figures. The first step in such a proof is using variables to assign general coordinates to a figure using only what is known about the figure.

CC.9-12.G.GPE.4

2 EXAMPLE   Writing a Coordinate Proof

Prove that in a right triangle, the midpoint of the hypotenuse is equidistant from all three vertices.

A   Assign coordinates to the figure.

Let the triangle be $\triangle ABC$. Since the triangle is a right triangle, assume $\angle B$ is a right angle. Place $\angle B$ at the origin and place the legs along the positive x- and y-axes.

Since the proof involves a midpoint, use multiples of 2 in assigning coordinates to A and C, as shown.

B   Let M be the midpoint of the hypotenuse, $\overline{AC}$. Use the midpoint formula to find the coordinates of M.

$$M\left(\frac{2a + 0}{2}, \frac{0 + 2c}{2} \right) = M\left(\boxed{a}, \boxed{c} \right)$$

C   Use the distance formula to find MA, MB, and MC.

$$MA = \sqrt{\left(2a - \boxed{a} \right)^2 + \left(0 - \boxed{c} \right)^2} = \sqrt{\boxed{a}^2 + \boxed{c}^2}$$

$$MB = \sqrt{\left(\boxed{a} - 0 \right)^2 + \left(\boxed{c} - 0 \right)^2} = \sqrt{\boxed{a}^2 + \boxed{c}^2}$$

$$MB = \sqrt{\left(\boxed{a} - 0 \right)^2 + \left(\boxed{c} - 2c \right)^2} = \sqrt{\boxed{a}^2 + \boxed{c}^2}$$

So, the midpoint of the hypotenuse is equidistant from all three vertices because

$MA = MB = MC.$

EXTRA EXAMPLE

Use the coordinates shown below to prove that in a right triangle, the midpoint of the hypotenuse is equidistant from all three vertices.

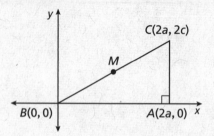

Let M be the midpoint of the hypotenuse, $\overline{BC}$. Then by the midpoint formula, the coordinates of M are $M(a, c)$.

By the distance formula,

$$MA = \sqrt{(2a - a)^2 + (0 - c)^2} = \sqrt{a^2 + c^2},$$

$$MB = \sqrt{(a - 0)^2 + (c - 0)^2} = \sqrt{a^2 + c^2},$$

$$MC = \sqrt{(2a - a)^2 + (2c - c)^2} = \sqrt{a^2 + c^2}.$$

So the midpoint of the hypotenuse is equidistant from all three vertices because $MA = MB = MC$.

MATHEMATICAL PRACTICE — Highlighting the Standards

Exercise 4 gives students experience critiquing the work of another student. This is an important element of Standard 3 (Construct viable arguments and critique the reasoning of others). In this exercise, students must pinpoint the aspect of the student's proof that is incorrect. Students should recognize that some parts of an argument may be correct (i.e., a correct calculation using the distance formula) while other parts of the argument may be incorrect (i.e., an incorrect assignment of coordinates for the figure).

Essential Question

How do you write a coordinate proof?

To write a coordinate proof, you use variables to assign general coordinates to a figure and then use the distance formula, the midpoint formula, and/or other algebraic facts to construct a logical argument.

Summarize

Have students write a journal entry in which they explain how to assign coordinates to a figure in a coordinate proof. Encourage them to discuss general triangles as well as right triangles, and ask students to include examples of triangles that have been assigned coordinates.

PRACTICE

Where skills are taught	Where skills are practiced
1 EXAMPLE	EXS. 1–3
2 EXAMPLE	EX. 4

Exercise 5: Students use reasoning to critique an incorrect coordinate proof.

© Houghton Mifflin Harcourt Publishing Company

> **REFLECT**
>
> **2a.** Explain why it is more convenient to assign the coordinates as $A(2a, 0)$ and $C(0, 2c)$ rather than $A(a, 0)$ and $C(0, c)$.
>
> This choice eliminates the need for fractions in the coordinates of M.
>
> **2b.** Can you write the proof by assigning the coordinates as $A(2n, 0)$ and $C(0, 2n)$?
>
> No; this would assume the triangle is isosceles. The statement to be
>
> proved applies to all right triangles, not just isosceles right triangles.

PRACTICE

1. Prove or disprove that the triangle with vertices $R(-2, -2)$, $S(1, 4)$, and $T(4, -5)$ is an equilateral triangle.

By the distance formula, $RS = \sqrt{45}$, $RT = \sqrt{45}$,

and $ST = \sqrt{90}$. Since the three sides do not

all have the same length, the triangle is not

equilateral.

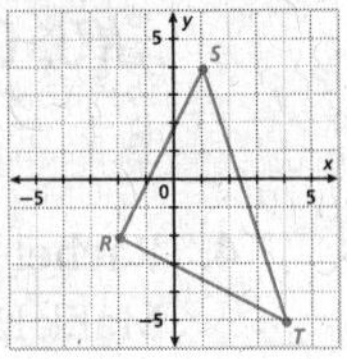

2. Refer to the triangle you drew in Exercise 1 to prove or disprove that the triangle with vertices $R(-2, -2)$, $S(1, 4)$, and $T(4, -5)$ is a right triangle.

By the slope formula, the slope of $\overline{RS}$ is 2 and the slope of $\overline{RT}$ is $-\frac{1}{2}$.

Because the product of these slopes is -1, the angle formed by $\overline{RS}$ and $\overline{RT}$

is a right angle, and so the triangle is a right triangle.

3. $\triangle ABC$ has vertices $A(-4, 1)$, $B(-3, 4)$, and $C(-1, 1)$. $\triangle DEF$ has vertices $D(2, -3)$, $E(5, -2)$, and $F(2, 0)$. Prove or disprove that the triangles are congruent.

By the distance formula, $AC = DF = 3$,

$AB = DE = \sqrt{10}$, and $BC = EF = \sqrt{13}$. Therefore,

$\triangle ABC \cong \triangle DEF$ by the SSS Congruence Criterion.

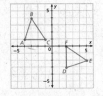

© Houghton Mifflin Harcourt Publishing Company

---

4. Write a coordinate proof to prove that the diagonals of a rectangle are congruent. Use the space at right to show how to assign coordinates. Then write the proof below.

Assign coordinates as shown. By the

distance formula, $BD = \sqrt{a^2 + c^2}$ and

$AC = \sqrt{a^2 + c^2}$. Therefore $\overline{BD} \cong \overline{AC}$, so the

diagonals are congruent.

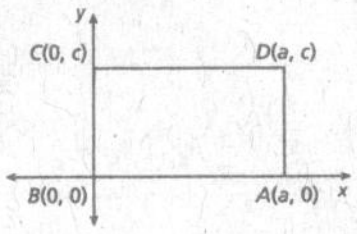

5. **Error Analysis** A student proves that every right triangle is isosceles by assigning coordinates as shown at right and by using the distance formula to show that $PQ = a$ and $RQ = a$. Explain the error in the student's proof.

The proof is not correct because the assigned

coordinates do not result in a general right

triangle. The coordinates of R should be (a, b).

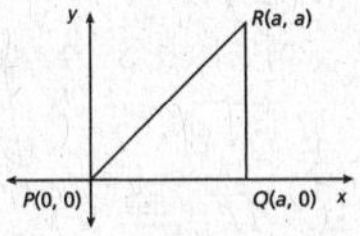

© Houghton Mifflin Harcourt Publishing Company

Assign these pages to help your students practice and apply important lesson concepts. For additional exercises, see the Student Edition.

Answers

Additional Practice

1.
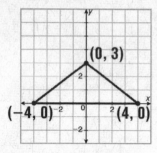

2.
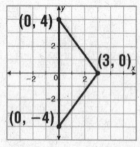

3. Possible answer: *ABCD* is a rectangle with width *AD* and length *DC*. The area of *ABCD* is (*AD*)(*DC*) or (4)(6) = 24 square units. By the Midpoint Formula, the coordinates of *E* are $\left(\dfrac{0+6}{2}, \dfrac{0+0}{2}\right) =$ (3, 0) and the coordinates of *F* are $\left(\dfrac{0+0}{2}, \dfrac{0+4}{2}\right) = (0, 2)$. The *x*-coordinate of *E* is the length of rectangle *DEGF*, and the *y*-coordinate of *F* is the width. So the area of *DEGF* is (3)(2) = 6 square units. Since $6 = \dfrac{1}{4}(24)$, the area of rectangle *DEGF* is one-fourth the area of rectangle *ABCD*.

Problem Solving

1. about 4.2 yd   2. about 338.9 m

3.
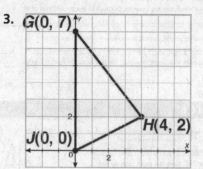

4. Rachel had ridden farther, about 3.2 miles; Malik had ridden about 2.2 miles.

5. D   6. J

Additional Practice

Position an isosceles triangle with sides of 8 units, 5 units, and 5 units in the coordinate plane. Label the coordinates of each vertex.
(*Hint:* Use the Pythagorean Theorem.)

1. Center the long side on the *x*-axis at the origin.

2. Place the long side on the *y*-axis centered at the origin.

Write a coordinate proof.

3. **Given:** Rectangle *ABCD* has vertices *A*(0, 4), *B*(6, 4), *C*(6, 0), and *D*(0, 0). *E* is the midpoint of $\overline{DC}$. *F* is the midpoint of $\overline{DA}$.

   Prove: The area of rectangle *DEGF* is one-fourth the area of rectangle *ABCD*.

Problem Solving

Round to the nearest tenth for Exercises 1 and 2.

1. A fountain is at the center of a square courtyard. If one grid unit represents one yard, what is the distance from the fountain at (0, 0) to each corner of the courtyard?

   _____

2. Noah started at his home at *A*(0, 0), walked with his dog to the park at *B*(4, 2), walked to his friend's house at *C*(8, 0), then walked home. If one grid unit represents 20 meters, what is the distance that Noah and his dog walked?

   _____

Use the following information for Exercises 3 and 4.

Rachel started her cycling trip at *G*(0, 7). Malik started his trip at *J*(0, 0). Their paths crossed at *H*(4, 2).

3. Draw their routes in the coordinate plane.

4. If one grid unit represents $\frac{1}{2}$ mile, who had ridden farther when their paths crossed? Explain.

   _____

Choose the best answer.

5. Two airplanes depart from an airport at *A*(9, 11). The first airplane travels to a location at *N*(−250, 80), and the second airplane travels to a location at *P*(105, −400). Each unit represents 1 mile. What is the distance, to the nearest mile, between the two airplanes?

   A 335.3 mi   C 490.3 mi
   B 477.9 mi   D 597.0 mi

6. A corner garden has vertices at *Q*(0, 0), *R*(0, 2*d*), and *S*(2*c*, 0). A brick walkway runs from point *Q* to the midpoint *M* of $\overline{RS}$. What is *QM*?

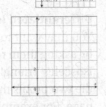

   F (*c*, *d*)   H $\sqrt{c+d}$
   G $c^2 + d^2$ J $\sqrt{c^2 + d^2}$

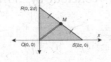

Isosceles and Equilateral Triangles
Focus on Reasoning

Essential question: *What special relationships exist among the sides and angles of isosceles triangles?*

COMMON CORE **Standards for Mathematical Content**

CC.9-12.G.CO.10 Prove theorems about triangles.

Vocabulary
legs

vertex angle

base

base angles

Prerequisites
Reflected Points on an Angle Theorem

Triangle congruence criteria

Triangle Sum Theorem

Math Background
This Focus on Reasoning lesson gives students the opportunity to investigate the Isosceles Triangle Theorem from both an inductive and deductive perspective. In particular, the opening activity leads students to make a conjecture about the measures of the base angles of an isosceles triangle. Students prove their conjecture and its converse in the remainder of the lesson.

INTRODUCE

Students should already be familiar with isosceles triangles from earlier grades. Ask a volunteer to define *isosceles triangle* and have students give real-world examples of isosceles triangles. If possible, you might display a photo of the Transamerica Pyramid in San Francisco, whose faces are isosceles triangles, or show the class a football pennant or other flag in the shape of an isosceles triangle. Tell students they will be investigating properties of isosceles triangles in this lesson.

TEACH

1 Investigate isosceles triangles.

Questioning Strategies
- What must be true about the triangles you construct in order for them to be isosceles triangles? **They must have at least two congruent sides.**
- How could you draw isosceles triangles without using a compass? **Possible answer: Draw $\angle A$ and plot point B on one side of $\angle A$. Then use a ruler to measure $\overline{AB}$ and plot point C on the other side of $\angle A$ so that $AC = AB$.**

2 Prove the Isosceles Triangle Theorem.

Questioning Strategies
- What can you say about an isosceles triangle, $\triangle ABC$, with base angles $\angle B$ and $\angle C$, if you know that $m\angle A = 100°$? Explain. **By the Isosceles Triangle Theorem, $\angle B \cong \angle C$, and $m\angle B + m\angle C = 80°$ by the Triangle Sum Theorem, so $m\angle B = m\angle C = 40°$.**
- What can you say about the angles of an isosceles right triangle? **The angles of the triangle measure 90°, 45°, and 45°.**

Differentiated Instruction
You may want to challenge advanced students by asking them to come up with a proof of the Isosceles Triangle Theorem that is different from the two proofs that are presented on the student page. For example, students might draw the bisector of $\angle A$ and then use the SAS Congruence Criterion to show that the two triangles formed by the bisector are congruent. Such a proof would conclude by showing that $\angle B \cong \angle C$ by CPCTC.

Name _____ Class _____ Date _____

4-9

Isosceles and Equilateral Triangles
Focus on Reasoning

Essential question: *What special relationships exist among the sides and angles of isosceles triangles?*

COMMON CORE
CC.9-12.G.CO.10

Recall that an *isosceles* triangle is a triangle with at least two congruent sides. The congruent sides are called the **legs** of the triangle. The angle formed by the legs is the **vertex angle**. The side of the triangle opposite the vertex angle is the **base**. The angles that have the base as a side are the **base angles**.

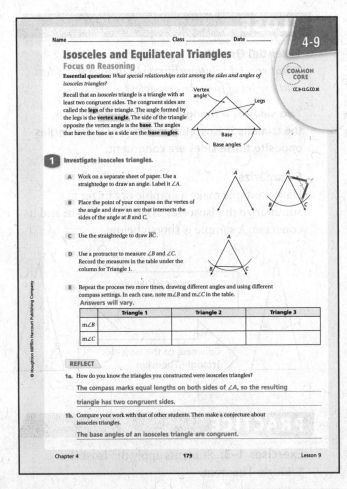

1 Investigate isosceles triangles.

A Work on a separate sheet of paper. Use a straightedge to draw an angle. Label it ∠A.

B Place the point of your compass on the vertex of the angle and draw an arc that intersects the sides of the angle at B and C.

C Use the straightedge to draw $\overline{BC}$.

D Use a protractor to measure ∠B and ∠C. Record the measures in the table under the column for Triangle 1.

E Repeat the process two more times, drawing different angles and using different compass settings. In each case, note m∠B and m∠C in the table. **Answers will vary.**

	Triangle 1	Triangle 2	Triangle 3
m∠B			
m∠C			

REFLECT

1a. How do you know the triangles you constructed were isosceles triangles?

The compass marks equal lengths on both sides of ∠A, so the resulting

triangle has two congruent sides.

1b. Compare your work with that of other students. Then make a conjecture about isosceles triangles.

The base angles of an isosceles triangle are congruent.

Chapter 4   179   Lesson 9

---

2 Prove the Isosceles Triangle Theorem.

The base angles of an isosceles triangle are congruent.

Given: $\overline{AB} \cong \overline{AC}$
Prove: ∠B ≅ ∠C

Complete the proof.

Draw line *m*, which is the bisector of ∠A. Consider the reflection across line *m*.

Because AB = AC, you can conclude that B and C are images of each other under the reflection across line *m*. This is justified by

the Reflected Points on an Angle Theorem.

So, ∠B and ∠C are images of each other and therefore ∠B ≅ ∠C, because

reflections preserve angle measure.

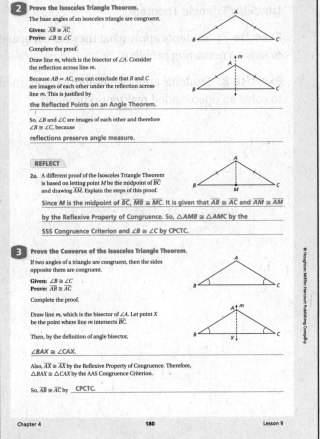

REFLECT

2a. A different proof of the Isosceles Triangle Theorem is based on letting point M be the midpoint of $\overline{BC}$ and drawing $\overline{AM}$. Explain the steps of this proof.

Since M is the midpoint of $\overline{BC}$, $\overline{MB} \cong \overline{MC}$. It is given that $\overline{AB} \cong \overline{AC}$ and $\overline{AM} \cong \overline{AM}$

by the Reflexive Property of Congruence. So, △AMB ≅ △AMC by the

SSS Congruence Criterion and ∠B ≅ ∠C by CPCTC.

3 Prove the Converse of the Isosceles Triangle Theorem.

If two angles of a triangle are congruent, then the sides opposite them are congruent.

Given: ∠B ≅ ∠C
Prove: $\overline{AB} \cong \overline{AC}$

Complete the proof.

Draw line *m*, which is the bisector of ∠A. Let point X be the point where line *m* intersects $\overline{BC}$.

Then, by the definition of angle bisector,

∠BAX ≅ ∠CAX.

Also, $\overline{AX} \cong \overline{AX}$ by the Reflexive Property of Congruence. Therefore, △BAX ≅ △CAX by the AAS Congruence Criterion.

So, $\overline{AB} \cong \overline{AC}$ by   CPCTC.

Chapter 4   180   Lesson 9

3 Prove the Converse of the Isosceles Triangle Theorem.

Questioning Strategies

• Is it possible to prove that $\triangle BAX \cong \triangle CAX$ by the ASA Congruence Criterion? Why or why not? **No; you do not yet know that $\overline{AB} \cong \overline{AC}$. This is what you are trying to prove, so you cannot assume it is true in the proof.**

Avoid Common Errors

In this lesson, students learn a fourth congruence criterion, the AAS Congruence Criterion. Having seen this new congruence criterion, students may assume that there is an SSA Congruence Criterion. Be sure students understand that SSA conditions do not guarantee a unique triangle, and tell them they will learn more about this in Lesson 6-6 when they study the Law of Sines.

MATHEMATICAL PRACTICE

Highlighting the Standards

Exercise 8 offers an opportunity to address Standard 1 (Make sense of problems and persevere in solving them). Specifically, students will need to look for entry points in order to get started solving the problem. Encourage students to identify information that is needed to solve part (a) of the problem, and suggest that they highlight or underline this information. Later, students can reread the problem to identify additional information that is needed for part (b).

Essential Question

What special relationships exist among the sides and angles of isosceles triangles?

Two sides of a triangle are congruent (that is, the triangle is isosceles) if and only if the angles opposite those sides are congruent.

Summarize

Have students make a graphic organizer to summarize the Isosceles Triangle Theorem and its converse. A sample is shown below.

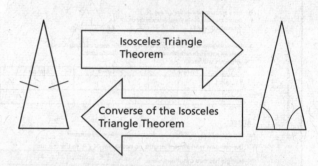

PRACTICE

Exercises 1–3: Students apply the Isosceles Triangle Theorem.

Exercises 4–6: Students apply the Converse of the Isosceles Triangle Theorem.

Exercise 7: Students apply what they have learned to solve a reasoning problem.

Exercise 8: Students apply what they have learned to solve an open-ended real-world problem.

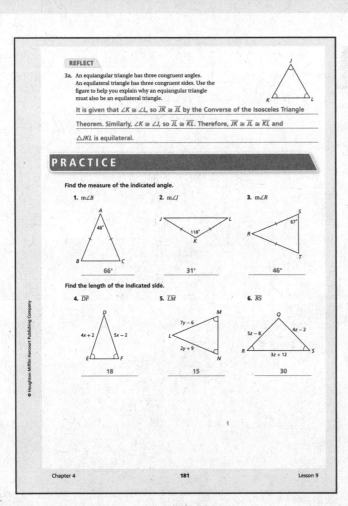

REFLECT

3a. An equiangular triangle has three congruent angles. An equilateral triangle has three congruent sides. Use the figure to help you explain why an equiangular triangle must also be an equilateral triangle.

It is given that $\angle K \cong \angle L$, so $\overline{JK} \cong \overline{JL}$ by the Converse of the Isosceles Triangle

Theorem. Similarly, $\angle K \cong \angle J$, so $\overline{JL} \cong \overline{KL}$. Therefore, $\overline{JK} \cong \overline{JL} \cong \overline{KL}$ and

$\triangle JKL$ is equilateral.

PRACTICE

Find the measure of the indicated angle.

1. $m\angle B$
66°

2. $m\angle J$
31°

3. $m\angle R$
46°

Find the length of the indicated side.

4. $\overline{DF}$
18

5. $\overline{LM}$
15

6. $\overline{RS}$
30

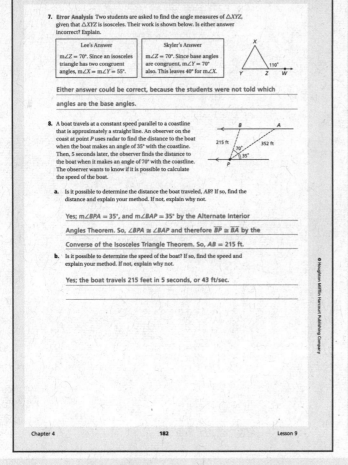

7. **Error Analysis** Two students are asked to find the angle measures of $\triangle XYZ$, given that $\triangle XYZ$ is isosceles. Their work is shown below. Is either answer incorrect? Explain.

Lee's Answer	Skyler's Answer
$m\angle Z = 70°$. Since an isosceles triangle has two congruent angles, $m\angle X = m\angle Y = 55°$.	$m\angle Z = 70°$. Since base angles are congruent, $m\angle Y = 70°$ also. This leaves 40° for $m\angle X$.

Either answer could be correct, because the students were not told which

angles are the base angles.

8. A boat travels at a constant speed parallel to a coastline that is approximately a straight line. An observer on the coast at point P uses radar to find the distance to the boat when the boat makes an angle of 35° with the coastline. Then, 5 seconds later, the observer finds the distance to the boat when it makes an angle of 70° with the coastline. The observer wants to know if it is possible to calculate the speed of the boat.

a. Is it possible to determine the distance the boat traveled, AB? If so, find the distance and explain your method. If not, explain why not.

Yes; $m\angle BPA = 35°$, and $m\angle BAP = 35°$ by the Alternate Interior

Angles Theorem. So, $\angle BPA \cong \angle BAP$ and therefore $\overline{BP} \cong \overline{BA}$ by the

Converse of the Isosceles Triangle Theorem. So, $AB = 215$ ft.

b. Is it possible to determine the speed of the boat? If so, find the speed and explain your method. If not, explain why not.

Yes; the boat travels 215 feet in 5 seconds, or 43 ft/sec.

ADDITIONAL PRACTICE AND PROBLEM SOLVING

Assign these pages to help your students practice and apply important lesson concepts. For additional exercises, see the Student Edition.

Answers

Additional Practice

1. Possible answer: It is given that $\overline{HI}$ is congruent to $\overline{HJ}$, so $\angle I$ must be congruent to $\angle J$ by the Isosceles Triangle Theorem. $\angle IKH$ and $\angle JKH$ are both right angles by the definition of perpendicular lines, and all right angles are congruent. Thus by AAS, $\triangle HKI$ is congruent to $\triangle HKJ$. $\overline{IK}$ is congruent to $\overline{KJ}$ by CPCTC, so $\overline{HK}$ bisects $\overline{IJ}$ by the definition of segment bisector.

2. 58.1 ft
3. 45°
4. $\sqrt{2}$
5. 36 or 9
6. 76°
7. $\frac{4}{3}$
8. 10
9. 30°
10. 89

Problem Solving

1. 14 in.
2. 40°
3. 11 ft; $m\angle GJH = 72° - 36° = 36°$. $m\angle GHJ = 36°$ by Alt. Int. ∠s Thm. By Converse of Isosceles Triangle Theorem, $GJ = GH = 11$ ft.
4. D
5. G
6. C
7. H

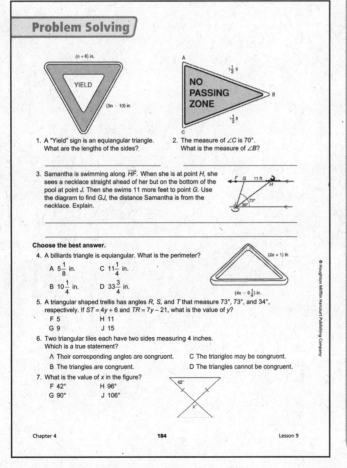

Additional Practice

Name_____ Class_____ Date_____

4-9

An altitude of a triangle is a perpendicular segment from a vertex to the line containing the opposite side. Write a paragraph proof that the altitude to the base of an isosceles triangle bisects the base.

1. **Given:** $\overline{HI} \cong \overline{HJ}, \overline{HK} \perp \overline{IJ}$

   Prove: $\overline{HK}$ bisects $\overline{IJ}$.

2. An *obelisk* is a tall, thin, four-sided monument that tapers to a pyramidal top. The most well-known obelisk to Americans is the Washington Monument on the National Mall in Washington, D.C. Each face of the pyramidal top of the Washington Monument is an isosceles triangle. The height of each triangle is 55.5 feet, and the base of each triangle measures 34.4 feet. Find the length, to the nearest tenth of a foot, of one of the two equal legs of the triangle. _____

Find each value.

3. $m\angle X =$ _____

4. $BC =$ _____

5. $PQ =$ _____

6. $m\angle K =$ _____

7. $t =$ _____

8. $n =$ _____

9. $m\angle A =$ _____

10. $x =$ _____

Chapter 4   183   Lesson 9

Problem Solving

1. A "Yield" sign is an equiangular triangle. What are the lengths of the sides?

2. The measure of $\angle C$ is 70°. What is the measure of $\angle B$?

3. Samantha is swimming along $\overline{HF}$. When she is at point H, she sees a necklace straight ahead of her but on the bottom of the pool at point J. Then she swims 11 more feet to point G. Use the diagram to find GJ, the distance Samantha is from the necklace. Explain.

_____

Choose the best answer.

4. A billiards triangle is equiangular. What is the perimeter?

   A $5\frac{1}{8}$ in.   C $11\frac{1}{4}$ in.

   B $10\frac{1}{4}$ in.   D $33\frac{3}{4}$ in.

5. A triangular shaped trellis has angles R, S, and T that measure 73°, 73°, and 34°, respectively. If $ST = 4y + 6$ and $TR = 7y - 21$, what is the value of y?

   F 5   H 11

   G 9   J 15

6. Two triangular tiles each have two sides measuring 4 inches. Which is a true statement?

   A Their corresponding angles are congruent.   C The triangles may be congruent.

   B The triangles are congruent.   D The triangles cannot be congruent.

7. What is the value of x in the figure?

   F 42°   H 96°

   G 90°   J 106°

Chapter 4   184   Lesson 9

© Houghton Mifflin Harcourt Publishing Company

Notes

© Houghton Mifflin Harcourt Publishing Company

This page provides students with the opportunity to apply concepts from the Common Core in real-world problem situations. There are three different levels of performance tasks:

⭐ **Novice:** These are short word problems that require students to apply the math they have learned in straightforward, real-world situations.

⭐⭐ **Apprentice:** These are more involved problems that guide students step-by-step through more complex tasks. These exercises include more complicated reasoning, writing, and open-ended elements.

⭐⭐⭐ **Expert:** These are open-ended, non-routine problems that, instead of stepping the students through, ask them to choose their own methods for solving and justify their answers and reasoning.

Sample answers

1. Yes; he needs at least one more piece of information, for example the measure of the third side to satisfy SSS or the measure of the angle between the two sides he measured to satisfy SAS.

2. Yes; the third angle of the green tabletop measures 95°. The third angle of the blue tabletop measures 35°. The shortest side of each measures 30 inches. All pairs of corresponding angles are congruent and a pair of corresponding sides is congruent. The tabletops are congruent by AAS or ASA.

3. Scoring Guide:

Task	Possible points
a	1 point for correctly stating that, to prove $\overline{AB} \parallel \overline{DC}$, use alternate interior angles, either $\angle A \cong \angle C$ or $\angle B \cong D$
b	2 points for writing a solid plan for proof. Possible answer: First prove $\triangle BKA \cong \triangle DKC$ by SAS, and then use CPCTC to prove $\angle A \cong \angle C$.
c	3 points for correctly proving the lines parallel: 1) $\overline{AK} \cong \overline{CK}$ and $\overline{BK} \cong \overline{DK}$ (def. of bisect); 2) $\angle AKB \cong \angle CKD$(vert. $\angle s \cong$); 3) $\triangle BKA \cong \triangle DKC$ (SAS); 4) $\angle A \cong \angle C$ (CPCTC); 5) $\overline{AB} \parallel \overline{DC}$ ($\cong$ alt. int. $\angle s \Rightarrow \parallel$ lines)

Total possible points: 6

CHAPTER 4

Performance Tasks

COMMON CORE
CC.9-12.G.CO.10
CC.9-12.G.SRT.5
CC.9-12.G.GPE.4

⭐ **1.** The Pep Club wants to duplicate the school pennant. The pennant is in the shape of a triangle. Two of the sides have the same measure of 22 inches. Does the club need to make any other measurements to create the duplicate? If so, what does the club need to measure? Explain your answer.

⭐ **2.** Two angles of a triangular tabletop measure 35° and 50°. The shortest side of the table measures 30 inches. Two angles of a second triangular tabletop measure 50° and 95°. The shortest side of this tabletop also measures 30 inches. Are the two tabletops congruent? Justify your answer.

⭐ **3.** In the diagram, $\overline{AC}$ bisects $\overline{BD}$ at K and $\overline{BD}$ bisects $\overline{AC}$ at K.

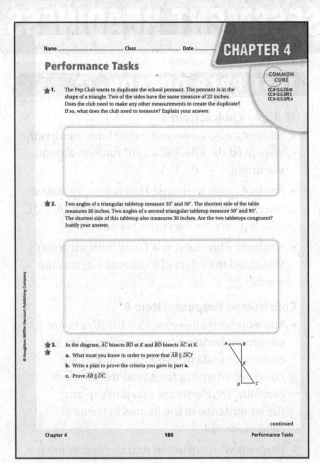

　　a. What must you know in order to prove that $\overline{AB} \parallel \overline{DC}$?

　　b. Write a plan to prove the criteria you gave in part **a.**

　　c. Prove $\overline{AB} \parallel \overline{DC}$.

continued

⭐ **4.** The vertices of a triangle are $X(2, 2)$, $Y(5, 6)$, and $Z(8, 2)$.

　　a. Prove that point Y lies on the perpendicular bisector of $\overline{XZ}$.

　　b. After a transformation, the images of points X and Z are $X'(-2, -2)$ and $Z'(-2, -8)$. The transformation preserves distance and angle. Name two possibilities for the coordinates of point Y'.

　　c. Choose either of the possibilities for the location of point Y' you named in part **b.** Use it to prove that $\triangle XYZ \cong \triangle X'Y'Z'$.

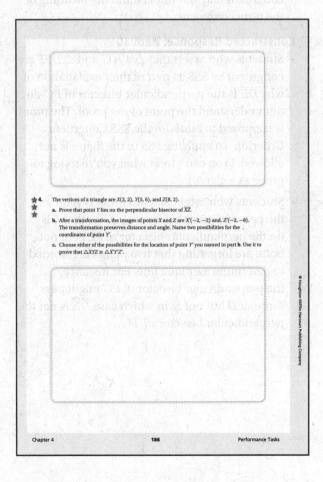

4. Scoring Guide:

Task	Possible points
a	2 points for giving a correct proof, for example: By the Distance Formula, $XY = \sqrt{(5-2)^2 + (6-2)^2} = 5$ and $ZY = \sqrt{(5-8)^2 + (6-2)^2} = 5$, so Y must be on the perp. bisector of $\overline{XZ}$.
b	1 point for finding $(2, -5)$, and 1 point for finding $(-6, -5)$
c	2 points for a correct proof, for example: Use the Distance Formula to show $XY = X'Y' = 5$, $ZY = Z'Y' = 5$, and $XZ = X'Z' = 6$, so $\triangle XYZ \cong X'Y'Z'$ by SSS.

Total possible points: 6

COMMON CORE CORRELATION

Standard	Items
CC.9-12.G.CO.5	4
CC.9-12.G.CO.6	8
CC.9-12.G.CO.7	9
CC.9-12.G.CO.8	10
CC.9-12.G.CO.10	2
CC.9-12.G.SRT.5	1, 3, 7
CC.9-12.G.GPE.4	5
CC.9-12.G.GPE.7*	6

TEST PREP DOCTOR ⊕

Multiple Choice: Item 4

- Students who answered **F** may have incorrectly visualized the effect of a 180° rotation around the origin.

- Students who answered **H** may have mistaken the given vector, $\langle -2, 0 \rangle$, for the vector $\langle 0, -2 \rangle$, which produces the correct result.

- Students who answered **J** may have incorrectly visualized the effect of a reflection across the x-axis.

Constructed Response: Item 8

- Students who answered that the figures are congruent because corresponding sides are congruent and corresponding angles are congruent may not have read the problem carefully. (Students are asked to explain the congruence of the figures in terms of *rigid motions*.)

- Students who answered that the figures are not congruent may not understand the meaning of the term *congruent*.

Constructed Response: Item 10

- Students who assert that $\triangle A'B'C'$ and $\triangle DEF$ are congruent by SSS as part of their explanation of why $\overline{DE}$ is the perpendicular bisector of $\overline{FC'}$ do not understand the point of the proof. The proof is supposed to *establish* the SSS Congruence Criterion, so applying SSS to the figure is not allowed. (You can't treat what you're trying to prove as a given.)

- Students who establish either that D is on the perpendicular bisector of $\overline{FC'}$ or that E is on the perpendicular bisector of $\overline{FC'}$, but not both, are forgetting that two points are needed to determine a unique line. For instance, the perpendicular bisector of $\overline{FC'}$ might pass through D but not E, in which case $\overline{DE}$ is not the perpendicular bisector of $\overline{FC'}$.

CHAPTER 4 COMMON CORE ASSESSMENT READINESS

Name _____ Class _____ Date _____

MULTIPLE CHOICE

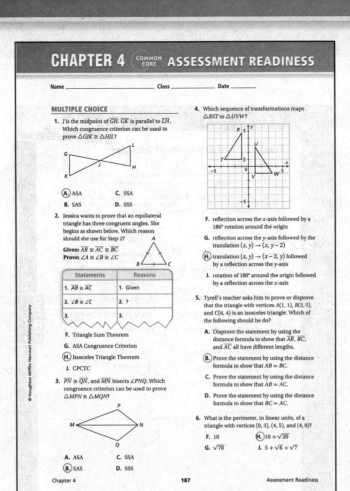

1. *J* is the midpoint of $\overline{GH}$. $\overline{GK}$ is parallel to $\overline{LH}$. Which congruence criterion can be used to prove $\triangle GJK \cong \triangle HJL$?

- (A.) ASA
- B. SAS
- C. SSA
- D. SSS

2. Jessica wants to prove that an equilateral triangle has three congruent angles. She begins as shown below. Which reason should she use for Step 2?

Given: $\overline{AB} \cong \overline{AC} \cong \overline{BC}$
Prove: $\angle A \cong \angle B \cong \angle C$

Statements	Reasons
1. $\overline{AB} \cong \overline{AC}$	1. Given
2. $\angle B \cong \angle C$	2. ?
3.	3.

- F. Triangle Sum Theorem
- G. ASA Congruence Criterion
- (H.) Isosceles Triangle Theorem
- J. CPCTC

3. $\overline{PN} \cong \overline{QN}$, and $\overline{MN}$ bisects $\angle PNQ$. Which congruence criterion can be used to prove $\triangle MPN \cong \triangle MQN$?

- A. ASA
- (B.) SAS
- C. SSA
- D. SSS

4. Which sequence of transformations maps $\triangle RST$ to $\triangle UVW$?

- F. reflection across the *x*-axis followed by a 180° rotation around the origin
- G. reflection across the *y*-axis followed by the translation $(x, y) \rightarrow (x, y - 2)$
- (H.) translation $(x, y) \rightarrow (x - 2, y)$ followed by a reflection across the *y*-axis
- J. rotation of 180° around the origin followed by a reflection across the *x*-axis

5. Tyrell's teacher asks him to prove or disprove that the triangle with vertices $A(1, 1)$, $B(2, 5)$, and $C(6, 4)$ is an isosceles triangle. Which of the following should he do?

- A. Disprove the statement by using the distance formula to show that $\overline{AB}$, $\overline{BC}$, and $\overline{AC}$ all have different lengths.
- (B.) Prove the statement by using the distance formula to show that $AB = BC$.
- C. Prove the statement by using the distance formula to show that $AB = AC$.
- D. Prove the statement by using the distance formula to show that $BC = AC$.

6. What is the perimeter, in linear units, of a triangle with vertices $(0, 3)$, $(4, 5)$, and $(4, 0)$?

- F. 10
- G. $\sqrt{70}$
- (H.) $10 + \sqrt{20}$
- J. $5 + \sqrt{6} + \sqrt{7}$

CONSTRUCTED RESPONSE

7. To find the distance *AB* across a pond, you locate points as follows.

Starting at *A* and walking along a straight path, you walk 28 feet and put a marker at *C*. Then you walk 28 feet farther and put a marker at *D*.

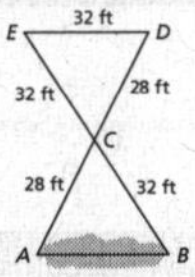

Starting at *B*, you walk to *C*, measuring the distance you walked (32 feet). Then you walk 32 feet farther and put a marker at *E*. Finally, you measure the distance from *D* to *E*, as shown. Explain how to use this information to find *AB*.

$\triangle ABC \cong \triangle DEC$ by SAS, so $AB = 32$ ft
by CPCTC.

8. Determine whether the figures shown below are congruent. Explain your answer using rigid motions.

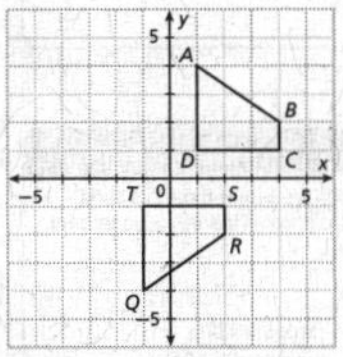

The figures are congruent because
there is a sequence of rigid motions
(translation $(x, y) \rightarrow (x + 2, y)$, then
reflection across the *x*-axis) that maps
QRST to *ABCD*.

9. Given that $\triangle JKL \cong \triangle MNP$, use the definition of congruence in terms of rigid motions to explain why $\overline{KL}$ must be congruent to $\overline{NP}$.

There are rigid motions that map
$\triangle JKL$ to $\triangle MNP$. This sequence maps
$\overline{KL}$ onto $\overline{NP}$. By the definition of
congruence, $\overline{KL} \cong \overline{NP}$.

10. You are writing a proof that the SSS Congruence Criterion follows from the definition of congruence in terms of rigid motions. You start with two triangles, $\triangle ABC$ and $\triangle DEF$, such that $\overline{AB} \cong \overline{DE}$, $\overline{BC} \cong \overline{EF}$, and $\overline{AC} \cong \overline{DF}$.

You use the fact that $\overline{AB} \cong \overline{DE}$ to conclude that there is a sequence of rigid motions that maps $\overline{AB}$ onto $\overline{DE}$. Applying this sequence of rigid motions to $\triangle ABC$ leads to this figure.

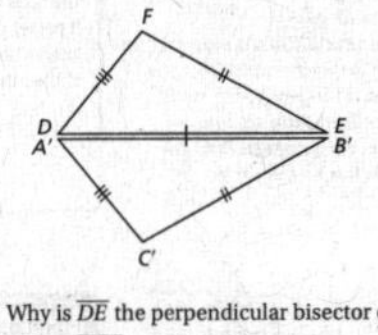

Why is $\overline{DE}$ the perpendicular bisector of $\overline{FC'}$?

Since $\overline{A'C'} \cong \overline{DF}$, D lies on the
perpendicular bisector of $\overline{FC'}$ by the
Perpendicular Bisector Theorem.
Similarly, $\overline{B'C'} \cong \overline{EF}$, so E lies on
the perpendicular bisector of $\overline{FC'}$.
Therefore, $\overline{DE}$ is the perpendicular
bisector of $\overline{FC'}$.

© Houghton Mifflin Harcourt Publishing Company

Properties and Attributes of Triangles

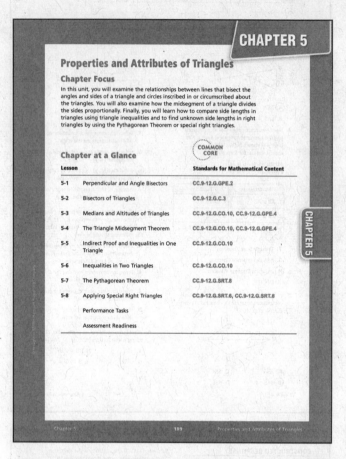

Properties and Attributes of Triangles

CHAPTER 5

Chapter Focus

In this unit, you will examine the relationships between lines that bisect the angles and sides of a triangle and circles inscribed in or circumscribed about the triangles. You will also examine how the midsegment of a triangle divides the sides proportionally. Finally, you will learn how to compare side lengths in triangles using triangle inequalities and to find unknown side lengths in right triangles by using the Pythagorean Theorem or special right triangles.

Chapter at a Glance

COMMON CORE

Lesson		Standards for Mathematical Content
5-1	Perpendicular and Angle Bisectors	CC.9-12.G.GPE.2
5-2	Bisectors of Triangles	CC.9-12.G.C.3
5-3	Medians and Altitudes of Triangles	CC.9-12.G.CO.10, CC.9-12.G.GPE.4
5-4	The Triangle Midsegment Theorem	CC.9-12.G.CO.10, CC.9-12.G.GPE.4
5-5	Indirect Proof and Inequalities in One Triangle	CC.9-12.G.CO.10
5-6	Inequalities in Two Triangles	CC.9-12.G.CO.10
5-7	The Pythagorean Theorem	CC.9-12.G.SRT.8
5-8	Applying Special Right Triangles	CC.9-12.G.SRT.6, CC.9-12.G.SRT.8
	Performance Tasks	
	Assessment Readiness	

Chapter 5   189   Properties and Attributes of Triangles

COMMON CORE PROFESSIONAL DEVELOPMENT **CC.9-12.G.C.3**

Students use paper folding and construction to explore relationships inside and outside of a triangle. For example, by induction students may be convinced that perpendicular bisectors of a triangle are concurrent at a circumcenter, which is the center of a circumscribed circle. Although this may be convincing, remind students that inductive reasoning does not constitute a proof. Likewise, students also see that the medians of a triangle are concurrent at the centroid, which is considered a physical balance point having great scientific properties.

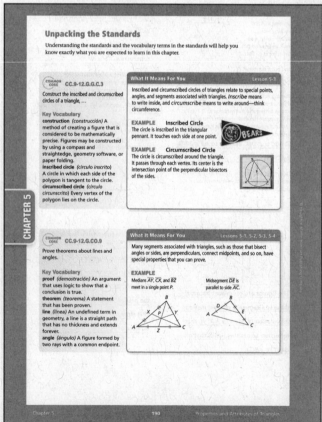

Unpacking the Standards

Understanding the standards and the vocabulary terms in the standards will help you know exactly what you are expected to learn in this chapter.

COMMON CORE CC.9-12.G.G.C.3

Construct the inscribed and circumscribed circles of a triangle, ...

Key Vocabulary
construction *(construcción)* A method of creating a figure that is considered to be mathematically precise. Figures may be constructed by using a compass and straightedge, geometry software, or paper folding.
inscribed circle *(círculo inscrito)* A circle in which each side of the polygon is tangent to the circle.
circumscribed circle *(círculo circunscrito)* Every vertex of the polygon lies on the circle.

What It Means For You   Lesson 5-3

Inscribed and circumscribed circles of triangles relate to special points, angles, and segments associated with triangles. *Inscribe* means to write inside, and *circumscribe* means to write around—think circumference.

EXAMPLE   Inscribed Circle
The circle is inscribed in the triangular pennant. It touches each side at one point.

EXAMPLE   Circumscribed Circle
The circle is circumscribed around the triangle. It passes through each vertex. Its center is the intersection point of the perpendicular bisectors of the sides.

COMMON CORE CC.9-12.G.CO.9

Prove theorems about lines and angles.

Key Vocabulary
proof *(demostración)* An argument that uses logic to show that a conclusion is true.
theorem *(teorema)* A statement that has been proven.
line *(línea)* An undefined term in geometry, a line is a straight path that has no thickness and extends forever.
angle *(ángulo)* A figure formed by two rays with a common endpoint.

What It Means For You   Lessons 5-1, 5-2, 5-3, 5-4

Many segments associated with triangles, such as those that bisect angles or sides, are perpendiculars, connect midpoints, and so on, have special properties that you can prove.

EXAMPLE
Medians $\overline{AY}$, $\overline{CX}$, and $\overline{BZ}$ meet in a single point P.

Midsegment $\overline{DE}$ is parallel to side $\overline{AC}$.

Chapter 5   190   Properties and Attributes of Triangles

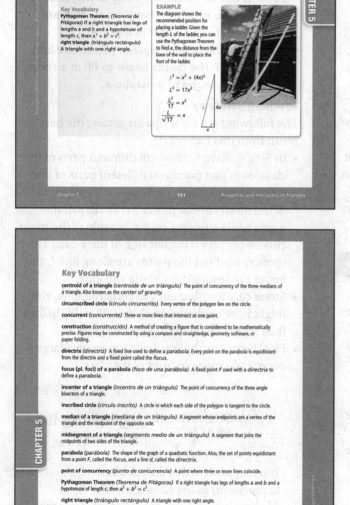

CC.9-12.G.SRT.8*

Students extend previous knowledge about the Pythagorean Theorem in this chapter. The Pythagorean Theorem describes a relationship that has been known for thousands of years, and there are many different proofs of it. In this chapter, students use an area proof to establish the validity of the Pythagorean Theorem, and then use it and its converse to solve problems. Students extend the Pythagorean Theorem further to establish through sound logical argument that you can classify a triangle as acute or obtuse given only its side lengths.

CHAPTER 5

Left panel content:

COMMON CORE CC.9-12.G.CO.10
Prove theorems about triangles.

Key Vocabulary
proof *(demostración)* An argument that uses logic to show that a conclusion is true.
theorem *(teorema)* A statement that has been proven.
triangle *(triángulo)* A three-sided polygon.

What It Means For You Lessons 5-3, 5-4, 5-5, 5-6
You can prove theorems about the relationships among side lengths and angle measures within a single triangle and between two or more triangles.

EXAMPLE Relationships within a triangle
Because $m\angle PSQ = 51°$ by the Triangle Sum Theorem, it is the smallest angle in $\triangle PSQ$. So, the opposite side, $\overline{PQ}$, is the shortest side of $\triangle PSQ$.

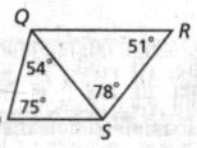

EXAMPLE Relationships between triangles
By the Hinge Theorem, if $m\angle B > m\angle E$ in the two triangles shown with congruent sides as marked, then $AC > DF$.

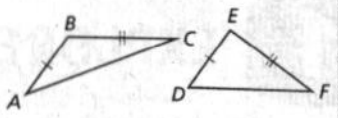

COMMON CORE CC.9-12.G.SRT.8
Use ... the Pythagorean Theorem to solve right triangles in applied problems.

Key Vocabulary
Pythagorean Theorem *(Teorema de Pitágoras)* If a right triangle has legs of lengths a and b and a hypotenuse of length c, then $a^2 + b^2 = c^2$.
right triangle *(triángulo rectángulo)* A triangle with one right angle.

What It Means For You Lessons 5-7, 5-8
You can use the relationship between the side lengths of a right triangle to solve real-world problems.

EXAMPLE
The diagram shows the recommended position for placing a ladder. Given the length L of the ladder, you can use the Pythagorean Theorem to find x, the distance from the base of the wall to place the foot of the ladder.

$$L^2 = x^2 + (4x)^2$$
$$L^2 = 17x^2$$
$$\frac{L^2}{17} = x^2$$
$$\frac{L}{\sqrt{17}} = x$$

Chapter 5   191   Properties and Attributes of Triangles

Second panel content:

Key Vocabulary

centroid of a triangle *(centroide de un triángulo)* The point of concurrency of the three medians of a triangle. Also known as the *center of gravity*.

circumscribed circle *(círculo circunscrito)* Every vertex of the polygon lies on the circle.

concurrent *(concurrente)* Three or more lines that intersect at one point.

construction *(construcción)* A method of creating a figure that is considered to be mathematically precise. Figures may be constructed by using a compass and straightedge, geometry software, or paper folding.

directrix *(directriz)* A fixed line used to define a *parabola*. Every point on the parabola is equidistant from the directrix and a fixed point called the *focus*.

focus (pl. foci) of a parabola *(foco de una parábola)* A fixed point F used with a *directrix* to define a *parabola*.

incenter of a triangle *(incentro de un triángulo)* The point of concurrency of the three angle bisectors of a triangle.

inscribed circle *(círculo inscrito)* A circle in which each side of the polygon is tangent to the circle.

median of a triangle *(mediana de un triángulo)* A segment whose endpoints are a vertex of the triangle and the midpoint of the opposite side.

midsegment of a triangle *(segmento medio de un triángulo)* A segment that joins the midpoints of two sides of the triangle.

parabola *(parábola)* The shape of the graph of a quadratic function. Also, the set of points equidistant from a point F, called the *focus*, and a line d, called the *directrix*.

point of concurrency *(punto de concurrencia)* A point where three or more lines coincide.

Pythagorean Theorem *(Teorema de Pitágoras)* If a right triangle has legs of lengths a and b and a hypotenuse of length c, then $a^2 + b^2 = c^2$.

right triangle *(triángulo rectángulo)* A triangle with one right angle.

Chapter 5   192   Properties and Attributes of Triangles

CHAPTER 5

Perpendicular and Angle Bisectors
Extension: Perpendicular Bisectors and Parabolas

Essential question: *How do you write the equation of a parabola given its focus and directrix?*

COMMON CORE Standards for Mathematical Content

CC.9-12.G.GPE.2 Derive the equation of a parabola given a focus and directrix.

Vocabulary
parabola

focus

directrix

Prerequisites
Distance formula

Math Background
A *locus* is a collection of points that share a property or satisfy a given condition. For instance, a circle may be defined as the locus of points in a plane that are a fixed distance from a given point. In this lesson, students explore parabolas. A parabola is the locus of points in a plane that are equidistant from a given point and a given line.

INTRODUCE

Begin by discussing the idea of the distance from a point to a line. Draw a point, *P*, and a line, *m*, on the board and ask students how they would define the distance between point *P* and line *m*. Students may mention that the distance should be the length of a line segment from *P* to line *m*. Explain that there are infinitely many such line segments, some of which are shown in the figure. Tell students that the distance is defined to be the length of the *shortest* segment from *P* to line *m*. This is the perpendicular segment from *P* to line *m*.

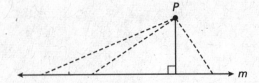

TEACH

1 EXPLORE

Materials: compass, straightedge

Questioning Strategies
- Will everyone in the class construct the same point in this investigation? Why or why not? No; there are infinitely many points that are equidistant from point *P* to line ℓ.
- What happens as your teacher plots more and more points? The points begin to fill in a curve that has the shape of a parabola.

Teaching Strategy
The following are a few tips for getting the best result from this Explore.
- In Step A, have students in different parts of the classroom plot points on different parts of line ℓ. For example, have students on the right side of the room choose points to the right of the *y*-axis while students on the left side of the room choose points on the left side of the *y*-axis. The more spread out the points are along line ℓ, the better the resulting parabola will look.
- Stress care and accuracy in constructions. You might have students check that $PX = PQ$ before they report their coordinates for point *X*.
- Plot the points that students report on a large coordinate plane in front of the class.

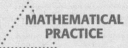

MATHEMATICAL PRACTICE | **Highlighting the Standards**

You may wish to discuss Standard 6 (Attend to precision) as the class completes this Explore. In particular, the standard states that students should "express numerical answers with a degree of precision appropriate for the problem context." To that end, ask students whether it would make sense for a student to report the approximate coordinates of his or her point *x* as (1, 0.793). Then discuss levels of precision that do make sense for this activity.

Name _____ Class _____ Date _____

5-1

Perpendicular and Angle Bisectors
Extension: Perpendicular Bisectors and Parabolas

Essential question: *How do you write the equation of a parabola given its focus and directrix?*

Video Tutor

The distance from a point to a line is the length of the perpendicular segment from the point to the line. In the figure, the distance from point A to line ℓ is AB.

You will use the idea of the distance from a point to a line below.

CC.9-12.G.GPE.2

1 EXPLORE   Creating a Parabola

Follow these instructions to plot a point. You will report the approximate coordinates of the point to your teacher, who will create a graph consisting of all points from everyone in the class. Be sure to work as accurately as possible.

   A   Choose a point on line ℓ. Plot a point Q at this location.

   B   Using a straightedge, draw a perpendicular to ℓ that passes through point Q. Label this line m.

   C   Use the straightedge to draw $\overline{PQ}$. Then use a compass and straightedge to construct the perpendicular bisector of $\overline{PQ}$.

   D   Plot a point X where the perpendicular bisector intersects line m.

   E   Write the approximate coordinates of point X and report the coordinates to your teacher.
     Possible answer: $\left(4, 1\frac{1}{3}\right)$

Sample construction shown.

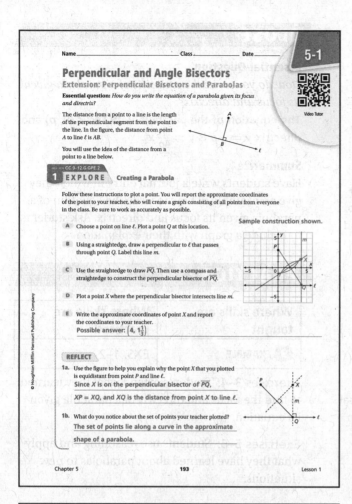

REFLECT

1a. Use the figure to help you explain why the point X that you plotted is equidistant from point P and line ℓ.
Since X is on the perpendicular bisector of $\overline{PQ}$,
$XP = XQ$, and XQ is the distance from point X to line ℓ.

1b. What do you notice about the set of points your teacher plotted?
The set of points lie along a curve in the approximate shape of a parabola.

Chapter 5   193   Lesson 1

A **parabola** is the set of all points P in a plane that are equidistant from a given point, called the **focus**, and a given line, called the **directrix**.

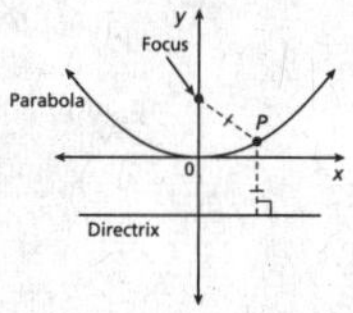

To derive the general equation of a parabola, you can use the above definition, the distance formula, and the idea that the distance from a point to a line is the length of the perpendicular segment from the point to the line.

CC.9-12.G.GPE.2

2 EXPLORE   Deriving the Equation of a Parabola

   A   Let the focus of the parabola be $F(0, p)$ and let the directrix be the line $y = -p$. Let P be a point on the parabola with coordinates (x, y).

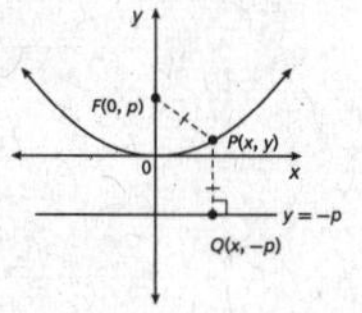

   B   Let Q be the point of intersection of the perpendicular from P and the directrix. Then the coordinates of Q are $(x, -p)$.

   C   By the definition of a parabola, $FP = QP$.

By the distance formula,
$FP = \sqrt{(x-0)^2 + (y-p)^2} = \sqrt{x^2 + (y-p)^2}$
and $QP = \sqrt{(x-x)^2 + (y-(-p))^2} = \sqrt{0 + (y+p)^2} = |y+p|$.

$\sqrt{x^2 + (y-p)^2}$ =	$\|y+p\|$	Set FP equal to QP.
$x^2 + (y-p)^2$ =	$\|y+p\|^2$	Square both sides.
$x^2 + y^2 - 2py + p^2$ =	$y^2 + 2py + p^2$	Expand the squared terms.
$x^2 - 2py$ =	$2py$	Subtract y^2 and p^2 from both sides.
x^2 =	$4py$	Add $2py$ to both sides.
$\frac{1}{4p}x^2$ =	y	Solve for y.

REFLECT

2a. Explain how the value of p determines whether the parabola opens up or down.
When p is positive, the focus is on the positive y-axis and the directrix is a horizontal line below the x-axis, so the parabola opens up; when p is negative, the focus is on the negative y-axis and the directrix is a horizontal line above the x-axis, so the parabola opens down.

2b. Explain why the origin $(0, 0)$ is always a point on a parabola with focus $F(0, p)$ and directrix $y = -p$.
The distance from $(0, 0)$ to $(0, p)$ is $|p|$, and the distance from $(0, 0)$ to the directrix is also $|p|$, so $(0, 0)$ is on the parabola by definition.

Chapter 5   194   Lesson 1

Questioning Strategies

- How can you find the distance QP without using the distance formula? **Because $\overline{QP}$ is vertical, you can find the length of the segment by subtracting the y-coordinates of Q and P and taking the absolute value of the result.**

- How do you know that the origin is a point on this parabola? **Its distance from the focus, $(0, p)$ is $|p|$ and its distance from the directrix, $y = -p$, is also $|p|$, so it is equidistant from the focus and the directrix.**

3 EXAMPLE

Questioning Strategies

- What does the value of p tell you about the parabola? **Because p is negative, the parabola will open down.**

- What is the domain and range for the function described by this parabola? **The domain is all real numbers; the range is all real numbers less than or equal to zero.**

EXTRA EXAMPLE

Write the equation of the parabola with focus $(0, -1)$ and directrix $y = 1$. Then, graph the parabola.

$y = -\frac{1}{4}x^2$

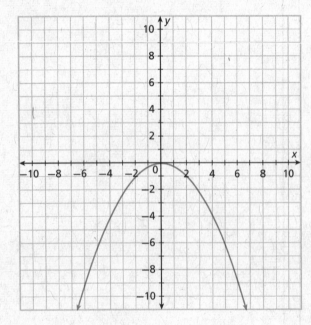

CLOSE

Essential Question

How do you write the equation of a parabola given its focus and directrix?

The equation of the parabola with focus $(0, p)$ and directrix $y = -p$ is $y = \frac{1}{4p}x^2$.

Summarize

Have students write a journal entry in which they give an example of how to write the equation of a parabola given its focus and directrix. Ask students to include a graph with their explanation.

PRACTICE

Where skills are taught	Where skills are practiced
3 EXAMPLE	EXS. 1–2

Exercises 3–4: Students extend what they learned to find the focus and directrix of a parabola given its equation.

Exercises 5–6: Students use reasoning and apply what they have learned about parabolas to new situations.

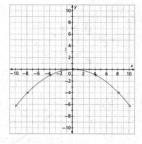

CC.9-12.G.GPE.2

3 EXAMPLE Writing the Equation of a Parabola

Write the equation of the parabola with focus $(0, -4)$ and directrix $y = 4$.
Then graph the parabola.

A The focus of the parabola is $(0, p)$, so $p = $ _____ -4 _____.

The general equation of a parabola is $y = \frac{1}{4p}x^2$.

So, the equation of this parabola is _____ $y = -\frac{1}{16}x^2$ _____

B To graph the parabola, complete the table of
values. Then plot points and draw the curve.

x	y
-8	-4
-4	-1
0	0
4	-1
8	-4

REFLECT

3a. The *vertex* of a parabola is the midpoint of the perpendicular segment from the
focus to the directrix. What is the vertex of the parabola you graphed?

$(0, 0)$

3b. Does your graph lie above or below the *x*-axis? Why does this make sense based on
the parabola's equation?

Below; x^2 is always greater than or equal to 0, so $-\frac{1}{16}x^2$ is always less than or

equal to 0. Therefore, the function's *y*-values are always less than or equal to 0.

3c. Describe any symmetry your graph has. Why does this make sense based on the
parabola's equation?

The parabola has reflection symmetry, with the *y*-axis as the line of symmetry.

This makes sense because every value of *x* and its opposite have the same *y*-value:

$-\frac{1}{16}x^2 = -\frac{1}{16}(-x)^2$.

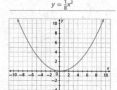

© Houghton Mifflin Harcourt Publishing Company

PRACTICE

Write the equation of the parabola with the given focus and directrix. Then
graph the parabola.

1. focus: $(0, 2)$; directrix: $y = -2$

$y = \frac{1}{8}x^2$

2. focus: $(0, -5)$; directrix: $y = 5$

$y = -\frac{1}{20}x^2$

Find the focus and directrix of the parabola with the given equation.

3. $y = -\frac{1}{24}x^2$

focus: $(0, -6)$; directrix: $y = 6$

4. $y = 2x^2$

focus: $\left(0, \frac{1}{8}\right)$; directrix: $y = -\frac{1}{8}$

5. Complete the table by writing the equation of each parabola. Then use a
calculator to graph the equations in the same window to help you make a
conjecture: What happens to the graph of a parabola as the focus and directrix
move apart?

Focus	(0, 1)	(0, 2)	(0, 3)	(0, 4)
Directrix	$y = -1$	$y = -2$	$y = -3$	$y = -4$
Equation	$y = \frac{1}{4}x^2$	$y = \frac{1}{8}x^2$	$y = \frac{1}{12}x^2$	$y = \frac{1}{16}x^2$

As the focus and directrix move apart, the parabola is vertically compressed.

6. Find the length of the line segment that is parallel to the directrix
of a parabola, that passes through the focus, and that has endpoints
on the parabola.

$|4p|$, because the endpoints are $(-2p, p)$ and $(2p, p)$.

© Houghton Mifflin Harcourt Publishing Company

© Houghton Mifflin Harcourt Publishing Company

Assign these pages to help your students practice and apply important lesson concepts. For additional exercises, see the Student Edition.

Answers

Additional Practice

1. $y = \frac{1}{40}x^2$ **2.** $y = -\frac{1}{24}x^2$

3. $y = -\frac{1}{52}x^2$ **4.** $y = \frac{1}{6}x^2$

5. $y = -\frac{1}{12}x^2$ **6.** $y = -\frac{1}{22}x^2$

7. $-3, (0, -3), y = 3$

8. $8, (0, 8), y = -8$

9. $-9, (0, -9), y = 9$

10. $2, (0, 2), y = -2$

11. $12, (0, 12), y = -12$

12. $-2.5, (0, -2.5), y = 2.5$

13. $-7, (0, -7), y = 7$

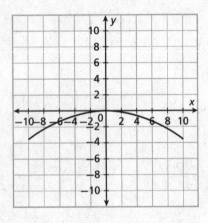

Problem Solving

1. a. $(0, 0)$

b. $4p = 96, p = 24$

c. $(0, 24)$

d. $y = -24$

e.

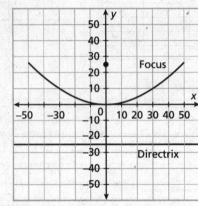

2. $y = \frac{1}{72}x^2$

3. A   **4.** J

Additional Practice

Write the equation of the parabola with the given focus and directrix.

1. focus: (0, 10), directrix: $y = -10$

_____

2. focus (0, –6), directrix: $y = 6$

_____

3. focus (0, –13), directrix: $y = 13$

_____

4. focus (0, 1.5), directrix: $y = -1.5$

_____

5. focus (0, –3), directrix: $y = 3$

_____

6. focus (0, –5.5), directrix: $y = 5.5$

_____

Find the value of p, the focus, and the directrix of the parabola with the given equation.

7. $y = -\frac{1}{12}x^2$

_____

8. $y = \frac{1}{32}x^2$

_____

9. $y = -\frac{1}{36}x^2$

_____

10. $y = \frac{1}{8}x^2$

_____

11. $y = \frac{1}{48}x^2$

_____

12. $y = -\frac{1}{10}x^2$

_____

13. Find the value of p, the focus, and the directrix of the parabola with equation $y = -\frac{1}{28}x^2$. Then graph the parabola.

_____

© Houghton Mifflin Harcourt Publishing Company

Problem Solving

A model of a parabolic mirror has a cross section that can be modeled by the equation $y = \frac{1}{96}x^2$.

1. You want to graph the equation of the cross section of the model.
   a. What are the coordinates of the vertex of the parabola?

   _____

   b. Find the distance, p, from the vertex to both the focus and the directrix of the parabola.

   _____

   c. Find the coordinates of the focus.

   _____

   d. Write the equation of the directrix.

   _____

   e. Sketch a graph of the cross section of the model including the focus and the directrix.

2. You want to construct a model of a different parabolic mirror. For this model, you want the focus to be (0, 18) and the directrix to be $y = -18$. Write the equation of the new parabola.

_____

Choose the letter for the best answer.

3. Melissa wrote the equation of a parabola with focus (0, –5) and directrix $y = 5$. Which equation should Melissa have written?

   A $y = -\frac{1}{20}x^2$

   B $y = \frac{1}{20}x^2$

   C $y = -\frac{1}{5}x^2$

   D $y = \frac{1}{5}x^2$

4. A solar trough used to collect solar energy has a reflective surface. The surface has a cross section that is a parabola with equation $y = \frac{1}{24}x^2$. What is the focus of the parabola?

   F (0, –6)

   G (–6, 0)

   H (6, 0)

   J (0, 6)

© Houghton Mifflin Harcourt Publishing Company

Notes

Bisectors of Triangles
Going Deeper

Essential question: *How do you construct the circle that circumscribes a triangle, and how do you inscribe a circle in a triangle?*

Standards for Mathematical Content

CC.9-12.G.C.3 Construct the inscribed and circumscribed circles of a triangle ...

Vocabulary

circumscribe

circumcircle

circumcenter

inscribed

incenter

incircle

Prerequisites

Constructing the perpendicular bisector of a segment

Constructing the bisector of an angle

Math Background

For any triangle, the perpendicular bisectors of the sides are concurrent at a point called the circumcenter of the triangle, and the angle bisectors are concurrent at a point called the incenter of the triangle. These are two of four concurrency points of a triangle. The other two are the centroid (the point of concurrency of the medians) and the orthocenter (the point of concurrency of the altitudes).

INTRODUCE

Draw a triangle on the board. Ask students whether they think it is possible to draw a circle that passes through all three of the triangle's vertices. Then, ask students whether they think it is possible to draw such a circle for *any* given triangle. Students may be surprised to learn that every triangle, whatever its shape, may be circumscribed by a circle.

Now draw a triangle on the board. Ask students what it would mean for a circle to be inscribed in the triangle. Tell students that when a circle is inscribed, each side of the triangle is a tangent to the circle. Ask students if they think it is possible to inscribe a circle in any triangle, regardless of its shape or size. Explain to students that they will learn a technique for locating the center of the inscribed circle that works for any triangle.

TEACH

1 EXAMPLE

Questioning Strategies

• What do you have to do to construct a circumcircle of $\triangle PQR$? **Find a point that is equidistant from P, Q, and R. This point is the center of the required circle.**

EXTRA EXAMPLE

Construct the circumcircle of $\triangle JKL$.

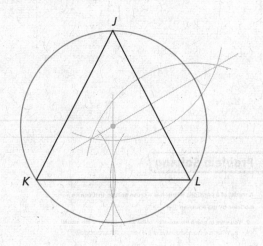

Name _____ Class _____ Date _____

5-2

Bisectors of Triangles
Going Deeper

Essential question: *How do you construct the circle that circumscribes a triangle, and how do you inscribe a circle in a triangle?*

Video Tutor

A circle is said to **circumscribe** a polygon if the circle passes through all of the polygon's vertices. In the figure, circle C circumscribes $\triangle XYZ$ and this circle is called the **circumcircle** of $\triangle XYZ$.

In order to construct the circumcircle of a triangle, you need to find the center of the circle. This point is called the **circumcenter** of the triangle. The following example will guide you through the reasoning process to do this.

CC.9-12.G.C.3

1 EXAMPLE Constructing a Circumscribed Circle

Work directly on the figure to construct the circumcircle of $\triangle PQR$.

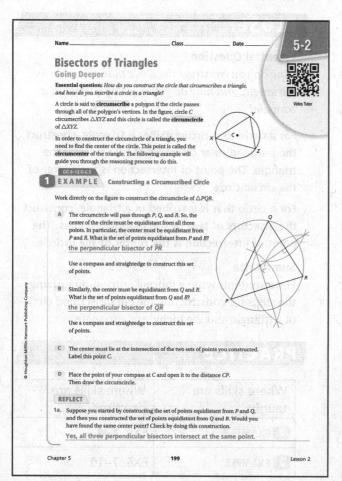

A. The circumcircle will pass through P, Q, and R. So, the center of the circle must be equidistant from all three points. In particular, the center must be equidistant from P and R. What is the set of points equidistant from P and R?

the perpendicular bisector of $\overline{PR}$

Use a compass and straightedge to construct this set of points.

B. Similarly, the center must be equidistant from Q and R. What is the set of points equidistant from Q and R?

the perpendicular bisector of $\overline{QR}$

Use a compass and straightedge to construct this set of points.

C. The center must lie at the intersection of the two sets of points you constructed. Label this point C.

D. Place the point of your compass at C and open it to the distance CP. Then draw the circumcircle.

REFLECT

1a. Suppose you started by constructing the set of points equidistant from P and Q, and then you constructed the set of points equidistant from Q and R. Would you have found the same center point? Check by doing this construction.

Yes, all three perpendicular bisectors intersect at the same point.

Chapter 5   199   Lesson 2

A circle is **inscribed** in a polygon if each side of the polygon is tangent to the circle. In the figure, circle C is inscribed in quadrilateral $WXYZ$ and this circle is called the **incircle** of the quadrilateral.

In order to construct the incircle of a triangle, you need to find the center of the circle. This point is called the **incenter** of the triangle. The following example will guide you through the reasoning process for constructing an inscribed circle in a triangle.

CC.9-12.G.C.3

2 EXAMPLE Constructing an Inscribed Circle

Work directly on the figure to inscribe a circle in $\triangle PQR$.

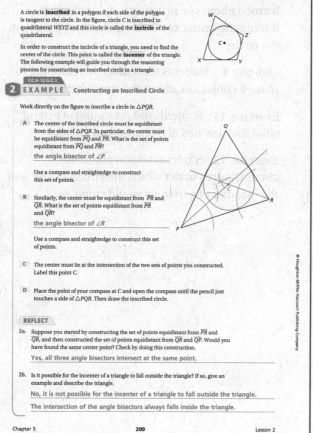

A. The center of the inscribed circle must be equidistant from the sides of $\triangle PQR$. In particular, the center must be equidistant from $\overline{PQ}$ and $\overline{PR}$. What is the set of points equidistant from $\overline{PQ}$ and $\overline{PR}$?

the angle bisector of $\angle P$

Use a compass and straightedge to construct this set of points.

B. Similarly, the center must be equidistant from $\overline{PR}$ and $\overline{QR}$. What is the set of points equidistant from $\overline{PR}$ and $\overline{QR}$?

the angle bisector of $\angle R$

Use a compass and straightedge to construct this set of points.

C. The center must lie at the intersection of the two sets of points you constructed. Label this point C.

D. Place the point of your compass at C and open the compass until the pencil just touches a side of $\triangle PQR$. Then draw the inscribed circle.

REFLECT

2a. Suppose you started by constructing the set of points equidistant from $\overline{PR}$ and $\overline{QR}$, and then constructed the set of points equidistant from $\overline{QR}$ and $\overline{QP}$. Would you have found the same center point? Check by doing this construction.

Yes, all three angle bisectors intersect at the same point.

2b. Is it possible for the incenter of a triangle to fall outside the triangle? If so, give an example and describe the triangle.

No, it is not possible for the incenter of a triangle to fall outside the triangle.

The intersection of the angle bisectors always falls inside the triangle.

Chapter 5   200   Lesson 2

© Houghton Mifflin Harcourt Publishing Company

Questioning Strategies
- How many angle bisectors does a triangle have? 3
- What is true about the points on the bisector of an angle? The points are all equidistant from the sides of the angle.

EXTRA EXAMPLE
Construct the inscribed circle for the triangle.

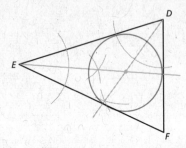

MATHEMATICAL PRACTICE **Highlighting the Standards**

The constructions in this lesson provide an opportunity to address Standard 6 (Attend to precision). In order for students to locate the center of the circumcircle or incircle, students must carefully construct perpendicular bisectors or angle bisectors. Fortunately, the constructions provide self-checks because students can see whether the circle they draw actually passes through the triangle's vertices (circumcircle) or is tangent to the triangle's sides (incenter).

CLOSE

Essential Question
How do you construct the circle that circumscribes a triangle, and how do you inscribe a circle in a triangle?

For a circle that circumscribes a triangle, construct the perpendicular bisectors of two sides of the triangle. The point of intersection is the center of the circumcircle.

For a circle that is inscribed in a triangle, construct the bisectors of two of the triangle's angles. The point of intersection is the center of the incircle.

Summarize
Have students write a journal entry summarizing the steps for constructing the circumscribed circle of a triangle and the incircle of a triangle.

PRACTICE

Where skills are taught	Where skills are practiced
1 EXAMPLE	EXS. 1–4
2 EXAMPLE	EXS. 7–10

Exercise 5: Students extend what they have learned about constructing a circumcircle to finding the center of a circle given three points on the circle.

Exercise 6: Students use inductive reasoning to make a conjecture about the circumcenter.

Exercise 11: Students use reasoning to extend what they learned about inscribed circles.

Exercise 12: Students reason about the circumstances under which the circumcenter and the incenter of a triangle would coincide.

PRACTICE

Construct the circumcircle of each triangle.

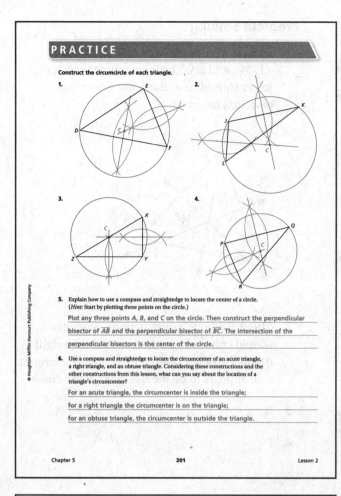

1.

2.

3.

4.

5. Explain how to use a compass and straightedge to locate the center of a circle.
(*Hint:* Start by plotting three points on the circle.)

Plot any three points A, B, and C on the circle. Then construct the perpendicular

bisector of $\overline{AB}$ and the perpendicular bisector of $\overline{BC}$. The intersection of the

perpendicular bisectors is the center of the circle.

6. Use a compass and straightedge to locate the circumcenter of an acute triangle,
a right triangle, and an obtuse triangle. Considering these constructions and the
other constructions from this lesson, what can you say about the location of a
triangle's circumcenter?

For an acute triangle, the circumcenter is inside the triangle;

for a right triangle the circumcenter is on the triangle;

for an obtuse triangle, the circumcenter is outside the triangle.

Construct the inscribed circle for each triangle.

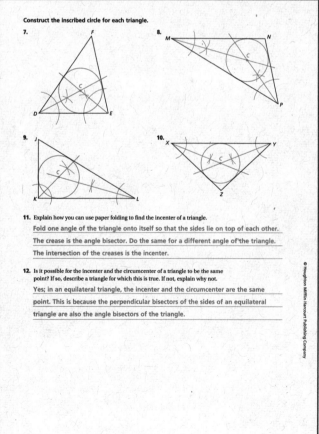

7.

8.

9.

10.

11. Explain how you can use paper folding to find the incenter of a triangle.

Fold one angle of the triangle onto itself so that the sides lie on top of each other.

The crease is the angle bisector. Do the same for a different angle of the triangle.

The intersection of the creases is the incenter.

12. Is it possible for the incenter and the circumcenter of a triangle to be the same
point? If so, describe a triangle for which this is true. If not, explain why not.

Yes; in an equilateral triangle, the incenter and the circumcenter are the same

point. This is because the perpendicular bisectors of the sides of an equilateral

triangle are also the angle bisectors of the triangle.

ADDITIONAL PRACTICE AND PROBLEM SOLVING

Assign these pages to help your students practice and apply important lesson concepts. For additional exercises, see the Student Edition.

Answers

Additional Practice

1–4. Check students' constructions.

5. circumcenter

6. incenter

7. Possible answer: Raleigh needs to find the circumcircle of the triangle. The circumcircle just touches all three vertices of the triangle, so it fits just around it. The circumcenter can be found by drawing the perpendicular bisectors of the sides of the triangle. The circumcircle is drawn with the circumcenter as center and a radius equal to the distance from the center to one of the vertices.

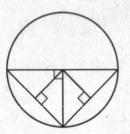

Problem Solving

1. Draw the perpendicular bisectors of $\overline{XY}$, $\overline{YZ}$, and $\overline{ZX}$. The location of the water tower should be at the point where the bisectors intersect.

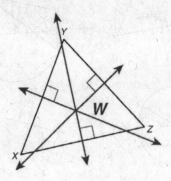

2. Check students' constructions. Students should construct the circumcircle of a right triangle and get Paulo's result, that the longest side appears to be the diameter of the circle.

3. B

4. F

5-2

Additional Practice

Construct the circumcircle of each triangle.

1.

2.

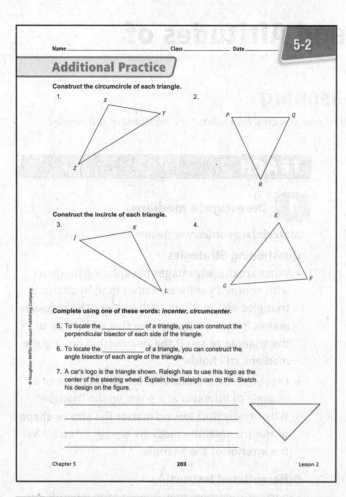

Construct the incircle of each triangle.

3.

4.

Complete using one of these words: *incenter, circumcenter*.

5. To locate the _____ of a triangle, you can construct the perpendicular bisector of each side of the triangle.

6. To locate the _____ of a triangle, you can construct the angle bisector of each angle of the triangle.

7. A car's logo is the triangle shown. Raleigh has to use this logo as the center of the steering wheel. Explain how Raleigh can do this. Sketch his design on the figure.

_____

_____

_____

Problem Solving

1. The diagram shows the locations of three cities, labeled X, Y, and Z. Explain how to use a compass and straightedge to mark a location for a new water tower that will be the same distance from each of the three cities. Then perform the construction.

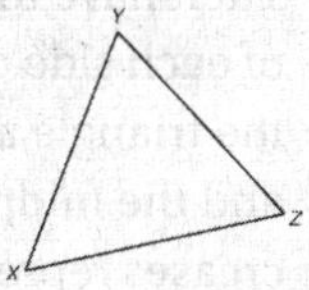

_____

_____

_____

2. Paulo drew a right triangle by using a corner of a piece of paper to draw the right angle. Then he constructed the circumcircle of his right triangle. He noticed that the longest side of the triangle appeared to be the diameter of the triangle. Draw your own right triangle. Then construct its circumcircle. Do you get the same result as Paulo?

_____

Choose the best answer.

3. An architect draws △ JKL to represent a triangular sitting area in a mall. The architect then constructs the angle bisectors of the angles of the triangle and finds that the bisectors intersect at a point 5 centimeters from $\overline{JK}$. On the architect's drawing, what is the distance of this point from $\overline{KL}$?

   A 2.5 cm   B 5 cm   C 7.5 cm   D 10 cm

4. A new gym is to be located the same distance from three schools. You have a compass and straightedge and a map with points A, B, and C representing the three schools. How can you locate the new gym?

   F Construct the perpendicular bisectors of the sides of △ ABC and find the point where the perpendicular bisectors intersect.

   G Construct the bisectors of the angles of △ ABC and find the point where the bisectors intersect.

   H Construct an inscribed circle inside △ ABC.

   J Construct the incircle of △ ABC.

Medians and Altitudes of Triangles
Focus on Reasoning

Essential question: *What can you conclude about the medians of a triangle?*

COMMON CORE Standards for Mathematical Content

CC.9-12.G.CO.10 Prove theorems about triangles.

CC.9-12.G.GPE.4 Use coordinates to prove simple geometric theorems algebraically.

Vocabulary
median

concurrent

point of concurrency

centroid

Prerequisites
Midpoint formula

Writing coordinate proofs

The equation of a line

Math Background
In this Focus on Reasoning lesson, students use geometry software to explore the medians of a triangle. They use inductive reasoning to make the conjecture that the medians of a triangle are concurrent and then they use deductive reasoning to complete a coordinate proof of this fact.

INTRODUCE

Discuss the use of the word *median* in mathematics and in everyday situations. Students should already be familiar with medians from their study of data and statistics in earlier grades. Explain that there is another use of the term *median* in mathematics. Then define the median of a triangle. Make a sketch on the board showing students how to draw a median, and point out that every triangle has three medians. Tell students they will use geometry software and inductive reasoning to make a conjecture about medians.

TEACH

1 Investigate medians.

Materials: geometry software

Questioning Strategies

- What are the advantages to exploring medians with geometry software rather than by drawing triangles and medians with a ruler? The software makes it easy to change the size and shape of the triangle to see if the relationship among the medians still holds.

- Do you think it is possible for the medians of a triangle to intersect at a point on the triangle? Why or why not? No; no matter the size or shape of the triangle, the medians always intersect in the interior of the triangle.

Differentiated Instruction

Kinesthetic learners may benefit from a hands-on approach to the investigation. Have students draw a large triangle on a sheet of paper and cut it out. Then have them use a ruler to find the midpoint of each side of the triangle. Students can then fold the triangle along the line through each vertex and the midpoint of the opposite side. The three creases represent the medians of the triangle and students should find that the creases intersect at a common point.

Name _____ Class _____ Date _____

5-3

Medians and Altitudes of Triangles
Focus on Reasoning

Essential question: *What can you conclude about the medians of a triangle?*

COMMON CORE

CC.9-12.G.CO.10,
CC.9-12.G.GPE.4

A **median** of a triangle is a line segment whose endpoints are a vertex of the triangle and the midpoint of the opposite side. Every triangle has three medians. In the figure, $\overline{LM}$ is a median of $\triangle JKL$.

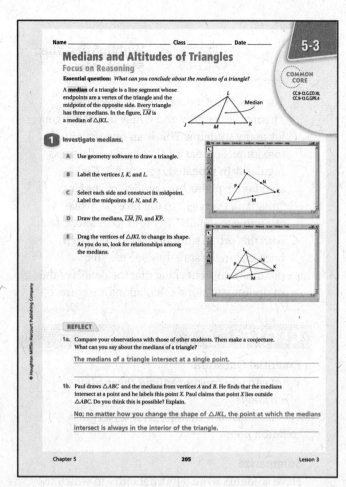

1 **Investigate medians.**

A Use geometry software to draw a triangle.

B Label the vertices *J*, *K*, and *L*.

C Select each side and construct its midpoint. Label the midpoints *M*, *N*, and *P*.

D Draw the medians, $\overline{LM}$, $\overline{JN}$, and $\overline{KP}$.

E Drag the vertices of $\triangle JKL$ to change its shape. As you do so, look for relationships among the medians.

REFLECT

1a. Compare your observations with those of other students. Then make a conjecture. What can you say about the medians of a triangle?

The medians of a triangle intersect at a single point.

1b. Paul draws $\triangle ABC$ and the medians from vertices *A* and *B*. He finds that the medians intersect at a point and he labels this point *X*. Paul claims that point *X* lies outside $\triangle ABC$. Do you think this is possible? Explain.

No; no matter how you change the shape of $\triangle JKL$, the point at which the medians

intersect is always in the interior of the triangle.

Chapter 5   205   Lesson 3

Three or more lines are said to be **concurrent** when they intersect at a point. The point is called the **point of concurrency**. You have seen that the medians of a triangle are concurrent. The point of concurrency of the medians of a triangle is called the **centroid** of the triangle.

Concurrency of Medians Theorem

The medians of a triangle are concurrent.

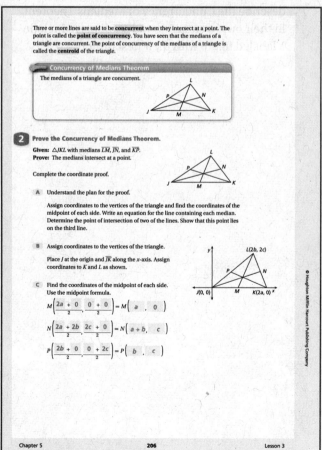

2 **Prove the Concurrency of Medians Theorem.**

Given: $\triangle JKL$ with medians $\overline{LM}$, $\overline{JN}$, and $\overline{KP}$.
Prove: The medians intersect at a point.

Complete the coordinate proof.

A Understand the plan for the proof.

Assign coordinates to the vertices of the triangle and find the coordinates of the midpoint of each side. Write an equation for the line containing each median. Determine the point of intersection of two of the lines. Show that this point lies on the third line.

B Assign coordinates to the vertices of the triangle.

Place *J* at the origin and $\overline{JK}$ along the *x*-axis. Assign coordinates to *K* and *L* as shown.

C Find the coordinates of the midpoint of each side. Use the midpoint formula.

$$M\left(\frac{2a + 0}{2}, \frac{0 + 0}{2}\right) = M\left(\boxed{a}, \boxed{0}\right)$$

$$N\left(\frac{2a + 2b}{2}, \frac{2c + 0}{2}\right) = N\left(\boxed{a+b}, \boxed{c}\right)$$

$$P\left(\frac{2b + 0}{2}, \frac{0 + 2c}{2}\right) = P\left(\boxed{b}, \boxed{c}\right)$$

© Houghton Mifflin Harcourt Publishing Company

Chapter 5   206   Lesson 3

2 Prove the Concurrency of Medians Theorem.

Questioning Strategies

- What type of proof is used to prove the Concurrency of Medians Theorem? It is a coordinate proof.

- In the proof, why do you write equations for the lines containing the medians? This allows you to determine the point of intersection of two of the lines. Then you can show that this intersection point lies on the third line.

Avoid Common Errors

Students may get lost in the algebra that is required to complete the proof and lose track of the overall structure of the proof. To help students stay on track, you may want to have students write the main steps of the proof and then check off the steps as they complete them.

1. Assign coordinates to the vertices.

2. Find the coordinates of the midpoint of each side.

3. Write equations for the lines containing the medians.

4. Find the point of intersection of two of the lines.

5. Show that the point of intersection lies on the third line.

The proof the Concurrency of Medians Theorem is lengthy and it may be challenging for many students. This is an opportunity to address Standard 8 (Look for and express regularity in repeated reasoning). The standard explains how proficient students "maintain oversight of the process, while attending to details." In order to be successful with this proof, students will need to step back and make sure they see the "big picture," while checking that the details of the midpoint and slope calculations are correct.

CLOSE

Essential Question

What can you conclude about the medians of a triangle?
The medians of a triangle all intersect at a common point.

Summarize

Have students write a journal entry in which they describe the Concurrency of Medians Theorem in their own words. Remind students to include a labeled figure with their description.

© Houghton Mifflin Harcourt Publishing Company

D Write the equation for the line containing $\overleftrightarrow{JN}$. To do so, use the *point-slope form* of the equation of a line: If a line has slope m and passes through (x_0, y_0), then the line's equation is $y - y_0 = m(x - x_0)$.

Slope of $\overleftrightarrow{JN} = \frac{c - 0}{a + b - 0} = \frac{c}{a + b}$

To write the equation of $\overleftrightarrow{JN}$, use the fact that the line passes through $(0, 0)$.

Equation of $\overleftrightarrow{JN}$: $y - 0 = \frac{c}{a + b}(x - 0)$ or $y = \frac{c}{a + b}x$

E Write the equations for the lines containing $\overleftrightarrow{LM}$ and $\overleftrightarrow{PK}$.

Slope of $\overleftrightarrow{LM} = \frac{2c - 0}{2b - a} = \frac{2c}{2b - a}$

Equation of $\overleftrightarrow{LM}$: $y - 0 = \frac{2c}{2b - a}(x - a)$ or $y = \frac{2c}{2b - a}(x - a)$

Slope of $\overleftrightarrow{PK} = \frac{c - 0}{b - 2a} = \frac{c}{b - 2a}$

Equation of $\overleftrightarrow{PK}$: $y - 0 = \frac{c}{b - 2a}(x - 2a)$ or $y = \frac{c}{b - 2a}(x - 2a)$

F Find the point of intersection of $\overleftrightarrow{JN}$ and $\overleftrightarrow{LM}$. To do so, set the right side of the equation for $\overleftrightarrow{JN}$ equal to the right side of the equation for $\overleftrightarrow{LM}$. Then solve for x, to find the x-coordinate of the point of intersection.

$\frac{c}{a + b}x = \frac{2c}{2b - a}(x - a)$	Write the equation for x.
$cx(2b - a) = 2c(x - a)(a + b)$	Multiply both sides by $(a + b)(2b - a)$.
$2bcx - acx = (2cx - 2ac)(a + b)$	Multiply.
$2bcx - acx = 2acx - 2a^2c + 2bcx - 2abc$	Multiply on right side of equation.
$-acx = 2acx - 2a^2c - 2abc$	Subtract $2bcx$ from both sides.
$-3acx = -2a^2c - 2abc$	Subtract $2acx$ from both sides.
$-3x = -2a - 2b$	Factor out ac; divide both sides by ac.
$x = \frac{2a + 2b}{3}$	Divide both sides by -3.

To find the y-coordinate of the point of intersection, substitute this value of x into the equation for $\overleftrightarrow{JN}$ and solve for y.

$y = \frac{c}{a + b}x = \frac{c}{a + b} \cdot \frac{2a + 2b}{3} = \frac{2c}{3}$

The coordinates of the point of intersection of $\overleftrightarrow{JN}$ and $\overleftrightarrow{LM}$ are $\left(\frac{2a + 2b}{3}, \frac{2c}{3}\right)$.

© Houghton Mifflin Harcourt Publishing Company

G Now show that the point you found in Step F lies on $\overleftrightarrow{PK}$. To do so, substitute the x-coordinate of the point into the equation for $\overleftrightarrow{PK}$. Then simplify to show that the corresponding y-value is the same as the y-coordinate you calculated in Step F.

$y = \frac{c}{b - 2a}(x - 2a)$	Write the equation for $\overleftrightarrow{PK}$.
$y = \frac{c}{b - 2a}\left(\frac{2a + 2b}{3} - 2a\right)$	Substitute the x-coordinate of the point.
$y = \frac{c}{b - 2a}\left(\frac{2b - 4a}{3}\right)$	Subtract inside the parentheses.
$y = \frac{c}{b - 2a}\left(\frac{2(b - 2a)}{3}\right)$	Factor the numerator inside the parentheses.
$y = \frac{c}{1}\left(\frac{2}{3}\right)$	Divide to remove common factors.
$y = \frac{2c}{3}$	Simplify.

Because this y-value is the same as the y-coordinate of the point of intersection from Step F, the point also lies on $\overleftrightarrow{PK}$. This shows that the medians are concurrent.

REFLECT

2a. Explain how you can find the coordinates of the centroid of a triangle with vertices $R(0, 0)$, $S(6, 0)$, and $T(3, 9)$.

Comparing to the generic coordinates shows that $2a = 6$, $2b = 3$, and $2c = 9$, so

substitute the values $a = 3$, $b = \frac{3}{2}$, and $c = \frac{9}{2}$ in the expressions for the coordinates

of the point of intersection. The centroid is (3, 3).

2b. A student proves the Concurrency of Medians Theorem by first assigning coordinates to the vertices of $\triangle JKL$ as $J(0, 0)$, $K(2a, 0)$, and $L(2a, 2c)$. The students says that this choice of coordinates makes the algebra in the proof a bit easier. Do you agree with the student's choice of coordinates? Explain.

No; these coordinates result in a triangle that is a right triangle, so the proof

would not hold for triangles in general.

2c. A student claims that the averages of the x-coordinates and of the y-coordinates of the vertices of a triangle are the x- and y-coordinates of the centroid. Does the coordinate proof of the Concurrency of Medians Theorem support the claim? Explain.

Yes. The x-coordinates of the vertices are 0, $2a$, and $2b$; their average is $\frac{(2a + 2b)}{3}$.

The y-coordinates of the vertices are 0, 0, and $2c$; their average is $\frac{2c}{3}$. This agrees

with the expressions for the coordinates of the centroid.

© Houghton Mifflin Harcourt Publishing Company

© Houghton Mifflin Harcourt Publishing Company

Assign these pages to help your students practice and apply important lesson concepts. For additional exercises, see the Student Edition.

Answers

Additional Practice

1. $6\frac{1}{3}$ **2.** 19

3. $3\frac{1}{3}$ **4.** $6\frac{2}{3}$

5. 1, 1.9   **6.** 2, 5

7. 2, −3   **8.** 36 m^2

9. 10.25 m

10. Possible answer:

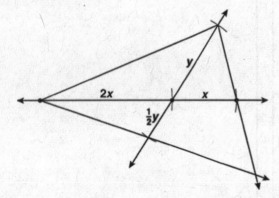

Problem Solving

1. $\left(4, \frac{14}{3}\right)$ **2.** $\left(9\frac{2}{3}, 6\right)$

3. $\left(-1\frac{4}{5}, 5\frac{4}{5}\right); \left(-\frac{1}{3}, 4\frac{1}{3}\right)$ **4.** B

5. H   **6.** B

5-3

Additional Practice

Use the figure for Exercises 1–4. $GB = 12\frac{2}{3}$ and $CD = 10$.

Find each length.

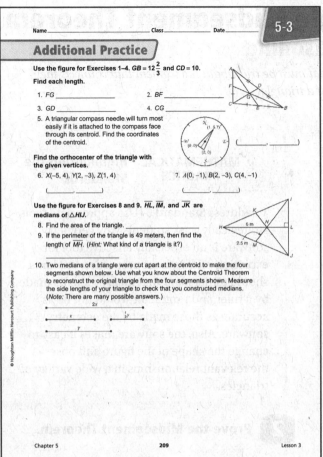

1. FG _____

2. BF _____

3. GD _____

4. CG _____

5. A triangular compass needle will turn most easily if it is attached to the compass face through its centroid. Find the coordinates of the centroid.

(_____ , _____)

Find the orthocenter of the triangle with the given vertices.

6. $X(-5, 4)$, $Y(2, -3)$, $Z(1, 4)$

(_____ , _____)

7. $A(0, -1)$, $B(2, -3)$, $C(4, -1)$

(_____ , _____)

Use the figure for Exercises 8 and 9. $\overline{HL}, \overline{IM}$, and $\overline{JK}$ are medians of $\triangle HIJ$.

8. Find the area of the triangle. _____

9. If the perimeter of the triangle is 49 meters, then find the length of $\overline{MH}$. (*Hint:* What kind of a triangle is it?)

_____

10. Two medians of a triangle were cut apart at the centroid to make the four segments shown below. Use what you know about the Centroid Theorem to reconstruct the original triangle from the four segments shown. Measure the side lengths of your triangle to check that you constructed medians. (*Note:* There are many possible answers.)

Problem Solving

1. The diagram shows the coordinates of the vertices of a triangular patio umbrella. The umbrella will rest on a pole that will support it. Where should the pole be attached so that the umbrella is balanced?

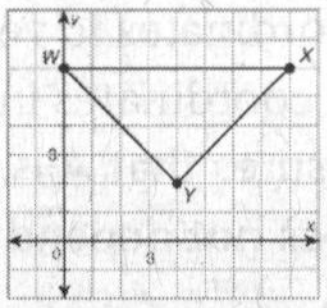

_____

2. In a plan for a triangular wind chime, the coordinates of the vertices are $J(10, 2)$, $K(7, 6)$, and $L(12, 10)$. At what coordinates should the manufacturer attach the chain from which it will hang in order for the chime to be balanced?

_____

3. Triangle PQR has vertices at $P(-3, 5)$, $Q(-1, 7)$, and $R(3, 1)$. Find the coordinates of the orthocenter and the centroid.

_____

Choose the best answer.

4. A triangle has coordinates at $A(0, 6)$, $B(8, 6)$, and $C(5, 0)$. $\overline{CD}$ is a median of the triangle, and $\overline{CE}$ is an altitude of the triangle. Which is a true statement?

  A The coordinates of D and E are the same.

  B The distance between D and E is 1 unit.

  C The distance between D and E is 2 units.

  D D is on the triangle, and E is outside the triangle.

5. Lines j and k contain medians of $\triangle DEF$. Find y and z.

  F $y = 16$; $z = 4$ H $y = 64$; $z = 4.8$

  G $y = 32$; $z = 4$ J $y = 108$; $z = 8$

6. An inflatable triangular raft is towed behind a boat. The raft is an equilateral triangle. To maintain balance, the seat is at the centroid B of the triangle. What is AB, the distance from the seat to the tow rope? Round to the nearest tenth.

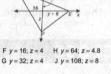

  A 18.7 in.

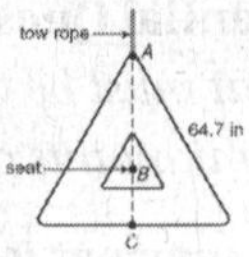

  B 37.4 in.

  C 43.1 in.

  D 56.0 in.

The Triangle Midsegment Theorem
Focus on Reasoning

Essential question: *What must be true about the segment that connects the midpoints of two sides of a triangle?*

COMMON CORE Standards for Mathematical Content

CC.9-12.G.CO.10 Prove theorems about triangles.

CC.9-12.G.GPE.4 Use coordinates to prove simple geometric theorems algebraically.

Vocabulary
midsegment

Prerequisites
Distance and midpoint formulas

Writing coordinate proofs

Slope of parallel lines

Math Background
A major goal of geometry is understanding properties that are true for every triangle. Students have already seen the Triangle Sum Theorem and the Concurrency of Medians Theorem. This lesson focuses on facts about triangle midsegments. Note that the results are proved here using coordinate methods. They can also be proved using the SAS Similarity Criterion (discussed in a later lesson).

INTRODUCE

Define *midsegment*. Make a sketch on the board showing students how to draw a midsegment, and point out that every triangle has three midsegments. Explain that in this lesson, students will primarily work with one midsegment at a time.

TEACH

1 Investigate midsegments.

Questioning Strategies
- What is the name for the angle pair consisting of ∠ADE and ∠ABC? **corresponding angles**
- What theorems do you know about this type of angle pair? **If two lines are cut by a transversal so that a pair of corresponding angles have the same measure, then the lines are parallel.**

MATHEMATICAL PRACTICE · Highlighting the Standards

To address Standard 5 (Use appropriate tools strategically), ask students why geometry software is an especially effective tool for exploring midsegment properties. Students should understand that measurements made by a ruler and protractor would not be as accurate as those made by the geometry software. Also, the software makes it easy to change the shape of the figure and observe the relevant relationships in a wide variety of triangles.

2 Prove the Midsegment Theorem.

Questioning Strategies
- Once you assign vertex B the coordinates $(0, 0)$ and vertex C the coordinates $(2p, 0)$, why do you use the new variables q and r to assign coordinates to vertex A, rather than writing its coordinates in terms of the variable p? **This ensures that A is a general point whose location does not depend upon the other points.**
- What are some ways you can prove that two line segments are parallel? Which of these methods may work best in a coordinate proof? **Show corresponding angles have the same measure, show the lines have the same slope, etc. In a coordinate proof, it may be easiest to show that the lines have the same slope.**

CLOSE

Essential Question
What must be true about the segment that connects the midpoints of two sides of a triangle?

The segment is parallel to the third side of the triangle and half as long as the third side.

Summarize
Have students write a journal entry stating the Midsegment Theorem in their own words.

© Houghton Mifflin Harcourt Publishing Company

Name _____ Class _____ Date _____

The Triangle Midsegment Theorem
Focus on Reasoning

Essential question: *What must be true about the segment that connects the midpoints of two sides of a triangle?*

A **midsegment** of a triangle is a line segment that connects the midpoints of two sides of the triangle.

COMMON CORE
CC.9-12.G.CO.10,
CC.9-12.G.GPE.4

1 Investigate midsegments.

A Use geometry software to draw a triangle.

B Label the vertices *A*, *B*, and *C*.

C Select $\overline{AB}$ and construct its midpoint.
Select $\overline{AC}$ and construct its midpoint.
Label the midpoints *D* and *E*.

D Draw the midsegment, $\overline{DE}$.

E Measure the lengths of $\overline{DE}$ and $\overline{BC}$.

F Measure $\angle ADE$ and $\angle ABC$.

G Drag the vertices of $\triangle ABC$ to change
its shape. As you do so, look for
relationships in the measurements.

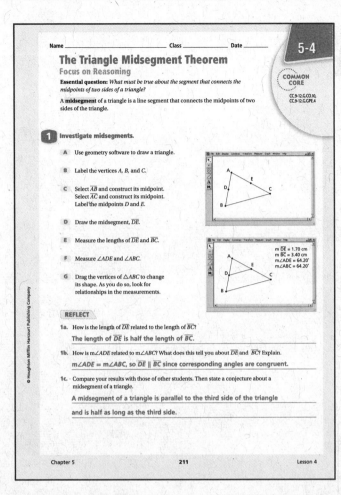

m $\overline{DE}$ = 1.70 cm
m $\overline{BC}$ = 3.40 cm
m$\angle ADE$ = 64.20°
m$\angle ABC$ = 64.20°

REFLECT

1a. How is the length of $\overline{DE}$ related to the length of $\overline{BC}$?

The length of $\overline{DE}$ is half the length of $\overline{BC}$.

1b. How is m$\angle ADE$ related to m$\angle ABC$? What does this tell you about $\overline{DE}$ and $\overline{BC}$? Explain.

m$\angle ADE$ = m$\angle ABC$, so $\overline{DE} \parallel \overline{BC}$ since corresponding angles are congruent.

1c. Compare your results with those of other students. Then state a conjecture about a midsegment of a triangle.

A midsegment of a triangle is parallel to the third side of the triangle

and is half as long as the third side.

Chapter 5   211   Lesson 4

© Houghton Mifflin Harcourt Publishing Company

---

2 Prove the Midsegment Theorem.

A midsegment of a triangle is parallel to the third side
of the triangle and is half as long as the third side.

Given: $\overline{DE}$ is a midsegment of $\triangle ABC$.
Prove: $\overline{DE} \parallel \overline{BC}$ and $DE = \frac{1}{2} BC$.

A Use a coordinate proof. Place $\triangle ABC$ on a
coordinate plane so that one vertex is at the origin
and one side lies on the *x*-axis, as shown. For
convenience, assign vertex *C* the coordinates
$(2p, 0)$ and assign vertex *A* the coordinates $(2q, 2r)$.

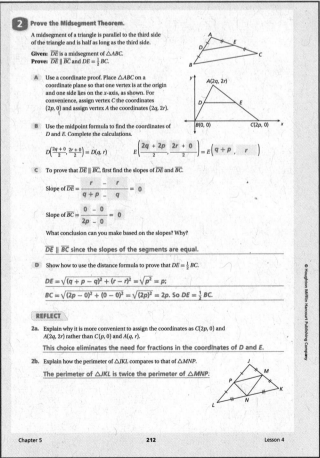

B Use the midpoint formula to find the coordinates of
D and *E*. Complete the calculations.

$$D\left(\frac{2q+0}{2}, \frac{2r+0}{2}\right) = D(q, r) \qquad E\left(\frac{2q+2p}{2}, \frac{2r+0}{2}\right) = E\left(\boxed{q+p}, \boxed{r}\right)$$

C To prove that $\overline{DE} \parallel \overline{BC}$, first find the slopes of $\overline{DE}$ and $\overline{BC}$.

Slope of $\overline{DE} = \dfrac{r - r}{q+p - q} = 0$

Slope of $\overline{BC} = \dfrac{0 - 0}{2p - 0} = 0$

What conclusion can you make based on the slopes? Why?

$\overline{DE} \parallel \overline{BC}$ since the slopes of the segments are equal.

D Show how to use the distance formula to prove that $DE = \frac{1}{2} BC$.

$DE = \sqrt{(q+p-q)^2 + (r-r)^2} = \sqrt{p^2} = p;$

$BC = \sqrt{(2p-0)^2 + (0-0)^2} = \sqrt{(2p)^2} = 2p.$ So $DE = \frac{1}{2} BC.$

REFLECT

2a. Explain why it is more convenient to assign the coordinates as $C(2p, 0)$ and
$A(2q, 2r)$ rather than $C(p, 0)$ and $A(q, r)$.

This choice eliminates the need for fractions in the coordinates of *D* and *E*.

2b. Explain how the perimeter of $\triangle JKL$ compares to that of $\triangle MNP$.

The perimeter of $\triangle JKL$ is twice the perimeter of $\triangle MNP$.

Chapter 5   212   Lesson 4

© Houghton Mifflin Harcourt Publishing Company

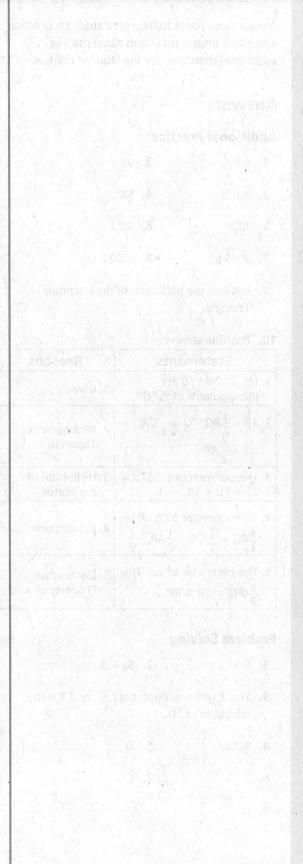

ADDITIONAL PRACTICE AND PROBLEM SOLVING

Assign these pages to help your students practice and apply important lesson concepts. For additional exercises, see the Student Edition.

Answers

Additional Practice

1. 9.1 **2.** 35

3. 9.1 **4.** 58°

5. 122° **6.** 58°

7. 3045 mi **8.** 1522.5 mi

9. It is half the perimeter of the Bermuda Triangle.

10. Possible answer:

Statements	Reasons
1. $\overline{US}$, $\overline{ST}$, and $\overline{TU}$ are midsegments of $\triangle PQR$.	1. Given
2. $ST = \frac{1}{2}PQ$, $TU = \frac{1}{2}QR$, $US = \frac{1}{2}RP$	2. Midsegment Theorem
3. The perimeter of $\triangle STU = ST + TU + US$.	3. Definition of perimeter
4. The perimeter of $\triangle STU = \frac{1}{2}PQ + \frac{1}{2}QR + \frac{1}{2}RP$.	4. Substitution
5. The perimeter of $\triangle STU = \frac{1}{2}(PQ + QR + RP)$.	5. Distributive Property of =

Problem Solving

1. 9.5 **2.** $5x + 2$

3. Yes; X is the midpoint of $\overline{LN}$, and Y is the midpoint of $\overline{ML}$.

4. 9.2 mi **5.** D

6. F **7.** C

8. G

Name _____ **Class** _____ **Date** _____   **5-4**

Additional Practice

Use the figure for Exercises 1–6. Find each measure.

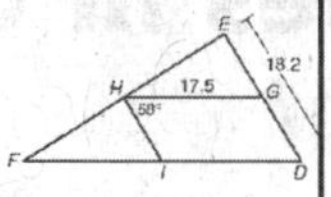

1. *HI* _____   2. *DF* _____

3. *GE* _____   4. m∠*HIF* _____

5. m∠*HGD* _____   6. m∠*D* _____

The Bermuda Triangle is a region in the
Atlantic Ocean off the southeast coast of
the United States. The triangle is bounded
by Miami, Florida; San Juan, Puerto Rico;
and Bermuda. In the figure, the dotted lines
are midsegments.

	Dist. (mi)
Miami to San Juan	1038
Miami to Bermuda	1042
Bermuda to San Juan	965

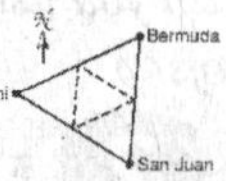

7. Use the distances in the chart to find the perimeter of
   the Bermuda Triangle. _____

8. Find the perimeter of the midsegment triangle within
   the Bermuda Triangle. _____

9. How does the perimeter of the midsegment triangle compare to
   the perimeter of the Bermuda Triangle?

   _____

Write a two-column proof that the perimeter of a
midsegment triangle is half the perimeter of the triangle.

10. **Given:** $\overline{US}$, $\overline{ST}$, and $\overline{TU}$ are midsegments of △*PQR*.

    Prove: The perimeter of $\triangle STU = \frac{1}{2}(PQ + QR + RP)$.

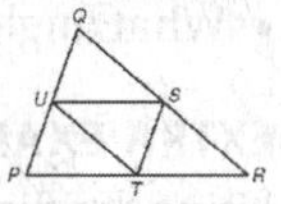

Problem Solving

1. The vertices of △*JKL* are *J*(–9, 2), *K*(10, 1),
   and *L*(5, 6). $\overline{CD}$ is the midsegment parallel
   to $\overline{JK}$. What is the length of $\overline{CD}$? Round to
   the nearest tenth.

2. In △*QRS*, *QR* = 2*x* + 5, *RS* = 3*x* – 1,
   and *SQ* = 5*x*. What is the perimeter of
   the midsegment triangle of △*QRS*?

3. Is *XY* a midsegment of △*LMN* if its endpoints
   are *X*(8, 2.5) and *Y*(6.5, –2)? Explain.

   _____

   _____

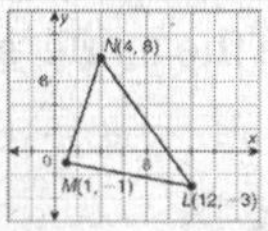

4. The diagram at right shows horseback riding trails. Point *B*
   is the halfway point along path $\overline{AC}$. Point *D* is the halfway
   point along path $\overline{CE}$. The paths along $\overline{BD}$ and $\overline{AE}$
   are parallel. If riders travel from *A* to *B* to *D* to *E*, and then
   back to *A*, how far do they travel?

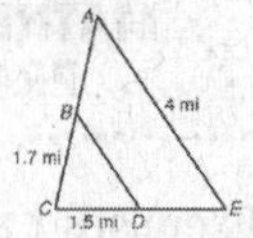

   _____

Choose the best answer.

5. Right triangle *FGH* has midsegments of
   length 10 centimeters, 24 centimeters,
   and 26 centimeters. What is the area of
   △*FGH*?

   A 60 cm²   C 240 cm²
   B 120 cm²   D 480 cm²

6. In triangle *HJK*, m∠*H* = 110°, m∠*J* = 30°,
   and m∠*K* = 40°. If *R* is the midpoint of
   $\overline{JK}$, and *S* is the midpoint of $\overline{HK}$, what is
   m∠*JRS*?

   F 150°   H 110°
   G 140°   J 30°

Use the diagram for Exercises 7 and 8.

On the balance beam, *V* is the midpoint of $\overline{AB}$,
and *W* is the midpoint of $\overline{YB}$.

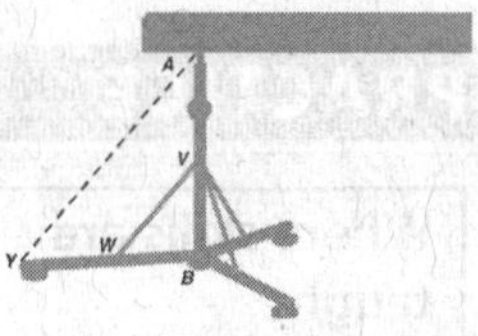

7. The length of $\overline{VW}$ is $1\frac{7}{8}$ feet. What is *AY*?

   A $\frac{7}{8}$ ft   C $3\frac{3}{4}$ ft
   B $\frac{15}{16}$ ft   D $7\frac{1}{2}$ ft

8. The measure of ∠*AYW* is 50°. What is the
   measure of ∠*VWB*?

   F 45°   H 90°
   G 50°   J 130°

Indirect Proof and Inequalities in One Triangle
Going Deeper

Essential question: How can you use inequalities related to triangle side lengths and angle measures in proofs?

COMMON CORE Standards for Mathematical Content

CC.9-12.G.CO.10 Prove theorems about triangles.

Prerequisites

Triangle Sum Theorem

Math Background

The two angle-side relationships stated in this lesson are converses. They allow you to draw conclusions about side-length relationships in a triangle given angle measures or about angle-measure relationships given side lengths. To apply these relationships to two or more triangles, you use the Transitive Property of Inequality.

INTRODUCE

Be sure students understand the Transitive Property of Inequality: If $a < b$ and $b < c$, then $a < c$. A simple case of using this inequality would be as follows: Any negative number is less than 0 and 0 is less than any positive number, so any negative number is less than any positive number.

TEACH

1 EXAMPLE

Questioning Strategies

• What side do triangles $\triangle KLN$ and $\triangle LMN$ share? How does this side enter into the proof? $\overline{LN}$; by showing that $KL < LN$ in $\triangle KLN$ and that $LN < MN$ in $\triangle LMN$, you can conclude that $KL < MN$.

EXTRA EXAMPLE

Prove that $XW < XY$.

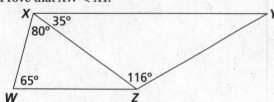

$m\angle XZW = 35°$ and $m\angle XYZ = 29°$. $XW < XZ$ because $35° < 65°$. $XZ < XY$ because $29° < 116°$. So, $XW < XY$ by the Trans. Prop. of Ineq.

2 EXAMPLE

Questioning Strategies

• Which two triangles should you consider to prove that $m\angle BCA < m\angle BAD$? $\triangle ABC$ and $\triangle ABD$

• What angle do the two triangles share? $\angle ABC$

EXTRA EXAMPLE

Using the diagram for **2 EXAMPLE**, show that $m\angle ABC < m\angle ACD$. $AB < AC$ in $\triangle ABC$, so $m\angle BCA < m\angle ABC$. $AC < AD$ in $\triangle ACD$, so $m\angle ABC < m\angle ACD$. By the Trans. Prop. of Ineq. $m\angle BCA < m\angle ACD$.

CLOSE

Essential Question

How can you use inequalities related to triangle side lengths and angle measures in proofs?
Given triangles sharing a common side or angle, write inequalities linking the measure of the common side or angle with the measures of the sides or angles for which you seek a relationship. Then use the Trans. Prop. of Ineq.

Summarize

Have students use diagrams in their journals to illustrate the angle–side relationships in triangles.

MATHEMATICAL PRACTICE   **Highlighting the Standards**

Exercises 1 and 2 involve Standard 3 (Construct viable arguments) and Standard 7 (Look for and make use of structure), challenging students to combine algebraic skills with inequalities and geometric argument.

PRACTICE

Where skills are taught	Where skills are practiced
1 EXAMPLE	EX. 1
2 EXAMPLE	EX. 2

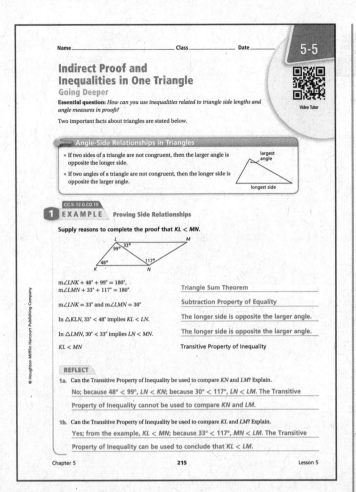

Name_____ Class_____ Date_____

5-5

Indirect Proof and Inequalities in One Triangle
Going Deeper

Essential question: *How can you use inequalities related to triangle side lengths and angle measures in proofs?*

Two important facts about triangles are stated below.

Angle-Side Relationships in Triangles

- If two sides of a triangle are not congruent, then the larger angle is opposite the longer side.
- If two angles of a triangle are not congruent, then the longer side is opposite the larger angle.

CC.9-12.G.CO.10
1 EXAMPLE Proving Side Relationships

Supply reasons to complete the proof that $KL < MN$.

$m\angle LNK + 48° + 99° = 180°$,
$m\angle LMN + 33° + 117° = 180°$ .... Triangle Sum Theorem

$m\angle LNK = 33°$ and $m\angle LMN = 30°$ .... Subtraction Property of Equality

In $\triangle KLN$, $33° < 48°$ implies $KL < LN$. .... The longer side is opposite the larger angle.

In $\triangle LMN$, $30° < 33°$ implies $LN < MN$. .... The longer side is opposite the larger angle.

$KL < MN$ .... Transitive Property of Inequality

REFLECT

1a. Can the Transitive Property of Inequality be used to compare KN and LM? Explain.

No; because $48° < 99°$, $LN < KN$; because $30° < 117°$, $LN < LM$. The Transitive Property of Inequality cannot be used to compare KN and LM.

1b. Can the Transitive Property of Inequality be used to compare KL and LM? Explain.

Yes; from the example, $KL < MN$; because $33° < 117°$, $MN < LM$. The Transitive Property of Inequality can be used to conclude that $KL < LM$.

Chapter 5   215   Lesson 5

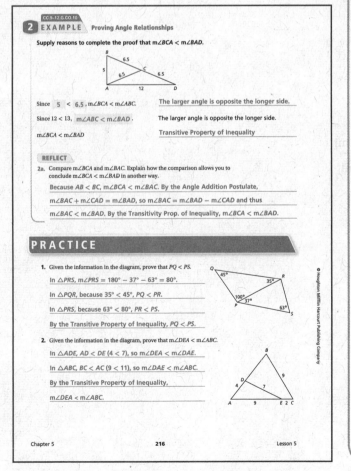

CC.9-12.G.CO.10
2 EXAMPLE Proving Angle Relationships

Supply reasons to complete the proof that $m\angle BCA < m\angle BAD$.

Since $5 < 6.5$, $m\angle BCA < m\angle ABC$. .... The larger angle is opposite the longer side.

Since $12 < 13$, $m\angle ABC < m\angle BAD$. .... The larger angle is opposite the longer side.

$m\angle BCA < m\angle BAD$ .... Transitive Property of Inequality

REFLECT

2a. Compare $m\angle BCA$ and $m\angle BAC$. Explain how the comparison allows you to conclude $m\angle BCA < m\angle BAD$ in another way.

Because $AB < BC$, $m\angle BCA < m\angle BAC$. By the Angle Addition Postulate, $m\angle BAC + m\angle CAD = m\angle BAD$, so $m\angle BAC = m\angle BAD - m\angle CAD$ and thus $m\angle BAC < m\angle BAD$. By the Transitivity Prop. of Inequality, $m\angle BCA < m\angle BAD$.

PRACTICE

1. Given the information in the diagram, prove that $PQ < PS$.

In $\triangle PRS$, $m\angle PRS = 180° - 37° - 63° = 80°$.

In $\triangle PQR$, because $35° < 45°$, $PQ < PR$.

In $\triangle PRS$, because $63° < 80°$, $PR < PS$.

By the Transitive Property of Inequality, $PQ < PS$.

2. Given the information in the diagram, prove that $m\angle DEA < m\angle ABC$.

In $\triangle ADE$, $AD < DE$ ($4 < 7$), so $m\angle DEA < m\angle DAE$.

In $\triangle ABC$, $BC < AC$ ($9 < 11$), so $m\angle DAE < m\angle ABC$.

By the Transitive Property of Inequality,

$m\angle DEA < m\angle ABC$.

Chapter 5   216   Lesson 5

ADDITIONAL PRACTICE AND PROBLEM SOLVING

Assign these pages to help your students practice and apply important lesson concepts. For additional exercises, see the Student Edition.

Answers

Additional Practice

1. $m\angle 1 + m\angle 2 + m\angle 3 > 180°$
2. Possible answer: Assume that $m\angle 1 + m\angle 2 + m\angle 3 > 180°$. $\angle 4$ is an exterior angle of $\triangle ABC$, so by the Exterior Angle Theorem, $m\angle 1 + m\angle 2 = m\angle 4$. $\angle 3$ and $\angle 4$ are a linear pair, so by the Linear Pair Theorem, $m\angle 3 + m\angle 4 = 180°$. Substitution leads to the conclusion that $m\angle 1 + m\angle 2 + m\angle 3 = 180°$, which contradicts the assumption. Thus the assumption is false, and the sum of the angle measures of a triangle cannot add to more than 180°.
3. $\angle F$; $\angle D$; $\angle E$
4. $\overline{HI}$; $\overline{GH}$; $\overline{GI}$
5. no; $8 + 8 = 16$
6. yes
7. yes
8. yes
9. no; $12 + 20 < 36$
10. $4.7 \text{ m} < s < 11.7 \text{ m}$
11. $121 \text{ ft} < s < 475 \text{ ft}$
12. $\frac{1}{2} \text{ mi} < s < 7\frac{1}{2} \text{ mi}$
13. Renaldo could travel between 8562 miles and 15,502 miles.

Problem Solving

1. Fairbanks to Nome
2. towers *K* and *L*
3. targets 2 and 3
4. targets 1 and 4
5. C
6. J
7. A

Additional Practice

Write an indirect proof that the angle measures of a triangle cannot add to more than 180°.

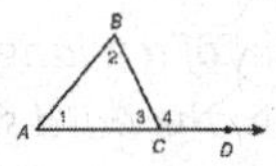

1. State the assumption that starts the indirect proof.

_____

2. Use the Exterior Angle Theorem and the Linear Pair Theorem to write the indirect proof.

3. Write the angles of △DEF in order from smallest to largest.

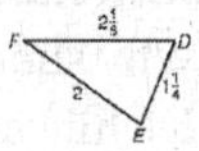

4. Write the sides of △GHI in order from shortest to longest.

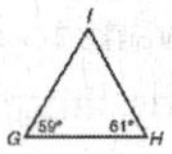

Tell whether a triangle can have sides with the given lengths. If not, explain why not.

5. 8, 8, 16 _____ 6. 0.5, 0.7, 0.3 _____ 7. $10\frac{1}{2}$, 4, 14 _____

8. $3x + 2$, x^2, $2x$ when $x = 4$ _____

9. $3x + 2$, x^2, $2x$ when $x = 6$ _____

The lengths of two sides of a triangle are given. Find the range of possible lengths for the third side.

10. 8.2 m, 3.5 m 11. 298 ft, 177 ft 12. $3\frac{1}{2}$ mi, 4 mi

_____ _____ _____

13. The annual Cheese Rolling happens in May at Gloucestershire, England. As the name suggests, large, 7–9 pound wheels of cheese are rolled down a steep hill, and people chase after them. The first person to the bottom wins cheese. Renaldo wants to go to the Cheese Rolling. He plans to leave from Atlanta and fly into London (4281 miles). On the return, he will fly back from London to New York City (3470 miles) to visit his aunt. Then Renaldo heads back to Atlanta. Atlanta, New York City, and London do not lie on the same line. Find the range of the total distance Renaldo could travel on his trip.

Problem Solving

1. A charter plane travels from Barrow, Alaska, to Fairbanks. From Fairbanks, it flies to Nome, and then back to its starting point in Barrow. Which of the three legs of the trip is the longest?

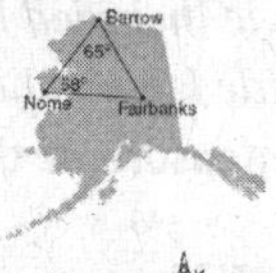

_____

2. Three cell phone towers are shown at the right. The measure of ∠M is 10° less than the measure of ∠K. The measure of ∠L is 1° greater than the measure of ∠K. Which two towers are closest together?

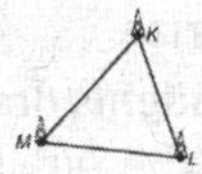

_____

Use the figure for Exercises 3 and 4.

In disc golf, a player tries to throw a disc into a metal basket target. Four disc golf targets on a course are shown at right.

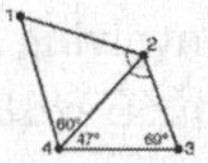

3. Which two targets are closest together?

_____

4. Which two targets are farthest apart?

_____

Choose the best answer.

5. The distance from Jacksonville to Tampa is 171 miles. The distance from Tampa to Miami is 206 miles. Use the Triangle Inequality Theorem to find the range for the distance from Jacksonville to Miami.

A 0 mi < d < 35 mi
B 0 mi < d < 377 mi
C 35 mi < d < 377 mi
D −35 mi < d < 377 mi

6. In Jessica's room, the distance from the door D to the closet C is 4 feet. The distance from the closet to the window W is 6 feet. The distance from the window to the door is 8 feet. On a floor plan of her room, △CDW is drawn. Order the angles from least to greatest measure.

F ∠C, ∠D, ∠W   H ∠W, ∠C, ∠D
G ∠D, ∠C, ∠W   J ∠W, ∠D, ∠C

7. Walking paths at a park are shown. Which route represents the greatest distance?

A A to B to D   C C to B to D
B A to D to B   D C to D to B

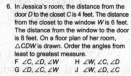

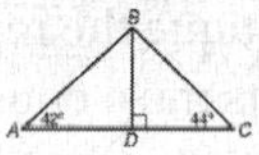

Notes

Inequalities in Two Triangles
Going Deeper

Essential question: When two sides of a triangle have fixed lengths and the angle included by them changes, how does the third side length change?

COMMON CORE Standards for Mathematical Content

CC.9-12.G.CO.10 Prove theorems about triangles.

Prerequisites
Measuring angles and line segments

Math Background
In this lesson, students investigate the Hinge Theorem, first by exploring triangles that are isosceles and then by exploring triangles that are scalene.

INTRODUCE

Ask students to think about a compass. As they increase the angle formed by the arm with the sharp point and the arm that holds the pencil, they should realize that the distance between the sharp point and the tip of the pencil also increases.

TEACH

1 EXPLORE

Questioning Strategies
- In what sequence of steps will you construct the desired triangle? **Construct the angle first, and then construct congruent segments along the sides of the angle.**
- Under what conditions will the triangle you form be isosceles but not equilateral? **when the third side is longer or shorter than the congruent sides**
- How can you determine the range of possible lengths of the third side? **Consider the two extreme cases: When the two congruent sides form a 0° angle, the third side has a length of 0. When the two congruent sides form a 180° angle, the third side has a length of $a + a = 2a$.**

2 EXPLORE

Questioning Strategies
- Why shouldn't you vary your choices for a and b while changing the measure of the angle? **You want to know how angle measure alone affects the length of the third side. Changing a and b varies the third side even with the angle fixed, so you would not be able to isolate the relationship between angle measure and third side length.**
- How can you determine the range of possible lengths of the third side? **Consider the two extreme cases: When the two sides of fixed length form a 0° angle, the length of the third side is the difference of the longer fixed length and the shorter fixed length. When the two sides of fixed length form a 180° angle, the length of the third side is the sum of the fixed lengths.**

CLOSE

Essential Question
When two sides of a triangle have fixed lengths and the angle included by them changes, how does the third side length change? **Increasing the included angle measure of the increases the length third side.**

Summarize
Have students draw $\triangle ABC$ where $AC = 3$, $BC = 4$, and m$\angle C = 90°$. Have them find AB, then write inequalities involving AB when $0° <$ m$\angle C < 90°$ and when $90° <$ m$\angle C < 180°$. **5; 1 < AB < 5 ; 5 < AB < 7**

MATHEMATICAL PRACTICE | **Highlighting the Standards**

Reflect questions 1c and 2c can involve Standard 3 (Construct viable arguments and critique the reasoning of others). Here, students must consider extreme cases (degenerate triangles) in order to establish limits on the possible lengths of the third side.

© Houghton Mifflin Harcourt Publishing Company

Name _____ Class _____ Date _____

5-6

Inequalities in Two Triangles
Going Deeper

Essential question: When two sides of a triangle have fixed lengths and the angle included by them changes, how does the third side length change?

Video Tutor

1 EXPLORE Comparing Triangles with Two Congruent Sides

A Using a protractor, draw an angle. Along each side, measure a distance *a* of your choice. Then join the three points obtained to form a triangle like the one below, △XYZ. Draw several such triangles, using various angle measures, such as 30°, 60°, 90°, 120°, and 150°, but keeping the distance *a* the same.

B In each triangle you construct, measure the length of the third side, *XZ*. Label the lengths on your diagrams.

C Record your results in the table. Possible answers are shown.

Angle measure	30°	60°	90°	120°	150°
Distance *a*	15 cm	15 cm	15 cm	15 cm	15 cm
Length of third side	7.8 cm	15 cm	21.2 cm	26.0 cm	29.0 cm

REFLECT

1a. Classify the triangles you drew.

The triangles are all isosceles, because they have two sides that are the same length. If the included angle is 60°, the triangle is also equilateral.

1b. In general terms, how does changing the included angle affect the length of the third side? Conversely, as the length of the third side increases, how is the angle opposite the third side affected?

As the included angle increases, the length of the third side increases. As the length of the third side increases, the included angle measure increases.

1c. What is the range of possible values for the third side?

The third side length will be between 0 and 2a, where a is the length of each of the two fixed sides.

2 EXPLORE Comparing Triangles with Different Side Lengths

A Repeat the steps of the previous Explore, but use two different distances, *a* and *b*, of your choice. Draw several triangles, using various angle measures, such as 30°, 60°, 90°, 120°, and 150°, but keeping the distances *a* and *b* the same each time.

B In each triangle you construct, measure the length of the third side, *XZ*. Label the lengths on your diagrams.

C Record your results in the table. Possible answers are shown.

Angle measure	30°	60°	90°	120°	150°
Distance *a*	18 cm	18 cm	18 cm	18 cm	18 cm
Distance *b*	24 cm	24 cm	24 cm	24 cm	24 cm
Length of third side	22.9 cm	26.2 cm	30 cm	33.4 cm	35.7 cm

REFLECT

2a. Classify the triangles you drew.

Possible answer: The triangles are scalene. That is, the three side lengths are different from one another.

2b. How do your results compare with Explore 1?

The general result is the same: Increasing the measure of the included angle increases the length of the third side.

2c. What is the range of possible values for the third side? Explain.

Possible answer: If the two fixed side lengths are a and b and a < b, the third side length is between b − a and b + a.

2d. If side lengths a and b are different, is it possible to adjust the angle between them to make an isosceles triangle? Under what conditions is this possible?

Possible answer: You can form an isosceles triangle with a third side length of a when b < 2a, or with a third side length of b when a < 2b.

ADDITIONAL PRACTICE AND PROBLEM SOLVING

Assign these pages to help your students practice and apply important lesson concepts. For additional exercises, see the Student Edition.

Answers

Additional Practice

1. $m\angle K < m\angle M$
2. $AB < DE$
3. $QR > ST$
4. $7 < x < 58$
5. $\frac{5}{3} < x < \frac{17}{2}$
6. $-2 < x < 10.5$
7. $x > 4$
8. Possible answer: The legs of a compass and the length spanned by it form a triangle, but the lengths of the legs cannot change. Therefore any two settings of the compass are subject to the Hinge Theorem. To draw a largerdiameter circle, the measure of the hinge angle must be made larger. To draw a smaller-diameter circle, the measure of the hinge angle must be made smaller.

Problem Solving

1. Greatest at relaxed position; least at writing position; the length of his leg and the length of his body are the same in all three triangles. So, by the Converse of the Hinge Thm., the larger included ∠ is across from the longer third side.
2. the second cyclist
3. The ∠ formed by the compass when drawing the first circle is smaller. So the distance between the points of the compass is greater for the second circle.
4. B
5. G

Name _______________ Class _______________ Date _______________

5-6

Additional Practice

Compare the given measures.

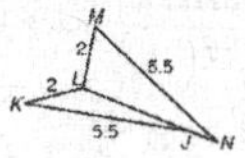
M
2
8.5
2
K
5.5
J
N

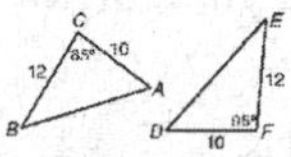
C
12
85°
10
A
B
E
12
D
85°
10
F

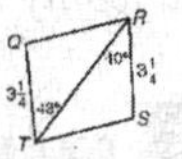
Q
R
10°
$3\frac{1}{4}$
$3\frac{1}{4}$
48°
T
S

1. m∠K and m∠M ____________

2. AB and DE ____________

3. QR and ST ____________

Find the range of values for x.

4. 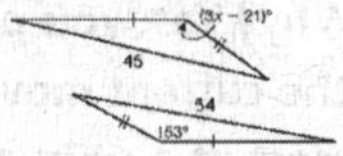
(3x − 21)°
45
54
153°

____

6. 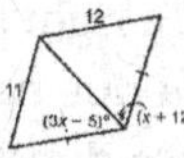
12
11
(3x − 5)°
(x + 12)°

____

5. 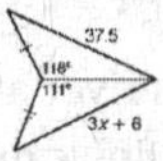
37.5
118°
111°
3x + 6

____

7. 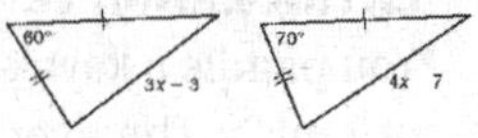
60°
3x − 3
70°
4x
7

____

8. You have used a compass to copy and bisect segments and angles and to draw arcs and circles. A compass has a drawing leg, a pivot leg, and a hinge at the angle between the legs. Explain why and how the measure of the angle at the hinge changes if you draw two circles with different diameters.

____

Problem Solving

1. The angle that a person makes as he or she is sitting changes with the task. The diagram shows the position of a student at his desk. In which position is the angle measure $a°$ at which he is sitting the greatest? The least? Explain.

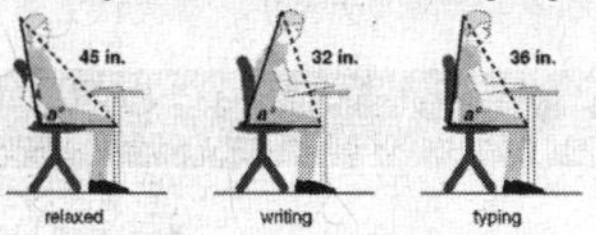
45 in.
32 in.
36 in.
relaxed
writing
typing

____

2. Two cyclists start from the same location and travel in opposite directions for 2 miles each. Then the first cyclist turns right 90° and continues for another mile. At the same time, the second cyclist turns 45° left and continues for another mile. At this point, which cyclist is closer to the original starting point?

____

3. A compass is used to draw a circle. Then the compass is opened wider and another circle is drawn. Explain how this illustrates the Hinge Theorem.

____

Choose the best answer.

4. Two sides of each triangle in the circle are formed from the radii of the circle. Compare EF and FG.

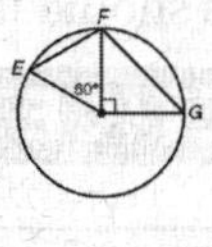
F
E
80°
G

A EF = FG

B EF < FG

C EF > FG

D Not enough information is given.

5. Compare m∠Y and m∠M.

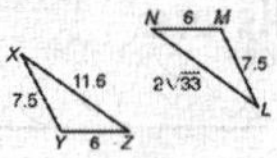
N
6
M
7.5
$2\sqrt{33}$
L
X
11.6
7.5
Y
6
Z

F m∠Y = m∠M

G m∠Y > m∠M

H m∠Y < m∠M

J Not enough information is given.

Notes

The Pythagorean Theorem
Going Deeper

Essential question: How can you apply the Pythagorean Theorem?

COMMON CORE Standards for Mathematical Content

CC.9-12.G.SRT.8 Use ... the Pythagorean Theorem to solve right triangles in applied problems.

Prerequisites
The Pythagorean Theorem

Math Background
The Pythagorean Theorem states that for any right triangle with legs of length a and b and hypotenuse of length c, $a^2 + b^2 = c^2$. Therefore, the Pythagorean Theorem can be used to find the length of any side of a right triangle if the lengths of the other two sides are known.

INTRODUCE

Remind students that $a^2 + b^2 = c^2$ for any right triangle. Be sure to stress that c represents the length of the hypotenuse (the side opposite the right angle), which is always the longest side of a right triangle.

TEACH

1 EXAMPLE

Questioning Strategies
• Do you expect the distance BC to be greater than or less than the length of the brace? Why? **less than; the brace is the hypotenuse of the right triangle, so it must be longer than either leg.**

EXTRA EXAMPLE
Rasheed is building a shelf that folds down from the wall. When it is lowered, the shelf will extend 14 inches from the wall and will be supported by a 17-inch-long chain. To the nearest tenth of an inch, how far above the shelf should the chain be attached to the wall?

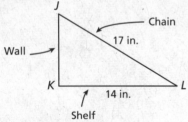

9.6 in.

2 EXAMPLE

Questioning Strategies
• Is $\triangle ABC$ a right triangle? Why? **Yes; you paddle the canoe due north, and the current moves due east. These directions intersect at a right angle.**

EXTRA EXAMPLE
You paddle a kayak due north across a river at a rate of 2 mi/h. The river has a current that flows due west at a rate of 0.5 mi/h. What is the kayak's actual speed? **≈2.1 mi/h**

MATHEMATICAL PRACTICE   **Highlighting the Standards**

Example 2 provides an opportunity to address Standard 4 (Model with mathematics). Students may not be aware that when a speed has a direction associated with it, a useful model is an arrow (where the arrow points in the direction of motion and the length of the arrow is the speed). The Pythagorean Theorem can be applied in cases, like this one, where the arrows form a right triangle.

CLOSE

Essential Question
How can you apply the Pythagorean Theorem?
When a real-world problem involves a right triangle with two side lengths known, you can use the Pythagorean Theorem to find the missing side length.

Summarize
Have students write a journal entry in which they create a real-world problem that involves finding a missing side length of a right triangle. Students should include a solution of the problem.

PRACTICE

Where skills are taught	Where skills are practiced
1 EXAMPLE	EXS. 1–8
2 EXAMPLE	EX. 9

Name_____ Class_____ Date_____ **5-7**

The Pythagorean Theorem
Going Deeper

Essential question: *How can you apply the Pythagorean Theorem?*

CC.9–12.G.SRT.8

1 EXAMPLE Using the Pythagorean Theorem with Lengths

A shelf extends perpendicularly 24 cm from a wall. You want to place a 28-cm brace under the shelf, as shown. To the nearest tenth of a centimeter, how far below the shelf will the brace be attached to the wall?

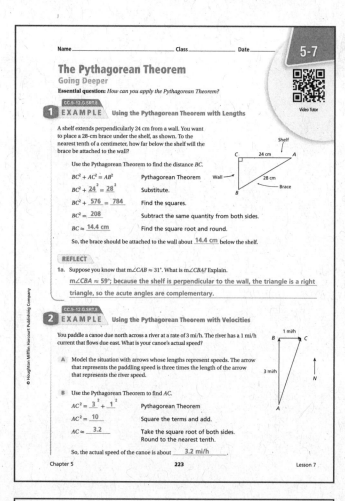

Use the Pythagorean Theorem to find the distance BC.

$BC^2 + AC^2 = AB^2$ Pythagorean Theorem

$BC^2 + \underline{24}^2 = \underline{28}^2$ Substitute.

$BC^2 + \underline{576} = \underline{784}$ Find the squares.

$BC^2 = \underline{208}$ Subtract the same quantity from both sides.

$BC \approx \underline{14.4}$ cm   Find the square root and round.

So, the brace should be attached to the wall about __14.4 cm__ below the shelf.

REFLECT

1a. Suppose you know that m∠CAB ≈ 31°. What is m∠CBA? Explain.

m∠CBA ≈ 59°; because the shelf is perpendicular to the wall, the triangle is a right triangle, so the acute angles are complementary.

CC.9–12.G.SRT.8

2 EXAMPLE Using the Pythagorean Theorem with Velocities

You paddle a canoe due north across a river at a rate of 3 mi/h. The river has a 1 mi/h current that flows due east. What is your canoe's actual speed?

A   Model the situation with arrows whose lengths represent speeds. The arrow that represents the paddling speed is three times the length of the arrow that represents the river speed.

B   Use the Pythagorean Theorem to find AC.

$AC^2 = \underline{3}^2 + \underline{1}^2$ Pythagorean Theorem

$AC^2 = \underline{10}$ Square the terms and add.

$AC \approx \underline{3.2}$ Take the square root of both sides. Round to the nearest tenth.

So, the actual speed of the canoe is about __3.2 mi/h__.

© Houghton Mifflin Harcourt Publishing Company

REFLECT

2a. Why does it make sense that the canoe's actual speed is greater than both the speed at which you paddle and the speed of the current?

The speed is represented by the hypotenuse of a right triangle, which must be longer than either of the legs.

PRACTICE

Use the Pythagorean Theorem to find the missing side length. Round to the nearest tenth.

1.   __25__

2.   __13.5__

3.   __12__

4.   __50.0__

5.   __12.1__

6.   __93.0__

7. A ladder leans against a wall and reaches a point 15 feet up the wall. The base of the ladder is 3.9 feet from the wall. To the nearest tenth of a foot, what is the length of the ladder?

Length of ladder: 15.5 ft

8. A 7.2-meter guy wire goes from the top of a utility pole to a point on the ground that is 3 meters from the base of the pole. To the nearest tenth of a meter, how tall is the utility pole?

Height of pole: 6.5 m

9. A plane flies due north at 500 mi/h. There is a crosswind blowing due east at 60 mi/h. What is the plane's actual speed to the nearest tenth?

Actual speed: 503.6 mi/h

© Houghton Mifflin Harcourt Publishing Company

ADDITIONAL PRACTICE AND PROBLEM SOLVING

Assign these pages to help your students practice and apply important lesson concepts. For additional exercises, see the Student Edition.

Answers

Additional Practice

1. $\sqrt{61}$
2. $2\sqrt{14}$
3. 48
4. height: 25.2 in.; width: 33.6 in.
5. 51.4 in.
6. 2.5; no
7. 25; yes
8. $3\sqrt{10}$; no
9. yes; acute
10. yes; obtuse
11. yes; obtuse
12. Possible answer: The triangle is obtuse, so Kitty is correct. But Kitty did not use the Pythagorean Inequalities Theorem correctly. The measure of the longest side should be substituted for c, so $169 + 64 < 256$ is the inequality that shows that the triangle is obtuse.

Problem Solving

1. 18.9 ft
2. 4.1 ft
3. 38 ft
4. width = 36.6 in.; height = 20.6 in.
5. C
6. J
7. A
8. H

Name_____ Class_____ Date_____

Additional Practice

Find the value of x. Give your answer in simplest radical form.

1.

2.

3.

4. The aspect ratio of a TV screen is the ratio of the width to the height of the image. A regular TV has an aspect ratio of 4 : 3. Find the height and width of a 42-inch TV screen to the nearest tenth of an inch. (The measure given is the length of the diagonal across the screen.)

_____

5. A "wide-screen" TV has an aspect ratio of 16 : 9. Find the length of a diagonal on a wide-screen TV screen that has the same height as the screen in Exercise 4.

_____

Find the missing side lengths. Give your answer in simplest radical form. Tell whether the side lengths form a Pythagorean Triple.

6.

7.

8.

Tell whether the measures can be the side lengths of a triangle. If so, classify the triangle as acute, obtuse, or right.

9. 15, 18, 20 _____

10. 7, 8, 11 _____

11. 6, 7, $3\sqrt{13}$ _____

12. Kitty has a triangle with sides that measure 16, 8, and 13. She does some calculations and finds that 256 + 64 > 169. Kitty concludes that the triangle is obtuse. Evaluate Kitty's conclusion and Kitty's reasoning.

_____

_____

_____

Chapter 5   225   Lesson 7

Problem Solving

1. It is recommended that for a height of 20 inches, a wheelchair ramp be 19 feet long. What is the value of x to the nearest tenth?

2. Find x, the length of the weight-lifting incline bench. Round to the nearest tenth.

3. A ladder 15 feet from the base of a building reaches a window that is 35 feet high. What is the length of the ladder to the nearest foot?

4. In a wide-screen television, the ratio of width to height is 16 : 9. What are the width and height of a television that has a diagonal measure of 42 inches? Round to the nearest tenth.

Choose the best answer.

5. The distance from Austin to San Antonio is about 74 miles, and the distance from San Antonio to Victoria is about 102 miles. Find the approximate distance from Austin to Victoria.

   A 28 mi   C 126 mi
   B 70 mi   D 176 mi

6. What is the approximate perimeter of △DEC if rectangle ABCD has a length of 4.6 centimeters?

   F 5.1 cm
   G 6.5 cm
   H 9.8 cm
   J 11.1 cm

7. The legs of a right triangle measure 3x and 15. If the hypotenuse measures 3x + 3, what is the value of x?

   A 12   C 36
   B 16   D 221

8. A cube has edge lengths of 6 inches. What is the approximate length of a diagonal d of the cube?

   F 6 in.   H 10.4 in.
   G 8.4 in.   J 12 in.

Chapter 5   226   Lesson 7

Applying Special Right Triangles
Going Deeper

Essential question: *What can you say about the side lengths associated with special right triangles?*

COMMON CORE **Standards for Mathematical Content**

CC.9-12.G.SRT.6 Understand that by similarity, side ratios in right triangles are properties of the angles in the triangle, leading to definitions of trigonometric ratios for acute angles.

CC.9-12.G.SRT.8 Use ... the Pythagorean Theorem to solve right triangles in applied problems.

Prerequisites
The Pythagorean Theorem

Math Background
This lesson begins with two investigations in which students explore 45°-45°-90° and 30°-60°-90° triangles. These special right triangles occur so often in mathematical and real-world problems that it is well worth spending some time understanding the relationships among the sides of these triangles.

INTRODUCE

Ask students to use a compass and straightedge to construct an isosceles right triangle. Then, ask students to use a protractor to measure the acute angles of the triangle. Students should find that both acute angles of the triangle measure 45°.

Likewise, have students use a compass and straightedge to construct an equilateral triangle and drop a perpendicular from one vertex. Then, have students use a protractor to measure the acute angles of one of the two triangles into which the perpendicular divides the equilateral triangle. Students should find that the acute angles measure 30° and 60°.

TEACH

1 EXPLORE

Questioning Strategies
- How can you find the length of the hypotenuse of an isosceles right triangle if you know the length of one of the legs? Multiply the length of the leg by $\sqrt{2}$.
- How can you find the length of the legs of an isosceles right triangle if you know the length of the hypotenuse? Divide the length of the hypotenuse by $\sqrt{2}$.

Differentiated Instruction
Kinesthetic learners may benefit from verifying the results of the Explore via a simple paper folding activity. Have students take a square piece of paper and fold it in half diagonally. This creates an isosceles right triangle. Then ask students to measure one leg of the triangle to the nearest millimeter, and have them use this information and the results of the Explore to predict the length of the hypotenuse. Finally, have students measure the length of the hypotenuse to check their predictions.

2 EXPLORE

Questioning Strategies
- What can you say about the angles of an equilateral triangle? All three angles measure 60°.
- How can you find the length of the hypotenuse of a 30°-60°-90° triangle if you know the length of the shorter leg? Multiply the length of the shorter leg by 2.
- What is the ratio of the length of the hypotenuse to the length of the shorter leg in any 30°-60°-90° triangle? The ratio is 2 to 1.

© Houghton Mifflin Harcourt Publishing Company

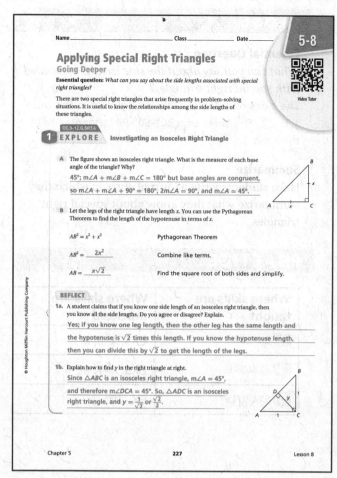

Name _____ Class _____ Date _____

5-8

Video Tutor

Applying Special Right Triangles
Going Deeper

Essential question: *What can you say about the side lengths associated with special right triangles?*

There are two special right triangles that arise frequently in problem-solving situations. It is useful to know the relationships among the side lengths of these triangles.

CC.9-12.G.SRT.6

1 EXPLORE Investigating an Isosceles Right Triangle

A The figure shows an isosceles right triangle. What is the measure of each base angle of the triangle? Why?

45°; $m\angle A + m\angle B + m\angle C = 180°$ but base angles are congruent, so $m\angle A + m\angle A + 90° = 180°$, $2m\angle A = 90°$, and $m\angle A = 45°$.

B Let the legs of the right triangle have length x. You can use the Pythagorean Theorem to find the length of the hypotenuse in terms of x.

$AB^2 = x^2 + x^2$ Pythagorean Theorem

$AB^2 = \underline{2x^2}$ Combine like terms.

$AB = \underline{x\sqrt{2}}$ Find the square root of both sides and simplify.

REFLECT

1a. A student claims that if you know one side length of an isosceles right triangle, then you know all the side lengths. Do you agree or disagree? Explain.

Yes; if you know one leg length, then the other leg has the same length and the hypotenuse is $\sqrt{2}$ times this length. If you know the hypotenuse length, then you can divide this by $\sqrt{2}$ to get the length of the legs.

1b. Explain how to find y in the right triangle at right.

Since $\triangle ABC$ is an isosceles right triangle, $m\angle A = 45°$, and therefore $m\angle DCA = 45°$. So, $\triangle ADC$ is an isosceles right triangle, and $y = \frac{1}{\sqrt{2}}$ or $\frac{\sqrt{2}}{2}$.

© Houghton Mifflin Harcourt Publishing Company

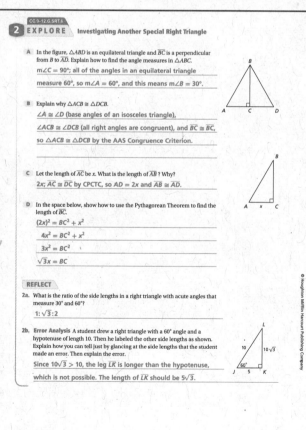

CC.9-12.G.SRT.6

2 EXPLORE Investigating Another Special Right Triangle

A In the figure, $\triangle ABD$ is an equilateral triangle and $\overline{BC}$ is a perpendicular from B to $\overline{AD}$. Explain how to find the angle measures in $\triangle ABC$.

$m\angle C = 90°$; all of the angles in an equilateral triangle measure 60°, so $m\angle A = 60°$, and this means $m\angle B = 30°$.

B Explain why $\triangle ACB \cong \triangle DCB$.

$\angle A \cong \angle D$ (base angles of an isosceles triangle), $\angle ACB \cong \angle DCB$ (all right angles are congruent), and $\overline{BC} \cong \overline{BC}$, so $\triangle ACB \cong \triangle DCB$ by the AAS Congruence Criterion.

C Let the length of $\overline{AC}$ be x. What is the length of $\overline{AB}$? Why?

$2x$; $\overline{AC} \cong \overline{DC}$ by CPCTC, so $AD = 2x$ and $\overline{AB} \cong \overline{AD}$.

D In the space below, show how to use the Pythagorean Theorem to find the length of $\overline{BC}$.

$(2x)^2 = BC^2 + x^2$

$4x^2 = BC^2 + x^2$

$3x^2 = BC^2$

$\sqrt{3}x = BC$

REFLECT

2a. What is the ratio of the side lengths in a right triangle with acute angles that measure 30° and 60°?

$1 : \sqrt{3} : 2$

2b. **Error Analysis** A student drew a right triangle with a 60° angle and a hypotenuse of length 10. Then he labeled the other side lengths as shown. Explain how you can tell just by glancing at the side lengths that the student made an error. Then explain the error.

Since $10\sqrt{3} > 10$, the leg $\overline{LK}$ is longer than the hypotenuse, which is not possible. The length of $\overline{LK}$ should be $5\sqrt{3}$.

© Houghton Mifflin Harcourt Publishing Company

MATHEMATICAL PRACTICE — Highlighting the Standards

You can address Standard 7 (Look for and make use of structure) as you teach this lesson. Emphasize to students that some geometric figures have inherent properties or relationships that are useful in solving problems. For example, in order to find the height x of a 6-foot skateboard ramp that makes a 30° angle with the ground, students who are familiar with right-triangle trigonometry could set up and solve the equation $\sin 30° = \frac{x}{6}$. However, recognizing the 30°-60°-90° triangle in this problem means that a quicker solution is available. That is, the length of the shorter leg of a 30°-60°-90° triangle is half the length of the hypotenuse, so the height is 3 feet.

3 EXAMPLE

Questioning Strategies

- In part A, are you given the length of a leg or the length of the hypotenuse? What do you have to do to find the lengths of the other sides? leg; the other leg has the same length, while the hypotenuse has a length that is $\sqrt{2}$ times the given leg length.

- In part B, are you given the length of the shorter leg, the longer leg, or the hypotenuse? What do you have to do to find the lengths of the other sides? hypotenuse; the shorter leg is half as long as the hypotenuse, while the length of the longer leg is $\sqrt{3}$ times the length of the shorter leg.

EXTRA EXAMPLE

A. In $\triangle ABC$, $m\angle A = m\angle B = 45°$ and $m\angle C = 90°$. If $AB = 6$, what are BC and AC? $AC = BC = 3\sqrt{2}$

B. In $\triangle ABC$, $m\angle A = 30°$, $m\angle B = 60°$, and $m\angle C = 90°$. If $BC = 9$, what are AB and AC? $AB = 6\sqrt{3}$; $AC = 3\sqrt{3}$

CLOSE

Essential Question
What can you say about the side lengths associated with special right triangles?
The sides of a 45°-45°-90° triangle are in the ratio $1:1:\sqrt{2}$. The sides of a 30°-60°-90° triangle are in the ratio $1:\sqrt{3}:2$.

Summarize
Have students write a journal entry in which they summarize what they know about special right triangles.

PRACTICE

Where skills are taught	Where skills are practiced
1 EXPLORE	EXS. 1–3, 8
2 EXPLORE	EXS. 4–7, 9
3 EXAMPLE	EX. 10

The right triangles you investigated are sometimes called 45°-45°-90° and 30°-60°-90° right triangles. The side-length relationships that you discovered can be used to find lengths in any such triangles.

3 EXAMPLE   Solving Special Right Triangles

A   Refer to the diagram of the 45°-45°-90° triangle. Fill in the calculations that help you find the missing side lengths. Give answers in simplest radical form.

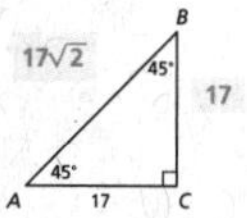

$AC = \underline{17}$

$BC = AC \cdot \underline{1} = \underline{17}$

$AB = AC \cdot \sqrt{2} = \underline{17\sqrt{2}}$

B   Refer to the diagram of the 30°-60°-90° triangle. Fill in the calculations that help you find the missing side lengths. Give answers in simplest radical form.

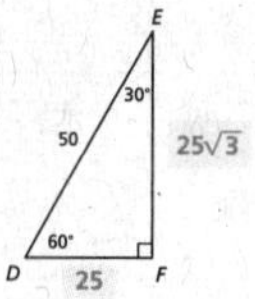

$DE = \underline{50}$

$DF = DE \div \underline{2} = \underline{25}$

$EF = DF \cdot \sqrt{3} = \underline{25\sqrt{3}}$

C   Add the side lengths you calculated to the diagrams.

REFLECT

3a. Suppose you are given the length of the hypotenuse of a 45°-45°-90° triangle. How can you calculate the length of a leg?

Divide the hypotenuse length by $\sqrt{2}$.

3b. Suppose you are given the length of the longer leg of a 30°-60°-90° triangle. How can you calculate the length of the shorter leg?

Divide the longer leg length by $\sqrt{3}$.

3c. When finding a leg length in a 45°-45°-90° triangle, one student gave the answer $\frac{30}{\sqrt{2}}$ and another gave the answer $15\sqrt{2}$. Show the answers are equivalent.

The first answer can be rewritten in simplest radical form to obtain the second answer: $\frac{30}{\sqrt{2}} = \frac{30}{\sqrt{2}} \cdot \frac{\sqrt{2}}{\sqrt{2}} = \frac{30\sqrt{2}}{2} = 15\sqrt{2}.$

PRACTICE

Find the value of x. Give your answer in simplest radical form.

1.

$3\sqrt{2}$

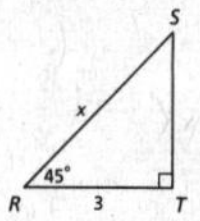

2.

$7\sqrt{2}$

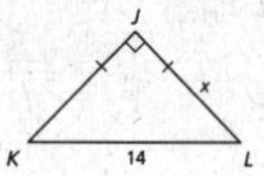

3.
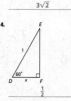
2

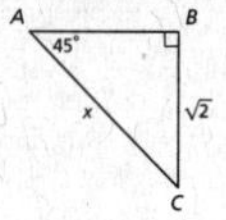

4.

$\frac{1}{2}$

5.

$5\sqrt{3}$

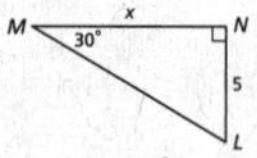

6.

$6\sqrt{3}$

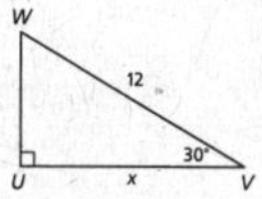

7.

14

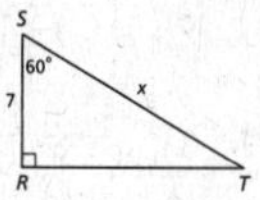

8.

$\frac{15}{2}\sqrt{2}$

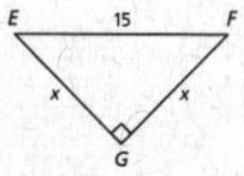

9.

12

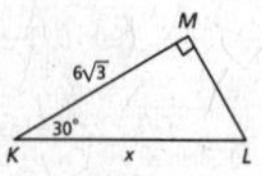

10. **Error Analysis** Two students were asked to find the value of x in the figure at right. Which student's work is correct? Explain the other student's error.

Roberto's Work	Aaron's Work
In a 30°-60°-90° triangle, the hypotenuse is twice as long as the shorter leg, so $BC = 4$. The ratio of the lengths of the legs is $1:\sqrt{3}$, so $x = 4\sqrt{3}$.	In a 30°-60°-90° triangle, the side lengths are in a ratio of $1:\sqrt{3}:2$, so x must be $\sqrt{3}$ times the length of $\overline{AB}$. Therefore, $x = 8\sqrt{3}$.

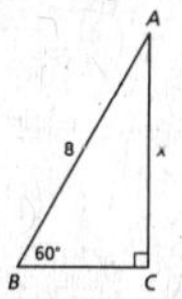

Roberto's work is correct. Aaron had the correct ratios for the

side lengths, but applied them incorrectly to the given triangle.

$AB = 8$, so $BC = 4$ and $AC = \sqrt{3} \cdot BC = 4\sqrt{3}.$

ADDITIONAL PRACTICE AND PROBLEM SOLVING

Assign these pages to help your students practice and apply important lesson concepts. For additional exercises, see the Student Edition.

Answers

Additional Practice

1. 16
2. $\frac{7\sqrt{2}}{2}$
3. 2
4. 30; $20\sqrt{3}$
5. $4\sqrt{3}$; $8\sqrt{3}$
6. $\sqrt{3}$; 3
7. Possible answer: Lucia's hypothesis cannot be correct. The base of the alcove is $\frac{57\sqrt{2}}{4}$ inches or just over 20 inches long, so a $22\frac{1}{8}$-inch tabletcould not fit.
8. Possible answer: To find the height of a 45°-45°-90° triangle, draw a perpendicular to the hypotenuse. This makes another smaller 45°-45°-90 triangle whose hypotenuse is the length of one of the legs of the larger triangle. The height of the alcove is $\frac{57\sqrt{2}}{8}$ inches or about 10 inches, so the statues could have been placed in the alcoves.

Problem Solving

1. $12\sqrt{3}$ in. or about 20.8 in.
2. $32\sqrt{3}$ in. or about 55.4 in.
3. $3\sqrt{2}$ in. or about 4.2 in.
4. $\frac{8\sqrt{3}}{3}$ in. or about 4.6 in.
5. $14\sqrt{3}$ in.
6. $19\sqrt{2}$ cm
7. B
8. F

Name_____ Class_____ Date_____   **5-8**

Additional Practice

Find the value of *x* in each figure. Give your answer in simplest radical form.

1.

2.

3.

_____   _____   _____

Find the values of *x* and *y*. Give your answers in simplest radical form.

4.

5.

6.

4. *x* = _____ *y* = _____   5. *x* = _____ *y* = _____   6. *x* = _____ *y* = _____

Lucia is an archaeologist trekking through the jungle of the Yucatan Peninsula. She stumbles upon a stone structure covered with creeper vines and ferns. She immediately begins taking measurements of her discovery. (*Hint:* Drawing some figures may help.)

7. Around the perimeter of the building, Lucia finds small alcoves at regular intervals carved into the stone. The alcoves are triangular in shape with a horizontal base and two sloped equal-length sides that meet at a right angle. Each of the sloped sides measures $14\frac{1}{4}$ inches. Lucia has also found several stone tablets inscribed with characters. The stone tablets measure $22\frac{1}{8}$ inches long. Lucia hypothesizes that the alcoves once held the stone tablets. Tell whether Lucia's hypothesis may be correct. Explain your answer.

_____

_____

8. Lucia also finds several statues around the building. The statues measure $9\frac{7}{16}$ inches tall. She wonders whether the statues might have been placed in the alcoves. Tell whether this is possible. Explain your answer.

_____

_____

_____

_____

© Houghton Mifflin Harcourt Publishing Company

Problem Solving

For Exercises 1–6, give your answers in simplest radical form.

1. In bowling, the pins are arranged in a pattern based on equilateral triangles. What is the distance between pins 1 and 5?

2. To secure an outdoor canopy, a 64-inch cord is extended from the top of a vertical pole to the ground. If the cord makes a 60° angle with the ground, how tall is the pole?

_____

Find the length of $\overline{AB}$ in each quilt pattern.

3.

4.

_____   _____

Choose the best answer.

5. An equilateral triangle has an altitude of 21 inches. What is the side length of the triangle?

_____

6. A shelf is an isosceles right triangle, and the longest side is 38 centimeters. What is the length of each of the other two sides?

_____

Use the figure for Exercises 7 and 8.
Assume △*JKL* is in the first quadrant, with m∠*K* = 90°.

7. Suppose that $\overline{JK}$ is a leg of △*JKL*, a 45°-45°-90° triangle. What are possible coordinates of point *L*?

  A (6, 4.5)   C (6, 2)

  B (7, 2)   D (8, 7)

8. Suppose △*JKL* is a 30°-60°-90° triangle and $\overline{JK}$ is the side opposite the 60° angle. What are the approximate coordinates of point *L*?

  F (4.9, 2)   H (8.7, 2)

  G (4.5, 2)   J (7.1, 2)

© Houghton Mifflin Harcourt Publishing Company

This page provides students with the opportunity to apply concepts from the Common Core in real-world problem situations. There are three different levels of performance tasks:

⭐**Novice:** These are short word problems that require students to apply the math they have learned in straightforward, real-world situations.

⭐⭐**Apprentice:** These are more involved problems that guide students step-by-step through more complex tasks. These exercises include more complicated reasoning, writing, and open-ended elements.

⭐⭐⭐**Expert:** These are open-ended, non-routine problems that, instead of stepping the students through, ask them to choose their own methods for solving and justify their answers and reasoning.

Sample answers

1. The tailor should make the vertex angle less than 26°. The skirts are identical in length, so according to the Hinge Theorem, the gore with the smaller angle will have a shorter base. The gore with the shorter base will flare out less.

2. 280 ft

3. Scoring Guide:

Task	Possible points
a	2 points for correctly finding the lengths of 12 in., 24 in., and 36 in.
b	1 point for correctly finding the total length of 10 ft
c	1 point for correctly stating he needs 2 planks, and 1 point for a correct explanation, for example: One 6-foot plank can be cut into the 12 in. and 48 in. shelves, and the other can be cut into the 24 in. and 36 in. shelves
d	1 point for correctly stating that he will have a total of 23 in. left over

Total possible points: 6

CHAPTER 5

Performance Tasks

COMMON CORE
CC.9-12.G.CO.9
CC.9-12.G.CO.10
CC.9-12.G.SRT.4
CC.9-12.G.C.3
CC.9-12.G.MG.3

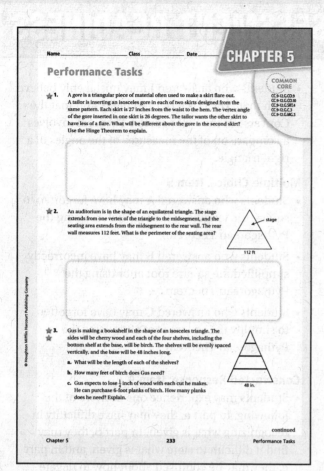

★ 1. A *gore* is a triangular piece of material often used to make a skirt flare out. A tailor is inserting an isosceles gore in each of two skirts designed from the same pattern. Each skirt is 27 inches from the waist to the hem. The vertex angle of the gore inserted in one skirt is 26 degrees. The tailor wants the other skirt to have less of a flare. What will be different about the gore in the second skirt? Use the Hinge Theorem to explain.

★ 2. An auditorium is in the shape of an equilateral triangle. The stage extends from one vertex of the triangle to the midsegment, and the seating area extends from the midsegment to the rear wall. The rear wall measures 112 feet. What is the perimeter of the seating area?

stage

112 ft

★ 3. Gus is making a bookshelf in the shape of an isosceles triangle. The sides will be cherry wood and each of the four shelves, including the bottom shelf at the base, will be birch. The shelves will be evenly spaced vertically, and the base will be 48 inches long.

   a. What will be the length of each of the shelves?

   b. How many feet of birch does Gus need?

   c. Gus expects to lose $\frac{1}{4}$ inch of wood with each cut he makes. He can purchase 6-foot planks of birch. How many planks does he need? Explain.

48 in.

continued

---

   d. After Gus makes all the necessary cuts, what is the total length of the piece(s) of birch he will have left over?

★ 4. Three people are repairing a fence around a rectangular field. They need to share tools, so they want to leave the tools they are not using in a place equidistant from the places they are repairing. Person *A* is working 700 feet north of the southwest corner. Person *B* is working 1200 feet east and 1000 feet north of the southwest corner. Person *C* is working 1500 feet east of the southwest corner. Find the point that is equidistant from all three points. Round to the nearest foot, and describe the point with distances relative to the southwest corner. Show your work.

4. Scoring Guide:

Task	Possible points
a	2 points for correctly finding the point to be 734 ft east and 315 ft north of the southwest corner, and 4 points for showing appropriate work, which should involve finding the circumcenter of the triangle formed by the three workers.

Total possible points: 6

COMMON CORE CORRELATION

Standard	Items
CC.9-12.G.CO.10	4, 9
CC.9-12.G.SRT.8*	5, 6, 7
CC.9-12.G.C.3	3, 8
CC.9-12.G.GPE.2	1, 2

TEST PREP DOCTOR ✚

Multiple Choice: Item 2
- Students who answered **F** or **G** may have confused the equations of parabolas that have horizontal axes of symmetry and the equations of parabolas that have vertical axes of symmetry.
- Students who answered **H** may have incorrectly substituted -2 rather than $-(-2)$ for p in the equation for the parabola.

Multiple Choice: Item 3
- Students who answered **B** may have confused the circumcircle of $\triangle PQR$ with the incircle of $\triangle PQR$. The center of the circumcircle is the intersection of the perpendicular bisectors of the sides.
- Students who answered **C** may mistakenly believe that the center of the inscribed circle is the intersection of the altitudes of the triangle.
- Students who answered **D** may mistakenly believe that the center of the inscribed circle is the intersection of the medians of the triangle.

Multiple Choice: Item 4
- Students who answered **G** may have confused the Hinge Theorem and the Triangle Inequality Theorem (The sum of the lengths of any two sides of a triangle is greater than the length of the third side.)
- Students who answered **H** may be confused about the converse of the Hinge Theorem, and may mistakenly believe it reverses the order of the measures of the angles.

- Students who answered **J** may mistakenly believe both that $\triangle BCD$ is a right triangle, and that the Converse of the Pythagorean Theorem involves a comparison of the measures of the angles of a right triangle.

Multiple Choice: Item 5
- Students who answered **A** may have forgotten to square the lengths of the legs before using the Pythagorean Theorem.
- Students who answered **B** may have incorrectly simplified the square root after using the Pythagorean Theorem.
- Students who answered **C** may have forgotten to simplify the square root after using the Pythagorean Theorem.

Constructed Response: Item 9
- Students may experience one or more of the following. In part **a**, they may have difficulty in recognizing what is given. In part **b**, they may find it difficult to state what is given, and in part **c**, they may be confused about how to negate the statement they composed in part **b**. Some students may have trouble in part **d** if they do not have a sound understanding of the properties of equality and inequality. In part **d**, some students may not recognize that the measure of an angle in a triangle must be greater than 0°. As a result, they may not realize they have actually found the contradiction that completes the indirect proof.

CHAPTER 5 · COMMON CORE · ASSESSMENT READINESS

Name _____ Class _____ Date _____

MULTIPLE CHOICE

1. What is an equation of the parabola with focus $F(0, -6)$ and directrix $y = 6$?

   A. $y = \frac{1}{24}x^2$

   B. $x = \frac{1}{24}y^2$

   C. $x = -\frac{1}{24}y^2$

   (D.) $y = -\frac{1}{24}x^2$

2. Write an equation in standard form for the parabola whose graph is shown.

   F. $y = -\frac{1}{8}x^2$

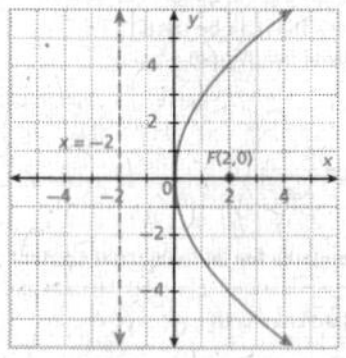

   G. $y = \frac{1}{8}x^2$

   (H.) $x = \frac{1}{8}y^2$

   J. $x = -\frac{1}{8}y^2$

3. Jessica is using a compass and straightedge to construct the inscribed circle for $\triangle PQR$. Which of the following should be her first step?

   (A.) Construct the bisector of $\angle Q$.

   B. Construct the perpendicular bisector of $\overline{QR}$.

   C. Construct the perpendicular from P to $\overline{QR}$.

   D. Construct the midpoint of $\overline{PR}$.

4. What can you conclude about $m\angle ABC$ and $m\angle CBD$ and why?

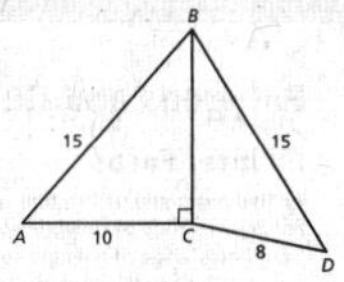

   (F.) $m\angle ABC > m\angle CBD$
   (Hinge Theorem)

   G. $m\angle ABC > m\angle CBD$
   (Triangle Inequality theorem)

   H. $m\angle ABC < m\angle CBD$
   (Converse of the Hinge Theorem)

   J. $m\angle ABC < m\angle CBD$
   (Converse of the Pythagorean Theorem)

5. The lengths of the two legs of a right triangle are 2 inches and 4 inches. What is the length of the hypotenuse in simplest radical form?

   A. $\sqrt{6}$ inches

   B. $2\sqrt{3}$ inches

   (C.) $2\sqrt{5}$ inches

   D. $\sqrt{20}$ inches

6. A square courtyard has a straight walkway from one corner to the opposite corner. If each wall of the courtyard is 20 feet long, what is the length of the walkway?

   F. 10 feet

   G. 20 feet

   (H.) $20\sqrt{2}$ feet

   J. $20\sqrt{3}$ feet

---

7. The sides of an equilateral triangle are 40 inches long. What is the height of the triangle?

   A. 20 feet

   B. 80 feet

   (C.) $20\sqrt{3}$ feet

   D. $40\sqrt{3}$ feet

CONSTRUCTED RESPONSE

8. The diagram below shows the first several steps of a construction.

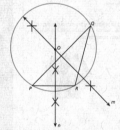

   a. What is line m in relation to the triangle?

   Line m is the perpendicular

   bisector of $\overline{PQ}$.

   b. What is line n in relation to the triangle?

   Line n is the perpendicular bisector

   of $\overline{PR}$.

   c. Draw a circle centered at O that passes through point P. Identify the circle in relation to $\triangle PQR$.

   Circle O with radius OP is the

   circumcircle of $\triangle PQR$.

9. In an indirect proof, you begin by assuming that the conclusion is false. Then you show that this assumption leads to a contradiction.

   Suppose that you want to prove that obtuse $\triangle RST$ does not have a right angle.

   a. What is the given information?

   $\triangle RST$ is an obtuse triangle.

   b. What are you trying to conclude?

   $\triangle RST$ does not have a right angle.

   c. If you assume that the conclusion is false, what must be true instead?

   $\triangle RST$ does have a right angle.

   d. Let $\angle R$ be a right angle. Assume $\angle S$ is a right or obtuse angle. Justify each statement.

Statements	
1. $m\angle R = 90°$, $m\angle S \geq 90°$	1. Definition of right and obtuse angles
2. $m\angle R + m\angle S + m\angle T = 180°$	2. Sum of interior angles of a triangle
3. $90° + m\angle S + m\angle T = 180°$	3. Substitution Property of Equality
4. $m\angle S = 90° - m\angle T$	4. Subtraction Property of Equality
5. $90° \leq 90° - m\angle T$	5. Substitution Property of Inequality
6. $m\angle T \leq 0°$	6. Addition Property of Inequality

   e. What is the contradicion?

   The measure of an angle in a

   triangle cannot be 0 or negative.

   Therefore, $m\angle S$ must be less than

   90°, or acute.

CHAPTER 6

Polygons and Quadrilaterals

COMMON CORE PROFESSIONAL DEVELOPMENT

CC.9-12.G.CO.13

Students use a compass and straightedge to construct various regular polygons, such as a square, a regular hexagon, and a regular pentagon. It is also possible to use geometry software to perform the constructions. Students may be able to benefit more from using technology, as they can easily reconstruct quickly to create smaller and larger regular polygons. Performing these constructions provides students with opportunities to make connections between the construction methods and the number of sides a polygon has, which also helps students understand the properties of regular polygons.

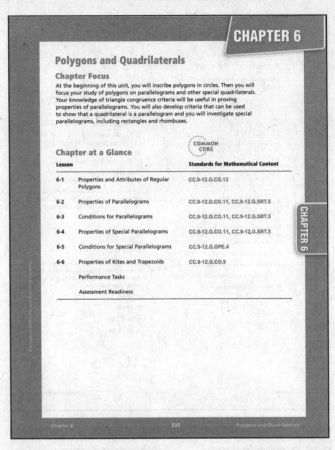

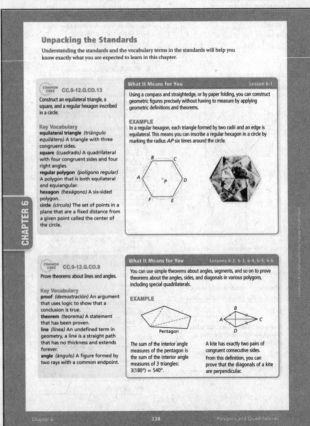

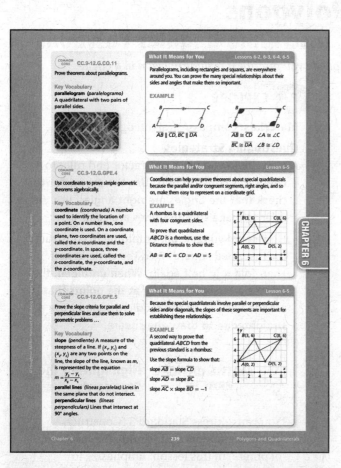

COMMON CORE CC.9-12.G.CO.11
Prove theorems about parallelograms.

Key Vocabulary
parallelogram *(paralelogramo)*
A quadrilateral with two pairs of parallel sides.

What It Means for You   Lessons 6-2, 6-3, 6-4, 6-5
Parallelograms, including rectangles and squares, are everywhere around you. You can prove the many special relationships about their sides and angles that make them so important.

EXAMPLE

$\overline{AB} \parallel \overline{CD}, \overline{BC} \parallel \overline{DA}$

$\overline{AB} \cong \overline{CD}$ $\angle A \cong \angle C$
$\overline{BC} \cong \overline{DA}$ $\angle B \cong \angle D$

COMMON CORE CC.9-12.G.GPE.4
Use coordinates to prove simple geometric theorems algebraically.

Key Vocabulary
coordinate *(coordenada)* A number used to identify the location of a point. On a number line, one coordinate is used. On a coordinate plane, two coordinates are used, called the x-coordinate and the y-coordinate. In space, three coordinates are used, called the x-coordinate, the y-coordinate, and the z-coordinate.

What It Means for You   Lesson 6-5
Coordinates can help you prove theorems about special quadrilaterals because the parallel and/or congruent segments, right angles, and so on, make them easy to represent on a coordinate grid.

EXAMPLE
A rhombus is a quadrilateral with four congruent sides.
To prove that quadrilateral ABCD is a rhombus, use the Distance Formula to show that:
$AB = BC = CD = AD = 5$

COMMON CORE CC.9-12.G.GPE.5
Prove the slope criteria for parallel and perpendicular lines and use them to solve geometric problems …

Key Vocabulary
slope *(pendiente)* A measure of the steepness of a line. If (x_1, y_1) and (x_2, y_2) are any two points on the line, the slope of the line, known as m, is represented by the equation $m = \frac{y_2 - y_1}{x_2 - x_1}$.
parallel lines *(líneas paralelas)* Lines in the same plane that do not intersect.
perpendicular lines *(líneas perpendiculares)* Lines that intersect at 90° angles.

What It Means for You   Lesson 6-5
Because the special quadrilaterals involve parallel or perpendicular sides and/or diagonals, the slopes of these segments are important for establishing these relationships.

EXAMPLE
A second way to prove that quadrilateral ABCD from the previous standard is a rhombus:
Use the slope formula to show that:
slope $\overline{AB}$ = slope $\overline{CD}$
slope $\overline{AD}$ = slope $\overline{BC}$
slope $\overline{AC} \times$ slope $\overline{BD} = -1$

Chapter 6   239   Polygons and Quadrilaterals

CHAPTER 6

COMMON CORE PROFESSIONAL DEVELOPMENT **CC.9-12.G.CO.11**

Many different types of polygons are considered parallelograms. In fact, any quadrilateral whose opposite sides are parallel is classified as a parallelogram. In this chapter, students learn to classify subsets of parallelograms based on their properties. Using the fact that a definition is a biconditional statement, students use conditional statements and their converses to prove and apply properties of parallelograms. This chapter provides ample practice in using logic and deductive reasoning to apply mathematical principles.

CHAPTER 6

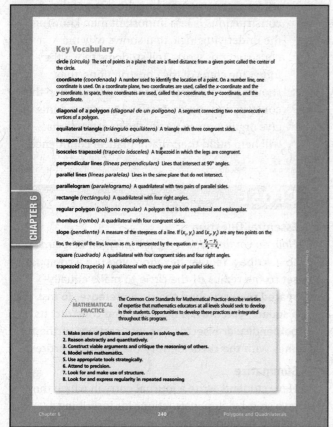

Key Vocabulary

circle *(círculo)* The set of points in a plane that are a fixed distance from a given point called the center of the circle.

coordinate *(coordenada)* A number used to identify the location of a point. On a number line, one coordinate is used. On a coordinate plane, two coordinates are used, called the x-coordinate and the y-coordinate. In space, three coordinates are used, called the x-coordinate, the y-coordinate, and the z-coordinate.

diagonal of a polygon *(diagonal de un polígono)* A segment connecting two nonconsecutive vertices of a polygon.

equilateral triangle *(triángulo equilátero)* A triangle with three congruent sides.

hexagon *(hexágono)* A six-sided polygon.

isosceles trapezoid *(trapecio isósceles)* A trapezoid in which the legs are congruent.

perpendicular lines *(líneas perpendiculares)* Lines that intersect at 90° angles.

parallel lines *(líneas paralelas)* Lines in the same plane that do not intersect.

parallelogram *(paralelogramo)* A quadrilateral with two pairs of parallel sides.

rectangle *(rectángulo)* A quadrilateral with four right angles.

regular polygon *(polígono regular)* A polygon that is both equilateral and equiangular.

rhombus *(rombo)* A quadrilateral with four congruent sides.

slope *(pendiente)* A measure of the steepness of a line. If (x_1, y_1) and (x_2, y_2) are any two points on the line, the slope of the line, known as m, is represented by the equation $m = \frac{y_2 - y_1}{x_2 - x_1}$.

square *(cuadrado)* A quadrilateral with four congruent sides and four right angles.

trapezoid *(trapecio)* A quadrilateral with exactly one pair of parallel sides.

MATHEMATICAL PRACTICE
The Common Core Standards for Mathematical Practice describe varieties of expertise that mathematics educators at all levels should seek to develop in their students. Opportunities to develop these practices are integrated throughout this program.

1. Make sense of problems and persevere in solving them.
2. Reason abstractly and quantitatively.
3. Construct viable arguments and critique the reasoning of others.
4. Model with mathematics.
5. Use appropriate tools strategically.
6. Attend to precision.
7. Look for and make use of structure.
8. Look for and express regularity in repeated reasoning

Chapter 6   240   Polygons and Quadrilaterals

CHAPTER 6

© Houghton Mifflin Harcourt Publishing Company

Properties and Attributes of Regular Polygons
Connection: Inscribing Regular Polygons

Essential question: *How do you inscribe a regular polygon in a circle?*

COMMON **Standards for**
CORE **Mathematical Content**

CC.9-12.G.CO.13 Construct an equilateral triangle, a square, and a regular hexagon inscribed in a circle.

Vocabulary
inscribed

Prerequisites
Constructing the perpendicular bisector of a segment

Math Background
In a previous lesson, students learned to circumscribe a circle about a given triangle. In this lesson, the process is reversed. Now, the circle is the starting point, and students must construct a specified inscribed polygon. As you discuss the constructions in this lesson, highlight the dual nature of inscribing and circumscribing.

INTRODUCE

Explain what it means for a polygon to be inscribed in a figure. You may wish to draw some examples and non-examples on the board to be sure students understand that all vertices of the inscribed polygon must lie on the circle.

TEACH

1 EXPLORE

Materials: compass, straightedge
Questioning Strategies
- How many points do you need to locate on the circle to draw the hexagon? 6
- What must be true about the points for the hexagon to be a regular hexagon? The points must be equally spaced around the circle.
- If A and B are two vertices of the hexagon and O is the center of the circle, what do you know about m$\angle AOB$? Why? This angle measures 60° because it is one of 6 congruent angles that surround the center and completely fill the circle.

2 EXPLORE

Materials: compass, straightedge
Questioning Strategies
- How could you use a protractor and ruler to check this construction? Use the protractor to check that the angles are right angles; use the ruler to make sure the sides are congruent.
- How could you use paper folding to construct the inscribed square? Fold the circle in half. Then fold it in half again. When unfolded, the creases intersect the circle at the points that are the vertices of the required square. Use a straightedge to draw the square.

MATHEMATICAL **Highlighting the**
PRACTICE **Standards**

You can address Standard 3 (Construct viable arguments and critique the reasoning of others) in this lesson. Emphasize to students that memorizing the steps of the constructions is less important than knowing the underlying logic that shows why the constructions work. Tell students that if they forget the steps of the constructions, they should be able to use reasoning to develop the constructions on their own. Having students give arguments to justify the constructions will help build their mathematical confidence.

CLOSE

Essential Question
How do you inscribe a regular polygon in a circle?
To inscribe a regular hexagon, you use a compass set to the radius of the circle to make equally-spaced marks around the circumference. To inscribe a square, you draw a diameter and construct its perpendicular bisector. The intersections of these lines with the circle identify the square's vertices.

Summarize
Have students write a journal entry in which they give step-by-step instructions for inscribing a regular hexagon and square in a circle.

Name_____ Class_____ Date_____

6-1

Properties and Attributes of Regular Polygons
Connection: Inscribing Regular Polygons

Essential question: *How do you inscribe a regular polygon in a circle?*

A polygon is said to be **inscribed** in a circle if all of the polygon's vertices lie on the circle. In the figure, △XYZ is inscribed in circle C. You can also say that circle C circumscribes △XYZ.

In this lesson, you will use a compass and straightedge to inscribe regular polygons in a circle.

CC.9-12.G.CO.13

1 EXPLORE   Inscribing a Regular Hexagon

Use the space at right to inscribe a regular hexagon in a circle.

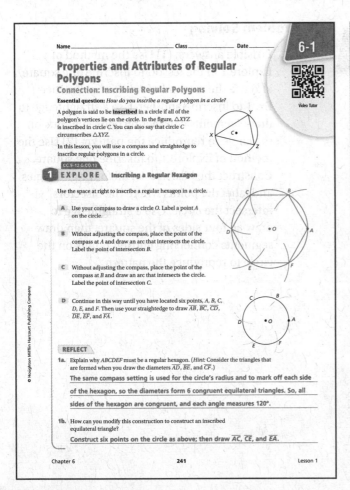

A Use your compass to draw a circle O. Label a point A on the circle.

B Without adjusting the compass, place the point of the compass at A and draw an arc that intersects the circle. Label the point of intersection B.

C Without adjusting the compass, place the point of the compass at B and draw an arc that intersects the circle. Label the point of intersection C.

D Continue in this way until you have located six points, A, B, C, D, E, and F. Then use your straightedge to draw $\overline{AB}$, $\overline{BC}$, $\overline{CD}$, $\overline{DE}$, $\overline{EF}$, and $\overline{FA}$.

REFLECT

1a. Explain why ABCDEF must be a regular hexagon. (*Hint:* Consider the triangles that are formed when you draw the diameters $\overline{AD}$, $\overline{BE}$, and $\overline{CF}$.)

The same compass setting is used for the circle's radius and to mark off each side

of the hexagon, so the diameters form 6 congruent equilateral triangles. So, all

sides of the hexagon are congruent, and each angle measures 120°.

1b. How can you modify this construction to construct an inscribed equilateral triangle?

Construct six points on the circle as above; then draw $\overline{AC}$, $\overline{CE}$, and $\overline{EA}$.

© Houghton Mifflin Harcourt Publishing Company

Chapter 6   241   Lesson 1

CC.9-12.G.CO.13

2 EXPLORE   Inscribing a Square

Use the space at right to inscribe a square in a circle.

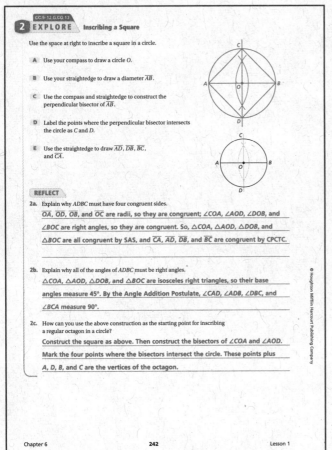

A Use your compass to draw a circle O.

B Use your straightedge to draw a diameter $\overline{AB}$.

C Use the compass and straightedge to construct the perpendicular bisector of $\overline{AB}$.

D Label the points where the perpendicular bisector intersects the circle as C and D.

E Use the straightedge to draw $\overline{AD}$, $\overline{DB}$, $\overline{BC}$, and $\overline{CA}$.

REFLECT

2a. Explain why ADBC must have four congruent sides.

$\overline{OA}$, $\overline{OD}$, $\overline{OB}$, and $\overline{OC}$ are radii, so they are congruent; ∠COA, ∠AOD, ∠DOB, and

∠BOC are right angles, so they are congruent. So, △COA, △AOD, △DOB, and

△BOC are all congruent by SAS, and $\overline{CA}$, $\overline{AD}$, $\overline{DB}$, and $\overline{BC}$ are congruent by CPCTC.

2b. Explain why all of the angles of ADBC must be right angles.

△COA, △AOD, △DOB, and △BOC are isosceles right triangles, so their base

angles measure 45°. By the Angle Addition Postulate, ∠CAD, ∠ADB, ∠DBC, and

∠BCA measure 90°.

2c. How can you use the above construction as the starting point for inscribing a regular octagon in a circle?

Construct the square as above. Then construct the bisectors of ∠COA and ∠AOD.

Mark the four points where the bisectors intersect the circle. These points plus

A, D, B, and C are the vertices of the octagon.

© Houghton Mifflin Harcourt Publishing Company

Chapter 6   242   Lesson 1

© Houghton Mifflin Harcourt Publishing Company

Assign these pages to help your students practice and apply important lesson concepts. For additional exercises, see the Student Edition.

Answers

Additional Practice

1-4.

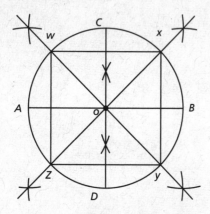

Possible answer: The triangles *WOX, XOY, ZOY,* and *WOZ* are all congruent by SAS, so the sides of *WXYZ* are congruent. Each angle of *WXYZ* is composed of two adjacent 45° angles, so each angle is a right angle.

5-8.

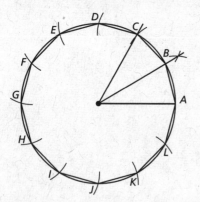

Possible answer: The same compass opening was used to draw all the arcs, so all the sides of *ABCDEFGHIJKL* are congruent. All the triangles with one vertex *O* and the other vertices consecutive points on the circle are congruent by SSS. All the angles of the dodecahedron are composed of two adjacent congruent angles, so they are congruent.

Problem Solving

1. Possible answers: (1) Use the method of Explore 1 in the lesson to inscribe one square, and use the method of Additional Practice Ex. 1 to inscribe another. Use a straightedge to draw segments connecting chosen points on the circle to reproduce the pattern. (2) Use the method of Explore 1 to inscribe one square. Construct the bisectors of all four right angles and label the points where the bisectors intersect the circle. Use a straightedge to draw all four sides of the square, then draw segments connecting chosen points on the circle to reproduce the pattern.

2. D

3. G

Notes

Additional Practice

In Exercises 1–4, you will inscribe a square in a circle. Use the space at the right to complete your sketch.

1. Use the method of Explore 2 of the lesson to draw circle O and diameter $\overline{AB}$, and to construct $\overline{CD}$, the perpendicular bisector of $\overline{AB}$.

2. Construct the bisector of $\angle AOC$. Label the point where the bisector intersects the circle W.

3. Construct the bisectors of $\angle COB$, $\angle BOD$, and $\angle AOD$, in that order. Label the points where the bisectors intersect the circle X, Y, and Z (in that order).

4. Use your straightedge to draw WXYZ. Explain how you know that WXYZ is a square.

_____
_____
_____

A dodecahedron is a twelve-sided polygon. In Exercises 5–8, you will inscribe a regular dodecahedron in a circle.

5. Use the method of Explore 1 from the lesson to draw a circle O and label point A. Draw the first arc and label the point of intersection C. Draw the remaining indicated arcs, but do not label the points.

6. Use your straightedge to draw $\overline{OA}$ and $\overline{OC}$, construct the bisector of $\angle COA$. Label the point where the bisector intersects the circle B..

7. Place the point of your compass at point B and open the compass until the pencil just touches point C. Without adjusting the compass, place the point of the compass at C and draw an arc that intersects the circle. Label the point of intersection D. Continue in this way until you have located 12 points lettered A through L.

8. Use your straightedge to draw ABCDEFGHIJKL. Explain how you know that ABCDEFGHIJKL is a regular dodecahedron.

_____
_____

Problem Solving

Write the correct answer.

1. Charlene is planning to paint a circular mirror to look like stained glass. She has chosen the design shown. Explain two different methods Charlene can use to inscribe regular polygons in the circle and produce her desired result.

_____
_____
_____
_____
_____

Harry is designing an advertising logo. He originally sketched a pattern for a dodecagon (a twelve-sided figure) inscribed in a circle, as shown. He is considering using a different inscribed polygon instead. Choose the best answer.

2. For which inscribed polygon can Harry *not* use the existing pattern without performing any additional construction?

  A equilateral triangle

  B square

  C regular hexagon

  D regular octagon

3. Harry decides to inscribe a regular 24-sided polygon in the circle. Instead of starting over from scratch, he decides to use his existing pattern but leaves the labeled points. What would be a good next step?

  F Draw segments connecting every two consecutive points (for instance, A and C, and C and E).

  G Construct the bisector of $\angle AOB$.

  H Construct the bisector of $\angle LOD$.

  J Construct the perpendicular bisector of $\overline{GA}$.

6-2 Properties of Parallelograms
Focus on Reasoning

Essential question: *What can you conclude about the sides, angles, and diagonals of a parallelogram?*

COMMON CORE Standards for Mathematical Content

CC.9-12.G.CO.11 Prove theorems about parallelograms.

CC.9-12.G.SRT.5 Use congruence ... criteria for triangles to solve problems and to prove relationships in geometric figures.

Vocabulary
diagonal

Prerequisites
Theorems about parallel lines cut by a transversal

Triangle congruence criteria

Math Background
In this lesson, students extend their earlier work with triangle congruence criteria and triangle properties to prove facts about parallelograms. This lesson gives students a chance to use inductive and deductive reasoning to investigate properties of the sides, angles, and diagonals of parallelograms.

INTRODUCE

Students have encountered parallelograms in earlier grades. Ask a volunteer to define *parallelogram*. Students may have only an informal idea of what a parallelogram is (e.g., "a slanted rectangle"), so be sure they understand that the mathematical definition of a parallelogram is a quadrilateral with two pairs of parallel sides. You may want to show students how they can make a parallelogram by drawing lines on either side of a ruler, changing the position of the ruler, and drawing another pair of lines. Ask students to explain why this method creates a parallelogram.

TEACH

1 Investigate parallelograms.

Materials: geometry software

Questioning Strategies

- As you use the software to drag points *A, B, C,* and/or *D*, does the quadrilateral remain a parallelogram? Why? **Yes; the lines that form opposite sides remain parallel.**

- What do you notice about consecutive angles in the parallelogram? Why does this make sense? **Consecutive angles are supplementary. This makes sense because opposite sides are parallel, so consecutive angles are same-side interior angles. By the Same-Side Interior Angles Postulate, these angles are supplementary.**

Teaching Strategy
Some students may have difficulty with terms like *opposite sides* or *consecutive angles*. Remind students that opposite sides of a quadrilateral do not share a vertex (that is, they do not intersect). Consecutive sides of a quadrilateral do share a vertex (that is, they intersect). Opposite angles of a quadrilateral do not share a side. Consecutive angles of a quadrilateral do share a side. You may want to help students draw and label a quadrilateral for reference.

2 Prove that opposite sides of a parallelogram are congruent.

Questioning Strategies

- Why do you think the proof is based on drawing the diagonal $\overline{DB}$? **Drawing the diagonal creates two triangles; then you can use triangle congruence criteria and CPCTC.**

Name _____ Class _____ Date _____

6-2

Properties of Parallelograms
Focus on Reasoning

COMMON CORE
CC.9-12.G.CO.11,
CC.9-12.G.SRT.5

Essential question: *What can you conclude about the sides, angles, and diagonals of a parallelogram?*

Recall that a *parallelogram* is a quadrilateral that has two pairs of parallel sides. You use the symbol ▱ to name a parallelogram. For example, the figure shows ▱*ABCD*.

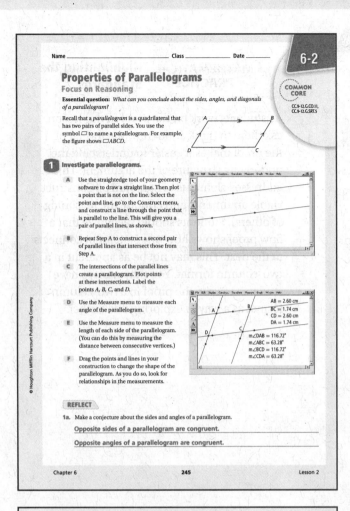

1 Investigate parallelograms.

A   Use the straightedge tool of your geometry software to draw a straight line. Then plot a point that is not on the line. Select the point and line, go to the Construct menu, and construct a line through the point that is parallel to the line. This will give you a pair of parallel lines, as shown.

B   Repeat Step A to construct a second pair of parallel lines that intersect those from Step A.

C   The intersections of the parallel lines create a parallelogram. Plot points at these intersections. Label the points *A*, *B*, *C*, and *D*.

D   Use the Measure menu to measure each angle of the parallelogram.

E   Use the Measure menu to measure the length of each side of the parallelogram. (You can do this by measuring the distance between consecutive vertices.)

F   Drag the points and lines in your construction to change the shape of the parallelogram. As you do so, look for relationships in the measurements.

REFLECT

1a.   Make a conjecture about the sides and angles of a parallelogram.

Opposite sides of a parallelogram are congruent.

Opposite angles of a parallelogram are congruent.

© Houghton Mifflin Harcourt Publishing Company

You may have discovered the following theorem about parallelograms.

> **Theorem**
>
> If a quadrilateral is a parallelogram, then opposite sides are congruent.

2 Prove that opposite sides of a parallelogram are congruent.

Complete the proof.

Given: *ABCD* is a parallelogram.

Prove: $\overline{AB} \cong \overline{CD}$ and $\overline{AD} \cong \overline{BC}$

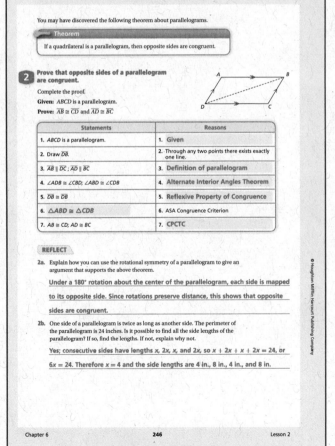

Statements	Reasons
1. *ABCD* is a parallelogram.	1. Given
2. Draw $\overline{DB}$.	2. Through any two points there exists exactly one line.
3. $\overline{AB} \parallel \overline{DC}$; $\overline{AD} \parallel \overline{BC}$	3. **Definition of parallelogram**
4. $\angle ADB \cong \angle CBD$; $\angle ABD \cong \angle CDB$	4. **Alternate Interior Angles Theorem**
5. $\overline{DB} \cong \overline{DB}$	5. **Reflexive Property of Congruence**
6. $\triangle ABD \cong \triangle CDB$	6. ASA Congruence Criterion
7. $AB \cong CD$; $AD \cong BC$	7. CPCTC

REFLECT

2a.   Explain how you can use the rotational symmetry of a parallelogram to give an argument that supports the above theorem.

Under a 180° rotation about the center of the parallelogram, each side is mapped

to its opposite side. Since rotations preserve distance, this shows that opposite

sides are congruent.

2b.   One side of a parallelogram is twice as long as another side. The perimeter of the parallelogram is 24 inches. Is it possible to find all the side lengths of the parallelogram? If so, find the lengths. If not, explain why not.

Yes; consecutive sides have lengths *x*, 2*x*, *x*, and 2*x*, so *x* + 2*x* + *x* + 2*x* = 24, or

6*x* = 24. Therefore *x* = 4 and the side lengths are 4 in., 8 in., 4 in., and 8 in.

© Houghton Mifflin Harcourt Publishing Company

Investigate diagonals of parallelograms.

Materials: geometry software

Questioning Strategies

- How many diagonals does a parallelogram have? Is this true for every quadrilateral? Two; yes

- If a quadrilateral is named *PQRS*, what are the diagonals? $\overline{PR}$ and $\overline{QS}$

- Are the diagonals of a parallelogram ever congruent? If so, when does this appear to happen? Yes; when the parallelogram is a rectangle

 Prove diagonals of a parallelogram bisect each other.

Questioning Strategies

- Why do you think this theorem was introduced after the theorems about the sides and angles of a parallelogram? The proof of this theorem depends upon the fact that opposite sides of a parallelogram are congruent.

MATHEMATICAL PRACTICE · Highlighting the Standards

As students work on the proof in this lesson, ask them to think about how the format of the proof makes it easier to understand the underlying structure of the argument. This addresses elements of Standard 3 (Construct viable arguments and critique the reasoning of others). Students should recognize that a flow proof shows how one statement connects to the next. This may not be as apparent in a two-column format. You may want to have students rewrite the proof in a two-column format as a way of exploring this further.

Essential question: *What can you conclude about the diagonals of a parallelogram?*

A segment that connects any two nonconsecutive
vertices of a polygon is a **diagonal**. A
parallelogram has two diagonals. In the figure,
$\overline{AC}$ and $\overline{BD}$ are diagonals of $\square ABCD$.

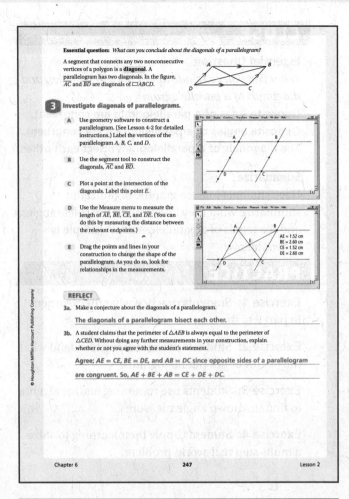

3 Investigate diagonals of parallelograms.

A   Use geometry software to construct a
parallelogram. (See Lesson 4-2 for detailed
instructions.) Label the vertices of the
parallelogram *A, B, C,* and *D.*

B   Use the segment tool to construct the
diagonals, $\overline{AC}$ and $\overline{BD}$.

C   Plot a point at the intersection of the
diagonals. Label this point *E.*

D   Use the Measure menu to measure the
length of $\overline{AE}$, $\overline{BE}$, $\overline{CE}$, and $\overline{DE}$. (You can
do this by measuring the distance between
the relevant endpoints.)

E   Drag the points and lines in your
construction to change the shape of the
parallelogram. As you do so, look for
relationships in the measurements.

> AE = 1.52 cm
> BE = 2.60 cm
> CE = 1.52 cm
> DE = 2.60 cm

REFLECT

3a. Make a conjecture about the diagonals of a parallelogram.

The diagonals of a parallelogram bisect each other.

3b. A student claims that the perimeter of $\triangle AEB$ is always equal to the perimeter of
$\triangle CED$. Without doing any further measurements in your construction, explain
whether or not you agree with the student's statement.

Agree; $AE = CE$, $BE = DE$, and $AB = DC$ since opposite sides of a parallelogram

are congruent. So, $AE + BE + AB = CE + DE + DC.$

© Houghton Mifflin Harcourt Publishing Company

You may have discovered the following theorem about parallelograms.

> **Theorem**
>
> If a quadrilateral is a parallelogram, then the diagonals bisect each other.

4 Prove diagonals of a parallelogram bisect each other.
Complete the proof.
Given: ABCD is a parallelogram.
Prove: $\overline{AE} \cong \overline{CE}$ and $\overline{BE} \cong \overline{DE}$.

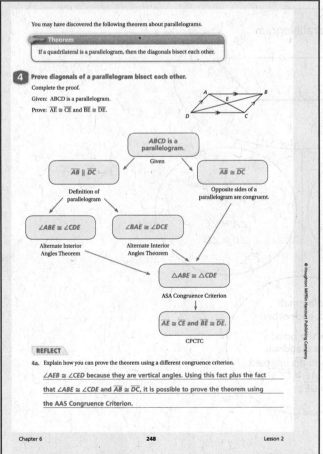

ABCD is a
parallelogram.

Given

$\overline{AB} \parallel \overline{DC}$

Definition of
parallelogram

$\overline{AB} \cong \overline{DC}$

Opposite sides of a
parallelogram are congruent.

$\angle ABE \cong \angle CDE$

Alternate Interior
Angles Theorem

$\angle BAE \cong \angle DCE$

Alternate Interior
Angles Theorem

$\triangle ABE \cong \triangle CDE$

ASA Congruence Criterion

$\overline{AE} \cong \overline{CE}$ and $\overline{BE} \cong \overline{DE}$.

CPCTC

REFLECT

4a. Explain how you can prove the theorem using a different congruence criterion.

$\angle AEB \cong \angle CED$ because they are vertical angles. Using this fact plus the fact

that $\angle ABE \cong \angle CDE$ and $\overline{AB} \cong \overline{DC}$, it is possible to prove the theorem using

the AAS Congruence Criterion.

© Houghton Mifflin Harcourt Publishing Company

Teaching Strategy

The lesson concludes with the theorem that states that opposite angles of a parallelogram are congruent. The proof of this theorem is left as an exercise (Exercise 1). Be sure students recognize that the proof of this theorem is similar to the proof that opposite sides of a parallelogram are congruent. Noticing such similarities is an important problem-solving skill.

MATHEMATICAL PRACTICE	Highlighting the Standards

Exercise 4 is a multi-part exercise that includes opportunities for mathematical modeling, reasoning, and communication. It is a good opportunity to address Standard 4 (Model with mathematics). Draw students' attention to the way they interpret their mathematical results in the context of the real-world situation. Specifically, ask students to explain what their mathematical findings tell them about the appearance and layout of the park.

CLOSE

Essential Question

What can you conclude about the sides, angles, and diagonals of a parallelogram?

Opposite sides of a parallelogram are congruent.
Opposite angles of a parallelogram are congruent.
The diagonals of a parallelogram bisect each other.

Summarize

Have students make a graphic organizer to summarize what they know about the sides, angles, and diagonals of a parallelogram. A sample is shown below.

PRACTICE

Exercise 1: Students practice what they learned in part 2 of the lesson.

Exercise 2: Students use reasoning to extend what they know about parallelograms.

Exercise 3: Students use reasoning and/or algebra to find unknown angle measures.

Exercise 4: Students apply their learning to solve a multi-step real-world problem.

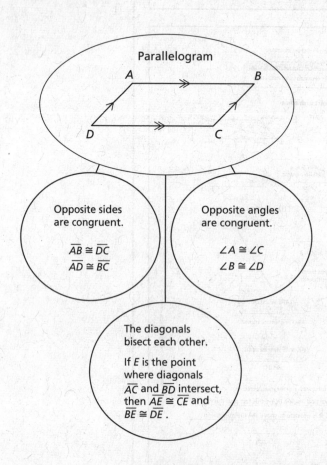

The angles of a parallelogram also have an important property. It is stated in the following theorem, which you will prove as an exercise.

> **Theorem**
>
> If a quadrilateral is a parallelogram, then opposite angles are congruent.

PRACTICE

1. Prove the above theorem about opposite angles of a parallelogram.

Given: *ABCD* is a parallelogram.
Prove: $\angle A \cong \angle C$ and $\angle B \cong \angle D$

(*Hint:* You only need to prove that $\angle A \cong \angle C$. A similar argument can be used to prove that $\angle B \cong \angle D$. Also, you may or may not need to use all the rows of the table in your proof.)

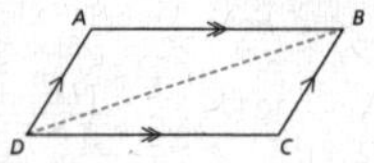

Statements	Reasons
1. *ABCD* is a parallelogram.	1. Given
2. Draw $\overline{DB}$.	2. Through any two points there exists exactly one line.
3. $AB \parallel DC$; $AD \parallel BC$	3. Definition of parallelogram
4. $\angle ADB \cong \angle CBD$; $\angle ABD \cong \angle CDB$	4. Alternate Interior Angles Theorem
5. $\overline{DB} \cong \overline{DB}$	5. Reflexive Property of Congruence
6. $\triangle ABD \cong \triangle CDB$	6. ASA Congruence Criterion
7. $\angle A \cong \angle C$	7. CPCTC

2. Explain why consecutive angles of a parallelogram are supplementary.

Consecutive angles of a parallelogram are same-side interior angles for a

pair of parallel lines (the opposite sides of the parallelogram), so the angles

are supplementary by the Same-Side Interior Angles Postulate.

3. In the figure, *JKLM* is a parallelogram. Find the measure of each of the numbered angles.

$m\angle 1 = 19°$; $m\angle 2 = 43°$; $m\angle 3 = 118°$;

$m\angle 4 = 118°$; $m\angle 5 = 19°$

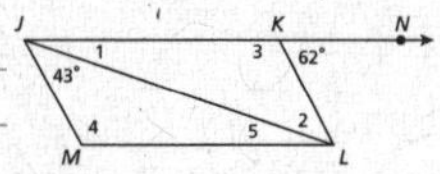

---

4. A city planner is designing a park in the shape of a parallelogram. As shown in the figure, there will be two straight paths through which visitors may enter the park. The paths are bisectors of consecutive angles of the parallelogram, and the paths intersect at point *P*.

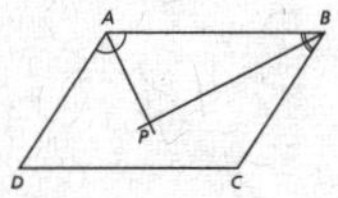

a. Work directly on the parallelograms below and use a compass and straightedge to construct the bisectors of $\angle A$ and $\angle B$. Then use a protractor to measure $\angle APB$ in each case.

 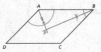

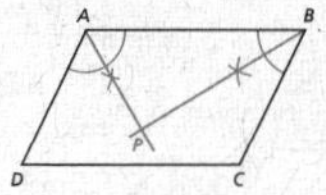

Make a conjecture about $\angle APB$.

$\angle APB$ is a right angle.

b. Write a paragraph proof to show that your conjecture is always true. (*Hint:* Suppose $m\angle BAP = x°$, $m\angle ABP = y°$, and $m\angle APB = z°$. What do you know about $x + y + z$? What do you know about $2x + 2y$?)

By the Triangle Sum Theorem, $x + y + z = 180$. Also, $m\angle DAB = (2x)°$ and

$m\angle ABC = (2y)°$. By the Same-Side Interior Angles Postulate $m\angle DAB +$

$m\angle ABC = 180°$. So $2x + 2y = 180$ and $x + y = 90$. Substituting this in the

first equation gives $90 + z = 180$ and $z = 90$.

c. When the city planner takes into account the dimensions of the park, she finds that point *P* lies on $\overline{DC}$, as shown. Explain why it must be the case that $DC = 2AD$. (*Hint:* Use congruent base angles to show that $\triangle DAP$ and $\triangle CPB$ are isosceles.)

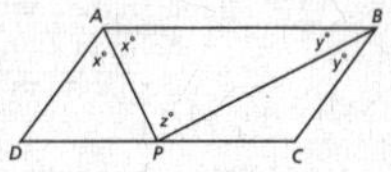

$\angle DAP \cong \angle BAP$ since $\overline{AP}$ is an angle bisector. Also, $\angle DPA \cong \angle BAP$ by the

Alternate Interior Angles Theorem. Therefore, $\angle DAP \cong \angle DPA$. This means

$\triangle DAP$ is isosceles, with $\overline{AD} \cong \overline{DP}$. Similarly, $\overline{BC} \cong \overline{PC}$. Also, $\overline{BC} \cong \overline{AD}$ as

opposite sides of a parallelogram. So, $DC = DP + PC = AD + BC = AD +$

$AD = 2AD$.

ADDITIONAL PRACTICE AND PROBLEM SOLVING

Assign these pages to help your students practice and apply important lesson concepts. For additional exercises, see the Student Edition.

Answers

Sec 6.2 P251

Additional Practice

1. 108.8 cm

2. 91 cm

3. 217.6 cm

4. 123°

5. 123°

6. 57°

7. 117°

8. 63°

9. 71

10. 21

11. 10.5

12. 15

13. 30

14. (0, −3)

15. Possible answer:

Statements	Reasons
1. *DEFG* is a parallelogram.	1. Given
2. m∠*EDG* = m∠*EDH* + m∠*GDH*, m∠*FGD* = m∠*FGH* + m∠*DGH*	2. Angle Add. Post.
3. m∠*EDG* + m∠*FGD* = 180°	3. ▱ → cons. ∠s supp.
4. m∠*EDH* + m∠*GDH* + m∠*FGH* + m∠*DGH* = 180°	4. Subst. (Steps 2, 3)
5. m∠*GDH* + m∠*DGH* + m∠*DHG* = 180°	5. Triangle Sum Thm.
6. m∠*GDH* + m∠*DGH* + m∠*DHG* = m∠*EDH* + m∠*GDH* + m∠*FGH* + m∠*DGH*	6. Trans. Prop. of =
7. m∠*DHG* = m∠*EDH* + m∠*FGH*	7. Subtr. Prop. of =

Problem Solving P252

1. m∠*C* = 135°; m∠*D* = 45°

2. 15 in.

3. 4.5 ft

4. 65°

5. B

6. H

7. D

6-2

Additional Practice

A gurney is a wheeled cot or stretcher used in hospitals. Many gurneys are made so that the base will fold up for easy storage in an ambulance. When partially folded, the base forms a parallelogram. In □ *STUV*, *VU* = 91 centimeters, *UW* = 108.8 centimeters, and m∠*TSV* = 57°. Find each measure.

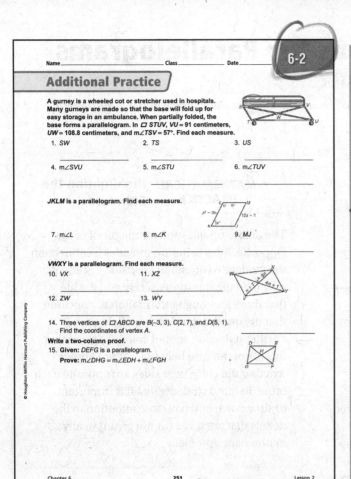

1. *SW* _____

2. *TS* _____

3. *US* _____

4. m∠*SVU* _____

5. m∠*STU* _____

6. m∠*TUV* _____

JKLM is a parallelogram. Find each measure.

7. m∠*L* _____

8. m∠*K* _____

9. *MJ* _____

VWXY is a parallelogram. Find each measure.

10. *VX* _____

11. *XZ* _____

12. *ZW* _____

13. *WY* _____

14. Three vertices of □ *ABCD* are *B*(–3, 3), *C*(2, 7), and *D*(5, 1). Find the coordinates of vertex *A*.

Write a two-column proof.

15. **Given:** *DEFG* is a parallelogram.

   Prove: m∠*DHG* = m∠*EDH* + m∠*FGH*

© Houghton Mifflin Harcourt Publishing Company

Problem Solving

Use the diagram for Exercises 1 and 2.

The wall frames on the staircase wall form parallelograms *ABCD* and *EFGH*.

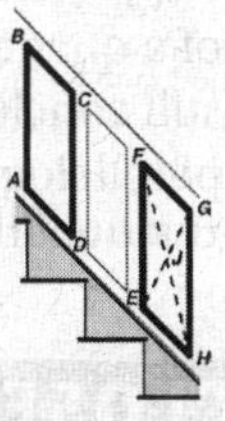

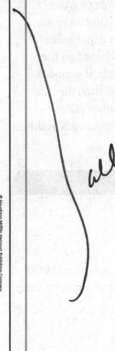

1. In □ *ABCD*, the measure of ∠*A* is three times the measure of ∠*B*. What are the measures of ∠*C* and ∠*D*?

   _____

2. In □ *EFGH*, *FH* = 5*x* inches, *EG* = (2*x* + 4) inches, and *JG* = 8 inches. What is the length of *JH*?

   _____

3. The diagram shows a section of the support structure of a roller coaster. In □ *JKLM*, *JK* = (3*z* – 0.9) feet, and *LM* = (*z* + 2.7) feet. Find *JK*.

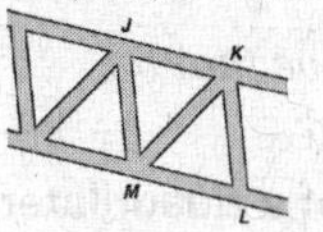

   _____

4. In □ *TUVW*, part of a ceramic tile pattern, m∠*TUV* = (8*x* + 1)° and m∠*UVW* = (12*x* + 19)°. Find m∠*TUV*.

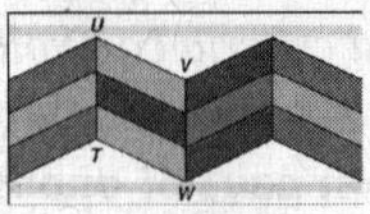

   _____

Choose the best answer.

5. What is the measure of ∠*Z* in parallelogram *WXYZ*?

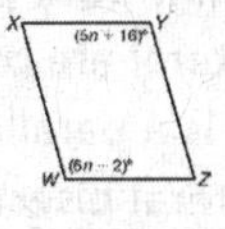

   A 18°

   B 74°

   C 106°

   D 108°

6. The perimeter of □ *CDEF* is 54 centimeters. Find the length of *FC* if *DE* is 5 centimeters longer than *EF*.

   F 11 cm

   G 14 cm

   H 16 cm

   J 44 cm

7. In □ *PQRS*, *QT* = 7*x*, *TS* = 2*x* + 2.5, *RT* = 2*y*, and *TP* = *y* + 3. Find the perimeter of △*PTS*.

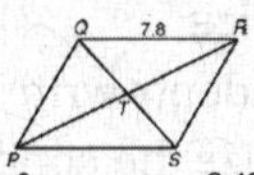

   A 6

   B 9.5

   C 12

   D 17.3

© Houghton Mifflin Harcourt Publishing Company

Conditions for Parallelograms
Going Deeper

Essential question: *What criteria can you use to prove that a quadrilateral is a parallelogram?*

COMMON **Standards for**
CORE **Mathematical Content**

CC.9-12.G.CO.11 Prove theorems about parallelograms.

CC.9-12.G.SRT.5 Use congruence ... criteria for triangles to solve problems and to prove relationships in geometric figures.

Prerequisites

Converses of theorems about parallel lines cut by a transversal

Triangle congruence criteria

Math Background

In the previous lesson, students learned about three properties of parallelograms: opposite sides are congruent, opposite angles are congruent, and the diagonals bisect each other. As students will see in this lesson, each of these conditions is sufficient to conclude that a quadrilateral is a parallelogram.

INTRODUCE

Remind students of the criteria they know for determining when two triangles are congruent (SSS, SAS, ASA, and AAS). Explain that there are also criteria for determining when a quadrilateral is a parallelogram. One of these is based on the definition of a parallelogram. That is, if opposite sides of a quadrilateral are parallel, then the quadrilateral is a parallelogram. Other criteria are based on the converses of the theorems in the previous lesson.

TEACH

PROOF

Questioning Strategies

• What must you do in order to prove that *ABCD* is a parallelogram? Show that the opposite sides are parallel.

MATHEMATICAL **Highlighting the**
PRACTICE **Standards**

The follow-up question for the proof of the Opposite Sides Criterion provides a connection to Standard 6 (Attend to precision). Students may read the question quickly and decide that there is enough information to conclude that the quadrilateral is a parallelogram. Further reflection should convince them that this is not the case because it is not known whether the congruent sides are opposite each other. Remind students that it is important to slow down and pay close attention to the details that are given (or not given) in any mathematics problem.

2 PROOF

Questioning Strategies

• Suppose only one pair of opposite angles of a quadrilateral are congruent. Can you still conclude that the quadrilateral is a parallelogram? Explain. No; in this case, the quadrilateral could be a kite.

CLOSE

Essential Question

What criteria can you use to prove that a quadrilateral is a parallelogram?

If both pairs of opposite sides of a quadrilateral are congruent, then the quadrilateral is a parallelogram. If both pairs of opposite angles of a quadrilateral are congruent, then the quadrilateral is a parallelogram. If the diagonals of a quadrilateral bisect each other, then the quadrilateral is a parallelogram.

Summarize

Have students write a journal entry in which they summarize the conditions that guarantee that a quadrilateral is a parallelogram.

© Houghton Mifflin Harcourt Publishing Company

Name_____ Class_____ Date_____

6-3
Video Tutor

Conditions for Parallelograms
Going Deeper

Essential question: *What criteria can you use to prove that a quadrilateral is a parallelogram?*

The converses of the theorems you developed in the last two lessons are all true. These provide several criteria that can be used to prove that a quadrilateral is a parallelogram.

> **Opposite Sides Criterion for a Parallelogram**
> If both pairs of opposite sides of a quadrilateral are congruent, then the quadrilateral is a parallelogram.

CC.9-12.G.SRT.5

1 PROOF   Opposite Sides Criterion for a Parallelogram

Complete the proof.

Given: $\overline{AB} \cong \overline{DC}$ and $\overline{AD} \cong \overline{BC}$

Prove: *ABCD* is a parallelogram.

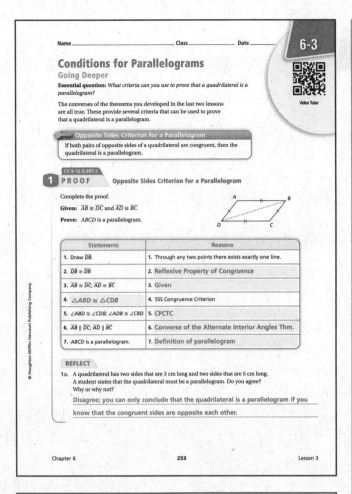

Statements	Reasons
1. Draw $\overline{DB}$.	1. Through any two points there exists exactly one line.
2. $\overline{DB} \cong \overline{DB}$	2. Reflexive Property of Congruence
3. $\overline{AB} \cong \overline{DC}$; $\overline{AD} \cong \overline{BC}$	3. Given
4. $\triangle ABD \cong \triangle CDB$	4. SSS Congruence Criterion
5. $\angle ABD \cong \angle CDB$; $\angle ADB \cong \angle CBD$	5. CPCTC
6. $\overline{AB} \parallel \overline{DC}$; $\overline{AD} \parallel \overline{BC}$	6. Converse of the Alternate Interior Angles Thm.
7. *ABCD* is a parallelogram.	7. Definition of parallelogram

REFLECT

1a. A quadrilateral has two sides that are 3 cm long and two sides that are 5 cm long. A student states that the quadrilateral must be a parallelogram. Do you agree? Why or why not?

Disagree; you can only conclude that the quadrilateral is a parallelogram if you

know that the congruent sides are opposite each other.

Chapter 6   253   Lesson 3

> **Opposite Angles Criterion for a Parallelogram**
> If both pairs of opposite angles of a quadrilateral are congruent, then the quadrilateral is a parallelogram.

CC.9-12.G.CO.11

2 PROOF   Opposite Angles Criterion for a Parallelogram

Complete the paragraph proof.

Given: $\angle A \cong \angle C$ and $\angle B \cong \angle D$.

Prove: *ABCD* is a parallelogram.

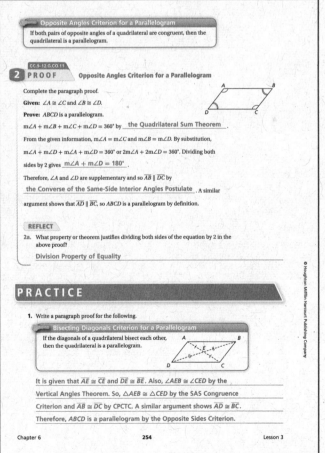

$m\angle A + m\angle B + m\angle C + m\angle D = 360°$ by   the Quadrilateral Sum Theorem .

From the given information, $m\angle A = m\angle C$ and $m\angle B = m\angle D$. By substitution,

$m\angle A + m\angle D + m\angle A + m\angle D = 360°$ or $2m\angle A + 2m\angle D = 360°$. Dividing both

sides by 2 gives $m\angle A + m\angle D = 180°$.

Therefore, $\angle A$ and $\angle D$ are supplementary and so $\overline{AB} \parallel \overline{DC}$ by

the Converse of the Same-Side Interior Angles Postulate . A similar

argument shows that $\overline{AD} \parallel \overline{BC}$, so *ABCD* is a parallelogram by definition.

REFLECT

2a. What property or theorem justifies dividing both sides of the equation by 2 in the above proof?

Division Property of Equality

PRACTICE

1. Write a paragraph proof for the following.

> **Bisecting Diagonals Criterion for a Parallelogram**
> If the diagonals of a quadrilateral bisect each other, then the quadrilateral is a parallelogram.

It is given that $\overline{AE} \cong \overline{CE}$ and $\overline{DE} \cong \overline{BE}$. Also, $\angle AEB \cong \angle CED$ by the

Vertical Angles Theorem. So, $\triangle AEB \cong \triangle CED$ by the SAS Congruence

Criterion and $\overline{AB} \cong \overline{DC}$ by CPCTC. A similar argument shows $\overline{AD} \cong \overline{BC}$.

Therefore, *ABCD* is a parallelogram by the Opposite Sides Criterion.

Chapter 6   254   Lesson 3

ADDITIONAL PRACTICE AND PROBLEM SOLVING

Assign these pages to help your students practice and apply important lesson concepts. For additional exercises, see the Student Edition.

Answers

Additional Practice

1. $ABCD$ is a parallelogram. $m\angle A = m\angle C = 72°$ and $m\angle B = m\angle D = 108°$

2. $EFGH$ is not a parallelogram. $HI = 8.6$ and $FI = 7.6$. $\overline{EG}$ does not bisect $\overline{HF}$.

3. No, the diagonals do not necessarily bisect each other.

4. Yes, the triangles with numbered angles are $\cong$ by AAS. By CPCTC, the parallel sides are congruent.

5. No, $x° + x°$ may not be 180°.

6. slope of $\overline{JK}$ = slope of $\overline{LM} = 1$; slope of $\overline{KL}$ = slope of $\overline{JM} = -\frac{2}{3}$; $JKLM$ is a parallelogram.

7. $PQ = RS = \sqrt{26}$; $QR = PS = 5\sqrt{2}$; $PQRS$ is a parallelogram.

8. Possible answer: $UV = TW = 2\sqrt{5}$; slope of $\overline{UV}$ = slope of $\overline{TW} = 2$; $TUVW$ is a parallelogram.

Problem Solving P256

1. Yes; both pairs of opposite sides of quadrilateral $LMNP$ remain congruent, so $LMNP$ is always a ▱.

2. 56°

3. Possible answer: $m\angle F = 120°$

4. Possible answer: $y = -x + 1$; both pairs of opposite sides have the same slope, so they are parallel.

5. C

6. H

Notes

) prep?

Name_____ Class_____ Date_____   **6-3**

Additional Practice

For Exercises 1 and 2, determine whether the figure is a parallelogram for the given values of the variables. Explain your answers.

1. $x = 9$ and $y = 11$

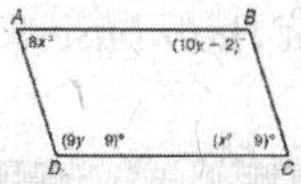

2. $a = 4.3$ and $b = 13$

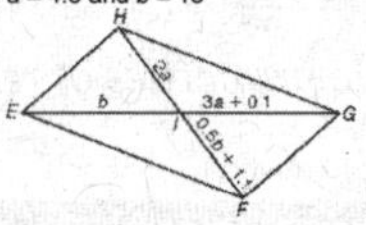

_____   _____

_____   _____

_____   _____

Determine whether each quadrilateral must be a parallelogram. Justify your answers.

3.   4. 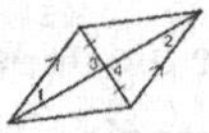   5.

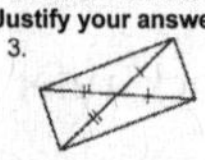

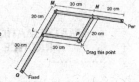

_____   _____   _____

_____   _____   _____

_____   _____   _____

_____   _____   _____

Use the given method to determine whether the quadrilateral with the given vertices is a parallelogram.

6. Find the slopes of all four sides: $J(-4, -1)$, $K(-7, -4)$, $L(2, -10)$, $M(5, -7)$

_____

7. Find the lengths of all four sides: $P(2, 2)$, $Q(1, -3)$, $R(-4, 2)$, $S(-3, 7)$

_____

8. Find the slopes and lengths of one pair of opposite sides:

$T\left(\frac{3}{2}, -2\right), U\left(\frac{3}{2}, 4\right), V\left(-\frac{1}{2}, 0\right), W\left(-\frac{1}{2}, -6\right)$

_____

Problem Solving

Use the diagram for Exercises 1 and 2.

A *pantograph* is a drawing instrument used to magnify figures.

1. If you drag the point at P so that the angle measures change, will $LMNP$ continue to be a parallelogram? Explain.

_____

_____

2. If you drag the point at P so that m∠$LMN = 56°$, what will be the measure of ∠QLP?

3. In the state flag of Maryland, m∠$G = 60°$ and m∠$H = 120°$. Name one more condition that would allow you to conclude that $EFGH$ is a parallelogram.

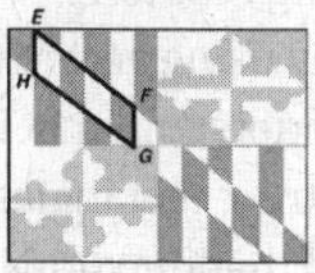

4. The graphs of $y = 2x$, $y = 2x - 5$, and $y = -x$ in the coordinate plane contain three sides of a quadrilateral. Give an equation of a line whose graph contains a segment that can complete the quadrilateral to form a parallelogram. Explain.

_____

_____

_____

Choose the best answer.

5. For which value of n is $QRST$ a parallelogram?

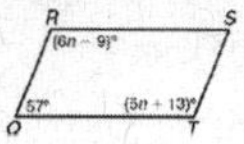

A 15.5
B 20.6
C 22
D 25

6. Under what conditions must $ABCD$ be a parallelogram?

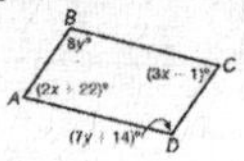

F $x = 23$
G $y = 14$
H $x = 23$ and $y = 14$
J $x = 14$ and $y = 23$

Slip# 4

Properties of Special Parallelograms
Focus on Reasoning

Essential question: *What are the properties of rectangles and rhombuses?*

COMMON CORE Standards for Mathematical Content

CC.9-12.G.CO.11 Prove theorems about parallelograms.

CC.9-12.G.SRT.5 Use congruence ... criteria for triangles to solve problems and to prove relationships in geometric figures.

Vocabulary
rectangle

rhombus

Prerequisites
Triangle congruence criteria

Properties of parallelograms

Conditions for parallelograms

Math Background
A rectangle is a quadrilateral with four right angles (or, equivalently, four congruent angles). A rhombus is a quadrilateral with four congruent sides. As students learn in this lesson, both types of quadrilaterals are parallelograms. Note that a square is a quadrilateral with four right angles and four congruent sides. This means a square is both a rectangle and a rhombus, as well as a parallelogram.

INTRODUCE

Ask students to point out examples of rectangles in the classroom (windows, desktops, textbook covers, and so forth). Then ask students if they can define *rectangle*. Students may have the misconception that rectangles are defined to be parallelograms with four right angles. Explain that the definition states that a rectangle is a quadrilateral with four right angles. The fact that a rectangle is a parallelogram is something that must be proved.

TEACH

1 Investigate properties of rectangles.

Materials: square tile or pattern block, ruler

Questioning Strategies
- Why does tracing along the edges of a square tile or pattern block guarantee that the figure you create is a rectangle? **Using the tile or pattern block in this way guarantees that the resulting quadrilateral has four right angles.**
- Suppose quadrilateral *PQRS* is a rectangle. What statements about congruent segments do you think are true? $\overline{PQ} \cong \overline{RS}$, $\overline{PS} \cong \overline{QR}$, $\overline{PR} \cong \overline{QS}$

Differentiated Instruction
If some students have difficulty following the instructions to draw rectangles, you might have these students trace the outline of rectangular objects such as index cards, pads of sticky notes, book covers, etc. Then have them continue with Step B of the investigation.

MATHEMATICAL PRACTICE   Highlighting the Standards

You can address Standard 5 (Use appropriate tools strategically) in a class discussion about the hands-on investigation. Ask students to describe the advantages of creating a rectangle by using the drawing method presented here rather than by using geometry software. Students should understand that it can be cumbersome to construct rectangles using geometry software and that the drawing method described here may give a more immediate entry point into the investigation.

Name _____ Class _____ Date _____

6-4

Properties of Special Parallelograms
Focus on Reasoning

COMMON CORE

CC.9-12.G.CO.11, CC.9-12.G.SRT.5

Essential question: *What are the properties of rectangles and rhombuses?*

A **rectangle** is a quadrilateral with four right angles. The figure shows rectangle *ABCD*.

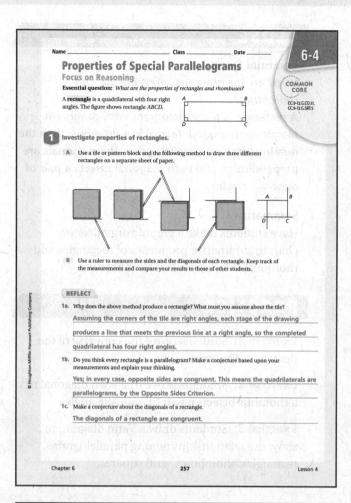

1 Investigate properties of rectangles.

A Use a tile or pattern block and the following method to draw three different rectangles on a separate sheet of paper.

B Use a ruler to measure the sides and the diagonals of each rectangle. Keep track of the measurements and compare your results to those of other students.

REFLECT

1a. Why does the above method produce a rectangle? What must you assume about the tile?

Assuming the corners of the tile are right angles, each stage of the drawing

produces a line that meets the previous line at a right angle, so the completed

quadrilateral has four right angles.

1b. Do you think every rectangle is a parallelogram? Make a conjecture based upon your measurements and explain your thinking.

Yes; in every case, opposite sides are congruent. This means the quadrilaterals are

parallelograms, by the Opposite Sides Criterion.

1c. Make a conjecture about the diagonals of a rectangle.

The diagonals of a rectangle are congruent.

You may have discovered the following theorem about rectangles.

Rectangle Theorem

A rectangle is a parallelogram with congruent diagonals.

In order to prove the above theorem, it is convenient to use a theorem that states that all right angles are congruent. The proof of this theorem is straightforward: If $\angle X$ and $\angle Y$ are right angles, then m$\angle X$ = 90° and m$\angle Y$ = 90° so m$\angle X$ = m$\angle Y$ and $\angle X \cong \angle Y$.

2 Prove the Rectangle Theorem.

Complete the proof.

Given: *ABCD* is a rectangle.
Prove: *ABCD* is a parallelogram; $\overline{AC} \cong \overline{BD}$.

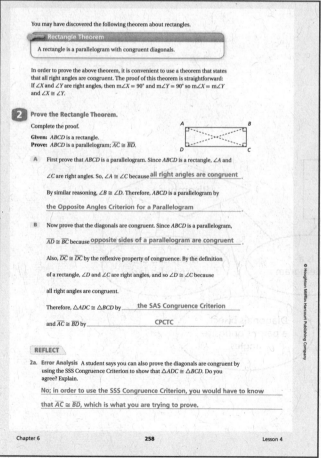

A First prove that *ABCD* is a parallelogram. Since *ABCD* is a rectangle, $\angle A$ and

$\angle C$ are right angles. So, $\angle A \cong \angle C$ because all right angles are congruent.

By similar reasoning, $\angle B \cong \angle D$. Therefore, *ABCD* is a parallelogram by

the Opposite Angles Criterion for a Parallelogram

B Now prove that the diagonals are congruent. Since *ABCD* is a parallelogram,

$\overline{AD} \cong \overline{BC}$ because opposite sides of a parallelogram are congruent

Also, $\overline{DC} \cong \overline{DC}$ by the reflexive property of congruence. By the definition

of a rectangle, $\angle D$ and $\angle C$ are right angles, and so $\angle D \cong \angle C$ because

all right angles are congruent.

Therefore, $\triangle ADC \cong \triangle BCD$ by _____the SAS Congruence Criterion_____

and $\overline{AC} \cong \overline{BD}$ by _____CPCTC_____

REFLECT

2a. **Error Analysis** A student says you can also prove the diagonals are congruent by using the SSS Congruence Criterion to show that $\triangle ADC \cong \triangle BCD$. Do you agree? Explain.

No; in order to use the SSS Congruence Criterion, you would have to know

that $\overline{AC} \cong \overline{BD}$, which is what you are trying to prove.

2 **Prove the Rectangle Theorem.**

Questioning Strategies
• What two things do you have to prove in order to prove the theorem? Prove *ABCD* is a parallelogram; prove the diagonals of *ABCD* are congruent.

Avoid Common Errors
Students may try to prove that a rectangle is a parallelogram by stating that $\overline{AB} \cong \overline{DC}$ and $\overline{AD} \cong \overline{BC}$, so *ABCD* is a parallelogram by the Opposite Sides Criterion for a Parallelogram. However, the given information states only that *ABCD* is a rectangle (that is, *ABCD* has four right angles). The fact that a rectangle has opposite sides that are congruent is a consequence of the fact that a rectangle is a parallelogram. In order to avoid circular reasoning, congruent opposite sides cannot be used as part of this proof.

3 **Prove diagonals of a rhombus are perpendicular.**

Questioning Strategies
• Why do the diagonals of a rhombus bisect each other? Since a rhombus is a parallelogram, the diagonals bisect each other.

• To prove that $\overline{JL} \perp \overline{MK}$, do you need to show that all four of the angles formed by the intersecting diagonals are right angles? Why or why not? No; you only need to show that one angle is a right angle. If one angle is a right angle, it's easy to see that the others must also be right angles by the Vertical Angles Theorem and the Linear Pair Theorem.

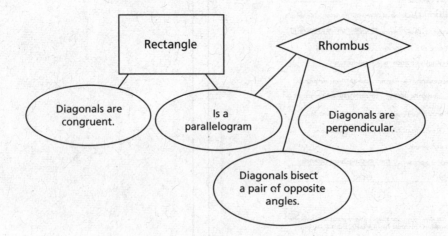

© Houghton Mifflin Harcourt Publishing Company

CLOSE

Essential Question
What are the properties of rectangles and rhombuses?
A rectangle is a parallelogram with congruent diagonals. If a quadrilateral is a rhombus, then the quadrilateral is a parallelogram, the diagonals are perpendicular, and each diagonal bisects a pair of opposite angles.

Summarize
Have students make a graphic organizer or chart to summarize properties of rectangles and rhombuses. A sample is shown below.

PRACTICE

Exercise 1: Students prove the converse of the Rectangle Theorem.

Exercise 2: Students prove that each diagonal of a rhombus bisects a pair of opposite angles.

Exercise 3: Students draw a Venn diagram to show the relationships among parallelograms, rectangles, rhombuses, and squares.

A **rhombus** is a quadrilateral with four congruent sides. The figure shows rhombus *JKLM*.

The following is a summary of some properties of rhombuses. You will prove these properties below and in the exercises.

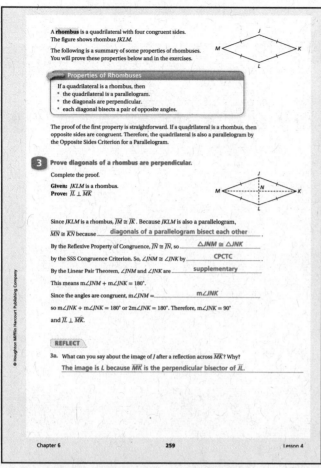

Properties of Rhombuses

If a quadrilateral is a rhombus, then
* the quadrilateral is a parallelogram.
* the diagonals are perpendicular.
* each diagonal bisects a pair of opposite angles.

The proof of the first property is straightforward. If a quadrilateral is a rhombus, then opposite sides are congruent. Therefore, the quadrilateral is also a parallelogram by the Opposite Sides Criterion for a Parallelogram.

3 Prove diagonals of a rhombus are perpendicular.

Complete the proof.

Given: *JKLM* is a rhombus.
Prove: $\overline{JL} \perp \overline{MK}$

Since *JKLM* is a rhombus, $\overline{JM} \cong \overline{JK}$. Because *JKLM* is also a parallelogram, $\overline{MN} \cong \overline{KN}$ because ___diagonals of a parallelogram bisect each other___

By the Reflexive Property of Congruence, $\overline{JN} \cong \overline{JN}$, so ___$\triangle JNM \cong \triangle JNK$___ by the SSS Congruence Criterion. So, $\angle JNM \cong \angle JNK$ by ___CPCTC___.

By the Linear Pair Theorem, $\angle JNM$ and $\angle JNK$ are ___supplementary___.

This means $m\angle JNM + m\angle JNK = 180°$.

Since the angles are congruent, $m\angle JNM =$ ___$m\angle JNK$___

so $m\angle JNK + m\angle JNK = 180°$ or $2m\angle JNK = 180°$. Therefore, $m\angle JNK = 90°$ and $\overline{JL} \perp \overline{MK}$.

REFLECT

3a. What can you say about the image of *J* after a reflection across $\overline{MK}$? Why?

The image is *L* because $\overline{MK}$ is the perpendicular bisector of $\overline{JL}$.

PRACTICE

1. Prove the converse of the Rectangle Theorem. That is, if a parallelogram has congruent diagonals, then the parallelogram is a rectangle.

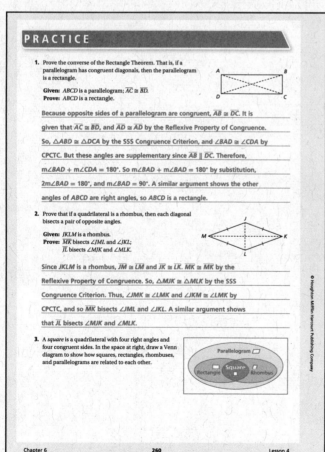

Given: *ABCD* is a parallelogram; $\overline{AC} \cong \overline{BD}$.
Prove: *ABCD* is a rectangle.

Because opposite sides of a parallelogram are congruent, $\overline{AB} \cong \overline{DC}$. It is given that $\overline{AC} \cong \overline{BD}$, and $\overline{AD} \cong \overline{AD}$ by the Reflexive Property of Congruence.

So, $\triangle ABD \cong \triangle DCA$ by the SSS Congruence Criterion, and $\angle BAD \cong \angle CDA$ by CPCTC. But these angles are supplementary since $\overline{AB} \parallel \overline{DC}$. Therefore, $m\angle BAD + m\angle CDA = 180°$. So $m\angle BAD + m\angle BAD = 180°$ by substitution, $2m\angle BAD = 180°$, and $m\angle BAD = 90°$. A similar argument shows the other angles of *ABCD* are right angles, so *ABCD* is a rectangle.

2. Prove that if a quadrilateral is a rhombus, then each diagonal bisects a pair of opposite angles.

Given: *JKLM* is a rhombus.
Prove: $\overline{MK}$ bisects $\angle JML$ and $\angle JKL$;
$\overline{JL}$ bisects $\angle MJK$ and $\angle MLK$.

Since *JKLM* is a rhombus, $\overline{JM} \cong \overline{LM}$ and $\overline{JK} \cong \overline{LK}$. $\overline{MK} \cong \overline{MK}$ by the Reflexive Property of Congruence. So, $\triangle MJK \cong \triangle MLK$ by the SSS Congruence Criterion. Thus, $\angle JMK \cong \angle LMK$ and $\angle JKM \cong \angle LKM$ by CPCTC, and so $\overline{MK}$ bisects $\angle JML$ and $\angle JKL$. A similar argument shows that $\overline{JL}$ bisects $\angle MJK$ and $\angle MLK$.

3. A *square* is a quadrilateral with four right angles and four congruent sides. In the space at right, draw a Venn diagram to show how squares, rectangles, rhombuses, and parallelograms are related to each other.

Notes

ADDITIONAL PRACTICE AND PROBLEM SOLVING

Assign these pages to help your students practice and apply important lesson concepts. For additional exercises, see the Student Edition.

Answers

Additional Practice

1. rectangle
2. square
3. rhombus
4. 9 feet
5. 4 ft
6. $\sqrt{97}$ feet
7. $\frac{\sqrt{97}}{2}$ ft
8. 36
9. 107°
10. 73°
11. 36.5°
12. $2\sqrt{13}$; $2\sqrt{13}$
    $-\frac{3}{2}$; $\frac{2}{3}$
    0, 1; 0, 1
13. Possible answer: $ABCD$ is a rectangle, so $\overline{AC}$ is congruent to $\overline{BD}$. Because $ABCD$ is a rectangle, it is also a parallelogram. Because $ABCD$ is a parallelogram, its diagonals bisect each other. By the definition of bisector, $EC = \frac{1}{2}AC$ and $ED = \frac{1}{2}BD$. But by the definition of congruent segments, $AC = BD$. So substitution and the Transitive Property of Equality show that $EC = ED$. Because $\overline{EC} \cong \overline{ED}$, $\triangle ECD$ is an isosceles triangle. The base angles of an isosceles triangle are congruent, so $\angle EDC \cong \angle ECD$.

Problem Solving

1. 8 yd
2. 25.3 ft
3. 106°
4. 2.6 m
5. 13 in. by $12\frac{1}{4}$ in.
6. B
7. F

Name________________________ Class______________ Date__________

6-4

Additional Practice

Tell whether each figure must be a rectangle, rhombus, or square based on the information given. Use the most specific name possible.

1. 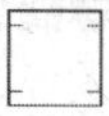
2. 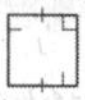
3. 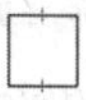

_______________ _______________ _______________

A modern artist's sculpture has rectangular faces. The face shown here is 9 feet long and 4 feet wide. Find each measure in simplest radical form. (*Hint:* Use the Pythagorean Theorem.)

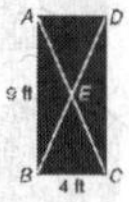

4. *DC* = _______________ 5. *AD* = _______________

6. *DB* = _______________ 7. *AE* = _______________

VWXY **is a rhombus. Find each measure.**

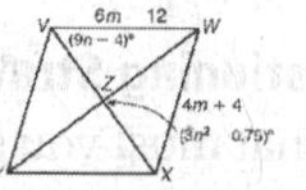

8. *XY* = _______________

9. m∠*YVW* = _______________

10. m∠*VYX* = _______________

11. m∠*XYZ* = _______________

12. The vertices of square *JKLM* are *J*(−2, 4), *K*(−3, −1), *L*(2, −2), and *M*(3, 3). Find each of the following to show that the diagonals of square *JKLM* are congruent perpendicular bisectors of each other.

JL = _______________ KM = _______________

slope of $\overline{JL}$ = _______________ slope of $\overline{KM}$ = _______________

midpoint of $\overline{JL}$ = (________, ________) midpoint of $\overline{KM}$ = (________, ________)

Write a paragraph proof.

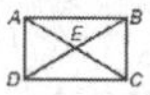

13. **Given:** *ABCD* is a rectangle.
Prove: ∠*EDC* ≅ ∠*ECD*

Problem Solving

Use the diagram for Exercises 1 and 2.

The soccer goalposts determine rectangle *ABCD*.

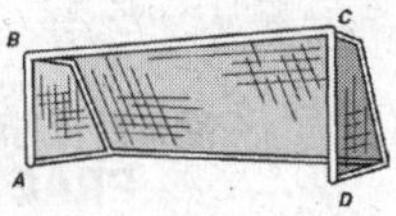

1. The distance between goalposts, *BC*, is three times the distance from the top of the goalpost to the ground. If the perimeter of *ABCD* is $21\frac{1}{3}$ yards, what is the length of $\overline{BC}$?

____

2. The distance from *B* to *D* is approximately (*x* + 10) feet, and the distance from *A* to *C* is approximately (2*x* − 5.3) feet. What is the approximate distance from *A* to *C*?

____

3. *MNPQ* is a rhombus. The measure of ∠*MRQ* is (13*t* − 1)°, and the measure of ∠*PQR* is (7*t* + 4)°. What is the measure of ∠*PQM*?

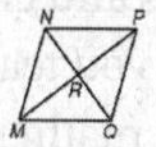

____

4. The *scissor lift* forms rhombus *PQRS* with *PQ* = (7*b* − 5) meters and *QR* = (2*b* − 0.5) meters. If *S* is the midpoint of $\overline{RT}$, what is the length of $\overline{RT}$?

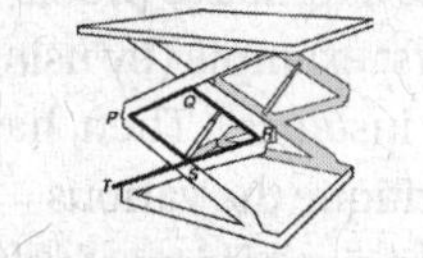

5. The diagram shows the lid of a rectangular case that holds 80 CDs. What are the dimensions of the case?

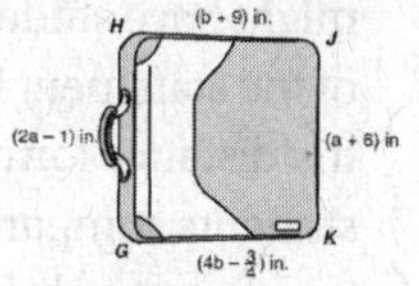

_______________________________ _______________________________

Choose the best answer.

6. What is the measure of ∠1 in the rectangle?

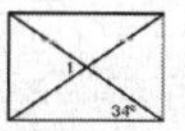

A 34° C 90°
B 68° D 146°

7. A square graphed on the coordinate plane has a diagonal with endpoints *E*(2, 3) and *F*(0, −3). What are the coordinates of the endpoints of the other diagonal?

F (4, −1) and (−2, 1)
G (4, 0) and (−2, 1)
H (4, −1) and (−3, 1)
J (3, −1) and (−2, 1)

Notes

Conditions for Special Parallelograms
Connection: Using Coordinate Methods

Essential question: *How can you use slope in coordinate proofs?*

© Houghton Mifflin Harcourt Publishing Company

Standards for Mathematical Content

CC.9-12.G.GPE.4 Use coordinates to prove simple geometric theorems algebraically.

Prerequisites
Writing coordinate proofs
Slopes of parallel and perpendicular lines

Math Background
Slope makes it possible to give a straightforward proof that a quadrilateral determined by four points is (or is not) a parallelogram. Although it is possible to prove that a quadrilateral is a parallelogram using the distance formula, this can be cumbersome, and the proof depends upon the theorem that says that if both pairs of opposite sides of a quadrilateral are congruent, then the quadrilateral is a parallelogram. Using slope, only the definition of a parallelogram is necessary.

INTRODUCE

Remind students of the slope criteria for parallel lines and for perpendicular lines. Explain that these criteria are often helpful in coordinate proofs. Explain that the criteria are especially useful when the proof requires showing that sides of a polygon are parallel or perpendicular.

TEACH

1 EXAMPLE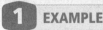

Questioning Strategies
- What must you show to prove that a quadrilateral is a parallelogram? Show that both pairs of opposite sides are parallel.
- How can you show this? Show that slopes of both pairs of opposite sides are equal.

EXTRA EXAMPLE
Prove or disprove that the quadrilateral determined by the points $R(-4, -1)$, $S(2, 2)$, $T(4, -1)$, and $U(-2, -4)$ is a parallelogram

slope of $\overline{RS}$ = slope of $\overline{TU} = \frac{1}{2}$

slope of $\overline{RU}$ = slope of $\overline{ST} = -\frac{3}{2}$

The slopes of opposite sides are equal, so opposite sides are parallel. So, quadrilateral *RSTU* is a parallelogram.

```
MATHEMATICAL PRACTICE
```
Highlighting the Standards

You can address Standard 3 (Construct viable arguments and critique the reasoning of others) as you teach this lesson. The standard states that mathematically proficient students should be able to "compare the effectiveness of two plausible arguments." To that end, you might have students write alternative proofs of the statement in the first example (by using the distance formula, for instance). Then, have students compare and critique the various proofs, not only from the point of view of valid reasoning, but also from the point of view of understandability and clarity.

Name _____ Class _____ Date _____

6-5

Conditions for Special Parallelograms
Connection: Using Coordinate Methods

Essential question: *How can you use slope in coordinate proofs?*

You have already used the distance formula and the midpoint formula in coordinate proofs. As you will see, slope is useful in coordinate proofs whenever you need to show that lines are parallel or perpendicular.

CC.9-12.G.GPE.4

1 EXAMPLE Proving a Quadrilateral Is a Parallelogram

Prove or disprove that the quadrilateral determined by the points $A(4, 4)$, $B(3, 1)$, $C(-2, -1)$, and $D(-1, 2)$ is a parallelogram.

A Plot the points on the coordinate plane at right.

Then draw quadrilateral $ABCD$.

B To determine whether $ABCD$ is a parallelogram, find the slope of each side of the quadrilateral.

Slope of $\overline{AB} = \frac{y_2 - y_1}{x_2 - x_1} = \frac{1 - 4}{3 - 4} = \frac{-3}{-1} = 3$

Slope of $\overline{BC} = \frac{y_2 - y_1}{x_2 - x_1} = \frac{-1 - 1}{-2 - 3} = \frac{-2}{-5} = \frac{2}{5}$

Slope of $\overline{CD} = \frac{y_2 - y_1}{x_2 - x_1} = \frac{2 - (-1)}{-1 - (-2)} = \frac{3}{1} = 3$

Slope of $\overline{DA} = \frac{y_2 - y_1}{x_2 - x_1} = \frac{4 - 2}{4 - (-1)} = \frac{2}{5} = \frac{2}{5}$

C Compare slopes. The slopes of opposite sides are ___equal___

This means opposite sides are ___parallel___

So, ___quadrilateral $ABCD$ is a parallelogram___

REFLECT

1a. Is there a way to write a proof that does not use slope? Explain.

Use the distance formula to show that $AB = CD$ and $BC = DA$. Then conclude that

$ABCD$ is a parallelogram using the Opposite Sides Criterion for a Parallelogram.

© Houghton Mifflin Harcourt Publishing Company

CC.9-12.G.GPE.4

2 EXAMPLE Proving a Quadrilateral Is a Rectangle

Prove or disprove that the quadrilateral determined by the points $Q(2, -3)$, $R(-4, 0)$, $S(-2, 4)$, and $T(4, 1)$ is a rectangle.

A Plot the points on the coordinate plane at right.

Then draw quadrilateral $QRST$.

B To determine whether $QRST$ is a rectangle, find the slope of each side of the quadrilateral.

Slope of $\overline{QR} = \frac{y_2 - y_1}{x_2 - x_1} = \frac{0 - (-3)}{-4 - 2} = \frac{3}{-6} = -\frac{1}{2}$

Slope of $\overline{RS} = \frac{y_2 - y_1}{x_2 - x_1} = \frac{4 - 0}{-2 - (-4)} = \frac{4}{2} = 2$

Slope of $\overline{ST} = \frac{y_2 - y_1}{x_2 - x_1} = \frac{1 - 4}{4 - (-2)} = \frac{-3}{6} = -\frac{1}{2}$

Slope of $\overline{TQ} = \frac{y_2 - y_1}{x_2 - x_1} = \frac{-3 - 1}{2 - 4} = \frac{-4}{-2} = 2$

C Find the product of the slopes of adjacent sides.

(slope of $\overline{QR}$)(slope of $\overline{RS}$) = $-\frac{1}{2} \cdot 2 = -1$

(slope of $\overline{RS}$)(slope of $\overline{ST}$) = $2 \cdot -\frac{1}{2} = -1$

(slope of $\overline{ST}$)(slope of $\overline{TQ}$) = $-\frac{1}{2} \cdot 2 = -1$

(slope of $\overline{TQ}$)(slope of $\overline{QR}$) = $2 \cdot -\frac{1}{2} = -1$

You can conclude that adjacent sides are ___perpendicular___

So, ___quadrilateral $QRST$ is a rectangle___

REFLECT

2a. What would you expect to find if you used the distance formula to calculate SQ and RT? Explain.

$SQ = RT$, since the diagonals of a rectangle are congruent.

2b. Explain how to prove that $QRST$ is not a square.

Use the distance formula to compare adjacent sides; because the

sides are not all congruent, $QRST$ is not a square.

© Houghton Mifflin Harcourt Publishing Company

Questioning Strategies

- What must you show to prove that a quadrilateral is a rectangle? Show that the quadrilateral has four right angles (i.e., that adjacent sides are perpendicular).

- How can you show this? Show that the product of the slopes of adjacent sides is −1.

EXTRA EXAMPLE

Prove or disprove that the quadrilateral determined by the points $J(-4, -1)$, $K(-2, 5)$, $L(1, 4)$, and $M(-1, -2)$ is a rectangle.

slope of $\overline{JK}$ = slope of $\overline{LM}$ = 3

slope of $\overline{KL}$ = slope of $\overline{JM}$ = $-\frac{1}{3}$

The product of the slopes of adjacent sides is −1, so adjacent sides are perpendicular. So, quadrilateral *JKLM* is a rectangle.

Differentiated Instruction

Some students may have difficulty using the formula to calculate slopes. You might suggest that these students try a more visual approach. For example, to find the slope of $\overline{TQ}$, the rise and run can be determined from the graph, as shown below.

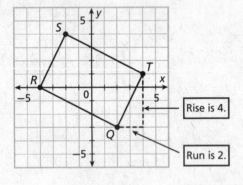

Rise is 4.

Run is 2.

CLOSE

Essential Question

How can you use slope in coordinate proofs?
You can use slope to show that opposite sides of a quadrilateral have the same slope. This shows that the opposite sides are parallel, so the quadrilateral is a parallelogram. You can also use slope to show that the product of the slopes of any pair of adjacent sides of a quadrilateral is −1. This shows that the adjacent sides are perpendicular, so the quadrilateral is a rectangle.

Summarize

Have students write a journal entry in which they give the coordinates of four points and then prove or disprove that the quadrilateral determined by the points is a parallelogram or rectangle.

PRACTICE

Where skills are taught	Where skills are practiced
1 EXAMPLE	EXS. 1–2
2 EXAMPLE	EXS. 3–4

Exercise 5: Students apply what they learned to prove that a quadrilateral is a trapezoid.

Exercise 6: Students use reasoning to find the coordinates of a point that makes a quadrilateral a parallelogram.

Exercise 7: Students connect what they learned in this lesson to what they know about translations in a coordinate plane.

Exercise 8: Students prove that the diagonals of a rhombus are perpendicular by using slopes.

1. Prove or disprove that the quadrilateral determined by the points $J(-3, 1)$, $K(3, 3)$, $L(2, -1)$, and $M(-4, -3)$ is a parallelogram.

   Slope of $\overline{JK}$ = slope of $\overline{LM} = \frac{1}{3}$; slope of $\overline{MJ}$ = slope of $\overline{KL}$ = 4. Since the slopes of

   opposite sides are equal, opposite sides are parallel and quadrilateral $JKLM$ is a

   parallelogram.

2. Prove or disprove that the quadrilateral determined by the points $A(-2, 3)$, $B(5, 3)$, $C(3, -1)$, and $D(-3, -1)$ is a parallelogram.

   Slope of $\overline{AB}$ = slope of $\overline{CD}$ = 0; slope of $\overline{DA}$ = 4; slope of $\overline{BC}$ = 2. Since the slopes

   of one pair of opposite sides are not equal, these opposite sides are not parallel,

   and quadrilateral $ABCD$ is not a parallelogram.

3. Prove or disprove that the quadrilateral determined by the points $Q(-3, 4)$, $R(5, 2)$, $S(4, -1)$, and $T(-4, 1)$ is a rectangle.

   Slope of $\overline{TQ}$ = slope of $\overline{RS}$ = 3; slope of $\overline{QR}$ = slope of $\overline{ST} = -\frac{1}{4}$. The product of

   the slopes of adjacent sides is not -1, so adjacent sides are not perpendicular and

   quadrilateral $QRST$ is not a rectangle.

4. Prove or disprove that the quadrilateral determined by the points $W(1, 5)$, $X(4, 4)$, $Y(2, -2)$, and $Z(-1, -1)$ is a rectangle.

   Slope of $\overline{WX}$ = slope of $\overline{YZ} = -\frac{1}{3}$; slope of $\overline{XY}$ = slope of $\overline{ZW}$ = 3. The product

   of the slopes of adjacent sides is -1, so adjacent sides are perpendicular, and

   quadrilateral $WXYZ$ is a rectangle.

5. Prove or disprove that the quadrilateral determined by the points $D(-2, 3)$, $E(3, 4)$, $F(0, -2)$, and $G(-4, -1)$ has exactly two parallel sides.

   Slope of $\overline{DE} = \frac{1}{5}$; slope of $\overline{EF}$ = 2; slope of $\overline{FG} = -\frac{1}{4}$; slope of $\overline{GD}$ = 2.

   Exactly one pair of opposite sides have the same slope, so these sides are

   parallel, and quadrilateral $DEFG$ has exactly two parallel sides.

---

6. Consider points $L(3, -4)$, $M(1, -2)$, and $N(5, 2)$.

   a. Find the coordinates of point P so that the quadrilateral determined by points $L, M, N,$ and P is a parallelogram. Is there more than one possibility? Explain.

   The coordinates of P may be (7, 0), (3, 4), or $(-1, -8)$. These coordinates result

   in a parallelogram, because opposite sides have equal slopes.

   b. Are any of the parallelograms a rectangle? Why?

   When the coordinates of P are (7, 0), the quadrilateral is a rectangle, because

   the product of the slopes of adjacent sides is -1.

7. You are using a coordinate plane to create a quadrilateral. You start by drawing $\overline{MN}$, as shown.

   a. You decide to translate $\overline{MN}$ by the translation $(x, y) \rightarrow (x + 3, y + 2)$. What type of quadrilateral is $MM'N'N$? Why?

   Parallelogram; opposite sides of the quadrilateral have

   the same slope.

   b. Do you get the same type of quadrilateral for any translation of $\overline{MN}$ that results in a quadrilateral $MM'N'N$? Explain. (*Hint:* Find the coordinates of M' and N' under a general translation, $(x, y) \rightarrow (x + a, y + b)$. Then consider the slopes of the sides of quadrilateral $MM'N'N$.)

   The coordinates of M' are $M'(-2 + a, 2 + b)$ and the coordinates of N' are

   $N'(a, -4 + b)$. Slope of $\overline{MN}$ = slope of $\overline{M'N'}$ = -3; slope of $\overline{MM'}$ = slope of

   $\overline{NN'} = \frac{b}{a}$, assuming $a \neq 0$. If $a = 0$, $\overline{MM'}$ and $\overline{NN'}$ are vertical segments. So

   for all values of a and b, opposite sides have equal slopes and $MM'N'N$ is a

   parallelogram.

   c. You decide you want $MM'N'N$ to be a rectangle. What translations can you use? (*Hint:* What must be true about a and b?)

   Any translation $(x, y) \rightarrow (x + a, y + b)$ such that $a = 3b$ gives a rectangle.

8. Rhombus $OPQR$ has vertices $O(0, 0)$, $P(a, b)$, $Q(a + b, a + b)$, and $R(b, a)$.

   Prove the diagonals of the rhombus are perpendicular.

   The slope of one diagonal is $\frac{a + b}{a + b} = 1$, and the slope of the other diagonal

   is $\frac{b - a}{a - b} = -1$; because the product of 1 and -1 is -1, the diagonals of the

   rhombus are perpendicular.

Notes

ADDITIONAL PRACTICE AND PROBLEM SOLVING

Assign these pages to help your students practice and apply important lesson concepts. For additional exercises, see the Student Edition.

Answers

Additional Practice

1. Possible answer: To know that the reflecting pool is a parallelogram, the congruent sides must be opposite each other. If this is true, then knowing that one angle in the pool is a right angle or that the diagonals are congruent proves that the pool is a rectangle.

2. Not valid; possible answer: you need to know that $\overline{AC} \perp \overline{BD}$.

3. possible answer: you need to know that $\overline{AC}$ and $\overline{BD}$ bisect each other.

4. valid

5. Not valid; possible answer: you need to know that $\overline{AD} \parallel \overline{BC}$.

6. rectangle, rhombus, square

   $\sqrt{26}; \sqrt{26}$

   $-5, \frac{1}{5}$

7. rhombus

   $\sqrt{2}; 3\sqrt{2}$

   $1; -1$

Problem Solving

1. Diagonals bisect each other, so the quad. is a ▱. The diagonals are ≅, so *EFGH* is a rect. because ▱ with diags. ≅ → rect.

2. No; from the given information, you can conclude only that *ABCD* is a rhombus.

3. Both pairs of opposite sides are ≅, so *STUV* is a ▱. *STUV* is a rectangle because ▱ with diags. ≅ → rect.

4. A
5. F
6. D
7. G

Notes

Additional Practice

1. On the National Mall in Washington, D.C., a reflecting pool lies between the Lincoln Memorial and the World War II Memorial. The pool has two 2300-foot-long sides and two 150-foot-long sides. Tell what additional information you need to know in order to determine whether the reflecting pool is a rectangle. (*Hint:* Remember that you have to show it is a parallelogram first.)

_____

_____

_____

Use the figure for Exercises 2–5. Determine whether each conclusion is valid. If not, tell what additional information is needed to make it valid.

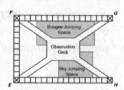

2. **Given:** $\overline{AC}$ and $\overline{BD}$ bisect each other. $\overline{AC} \cong \overline{BD}$
   Conclusion: ABCD is a square.

   _____

3. **Given:** $\overline{AC} \perp \overline{BD}$, $\overline{AB} \cong \overline{BC}$
   Conclusion: ABCD is a rhombus.

   _____

4. **Given:** $\overline{AB} \cong \overline{DC}$, $\overline{AD} \cong \overline{BC}$, m$\angle ADB$ = m$\angle ABD$ = 45°
   Conclusion: ABCD is a square.

   _____

5. **Given:** $\overline{AB} \parallel \overline{DC}$, $\overline{AD} \cong \overline{BC}$, $\overline{AC} \cong \overline{BD}$
   Conclusion: ABCD is a rectangle.

   _____

Find the lengths and slopes of the diagonals to determine whether a parallelogram with the given vertices is a rectangle, rhombus, or square. Give all names that apply.

6. E(−2, −4), F(0, −1), G(−3, 1), H(−5, −2)

   EG = _____   FH = _____

   slope of $\overline{EG}$ = _____   slope of $\overline{FH}$ = _____

7. P(−1, 3), Q(−2, 5), R(0, 4), S(1, 2)

   PR = _____   QS = _____

   slope of $\overline{PR}$ = _____   slope of $\overline{QS}$ = _____

Problem Solving

1. An amusement park has a rectangular observation deck with walkways above the bungee jumping and sky jumping. The distance from the center of the deck to points E, F, G, and H is 15 meters. Explain why EFGH must be a rectangle.

   _____

   _____

   _____

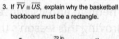

2. In the mosaic, $\overline{AB} \parallel \overline{CD}$ and $\overline{BC} \parallel \overline{DA}$. If AB = 4 inches and BC = 4 inches, can you conclude that ABCD is a square? Explain.

3. If $\overline{TV} \cong \overline{US}$, explain why the basketball backboard must be a rectangle.

   _____

   _____

Choose the best answer.

4. The vertices of a parallelogram are N(0, −4), P(6, −1), Q(4, 3), and R(−2, 0). Classify the parallelogram as specifically as possible.

   A rectangle only
   B square
   C rhombus only
   D quadrilateral

5. Choose the best description for the quadrilateral.

   F parallelogram
   G parallelogram and rectangle
   H parallelogram and rhombus
   J parallelogram and square

6. In parallelogram KLMN, m$\angle L$ = (4w + 5)°. Choose the value of w that makes KLMN a rectangle.

   A 90   C 43.75
   B 85   D 21.25

7. The coordinates of three vertices of quadrilateral ABCD are A(3, −1), B(10, 0), and C(5, 5). For which coordinates of D will the quadrilateral be a rhombus?

   F (−1, 4)   H (−1, 3)
   G (−2, 4)   J (−2, 3)

Properties of Kites and Trapezoids
Going Deeper

Essential question: How can auxiliary segments be used in proof?

© Houghton Mifflin Harcourt Publishing Company

COMMON CORE **Standards for Mathematical Content**

CC.9-12.G.CO.9 Prove theorems about lines and angles.

Prerequisites

Angles formed by parallel lines and transversals
Properties of parallelograms

Math Background

Inserting auxiliary segments into a diagram is not only permissible, but also advantageous. In the case of the proofs in this lesson, introducing a line segment that is parallel to one of the legs of a trapezoid allows you to divide the trapezoid into a parallelogram and a triangle.

INTRODUCE

Ask students to construct a trapezoid having a pair of congruent base angles. By folding their paper so that the vertices of the congruent angles coincide, students should see that the legs of the triangle also coincide, which indicates that the trapezoid is isosceles and motivates the first theorem in this lesson.

TEACH

 1 PROOF

Questioning Strategies

- What polygons does the auxiliary line segment $\overline{CE}$ determine? **The line segment separates the trapezoid into a parallelogram and what appears to be an isosceles triangle next to it.**

- After the auxiliary line segment is drawn, what three angles along the base of the trapezoid appear to be congruent? **∠BAD, ∠CED, and ∠CDE**

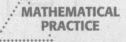 **2** PROOF

Questioning Strategies

- How are the diagrams for each proof the same and how are they different? **Each diagram shows the same trapezoid. In the diagram for the first proof, the base angles are marked as congruent. In the diagram for the second proof, the nonparallel sides are marked as congruent. The diagrams show what is given.**

- How is the isosceles triangle in this proof used differently than it was in the first proof? **In the second proof, congruent sides are used to show that base angles in the isosceles triangle are congruent. In the first proof, congruent base angles in the isosceles triangle are used to show that two sides of the triangle are congruent.**

CLOSE

Essential Question

How can auxiliary segments be used in proof?
As the proofs in this lesson illustrate, introducing an auxiliary segment allows you to take advantage of properties of familiar figures when proving properties of unfamiliar figures.

Summarize

Have students describe how the Isosceles Triangle Theorem and its converse play a key role in proving this lesson's theorems about trapezoids.

MATHEMATICAL PRACTICE | **Highlighting the Standards**

The proofs in this lesson provide opportunities to address Standard 7 (Look for and make use of structure). Students see that the use of an auxiliary line segment allows them to prove theorems about a complex figure (a trapezoid) by breaking it into simpler figures (a parallelogram and a triangle) whose properties they already know.

Name_____ Class_____ Date_____

6-6

Properties of Kites and Trapezoids
Going Deeper

Essential Question: *How can auxiliary segments be used in proofs?*

Proof of a theorem may require the use of an auxiliary segment or line added to a geometric diagram to help you.

> **Theorem**
>
> If a trapezoid has one pair of congruent base angles, then the trapezoid is isosceles.
>
> If $\angle A \cong \angle D$, then $\overline{AB} \cong \overline{DC}$.

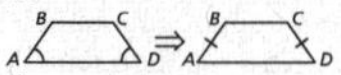

CC.9-12.G.CO.9

1 PROOF   Reasoning from Congruent Angles to Congruent Sides

Complete the proof.

Given: $ABCD$ is a trapezoid with $\overline{BC} \parallel \overline{AD}$, $\angle A \cong \angle D$, as shown in the diagram.

Prove: $ABCD$ is an isosceles trapezoid.

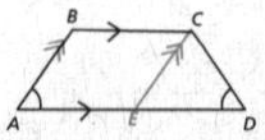

Statements	Reasons
1. $\overline{BC} \parallel \overline{AD}$	1. Given
2. Draw $\overline{CE} \parallel \overline{AB}$ intersecting $\overline{AD}$ at E.	2. Parallel Postulate
3. $ABCE$ is a parallelogram.	3. Definition of parallelogram
4. $\overline{AB} \cong \overline{CE}$	4. If a quadrilateral is a parallelogram, then its opposite sides are congruent
5. $\angle A \cong \angle CED$	5. Corresponding Angles Postulate
6. $\angle A \cong \angle D$	6. Given
7. $\angle D \cong \angle CED$	7. Substitution (Steps 5, 6)
8. $\overline{CE} \cong \overline{CD}$	8. Converse of Isosceles Triangle Theorem
9. $\overline{AB} \cong \overline{CD}$	9. Transitive Prop. of Cong. (Steps 4, 8)
10. $ABCD$ is an isosceles trapezoid.	10. Definition of isosceles trapezoid

REFLECT

1a. What are the parallel lines and transversal involved in Step 5 of the proof?

$\overleftrightarrow{AB}$ and $\overleftrightarrow{CE}$ are the parallel lines, and $\overleftrightarrow{AD}$ is the transversal.

1b. Can you prove the theorem on the previous page if you are given $\angle B \cong \angle C$ instead of $\angle A \cong \angle D$? Explain a possible approach.

Possible answer: Use the Same-Side Interior Angles Theorem to show that $\angle B$ and

$\angle A$ are supplementary, and $\angle C$ and $\angle D$ are supplementary; $\angle A \cong \angle D$ because

supplements of congruent angles are congruent. Then use the proof already shown.

The converse of the theorem on the preceding page is also true.

CC.9-12.G.CO.9

2 PROOF   Reasoning from Congruent Sides to Congruent Angles

Complete the proof.

Given: $ABCD$ is an isosceles trapezoid with $\overline{BC} \parallel \overline{AD}$, $\overline{AB} \cong \overline{CD}$, as shown in the diagram.

Prove: $\angle A \cong \angle D$

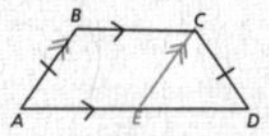

Statements	Reasons
1. $\overline{BC} \parallel \overline{AD}$	1. Given
2. Draw $\overline{CE} \parallel \overline{AB}$ intersecting $\overline{AD}$ at E.	2. Parallel Postulate
3. $\angle A \cong \angle CED$	3. Corresponding Angles Postulate
4. $ABCE$ is a parallelogram.	4. Definition of parallelogram
5. $\overline{AB} \cong \overline{CE}$	5. If a quadrilateral is a parallelogram, then its opposite sides are congruent.
6. $\overline{AB} \cong \overline{CD}$	6. Given
7. $\overline{CD} \cong \overline{CE}$	7. Substitution (Steps 5, 6)
8. $\angle CED \cong \angle D$	8. Isosceles Triangle Theorem
9. $\angle A \cong \angle D$	9. Transitive Prop. of Congruence (Steps 3, 8)

REFLECT

2a. Given that $\angle A \cong \angle D$ as proved above, how can you prove that $\angle B \cong \angle C$ in the isosceles trapezoid?

Possible answer: By the Same-Side Interior Angles Thm., $\angle B$ is supplementary to

$\angle A$, and $\angle C$ is supplementary to $\angle D$. Since $\angle A \cong \angle D$ by the proof above, $\angle B \cong \angle C$

by the Congruent Supplements Theorem.

© Houghton Mifflin Harcourt Publishing Company

ADDITIONAL PRACTICE AND PROBLEM SOLVING

Assign these pages to help your students practice and apply important lesson concepts. For additional exercises, see the Student Edition.

Answers

Additional Practice

1. (3) Alternate Interior Angles

   (7) ASA

   (9) N is the midpoint of $\overline{BE}$.

   (12) Congruent Supplements Theorem

2. By the Triangle Midsegment Theorem, $MN = \frac{1}{2}(AE) = \frac{1}{2}(AD + DE) = \frac{1}{2}(AD + BC)$.

Problem Solving p272

1. $\overline{AC}$

2. $\overline{AC}$ divides the kite into $\triangle ABC$ and $\triangle ADC$. AB ≅ AD and $\overline{BC} \cong \overline{BD}$ because $ABCD$ is a kite, and $\overline{AC} \cong \overline{AC}$ by the Reflexive Property. So, $\triangle ABC \cong \triangle ADC$ by SSS.

3. Possible answer: $\triangle ABC \cong \triangle ADC$, so $\angle BAC \cong \angle DAC$. Let E be the intersection of $\overline{AC}$ and $\overline{BD}$. $\triangle ABD$ is isosceles, so $\angle ABE \cong \angle ADE$. Then $\angle AEB$ and $\angle AED$ form a linear pair of congruent angles, so each is a right angle, and $\overline{AC} \perp \overline{BD}$.

4. C

5. G

6. B

Additional Practice

The midsegment of a trapezoid is the segment whose endpoints are the midpoints of the legs. According to the Trapezoid Midsegment Theorem, (1) the midsegment of a trapezoid is parallel to each base, and (2) its length is one half the sum of the lengths of the bases.

1. Complete this proof of Part 1 of the theorem.

   Given: $ABCD$ is a trapezoid with $\overline{BC} \parallel \overline{AD}$,

   M is the midpoint of $\overline{AB}$, N is the midpoint of $\overline{CD}$.

   Prove: $\overline{MN} \parallel \overline{AD}$, $\overline{MN} \parallel \overline{BC}$

1. $\overline{BC} \parallel \overline{AD}$	1. Given
2. Draw $\overrightarrow{BN}$ intersecting $\overrightarrow{AD}$ in point E.	2. Through any two points there is exactly one line; if two lines intersect, they intersect in exactly one point.
3. $\angle BCD \cong \angle CDE$	3.
4. $\angle BNC \cong \angle END$	4. Vertical Angles
5. N is the midpoint of $\overline{CD}$.	5. Given
6. $\overline{NC} \cong \overline{ND}$	6. Definition of midpoint
7. $\triangle BNC \cong \triangle END$	7.
8. $\overline{BN} \cong \overline{NE}$	8. CPCTC
9.	9. Definition of midpoint
10. $\overline{MN} \parallel \overline{AD}$	10. Triangle Midsegment Theorem
11. $\angle ABC$ and $\angle BAD$ are supplementary; $\angle NMA$ and $\angle BAD$ are supplementary.	11. Same-side interior angles
12. $\angle ABC \cong \angle NMA$	12.
13. $\overline{MN} \parallel \overline{BC}$	13. Converse of Corresponding Angles

2. Describe how you could use the Triangle Midsegment Theorem to

   prove Part 2 of the theorem, that is, $MN = \frac{1}{2}(AD + BC)$?

   _____

   _____

© Houghton Mifflin Harcourt Publishing Company

Problem Solving

A kite is a quadrilateral with exactly two pairs of congruent consecutive sides. Anil is making a kite for a kite-flying contest. For Exercises 1–3, use the kite pattern that he drew.

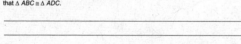

1. What auxiliary line could you use to prove that $\triangle ABC \cong \triangle ADC$?

   _____

2. Describe how you would use the auxiliary line in your answer to Exercise 1 to complete the proof that $\triangle ABC \cong \triangle ADC$.

   _____

   _____

   _____

3. The diagonals of a kite are perpendicular. Describe how you could prove that in kite $ABCD$, $\overline{AC} \perp \overline{BD}$.

   _____

   _____

   _____

Choose the best answer.

4. Trapezoid $PQRS$ has base angles that measure $(9r + 21)°$ and $(15r - 21)°$. Find the value of r so that $PQRS$ is isosceles. H

   A 3
   B 5
   C 7
   D 14

5. In kite $KLMN$, find the measure of $\angle M$.

   F 100.5°
   G 101°
   H 122°
   J 130°

6. In the design, eight isosceles trapezoids surround a regular octagon. What is the measure of $\angle B$ in trapezoid $ABCD$?

   A 35°
   B 45°
   C 55°
   D 65°

© Houghton Mifflin Harcourt Publishing Company

4-6 all

This page provides students with the opportunity to apply concepts from the Common Core in real-world problem situations. There are three different levels of performance tasks:

⭐ **Novice:** These are short word problems that require students to apply the math they have learned in straightforward, real-world situations.

⭐⭐ **Apprentice:** These are more involved problems that guide students step-by-step through more complex tasks. These exercises include more complicated reasoning, writing, and open-ended elements.

⭐⭐⭐ **Expert:** These are open-ended, non-routine problems that, instead of stepping the students through, ask them to choose their own methods for solving and justify their answers and reasoning.

Sample answers

1. $(3, -2)$; possible justification: Since C is 3 units right and 2 units down from B, point D must be 3 units right and 2 units down from A so that $\overline{AD}$ will be parallel and congruent to $\overline{BC}$.

2. A square, a rectangle, and an isosceles trapezoid are possible. The legs of the ironing board are equivalent to the diagonals of the quadrilateral, and only these quadrilaterals have congruent diagonals.

3. Scoring Guide:

Task	Possible points
a	1 point for correctly stating that the diagonals are not congruent because, by the Distance Formula, $WY = \sqrt{125}$ and $XZ = \sqrt{80}$
b	2 points for correctly stating that the diagonals are perpendicular because the slope of $\overline{WY}$ is -2, and the slope of $\overline{XZ}$ is $\frac{1}{2}$, so they are negative reciprocals
c	2 points for correctly stating that $\overline{WY}$ bisects $\overline{XZ}$ but not vice versa, since the midpoint of $\overline{WY}$ is $(9.5, 7)$ which is not on $\overline{XZ}$, and the midpoint of $\overline{XZ}$ is $(8, 10)$ which is on $\overline{WY}$
d	1 point for correctly identifying the quadrilateral as a kite

Total possible points: 6

Name_____ Class_____ Date_____

Performance Tasks

COMMON CORE
CC.9-12.G.CO.11
CC.9-12.G.GPE.4
CC.9-12.G.MG.3

⭐ 1. An architect is drawing a floor plan for a garage on a coordinate plane. The architect has located three corners of the garage at $A(0, 0)$, $B(4, 6)$, and $C(7, 4)$. If the garage must be in the shape of a rectangle, what are the coordinates of point D? Justify your answer.

⭐ 2. An ironing board manufacturer designs a folding ironing board with two legs. Each leg runs diagonally under the board from one end of the board to the floor, crossing over the other leg in the middle. Both legs are the same length. The designer connects the endpoints of the legs to form a quadrilateral. Which specific quadrilaterals could be formed? Explain your answer.

⭐⭐ 3. The endpoints of one diagonal of quadrilateral $WXYZ$ are $W(7, 12)$ and $Y(12, 2)$. The endpoints of the other diagonal are $X(12, 12)$ and $Z(4, 8)$.

   a. Are the diagonals congruent? How do you know?

   b. Are the diagonals perpendicular? Explain.

   c. Do the diagonals bisect each other? Explain.

   d. What is the most descriptive name for quadrilateral $WXYZ$?

continued

© Houghton Mifflin Harcourt Publishing Company

⭐⭐⭐ 4. The four vertices of a quadrilateral are given as $A(11, 7)$, $B(13, 4)$, $C(0, -7)$ and $D(x, y)$. Choose values for x and y such that $ABCD$ is a trapezoid, and then prove that your figure is a trapezoid.

© Houghton Mifflin Harcourt Publishing Company

---

4. Scoring Guide:

Task	Possible points
	2 points for correctly choosing a point that makes the figure a trapezoid, and 4 points for correctly proving it. For example, $D(-4, -1)$. The slope of $\overline{AB}$ is $-\frac{3}{2}$, the slope of $\overline{BC}$ is $\frac{11}{13}$, the slope of $\overline{CD}$ is $-\frac{3}{2}$, and the slope of $\overline{AD}$ is $\frac{8}{15}$. Equal slopes indicate parallel lines. Only one pair of sides has equal slopes, so only one pair of opposite sides is parallel. Therefore, by definition of trapezoid, the figure is a trapezoid.

Total possible points: 6

COMMON CORE CORRELATION

Standard	Items
CC.9–12.G.CO.11	1, 2, 3, 4
CC.9–12.G.CO.13	5, 6
CC.9–12.G.SRT.5	1, 3, 8
CC.9-12.GPE.4	7

TEST PREP DOCTOR ⊕

Multiple Choice: Item 1

- Students who answered **A** or **B** may not realize that although it is true that $\overline{LP} \cong \overline{MN}$ and that $\overline{LN} \cong \overline{MP}$, neither statement is helpful in combination with the fact that $\overline{LM} \cong \overline{PN}$ in proving that $LQM \cong NQP$.

- Students who answered **C** may not realize that although the given congruences are true, using them to prove that $LQM \cong NQP$ is unnecessarily complicated. On the other hand, the congruences in part **D** combined with Rosa's initial statement complete the desired proof.

Multiple Choice: Item 2

- Students who answered **G** may have incorrectly assumed that because a transversal is involved, the next step must involve angles formed by the transversal and the parallel lines.

- Students who answered **H** may not understand the Reflexive Property of Congruence.

- Students who answered **J** may have confused Step 3 with the final step of the proof, for which it would be reasonable to assume that the reason is CPCTC.

Multiple Choice: Item 4

- Students who answered **F**, **G**, or **J** may need to review the properties of parallelograms.

Constructed Response: Item 8

- Students who provide a "proof" that the quadrilateral is a parallelogram may make the assumption that that is the case, then attempt to justify their assumptions. For instance, they may note correctly that the slopes of $\overline{BC}$ and $\overline{DA}$ are -4, then mistakenly assert that the slopes of $\overline{AB}$ and $\overline{CD}$ must be $-\frac{1}{4}$.

CHAPTER 6 COMMON CORE ASSESSMENT READINESS

Name _____ Class _____ Date _____

MULTIPLE CHOICE

1. Rosa is using the figure below to prove that the diagonals of a parallelogram bisect each other. She starts by stating that $\overline{LM} \cong \overline{PN}$ since opposite sides of a parallelogram are congruent. What should she show next in order to prove that $\triangle LQM \cong \triangle NQP$?

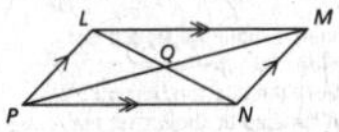

A. $\overline{LP} \cong \overline{MN}$

B. $\overline{LN} \cong \overline{MP}$

C. $\angle QLP \cong \angle QNM$ and $\angle QPL \cong \angle QMN$

(D.) $\angle MLQ \cong \angle PNQ$ and $\angle LMQ \cong \angle NPQ$

2. Ming is proving that opposite sides of a parallelogram are congruent. He begins as shown. Which reason should he use for Step 3?

Given: $PQRS$ is a parallelogram.
Prove: $\overline{PQ} \cong \overline{RS}$; $\overline{PS} \cong \overline{QR}$

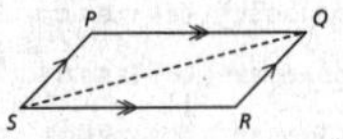

Statements	Reasons
1. $PQRS$ is a parallelogram	1. Given
2. Draw $\overline{SQ}$.	2. Through 2 pts. there is exactly one line.
3. $\overline{PQ} \parallel \overline{RS}$; $\overline{PS} \parallel \overline{QR}$	3. ?

(F.) Definition of parallelogram

G. Alternate Interior Angles Theorem

H. Reflexive Property of Congruence

J. CPCTC

3. $DEFG$ is a rhombus. You want to prove the property that a diagonal of a rhombus bisects a pair of opposite angles. To prove that $\overline{DF}$ bisects $\angle GDE$, you first show that $\triangle GDF \cong \triangle EDF$ using the definition of rhombus, the Reflexive Property of Congruence, and the SSS Congruence Criterion. What other reasons are needed to complete the proof?

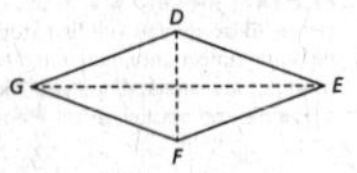

A. Isosceles Triangle Theorem; SAS Congruence Criterion

B. Definition of perpendicular; Triangle Sum Theorem

C. If a quadrilateral is a parallelogram, then opposite angles are congruent; definition of angle bisector

(D.) Congruent Parts of Congruent Triangles are Congruent; definition of angle bisector

4. Which property of rectangles is not true for all parallelograms?

F. opposite sides are parallel

G. opposite sides are congruent

(H.) diagonals are congruent

J. diagonals bisect each other

© Houghton Mifflin Harcourt Publishing Company

CONSTRUCTED RESPONSE

5. Use a compass and straightedge to construct a regular hexagon that is inscribed in circle O.

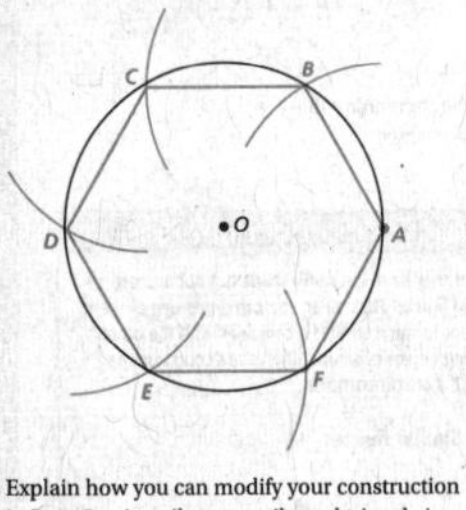

6. Explain how you can modify your construction in Item 5 to inscribe an equilateral triangle in circle O.

After completing the construction, use

a straightedge to draw $\overline{AC}$, $\overline{CE}$, and

$\overline{EA}$. $\triangle ACE$ is an equilateral triangle.

7. Prove or disprove that the quadrilateral determined by the points $A(-3, 1)$, $B(3, 3)$, $C(4, -1)$, and $D(-2, -3)$ is a rectangle.

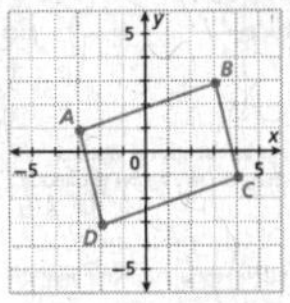

Slope of $\overline{AB}$ = slope of $\overline{CD}$ = $\frac{1}{3}$

Slope of $\overline{BC}$ = slope of $\overline{DA}$ = -4

The product of the slopes of adjacent

sides is not -1, so adjacent sides are

not perpendicular and quadrilateral

$ABCD$ is not a rectangle.

8. Prove the following. You may not need all the rows of the table in your proof.

Given: $ABCD$ is a rectangle. $\overline{AE} \cong \overline{FB}$
Prove: $\triangle DAF \cong \triangle CBE$

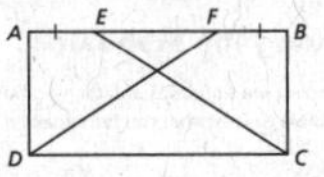

Statements	Reasons
1. $\overline{AE} \cong \overline{FB}$	1. Given
2. $\overline{AF} \cong \overline{EB}$	2. Common Segments Theorem
3. $ABCD$ is a rectangle.	3. Given
4. $ABCD$ is a parallelogram.	4. Rectangle Theorem
5. $\overline{AD} \cong \overline{BC}$	5. Opposite sides of a parallelogram are congruent.
6. $\angle A$ and $\angle B$ are right angles.	6. Definition of rectangle
7. $\angle A \cong \angle B$	7. All right angles are congruent.
8. $\triangle DAF \cong \triangle CBE$	8. SAS Congruence Criterion

© Houghton Mifflin Harcourt Publishing Company

Similarity

COMMON CORE PROFESSIONAL DEVELOPMENT **CC.9-12.G.SRT.2**

Students studied ratio and proportion extensively in earlier grades. Later, students began making connections between equivalent ratios (in the form of constant rates) to linear relationships. In this chapter, students make solid connections between equivalent ratios and the proportional side lengths of similar polygons. Students study many aspects of similarity—mathematical and non-mathematical definitions, identifying similarity transformations, verifying and proving similarity relationships in polygons and in real-world scenarios, and performing dilations in the coordinate plane. It is important for students to understand that just as two figures can be defined as congruent if obtained from a sequence of rigid transformations, two figures can be defined as similar if obtained by a sequence of transformations that includes a dilation.

CHAPTER 7

Similarity

Chapter Focus

Informally speaking, two figures are similar if they have the same shape, but not necessarily the same size. In this unit, you will put this idea into mathematical terms. To do so, you will first study a new transformation, the dilation. As you did with congruence, you will develop criteria that can be used to show that two triangles are similar. Then you will apply similarity to a wide range of real-world problems and mathematical theorems.

Chapter at a Glance

COMMON CORE

Lesson		Standards for Mathematical Content
7-1	Ratios in Similar Polygons	Prep for CC.9-12.G.SRT.1b, Prep for CC.9-12.G.SRT.2
7-2	Similarity and Transformations	CC.9-12.G.CO.2, CC.9-12.G.SRT.1, CC.9-12.G.SRT.2, CC.9-12.G.C.1
7-3	Triangle Similarity AA, SSS, SAS	CC.9-12.G.SRT.2, CC.9-12.G.SRT.3
7-4	Applying Properties of Similar Triangles	CC.9-12.G.SRT.4, CC.9-12.G.SRT.5
7-5	Using Proportional Relationships	CC.9-12.G.SRT.5, CC.9-12.G.MG.3
7-6	Dilations and Similarity in the Coordinate Plane	CC.9-12.G.CO.2
	Performance Tasks	
	Assessment Readiness	

Unpacking the Standards

Understanding the standards and the vocabulary terms in the standards will help you know exactly what you are expected to learn in this chapter.

COMMON CORE CC.9-12.G.SRT.2

Given two figures, … decide if they are similar; explain using similarity transformations the meaning of similarity for triangles as the equality of all corresponding pairs of angles and the proportionality of all corresponding pairs of sides.

Key Vocabulary

similar polygons *(polígonos semejantes)* Two polygons whose corresponding angles are congruent and whose corresponding side lengths are proportional.

similarity transformation *(transformación de semejanza)* A transformation that produces similar figures.

triangle *(triángulo)* A three-sided polygon.

corresponding angles of polygons *(ángulos correspondientes de los polígonos)* Angles in the same position in two different polygons that have the same number of angles.

corresponding sides of polygons *(lados correspondientes de los polígonos)* Sides in the same position in two different polygons that have the same number of sides.

What It Means For You   Lessons 7-1, 7-2, 7-3

Two figures are similar if they have the same shape but not necessarily the same size. When two figures are similar, you can dilate one of them and then slide, flip, and/or rotate it so that it coincides with the other. As a result, corresponding angles of similar figures are congruent and corresponding side lengths are proportional.

EXAMPLE   Similar figures

The figures are similar because you can multiply all the side lengths of the smaller figure by 1.2, rotate it 180°, and slide it so that it coincides with the larger figure.

NON-EXAMPLE   Non-similar figures

The rectangles are not similar. There is no combination of dilations, slides, flips, and/or rotations that will cause the two figures to coincide.

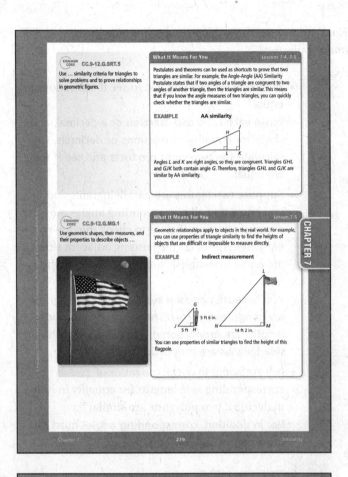

COMMON CORE CC.9-12.G.SRT.5
Use ... similarity criteria for triangles to solve problems and to prove relationships in geometric figures.

What It Means For You — Lessons 7-4, 7-5

Postulates and theorems can be used as shortcuts to prove that two triangles are similar. For example, the Angle-Angle (AA) Similarity Postulate states that if two angles of a triangle are congruent to two angles of another triangle, then the triangles are similar. This means that if you know the angle measures of two triangles, you can quickly check whether the triangles are similar.

EXAMPLE   AA similarity

Angles L and K are right angles, so they are congruent. Triangles GHL and GJK both contain angle G. Therefore, triangles GHL and GJK are similar by AA similarity.

COMMON CORE CC.9-12.G.MG.1
Use geometric shapes, their measures, and their properties to describe objects ...

What It Means For You — Lesson 7-5

Geometric relationships apply to objects in the real world. For example, you can use properties of triangle similarity to find the heights of objects that are difficult or impossible to measure directly.

EXAMPLE   Indirect measurement

5 ft 6 in.   5 ft   14 ft 2 in.

You can use properties of similar triangles to find the height of this flagpole.

Chapter 7 — 279 — Similarity

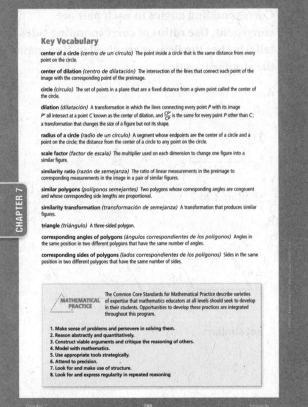

Key Vocabulary

center of a circle (*centro de un círculo*) The point inside a circle that is the same distance from every point on the circle.

center of dilation (*centro de dilatación*) The intersection of the lines that connect each point of the image with the corresponding point of the preimage.

circle (*círculo*) The set of points in a plane that are a fixed distance from a given point called the center of the circle.

dilation (*dilatación*) A transformation in which the lines connecting every point P with its image P' all intersect at a point C known as the center of dilation, and $\frac{CP'}{CP}$ is the same for every point P other than C; a transformation that changes the size of a figure but not its shape.

radius of a circle (*radio de un círculo*) A segment whose endpoints are the center of a circle and a point on the circle; the distance from the center of a circle to any point on the circle.

scale factor (*factor de escala*) The multiplier used on each dimension to change one figure into a similar figure.

similarity ratio (*razón de semejanza*) The ratio of linear measurements in the preimage to corresponding measurements in the image in a pair of similar figures.

similar polygons (*polígonos semejantes*) Two polygons whose corresponding angles are congruent and whose corresponding side lengths are proportional.

similarity transformation (*transformación de semejanza*) A transformation that produces similar figures.

triangle (*triángulo*) A three-sided polygon.

corresponding angles of polygons (*ángulos correspondientes de los polígonos*) Angles in the same position in two different polygons that have the same number of angles.

corresponding sides of polygons (*lados correspondientes de los polígonos*) Sides in the same position in two different polygons that have the same number of sides.

MATHEMATICAL PRACTICE
The Common Core Standards for Mathematical Practice describe varieties of expertise that mathematics educators at all levels should seek to develop in their students. Opportunities to develop these practices are integrated throughout this program.

1. Make sense of problems and persevere in solving them.
2. Reason abstractly and quantitatively.
3. Construct viable arguments and critique the reasoning of others.
4. Model with mathematics.
5. Use appropriate tools strategically.
6. Attend to precision.
7. Look for and make use of structure.
8. Look for and express regularity in repeated reasoning.

Chapter 7 — 280 — Similarity

CHAPTER 7

COMMON CORE PROFESSIONAL DEVELOPMENT CC.9-12.G.MG.1*

Indirect measurement involves using the properties of similar triangles to solve real-world problems, such as finding distances that cannot be measured directly. In previous courses, students have solved proportions to find unknown measures in similar triangles. In this chapter, students learn how to strategically position figures resulting in similar polygons, so that the properties of similar triangles can be used to solve for unknown measures without using direct measurement. Students are commonly surprised to learn of the numerous real-world scenarios in which indirect measurement using geometric properties is applied.

Ratios in Similar Polygons
Going Deeper

Essential question: How can you use ratios of corresponding side lengths to solve problems involving similar polygons?

COMMON **Standards for**
CORE **Mathematical Content**

Prep for CC.9-12.G.SRT.2 Given two figures, ... decide if they are similar ...

Prep for CC.9-12.G.SRT.1b The dilation of a line segment is longer or shorter in the ratio given by the scale factor.

Prerequisites
Writing and simplifying ratios

Math Background
There are several ways to define what is meant by *similar figures*. The most basic definition is that similar figures have the same shape but not necessarily the same size. A more precise definition, presented in this lesson and applied to polygons, is that all corresponding angles must be congruent and all corresponding side lengths must be proportional. In the next lesson, a definition based on similarity transformations (in particular, dilations) is presented. This lesson prepares for the next by connecting the ratio of corresponding side lengths to the scale factor used in a dilation.

INTRODUCE

Begin by describing two classes, one with 10 boys and 15 girls and the other with 12 boys and 18 girls. Point out that the ratios of boys to girls for the two classes are equal because both can be simplified to a ratio of 2 to 3. In this case, the number of boys is said to be *proportional* to the number of girls in the two classes.

TEACH

1 EXAMPLE

Questioning Strategies
• In part A, when checking the ratios of corresponding lengths and corresponding widths of rectangles *ABCD* and *WXYZ*, why is it incorrect to compare $\frac{BC}{XY}$ and $\frac{WX}{AB}$?
Both ratios must be formed by going in the same direction, either from rectangle *ABCD* to rectangle *WXYZ* or from rectangle *WXYZ* to rectangle *ABCD*.

• In what ways can you test to see if two ratios are equal?
Write each ratio as a fraction or a decimal, and check for equality of fractions or decimals. Or calculate the two cross products and see if they are equal.

• Suppose two figures are parallelograms and you know that all corresponding angles are congruent. Is it sufficient to check that the ratios of the lengths of corresponding adjacent sides are equal to establish similarity? Why or why not?
Yes; because opposite sides of a parallelogram are congruent, if corresponding adjacent side lengths are proportional, then all corresponding side lengths are proportional.

• Is it sufficient to check the ratios of corresponding side lengths for equality in order to decide if two polygons are similar?
No; in addition, corresponding angles must be congruent.

EXTRA EXAMPLE
Corresponding angles in each pair are congruent. Use ratios of corresponding sides to tell whether the figures are similar. If so, name the similarity ratio.

A.

similar; 3 to 2

B.

not similar

Name_____ Class_____ Date_____

7-1

Video Tutor

Ratios in Similar Polygons
Going Deeper

Essential question: *How can you use ratios of corresponding side lengths to solve problems involving similar polygons?*

Two polygons are **similar polygons** if and only if their corresponding angles are congruent and their corresponding side lengths are proportional. The *similarity ratio* of two similar figures is the ratio of any side length in the first figure to the corresponding side length in the second figure. To prove that two figures with corresponding angles congruent are similar, show that corresponding side lengths are proportional.

CC.9-12.G.SRT.2

1 EXAMPLE   Determining Polygon Similarity

Corresponding angles in each pair are congruent. Use ratios of corresponding side lengths to tell whether the figures are similar. If so, name the similarity ratio.

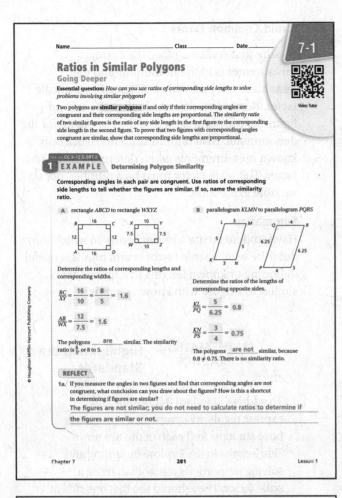

A rectangle *ABCD* to rectangle *WXYZ*

B parallelogram *KLMN* to parallelogram *PQRS*

Determine the ratios of corresponding lengths and corresponding widths.

$\dfrac{BC}{XY} = \dfrac{16}{10} = \dfrac{8}{5} = 1.6$

$\dfrac{AB}{WX} = \dfrac{12}{7.5} = 1.6$

The polygons ___are___ similar. The similarity ratio is $\frac{8}{5}$, or 8 to 5.

Determine the ratios of the lengths of corresponding opposite sides.

$\dfrac{KL}{PQ} = \dfrac{5}{6.25} = 0.8$

$\dfrac{KN}{PS} = \dfrac{3}{4} = 0.75$

The polygons ___are not___ similar, because $0.8 \neq 0.75$. There is no similarity ratio.

REFLECT

1a. If you measure the angles in two figures and find that corresponding angles are not congruent, what conclusion can you draw about the figures? How is this a shortcut in determining if figures are similar?

The figures are not similar; you do not need to calculate ratios to determine if the figures are similar or not.

Chapter 7   281   Lesson 1

1b. Describe how to find the *similarity ratio* of two similar figures when you are given lengths of corresponding sides.

Find the ratio of any side length in the first figure to the corresponding side length in the second figure. That is the similarity ratio.

CC.9-12.G.SRT.1b

2 EXPLORE   Finding Unknown Lengths in Similar Polygons

The trapezoids below are similar.

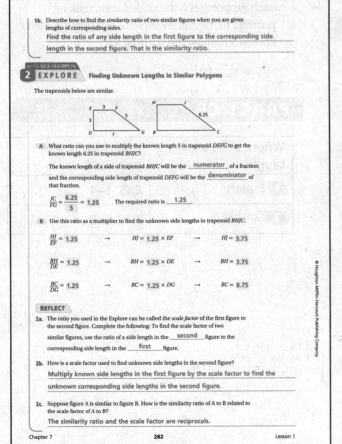

A What ratio can you use to multiply the known length 5 in trapezoid *DEFG* to get the known length 6.25 in trapezoid *BHJC*?

The known length of a side of trapezoid *BHJC* will be the ___numerator___ of a fraction and the corresponding side length of trapezoid *DEFG* will be the ___denominator___ of that fraction.

$\dfrac{JC}{FG} = \dfrac{6.25}{5} = 1.25$ The required ratio is ___1.25___

B Use this ratio as a multiplier to find the unknown side lengths in trapezoid *BHJC*.

$\dfrac{HJ}{EF} = 1.25$ → $HJ = 1.25 \times EF$ → $HJ = 3.75$

$\dfrac{BH}{DE} = 1.25$ → $BH = 1.25 \times DE$ → $BH = 3.75$

$\dfrac{BC}{DG} = 1.25$ → $BC = 1.25 \times DG$ → $BC = 8.75$

REFLECT

2a. The ratio you used in the Explore can be called the *scale factor* of the first figure to the second figure. Complete the following: To find the scale factor of two similar figures, use the ratio of a side length in the ___second___ figure to the corresponding side length in the ___first___ figure.

2b. How is a scale factor used to find unknown side lengths in the second figure?

Multiply known side lengths in the first figure by the scale factor to find the unknown corresponding side lengths in the second figure.

2c. Suppose figure A is similar to figure B. How is the similarity ratio of A to B related to the scale factor of A to B?

The similarity ratio and the scale factor are reciprocals.

Chapter 7   282   Lesson 1

Questioning Strategies

- Why is it useful to find the ratio of the known length of one side of trapezoid *BHJC* to the length of the corresponding side of trapezoid *DEFG*?

  This ratio can be used as a multiplier of the other sides of trapezoid *DEFG* to find the unknown side lengths in trapezoid *BHJC*.

- How could you find *HJ* by writing and solving a proportion?

  Write the proportion $\frac{JC}{FG} = \frac{HJ}{EF}$. Substituting known lengths gives $\frac{6.25}{5} = \frac{HJ}{3}$. Multiplying each side by 3 gives $HJ = 3\left(\frac{6.25}{5}\right) = 3.75$.

- How does the proportion method compare with the scale-factor method?

  Both methods give the same answer. That's because the scale factor, $\frac{6.25}{5}$ or 1.25, appears on the left side of the proportion.

- What can you say about the second figure if the scale factor is a number between 0 and 1?

  The second figure is smaller than the original.

- What can you say about the second figure if the scale factor is a number greater than 1?

  The second figure is larger than the original.

CLOSE

Essential Question

How can you use ratios of corresponding side lengths to solve problems involving similar polygons?

Suppose the lengths of all sides are known for the first figure and the length of only one side is known for the second figure. To find the unknown lengths of the second figure, form the ratio of the known side length in the second figure to the corresponding side length in the first figure, then use this ratio as a multiplier of each of the other known lengths in the first figure.

Avoid Common Errors

Be sure that students place the correct measurements in the numerator and the denominator of the ratio that specifies the scale factor. Remind students to look to the second figure for the numerator and the first figure for the denominator. Also remind students to use only known measurements when determining the scale factor. The scale factor must be a number, not a variable expression.

Summarize

Have students write a journal entry in which they describe what a scale factor is and how it is useful in finding unknown lengths in a figure that is similar to a figure with known lengths.

MATHEMATICAL PRACTICE | Highlighting the Standards

To address Standard 8 (Look for and express regularity in repeated reasoning), have students find each of the unknown side lengths in the Explore by writing and solving proportions rather than using a scale factor. They should see that one side of each proportion *is* the scale factor, making it possible to use the shortcut of multiplying each known length by the scale factor.

PRACTICE

Where skills are taught	Where skills are practiced
1 EXAMPLE	EXS. 1–4
2 EXPLORE	EXS. 5–8

PRACTICE

Corresponding angles in each pair are congruent. Use ratios of corresponding sides to tell whether the figures are similar. If so, identify the similarity ratio.

1. triangle *XYZ* to triangle *ABC*

Yes; $\frac{XY}{AB}: \frac{45}{15} = 3$, $\frac{XZ}{AC}: \frac{36}{12} = 3$, and

$\frac{YZ}{BC}: \frac{27}{9} = 3$. The ratios are all equal.

The similarity ratio is $\frac{3}{1}$.

2. trapezoid *JHLK* to trapezoid *DGFE*

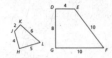

No; $\frac{JH}{DG}: \frac{4}{8} = \frac{1}{2}$, $\frac{JK}{DE}: \frac{2}{4} = \frac{1}{2}$, $\frac{HL}{GF}: \frac{5}{10} = \frac{1}{2}$, and

$\frac{KL}{EF}: \frac{6}{10} = \frac{3}{5}$. The ratios are not all equal.

There is no similarity ratio.

3. polygon *MNBCE* to polygon *RSTUV*

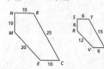

Yes; $\frac{NM}{SR}: \frac{10}{6} = \frac{5}{3}$, $\frac{ME}{RV}: \frac{20}{12} = \frac{5}{3}$, $\frac{EC}{VU}: \frac{10}{6} = \frac{5}{3}$,

$\frac{CB}{UT}: \frac{25}{15} = \frac{5}{3}$, and $\frac{BN}{TS}: \frac{10}{6} = \frac{5}{3}$. The ratios are

all equal. The similarity ratio is $\frac{5}{3}$.

4. The angles in rhombus A are congruent to the corresponding angles in rhombus B. The sides of rhombus A are 7 units long. The sides of rhombus B are 9 units long. Explain why the rhombuses are similar.

The ratio of any side length in rhombus A to the corresponding side length in

rhombus B will be $\frac{7}{9}$, because all sides of a rhombus are congruent.

The figures in each pair are similar. Find the lengths of the sides in the second figure. Show your work.

5. quadrilateral   quadrilateral
    ABCD   *PQRS*

$PQ = 8.4$, $PS = 22.4$, and $QR = 11.2$; the scale

factor of *ABCD* to *PQRS* is $\frac{RS}{CD}: \frac{14}{10} = 1.4$;

multiply the side lengths in *ABCD* by 1.4;

$PQ = 1.4 \times 6 = 8.4$, $PS = 1.4 \times 16 = 22.4$, and

$QR = 1.4 \times 8 = 11.2$.

6. polygon *BCHZRT*   polygon *ANGYPJ*

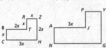

$PY = PJ = AN = 1.5x$, $AJ = YG = 3x$, and

$NG = 4.5x$; the scale factor of *BCHZRT* to

ANGYPJ is $\frac{3x}{2x}$, or 1.5. $AJ = YG = 1.5(2x) = 3x$,

and $NG = 1.5(3x) = 4.5x$

7. △*AED* ~ △*ABC*. In the diagram below, consider △*AED* to be the first triangle and △*ABC* to be the second triangle.

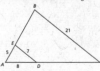

$AB = 15$ and $AC = 24$; the scale factor of

ABC to *AED* is $\frac{BC}{ED}$, or $\frac{21}{7} = 3$. Multiply the

side lengths in triangle *AED* by 3. $AB = 3(5)$

$= 15$ and $AC = 3(8) = 24$.

8. Polygons *WXYZ* and *DEFG* are similar and $k > 0$. Identify the similarity ratio of *WXYZ* to *DEFG* and the scale factor. Explain.

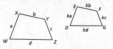

Similarity ratio: $\frac{1}{k}$. Compare lengths in *WXYZ*

to corresponding lengths in *DEFG*: $\frac{a}{ka} = \frac{1}{k}$,

$\frac{b}{kb} = \frac{1}{k}$, $\frac{c}{kc} = \frac{1}{k}$, and $\frac{d}{kd} = \frac{1}{k}$. Scale factor: k.

Compare lengths in *DEFG* to corresponding

lengths in *WXYZ*: $\frac{ka}{a} = k$, $\frac{kb}{b} = k$, $\frac{kc}{c} = k$,

and $\frac{kd}{d} = k$.

Notes

ADDITIONAL PRACTICE AND PROBLEM SOLVING

Assign these pages to help your students practice and apply important lesson concepts. For additional exercises, see the Student Edition.

Answers

Additional Practice

1. $\angle A \cong \angle X$; $\angle B \cong \angle Z$; $\angle C \cong \angle Y$;

   $\frac{AC}{XY} = \frac{AB}{XZ} = \frac{BC}{ZY} = \frac{2}{3}$

2. $\angle H \cong \angle Q$; $\angle I \cong \angle R$; $\angle J \cong \angle S$; $\angle K \cong \angle P$

   $\frac{KJ}{PS} = \frac{KH}{PQ} = \frac{HI}{QR} = \frac{JI}{SR} = \frac{5}{4}$

3. yes; $\frac{7}{5}$; Possible answer: $\square EFGH \sim \square WTUV$

4. No; sides cannot be matched to have corresponding sides proportional.

5. yes
6. yes
7. no
8. yes

Problem Solving

1. 6
2. 7 ft 10.5 in.
3. 50 m
4. yes; $\frac{8}{5}$ or $\frac{5}{8}$
5. C
6. G
7. C
8. J

7-1

Name_____ Class_____ Date_____

Additional Practice

Identify the pairs of congruent corresponding angles and the corresponding sides.

1.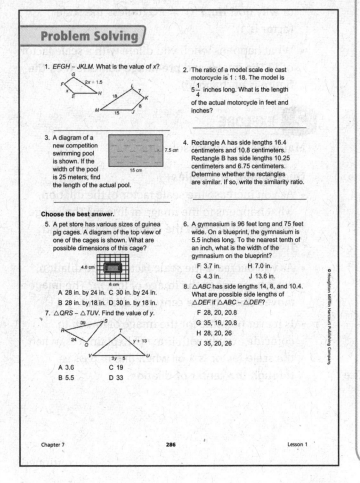

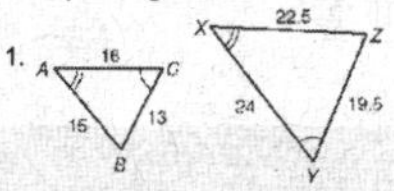

2.

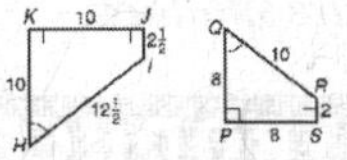

_____   _____
_____   _____
_____   _____

Determine whether the polygons are similar. If so, write the similarity ratio and a similarity statement. If not, explain why not.

3. parallelograms EFGH and TUVW

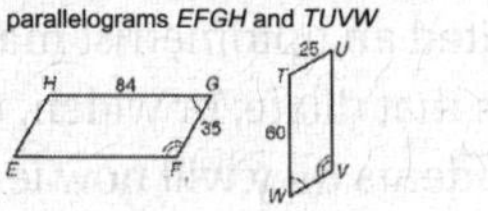

4. △CDE and △LMN

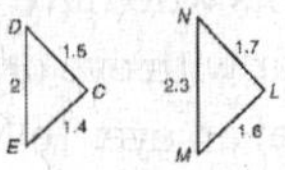

_____   _____
_____   _____

Tell whether the polygons must be similar based on the information given in the figures.

5.

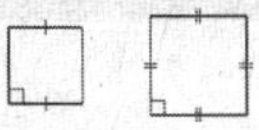

6.

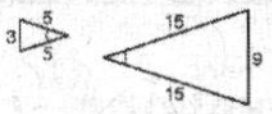

7.

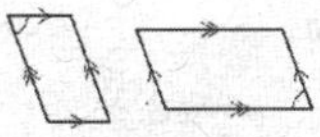

8.

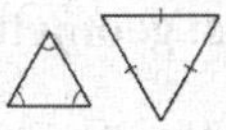

_____   _____

Problem Solving

1. EFGH ~ JKLM. What is the value of x?

2. The ratio of a model scale die cast motorcycle is 1 : 18. The model is $5\frac{1}{4}$ inches long. What is the length of the actual motorcycle in feet and inches?

3. A diagram of a new competition swimming pool is shown. If the width of the pool is 25 meters, find the length of the actual pool.
7.5 cm
15 cm

4. Rectangle A has side lengths 16.4 centimeters and 10.8 centimeters. Rectangle B has side lengths 10.25 centimeters and 6.75 centimeters. Determine whether the rectangles are similar. If so, write the similarity ratio.

_____

Choose the best answer.

5. A pet store has various sizes of guinea pig cages. A diagram of the top view of one of the cages is shown. What are possible dimensions of this cage?
4.8 cm
6 cm

  A 28 in. by 24 in. C 30 in. by 24 in.
  B 28 in. by 18 in. D 30 in. by 18 in.

6. A gymnasium is 96 feet long and 75 feet wide. On a blueprint, the gymnasium is 5.5 inches long. To the nearest tenth of an inch, what is the width of the gymnasium on the blueprint?

  F 3.7 in. H 7.0 in.
  G 4.3 in. J 13.6 in.

7. △QRS ~ △TUV. Find the value of y.
36
24
3y − 5
y + 13

  A 3.6 C 19
  B 5.5 D 33

8. △ABC has side lengths 14, 8, and 10.4. What are possible side lengths of △DEF if △ABC ~ △DEF?

  F 28, 20, 20.8
  G 35, 16, 20.8
  H 28, 20, 26
  J 35, 20, 26

Similarity and Transformations
Going Deeper

Essential question: *What are the key properties of dilations, and how can dilations be used to show figures are similar?*

© Houghton Mifflin Harcourt Publishing Company

COMMON CORE Standards for Mathematical Content

CC.9-12.G.CO.2 ... Compare transformations that preserve distance and angle to those that do not. (e.g., translation versus horizontal stretch).

CC.9-12.G.SRT.1 Verify experimentally the properties of dilations given by a center and a scale factor:

a. A dilation takes a line not passing through the center of the dilation to a parallel line, and leaves a line passing through the center unchanged.

b. The dilation of a line segment is longer or shorter in the ratio given by the scale factor.

CC.9-12.G.SRT.2 Given two figures, use the definition of similarity in terms of similarity transformations to decide if they are similar; ...

CC.9-12.G.C.1 Prove that all circles are similar.

Vocabulary
dilation
center of dilation
scale factor
similarity transformation
similar

Prerequisites
Transformations and rigid motions

Math Background
Dilations are the last of the major transformations that students will study in this course. Unlike earlier transformations (reflections, translations, and rotations), dilations are not rigid motions. That is, they do not preserve *both* the shape and the size of a figure. However, dilations do preserve the shape of a figure. Thus, every dilation is either an enlargement or a reduction.

Just as congruence was defined in terms of rigid motions so will similarity now be defined in terms of similarity transformations. Similarity transformations preserve the shape of a figure. The familiar AA Similarity Criterion follows from this definition of similarity.

INTRODUCE

Begin by discussing how the terms *dilate* and *dilation* are used in everyday situations. The word *dilate* means "make larger or cause to expand." Students who have visited an optometrist may be familiar with eye drops that dilate, or widen, the pupil of an eye. Tell students they will now learn about a transformation called a dilation.

TEACH

1 EXPLORE

Materials: geometry software

Questioning Strategies
- Do dilations appear to preserve angle measure? Why or why not? Yes; $m\angle P' = m\angle P$, $m\angle Q' = m\angle Q$, and $m\angle R' = m\angle R$.
- Do dilations appear to preserve distance? Why or why not? No; $P'Q' \neq PQ$ (unless the scale factor is 1).
- What happens when you dilate with a scale factor of 1? The image and pre-image coincide (i.e., the figure is unchanged).

2 EXPLORE

Materials: geometry software

Questioning Strategies
- As you increase the scale factor of the dilation, what happens to the image of line *m*? The image moves farther from the center of dilation and from line *m*.
- As you decrease the scale factor of the dilation, what happens to the image of line *m*? The image moves closer to the center of dilation.
- Is it ever possible for the image of line *m* to coincide exactly with line *m*? Explain. Yes; when the scale factor is 1 or when line *m* passes through the center of dilation.

continued

Name_____ Class_____ Date_____

7-2

Similarity and Transformations
Going Deeper

Essential question: *What are the key properties of dilations, and how can dilations be used to show figures are similar?*

You have already worked extensively with three transformations: reflections, translations, and rotations. Now you will focus on a fourth type of transformation: dilations. Dilations are defined as follows.

Let O be a point and let k be a positive real number. For any point P, let $D(P) = P'$, where P' is the point on $\overrightarrow{OP}$ such that $OP' = k \cdot OP$. Then D is the **dilation** with **center of dilation** O and **scale factor** k. If necessary, the center of dilation and scale factor can be included in the function notation by writing $D_{O,k}(P) = P'$.

The figure shows a dilation with scale factor 2 because $OP' = 2OP$ and $OQ' = 2OQ$.

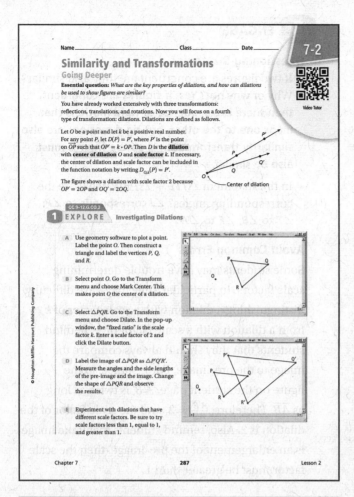

Center of dilation

CC.9-12.G.CO.2

1 EXPLORE   Investigating Dilations

A   Use geometry software to plot a point. Label the point O. Then construct a triangle and label the vertices P, Q, and R.

B   Select point O. Go to the Transform menu and choose Mark Center. This makes point O the center of a dilation.

C   Select $\triangle PQR$. Go to the Transform menu and choose Dilate. In the pop-up window, the "fixed ratio" is the scale factor k. Enter a scale factor of 2 and click the Dilate button.

D   Label the image of $\triangle PQR$ as $\triangle P'Q'R'$. Measure the angles and the side lengths of the pre-image and the image. Change the shape of $\triangle PQR$ and observe the results.

E   Experiment with dilations that have different scale factors. Be sure to try scale factors less than 1, equal to 1, and greater than 1.

Chapter 7   287   Lesson 2

REFLECT

1a. In general, how does a dilation transform a figure?

A dilation changes the size of a figure (unless the scale factor is 1) without changing its shape.

1b. Do you think dilations are rigid motions? Why or why not?

No; dilations change the size of a figure, so they are not rigid motions (unless the scale factor is 1).

1c. How does the value of k affect a dilation? What can you say about a dilation when $0 < k < 1$? when $k > 1$?

When $0 < k < 1$, the dilation reduces the figure. When $k > 1$, the dilation enlarges the figure.

CC.9-12.G.SRT.1

2 EXPLORE   Investigating Properties of Dilations

A   Use geometry software to plot a point. Label the point O. Then construct a straight line and label it m.

B   Construct the image of line m under a dilation with center O and scale factor 2.

C   Try dilations with different scale factors and try dragging the line to new positions. Notice what happens when the line passes through O.

D   Delete the line and its image. Construct a segment, $\overline{AB}$.

E   Construct the image of $\overline{AB}$ under a dilation with center O and scale factor 2. Label the image $\overline{A'B'}$.

AB = 1.94 cm
A'B' = 3.88 cm

F   Measure the length of $\overline{AB}$ and $\overline{A'B'}$.

G   Try dilations with different scale factors. In each case, compare the lengths of $\overline{AB}$ and $\overline{A'B'}$.

Chapter 7   288   Lesson 2

Technology

When students use geometry software to explore dilations, they should be careful that only one point (point O) is selected before they go to the Transform menu to mark the point as the center of dilation. Students should also make sure all of the triangle is selected (i.e., all three vertices and all three sides) before they apply the Dilate tool.

⟋MATHEMATICAL
PRACTICE   **Highlighting the Standards**

The Explores in this lesson offer opportunities for inductive reasoning, which is one aspect of Standard 3 (Construct viable arguments and critique the reasoning of others). For example, in Explore 1, students are asked to make a conjecture about the effect that the scale factor k has on a dilation. Students should base their conjectures upon their observations from working with geometry software. Encourage students to share their thinking with the class. Ask them to compare and, if necessary, refine their conjectures.

---

3 ENGAGE

Questioning Strategies

- If two figures are congruent are they also similar? Why or why not? **Yes; if figures are congruent, then there is a sequence of rigid motions that maps one to the other, but rigid motions are also similarity transformations, so the figures must also be similar.**

- In the statement $\triangle JTF \sim \triangle PBW$, what are the corresponding angles? **∠J corresponds to ∠P; ∠T to ∠B; ∠F to ∠W.**

Avoid Common Errors

Some students may have trouble determining scale factors. In particular, they may have difficulty distinguishing a dilation with a scale factor of k from a dilation with a scale factor of $\frac{1}{k}$. Remind students that they should always compare the image to the pre-image. For instance, in the figure on the student page, $\overline{A'B'}$ is twice as long as $\overline{AB}$. Therefore, $\frac{A'B'}{AB} = 2$, and the scale factor of the dilation is 2. Also, remind students that if the image is an enlargement of the pre-image, then the scale factor must be greater than 1.

REFLECT

2a. What can you say about the image of a straight line under a dilation? Does your answer depend upon the location of the line? Explain.

The image of a straight line m is a line parallel to line m. The only exception is when line m passes through the center of dilation. In that case, the dilation leaves the line unchanged.

2b. How is the length of a line segment related to the length of its image under a dilation with scale factor k?

The image of the line segment is longer or shorter in the ratio given by the scale factor. That is, $A'B' = k \cdot AB$.

2c. Suppose the points $A(x_1, y_1)$ and $B(x_2, y_2)$ are transformed by a dilation with scale factor k and center O. Give the coordinates of the image points A' and B'. Then show that the slope of $\overline{AB}$ equals the slope of $\overline{A'B'}$. What can you conclude about the segments?

The image points are $A'(kx_1, ky_1)$ and $B'(kx_2, ky_2)$.

Slope of $\overline{AB} = \frac{y_2 - y_1}{x_2 - x_1}$; slope of $\overline{A'B'} = \frac{ky_2 - ky_1}{kx_2 - kx_1} = \frac{k(y_2 - y_1)}{k(x_2 - x_1)} = \frac{y_2 - y_1}{x_2 - x_1}$.

The slopes of the segments are the same, so the segments are parallel.

You may have discovered that dilations preserve the shape, but not the size, of figures. The following summary describes the key properties of dilations.

> **Properties of Dilations**
>
> • Dilations preserve angle measure.
>
> • Dilations preserve betweenness.
>
> • Dilations preserve collinearity.
>
> • A dilation maps a line not passing through the center of dilation to a parallel line and leaves a line passing through the center unchanged.
>
> • The dilation of a line segment is longer or shorter in the ratio given by the scale factor.

---

3 **ENGAGE**   CC.9-12.G.SRT.2   **Introducing Similarity**

A **similarity transformation** is a transformation in which the image has the same shape as the pre-image. Specifically, the similarity transformations are the rigid motions (reflections, translations, and rotations) as well as dilations.

Two plane figures are **similar** if and only if one can be obtained from the other by similarity transformations (that is, by a sequence of reflections, translations, rotations, and/or dilations).

The symbol for similar is ~. As with congruence, it is customary to write a similarity statement so that corresponding vertices of the figures are listed in the same order. In the figure below, $\triangle A'B'C'$ is the image of $\triangle ABC$ after a dilation with center O and scale factor 2. Since a dilation is a similarity transformation, the two triangles are similar and you write $\triangle ABC \sim \triangle A'B'C'$.

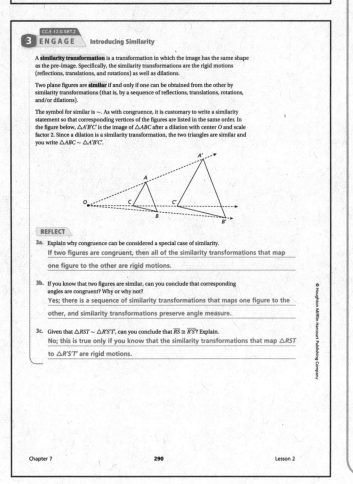

REFLECT

3a. Explain why congruence can be considered a special case of similarity.

If two figures are congruent, then all of the similarity transformations that map one figure to the other are rigid motions.

3b. If you know that two figures are similar, can you conclude that corresponding angles are congruent? Why or why not?

Yes; there is a sequence of similarity transformations that maps one figure to the other, and similarity transformations preserve angle measure.

3c. Given that $\triangle RST \sim \triangle R'S'T'$, can you conclude that $\overline{RS} \cong \overline{R'S'}$? Explain.

No; this is true only if you know that the similarity transformations that map $\triangle RST$ to $\triangle R'S'T'$ are rigid motions.

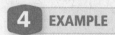

Questioning Strategies

- How can you tell which pairs of figures are likely to be similar? **Figures that appear to have the same shape are likely to be similar.**

EXTRA EXAMPLES

Use the definition of similarity in terms of similarity transformations to determine whether the two figures are similar. Explain your answer.

A.

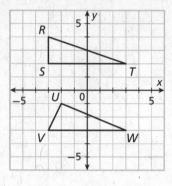

Not similar; there is no sequence of similarity transformations that maps $\triangle RST$ to $\triangle UVW$.

B.

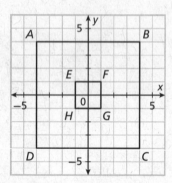

Similar; the dilation $(x, y) \rightarrow \left(\frac{1}{4}x, \frac{1}{4}y\right)$ maps $ABCD$ to $EFGH$.

C.

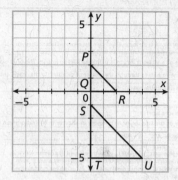

Similar; the dilation $(x, y) \rightarrow (2x, 2y)$ followed by the translation $(x, y) \rightarrow (x, y - 5)$ maps $\triangle PQR$ to $\triangle STU$.

5 PROOF

Questioning Strategies

- What do you have to do to show that two figures are similar? **You must show that there is a sequence of similarity transformations that map one figure to the other.**

- In the first step of the proof, why do you translate circle C along vector $\overline{CD}$? **This guarantees that the image of circle C will have the same center as that of circle D.**

4 EXAMPLE CC.9-12.G.SRT.2 Determining If Figures Are Similar

Use the definition of similarity in terms of similarity transformations to determine whether the two figures are similar. Explain your answer.

A △JKL and △MNP have different angle measures.

Since similarity transformations preserve angle measure, there is no sequence of similarity transformations that will map △JKL to △MNP.

Therefore, the figures are not similar .

B You can map △RST to △XYZ by the dilation that has the coordinate notation

$(x, y) \rightarrow (3x, 3y)$.

A dilation is a similarity transformation.

Therefore, the figures are similar .

C You can map ABCD to EFGH by the dilation that has the coordinate notation

$(x, y) \rightarrow (2x, 2y)$.

followed by the reflection that has the coordinate notation

$(x, y) \rightarrow (x, -y)$.

Dilations and reflections are similarity transformations.

Therefore, the figures are similar .

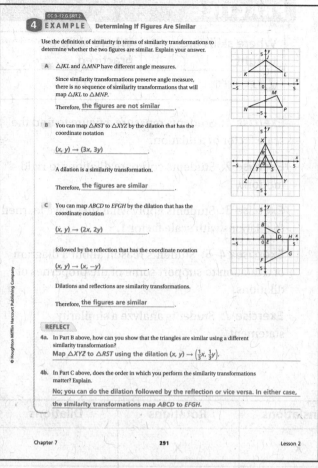

REFLECT

4a. In Part B above, how can you show that the triangles are similar using a different similarity transformation?

Map △XYZ to △RST using the dilation $(x, y) \rightarrow \left(\frac{1}{3}x, \frac{1}{3}y\right)$.

4b. In Part C above, does the order in which you perform the similarity transformations matter? Explain.

No; you can do the dilation followed by the reflection or vice versa. In either case, the similarity transformations map ABCD to EFGH.

You can use the definition of similarity to prove theorems about figures.

> **Theorem**
> All circles are similar.

5 PROOF CC.9-12.G.C.1 All Circles Are Similar

Complete the proof.

Given: Circle C with center C and radius r;
circle D with center D and radius s.

Prove: Circle C is similar to circle D.

To prove similarity, show that there is a sequence of similarity transformations that maps circle C to circle D.

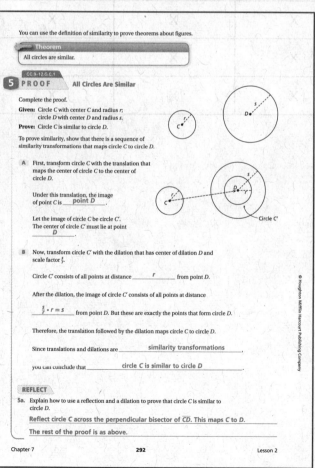

A First, transform circle C with the translation that maps the center of circle C to the center of circle D.

Under this translation, the image of point C is point D .

Let the image of circle C be circle C'.
The center of circle C' must lie at point D .

B Now, transform circle C' with the dilation that has center of dilation D and scale factor $\frac{s}{r}$.

Circle C' consists of all points at distance r from point D.

After the dilation, the image of circle C' consists of all points at distance

$\frac{s}{r} \cdot r = s$ from point D. But these are exactly the points that form circle D.

Therefore, the translation followed by the dilation maps circle C to circle D.

Since translations and dilations are similarity transformations

you can conclude that circle C is similar to circle D .

REFLECT

5a. Explain how to use a reflection and a dilation to prove that circle C is similar to circle D.

Reflect circle C across the perpendicular bisector of $\overline{CD}$. This maps C to D.

The rest of the proof is as above.

Essential Question

What are the key properties of dilations, and how can dilations be used to show figures are similar?

Dilations preserve angle measure, betweenness, and collinearity. A dilation maps a line not passing through the center of dilation to a parallel line and leaves a line passing through the center unchanged. The dilation of a line segment is longer or shorter in the ratio given by the scale factor.

To show two figures are similar, find a sequence of similarity transformations that maps one figure onto the other. Similarity transformations include dilations as well as the rigid motions (reflections, translations, and rotations).

Summarize

Have students make a graphic organizer or table to compare properties of reflections, translations, rotations, and dilations. A sample is shown below

Where skills are taught	Where skills are practiced
4 EXAMPLE	EXS. 8–13

Exercise 1: Students measure a figure to find the scale factor of a dilation.

Exercise 2: Students compare dilations to rigid motions.

Exercise 3: Students apply what they have learned to dilations with scale factor 1.

Exercises 4–6: Students reason about a diagram of a dilation to support some of the properties of dilations.

Exercise 7: Students analyze a similarity statement.

	Reflections	Translations	Rotations	Dilations
Preserves distance	X	X	X	
Preserves angle measure	X	X	X	X
Preserves betweenness	X	X	X	X
Preserves collinearity	X	X	X	X

PRACTICE

1. The figure shows the image A' of point A under a dilation with center O. Explain how you can use a ruler to find the scale factor of the dilation. Then find the scale factor.

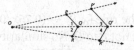

Measure OA' and OA. Find the ratio $\frac{OA'}{OA}$. In this case,

the scale factor is $\frac{1}{3}$.

2. Compare dilations to rigid motions. How are they similar? How are they different?

Dilations have the same properties as rigid motions, except for

preserving distance.

3. Describe the effect of a dilation with scale factor 1.

This dilation leaves every figure unchanged.

For Exercises 4–6, refer to the diagram of the dilation below.

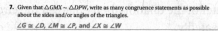

4. Suppose the points $P(x_1, y_1)$, $Q(x_2, y_2)$, and $R(x_3, y_3)$ are transformed by a dilation with scale factor k and center O. Show that the slope of $\overline{PQ}$ equals the slope of $\overline{P'Q'}$ and that the slope of $\overline{QR}$ equals the slope of $\overline{Q'R'}$.

The image points are $P'(kx_1, ky_1)$, $Q'(kx_2, ky_2)$, and $R'(kx_3, ky_3)$.

Slope of $\overline{PQ} = \dfrac{y_2 - y_1}{x_2 - x_1}$; slope of $\overline{P'Q'} = \dfrac{ky_2 - ky_1}{kx_2 - kx_1} = \dfrac{k(y_2 - y_1)}{k(x_2 - x_1)} = \dfrac{y_2 - y_1}{x_2 - x_1}$.

Slope of $\overline{QR} = \dfrac{y_3 - y_2}{x_3 - x_2}$; slope of $\overline{Q'R'} = \dfrac{ky_3 - ky_2}{kx_3 - kx_2} = \dfrac{k(y_3 - y_2)}{k(x_3 - x_2)} = \dfrac{y_3 - y_2}{x_3 - x_2}$.

5. Make a convincing argument for why $m\angle 1 = m\angle 3$ and $m\angle 2 = m\angle 4$. Use reasoning related to transversals and parallel lines.

The line containing O and Q' is a transversal that crosses parallels.

$\angle 1$ and $\angle 3$ are corresponding angles, so $m\angle 1 = m\angle 3$.

$\angle 2$ and $\angle 4$ are corresponding angles so $m\angle 2 = m\angle 4$.

6. Explain why $m\angle PQR = m\angle P'Q'R'$. What property of dilations does this reasoning support?

$m\angle PQR = m\angle 1 + m\angle 2 = m\angle 3 + m\angle 4 = m\angle P'Q'R'$ by the Substitution

Property of Equality, because $m\angle 1 = m\angle 3$ and $m\angle 2 = m\angle 4$. This

reasoning supports the property that dilations preserve angle measure.

© Houghton Mifflin Harcourt Publishing Company

---

7. Given that $\triangle GMX \sim \triangle DPW$, write as many congruence statements as possible about the sides and/or angles of the triangles.

$\angle G \cong \angle D$, $\angle M \cong \angle P$, and $\angle X \cong \angle W$

Use the definition of similarity in terms of similarity transformations to determine whether the two figures are similar. Explain your answer.

8.

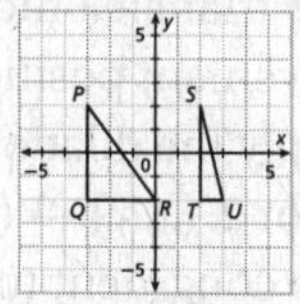

Not similar; there is no sequence of similarity transformations that maps $\triangle PQR$ to $\triangle STU$.

9.

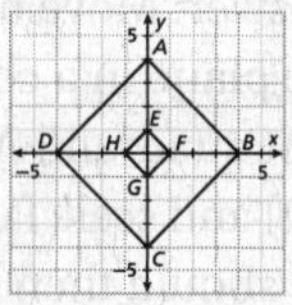

Similar; the dilation $(x, y) \rightarrow (4x, 4x)$ maps $EFGH$ to $ABCD$.

10.

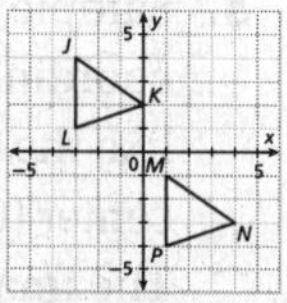

Similar; the translation $(x, y) \rightarrow (x + 4, y - 5)$ maps $\triangle JKL$ to $\triangle MNP$.

11.

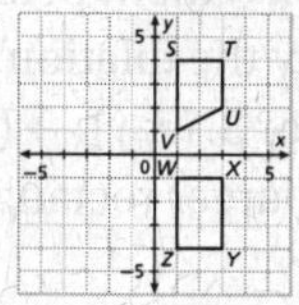

Not similar; there is no sequence of similarity transformations that maps $STUV$ to $WXYZ$.

12.

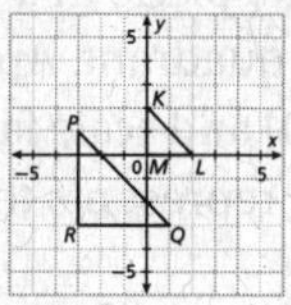

Similar; the dilation $(x, y) \rightarrow (2x, 2y)$ followed by the translation $(x, y) \rightarrow (x - 3, y - 3)$ maps $\triangle KLM$ to $\triangle PQR$.

13.

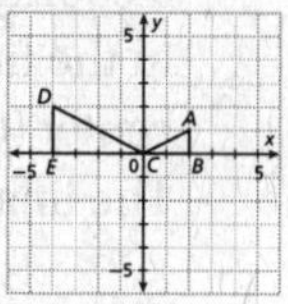

Similar; the dilation $(x, y) \rightarrow (2x, 2y)$ followed by the reflection $(x, y) \rightarrow (-x, y)$ maps $\triangle ABC$ to $\triangle DEC$.

© Houghton Mifflin Harcourt Publishing Company

ADDITIONAL PRACTICE AND PROBLEM SOLVING

Assign these pages to help your students practice and apply important lesson concepts. For additional exercises, see the Student Edition.

Answers

Additional Practice

1.

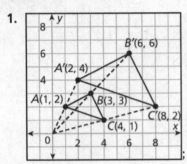

; dilation with center (0, 0) and scale factor 2

2.

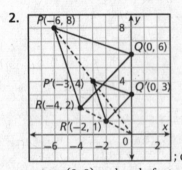

; dilation with center (0, 0) and scale factor $\frac{1}{2}$

3.

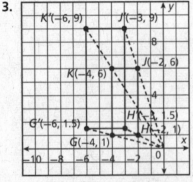

; dilation with center (0, 0) and scale factor 1.5

4.

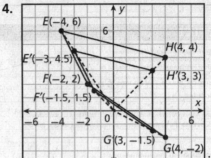

; dilation with center (0, 0) and scale factor 0.75

5. No: The rule $(x, y) \rightarrow (0.75x, 0.75y)$ maps *A* to *P*, but not *B* to *Q*. No similarity transformation maps *ABCDE* to *PQRST*.

6. Yes; $\triangle JKL$ can be mapped to $\triangle PQR$ by a dilation: $(x, y) \rightarrow (\frac{1}{2}x, \frac{1}{2}y)$. Then $\triangle PQR$ can be mapped to $\triangle STO$ by a translation: $(x, y) \rightarrow (x - 2, y - 2)$.

Problem Solving

1. Dilate the smaller triangle with a scale factor 2 and center at the vertex of the square border. Do the same at each vertex of the square border.

2. He used a point of the circle as the center of the dilation. He drew rays outward from the center of the dilation then enlarged the circles repeatedly.

3. Sample answer: Move one triangle onto a coordinate plane in a convenient position like the first quadrant. Apply the dilation with center (0, 0) and scale factor 2. $(x, y) \rightarrow (2x, 2y)$. The image should then be congruent to the image created with the graphics program.

4. Place the drawing of the smaller rectangle on a coordinate plane in a convenient position in the first quadrant. Apply the dilation with center (0, 0) and scale factor 3. $(x, y) \rightarrow (3x, 3y)$. The image represents the larger rectangle.

5. A

6. J

7-2

Additional Practice

Apply the dilation D to the polygon with the given vertices. Describe the dilation.

1. $D: (x, y) \rightarrow (2x, 2y)$
   $A(1, 2), B(3, 3), C(4, 1)$

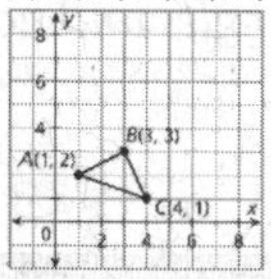

2. $D: (x, y) \rightarrow (\frac{1}{2}x, \frac{1}{2}y)$
   $P(-6, 8), Q(0, 6), R(-4, 2)$

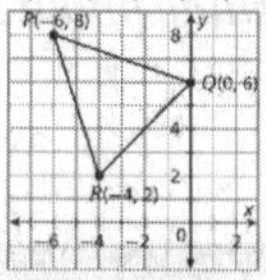

3. $D: (x, y) \rightarrow (1.5x, 1.5y)$
   $G(-4, 1), H(-2, 1), J(-2, 6), K(-4, 6)$

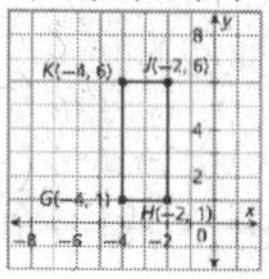

4. $D: (x, y) \rightarrow (0.75x, 0.75y)$
   $E(-4, 6), F(-2, 2), G(4, -2), H(4, 4)$

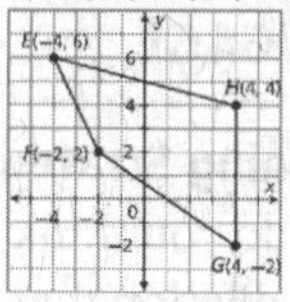

Determine whether the polygons with the given vertices are similar.

5. $A(-4, 4), B(0, 4), C(0, 0), D(-2, -2),$
   $E(-4, 0); P(-3, 3), Q(-1, 3), R(-1, 1),$
   $S(-2, 0), T(-3, 1)$

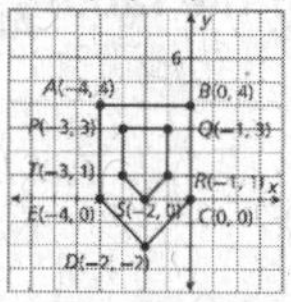

6. $J(-4, 6), K(4, 6), L(4, 4); P(-2, 3),$
   $Q(2, 3), R(2, 2); S(-4, 1), T(0, 1),$
   $O(0, 0)$

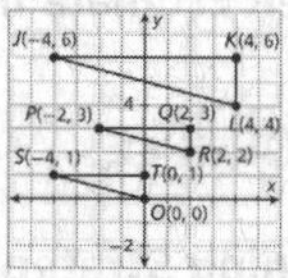

Problem Solving

1. Irena is designing a quilt. She started with a large square and then made this diagram to follow when making her quilt. Describe how she used dilations to make the pattern.

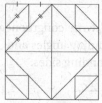

2. A crop circle is a large pattern formed by flattening or cutting crops so the design is apparent when viewed from above. Every year, Hector puts a crop circle into his corn field. This year's design is shown below. Describe how he used dilations to complete his design.

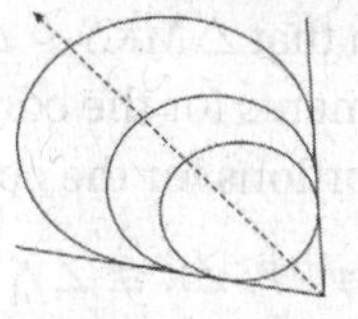

3. A graphic artist incorporated two similar right triangles into a logo with one triangle twice the size of the other. He used a computer graphics program to draw the first triangle and then used the enlargement tool of the program to draw the other triangle. How can he verify that the two triangles are similar?

4. A toy designer is planning to create a doll house. The design includes two similar rectangles with one being three times the size of the other. She cuts and traces the small rectangle onto grid paper first. Describe how she can use the tracing to make a pattern for the larger rectangle.

Choose the best answer.

5. Circle A with radius 4 and center (3, 0) is drawn in the coordinate plane. What is the scale factor that maps the circle with radius 3 and center (2, 3) onto circle A?

   A $\frac{4}{3}$

   B $\frac{3}{4}$

   C $\frac{7}{3}$

   D $\frac{3}{7}$

6. An art student uses dilations in all her art. She first plans the art piece on a coordinate grid. Determine the vertices of the image of the triangle with vertices $A(1, 1), B(2, 4),$ and $C(3, 9)$ after a dilation with scale factor 1.5.

   F $A'(1.5, 1.5), B'(3, 5), C'(4.5, 13.5)$

   G $A'(2.5, 2.5), B'(5, 10), C'(7.5, 22.5)$

   H $A'(1.5, 1.5), B'(4, 8), C'(6, 18)$

   J $A'(1.5, 1.5), B'(3, 6), C'(4.5, 13.5)$

Notes

Triangle Similarity: AA, SSS, and SAS
Going Deeper

Essential question: *What can you conclude about similar triangles and how can you prove triangles are similar?*

COMMON **Standards for**
CORE **Mathematical Content**

CC.9-12.G.SRT.2 ... explain using similarity transformations the meaning of similarity for triangles as the equality of all corresponding pairs of angles and the proportionality of all corresponding pairs of sides.

CC.9-12.G.SRT.3 Use the properties of similarity transformations to establish the AA criterion for two triangles to be similar.

Prerequisites
Similarity

Math Background
In this lesson, students study similar triangles. First, they learn that when two triangles are similar, the corresponding angles are congruent and the corresponding sides are proportional. This is the equivalent of the CPCTC theorem, but with the necessary changes for similarity rather than congruence. Then, students prove that the AA Similarity Criterion follows from the transformation-based definition of similarity.

INTRODUCE

Remind students that when they studied congruence, they first learned the definition of congruence in terms of rigid motions and then applied congruence to triangles. Specifically, students learned some shortcuts for proving that two triangles are congruent (SSS, SAS, ASA, AAS). Explain that in the same way, students will now consider what it means for two triangles to be similar. Tell students they will learn about some shortcuts for proving that two triangles are similar.

TEACH

1 ENGAGE

Questioning Strategies
- What do you think is the approximate scale factor of the dilation that maps $\triangle ABC$ to $\triangle A'B'C'$ in the figure? **Possible answer: approximately 1.5**
- How did you estimate the scale factor? **Possible answer: Estimate the value of the ratio $\frac{A'B'}{AB}$.**

2 EXAMPLE

Questioning Strategies
- Given a similarity statement about triangles, how many pairs of corresponding angles are there? How many pairs of corresponding sides are there? **There are three pairs of each.**
- How do you determine corresponding angles from a similarity statement? **Corresponding angles are named by letters in the same position in each triangle name.**

EXTRA EXAMPLE
Given that $\triangle MKS \sim \triangle PYC$, write congruence statements for the corresponding angles and proportions for the corresponding sides.

$\angle M \cong \angle P$, $\angle K \cong \angle Y$, $\angle S \cong \angle C$,

$\frac{MK}{PY} = \frac{KS}{YC} = \frac{MS}{PC}$

Avoid Common Errors
Remind students to write proportions by comparing the triangles in the same order. That is, the numerators should always give side lengths from one triangle and the denominators should always give side lengths from the other triangle. Thus, a proportion like $\frac{RS}{UV} = \frac{VW}{ST}$ is incorrect. Comparing $\triangle RST$ (numerators) to $\triangle UVW$ (denominators) gives the correct proportion, $\frac{RS}{UV} = \frac{ST}{VW}$.

© Houghton Mifflin Harcourt Publishing Company

7-3

Name_____ Class_____ Date_____

Triangle Similarity: AA, SSS, and SAS
Going Deeper

Essential question: *What can you conclude about similar triangles and how can you prove triangles are similar?*

CC.9-12.G.SRT.2

1 ENGAGE Applying Similarity to Triangles

Recall that when two figures are similar, there is a sequence of similarity transformations that maps one figure to the other. In particular, given $\triangle ABC \sim \triangle DEF$, you can first apply a dilation to $\triangle ABC$ to make both triangles the same size. Then you can apply a sequence of rigid motions to the dilated image of $\triangle ABC$ to map it to $\triangle DEF$.

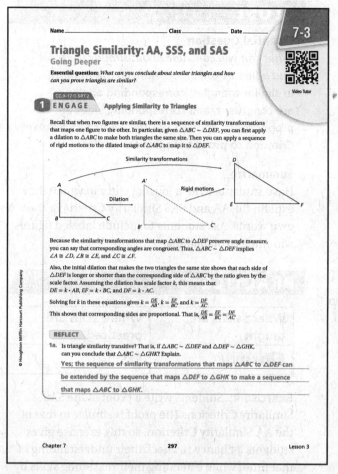

Because the similarity transformations that map $\triangle ABC$ to $\triangle DEF$ preserve angle measure, you can say that corresponding angles are congruent. Thus, $\triangle ABC \sim \triangle DEF$ implies $\angle A \cong \angle D$, $\angle B \cong \angle E$, and $\angle C \cong \angle F$.

Also, the initial dilation that makes the two triangles the same size shows that each side of $\triangle DEF$ is longer or shorter than the corresponding side of $\triangle ABC$ by the ratio given by the scale factor. Assuming the dilation has scale factor k, this means that $DE = k \cdot AB$, $EF = k \cdot BC$, and $DF = k \cdot AC$.

Solving for k in these equations gives $k = \frac{DE}{AB}$, $k = \frac{EF}{BC}$, and $k = \frac{DF}{AC}$.

This shows that corresponding sides are proportional. That is, $\frac{DE}{AB} = \frac{EF}{BC} = \frac{DF}{AC}$.

REFLECT

1a. Is triangle similarity transitive? That is, if $\triangle ABC \sim \triangle DEF$ and $\triangle DEF \sim \triangle GHK$, can you conclude that $\triangle ABC \sim \triangle GHK$? Explain.

Yes; the sequence of similarity transformations that maps $\triangle ABC$ to $\triangle DEF$ can

be extended by the sequence that maps $\triangle DEF$ to $\triangle GHK$ to make a sequence

that maps $\triangle ABC$ to $\triangle GHK$.

Chapter 7   297   Lesson 3

CC.9-12.G.SRT.2

2 EXAMPLE Identifying Congruent Angles and Proportional Sides

Given that $\triangle RST \sim \triangle UVW$, write congruence statements for the corresponding angles and proportions for the corresponding sides.

A Corresponding angles are listed in the same position in each triangle name.

$\angle R \cong \angle U$, $\angle S \cong \angle V$, $\angle T \cong \angle W$

B Corresponding sides are named by pairs of letters in the same position in each triangle name.

$\frac{UV}{RS} = \frac{VW}{ST} = \frac{UW}{RT}$

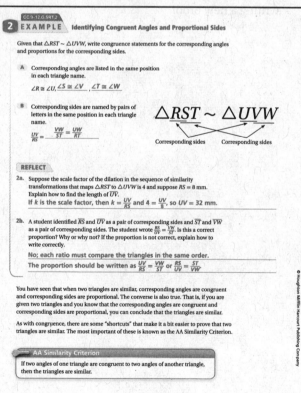

$$\triangle RST \sim \triangle UVW$$

Corresponding sides   Corresponding sides

REFLECT

2a. Suppose the scale factor of the dilation in the sequence of similarity transformations that maps $\triangle RST$ to $\triangle UVW$ is 4 and suppose $RS = 8$ mm. Explain how to find the length of $\overline{UV}$.

If k is the scale factor, then $k = \frac{UV}{RS}$ and $4 = \frac{UV}{8}$, so $UV = 32$ mm.

2b. A student identified $\overline{RS}$ and $\overline{UV}$ as a pair of corresponding sides and $\overline{ST}$ and $\overline{VW}$ as a pair of corresponding sides. The student wrote $\frac{RS}{UV} = \frac{VW}{ST}$. Is this a correct proportion? Why or why not? If the proportion is not correct, explain how to write it correctly.

No; each ratio must compare the triangles in the same order.

The proportion should be written as $\frac{UV}{RS} = \frac{VW}{ST}$ or $\frac{RS}{UV} = \frac{ST}{VW}$.

You have seen that when two triangles are similar, corresponding angles are congruent and corresponding sides are proportional. The converse is also true. That is, if you are given two triangles and you know that the corresponding angles are congruent and corresponding sides are proportional, you can conclude that the triangles are similar.

As with congruence, there are some "shortcuts" that make it a bit easier to prove that two triangles are similar. The most important of these is known as the AA Similarity Criterion.

AA Similarity Criterion

If two angles of one triangle are congruent to two angles of another triangle, then the triangles are similar.

Chapter 7   298   Lesson 3

© Houghton Mifflin Harcourt Publishing Company

Questioning Strategies

- How do you use the AA Similarity Criterion to show two triangles are similar? Show that two angles of one triangle are congruent to two angles of the other triangle. This lets you conclude that the two triangles are similar.

- How is this proof similar to those of the SSS, SAS, and ASA Congruence Criteria? You show that there is an appropriate sequence of transformations that maps one triangle to the other.

Teaching Strategies

Students will have practice using the AA Similarity Criterion in a later lesson. However, you may want to give students a quick example of how the criterion can be used. Draw the following figure on the board. Ask students whether the triangles are similar and why or why not. If necessary, help students understand that by the Triangle Sum Theorem, $m\angle C = 37°$ so the triangles are similar by the AA Similarity Criterion.

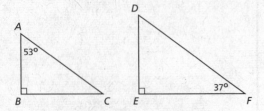

MATHEMATICAL PRACTICE · **Highlighting the Standards**

Exercise 4 requires students to write a complete proof. This is an opportunity to address Standard 6 (Attend to precision). In particular, every proof depends upon careful attention to mathematical definitions. Ask students to point out the definitions that are used in the proof. Have them explain how the definitions serve as elements of the overall deductive argument.

CLOSE

Essential Question

What can you conclude about similar triangles and how can you prove triangles are similar?
In similar triangles, corresponding angles are congruent, and corresponding sides are proportional. You can use the AA or SAS Similarity Criterion to prove triangles are similar.

Summarize

Have students write a journal entry in which they explain the AA and SAS Similarity Criteria in their own words. Ask students to include labeled figures with their explanations.

PRACTICE

Where skills are taught	Where skills are practiced
2 EXAMPLE	EXS. 1–3

Exercise 4: Students write a proof of the SAS Similarity Criterion. The proof is similar to that of the AA Similarity Criterion, so this exercise gives students a chance to check their understanding of that proof while extending their reasoning skills by writing a new proof.

3 PROOF CC.9–12.G.SRT.3 **AA Similarity Criterion**

Given: $\angle A \cong \angle X$ and $\angle B \cong \angle Y$
Prove: $\triangle ABC \sim \triangle XYZ$

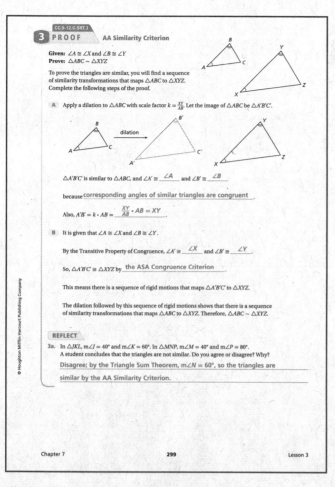

To prove the triangles are similar, you will find a sequence
of similarity transformations that maps $\triangle ABC$ to $\triangle XYZ$.
Complete the following steps of the proof.

A Apply a dilation to $\triangle ABC$ with scale factor $k = \frac{XY}{AB}$. Let the image of $\triangle ABC$ be $\triangle A'B'C'$.

$\triangle A'B'C'$ is similar to $\triangle ABC$, and $\angle A' \cong \underline{\quad \angle A \quad}$ and $\angle B' \cong \underline{\quad \angle B \quad}$

because $\underline{\text{corresponding angles of similar triangles are congruent}}$.

Also, $A'B' = k \cdot AB = \frac{XY}{AB} \cdot AB = XY$.

B It is given that $\angle A \cong \angle X$ and $\angle B \cong \angle Y$.

By the Transitive Property of Congruence, $\angle A' \cong \underline{\quad \angle X \quad}$ and $\angle B' \cong \underline{\quad \angle Y \quad}$.

So, $\triangle A'B'C' \cong \triangle XYZ$ by $\underline{\text{the ASA Congruence Criterion}}$.

This means there is a sequence of rigid motions that maps $\triangle A'B'C'$ to $\triangle XYZ$.

The dilation followed by this sequence of rigid motions shows that there is a sequence
of similarity transformations that maps $\triangle ABC$ to $\triangle XYZ$. Therefore, $\triangle ABC \sim \triangle XYZ$.

REFLECT

3a. In $\triangle JKL$, $m\angle J = 40°$ and $m\angle K = 60°$. In $\triangle MNP$, $m\angle M = 40°$ and $m\angle P = 80°$.
A student concludes that the triangles are not similar. Do you agree or disagree? Why?

$\underline{\text{Disagree; by the Triangle Sum Theorem, } m\angle N = 60°, \text{ so the triangles are}}$
$\underline{\text{similar by the AA Similarity Criterion.}}$

There is another criterion that can be used to show that two triangles are similar. You will
prove this criterion as an exercise.

SAS Similarity Criterion

If two sides of one triangle are proportional to two sides of another triangle
and their included angles are congruent, then the triangles are similar.

PRACTICE

For each similarity statement, write congruence statements for the
corresponding angles and proportions for the corresponding sides.

1. $\triangle GHJ \sim \triangle PQR$

$\angle G \cong \angle P$, $\angle H \cong \angle Q$,

$\angle J \cong \angle R$,

$\frac{PQ}{GH} = \frac{QR}{HJ} = \frac{PR}{GJ}$

2. $\triangle TWR \sim \triangle YSP$

$\angle T \cong \angle Y$, $\angle W \cong \angle S$,

$\angle R \cong \angle P$,

$\frac{YS}{TW} = \frac{SP}{WR} = \frac{YP}{TR}$

3. $\triangle PJL \sim \triangle WDM$

$\angle P \cong \angle W$, $\angle J \cong \angle D$,

$\angle L \cong \angle M$,

$\frac{WD}{PJ} = \frac{DM}{JL} = \frac{WM}{PL}$

4. Prove the SAS Similarity Criterion.

Given: $\frac{XY}{AB} = \frac{XZ}{AC}$ and $\angle A \cong \angle X$
Prove: $\triangle ABC \sim \triangle XYZ$
(*Hint:* The main steps of the proof
are similar to those of the proof of
the AA Similarity Criterion.)

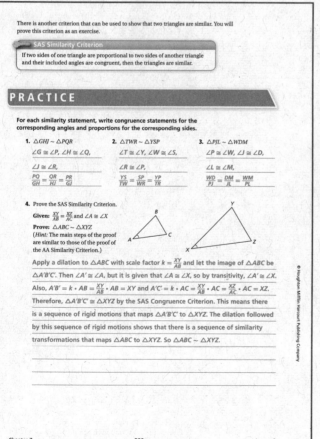

Apply a dilation to $\triangle ABC$ with scale factor $k = \frac{XY}{AB}$ and let the image of $\triangle ABC$ be

$\triangle A'B'C'$. Then $\angle A' \cong \angle A$, but it is given that $\angle A \cong \angle X$, so by transitivity, $\angle A' \cong \angle X$.

Also, $A'B' = k \cdot AB = \frac{XY}{AB} \cdot AB = XY$ and $A'C' = k \cdot AC = \frac{XY}{AB} \cdot AC = \frac{XZ}{AC} \cdot AC = XZ$.

Therefore, $\triangle A'B'C' \cong \triangle XYZ$ by the SAS Congruence Criterion. This means there

is a sequence of rigid motions that maps $\triangle A'B'C'$ to $\triangle XYZ$. The dilation followed

by this sequence of rigid motions shows that there is a sequence of similarity

transformations that maps $\triangle ABC$ to $\triangle XYZ$. So $\triangle ABC \sim \triangle XYZ$.

Notes

ADDITIONAL PRACTICE AND PROBLEM SOLVING

Assign these pages to help your students practice and apply important lesson concepts. For additional exercises, see the Student Edition.

Answers

Additional Practice

1. Possible answer: $\angle ACB$ and $\angle ECD$ are congruent vertical angles. $m\angle B = m\angle D = 100°$, so $\angle B \cong \angle D$. Thus, $\triangle ABC \sim \triangle EDC$ by AA $\sim$.

2. Possible answer: Every equilateral triangle is also equiangular, so each angle in both triangles measures 60°. Thus, $\triangle TUV \sim \triangle WXY$ by AA $\sim$.

3. Possible answer: It is given that $\angle JMN \cong \angle L$. $\frac{KL}{MN} = \frac{JL}{JM} = \frac{4}{3}$. Thus, $\triangle JLK \sim \triangle JMN$ by SAS $\sim$.

4. Possible answer: $\frac{PQ}{UT} = \frac{QR}{TS} = \frac{PR}{US} = \frac{3}{5}$. Thus, $\triangle PQR \sim \triangle UTS$ by SSS $\sim$.

5. Possible answer: $\angle C \cong \angle C$ by the Reflexive Property. $\angle CGD$ and $\angle F$ are right angles, so they are congruent. Thus, $\triangle CDG \sim \triangle CEF$ by AA $\sim$. $DE = 9.75$

Problem Solving

1. $\angle CBD \cong \angle CAE$ by Corr. $\measuredangle$ Thm. and $\angle C \cong \angle C$ by the Reflex. Prop. of $\cong$. So $\triangle CBD \sim \triangle CAE$ by AA $\sim$.

2. 46.7 in.

3. No; $\frac{WX}{XY} \neq \frac{XZ}{YZ}$

4. 15; $\triangle MNP \sim \triangle RQP$ by SAS $\sim$. Corr. sides of $\sim$ $\measuredangle$ are proportional.

5. B

6. F

7. C

7-3

Additional Practice

For Exercises 1 and 2, explain why the triangles are similar and write a similarity statement.

1.

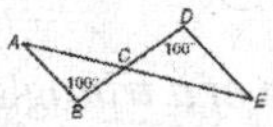

2.

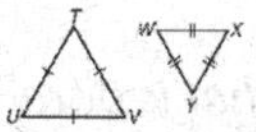

_____

_____

_____

_____

For Exercises 3 and 4, verify that the triangles are similar. Explain why.

3. $\triangle JLK$ and $\triangle JMN$

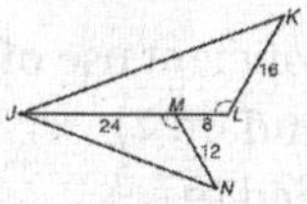

4. $\triangle PQR$ and $\triangle UTS$

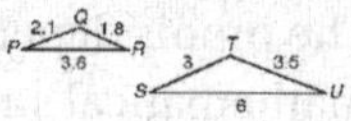

_____

_____

_____

For Exercise 5, explain why the triangles are similar and find the stated length.

5. DE

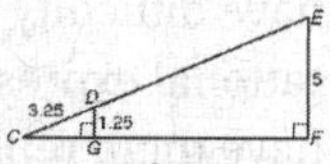

_____

_____

_____

Problem Solving

Use the diagram for Exercises 1 and 2.

In the diagram of the tandem bike, $\overline{AE} \parallel \overline{BD}$.

1. Explain why $\triangle CBD \sim \triangle CAE$.

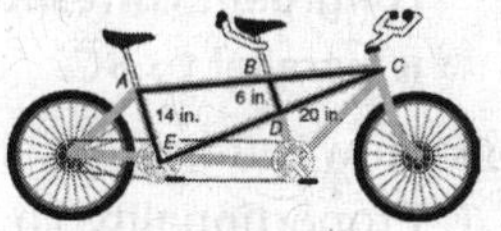

_____

_____

2. Find CE to the nearest tenth. _____

3. Is $\triangle WXZ \sim \triangle XYZ$? Explain.

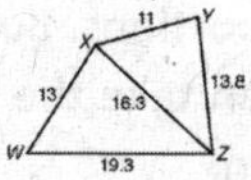

_____

_____

4. Find RQ. Explain how you found it.

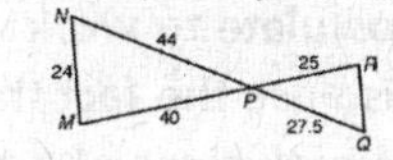

_____

_____

_____

Choose the best answer.

5. Find the value of x that makes $\triangle FGH \sim \triangle JKL$.

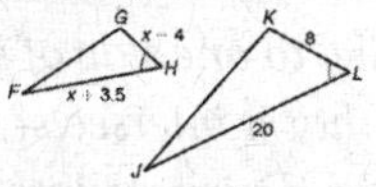

A 8   C 12
B 9   D 16

6. Triangle STU has vertices at $S(0, 0)$, $T(2, 6)$, and $U(8, 2)$. If $\triangle STU \sim \triangle WXY$ and the coordinates of W are $(0, 0)$, what are possible coordinates of X and Y?

F $X(1, 3)$ and $Y(4, 1)$
G $X(1, 3)$ and $Y(2, 0)$
H $X(3, 1)$ and $Y(2, 4)$
J $X(0, 3)$ and $Y(4, 0)$

7. To measure the distance EF across the lake, a surveyor at S locates points E, F, G, and H as shown. What is EF?

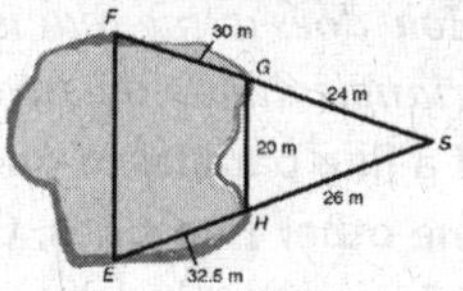

A 25 m   C 45 m
B 36 m   D 90 m

Applying Properties of Similar Triangles
Going Deeper

Essential question: *How does a line that is parallel to one side of a triangle divide the two sides that it intersects?*

COMMON CORE **Standards for Mathematical Content**

CC.9-12.G.SRT.4 Prove theorems about triangles.

CC.9-12.G.SRT.5 Use ... similarity criteria for triangles to solve problems and to prove relationships in geometric figures.

Prerequisites
Similarity and triangles

Math Background
The Triangle Proportionality Theorem and its converse may be stated as a single biconditional: A line that intersects two sides of a triangle is parallel to the third side of the triangle *if and only if* it divides the intersected sides proportionally.

INTRODUCE

Have students use a straightedge to draw $\triangle ABC$. Then, have them construct a line, $\overleftrightarrow{EF}$, parallel to $\overleftrightarrow{BC}$, as shown in the figure on the student page. Have students measure the required segments to calculate the ratios $\frac{AE}{EB}$ and $\frac{AF}{FC}$. Ask students what they notice, and check that all students got similar results. Tell students that the relationship they discovered is known as the Triangle Proportionality Theorem.

TEACH

1 PROOF

Questioning Strategies
- In the third line of Step B, where does the 1 on each side of the equation come from?
  On the left side of the equation and similarly,

  on the right side, it comes from writing

  $\frac{AE + EB}{AE} = \frac{AE}{AE} + \frac{EB}{AE}$ and using the fact that

  $\frac{AE}{AE} = 1$.

MATHEMATICAL PRACTICE — Highlighting the Standards

The proofs depend upon proficient use of mathematical structure (Standard 7). Specifically, students will need to use properties of fractions, such as $\frac{a}{a} = 1$ (for $a \neq 0$) and $\frac{a + b}{c} = \frac{a}{c} + \frac{b}{c}$ (for $c \neq 0$). If students have difficulty applying these properties to rational expressions that involve side lengths, have them replace the side lengths with lowercase variables. This may make it easier for students to recognize the underlying fraction operations.

2 PROOF

Questioning Strategies
- What are the main steps of the proof? **First, show that the two triangles, $\triangle AEF$ and $\triangle ABC$, are similar by the SAS Similarity Criterion. Then, use congruent corresponding angles to show that $\overleftrightarrow{EF}$ is parallel to $\overline{BC}$.**

- How is this proof similar to that of the Triangle Proportionality Theorem? **Both proofs use properties of fractions and the Segment Addition Postulate to work with proportions. Both proofs also use the fact that you can take the reciprocal of both sides of a proportion.**

CLOSE

Essential Question
How does a line that is parallel to one side of a triangle divide the two sides that it intersects?
If a line parallel to one side of a triangle intersects the other two sides, then it divides those sides proportionally.

Summarize
Have students write a journal entry in which they explain the Triangle Proportionality Theorem and its converse in their own words. Ask students to include figures with their explanation.

 © Houghton Mifflin Harcourt Publishing Company

Name _____ Class _____ Date _____

7-4

Applying Properties of Similar Triangles
Going Deeper

Essential question: *How does a line that is parallel to one side of a triangle divide the two sides that it intersects?*

The following theorem is sometimes known as the Side-Splitting Theorem. It describes what happens when a line that is parallel to one side of a triangle "splits" the other two sides.

Video Tutor

Triangle Proportionality Theorem

If a line parallel to one side of a triangle intersects the other two sides, then it divides those sides proportionally.

CC.9-12.G.SRT.4

1 PROOF   Triangle Proportionality Theorem

Given: $\overleftrightarrow{EF} \parallel \overline{BC}$

Prove: $\frac{AE}{EB} = \frac{AF}{FC}$

Complete the proof.

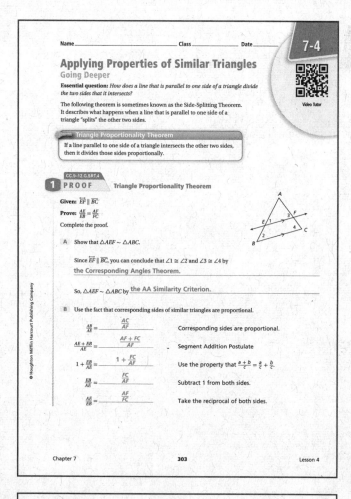

A   Show that $\triangle AEF \sim \triangle ABC$.

Since $\overleftrightarrow{EF} \parallel \overline{BC}$, you can conclude that $\angle 1 \cong \angle 2$ and $\angle 3 \cong \angle 4$ by the Corresponding Angles Theorem.

So, $\triangle AEF \sim \triangle ABC$ by the AA Similarity Criterion.

B   Use the fact that corresponding sides of similar triangles are proportional.

$\frac{AB}{AE} = \dfrac{AC}{AF}$ Corresponding sides are proportional.

$\frac{AE + EB}{AE} = \dfrac{AF + FC}{AF}$ Segment Addition Postulate

$1 + \frac{EB}{AE} = \dfrac{1 + \frac{FC}{AF}}{}$ Use the property that $\frac{a+b}{c} = \frac{a}{c} + \frac{b}{c}$.

$\frac{EB}{AE} = \dfrac{FC}{AF}$ Subtract 1 from both sides.

$\frac{AE}{EB} = \dfrac{AF}{FC}$ Take the reciprocal of both sides.

© Houghton Mifflin Harcourt Publishing Company

REFLECT

1a. Explain how you can conclude $\triangle AEF \sim \triangle ABC$ without using $\angle 3$ and $\angle 4$.

$\angle A \cong \angle A$ by the Reflexive Property of Congruence, and $\angle 1 \cong \angle 2$ since they are corresponding angles; $\triangle AEF \sim \triangle ABC$ by the AA Similarity Criterion.

Converse of the Triangle Proportionality Theorem

If a line divides two sides of a triangle proportionally, then it is parallel to the third side.

CC.9-12.G.SRT.5

2 PROOF   Converse of the Triangle Proportionality Theorem

Given: $\frac{AE}{EB} = \frac{AF}{FC}$

Prove: $\overleftrightarrow{EF} \parallel \overline{BC}$

Complete the proof.

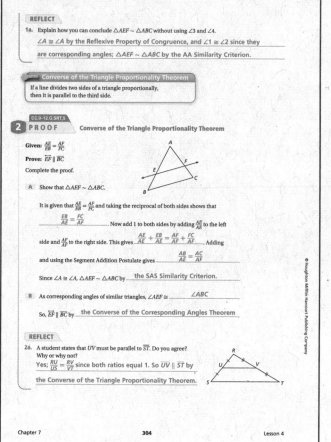

A   Show that $\triangle AEF \sim \triangle ABC$.

It is given that $\frac{AE}{EB} = \frac{AF}{FC}$ and taking the reciprocal of both sides shows that

$\frac{EB}{AE} = \dfrac{FC}{AF}$. Now add 1 to both sides by adding $\frac{AE}{AE}$ to the left

side and $\frac{AF}{AF}$ to the right side. This gives $\frac{AE}{AE} + \frac{EB}{AE} = \frac{AF}{AF} + \frac{FC}{AF}$. Adding

and using the Segment Addition Postulate gives $\frac{AB}{AE} = \dfrac{AC}{AF}$.

Since $\angle A \cong \angle A$, $\triangle AEF \sim \triangle ABC$ by the SAS Similarity Criterion.

B   As corresponding angles of similar triangles, $\angle AEF \cong \underline{\angle ABC}$

So, $\overleftrightarrow{EF} \parallel \overline{BC}$ by the Converse of the Corresponding Angles Theorem

REFLECT

2a. A student states that $\overline{UV}$ must be parallel to $\overline{ST}$. Do you agree? Why or why not?

Yes; $\frac{RU}{US} = \frac{RV}{VT}$ since both ratios equal 1. So $\overline{UV} \parallel \overline{ST}$ by the Converse of the Triangle Proportionality Theorem.

© Houghton Mifflin Harcourt Publishing Company

ADDITIONAL PRACTICE AND PROBLEM SOLVING

Assign these pages to help your students practice and apply important lesson concepts. For additional exercises, see the Student Edition.

Answers

Additional Practice

1. 5.4
2. 20
3. $PN = 66$ and $QM = 88$. $\frac{LP}{PN} = \frac{9}{66} = \frac{3}{22}$ and $\frac{LQ}{QM} = \frac{12}{88} = \frac{3}{22}$. Because $\frac{LP}{PN} = \frac{LQ}{QM}$, $\overline{PQ} \parallel \overline{NM}$ by the Conv. of the △ Proportionality Thm.
4. $\frac{FW}{WD} = \frac{1.5}{2.5} = \frac{3}{5}$ and $\frac{FX}{XE} = \frac{2.1}{3.5} = \frac{3}{5}$. Because $\frac{FW}{WD} = \frac{FX}{XE}$, $\overline{WX} \parallel \overline{DE}$ by the Conv. of the △ Proportionality Thm.
5. $SR = 56$; $RQ = 42$
6. $BE = 1.25$; $DE = 1$
7. isosceles

Problem Solving

1. No; $\frac{EH}{HG} \neq \frac{EJ}{JF}$
2. 0.24 km
3. 16
4. 79.8 ft
5. C
6. H
7. D

Name_____ Class_____ Date_____   **7-4**

Additional Practice

Find each length.

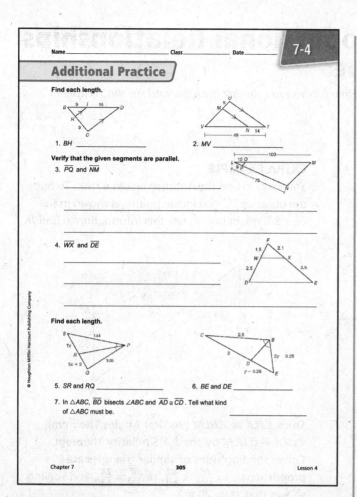

1. BH _____

2. MV _____

Verify that the given segments are parallel.

3. $\overline{PQ}$ and $\overline{NM}$

_____

_____

4. $\overline{WX}$ and $\overline{DE}$

_____

_____

_____

Find each length.

5. SR and RQ _____

6. BE and DE _____

7. In △ABC, $\overline{BD}$ bisects ∠ABC and $\overline{AD} \cong \overline{CD}$. Tell what kind
   of △ABC must be.

_____

Problem Solving

1. Is $\overleftrightarrow{GF} \parallel \overleftrightarrow{HJ}$ if x = 5? Explain.

_____

2. On the map, 5th Ave., 6th Ave., and
   7th Ave. are parallel. What is the length
   of Main St. between 5th Ave. and 6th Ave.?

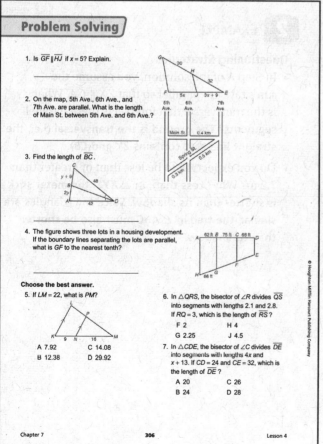

_____

3. Find the length of $\overline{BC}$.

_____

4. The figure shows three lots in a housing development.
   If the boundary lines separating the lots are parallel,
   what is GF to the nearest tenth?

_____

Choose the best answer.

5. If LM = 22, what is PM?

   A 7.92   C 14.08

   B 12.38   D 29.92

6. In △QRS, the bisector of ∠R divides $\overline{QS}$
   into segments with lengths 2.1 and 2.8.
   If RQ = 3, which is the length of $\overline{RS}$?

   F 2   H 4

   G 2.25   J 4.5

7. In △CDE, the bisector of ∠C divides $\overline{DE}$
   into segments with lengths 4x and
   x + 13. If CD = 24 and CE = 32, which is
   the length of $\overline{DE}$?

   A 20   C 26

   B 24   D 28

Using Proportional Relationships
Going Deeper

Essential question: *How can you use similar triangles and similar rectangles to solve problems?*

© Houghton Mifflin Harcourt Publishing Company

COMMON CORE **Standards for Mathematical Content**

CC.9-12.G.SRT.5 Use ... similarity criteria for triangles to solve problems and to prove relationships in geometric figures.

CC.9-12.G.MG.3 Apply geometric methods to solve design problems (e.g., ... working with typographic grid systems based on ratios).*

Prerequisites

Similarity and triangles

Math Background

In this lesson, students use similarity to solve a variety of real-world problems. The general process is the same for every problem: First, show that two figures are similar; then, use the fact that corresponding sides are proportional to find an unknown side length.

INTRODUCE

Remind students that they have already used congruence to solve real-world problems. For example, to find the distance across a pond, students showed that two triangles were congruent and then used CPCTC to find an unknown side length that corresponded to the distance across the pond. Tell students that this lesson presents similar problems (i.e., problems in which unknown lengths must be determined), but in this case students will use similarity and the proportionality of corresponding sides to find the unknown length.

TEACH

Questioning Strategies

• Do you expect *XY* to be less than or greater than 327 feet? Why? Less than; the side lengths of △*XYZ* are all less than the corresponding side lengths in △*VWZ*.

EXTRA EXAMPLE

You want to find the distance across a river. To find the distance *JK*, you locate points as shown in the figure. Explain how to use this information to find *JK*.

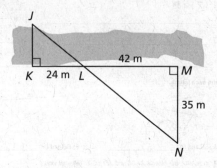

Since ∠*JLK* ≅ ∠*NLM* (Vertical Angles Theorem), △*JLK* ~ △*NLM* by the AA Similarity Theorem. Corresponding sides of similar triangles are proportional, so $\frac{JK}{NM} = \frac{KL}{ML}$, or $\frac{JK}{35} = \frac{24}{42}$, and solving shows that *JK* = 20 m.

2 EXAMPLE

Questioning Strategies

• In Step A of the solution, you assume the sun's rays are parallel so that $\overline{ZX} \parallel \overline{CA}$. What is the transversal that intersects these parallel segments? The ground is the transversal (i.e., the straight line that contains $\overline{ZY}$ and $\overline{CB}$).

• Do you expect *AB* to be less than or greater than 7.2 m? Why? Less than; in △*XYZ*, the meter stick is shorter than its shadow. Since the triangles are similar, the tree in △*ABC* must also be shorter than its shadow.

continued

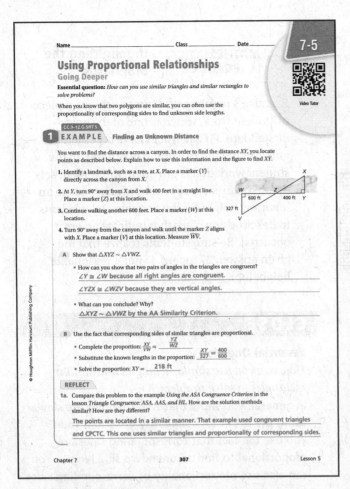

Name_____ Class_____ Date_____

7-5

Video Tutor

Using Proportional Relationships
Going Deeper

Essential question: *How can you use similar triangles and similar rectangles to solve problems?*

When you know that two polygons are similar, you can often use the proportionality of corresponding sides to find unknown side lengths.

CC.9-12.G.SRT.5

1 EXAMPLE Finding an Unknown Distance

You want to find the distance across a canyon. In order to find the distance XY, you locate points as described below. Explain how to use this information and the figure to find XY.

1. Identify a landmark, such as a tree, at X. Place a marker (Y) directly across the canyon from X.

2. At Y, turn 90° away from X and walk 400 feet in a straight line. Place a marker (Z) at this location.

3. Continue walking another 600 feet. Place a marker (W) at this location.

4. Turn 90° away from the canyon and walk until the marker Z aligns with X. Place a marker (V) at this location. Measure $\overline{WV}$.

A Show that $\triangle XYZ \sim \triangle VWZ$.

• How can you show that two pairs of angles in the triangles are congruent?

$\angle Y \cong \angle W$ because all right angles are congruent.

$\angle YZX \cong \angle WZV$ because they are vertical angles.

• What can you conclude? Why?

$\triangle XYZ \sim \triangle VWZ$ by the AA Similarity Criterion.

B Use the fact that corresponding sides of similar triangles are proportional.

• Complete the proportion: $\frac{XY}{VW} = \frac{YZ}{WZ}$

• Substitute the known lengths in the proportion: $\frac{XY}{327} = \frac{400}{600}$

• Solve the proportion: $XY = $ __218 ft__

REFLECT

1a. Compare this problem to the example *Using the ASA Congruence Criterion* in the lesson *Triangle Congruence: ASA, AAS, and HL.* How are the solution methods similar? How are they different?

The points are located in a similar manner. That example used congruent triangles

and CPCTC. This one uses similar triangles and proportionality of corresponding sides.

Chapter 7   307   Lesson 5

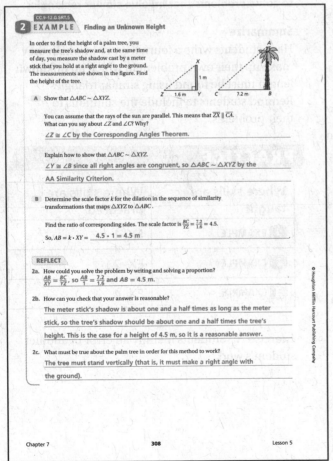

CC.9-12.G.SRT.5

2 EXAMPLE Finding an Unknown Height

In order to find the height of a palm tree, you measure the tree's shadow and, at the same time of day, you measure the shadow cast by a meter stick that you hold at a right angle to the ground. The measurements are shown in the figure. Find the height of the tree.

A Show that $\triangle ABC \sim \triangle XYZ$.

You can assume that the rays of the sun are parallel. This means that $\overline{ZX} \parallel \overline{CA}$. What can you say about $\angle Z$ and $\angle C$? Why?

$\angle Z \cong \angle C$ by the Corresponding Angles Theorem.

Explain how to show that $\triangle ABC \sim \triangle XYZ$.

$\angle Y \cong \angle B$ since all right angles are congruent, so $\triangle ABC \sim \triangle XYZ$ by the

AA Similarity Criterion.

B Determine the scale factor k for the dilation in the sequence of similarity transformations that maps $\triangle XYZ$ to $\triangle ABC$.

Find the ratio of corresponding sides. The scale factor is $\frac{BC}{YZ} = \frac{7.2}{1.6} = 4.5$.

So, $AB = k \cdot XY = $ __4.5 · 1 = 4.5 m__

REFLECT

2a. How could you solve the problem by writing and solving a proportion?

$\frac{AB}{XY} = \frac{BC}{YZ}$, so $\frac{AB}{1} = \frac{7.2}{1.6}$ and $AB = 4.5$ m.

2b. How can you check that your answer is reasonable?

The meter stick's shadow is about one and a half times as long as the meter

stick, so the tree's shadow should be about one and a half times the tree's

height. This is the case for a height of 4.5 m, so it is a reasonable answer.

2c. What must be true about the palm tree in order for this method to work?

The tree must stand vertically (that is, it must make a right angle with

the ground).

Chapter 7   308   Lesson 5

© Houghton Mifflin Harcourt Publishing Company

EXTRA EXAMPLE

To find the height of a building, you measure the building's shadow and, at the same time of day, you measure the shadow cast by a friend who is 6 feet tall. The measurements are shown in the figure. Find the height of the building.

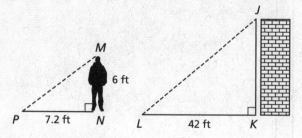

$JK = 35$ feet

3   **EXAMPLE**

Questioning Strategies

- How do you know when two rectangles are similar? They are similar if corresponding sides are proportional (or if they have the same ratio of length to width).

- Why is the number of horizontal 2-centimeter bands one more than the number of rows of rectangles? There is a band above each row of rectangles as well as an extra 2-cm band at the bottom of the poster.

EXTRA EXAMPLE

A designer wants to lay out a grid system for a poster that is 80 cm tall by 120 cm long. The grid must have margins of 5 cm along all edges and 5 cm between each horizontal row of rectangles. There must be 5 rows of rectangles, and each rectangle must be similar to the postcard itself. What are the dimensions of the rectangles? How many rectangles should appear in each row? How much space should be between the columns of rectangles?

10 cm tall and 15 cm long; 7 rectangles per row; $0.8\overline{3}$ cm between columns (or 10 cm tall and $6.\overline{6}$ cm long; 16 rectangles per row; $0.\overline{2}$ cm between columns).

⋮ MATHEMATICAL   **Highlighting the**
   PRACTICE   **Standards**

Exercise 3 requires students to critique a piece of student work, which is one of the goals of Standard 3 (Construct viable arguments and critique the reasoning of others). In the student work that is provided, the student sets up an incorrect proportion, which leads to an incorrect height for the flagpole. Ask students to describe any clues that indicate an error occurred. Be sure students realize that the given answer, 27 inches, is not a reasonable height for a flagpole.

CLOSE

Essential Question

How can you use similar triangles and similar rectangles to solve problems?

In general, you show that two triangles are similar using the AA or SAS Similarity Criterion. Then, you use the fact that corresponding sides are proportional to find an unknown side length. You can also use proportionality of corresponding sides to solve problems that involve similar rectangles.

Summarize

Have students write a journal entry in which they make up their own problem in which an unknown length must be found using similar triangles. Remind students to include the solutions to their problems.

PRACTICE

Where skills are taught	Where skills are practiced
1 EXAMPLE	EX. 1
2 EXAMPLE	EX. 2
3 EXAMPLE	EX. 4

Exercise 3: Students identify an error in another student's work.

3 EXAMPLE Solving a Problem About Similar Rectangles

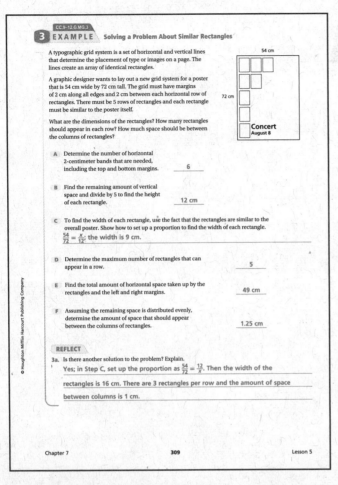

A typographic grid system is a set of horizontal and vertical lines that determine the placement of type or images on a page. The lines create an array of identical rectangles.

A graphic designer wants to lay out a new grid system for a poster that is 54 cm wide by 72 cm tall. The grid must have margins of 2 cm along all edges and 2 cm between each horizontal row of rectangles. There must be 5 rows of rectangles and each rectangle must be similar to the poster itself.

What are the dimensions of the rectangles? How many rectangles should appear in each row? How much space should be between the columns of rectangles?

A Determine the number of horizontal 2-centimeter bands that are needed, including the top and bottom margins.   6

B Find the remaining amount of vertical space and divide by 5 to find the height of each rectangle.   12 cm

C To find the width of each rectangle, use the fact that the rectangles are similar to the overall poster. Show how to set up a proportion to find the width of each rectangle.
$\frac{54}{72} = \frac{x}{12}$, the width is 9 cm.

D Determine the maximum number of rectangles that can appear in a row.   5

E Find the total amount of horizontal space taken up by the rectangles and the left and right margins.   49 cm

F Assuming the remaining space is distributed evenly, determine the amount of space that should appear between the columns of rectangles.   1.25 cm

REFLECT

3a. Is there another solution to the problem? Explain.
Yes; in Step C, set up the proportion as $\frac{54}{72} = \frac{12}{x}$. Then the width of the rectangles is 16 cm. There are 3 rectangles per row and the amount of space between columns is 1 cm.

PRACTICE

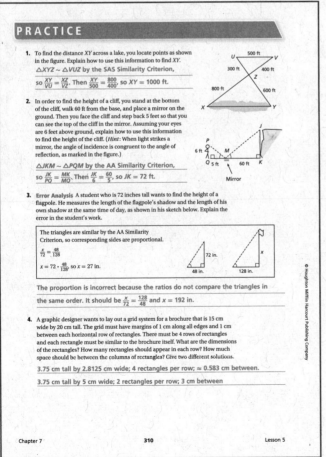

1. To find the distance XY across a lake, you locate points as shown in the figure. Explain how to use this information to find XY.
$\triangle XYZ \sim \triangle VUZ$ by the SAS Similarity Criterion,
so $\frac{XY}{VU} = \frac{XZ}{VZ}$. Then $\frac{XY}{500} = \frac{800}{400}$, so $XY = 1000$ ft.

2. In order to find the height of a cliff, you stand at the bottom of the cliff, walk 60 ft from the base, and place a mirror on the ground. Then you face the cliff and step back 5 feet so that you can see the top of the cliff in the mirror. Assuming your eyes are 6 feet above ground, explain how to use this information to find the height of the cliff. (*Hint:* When light strikes a mirror, the angle of incidence is congruent to the angle of reflection, as marked in the figure.)
$\triangle JKM \sim \triangle PQM$ by the AA Similarity Criterion,
so $\frac{JK}{PQ} = \frac{MK}{MQ}$. Then $\frac{JK}{6} = \frac{60}{5}$, so $JK = 72$ ft.

3. **Error Analysis** A student who is 72 inches tall wants to find the height of a flagpole. He measures the length of the flagpole's shadow and the length of his own shadow at the same time of day, as shown in his sketch below. Explain the error in the student's work.

> The triangles are similar by the AA Similarity Criterion, so corresponding sides are proportional.
> $\frac{x}{72} = \frac{48}{128}$
> $x = 72 \cdot \frac{48}{128}$, so $x = 27$ in.

The proportion is incorrect because the ratios do not compare the triangles in the same order. It should be $\frac{x}{72} = \frac{128}{48}$ and $x = 192$ in.

4. A graphic designer wants to lay out a grid system for a brochure that is 15 cm wide by 20 cm tall. The grid must have margins of 1 cm along all edges and 1 cm between each horizontal row of rectangles. There must be 4 rows of rectangles and each rectangle must be similar to the brochure itself. What are the dimensions of the rectangles? How many rectangles should appear in each row? How much space should be between the columns of rectangles? Give two different solutions.
3.75 cm tall by 2.8125 cm wide; 4 rectangles per row; ≈ 0.583 cm between.
3.75 cm tall by 5 cm wide; 2 rectangles per row; 3 cm between

ADDITIONAL PRACTICE AND PROBLEM SOLVING

Assign these pages to help your students practice and apply important lesson concepts. For additional exercises, see the Student Edition.

Answers

Additional Practice

1. Possible answer: Because the sun's rays are parallel, $\overline{BC} \parallel \overline{DE}$. $\angle ABC$ and $\angle ADE$ are congruent corresponding angles, and $\angle A$ is common to both triangles. So $\triangle ABC \sim \triangle ADE$ by AA $\sim$.

2. 5 ft 9 in.
3. 16 ft 4 in.
4. 10 ft
5. 14 ft
6. 2 ft
7. 12 ft^2
8. 42 mm
9. 90 mm^2

Problem Solving

1. 9 ft $7\frac{1}{2}$ in.
2. 1 in. : 4 yd
3. $181\frac{1}{4}$ ft
4. $3\frac{1}{2}$ in. by $2\frac{3}{4}$ in.
5. C
6. J
7. C
8. F

Name_____ Class_____ Date_____ **7-5**

Additional Practice

Refer to the figure for Exercises 1–3. A city is planning an outdoor concert for an Independence Day celebration. To hold speakers and lights, a crew of technicians sets up a scaffold with two platforms by the stage. The first platform is 8 feet 2 inches off the ground. The second platform is 7 feet 6 inches above the first platform. The shadow of the first platform stretches 6 feet 3 inches across the ground.

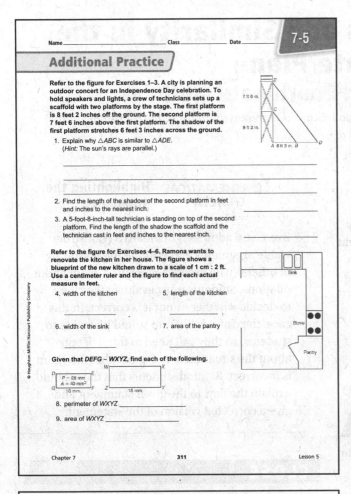

1. Explain why △ABC is similar to △ADE.
   (*Hint:* The sun's rays are parallel.)

   _____

   _____

2. Find the length of the shadow of the second platform in feet and inches to the nearest inch.

   _____

3. A 5-foot-8-inch-tall technician is standing on top of the second platform. Find the length of the shadow the scaffold and the technician cast in feet and inches to the nearest inch.

   _____

Refer to the figure for Exercises 4–6. Ramona wants to renovate the kitchen in her house. The figure shows a blueprint of the new kitchen drawn to a scale of 1 cm : 2 ft. Use a centimeter ruler and the figure to find each actual measure in feet.

4. width of the kitchen   5. length of the kitchen

   _____   _____

6. width of the sink   7. area of the pantry

   _____   _____

Given that *DEFG* ~ *WXYZ*, find each of the following.

8. perimeter of *WXYZ* _____

9. area of *WXYZ* _____

Problem Solving

1. A student is standing next to a sculpture. The figure shows the shadows that they cast. What is the height of the sculpture?

2. At the halftime show during a football game, a marching band is to form a rectangle 50 yards by 16 yards. The conductor wants to plan out the band members' positions using a 14- by 8.5-in. sheet of paper. What scale should she use to fit both dimensions of the rectangle on the page? (Use whole inches and yards.)

   _____

3. An artist makes a scale drawing of a new lion enclosure at the zoo. The scale is 1 in. : 25 ft. On the drawing, the length of the enclosure is $7\frac{1}{4}$ inches. What is the actual length of the lion enclosure?

   _____

4. A room is 14 feet long and 11 feet wide. If you made a scale drawing of the top view of the room using the scale $\frac{1}{2}$ in. = 2 ft, what would be the length and width of the room in your drawing?

   _____

Choose the best answer.

5. A visual-effects model maker for a movie draws a spaceship using a ratio of 1 : 24. The drawing of the spaceship is 22 inches long. What is the length of the spaceship in the movie?

   A 4 ft   C 44 ft
   B 8 ft   D 528 ft

6. A free-fall ride at an amusement park casts a shadow $43\frac{2}{3}$ feet long. At the same time, a 6-foot-tall person standing in line casts a shadow 2 feet long. What is the height of the ride?

   F $21\frac{5}{6}$ ft   H $98\frac{1}{4}$ ft
   G $65\frac{1}{2}$ ft   J 131 ft

7. The scale of the park map is 1.5 cm = 60 m. Which is the best estimate for the actual distance between the horse stables and the picnic area?

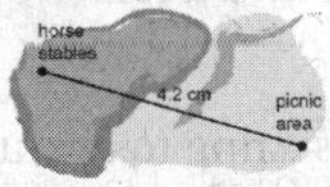

   A 21.4 m   C 168.0 m
   B 90.0 m   D 288.0 m

8. A hot-air balloon is 26.8 meters tall. Use the scale drawing to find the actual distance across the hot-air balloon.

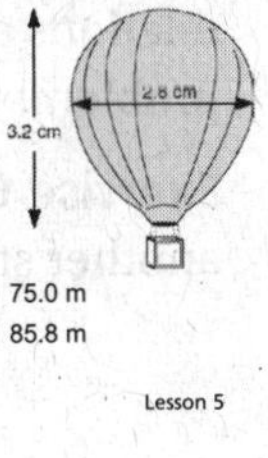

   F 23.45 m   H 75.0 m
   G 30.6 m   J 85.8 m

© Houghton Mifflin Harcourt Publishing Company

Dilations and Similarity in the Coordinate Plane
Connection: Coordinate Methods

Essential question: *How can you represent dilations in the coordinate plane?*

COMMON **Standards for**
CORE **Mathematical Content**

CC.9-12.G.CO.2 Represent transformations in the plane using, e.g., transparencies and geometry software; describe transformations as functions that take points in the plane as inputs and give other points as outputs ...

Prerequisites
Properties of dilations

Math Background
In this lesson, students perform dilations on a coordinate plane.

INTRODUCE

Remind students of the definition of *dilation* and the use of coordinate notation for transformations.

TEACH

1 EXAMPLE

Questioning Strategies
- Do you expect the image of *ABCDE* to be an enlargement or a reduction of the pre-image? Why? **Enlargement; the scale factor is > 1.**
- In which quadrant or quadrants will the image lie? Explain. **The pre-image lies in all four quadrants, so the image will also lie in all four quadrants.**

EXTRA EXAMPLE
Draw the image of the pentagon after a dilation with scale factor $\frac{1}{2}$.

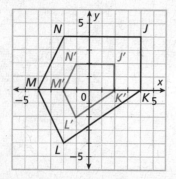

┊ MATHEMATICAL **Highlighting the**
┊ PRACTICE **Standards**

Exercise 6 addresses Standard 3 (Construct viable arguments and critique the reasoning of others). The exercise presents a claim about dilations. Students must evaluate the claim to decide whether or not it is correct. In this case, the claim is likely to sound plausible to students, so they will need to think deeply about the situation to recognize that the claim is incorrect. Remind students that they should explain the flaw in the given statement and give a corrected version of the statement.

CLOSE

Essential Question
How can you represent dilations in the coordinate plane?
For a dilation with scale factor k and center at the origin, you can represent the dilation using the coordinate notation $(x, y) \rightarrow (kx, ky)$.

Summarize
Have students write a journal entry in which they explain the steps for drawing a dilation image on a coordinate plane.

PRACTICE

Where skills are taught	Where skills are practiced
1 EXAMPLE	EXS. 1–4

Exercise 5: Students extend what they know about dilations and scale factors to solve a real-world problem.

Exercise 6: Students use reasoning to evaluate another student's claim about dilations.

Name _____ Class _____ Date _____

7-6

Dilations and Similarity in the Coordinate Plane
Connection: Coordinate Methods

Essential question: *How can you represent dilations in the coordinate plane?*

Video Tutor

When you work with dilations in the coordinate plane, you can assume the center of dilation is the origin. To find the image of a point after a dilation with scale factor k, multiply each coordinate of the point by k. Using coordinate notation, a dilation with scale factor k is written as follows: $(x, y) \rightarrow (kx, ky)$.

CC.9-12.G.CO.2

1 EXAMPLE Drawing a Dilation in a Coordinate Plane

Draw the image of the pentagon after a dilation with scale factor $\frac{3}{2}$.

A In the table below, list the vertices of the pentagon. Then use the rule for the dilation to write the vertices of the image.

Pre-image (x, y)	Image $\left(\frac{3}{2}x, \frac{3}{2}y\right)$
$A(3, 0)$	$A'\left(4\frac{1}{2}, 0\right)$
$B(0, 2)$	$B'(0, 3)$
$C(-2, 0)$	$C'(-3, 0)$
$D(-2, -2)$	$D'(-3, -3)$
$E(1, -2)$	$E'\left(1\frac{1}{2}, -3\right)$

B Plot the vertices of the image. Connect the vertices to complete the image.

REFLECT

1a. Explain how to use the distance formula to check that $\overline{B'C'}$ is the correct length.

By the distance formula, $BC = \sqrt{(0 - (-2))^2 + (2 - 0)^2} = \sqrt{8} = 2\sqrt{2}$ and $B'C' = \sqrt{(0 - (-3))^2 + (3 - 0)^2} = \sqrt{18} = 3\sqrt{2}$. So $B'C' = \frac{3}{2}BC$, which is correct.

1b. A student claims that under a dilation centered at the origin with scale factor k, a point and its image always lie in the same quadrant. Do you agree or disagree? Explain.

Agree; for example, if the point lies in Quadrant II, then its x-coordinate is negative and its y-coordinate is positive. Multiplying both coordinates by k does not change their signs, so the image also lies in Quadrant II.

© Houghton Mifflin Harcourt Publishing Company

PRACTICE

Draw the image of the figure after a dilation with the given scale factor.

1. scale factor: 2

2. scale factor: $\frac{1}{4}$

3. scale factor: $\frac{2}{3}$

4. scale factor: 3

5. Each centimeter on a scale drawing of a park represents three meters of actual distance. What is the scale factor of the dilation that maps the park to the scale drawing?

$\frac{1}{300}$

6. Error Analysis A student claims that a dilation with scale factor m and center of dilation O that is followed by a dilation with scale factor n and center of dilation O is equivalent to a single dilation with scale factor $m + n$ and center of dilation O. Do you agree or disagree? Explain.

Disagree; the first dilation multiplies lengths by m and the second dilation multiplies lengths by n, so the overall effect is to multiply lengths by mn, rather than $m + n$. The equivalent dilation has scale factor mn. The student is correct that the equivalent dilation has center of dilation O.

© Houghton Mifflin Harcourt Publishing Company

Assign these pages to help your students practice and apply important lesson concepts. For additional exercises, see the Student Edition.

Answers

Additional Practice

1.

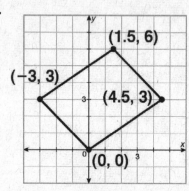

2.

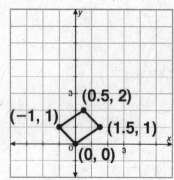

3. $\frac{4}{3}$; $(-20, 0)$ **4.** $\frac{1}{3}$; $(8, 0)$

Problem Solving

1. $\left(4, 6\frac{2}{3}\right)$ **2.** $G(21, 3)$; $\frac{3}{1}$

3. $L'(-25, 5)$, $M'(-10, 27.5)$, $N'(15, -15)$

4. $J'(0, 15)$; $\frac{3}{4}$ **5.** A

6. J   **7.** B

7-6

Notes

Additional Practice

A jeweler designs a setting that can hold a gem in the shape of a parallelogram. The figure shows the outline of the gem. The client, however, wants a gem and setting that is slightly larger.

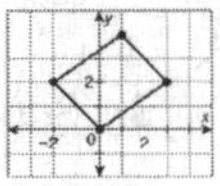

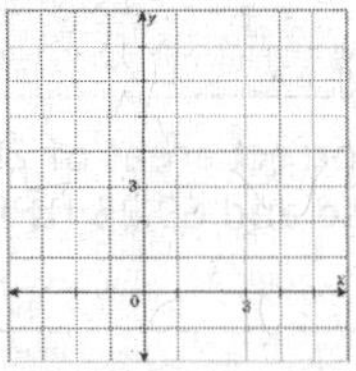

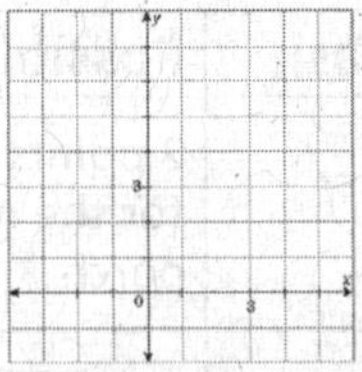

1. Draw the gem after a dilation with a scale factor of $\frac{3}{2}$.

2. The client is so pleased with her ring that she decides to have matching but smaller earrings made using the same pattern. Draw the gem after a dilation from the original pattern with a scale factor of $\frac{1}{2}$.

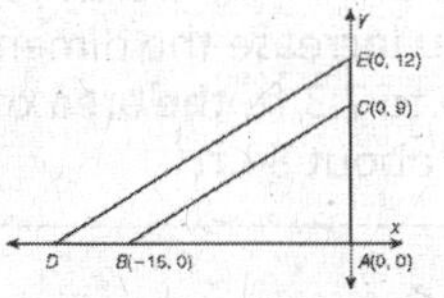

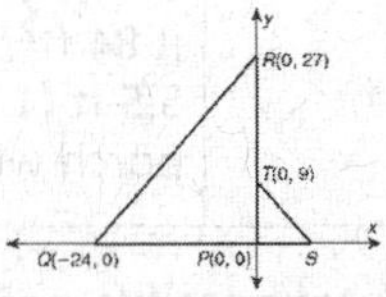

3. Given that $\triangle ABC \sim \triangle ADE$, find the scale factor and the coordinates of D.

_____

4. Given that $\triangle PQR \sim \triangle PST$, find the scale factor and the coordinates of S.

_____

$E(0, 12)$
$C(0, 8)$
D $B(-15, 0)$ $A(0, 0)$

$R(0, 27)$
$T(0, 9)$
$Q(-24, 0)$ $P(0, 0)$ S

© Houghton Mifflin Harcourt Publishing Company

Problem Solving

1. The figure shows a photograph on grid paper. What are the coordinates of C' if the photograph is enlarged with scale factor $\frac{4}{3}$?

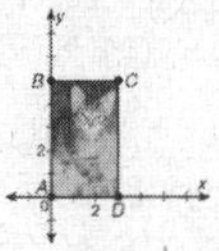

2. In the figure, $\triangle HFJ \sim \triangle EFG$. Find the coordinates of G and the scale factor.

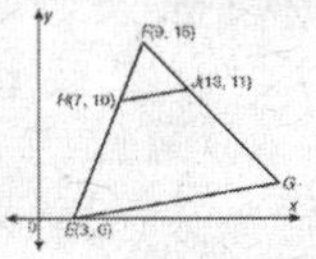

F(9, 16)
H(7, 10)   J(15, 11)
E(3, 6)   G

_____

3. Triangle LMN has vertices $L(-10, 2)$, $M(-4, 11)$, and $N(6, -6)$. Find the vertices of the image of $\triangle LMN$ after a dilation with scale factor $\frac{5}{2}$.

_____

4. Triangle HJM has vertices $H(-36, 0)$, $J(0, 20)$, and $M(0, 0)$. Triangle $H'J'M'$ has two vertices at $H'(-27, 0)$ and $M'(0, 0)$, and $\triangle H'J'M'$ is a dilation image of $\triangle HJM$. Find the coordinates of J' and the scale factor.

_____

Choose the best answer.

5. The arrow is cut from a logo. The artist needs to make a copy five times as large for a sign. If the coordinates of T are $T(3, 4.5)$, what are the coordinates of T' after the arrow is dilated with scale factor 5?

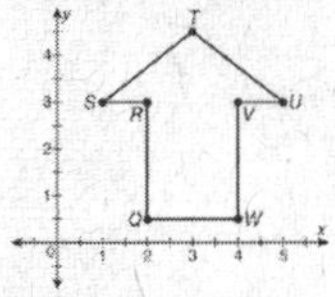

A $T'(15, 22.5)$
B $T'(7.5, 9)$
C $T'(4.5, 6.75)$
D $T'(2.5, 20)$

6. Triangle QRS has vertices $Q(-7, 3)$, $R(9, 8)$, and $S(2, 16)$. What is the scale factor if the vertices after a dilation are $Q'(-10.5, 4.5)$, $R'(13.5, 15)$, and $S'(3, 24)$?

F $\frac{1}{3}$

G $\frac{1}{2}$

H $\frac{2}{3}$

J $\frac{3}{2}$

7. A triangle has vertices $H(-4, 2)$, $J(-8, 6)$, and $K(0, 6)$. If $\triangle ABC \sim \triangle HJK$, what are possible vertices of $\triangle ABC$?
A $A(-4, 3), B(-2, 1), C(0, 3)$
B $A(-2, 1), B(-4, 3), C(0, 3)$
C $A(-2, 4), B(0, 6), C(-2, 8)$
D $A(-2, 4), B(-8, 6), C(-4, 2)$

© Houghton Mifflin Harcourt Publishing Company

This page provides students with the opportunity to apply concepts from the Common Core in real-world problem situations. There are three different levels of performance tasks:

⭐ **Novice:** These are short word problems that require students to apply the math they have learned in straightforward, real-world situations.

⭐⭐ **Apprentice:** These are more involved problems that guide students step-by-step through more complex tasks. These exercises include more complicated reasoning, writing, and open-ended elements.

⭐⭐⭐ **Expert:** These are open-ended, non-routine problems that, instead of stepping the students through, ask them to choose their own methods for solving and justify their answers and reasoning.

Sample answers

1. Answers will vary, but should involve comparing two ratios. Possible answer: student's head measures 9 in. and mouth measures 2.5 in., so ratio of Rushmore head to student head is 6.67 ft : 1 in., and ratio of Rushmore mouth to student mouth is 7.2 ft : 1 in. Since ratios are close, student's face is approximately similar to the carved faces.

2a. Scale factor of $\frac{5}{3}$

b.

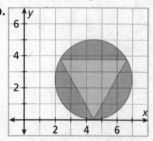

3. Scoring Guide:

Task	Possible points
a	2 points for the correct areas of 280 ft^2 for the main house and 63.25 ft^2 for the porch
b	1 point for explaining one change in dimension, and 3 points for explaining how it satisfies Alicia's goal, for example: 30% of 280 ft^2 is 84 ft^2, so increase one of the dimensions of the porch to make it 84 ft^2. If you increase the dimension of 5.5 ft (1.1 in.) to 7.3 ft, the area of the porch will be about 84 ft^2.

Total possible points: 6

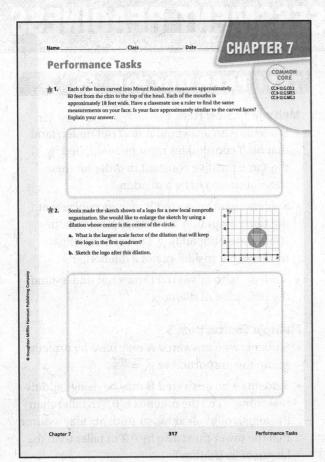

CHAPTER 7

Performance Tasks

COMMON CORE
CC.9-12.G.CO.2
CC.9-12.G.SRT.5
CC.9-12.G.MG.3

⭐ **1.** Each of the faces carved into Mount Rushmore measures approximately 60 feet from the chin to the top of the head. Each of the mouths is approximately 18 feet wide. Have a classmate use a ruler to find the same measurements on your face. Is your face approximately similar to the carved faces? Explain your answer.

⭐ **2.** Sonia made the sketch shown of a logo for a new local nonprofit organization. She would like to enlarge the sketch by using a dilation whose center is the center of the circle.

  a. What is the largest scale factor of the dilation that will keep the logo in the first quadrant?

  b. Sketch the logo after this dilation.

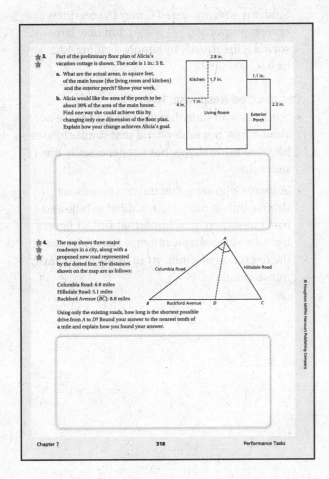

⭐ **3.** Part of the preliminary floor plan of Alicia's vacation cottage is shown. The scale is 1 in.: 5 ft.

  a. What are the actual areas, in square feet, of the main house (the living room and kitchen) and the exterior porch? Show your work.

  b. Alicia would like the area of the porch to be about 30% of the area of the main house. Find one way she could achieve this by changing only one dimension of the floor plan. Explain how your change achieves Alicia's goal.

⭐ **4.** The map shows three major roadways in a city, along with a proposed new road represented by the dotted line. The distances shown on the map are as follows:

Columbia Road: 6.8 miles
Hillsdale Road: 5.1 miles
Rockford Avenue ($\overline{BC}$): 8.8 miles

Using only the existing roads, how long is the shortest possible drive from A to D? Round your answer to the nearest tenth of a mile and explain how you found your answer.

4. Scoring Guide:

Task	Possible points
	2 points for finding a distance of about 8.9 miles, and 4 points for giving an appropriate explanation, which should include using the Triangle Angle Bisector Theorem to calculate $BD = 5$ miles and $DC = 3.8$ miles, adding the distances of the two possible routes, and then comparing

Total possible points: 6

© Houghton Mifflin Harcourt Publishing Company

COMMON CORE CORRELATION

Standard	Items
CC.9-12.G.CO.2	1, 6
CC.9-12.G.SRT.1	3
CC.9-12.G.SRT.2	7
CC.9-12.G.SRT.3	8
CC.9-12.G.SRT.4	2
CC.9-12.G.SRT.5	5
CC.9-12.G.C.1	9
CC.9-12.G.MG.3*	4

TEST PREP DOCTOR ✚

Multiple Choice: Item 1

- Students who answered **A** may not understand that both coordinates must be multiplied by the same positive constant in order for the transformation to be a dilation.
- Students who answered **B** may recognize that the same operation must be applied to both coordinates, but adding 2 to each coordinate results in a translation, not a dilation.
- Students who answered **D** may not understand the definition of *dilation*.

Multiple Choice: Item 5

- Students who answered **A** may have incorrectly set up the proportion as $\frac{x}{0.9} = \frac{40.2}{1.2}$.
- Students who answered **B** may be using "additive reasoning" (i.e., the mailbox is 0.3 m taller than the length of its shadow, so students may assume that the tower must also be 0.3 m taller than the length of its shadow).
- Students who answered **C** may have written a correct proportion $\left(\frac{x}{1.2} = \frac{40.2}{0.9}\right)$, but may have solved it incorrectly by simply dividing 40.2 by 0.9.

Constructed Response: Item 7

- Students who state that the two figures are not similar may not understand that similar figures have the same shape, but not necessarily the same size.
- Students who state that the two figures are similar, but do not specify a dilation followed by a translation, may know that similar figures have the same shape, but may not understand the definition of similarity in terms of similarity transformations.

CHAPTER 7 COMMON CORE ASSESSMENT READINESS

Name _____ Class _____ Date _____

MULTIPLE CHOICE

1. Which of the following transformations is a dilation?

A. $(x, y) \to (2x, y)$

B. $(x, y) \to (x + 2, y + 2)$

C. $(x, y) \to (2x, 2y)$

D. $(x, y) \to (x, y - 2)$

2. Juan is proving the Triangle Proportionality Theorem. Which reason should he use for Step 3?

Given: $\overline{XY} \parallel \overline{BC}$

Prove: $\frac{AX}{XB} = \frac{AY}{YC}$

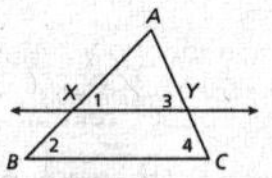

Statements	Reasons
1. $\overline{XY} \parallel \overline{BC}$	1. Given
2. $\angle 1 \cong \angle 2$; $\angle 3 \cong \angle 4$	2. Corresponding Angles Theorem
3. $\triangle AXY \sim \triangle ABC$	3. ?

F. ASA Congruence Criterion

G. Definition of corresponding angles

H. Definition of similarity

J. AA Similarity Criterion

3. Katie uses geometry software to draw a line ℓ and a point O that is not on line ℓ. Then she constructs the image of line ℓ under a dilation with center O and scale factor 4. Which of the following *best* describes the image of line ℓ?

A. a line parallel to line ℓ

B. a line perpendicular to line ℓ

C. a line passing through point O

D. a line that coincides with line ℓ

4. A graphic designer wants to lay out a grid system for a book cover that is 12 cm wide by 15 cm tall. The grid will have an array of identical rectangles, margins of 1 cm along all edges, and 1 cm between each horizontal row of rectangles. There must be 4 rows of rectangles and each rectangle must be similar to the cover itself. Which of the following are possible dimensions of the rectangles?

F. 2.5 cm tall by 2 cm wide

G. 2.75 cm tall by 2.2 cm wide

H. 3 cm tall by 2.4 cm wide

J. 3.25 cm tall by 2.6 cm wide

5. In order to find the height of a radio tower, you measure the tower's shadow and, at the same time of day, you measure the shadow cast by a mailbox that is 1.2 meters tall. The measurements are shown in the figure. What is the height of the tower?

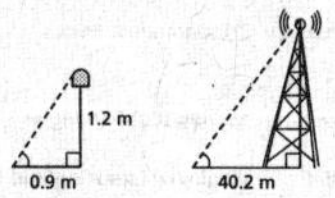

A. 30.15 m   C. 44.67 m

B. 40.5 m   D. 53.6 m

6. Which of the following is *not* preserved under a dilation?

F. angle measure

G. betweenness

H. collinearity

J. distance

CONSTRUCTED RESPONSE

7. Use the definition of similarity in terms of similarity transformations to determine whether the two figures are similar. Explain your answer.

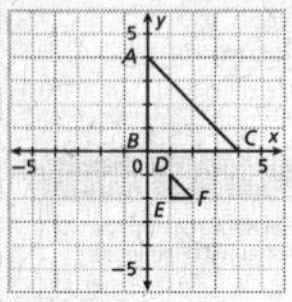

Similar; the dilation $(x, y) \to \left(\frac{1}{4}x, \frac{1}{4}y\right)$

followed by the translation $(x, y) \to$

$(x + 1, y - 2)$ maps $\triangle ABC$ to $\triangle DEF$.

8. You are proving that the AA Similarity Criterion follows from the definition of similarity in terms of similarity transformations.

Given: $\angle R \cong \angle U$ and $\angle S \cong \angle V$

Prove: $\triangle RST \sim \triangle UVW$

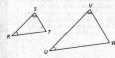

You begin by applying a dilation to $\triangle RST$. What is the scale factor k of the dilation? Why do you choose this scale factor?

$k = \frac{UV}{RS}$, this ensures that the image of

$\triangle RST$ is congruent to $\triangle UVW$ by the

ASA Congruence Criterion.

9. You are proving that all circles are similar. You start with the two circles shown below.

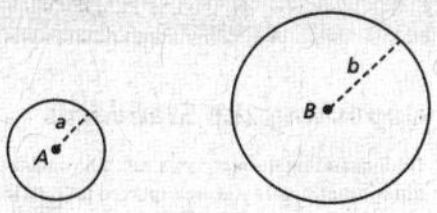

a. First you perform a transformation on circle A so that the image of point A is point B. Describe the transformation you use.

Translation along the vector $\overline{AB}$

b. The image of circle A is circle A', as shown.

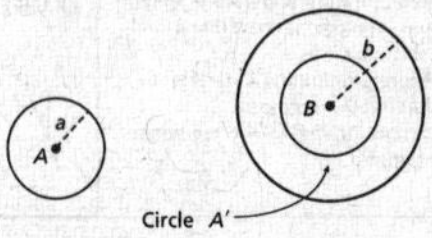

Circle A'

What transformation do you apply to circle A' in order to complete the proof? Why?

Dilation with center of dilation B

and scale factor $\frac{b}{a}$. The image of

circle A' will consist of all points at a

distance $\frac{b}{a} \cdot a = b$ from point B, and

these are the points that form circle B.

So this shows that there is a sequence

of similarity transformations

(translation followed by dilation) that

maps circle A to circle B.

CHAPTER 8

Right Triangles and Trigonometry

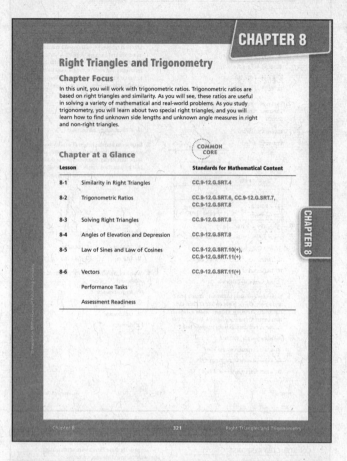

Right Triangles and Trigonometry

Chapter Focus

In this unit, you will work with trigonometric ratios. Trigonometric ratios are based on right triangles and similarity. As you will see, these ratios are useful in solving a variety of mathematical and real-world problems. As you study trigonometry, you will learn about two special right triangles, and you will learn how to find unknown side lengths and unknown angle measures in right and non-right triangles.

Chapter at a Glance

Lesson		COMMON CORE Standards for Mathematical Content
8-1	Similarity in Right Triangles	CC.9-12.G.SRT.4
8-2	Trigonometric Ratios	CC.9-12.G.SRT.6, CC.9-12.G.SRT.7, CC.9-12.G.SRT.8
8-3	Solving Right Triangles	CC.9-12.G.SRT.8
8-4	Angles of Elevation and Depression	CC.9-12.G.SRT.8
8-5	Law of Sines and Law of Cosines	CC.9-12.G.SRT.10(+), CC.9-12.G.SRT.11(+)
8-6	Vectors	CC.9-12.G.SRT.11(+)
	Performance Tasks	
	Assessment Readiness	

COMMON CORE PROFESSIONAL DEVELOPMENT — CC.9-12.G.SRT.6

Students have previously used the Pythagorean Theorem and properties of similar triangles to solve for missing information. In this chapter, students will use these concepts to derive the trigonometric ratios. Although students may have seen and used trigonometric ratios in previous courses, it is in this chapter that they are provided with the tools to prove the ratios are valid by using known relationships.

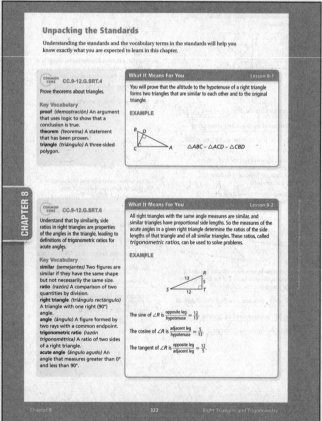

Unpacking the Standards

Understanding the standards and the vocabulary terms in the standards will help you know exactly what you are expected to learn in this chapter.

COMMON CORE CC.9-12.G.SRT.4

Prove theorems about triangles.

Key Vocabulary
proof *(demostración)* An argument that uses logic to show that a conclusion is true.
theorem *(teorema)* A statement that has been proven.
triangle *(triángulo)* A three-sided polygon.

What It Means For You — Lesson 8-1

You will prove that the altitude to the hypotenuse of a right triangle forms two triangles that are similar to each other and to the original triangle.

EXAMPLE

$\triangle ABC \sim \triangle ACD \sim \triangle CBD$

COMMON CORE CC.9-12.G.SRT.6

Understand that by similarity, side ratios in right triangles are properties of the angles in the triangle, leading to definitions of trigonometric ratios for acute angles.

Key Vocabulary
similar *(semejantes)* Two figures are similar if they have the same shape but not necessarily the same size.
ratio *(razón)* A comparison of two quantities by division.
right triangle *(triángulo rectángulo)* A triangle with one right (90°) angle.
angle *(ángulo)* A figure formed by two rays with a common endpoint.
trigonometric ratio *(razón trigonométrica)* A ratio of two sides of a right triangle.
acute angle *(ángulo agudo)* An angle that measures greater than 0° and less than 90°.

What It Means For You — Lesson 8-2

All right triangles with the same angle measures are similar, and similar triangles have proportional side lengths. So the measures of the acute angles in a given right triangle determine the ratios of the side lengths of that triangle and of all similar triangles. These ratios, called *trigonometric ratios*, can be used to solve problems.

EXAMPLE

The sine of $\angle R$ is $\dfrac{\text{opposite leg}}{\text{hypotenuse}} = \dfrac{12}{13}$

The cosine of $\angle R$ is $\dfrac{\text{adjacent leg}}{\text{hypotenuse}} = \dfrac{5}{13}$

The tangent of $\angle R$ is $\dfrac{\text{opposite leg}}{\text{adjacent leg}} = \dfrac{12}{5}$

COMMON CORE CC.9-12.G.SRT.8

Use trigonometric ratios and the Pythagorean Theorem to solve right triangles in applied problems.

Key Vocabulary

Pythagorean Theorem *(Teorema de Pitágoras)* If a right triangle has legs of lengths a and b and a hypotenuse of length c, then $a^2 + b^2 = c^2$.

What It Means For You Lessons 8-2, 8-3, 8-4

You can use trigonometric ratios and the Pythagorean theorem to find unknown angle measures and side lengths in right triangles.

EXAMPLE Using Trigonometric Ratios

Lombard Street is on a hill in San Francisco, California, that rises 45 feet for every 100 feet of horizontal distance. What angle does the hill make with a horizontal line? Round to the nearest degree.

The right triangle below represents the hill. $\angle A$ is the angle the hill makes with a horizontal line.

$$m\angle A = \tan^{-1}\left(\frac{45}{100}\right) \approx 27°$$

COMMON CORE CC.9-12.G.SRT.10(+)

Prove the Laws of Sines and Cosines and use them to solve problems.

Key Vocabulary

Law of Sines *(Ley de senos)* For $\triangle ABC$ with side lengths a, b, and c:

$$\frac{\sin A}{a} = \frac{\sin B}{b} = \frac{\sin C}{c}.$$

Law of Cosines *(Ley de cosenos)* For $\triangle ABC$ with side lengths a, b, and c:

$a^2 = b^2 + c^2 - 2bc \cos A$
$b^2 = a^2 + c^2 - 2ac \cos B$
$c^2 = a^2 + b^2 - 2ab \cos C$

What It Means For You Lesson 8-5

The Law of Sines and the Law of Cosines make it possible to find unknown angle measures and side lengths in any triangle, not just a right triangle, using measures that are known.

EXAMPLE Using the Law of Sines

Find DF to the nearest tenth.

$$\frac{\sin 105°}{18} = \frac{\sin 32°}{DF}$$

$$DF = \frac{18 (\sin 32°)}{\sin 105°}$$

$$DF \approx 9.9$$

EXAMPLE Using the Law of Cosines

Find BC to the nearest tenth.

$(BC)^2 = (AB)^2 + (AC)^2 - 2(AB)(AC)\cos A$
$(BC)^2 = 14^2 + 9^2 - 2(14)(9)\cos 62°$
$(BC)^2 \approx 158.69$
$BC \approx 12.6$

Chapter 8   323   Right Triangles and Trigonometry

COMMON CORE PROFESSIONAL DEVELOPMENT **CC.9-12.G.SRT.8***

After deriving and using trigonometric ratios of known angles to find lengths and distances, students will be introduced to trigonometric ratios as functions of an angle. By restricting domains, inverses of these functions can be defined and used to generate the angles for given lengths or distances of a right triangle. Armed with these tools, students can solve for every length and angle in a right triangle. Doing so is called *solving a right triangle*.

CHAPTER 8

Key Vocabulary

acute angle *(ángulo agudo)* An angle that measures greater than 0° and less than 90°.

angle of depression *(ángulo de depresión)* The angle formed by a horizontal line and a line of sight to a point below.

angle of elevation *(ángulo de elevación)* The angle formed by a horizontal line and a line of sight to a point above.

complementary angles *(ángulos complementarios)* Two angles whose measures have a sum of 90°.

cosine *(coseno)* In a right triangle, the cosine of angle A is the ratio of the length of the leg adjacent to angle A to the length of the hypotenuse. It is the reciprocal of the secant function.

initial point of a vector *(punto inicial de un vector)* The starting point of a vector.

Law of Sines *(Ley de senos)* For $\triangle ABC$ with side lengths a, b, and c, $\frac{\sin A}{a} = \frac{\sin B}{b} = \frac{\sin C}{c}$.

Law of Cosines *(Ley de cosenos)* For $\triangle ABC$ with side lengths a, b, and c:

$$a^2 = b^2 + c^2 - 2bc \cos A$$
$$b^2 = a^2 + c^2 - 2ac \cos B$$
$$c^2 = a^2 + b^2 - 2ab \cos C$$

leg of a right triangle *(cateto de un triángulo rectángulo)* One of the two sides of the right triangle that form the right angle.

Pythagorean Theorem *(Teorema de Pitágoras)* If a right triangle has legs of lengths a and b and a hypotenuse of length c, then $a^2 + b^2 = c^2$.

ratio *(razón)* A comparison of two quantities by division.

right triangle *(triángulo rectángulo)* A triangle with one right (90°) angle.

similar *(semejantes)* Two figures are similar if they have the same shape but not necessarily the same size.

sine *(seno)* In a right triangle, the ratio of the length of the leg opposite angle A to the length of the hypotenuse.

tangent of an angle *(tangente de un ángulo)* In a right triangle, the ratio of the length of the leg opposite angle A to the length of the leg adjacent to angle A.

terminal point of a vector *(punto terminal de un vector)* The endpoint of a vector.

triangle *(triángulo)* A three-sided polygon.

trigonometric ratio *(razón trigonométrica)* A ratio of two sides of a right triangle.

vector *(vector)* A quantity that has both magnitude and direction.

Chapter 8   324   Right Triangles and Trigonometry

Essential question: *How can you use triangle similarity to prove the Pythagorean Theorem?*

COMMON CORE **Standards for Mathematical Content**

CC.9-12.G.SRT.4 Prove theorems about triangles.

CC.9-12.G.SRT.5 Use ... similarity criteria for triangles to solve problems and to prove relationships in geometric figures.

Prerequisites

AA Similarity Criterion

Math Background

The Pythagorean Theorem was known in many ancient civilizations, including those of Egypt, India, and China. The oldest known axiomatic proof of the theorem, however, dates to Euclid's *Elements* (circa 300 BCE). Since then, hundreds of proofs have been given, including proofs that rely on area, proofs that use calculus, and the proof that is given in this lesson, which is based on similar triangles.

INTRODUCE

Review the Pythagorean Theorem, emphasizing that the theorem applies only to right triangles. You may want to show students a simple example, such as a 3-4-5 right triangle, in which it is easy to see that $3^2 + 4^2 = 5^2$.

TEACH

1 **PROOF**

Questioning Strategies

- The perpendicular from *C* to the hypotenuse creates two new triangles, $\triangle AXC$ and $\triangle CXB$. What can you say about these triangles and the original triangle? **All three triangles are similar to one another.**

- What is the hypotenuse of $\triangle AXC$? of $\triangle CXB$? $\overline{AC}$; $\overline{CB}$

Teaching Strategies

To be successful with this proof, students must be able to visualize the legs of $\triangle ACB$ as the hypotenuses of the smaller right triangles. It may be helpful for students to draw the three triangles separately, as shown below.

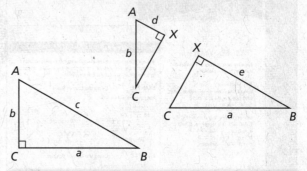

MATHEMATICAL PRACTICE **Highlighting the Standards**

Distinguishing correct logic from flawed logic is part of Standard 3 (Construct viable arguments and critique the reasoning of others). The question following the proof of the Pythagorean Theorem asks students to analyze an alternate proof of the theorem. This proof uses flawed logic because it assumes the result that is being proved. Discuss the perils of "circular reasoning" with the class and ask students to share additional examples of circular reasoning from daily life.

CLOSE

Essential Question

How can you use triangle similarity to prove the Pythagorean Theorem?

Draw a perpendicular from the right-angle vertex to the hypotenuse. Then, identify similar triangles, write proportions for corresponding sides, and use algebra to derive the Pythagorean Theorem.

Summarize

Have students write a journal entry in which they rewrite the proof of the Pythagorean Theorem in their own words.

Name_____ Class_____ Date_____

8-1

Similarity in Right Triangles
Going Deeper

Essential question: *How can you use triangle similarity to prove the Pythagorean Theorem?*

You have already used the Pythagorean Theorem in earlier courses and in earlier lessons of this book. There are many proofs of this familiar theorem. The proof in this lesson is based on using what you know about similar triangles.

Video Tutor

The Pythagorean Theorem

In a right triangle, the sum of the squares of the lengths of the legs is equal to the square of the length of the hypotenuse.

CC.9-12.G.SRT.4

1 PROOF The Pythagorean Theorem

Given: $\triangle ABC$ is a right triangle with legs of length a and b and hypotenuse of length c.

Prove: $a^2 + b^2 = c^2$

Complete the proof.

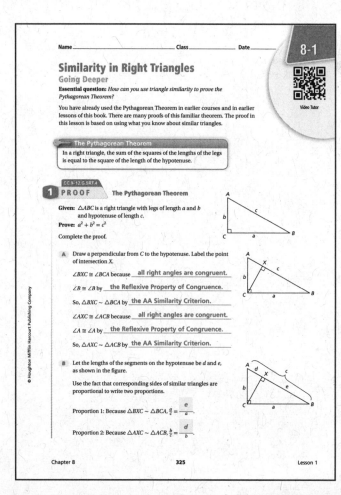

A Draw a perpendicular from C to the hypotenuse. Label the point of intersection X.

$\angle BXC \cong \angle BCA$ because ___all right angles are congruent.___

$\angle B \cong \angle B$ by ___the Reflexive Property of Congruence.___

So, $\triangle BXC \sim \triangle BCA$ by ___the AA Similarity Criterion.___

$\angle AXC \cong \angle ACB$ because ___all right angles are congruent.___

$\angle A \cong \angle A$ by ___the Reflexive Property of Congruence.___

So, $\triangle AXC \sim \triangle ACB$ by ___the AA Similarity Criterion.___

B Let the lengths of the segments on the hypotenuse be d and e, as shown in the figure.

Use the fact that corresponding sides of similar triangles are proportional to write two proportions.

Proportion 1: Because $\triangle BXC \sim \triangle BCA$, $\dfrac{a}{c} = \dfrac{e}{a}$.

Proportion 2: Because $\triangle AXC \sim \triangle ACB$, $\dfrac{b}{c} = \dfrac{d}{b}$.

Chapter 8   325   Lesson 1

C Now perform some algebra to complete the proof as follows.

Multiply both sides of Proportion 1 by ac. Write the resulting equation.

$a^2 = ce$

Multiply both sides of Proportion 2 by bc. Write the resulting equation.

$b^2 = cd$

Adding the above equations gives this: ___$a^2 + b^2 = ce + cd$___

Factor the right side of the equation: ___$a^2 + b^2 = c(e + d)$___

Finally, use the fact that $e + d =$ ___c___ by the Segment Addition

Postulate to rewrite the equation as ___$a^2 + b^2 = c^2$___.

REFLECT

1a. Error Analysis A student wrote a proof of the Pythagorean Theorem, as shown below.

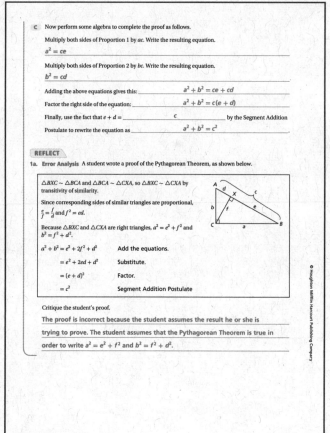

$\triangle BXC \sim \triangle BCA$ and $\triangle BCA \sim \triangle CXA$, so $\triangle BXC \sim \triangle CXA$ by transitivity of similarity.

Since corresponding sides of similar triangles are proportional, $\dfrac{e}{f} = \dfrac{f}{d}$ and $f^2 = ed$.

Because $\triangle BXC$ and $\triangle CXA$ are right triangles, $a^2 = e^2 + f^2$ and $b^2 = f^2 + d^2$.

$a^2 + b^2 = e^2 + 2f^2 + d^2$ Add the equations.

$= e^2 + 2ed + d^2$ Substitute.

$= (e + d)^2$ Factor.

$= c^2$ Segment Addition Postulate

Critique the student's proof.

The proof is incorrect because the student assumes the result he or she is

trying to prove. The student assumes that the Pythagorean Theorem is true in

order to write $a^2 = e^2 + f^2$ and $b^2 = f^2 + d^2$.

Chapter 8   326   Lesson 1

© Houghton Mifflin Harcourt Publishing Company

ADDITIONAL PRACTICE AND PROBLEM SOLVING

Assign these pages to help your students practice and apply important lesson concepts. For additional exercises, see the Student Edition.

Answers

Additional Practice

1. Possible answers: $\triangle JKL \sim \triangle JLM \sim \triangle LKM$

2. $\triangle DEF \sim \triangle GED \sim \triangle GDF$

3. $\triangle WXY \sim \triangle ZXW \sim \triangle ZWY$

4. 1

5. 15

6. $6\sqrt{2}$

7. $\frac{3\sqrt{2}}{2}$

8. $2\sqrt{35}$

9. 7

10. $\sqrt{35}$; $2\sqrt{15}$; $2\sqrt{21}$

11. 30; $10\sqrt{3}$; $20\sqrt{3}$

12. 2; $\sqrt{15}$; $\sqrt{10}$

13. $3\sqrt{10}$; $3\sqrt{35}$; $3\sqrt{14}$

14. 144; 60; 156

15. 12; $9\sqrt{13}$; $6\sqrt{13}$

16. 3,807 feet

17. $\frac{e}{b} = \frac{\boxed{c}}{e}$

18. $\frac{d}{b+c} = \frac{\boxed{e}}{a}$

19. $\frac{d}{\boxed{c}} = \frac{a}{e}$

Problem Solving

1. 7.7 ft

2. 351 mm^2

3. 28.2 cm

4. $10\frac{1}{4}$ ft

5. A

6. G

7. B

Additional Practice

Write a similarity statement comparing the three triangles in each diagram.

1. 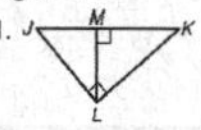 J, M, K, L

_____

2. 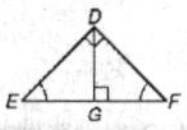 D, E, G, F

_____

3. 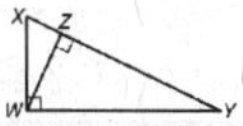 X, Z, W, Y

_____

Find the geometric mean of each pair of numbers. If necessary, give the answer in simplest radical form.

4. $\frac{1}{4}$ and 4 _____

5. 3 and 75 _____

6. 4 and 18 _____

7. $\frac{1}{2}$ and 9 _____

8. 10 and 14 _____

9. 4 and 12.25 _____

Find x, y, and z.

10.

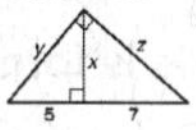

11.

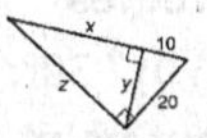

12.

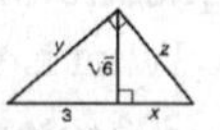

13.

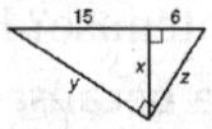

14.

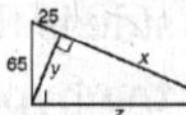

15.

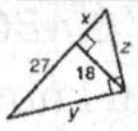

16. The Coast Guard has sent a rescue helicopter to retrieve passengers off a disabled ship. The ship has called in its position as 1.7 miles from shore. When the helicopter passes over a buoy that is known to be 1.3 miles from shore, the angle formed by the shore, the helicopter, and the disabled ship is 90°. Determine what the altimeter would read to the nearest foot when the helicopter is directly above the buoy.

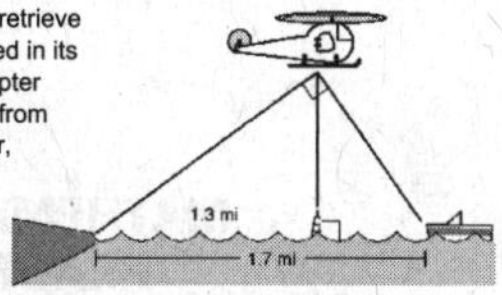

Use the diagram to complete each equation.

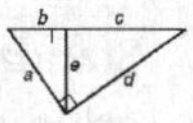

17. $\frac{e}{b}=\frac{\square}{e}$

18. $\frac{d}{b+c}=\frac{\square}{a}$

19. $\frac{d}{\square}=\frac{a}{e}$

Problem Solving

1. A sculpture is 10 feet long and 6 feet wide. The artist made the sculpture so that the height is the geometric mean of the length and the width. What is the height of the sculpture to the nearest tenth of a foot?

2. The altitude to the hypotenuse of a right triangle divides the hypotenuse into two segments that are 12 mm long and 27 mm long. What is the area of the triangle?

3. The perimeter of △ABC is 56.4 cm, and the perimeter of △GHJ is 14.1 cm. The perimeter of △DEF is the geometric mean of these two perimeters. What is the perimeter of △DEF?

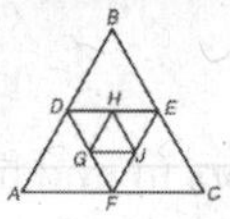

4. Tamara stands facing a painting in a museum. Her lines of sight to the top and bottom of the painting form a 90° angle. How tall is the painting?

Choose the best answer.

5. The altitude to the hypotenuse of a right triangle divides the hypotenuse into two segments that are x cm and 4x cm, respectively. What is the length of the altitude?

A 2x   C 5x
B 2.5x   D 4x²

6. Jack stands 9 feet from the primate enclosure at the zoo. His lines of sight to the top and bottom of the enclosure form a 90° angle. When he looks straight ahead at the enclosure, the vertical distance between his line of sight and the bottom of the enclosure is 5 feet. What is the height of the enclosure?

F 16.2 ft   H 23.8 ft
G 21.2 ft   J 28.8 ft

7. A surveyor sketched the diagram at right to calculate the distance across a ravine. What is x, the distance across the ravine, to the nearest tenth of a meter?

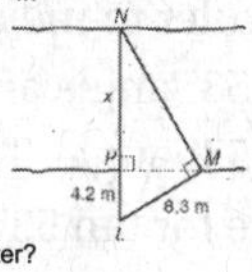

A 7.2 m   C 16.4 m
B 12.2 m   D 64.7 m

Trigonometric Ratios
Going Deeper

Essential question: *How do you find the tangent, sine, and cosine ratios for acute angles in a right triangle?*

COMMON CORE **Standards for Mathematical Content**

CC.9-12.G.SRT.6 Understand that by similarity, side ratios in right triangles are properties of the angles in the triangle, leading to definitions of trigonometric ratios for acute angles.

CC.9-12.G.SRT.7 Explain and use the relationship between the sine and cosine of complementary angles.

CC.9-12.G.SRT.8 Use trigonometric ratios ... to solve right triangles in applied problems.

Vocabulary

adjacent   trigonometric ratio
opposite   sine
tangent   cosine

Prerequisites

Similar triangles

Math Background

Students work with three trigonometric ratios in this lesson: tangent, sine, and cosine. The tangent ratio is treated by itself first to give students a chance to focus on the conceptual underpinnings of right-triangle trigonometry. That is, right triangles with a given acute angle, $\angle A$, are all similar, so the ratio of the length of the leg opposite $\angle A$ to the length of the leg adjacent to $\angle A$ is constant for all such triangles. Once students understand this concept, they should realize that it also applies to other ratios, such as the ratio of the length of the leg opposite $\angle A$ to the length of the hypotenuse (the sine ratio) and the ratio of the length of the leg adjacent to $\angle A$ to the length of the hypotenuse (the cosine ratio).

INTRODUCE

Draw a right triangle on the board and point out the hypotenuse and the two legs. Label an acute angle as $\angle A$ and show students the leg opposite $\angle A$ and the leg adjacent to $\angle A$. Draw right triangles in different orientations and have students identify the leg opposite $\angle A$ and the leg adjacent to $\angle A$.

TEACH

1 EXPLORE

Materials: geometry software

Questioning Strategies

- What is $m\angle A$? Why? 30°; the angle is formed by a 30° rotation about point A.

- In $\triangle ABC$, which side is the hypotenuse? How do you know? $\overline{AB}$ is the hypotenuse because it is opposite the right angle, $\angle C$.

MATHEMATICAL PRACTICE | **Highlighting the Standards**

Standard 3 (Construct viable arguments and critique the reasoning of others) includes communicating results to others. The Explore offers an opportunity for students to formulate and describe a conjecture. As students share their findings, ask questions to help them refine their statements. For example, students may state their conjecture as, "The ratios are equal." Prompt students to be more specific ("What ratios?"). Coaching students so they communicate their findings clearly and precisely will help them meet this standard for mathematical practice.

Teaching Strategies

Students can use their calculators to find tangent ratios of acute angles. (Remind students to check that their calculators are in Degree mode.) Students may wonder where these values come from. Tell them that they can find approximate tangent ratios themselves. For example, to find 53°, use a protractor and straightedge to draw any right triangle that has a 53° angle. Then use a ruler to measure the length of the side opposite the 53° angle and the length of the side adjacent to the 53° angle. The ratio of these lengths gives an estimate for tan 53°.

8-2

Trigonometric Ratios
Going Deeper

Essential question: *How do you find the tangent, sine, and cosine ratios for acute angles in a right triangle?*

In this chapter, you will be working extensively with right triangles, so some new vocabulary will be helpful. Given a right triangle, △ABC, with a right angle at vertex C, the leg **adjacent** to ∠A is the leg that forms one side of ∠A. The leg **opposite** ∠A is the leg that does not form a side of ∠A.

CC.9-12.G.SRT.6

1 EXPLORE Investigating a Ratio in a Right Triangle

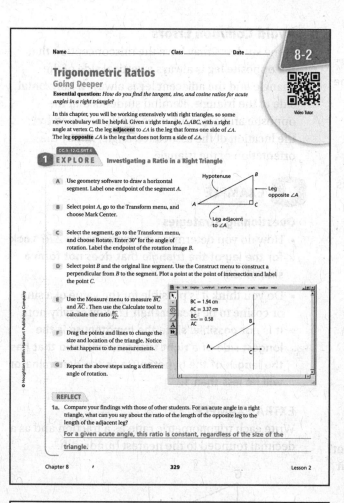

A   Use geometry software to draw a horizontal segment. Label one endpoint of the segment *A*.

B   Select point *A*, go to the Transform menu, and choose Mark Center.

C   Select the segment, go to the Transform menu, and choose Rotate. Enter 30° for the angle of rotation. Label the endpoint of the rotation image *B*.

D   Select point *B* and the original line segment. Use the Construct menu to construct a perpendicular from *B* to the segment. Plot a point at the point of intersection and label the point *C*.

E   Use the Measure menu to measure $\overline{BC}$ and $\overline{AC}$. Then use the Calculate tool to calculate the ratio $\frac{BC}{AC}$.

F   Drag the points and lines to change the size and location of the triangle. Notice what happens to the measurements.

G   Repeat the above steps using a different angle of rotation.

BC = 1.94 cm
AC = 3.37 cm
$\frac{BC}{AC}$ = 0.58

REFLECT

1a. Compare your findings with those of other students. For an acute angle in a right triangle, what can you say about the ratio of the length of the opposite leg to the length of the adjacent leg?

For a given acute angle, this ratio is constant, regardless of the size of the

triangle.

You may have discovered that in a right triangle the ratio of the length of the leg opposite an acute angle to the length of the leg adjacent to the angle is constant. You can use what you know about similarity to see why this is true.

Consider the right triangles △ABC and △DEF, in which ∠A ≅ ∠D, as shown. By the AA Similarity Criterion, △ABC ~ △DEF. This means the lengths of the sides of △DEF are each *k* times the lengths of the corresponding sides of △ABC.

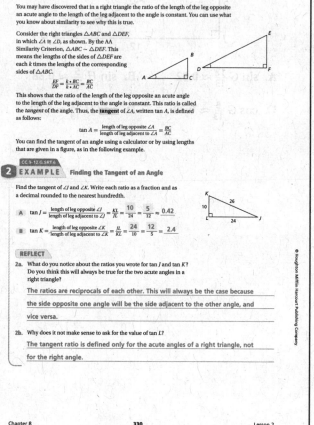

$$\frac{EF}{DF} = \frac{k \cdot BC}{k \cdot AC} = \frac{BC}{AC}$$

This shows that the ratio of the length of the leg opposite an acute angle to the length of the leg adjacent to the angle is constant. This ratio is called the *tangent* of the angle. Thus, the **tangent** of ∠A, written tan *A*, is defined as follows:

$$\tan A = \frac{\text{length of leg opposite } \angle A}{\text{length of leg adjacent to } \angle A} = \frac{BC}{AC}$$

You can find the tangent of an angle using a calculator or by using lengths that are given in a figure, as in the following example.

CC.9-12.G.SRT.6

2 EXAMPLE Finding the Tangent of an Angle

Find the tangent of ∠*J* and ∠*K*. Write each ratio as a fraction and as a decimal rounded to the nearest hundredth.

A $\tan J = \frac{\text{length of leg opposite } \angle J}{\text{length of leg adjacent to } \angle J} = \frac{KL}{JL} = \frac{10}{24} = \frac{5}{12} \approx 0.42$

B $\tan K = \frac{\text{length of leg opposite } \angle K}{\text{length of leg adjacent to } \angle K} = \frac{JL}{KL} = \frac{24}{10} = \frac{12}{5} = 2.4$

REFLECT

2a. What do you notice about the ratios you wrote for tan *J* and tan *K*? Do you think this will always be true for the two acute angles in a right triangle?

The ratios are reciprocals of each other. This will always be the case because

the side opposite one angle will be the side adjacent to the other angle, and

vice versa.

2b. Why does it not make sense to ask for the value of tan *L*?

The tangent ratio is defined only for the acute angles of a right triangle, not

for the right angle.

2 EXAMPLE

Questioning Strategies

- How do you identify the leg opposite ∠J? It is the leg that does not form a side of ∠J.

- How do you identify the leg adjacent to ∠J? It is the leg that forms a side of ∠J.

EXTRA EXAMPLE

Find the tangent of ∠M and ∠N. Write each ratio as a fraction and as a decimal rounded to the nearest hundredth.

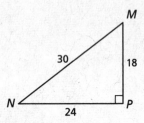

$\tan M = \frac{4}{3} \approx 1.33$; $\tan N = \frac{3}{4} = 0.75$

3 EXAMPLE

Questioning Strategies

- Is 14.9 feet a reasonable answer? Why or why not? It is reasonable because $\overline{BC}$ appears to be about twice as long as $\overline{AC}$, and $AC = 6$ ft.

EXTRA EXAMPLE

To help remove debris from the roof of a 30-foot building, workers use a straight chute, as shown in the figure. To the nearest tenth of a foot, how far from the base of the building does the chute touch the sidewalk? **12.7 ft**

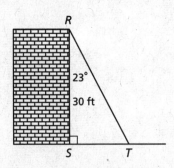

Avoid Common Errors

Some students may have the misconception that the opposite leg is always a vertical side of the triangle and the adjacent leg is always a horizontal side of the triangle. Remind students that the opposite and adjacent sides are determined by the location of the associated angle, not by the orientation of the triangle.

4 EXAMPLE

Questioning Strategies

- How do you determine the leg opposite ∠R? Look for the leg of the triangle that does not form a side of ∠R.

- Do you think it is possible for the value of a sine or cosine to be greater than 1? Why or why not? It is not possible; since the hypotenuse is the longest side of a right triangle, any ratio that has the length of the hypotenuse as the denominator will be less than 1.

EXTRA EXAMPLE

Write each trigonometric ratio as a fraction and as a decimal rounded to the nearest hundredth.

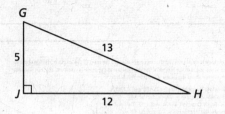

A. $\sin G \ \frac{12}{13} \approx 0.92$ **B.** $\sin H \ \frac{5}{13} \approx 0.38$

C. $\cos G \ \frac{5}{13} \approx 0.38$ **D.** $\cos H \ \frac{12}{13} \approx 0.92$

© Houghton Mifflin Harcourt Publishing Company

When you know the length of a leg of a right triangle and the measure of one of the acute angles, you can use the tangent to find the length of the other leg. This is especially useful in real-world problems.

CC.9-12.G.SRT.8

3 EXAMPLE Solving a Real-World Problem

A long ladder leans against a building and makes an angle of 68° with the ground. The base of the ladder is 6 feet from the building. To the nearest tenth of a foot, how far up the side of the building does the ladder reach?

A Write a tangent ratio that involves the unknown length, BC.

$$\tan A = \frac{\text{length of leg opposite } \angle A}{\text{length of leg adjacent to } \angle A} = \frac{BC}{6}$$

Use the fact that $m\angle A = 68°$ to write the equation as $\tan 68° = \frac{BC}{6}$.

B Solve for BC.

$6 \cdot \tan 68° = BC$ Multiply both sides by 6.

$6 \cdot \underline{2.475086853} = BC$ Use a calculator to find tan 68°. Do not round until the final step of the solution.

$\underline{14.9} \approx BC$ Multiply. Round to the nearest tenth.

So, the ladder reaches about $\underline{14.9\text{ feet}}$ up the side of the building.

REFLECT

3a. Why is it best to wait until the final step before rounding? What happens if you round the value of tan 68° to the nearest tenth before multiplying?

Rounding in the last step gives a more accurate answer. Rounding the tangent

to the nearest tenth before multiplying gives an answer of 15 feet.

3b. A student claims that it is possible to solve the problem using the tangent of $\angle B$. Do you agree or disagree? If it is possible, show the solution. If it is not possible, explain why not.

Agree; by the Triangle Sum Theorem, $m\angle B = 22°$, so tan $22° = \frac{6}{BC}$ and

$BC = \frac{6}{\tan 22°} \approx 14.9$.

© Houghton Mifflin Harcourt Publishing Company

A **trigonometric ratio** is a ratio of two sides of a right triangle. You have already seen one trigonometric ratio, the tangent. It is also possible to define two additional trigonometric ratios, the sine and the cosine, that involve the hypotenuse of a right triangle.

The **sine** of $\angle A$, written sin A, is defined as follows:

$$\sin A = \frac{\text{length of leg opposite } \angle A}{\text{length of hypotenuse}} = \frac{BC}{AB}$$

The **cosine** of $\angle A$, written cos A, is defined as follows:

$$\cos A = \frac{\text{length of leg adjacent to } \angle A}{\text{length of hypotenuse}} = \frac{AC}{AB}$$

CC.9-12.G.SRT.6

4 EXAMPLE Finding the Sine and Cosine of an Angle

Write each trigonometric ratio as a fraction and as a decimal rounded to the nearest hundredth.

A $\sin R = \frac{\text{length of leg opposite } \angle R}{\text{length of hypotenuse}} = \frac{PQ}{RQ} = \frac{20}{29} \approx 0.69$

B $\sin Q = \frac{\text{length of leg opposite } \angle Q}{\text{length of hypotenuse}} = \frac{RP}{RQ} = \frac{21}{29} \approx \underline{0.72}$

C $\cos R = \frac{\text{length of leg adjacent to } \angle R}{\text{length of hypotenuse}} = \frac{21}{29} \approx \underline{0.72}$

D $\cos Q = \frac{\text{length of leg adjacent to } \angle Q}{\text{length of hypotenuse}} = \frac{20}{29} \approx \underline{0.69}$

REFLECT

4a. What do you notice about the sines and cosines you found? Do you think this relationship will be true for any pair of acute angles in a right triangle? Explain.

sin R = cos Q and sin Q = cos R; this relationship always holds because the leg

opposite one acute angle is the leg adjacent to the other acute angle, so the

sine of one angle is the cosine of the other.

© Houghton Mifflin Harcourt Publishing Company

© Houghton Mifflin Harcourt Publishing Company

5 EXAMPLE

Questioning Strategies

- What does it mean for two angles to be complementary? **The sum of their measures is 90°.**

- How can you check your answer? **Use a calculator to check that cos 33° ≈ 0.839.**

EXTRA EXAMPLE

Given that $\cos 14° \approx 0.970$, write the cosine of a complementary angle.

$\sin 76° \approx 0.970$

6 EXAMPLE

Questioning Strategies

- Can you use either the sine or cosine ratio to find x? Explain. **Yes; you can solve $\sin 8° = \frac{x}{16}$ or you can solve $\cos 82° = \frac{x}{16}$.**

- Once you know that x is approximately 2.2 feet, how can you use the tangent ratio to find y? **Solve $\tan 8° = \frac{2.2}{y}$.**

EXTRA EXAMPLE

A 10-foot access ramp leads to the top of a platform, as shown in the figure. The ramp makes an angle of 6° with the ground. To the nearest tenth of a foot, what is the height of the platform? How far does the ramp extend in front of the platform?

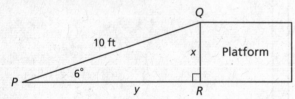

1.0 ft; 9.9 ft

MATHEMATICAL PRACTICE

Highlighting the Standards

You can address Standard 6 (Attend to precision) as you discuss Example 6. Ask students how their results would have been different if they had evaluated 16 sin 8° by evaluating sin 8°, rounding the result, and then multiplying by 16. Remind students that they will get the most accurate result by rounding *only* in the final step of the solution. This means they should evaluate an expression like 16 sin 8° by entering the entire expression into their calculator and then rounding the result.

You may have discovered a relationship between the sines and cosines of the acute angles in a right triangle. In particular, if $\angle A$ and $\angle B$ are the acute angles in a right triangle, then $\sin A = \cos B$ and $\sin B = \cos A$.

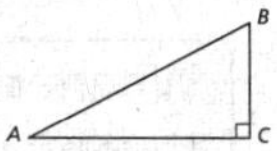

Note that the acute angles in a right triangle are complementary. The above observation leads to a more general fact: the sine of an angle is equal to the cosine of its complement, and the cosine of an angle is equal to the sine of its complement.

5 EXAMPLE CC.9-12.G.SRT.?   Using Complementary Angles

Given that $\sin 57° \approx 0.839$, write the cosine of a complementary angle.

A Find the measure x of an angle that is complementary to a 57° angle.

$x + 57° = 90°$, so $x = \underline{\quad 33° \quad}$

B Use the fact that the cosine of an angle is equal to the sine of its complement.

$\cos \underline{\quad 33° \quad} \approx 0.839$

Given that $\cos 60° = 0.5$, write the sine of a complementary angle.

C Find the measure y of an angle that is complementary to a 60° angle.

$y + 60° = 90°$, so $y = \underline{\quad 30° \quad}$

D Use the fact that the sine of an angle is equal to the cosine of its complement.

$\sin \underline{\quad 30° \quad} = 0.5$

REFLECT

5a. Is it possible to find $m\angle J$ in the figure? Explain.

$m\angle J \approx 57°$ since $\sin J = \frac{839}{1000} = 0.839$ and it is given

that $\sin 57° \approx 0.839$.

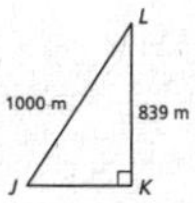

5b. What can you conclude about the sine and cosine of 45° ? Explain.

$\sin 45° = \cos 45°$ since a 45° angle is complementary to itself.

5c. Is it possible for the sine of an angle to equal 1? Why or why not?

No; the hypotenuse is always longer than the legs of a right triangle, so

the ratio of length of the opposite leg to the hypotenuse cannot equal 1.

---

6 EXAMPLE CC.9-12.G.SRT.8   Solving a Real-World Problem

A loading dock at a factory has a 16-foot ramp in front of it, as shown in the figure. The ramp makes an angle of 8° with the ground. To the nearest tenth of a foot, what is the height of the loading dock? How far does the ramp extend in front of the loading dock? (The figure is not drawn to scale, so you cannot measure it to solve the problem.)

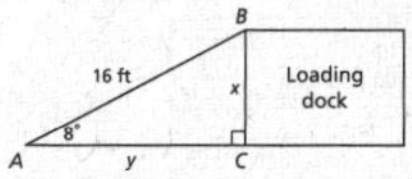

A Find the height x of the loading dock.

$\sin A = \frac{\text{length of leg opposite } \angle A}{\text{length of hypotenuse}} = \frac{x}{16}$, so $\sin 8° = \frac{x}{16}$.

Solve the equation for x.

$x = 16 \sin 8°$

Use a calculator to evaluate the expression, then round.

$x \approx \underline{\quad 2.2 \quad}$

So, the height of the loading dock is about $\underline{\quad 2.2 \text{ ft} \quad}$.

B Find the distance y that the ramp extends in front of the loading dock.

$\cos A = \frac{\text{length of leg adjacent to } \angle A}{\text{length of hypotenuse}} = \frac{y}{16}$, so $\cos 8° = \frac{y}{16}$.

Solve the equation for y.

$y = 16 \cos 8°$

Use a calculator to evaluate the expression, then round.

$y \approx \underline{\quad 15.8 \quad}$

So, the distance the ramp extends in front of the loading dock is about $\underline{\quad 15.8 \text{ ft} \quad}$.

REFLECT

6a. A student claimed that she found the height of the loading dock by using the cosine. Explain her thinking.

Since $\angle A$ and $\angle B$ are complementary, $m\angle B = 82°$. Then $\cos 82° = \frac{x}{16}$ and

$x = 16 \cos 82° \approx 2.2$.

6b. Suppose the owner of the factory decides to build a new ramp for the loading dock so that the new ramp makes an angle of 5° with the ground. How far will this ramp extend from the loading dock? Explain.

Approximately 25.1 ft; in this case, $\tan 5° = \frac{2.2}{y}$, so $y = \frac{2.2}{\tan 5°}$.

Evaluating the expression shows that $y \approx 25.1$.

© Houghton Mifflin Harcourt Publishing Company

Essential Question

How do you find the tangent, sine, and cosine ratios for acute angles in a right triangle?

The tangent of an acute angle in a right triangle is the ratio of the length of the leg opposite the angle to the length of the leg adjacent to the angle. The sine is the ratio of the length of the leg opposite the angle to the length of the hypotenuse. The cosine is the ratio of the length of the leg adjacent to the angle to the length of the hypotenuse.

Summarize

Have students make a graphic organizer to summarize the sine, cosine, and tangent ratios. A sample is shown below.

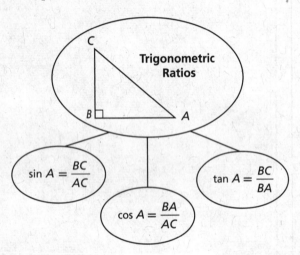

Where skills are taught	Where skills are practiced
2 EXAMPLE	EXS. 1–3
3 EXAMPLE	EXS. 4–8
4 EXAMPLE	EXS. 9–11
5 EXAMPLE	EXS. 12–13
6 EXAMPLE	EXS. 14–17

Exercise 18: Students use reasoning skills to critique other students' work.

PRACTICE

Find the tangent of ∠A and ∠B. Write each ratio as a fraction and as a decimal rounded to the nearest hundredth.

1.

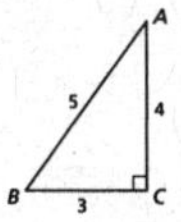

$\tan A = \frac{3}{4} = 0.75;$

$\tan B = \frac{4}{3} \approx 1.33$

2.

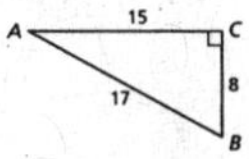

$\tan A = \frac{8}{15} \approx 0.53;$

$\tan B = \frac{15}{8} \approx 1.88$

3.

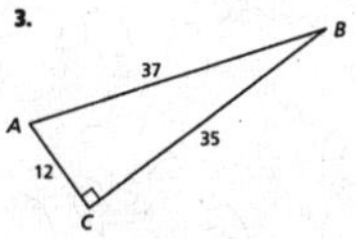

$\tan A = \frac{35}{12} \approx 2.92;$

$\tan B = \frac{12}{35} \approx 0.34$

Find the value of x to the nearest tenth.

4.

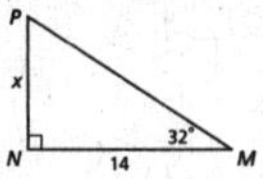

8.7

5.

5.5

6.

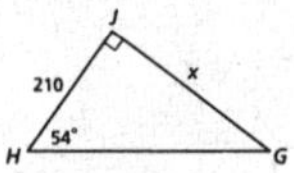

289.0

7. A hiker whose eyes are 5.5 feet above ground stands 25 feet from the base of a redwood tree. She looks up at an angle of 71° to see the top of the tree. To the nearest tenth of a foot, what is the height of the tree?

78.1 ft

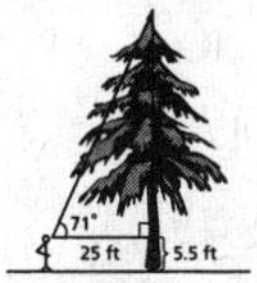

8. **Error Analysis** To find the distance XY across a large rock formation, a student stands facing one endpoint of the formation, backs away from it at a right angle for 20 meters, and then turns 55° to look at the other endpoint of the formation. The student's calculations are shown. Critique the student's work.

The student set up the tangent ratio incorrectly.

It should be $\tan 55° = \frac{XY}{20}$, which gives $XY \approx 28.6$.

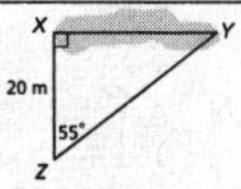

$\tan 55° = \frac{20}{XY}$

$XY \cdot \tan 55° = 20$

$XY = \frac{20}{\tan 55°} \approx 14.0 \text{ m}$

Find the given trigonometric ratios. Write each ratio as a fraction and as a decimal rounded to the nearest hundredth.

9. sin R, cos R

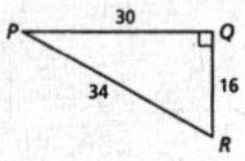

$\sin R = \frac{30}{34} \approx 0.88;$

$\cos R = \frac{16}{34} \approx 0.47$

10. cos D, cos E

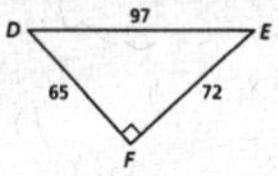

$\cos D = \frac{65}{97} \approx 0.67;$

$\cos E = \frac{72}{97} \approx 0.74$

11. sin M, sin N

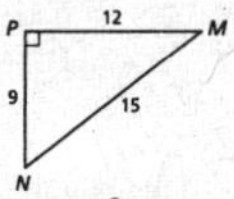

$\sin M = \frac{9}{15} = 0.6;$

$\sin N = \frac{12}{15} = 0.8$

12. Given that sin 15° ≈ 0.259, write the cosine of a complementary angle. cos 75° ≈ 0.259

13. Given that cos 62° ≈ 0.469, write the sine of a complementary angle. sin 28° ≈ 0.469

Find the value of x to the nearest tenth.

14.

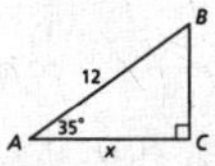

9.8

15.

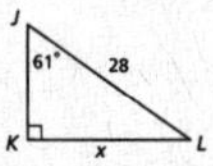

24.5

16.

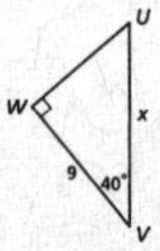

11.7

17. You are building a skateboard ramp from a piece of wood that is 3.1 meters long. You want the ramp to make an angle of 25° with the ground. To the nearest tenth of a meter, what is the length of the ramp's base? What is its height?

Length of base: 2.8 m; height: 1.3 m

18. **Error Analysis** Three students were asked to find the value of x in the figure. The equations they used are shown at right. Which students, if any, used a correct equation? Explain the other students' errors and then find the value of x.

Jamila's equation is correct. Lee should have

written $\sin 57° = \frac{15}{x}$. Tyler's equation has two errors;

he should have written $\cos 33° = \frac{15}{x}$.

$x \approx 17.9$

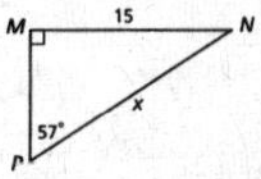

Lee's equation: $\sin 57° = \frac{x}{15}$

Jamila's equation: $\cos 33° = \frac{15}{x}$

Tyler's equation: $\sin 33° = \frac{x}{15}$

ADDITIONAL PRACTICE AND PROBLEM SOLVING

Assign these pages to help your students practice and apply important lesson concepts. For additional exercises, see the Student Edition.

Answers

Additional Practice

1. $\frac{7}{25}$; 0.28	**2.** $\frac{7}{25}$; 0.28
3. $\frac{24}{7}$; 3.43	**4.** $\frac{24}{25}$; 0.96
5. $\frac{24}{25}$; 0.96	**6.** $\frac{7}{24}$; 0.29
7. $\frac{1}{2}$	**8.** $\frac{\sqrt{3}}{2}$
9. 1	**10.** $\frac{\sqrt{3}}{3}$
11. $\frac{\sqrt{2}}{2}$	**12.** $\sqrt{3}$
13. 0.90	**14.** 0.53
15. 0.27	**16.** 14.03 in.
17. 57.36 cm	**18.** 0.36 mi
19. 8.68 km	**20.** 95.41 yd
21. 3.18 ft	

Problem Solving

1. 4.80 ft	**2.** 9.49 cm
3. 61.4 cm	**4.** 19 in^2
5. C	**6.** G
7. A	**8.** F

Name _____ Class _____ Date _____

8-2

Additional Practice

Use the figure for Exercises 1–6. Write each trigonometric ratio as a simplified fraction and as a decimal rounded to the nearest hundredth.

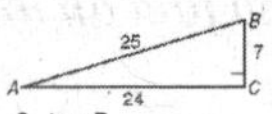

1. sin A

2. cos B

3. tan B

_____   _____   _____

4. sin B

5. cos A

6. tan A

_____   _____   _____

Use special right triangles to write each trigonometric ratio as a simplified fraction.

7. sin 30° _____

8. cos 30° _____

9. tan 45° _____

10. tan 30° _____

11. cos 45° _____

12. tan 60° _____

Use a calculator to find each trigonometric ratio. Round to the nearest hundredth.

13. sin 64° _____

14. cos 58° _____

15. tan 15° _____

Find each length. Round to the nearest hundredth.

16.

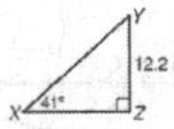

XZ _____

17.

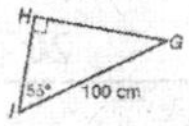

HI _____

18.

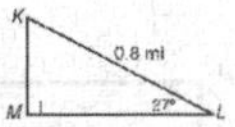

KM _____

19.

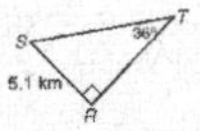

ST _____

20.

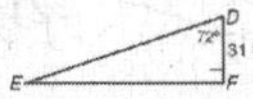

EF _____

21.

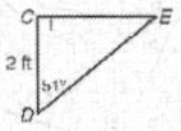

DE _____

Problem Solving

1. A ramp is used to load a 4-wheeler onto a truck bed that is 3 feet above the ground. The angle that the ramp makes with the ground is 32°. What is the horizontal distance covered by the ramp? Round to the nearest hundredth.

_____

2. Find the perimeter of the triangle. Round to the nearest hundredth.

_____

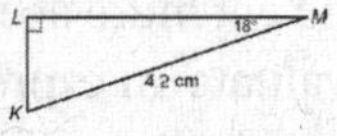

3. A right triangle has an angle that measures 55°. The leg adjacent to this angle has a length of 43 cm. What is the length of the other leg of the triangle? Round to the nearest tenth.

_____

4. The hypotenuse of a right triangle measures 9 inches, and one of the acute angles measures 36°. What is the area of the triangle? Round to the nearest square inch.

_____

Choose the best answer.

5. A 14-foot ladder makes a 62° angle with the ground. To the nearest foot, how far up the house does the ladder reach?

   A 6 ft

   B 7 ft

   C 12 ft

   D 16 ft

6. To the nearest inch, what is the length of the springboard shown below?

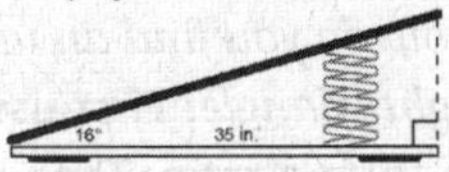

   F 24 in.

   G 36 in.

   H 38 in.

   J 127 in.

7. What is EF, the measure of the longest side of the sail on the model? Round to the nearest inch.

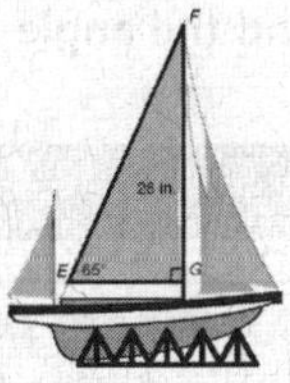

   A 31 in.

   B 35 in.

   C 40 in.

   D 60 in.

8. Right triangle ABC is graphed on the coordinate plane and has vertices at A(−1, 3), B(0, 5), and C(4, 3). What is the measure of ∠C to the nearest degree?

   F 27°

   G 29°

   H 32°

   J 43°

Solving Right Triangles
Going Deeper

Essential question: *How do you find an unknown angle measure in a right triangle?*

COMMON CORE **Standards for Mathematical Content**

CC.9-12.G.SRT.8 Use trigonometric ratios to solve right triangles ...

Vocabulary

inverse trigonometric ratio

Prerequisites

Trigonometric ratios

Math Background

When the lengths of two sides of a right triangle are known, the triangle is completely determined. The length of the third side can be found using the Pythagorean Theorem, and the measure of either acute angle can be found using an inverse trigonometric ratio.

INTRODUCE

Relate inverse trigonometric ratios to inverse operations. For example, the doubling operation takes the number 5 and gives the number 10, so the "inverse doubling" (or halving) operation takes the number 10 and gives the number 5.

TEACH

1 EXAMPLE

Questioning Strategies

• Is it possible to find m∠K before finding m∠J? If so, how? yes; m∠K = $\tan^{-1}\left(\frac{35}{12}\right)$.

EXTRA EXAMPLE

Find m∠A. Round to the nearest degree.

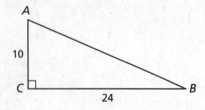

67°

2 EXAMPLE

Questioning Strategies

• If you want to find m∠S instead of m∠R, what inverse trigonometric ratio would you use? the inverse cosine ratio

EXTRA EXAMPLE

Find m∠F. Round to the nearest degree.

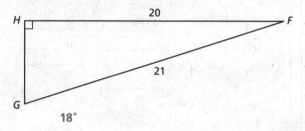

18°

> **MATHEMATICAL PRACTICE** **Highlighting the Standards**
>
> To address Standard 5 (Use appropriate tools strategically), discuss the use of calculators for finding inverse trigonometric ratios. In particular, students should recognize that they will get more accurate results if they directly evaluate an expression like $\tan^{-1}\left(\frac{1}{3}\right)$ rather than finding a decimal approximation for the fraction $\frac{1}{3}$, rounding, and evaluating $\tan^{-1}(0.33)$.

CLOSE

Essential Question

How do you find an unknown angle measure in a right triangle? First use two known side lengths to form a ratio. Then use the appropriate inverse trigonometric ratio to find the angle measure.

PRACTICE

Where skills are taught	Where skills are practiced
1 EXAMPLE	EXS. 1–6
2 EXAMPLE	EXS. 1–6

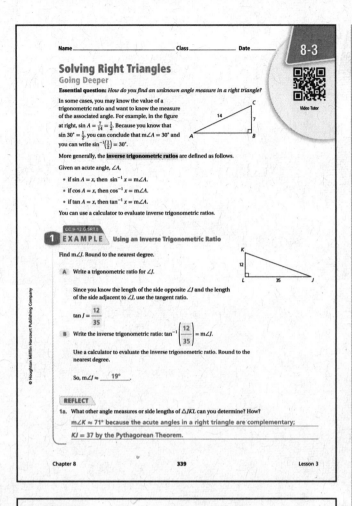

Name_____ Class_____ Date_____

8-3

Solving Right Triangles
Going Deeper

Essential question: *How do you find an unknown angle measure in a right triangle?*

In some cases, you may know the value of a trigonometric ratio and want to know the measure of the associated angle. For example, in the figure at right, $\sin A = \frac{7}{14} = \frac{1}{2}$. Because you know that $\sin 30° = \frac{1}{2}$, you can conclude that $m\angle A = 30°$ and you can write $\sin^{-1}\left(\frac{1}{2}\right) = 30°$.

More generally, the **inverse trigonometric ratios** are defined as follows.

Given an acute angle, $\angle A$,

- if $\sin A = x$, then $\sin^{-1} x = m\angle A$.
- if $\cos A = x$, then $\cos^{-1} x = m\angle A$.
- if $\tan A = x$, then $\tan^{-1} x = m\angle A$.

You can use a calculator to evaluate inverse trigonometric ratios.

CC.9-12.G.SRT.8
1 EXAMPLE   Using an Inverse Trigonometric Ratio

Find $m\angle J$. Round to the nearest degree.

A Write a trigonometric ratio for $\angle J$.

Since you know the length of the side opposite $\angle J$ and the length of the side adjacent to $\angle J$, use the tangent ratio.

$$\tan J = \frac{12}{35}$$

B Write the inverse trigonometric ratio: $\tan^{-1}\left(\dfrac{12}{35}\right) = m\angle J$.

Use a calculator to evaluate the inverse trigonometric ratio. Round to the nearest degree.

So, $m\angle J \approx$ ___19°___.

REFLECT

1a. What other angle measures or side lengths of $\triangle JKL$ can you determine? How?

$m\angle K \approx 71°$ because the acute angles in a right triangle are complementary;

$KJ = 37$ by the Pythagorean Theorem.

Chapter 8   339   Lesson 3

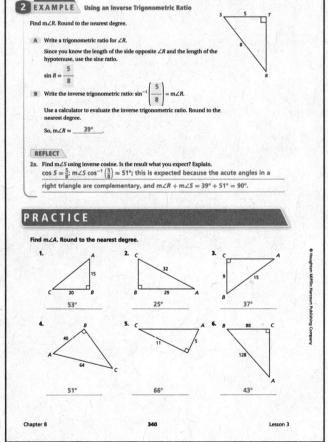

CC.9-12.G.SRT.8
2 EXAMPLE   Using an Inverse Trigonometric Ratio

Find $m\angle R$. Round to the nearest degree.

A Write a trigonometric ratio for $\angle R$.

Since you know the length of the side opposite $\angle R$ and the length of the hypotenuse, use the sine ratio.

$$\sin R = \frac{5}{8}$$

B Write the inverse trigonometric ratio: $\sin^{-1}\left(\dfrac{5}{8}\right) = m\angle R$.

Use a calculator to evaluate the inverse trigonometric ratio. Round to the nearest degree.

So, $m\angle R \approx$ ___39°___.

REFLECT

2a. Find $m\angle S$ using inverse cosine. Is the result what you expect? Explain.

$\cos S = \frac{5}{8}$; $m\angle S \cos^{-1}\left(\frac{5}{8}\right) \approx 51°$; this is expected because the acute angles in a

right triangle are complementary, and $m\angle R + m\angle S = 39° + 51° = 90°$.

PRACTICE

Find $m\angle A$. Round to the nearest degree.

1.   2.   3.
___53°___   ___25°___   ___37°___

4.   5.   6.
___51°___   ___66°___   ___43°___

Chapter 8   340   Lesson 3

ADDITIONAL PRACTICE AND PROBLEM SOLVING

Assign these pages to help your students practice and apply important lesson concepts. For additional exercises, see the Student Edition.

Answers

Additional Practice

1. $\angle 1$
2. $\angle 1$
3. $\angle 2$
4. $\angle 2$
5. $\angle 2$
6. $\angle 1$
7. 55°
8. 24°
9. 79°
10. 22°
11. 77°
12. 6°
13. $AB = 7.74$ in.; $m\angle A = 57°$; $m\angle B = 33°$
14. $EF = 2.73$ m; $m\angle D = 65°$; $m\angle F = 25°$
15. $GH = 7.64$ ft; $GI = 7.91$; $m\angle I = 44°$
16. $KL = 2.71$ yd; $JK = 2.84$ yd; $m\angle K = 17°$
17. $QP = 11.18$ cm; $m\angle Q = 42°$; $m\angle R = 48°$
18. $ST = 3.58$ yd; $m\angle S = 12°$; $m\angle T = 78°$
19. $BC = 8.60$; $BD = 7$; $CD = 5$; $m\angle B = 36°$; $m\angle C = 54°$; $m\angle D = 90°$
20. $LM = 2$; $LN = 7$; $MN = 7.28$; $m\angle L = 90°$; $m\angle M = 74°$; $m\angle N = 16°$
21. $XY = 1$; $XZ = 1.41$; $YZ = 1$; $m\angle X = 45°$; $m\angle Y = 90°$; $m\angle Z = 45°$

Problem Solving

1. 16°
2. 22° to 27°
3. 64°
4. 34.9 ft
5. A
6. G
7. D
8. F

8-3

Additional Practice

Use the given trigonometric ratio to determine which angle of the triangle is ∠A.

1. $\sin A = \dfrac{8}{17}$ _____

2. $\cos A = \dfrac{15}{17}$ _____

3. $\tan A = \dfrac{15}{8}$ _____

4. $\sin A = \dfrac{15}{17}$ _____

5. $\cos A = \dfrac{8}{17}$ _____

6. $\tan A = \dfrac{8}{15}$ _____

Use a calculator to find each angle measure to the nearest degree.

7. $\sin^{-1}(0.82)$ _____

8. $\cos^{-1}\left(\dfrac{11}{12}\right)$ _____

9. $\tan^{-1}(5.03)$ _____

10. $\sin^{-1}\left(\dfrac{3}{8}\right)$ _____

11. $\cos^{-1}(0.23)$ _____

12. $\tan^{-1}\left(\dfrac{1}{9}\right)$ _____

Find the unknown measures. Round lengths to the nearest hundredth and angle measures to the nearest degree.

13.

14.

15.

16.

17.

18.

For each triangle, find all three side lengths to the nearest hundredth and all three angle measures to the nearest degree.

19. B(−2, −4), C(3, 3), D(−2, 3)

20. L(−1, −6), M(1, −6), N(−1, 1)

21. X(−4, 5), Y(−3, 5), Z(−3, 4)

© Houghton Mifflin Harcourt Publishing Company

Problem Solving

1. A road has a grade of 28.4%. This means that the road rises 28.4 ft over a horizontal distance of 100 ft. What angle does the hill make with a horizontal line? Round to the nearest degree.

_____

2. Pet ramps for loading larger dogs into vehicles usually have slopes between $\dfrac{2}{5}$ and $\dfrac{1}{2}$. What is the range of angle measures that most pet ramps make with a horizontal line? Round to the nearest degree.

_____

Use the side view of a water slide for Exercises 3 and 4.

The ladder, represented by $\overline{AB}$, is 17 feet long.

3. What is the measure of angle A, the angle that the ladder makes with a horizontal line?

_____

4. What is BC, the length of the slide? Round to the nearest tenth of a foot.

_____

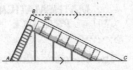

Choose the best answer.

5. Janelle sets her treadmill grade to 6%. What is the angle that the treadmill surface makes with a horizontal line? Round to the nearest degree.

   A 3°   C 12°

   B 4°   D 31°

6. The coordinates of the vertices of △RST are R(3, 3), S(8, 3), and T(8, −6). What is the measures of angle T? Round to the nearest degree.

   F 18°   H 61°

   G 29°   J 65°

7. If cos A = 0.28, which angle in the triangles below is ∠A?

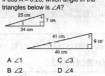

   A ∠1   C ∠3

   B ∠2   D ∠4

8. Find the measure of the acute angle formed by the graph of $y = \dfrac{3}{4}x$ and the x-axis. Round to the nearest degree.

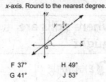

   F 37°   H 49°

   G 41°   J 53°

© Houghton Mifflin Harcourt Publishing Company

Angles of Elevation and Depression
Going Deeper

Essential question: *How can you use trigonometric ratios to solve problems involving angles of elevation and depression?*

© Houghton Mifflin Harcourt Publishing Company

COMMON CORE Standards for Mathematical Content

CC.9-12.G.SRT.8 Use trigonometric ratios ... to solve right triangles in applied problems.

Prerequisites

Angles formed by parallel lines and a transversal
Trigonometric ratios

Math Background

The problems presented in this lesson are similar to those in previous lessons involving trigonometric ratios. The difference here is that students must recognize the role that the angle of elevation or depression plays in forming a right triangle.

INTRODUCE

Begin the lesson by showing students how to create a simple device for measuring an angle of elevation or depression. The device consists of a semicircular protractor with a weighted string attached to the center of the circle. A distant object is sighted along the protractor's straight edge, and the string shows the angle of tilt (measured from the 90° mark).

TEACH

1 EXAMPLE

Questioning Strategies

• What three quantities will your equation involving a trigonometric ratio contain?
120 ft, 5°, and *x*

• Which trigonometric ratio involves 120 and *x*?
tangent

EXTRA EXAMPLE

A sightseer at the top of a 145-foot-tall cliff spots a small boat some distance away from the base of the cliff. The angle of depression is 8°. What is the horizontal distance between the base of the cliff and the boat? Round to the nearest foot.
1032 ft

2 EXAMPLE

Questioning Strategies

• How is a problem involving an angle of elevation different from one involving an angle of depression? The acute angle needed for the right triangle is given already. It doesn't need to be found using alternate interior angles.

EXTRA EXAMPLE

The line of sight to an airplane forms a 25° angle with the ground when the plane is 2400 feet above ground. How far is the viewer from the point on the ground directly below the plane? 5147 ft

CLOSE

Essential Question

How can you use trigonometric ratios to solve problems involving angles of elevation and depression? Since an acute angle in a right triangle is given or can be found and the length of a leg is also given, the tangent ratio can be used to find the length of the other leg.

Summarize

Have students write a problem involving an angle of elevation or depression. Students can work with a partner to solve each other's problem.

MATHEMATICAL PRACTICE	Highlighting the Standards

The exercises address Standard 4 (Model with mathematics). Drawing a diagram that accurately captures the given information is crucial for these problems.

PRACTICE

Where skills are taught	Where skills are practiced
1 EXAMPLE	EXS. 2, 3
2 EXAMPLE	EXS. 1, 4

Name _____ Class _____ Date _____

8-4

Angles of Elevation and Depression
Going Deeper

Essential question: *How can you use trigonometric ratios to solve problems involving angles of elevation and depression?*

The diagram shows what is meant by **angle of elevation** and **angle of depression**. These angles depend on your viewpoint, but because they are both measured relative to parallel horizontal lines, they are equal in measure.

Video Tutor

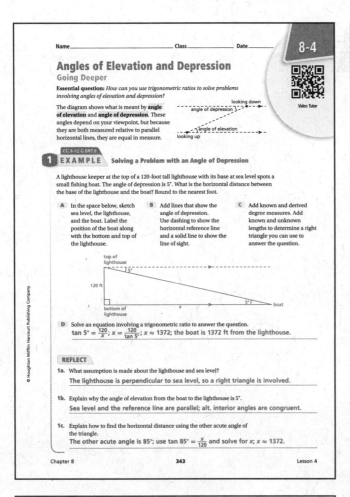

CC.9-12.G.SRT.8

1 EXAMPLE Solving a Problem with an Angle of Depression

A lighthouse keeper at the top of a 120-foot tall lighthouse with its base at sea level spots a small fishing boat. The angle of depression is 5°. What is the horizontal distance between the base of the lighthouse and the boat? Round to the nearest foot.

A In the space below, sketch sea level, the lighthouse, and the boat. Label the position of the boat along with the bottom and top of the lighthouse.

B Add lines that show the angle of depression. Use dashing to show the horizontal reference line and a solid line to show the line of sight.

C Add known and derived degree measures. Add known and unknown lengths to determine a right triangle you can use to answer the question.

D Solve an equation involving a trigonometric ratio to answer the question.
$\tan 5° = \frac{120}{x}$; $x = \frac{120}{\tan 5°}$; $x \approx 1372$; the boat is 1372 ft from the lighthouse.

REFLECT

1a. What assumption is made about the lighthouse and sea level?
The lighthouse is perpendicular to sea level, so a right triangle is involved.

1b. Explain why the angle of elevation from the boat to the lighthouse is 5°.
Sea level and the reference line are parallel; alt. interior angles are congruent.

1c. Explain how to find the horizontal distance using the other acute angle of the triangle.
The other acute angle is 85°; use $\tan 85° = \frac{x}{120}$ and solve for x; $x \approx 1372$.

Chapter 8   343   Lesson 4

CC.9-12.G.SRT.8

2 EXAMPLE Solving a Problem with an Angle of Elevation

A viewer watches a hot air balloon ascend. The viewer's line of sight forms a 20° angle with the ground when the balloon is 1200 feet above ground. How far is the viewer from where the balloon started its ascent?

A On the diagram at the right, add information that can be used to answer the question.

Show the right triangle and the angle of elevation. Label the diagram with known measures and use a variable for the unknown.

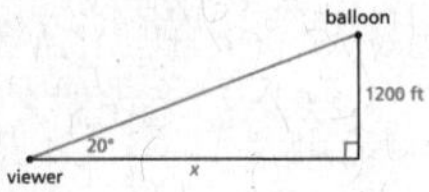

balloon

1200 ft

20°

viewer   x

B Write an equation you can use in this situation.
$\tan 20° = \frac{1200}{x}$

C Solve the equation to answer the question. Show your work.
$x = \frac{1200}{\tan 20°}$; $x \approx 3297$; the viewer is about 3297 feet from the starting point.

REFLECT

2a. Why is the sine ratio or cosine ratio not used in solving this Example?
Those ratios require the length of the hypotenuse, which is not given.

PRACTICE

Use a trigonometric ratio to solve. Give answers to the nearest foot.

1. A spectator looks up at an angle of 25° to the top of a building 500 feet away. How tall is the building?
$\tan 25° = \frac{x}{500}$; 233 ft

2. A worker looks down from the top of a bridge 240 feet above a river at a barge. The angle of depression is 60°. How far is the barge from the base of the bridge?
$\tan 60° = \frac{240}{x}$; 139 ft

3. A helicopter pilot hovers 500 feet above a straight and flat road. The pilot looks down at two cars using 24° and 28° as angles of depression. How far apart are the cars? Explain your work.
Let x and y be the distances from the cars to the point on the road below the helicopter; $\tan 24° = \frac{500}{x}$; $x \approx 1123$ ft; $\tan 28° = \frac{500}{y}$; $y \approx 940$ ft; $x - y \approx 183$ ft.

4. The string of a flying kite is 360 feet long and makes a 40° angle with the ground. Find the altitude of the kite and the horizontal distance between the kite flyer and the point on the ground directly below the kite.
altitude: $\sin 40° = \frac{y}{360}$; $v \approx 231$ ft; horizontal distance: $\cos 40° = \frac{h}{360}$; $h \approx 276$ ft

Chapter 8   344   Lesson 4

© Houghton Mifflin Harcourt Publishing Company

ADDITIONAL PRACTICE AND PROBLEM SOLVING

Assign these pages to help your students practice and apply important lesson concepts. For additional exercises, see the Student Edition.

Answers

Additional Practice

1. angle of elevation
2. angle of depression
3. angle of depression
4. angle of elevation
5. 34 ft 2 in.
6. 37 ft 1 in.
7. 31 ft 10 in.
8. 1.8 m
9. 65°
10. Mr. Shea lives above Lindsey.

Problem Solving

1. 120 ft
2. 154 m
3. 57 ft
4. A
5. H
6. C
7. J

Additional Practice

Marco breeds and trains homing pigeons on the roof of his building. Classify each angle as an angle of elevation or an angle of depression.

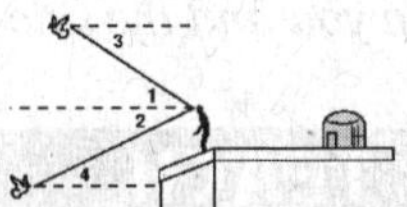

1. ∠1 _____

2. ∠2 _____

3. ∠3 _____

4. ∠4 _____

To attract customers to his car dealership, Frank tethers a large red balloon to the ground. In Exercises 5–7, give answers in feet and inches to the nearest inch. (Note: Assume the cord that attaches to the balloon makes a straight segment.)

5. The sun is directly overhead. The shadow of the balloon falls 14 feet 6 inches from the tether. Frank sights an angle of elevation of 67°. Find the height of the balloon. _____

6. Find the length of the cord that tethers the balloon. _____

7. The wind picks up and the angle of elevation changes to 59°. Find the height of the balloon. _____

Lindsey shouts down to Pete from her third-story window.

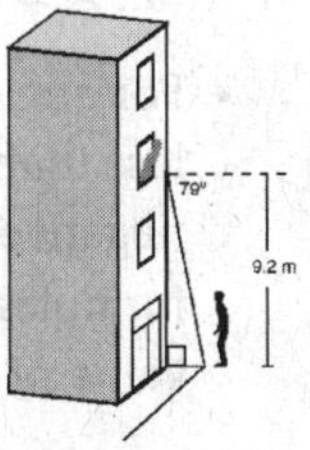

8. Lindsey is 9.2 meters up, and the angle of depression from Lindsey to Pete is 79°. Find the distance from Pete to the base of the building to the nearest tenth of a meter.

_____

9. To see Lindsey better, Pete walks out into the street so he is 4.3 meters from the base of the building. Find the angle of depression from Lindsey to Pete to the nearest degree.

_____

10. Mr. Shea lives in Lindsey's building. While Pete is still out in the street, Mr. Shea leans out his window to tell Lindsey and Pete to stop all the shouting. The angle of elevation from Pete to Mr. Shea is 72°. Tell whether Mr. Shea lives above or below Lindsey.

_____

Problem Solving

1. Mayuko is sitting 30 feet high in a football stadium. The angle of depression to the center of the field is 14°. What is the horizontal distance between Mayuko and the center of the field? Round to the nearest foot.

_____

2. A surveyor 50 meters from the base of a cliff measures the angle of elevation to the top of the cliff as 72°. What is the height of the cliff? Round to the nearest meter.

_____

3. Shane is 61 feet high on a ride at an amusement park. The angle of depression to the park entrance is 42°, and the angle of depression to his friends standing below is 80°. How far from the entrance are his friends standing? Round to the nearest foot.

_____

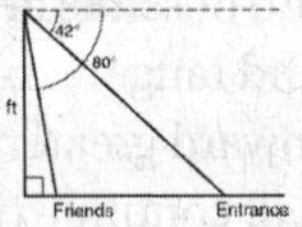

Choose the best answer.

4. The figure shows a person parasailing. What is x, the height of the parasailer, to the nearest foot?

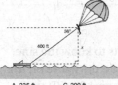

A 235 ft   C 290 ft
B 245 ft   D 323 ft

5. The elevation angle from the ground to the object to which the satellite dish is pointed is 32°. If x = 2.5 meters, which is the best estimate for y, the height of the satellite stand?

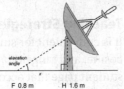

F 0.8 m   H 1.6 m
G 1.3 m   J 2.1 m

6. A lifeguard is in an observation chair and spots a person who needs help. The angle of depression to the person is 22°. The eye level of the lifeguard is 10 feet above the ground. What is the horizontal distance between the lifeguard and the person? Round to the nearest foot.

A 4 ft   C 25 ft
B 11 ft   D 27 ft

7. At a topiary garden, Emily is 8 feet from a shrub that is shaped like a dolphin. From where she is looking, the angle of elevation to the top of the shrub is 46°. If she is 5 feet tall, which is the best estimate for the height of the shrub?

F 6 ft   H 10 ft
G 8 ft   J 13 ft

8-5 Law of Sines and Law of Cosines
Going Deeper

Essential question: *How can you find the side lengths and angle measures of non-right triangles?*

CC.9-12.G.SRT.10(+) Prove the Laws of Sines and Cosines and use them to solve problems.

CC.9-12.G.SRT.11(+) Understand and apply the Law of Sines and the Law of Cosines to find unknown measurements in right and non-right triangles (e.g., surveying problems, resultant forces).

Prerequisites
Trigonometric ratios

Triangle Sum Theorem

Math Background
Previously, students learned various conditions that determine a unique triangle. For example, if you know the measure of two angles and the length of the included side (ASA), then the triangle is uniquely determined. That is, all triangles that satisfy these conditions will be congruent. This means it should be possible to calculate the remaining angle measure and the remaining side lengths. As students will learn in this lesson, the Law of Sines and the Law of Cosines make it possible to solve triangles when you are given three pieces of information that determine a unique triangle.

In order to apply the Law of Sines and the Law of Cosines to a non-right triangle that may have an obtuse angle, it is necessary to extend our definitions of the trigonometric ratios to include all angle measures between 0° and 180°. In Algebra 2, students will learn how to define trigonometric ratios for *any* angle measure by using the unit circle. In this lesson, the approach will be similar, but it will be restricted to angles whose terminal side lies in quadrants I and II.

INTRODUCE

Remind students that so far in this chapter they have worked exclusively with right triangles. Explain that the remaining lessons of the chapter deal with general triangles. However, to use trigonometric ratios with general triangles, it is first necessary to extend the definition of the sine, cosine, and tangent ratios to all angle measures between 0° and 180°.

TEACH

EXPLORE

Questioning Strategies

- In Step A, suppose m∠A = 45°. Do the formulas for sin A, cos A, and tan A give the expected values? Explain. Yes; In this case, $x = y = 1$, and the formulas give $\sin A = \frac{1}{\sqrt{2}}$, $\cos A = \frac{1}{\sqrt{2}}$, and $\tan A = 1$, all of which are correct.

- For angles whose measure is greater than 90° but less than 180°, why are the cosine and tangent negative? For these angles, x is negative in the formulas for cosine and tangent. This makes the value of the cosine and tangent negative.

> **MATHEMATICAL PRACTICE** **Highlighting the Standards**
>
> The Explore addresses Standard 8 (Look for and express regularity in repeated reasoning). As students extend the definitions of the sine, cosine, and tangent ratios, they use reasoning to develop formulas that are not only consistent with what they already know about these trigonometric ratios but also extend the possible arguments of the sine, cosine, and tangent. In this way, students are moving toward greater generalization. This process will continue (in Algebra 2) when students learn how to turn the trigonometric ratios into full-fledged trigonometric functions.

Teaching Strategies
It is convenient for students to know the sine, cosine, and tangent of 90°. In the figure on the student page that accompanies Step C, the coordinates of point B may be taken to be (0, 1) when ∠A is a right angle. Using the formulas for the trigonometric ratios with $x = 0$ and $y = 1$ shows that $\sin 90° = 1$, $\cos 90° = 0$, and $\tan 90°$ is undefined, since division by 0 is undefined.

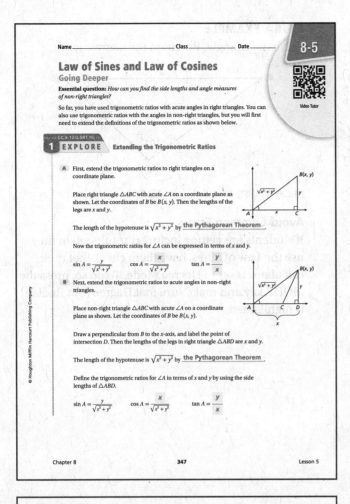

Name_____ Class_____ Date_____

8-5

Video Tutor

Law of Sines and Law of Cosines
Going Deeper

Essential question: *How can you find the side lengths and angle measures of non-right triangles?*

So far, you have used trigonometric ratios with acute angles in right triangles. You can also use trigonometric ratios with the angles in non-right triangles, but you will first need to extend the definitions of the trigonometric ratios as shown below.

CC.9-12.G.SRT.10(+)

1 EXPLORE Extending the Trigonometric Ratios

A First, extend the trigonometric ratios to right triangles on a coordinate plane.

Place right triangle $\triangle ABC$ with acute $\angle A$ on a coordinate plane as shown. Let the coordinates of B be $B(x, y)$. Then the lengths of the legs are x and y.

The length of the hypotenuse is $\sqrt{x^2 + y^2}$ by **the Pythagorean Theorem**

Now the trigonometric ratios for $\angle A$ can be expressed in terms of x and y.

$$\sin A = \frac{y}{\sqrt{x^2+y^2}} \qquad \cos A = \frac{x}{\sqrt{x^2+y^2}} \qquad \tan A = \frac{y}{x}$$

B Next, extend the trigonometric ratios to acute angles in non-right triangles.

Place non-right triangle $\triangle ABC$ with acute $\angle A$ on a coordinate plane as shown. Let the coordinates of B be $B(x, y)$.

Draw a perpendicular from B to the x-axis, and label the point of intersection D. Then the lengths of the legs in right triangle $\triangle ABD$ are x and y.

The length of the hypotenuse is $\sqrt{x^2 + y^2}$ by **the Pythagorean Theorem**

Define the trigonometric ratios for $\angle A$ in terms of x and y by using the side lengths of $\triangle ABD$.

$$\sin A = \frac{y}{\sqrt{x^2+y^2}} \qquad \cos A = \frac{x}{\sqrt{x^2+y^2}} \qquad \tan A = \frac{y}{x}$$

C Finally, extend the trigonometric ratios to obtuse angles in non-right triangles.

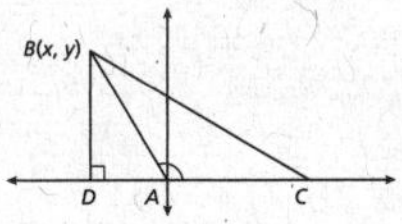

Place non-right triangle $\triangle ABC$ with obtuse $\angle A$ on a coordinate plane as shown. Let the coordinates of B be $B(x, y)$.

Draw a perpendicular from B to the x-axis, and label the point of intersection D. Then let the "lengths" of the legs in right triangle $\triangle ABD$ be x and y, where it is understood that $x < 0$.

The length of the hypotenuse, $\overline{AB}$, is $\sqrt{x^2 + y^2}$

Define the trigonometric ratios for $\angle A$ in terms of x and y by using the sides of $\triangle ABD$.

$$\sin A = \frac{y}{\sqrt{x^2+y^2}} \qquad \cos A = \frac{x}{\sqrt{x^2+y^2}} \qquad \tan A = \frac{y}{x}$$

D You can use a calculator to find trigonometric ratios for obtuse angles. Use a calculator to complete the table below. Round to the nearest hundredth.

Angle	Sine	Cosine	Tangent
97°	0.99	−0.12	−8.14
122°	0.85	−0.53	−1.60
165°	0.26	−0.97	−0.27

REFLECT

1a. Look for patterns in your table. Make a conjecture about the trigonometric ratios of obtuse angles.

For an obtuse angle, the sine is positive; the cosine and tangent are negative.

1b. Suppose $\angle A$ is obtuse. How do the definitions of the sine, cosine, and tangent for obtuse angles in Part C above explain why some of these trigonometric ratios are positive and some are negative?

In the definitions, $x < 0$, $y > 0$, and $\sqrt{x^2 + y^2} > 0$, so $\sin A = \frac{y}{\sqrt{x^2+y^2}} > 0$,

but $\cos A = \frac{x}{\sqrt{x^2+y^2}} < 0$ and $\tan A = \frac{y}{x} < 0$.

2 PROOF

Questioning Strategies

- In Step A of the proof, how do you solve the two equations for h? **Multiply both sides of $\sin A = \frac{h}{b}$ by b. Multiply both sides of $\sin B = \frac{h}{a}$ by a.**

- How can you state the Law of Sines in your own words? **Possible answer: The ratio of the sine of an angle to the length of the opposite side is constant for all three angles of a triangle.**

3 EXAMPLE

Questioning Strategies

- Does the Law of Sines apply to this problem? How do you know? **Yes; you are given ASA information, so you can use the Law of Sines to solve the triangle.**

- What part of the triangle can you solve without using the Law of Sines? Explain. **You can find $m\angle G$ by using the Triangle Sum Theorem.**

EXTRA EXAMPLE

Solve the triangle. Round to the nearest tenth.

$m\angle A = 36°$; $b = 9.3$; $c = 13.4$

Avoid Common Errors

If students are getting incorrect results when they use the Law of Sines, have them check that their calculator is set to Degree Mode. To do so, press the MODE key and make sure that Degree (not Radian) is highlighted.

© Houghton Mifflin Harcourt Publishing Company

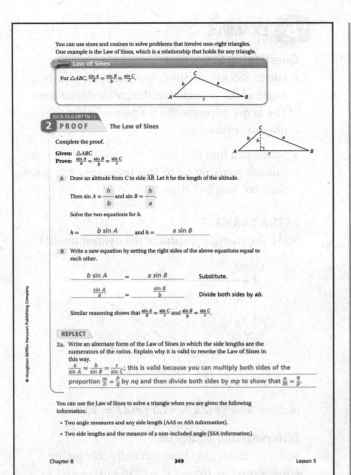

You can use sines and cosines to solve problems that involve non-right triangles. One example is the Law of Sines, which is a relationship that holds for any triangle.

Law of Sines

For $\triangle ABC$, $\dfrac{\sin A}{a} = \dfrac{\sin B}{b} = \dfrac{\sin C}{c}$.

CC.9-12.G.SRT.10(+)

2 PROOF   The Law of Sines

Complete the proof.

Given: $\triangle ABC$
Prove: $\dfrac{\sin A}{a} = \dfrac{\sin B}{b} = \dfrac{\sin C}{c}$

A Draw an altitude from C to side $\overline{AB}$. Let h be the length of the altitude.

Then $\sin A = \dfrac{h}{b}$ and $\sin B = \dfrac{h}{a}$.

Solve the two equations for h.

$h = \underline{\ b \sin A\ }$ and $h = \underline{\ a \sin B\ }$

B Write a new equation by setting the right sides of the above equations equal to each other.

$\underline{\ b \sin A\ } = \underline{\ a \sin B\ }$ Substitute.

$\underline{\ \dfrac{\sin A}{a}\ } = \underline{\ \dfrac{\sin B}{b}\ }$ Divide both sides by ab.

Similar reasoning shows that $\dfrac{\sin A}{a} = \dfrac{\sin C}{c}$ and $\dfrac{\sin B}{b} = \dfrac{\sin C}{c}$.

REFLECT

2a. Write an alternate form of the Law of Sines in which the side lengths are the numerators of the ratios. Explain why it is valid to rewrite the Law of Sines in this way.

$\dfrac{a}{\sin A} = \dfrac{b}{\sin B} = \dfrac{c}{\sin C}$; this is valid because you can multiply both sides of the

proportion $\dfrac{m}{n} = \dfrac{p}{q}$ by nq and then divide both sides by mp to show that $\dfrac{n}{m} = \dfrac{q}{p}$.

You can use the Law of Sines to solve a triangle when you are given the following information.

• Two angle measures and any side length (AAS or ASA information).
• Two side lengths and the measure of a non-included angle (SSA information).

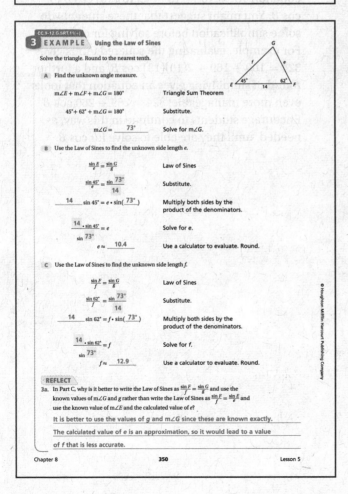

CC.9-12.G.SRT.11(+)

3 EXAMPLE   Using the Law of Sines

Solve the triangle. Round to the nearest tenth.

A Find the unknown angle measure.

$m\angle E + m\angle F + m\angle G = 180°$ Triangle Sum Theorem

$45° + 62° + m\angle G = 180°$ Substitute.

$m\angle G = \underline{\ 73°\ }$ Solve for $m\angle G$.

B Use the Law of Sines to find the unknown side length e.

$\dfrac{\sin E}{e} = \dfrac{\sin G}{g}$ Law of Sines

$\dfrac{\sin 45°}{e} = \dfrac{\sin 73°}{14}$ Substitute.

$14 \sin 45° = e \cdot \sin(73°)$ Multiply both sides by the product of the denominators.

$\dfrac{14 \cdot \sin 45°}{\sin 73°} = e$ Solve for e.

$e \approx \underline{\ 10.4\ }$ Use a calculator to evaluate. Round.

C Use the Law of Sines to find the unknown side length f.

$\dfrac{\sin F}{f} = \dfrac{\sin G}{g}$ Law of Sines

$\dfrac{\sin 62°}{f} = \dfrac{\sin 73°}{14}$ Substitute.

$14 \sin 62° = f \cdot \sin(73°)$ Multiply both sides by the product of the denominators.

$\dfrac{14 \cdot \sin 62°}{\sin 73°} = f$ Solve for f.

$f \approx \underline{\ 12.9\ }$ Use a calculator to evaluate. Round.

REFLECT

3a. In Part C, why is it better to write the Law of Sines as $\dfrac{\sin F}{f} = \dfrac{\sin G}{g}$ and use the known values of $m\angle G$ and g rather than write the Law of Sines as $\dfrac{\sin F}{f} = \dfrac{\sin E}{e}$ and use the known value of $m\angle E$ and the calculated value of e?

It is better to use the values of g and $m\angle G$ since these are known exactly.

The calculated value of e is an approximation, so it would lead to a value

of f that is less accurate.

© Houghton Mifflin Harcourt Publishing Company

Questioning Strategies
- What type of triangle is $\triangle ADC$? **right triangle**
- What are the legs in $\triangle ADC$? What is the hypotenuse? **The legs are $\overline{CD}$ and $\overline{AD}$; the hypotenuse is $\overline{AC}$.**
- What type of triangle is $\triangle CDB$? **right triangle**
- What are the legs in $\triangle CDB$? What is the hypotenuse? **The legs are $\overline{CD}$ and $\overline{DB}$; the hypotenuse is $\overline{CB}$.**

MATHEMATICAL PRACTICE **Highlighting the Standards**

You can address Standard 7 (Look for and make use of structure) while teaching students about the Law of Cosines. First have students compare the Law of Cosines to the Pythagorean Theorem. Students may notice that the Law of Cosines resembles the Pythagorean Theorem. In fact, the right side of the equation looks like the Pythagorean Theorem ($b^2 + c^2$) with a "correction factor" ($-2bc \cos A$). Furthermore, when $\angle A$ is a right angle, $\cos A = \cos 90° = 0$, and the Law of Cosines becomes the Pythagorean Theorem.

This discussion offers a perfect example of what the standard refers to as the ability to "see complicated things, such as some algebraic expressions, as single objects or as composed of several objects." That is, $-2bc \cos A$ may be viewed as a product of a number, two variables, and a cosine, or it may be viewed as a single entity that serves as a "correction factor" when $\angle A$ is not a right angle.

Questioning Strategies
- Given SSS information, how can you tell which angle of the triangle has the greatest measure? **The angle opposite the longest side has the greatest measure.**
- When you find that $\cos B \approx -0.2115$, what does this tell you about $\angle B$? **This means $m\angle B$ is greater than 90° and less than 180°.**

EXTRA EXAMPLE
Solve the triangle. Round to the nearest tenth.

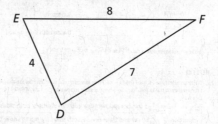

$m\angle D \approx 89.0°$; $m\angle E \approx 61.0°$; $m\angle F \approx 30.0°$

Differentiated Instruction
Some students may have difficulty solving the equation $18^2 = 10^2 + 13^2 - 2(10)(13) \cos B$ for $\cos B$. You might suggest that these students do some simplification before solving for $\cos B$. For example, evaluating the squared terms gives $324 = 100 + 169 - 2(10)(13) \cos B$, and a further round of simplifying gives an equation that looks even more manageable: $324 = 269 - 260 \cos B$. Encourage students to continue in this way, as needed, until they are able to solve for $\cos B$.

When you are given SSS or SAS information about a triangle, you cannot use the Law of Sines to solve the triangle. However, this information determines a unique triangle, so there should be some way to find the unknown side lengths and angle measures. The Law of Cosines is useful in this case.

Law of Cosines

For $\triangle ABC$,

$a^2 = b^2 + c^2 - 2bc \cos A,$

$b^2 = a^2 + c^2 - 2ac \cos B,$

$c^2 = a^2 + b^2 - 2ab \cos C.$

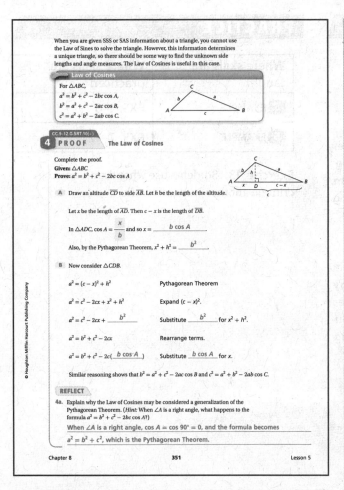

CC.9-12.G.SRT.10(+)

4 PROOF The Law of Cosines

Complete the proof.

Given: $\triangle ABC$
Prove: $a^2 = b^2 + c^2 - 2bc \cos A$

A Draw an altitude $\overline{CD}$ to side $\overline{AB}$. Let h be the length of the altitude.

Let x be the length of $\overline{AD}$. Then $c - x$ is the length of $\overline{DB}$.

In $\triangle ADC$, $\cos A = \dfrac{x}{b}$ and so $x = $ ___$b \cos A$___

Also, by the Pythagorean Theorem, $x^2 + h^2 = $ ___b^2___.

B Now consider $\triangle CDB$.

$a^2 = (c-x)^2 + h^2$	Pythagorean Theorem
$a^2 = c^2 - 2cx + x^2 + h^2$	Expand $(c-x)^2$.
$a^2 = c^2 - 2cx + $ ___b^2___	Substitute ___b^2___ for $x^2 + h^2$.
$a^2 = b^2 + c^2 - 2cx$	Rearrange terms.
$a^2 = b^2 + c^2 - 2c(\ $___$b \cos A$___$)$	Substitute ___$b \cos A$___ for x.

Similar reasoning shows that $b^2 = a^2 + c^2 - 2ac \cos B$ and $c^2 = a^2 + b^2 - 2ab \cos C$.

REFLECT

4a. Explain why the Law of Cosines may be considered a generalization of the Pythagorean Theorem. (*Hint:* When $\angle A$ is a right angle, what happens to the formula $a^2 = b^2 + c^2 - 2bc \cos A$?)

When $\angle A$ is a right angle, $\cos A = \cos 90° = 0$, and the formula becomes

$a^2 = b^2 + c^2$, which is the Pythagorean Theorem.

CC.9-12.G.SRT.11(+)

5 EXAMPLE Using the Law of Cosines

Solve the triangle. Round to the nearest tenth.

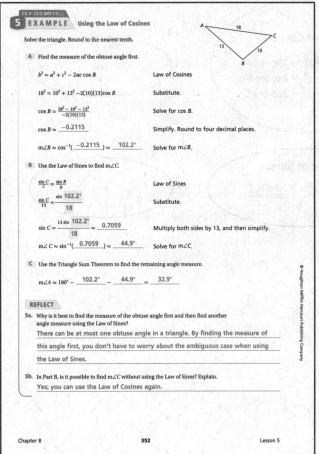

A Find the measure of the obtuse angle first.

$b^2 = a^2 + c^2 - 2ac \cos B$	Law of Cosines
$18^2 = 10^2 + 13^2 - 2(10)(13)\cos B$	Substitute.
$\cos B = \dfrac{18^2 - 10^2 - 13^2}{-2(10)(13)}$	Solve for $\cos B$.
$\cos B \approx $ ___-0.2115___	Simplify. Round to four decimal places.
$m\angle B \approx \cos^{-1}($___$-0.2115$___$) \approx $ ___$102.2°$___	Solve for $m\angle B$.

B Use the Law of Sines to find $m\angle C$.

$\dfrac{\sin C}{c} = \dfrac{\sin B}{b}$	Law of Sines
$\dfrac{\sin C}{13} = \dfrac{\sin 102.2°}{18}$	Substitute.
$\sin C = \dfrac{13 \sin 102.2°}{18} \approx $ ___0.7059___	Multiply both sides by 13, and then simplify.
$m\angle C \approx \sin^{-1}($___$0.7059$___$) \approx $ ___$44.9°$___	Solve for $m\angle C$.

C Use the Triangle Sum Theorem to find the remaining angle measure.

$m\angle A \approx 180° - $ ___$102.2°$___ $- $ ___$44.9°$___ $= $ ___$32.9°$___

REFLECT

5a. Why is it best to find the measure of the obtuse angle first and then find another angle measure using the Law of Sines?

There can be at most one obtuse angle in a triangle. By finding the measure of this angle first, you don't have to worry about the ambiguous case when using the Law of Sines.

5b. In Part B, is it possible to find $m\angle C$ without using the Law of Sines? Explain.

Yes; you can use the Law of Cosines again.

© Houghton Mifflin Harcourt Publishing Company

Essential Question

How can you find the side lengths and angle measures of non-right triangles?

To find the side lengths and angle measures of a non-right triangle, you need to know three measurements that determine the triangle uniquely. If you know ASA or AAS, you can find the missing angle measure by using the Triangle Sum Theorem, and you can find the missing side lengths by using the Law of Sines. If you know SSS, you can find two of the missing angle measures by using the Law of Cosines, and you can find the third angle measure by using the Triangle Sum Theorem. If you know SAS, you can find the missing side length by using the Law of Cosines, you can find one of the missing angles by using the Law of Sines, and you can find the other missing angle measure by using the Triangle Sum Theorem.

Summarize

Have students make a graphic organizer to summarize the Law of Sines, the Law of Cosines, and when each of the laws may be used. A sample is shown below.

Where skills are taught	Where skills are practiced
3 EXAMPLE	EXS. 1–6
5 EXAMPLE	EXS. 7–12

Exercise 13: Students use what they learned to critique another student's work.

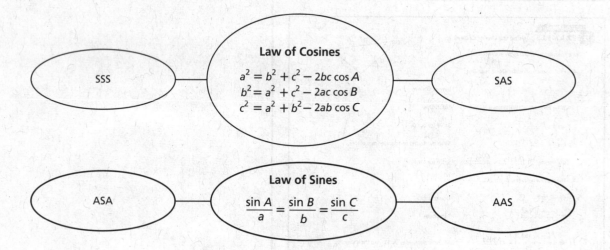

Law of Cosines

$$a^2 = b^2 + c^2 - 2bc \cos A$$
$$b^2 = a^2 + c^2 - 2ac \cos B$$
$$c^2 = a^2 + b^2 - 2ab \cos C$$

SSS   SAS

Law of Sines

$$\frac{\sin A}{a} = \frac{\sin B}{b} = \frac{\sin C}{c}$$

ASA   AAS

PRACTICE

Solve each triangle. Round to the nearest tenth.

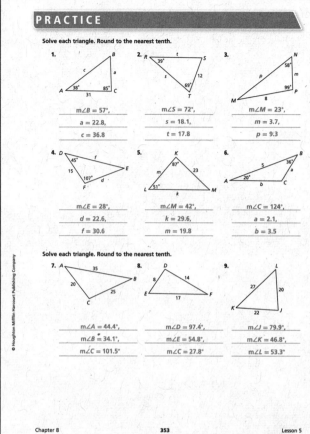

1.

m∠B = 57°,
a = 22.8,
c = 36.8

2.

m∠S = 72°,
s = 18.1,
t = 17.8

3.

m∠M = 23°,
m = 3.7,
p = 9.3

4.

m∠E = 28°,
d = 22.6,
f = 30.6

5.

m∠M = 42°,
k = 29.6,
m = 19.8

6.

m∠C = 124°,
a = 2.1,
b = 3.5

Solve each triangle. Round to the nearest tenth.

7.

m∠A = 44.4°,
m∠B = 34.1°,
m∠C = 101.5°

8.

m∠D = 97.4°,
m∠E = 54.8°,
m∠C = 27.8°

9.

m∠J = 79.9°,
m∠K = 46.8°,
m∠L = 53.3°

© Houghton Mifflin Harcourt Publishing Company

Solve each triangle. Round to the nearest tenth.

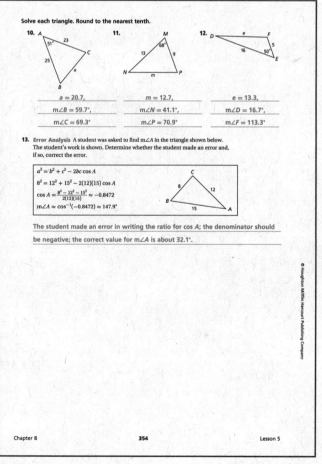

10.

a = 20.7,
m∠B = 59.7°,
m∠C = 69.3°

11.

m = 12.7,
m∠N = 41.1°,
m∠P = 70.9°

12.

e = 13.3,
m∠D = 16.7°,
m∠F = 113.3°

13. **Error Analysis** A student was asked to find m∠A in the triangle shown below. The student's work is shown. Determine whether the student made an error and, if so, correct the error.

$$a^2 = b^2 + c^2 - 2bc \cos A$$
$$8^2 = 12^2 + 15^2 - 2(12)(15) \cos A$$
$$\cos A = \frac{8^2 - 12^2 - 15^2}{2(12)(15)} \approx -0.8472$$
$$m\angle A \approx \cos^{-1}(-0.8472) \approx 147.9°$$

The student made an error in writing the ratio for cos A; the denominator should

be negative; the correct value for m∠A is about 32.1°.

© Houghton Mifflin Harcourt Publishing Company

ADDITIONAL PRACTICE AND PROBLEM SOLVING

Assign these pages to help your students practice and apply important lesson concepts. For additional exercises, see the Student Edition.

Answers

Additional Practice

1. 0.93 **2.** −0.87

3. −0.31 **4.** 1.00

5. −0.63 **6.** −6.31

7. 0.17 **8.** −0.10

9. −1.96 **10.** 17.0 m

11. 2.8 in. **12.** 61.1 km

13. 55° **14.** 85°

15. 18° **16.** 6.0 ft

17. 3.7 cm **18.** 10.0 mi

19. 144° **20.** 47°

21. 40°

Problem Solving

1. 23.3 mi **2.** 32.9 ft

3. 122° **4.** 60°

5. C **6.** G

7. B **8.** H

Additional Practice

Use a calculator to find each trigonometric ratio. Round to the nearest hundredth.

1. sin 111° _____
2. cos 150° _____
3. tan 163° _____
4. sin 92° _____
5. cos 129° _____
6. tan 99° _____
7. sin 170° _____
8. cos 96° _____
9. tan 117° _____

Use the Law of Sines to find each measure. Round lengths to the nearest tenth and angle measures to the nearest degree.

10.

BC _____

11.

DE _____

12.

GH _____

13.

m∠J _____

14.

m∠R _____

15.

m∠T _____

Use the Law of Cosines to find each measure. Round lengths to the nearest tenth and angle measures to the nearest degree.

16.

YZ _____

17.

BD _____

18.

EF _____

19.

m∠I _____

20.

m∠M _____

21.

m∠S _____

© Houghton Mifflin Harcourt Publishing Company

Problem Solving

1. The map shows three earthquake centers for one week in California. How far apart were the earthquake centers at points A and C ? Round to the nearest tenth.

Oceanside
San Diego

_____

2. A BMX track has a starting hill as shown in the diagram. What is the length of the hill, WY ? Round to the nearest tenth.

_____

3. The edges of a triangular cushion measure 8 inches, 3 inches, and 6 inches. What is the measure of the largest angle of the cushion to the nearest degree?

_____

4. The coordinates of the vertices of △HJK are H(0, 4), J(5, 7), and K(9, –1). Find the measure of ∠H to the nearest degree.

_____

Choose the best answer. Use the following information and diagram for Exercises 5 and 6.

To find the distance across a bay, a surveyor locates points Q, R, and S as shown.

5. What is QR to the nearest tenth?
   A 8 m   C 41.9 m
   B 35.2 m   D 55.4 m

6. What is m∠Q to the nearest degree?
   F 43°   H 67°
   G 49°   J 107°

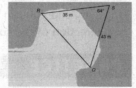

7. Two angles of a triangle measure 56° and 77°. The side opposite the 56° angle is 29 cm long. What is the measure of the shortest side? Round to the nearest tenth.
   A 23.4 cm   C 32.9 cm
   B 25.6 cm   D 34.1 cm

8. Which is the best estimate for the perimeter of a triangle if two sides measure 7 inches and 10 inches, and the included angle between the two sides is 82°?
   F 11.4 in.   H 28.4 in.
   G 12.2 in.   J 39.9 in.

© Houghton Mifflin Harcourt Publishing Company

Vectors
Connection: Applying the Law of Cosines and Law of Sines

Essential question: *How can you apply trigonometry to solve vector problems?*

COMMON Standards for
CORE Mathematical Content

CC.9-12.G.SRT.11(+) Understand and apply the Law of Sines and the Law of Cosines to find unknown measurements in right and non-right triangles (e.g., surveying problems, resultant forces).

Prerequisites
Trigonometric ratios
The Law of Cosines and the Law of Sines

Math Background
In physics, forces are represented by vectors. When two forces act on an object, the combined, or resultant, force is the sum of the vectors. Vectors are added geometrically by drawing one of the vectors, placing the initial point of the second vector at the terminal point of the first when drawing the second vector, and finally drawing the resultant from the initial point of the first to the terminal point of the second. This is the basis for the diagram in Example 1, where there are two forces acting on the plane: the propulsion force of the plane's engines and the force of the crosswind.

INTRODUCE

Begin by discussing with students a simple situation involving vectors. For instance, if you attempt to swim directly across a river, the river's current will carry you downstream, so you'll end up at a point farther down the other side of the river than you intended. The situation is similar for a plane flying into a crosswind.

TEACH

1 EXAMPLE

Questioning Strategies
- Do you expect the final speed of the plane to be greater than or less than 600 miles per hour? Why? **Greater than; the final speed is represented by the longest side of a triangle.**

- In the last step of the solution, why do you subtract m∠A from the original direction? **This gives the measure of the angle formed by the line pointing due north and the resultant vector (i.e., it gives the number of degrees east of north for the final direction of the plane).**

EXTRA EXAMPLE
A plane is flying at a rate of 520 miles per hour in the direction 70° west of north. There is an 80 miles per hour crosswind blowing due north. What is the final direction and speed of the plane? **about 62.2° west of north; about 552.5 mi/h**

MATHEMATICAL PRACTICE | **Highlighting the Standards**

This lesson offers an ideal opportunity to address Standard 4 (Model with mathematics) as students solve problems using the Law of Cosines and the Law of Sines. Part of the standard stresses that students "routinely interpret their mathematical results in the context of the situation and reflect on whether the results make sense." Students can hone these skills by solving the real-world problem in Example 1.

CLOSE

Essential Question
How can you apply trigonometry to solve vector problems? **When finding the sum of two vectors that represent forces acting on an object, you can use the Law of Cosines to find the magnitude of the sum, and you can use the Law of Sines to find the direction of the sum.**

PRACTICE

Where skills are taught	Where skills are practiced
1 EXAMPLE	EXS. 1–3

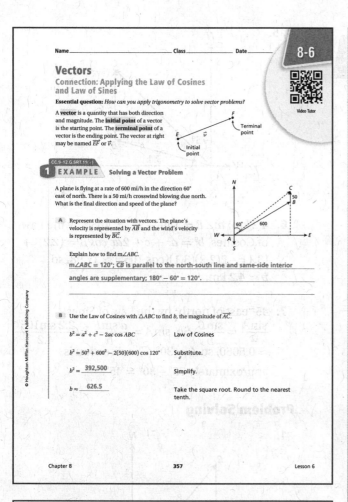

Vectors

Connection: Applying the Law of Cosines and Law of Sines

Essential question: *How can you apply trigonometry to solve vector problems?*

A **vector** is a quantity that has both direction and magnitude. The **initial point** of a vector is the starting point. The **terminal point** of a vector is the ending point. The vector at right may be named $\vec{EF}$ or $\vec{v}$.

CC.9-12.G.SRT.11(+)

1 EXAMPLE Solving a Vector Problem

A plane is flying at a rate of 600 mi/h in the direction 60° east of north. There is a 50 mi/h crosswind blowing due north. What is the final direction and speed of the plane?

A Represent the situation with vectors. The plane's velocity is represented by $\vec{AB}$ and the wind's velocity is represented by $\vec{BC}$.

Explain how to find m∠ABC.

m∠ABC = 120°; $\overline{CB}$ is parallel to the north-south line and same-side interior angles are supplementary; 180° − 60° = 120°.

B Use the Law of Cosines with △ABC to find b, the magnitude of $\vec{AC}$.

$b^2 = a^2 + c^2 - 2ac \cos ABC$ Law of Cosines

$b^2 = 50^2 + 600^2 - 2(50)(600) \cos 120°$ Substitute.

$b^2 = \underline{392{,}500}$ Simplify.

$b \approx \underline{626.5}$ Take the square root. Round to the nearest tenth.

© Houghton Mifflin Harcourt Publishing Company

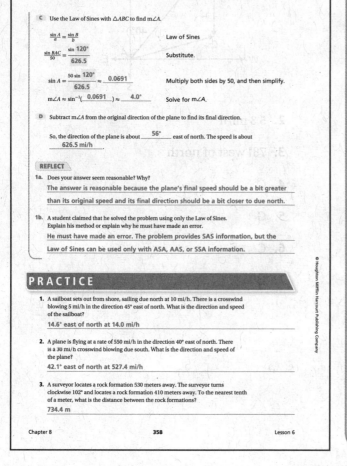

C Use the Law of Sines with △ABC to find m∠A.

$\frac{\sin A}{a} = \frac{\sin B}{b}$ Law of Sines

$\frac{\sin BAC}{50} = \frac{\sin 120°}{626.5}$ Substitute.

$\sin A = \frac{50 \sin 120°}{626.5} \approx \underline{0.0691}$ Multiply both sides by 50, and then simplify.

$m\angle A \approx \sin^{-1}(\underline{0.0691}) \approx \underline{4.0°}$ Solve for m∠A.

D Subtract m∠A from the original direction of the plane to find its final direction.

So, the direction of the plane is about ___56°___ east of north. The speed is about 626.5 mi/h

REFLECT

1a. Does your answer seem reasonable? Why?

The answer is reasonable because the plane's final speed should be a bit greater than its original speed and its final direction should be a bit closer to due north.

1b. A student claimed that he solved the problem using only the Law of Sines. Explain his method or explain why he must have made an error.

He must have made an error. The problem provides SAS information, but the Law of Sines can be used only with ASA, AAS, or SSA information.

PRACTICE

1. A sailboat sets out from shore, sailing due north at 10 mi/h. There is a crosswind blowing 5 mi/h in the direction 45° east of north. What is the direction and speed of the sailboat?

14.6° east of north at 14.0 mi/h

2. A plane is flying at a rate of 550 mi/h in the direction 40° east of north. There is a 30 mi/h crosswind blowing due south. What is the direction and speed of the plane?

42.1° east of north at 527.4 mi/h

3. A surveyor locates a rock formation 530 meters away. The surveyor turns clockwise 102° and locates a rock formation 410 meters away. To the nearest tenth of a meter, what is the distance between the rock formations?

734.4 m

© Houghton Mifflin Harcourt Publishing Company

Assign these pages to help your students practice and apply important lesson concepts. For additional exercises, see the Student Edition.

Answers

Additional Practice

1.

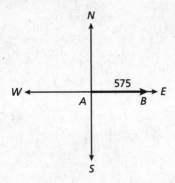

2.

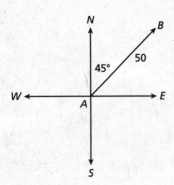

3.

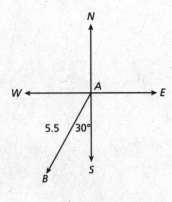

4, 5.

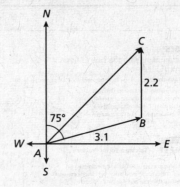

6. 4.2 km; $m\angle B = 180° - 75° = 105°$; by the Law of Cosines, $b^2 = a^2 + c^2 - 2ac \cos B = (2.2)^2 + (3.1)^2 - 2(2.2)(3.1)(\cos 105°) \approx 17.98$, so $b \approx 4.2$ km.

7. 45° east of north; by the Law of Sines, $\frac{\sin A}{a} = \frac{\sin B}{b}$. So, $\sin A = \frac{a \sin B}{b} = \frac{2.2 \sin 105°}{4.2} \approx 0.5060$, so $A \approx 30°$. The direction is approximately $75° - 30° = 45°$.

Problem Solving

1.

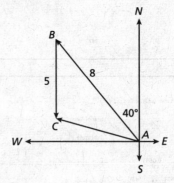

2. 5.3 mi/h

3. 78° west of north

4. C

5. G

6. C

7. H

Additional Practice

Represent the situation with a vector $\overline{AB}$.

1. An airplane flies at a rate of 575 mi/h due east.

2. A boat travels at a rate of 50 mi/h in the direction 45° east of north.

3. A hiker walks at a rate of 5.5 mi/h in the direction 30° west of south.

Use the information below for Exercises 4–7. In your answers, round distances to the nearest tenth and directions to the nearest degree.

Becky is researching her family history. She has found an old map that shows the site of her great-grandparents' farmhouse outside of town. To get to the site, Becky walks 3.1 km at a bearing of 75° east of north. Then she walks 2.2 km due north.

4. Represent the first part of Becky's path with a vector $\overline{AB}$ and the second part with a vector $\overline{BC}$.

5. Suppose you want to find the distance and direction Becky could have walked to get directly to the site. Draw the vector you could use to find that information.

6. Find the distance that Becky would have traveled if she chose the direct route. Explain how you found your answer.

_____

_____

7. Find the direction that Becky would have traveled if she chose the direct route. Explain how you found your answer.

_____

_____

Problem Solving

Use the following information for Exercises 1–3.

A sailboat is traveling under the conditions shown in the table.

	Direction	Rate
sailboat	40° west of north	8 mi/h
current	due south	5 mi/h

1. Represent the sailboat with a vector $\overline{AB}$, and the current with a vector $\overline{BC}$.

2. What is the sailboat's final speed? Round to the nearest tenth.

_____

3. What is the sailboat's final direction? Round to the nearest degree.

_____

Choose the best answer. Use the following information for Exercises 4–6.

A small plane is flying under the conditions shown in the table.

	Direction	Rate
plane	24° east of north	200 mi/h
wind	due east	28 mi/h

4. In a vector sketch of the situation, if $\overline{AB}$ represents the plane and $\overline{BC}$ represents the wind, what is m∠B?

  A 24°

  B 90° − 24° = 66°

  C 90° + 24° = 114°

  B 180° − 24° = 156°

5. What is the plane's final speed to the nearest mile per hour?

  F 202 mi/h   H 226 mi/h

  G 213 mi/h   J 45,339 mi/h

6. What is the direction of the plane to the nearest degree?

  A 7° east of north

  B 17° east of north

  C 31° east of north

  D 59° east of north

7. A person in a canoe leaves shore at a direction of 45° west of north and paddles at a constant speed of 2 mi/h. There is a current flowing 1.5 mi/h due west. What is the canoe's final speed?

  F 1.4 mi/h   H 3.2 mi/h

  G 2.0 mi/h   J 10.5 mi/h

This page provides students with the opportunity to apply concepts from the Common Core in real-world problem situations. There are three different levels of performance tasks:

⭐ **Novice:** These are short word problems that require students to apply the math they have learned in straightforward, real-world situations.

⭐⭐ **Apprentice:** These are more involved problems that guide students step-by-step through more complex tasks. These exercises include more complicated reasoning, writing, and open-ended elements.

⭐⭐⭐ **Expert:** These are open-ended, non-routine problems that, instead of stepping the students through, ask them to choose their own methods for solving and justify their answers and reasoning.

Sample answers

1a. Both angles are 45°.

 b. 38.2 in.

2. 6.8°; possible explanation: First, find the change in distance above sea level from the base of the hill to the top of the hill:
$2{,}108 - 545 = 1{,}563$ ft. Convert 2.5 mi to 13,200 ft, then find $\sin^{-1} \frac{1563}{13{,}200}$.

3. Scoring Guide:

Task	Possible points
a	1 point for correctly stating that two different lengths for the third side are possible, depending on whether the missing side is a leg or the hypotenuse of the right triangle
b	1 point for correctly finding the missing side lengths 5.4 ft and 20.5 ft, and 1 point for showing appropriate work
c	1 point for correctly stating that the farmer should choose 20.5 ft for the length of the third side and explaining that this triangle has an area of $0.5 \cdot 14 \cdot 15 = 105$ ft^2, while the other triangle has an area of $0.5 \cdot 5.4 \cdot 14 = 37.8$ ft^2
d	2 points for correctly using at least one trigonometric ratio to find the acute angles to be 43° and 47° Possible answer: $\tan^{-1} \frac{14}{15} \approx 43°$ for one acute angle, and the other is $90° - 43° = 47°$

Total possible points: 6

CHAPTER 8

Performance Tasks

COMMON CORE
CC 9-12.G.SRT.8

⭐ **1.** A bookcase fits diagonally into the corner of a room. The front of the bookcase is 54 inches wide. Each side of the bookcase uses the same amount of wall space.

   a. What angles are formed where the front of the bookcase touches the walls?

   b. Calculate how much wall space each side of the bookcase uses.

⭐ **2.** The base of a hill is 545 feet above sea level. The top of the hill is 2108 feet above sea level. A straight road from the base of the hill to the top of the hill is 2.5 miles long. What is the angle of elevation from the base of the hill to the top of the hill? Round to the nearest tenth of a degree. Explain how you found your answer.

⭐ **3.** A farmer is building a pen inside a barn. The pen will be in the shape of a right triangle. The farmer has 14 feet of barn wall to use for one side of the pen and wants another side of the pen to be 15 feet long.

   a. How many different lengths for the third side are possible? Explain.

   b. To the nearest tenth of a foot, find all possible lengths for the third side of the triangle. Show your work.

   c. The farmer wants the area of the pen to be as large as possible. What length should he choose for the third side? Justify your answer.

   d. Find the measure of the acute angles for the triangle you described in part **c**. Round to the nearest degree. Show how you used trigonometric ratios to find the angles.

continued

© Houghton Mifflin Harcourt Publishing Company

⭐ **4.** At 6 A.M., the angle of elevation of the sun from the horizon is 0 degrees. At noon, the angle of elevation of the sun is 87 degrees. At some time before noon, a flagpole 50 feet tall casts a shadow 24 feet 9 inches long. To the nearest minute, what is the time? Explain your work. Assume the angle of elevation of the sun increases at a constant rate.

4. Scoring Guide:

Task	Possible points
	2 points for correctly finding the time of 10:23 A.M., and 4 points for correctly explaining the solution: In 6 hours, the sun travels 87°, or 14.5° per hour. The shadow of the 50-ft flagpole is 24.75 feet long, so the elevation of the sun is $\tan^{-1}\frac{50}{24.75}$. The number of hours after 6 A.M. that this occurs is $\left(\tan^{-1}\frac{50}{24.75}\right) \div 14.5 \approx 4.39$, or approximately 10:23 A.M.

Total possible points: 6

© Houghton Mifflin Harcourt Publishing Company

COMMON CORE CORRELATION

Standards	Item
CC.9-12.G.SRT.6	5, 6
CC.9-12.G.SRT.7	1
CC.9-12.G.SRT.8*	4, 7
CC.9-12.G.SRT.10(+)	2, 3, 8, 9
CC.9-12.G.SRT.11(+)	3, 9

TEST PREP DOCTOR ✚

Multiple Choice: Item 4

- Students who answered **G** used the sine to solve the problem, but may have done so incorrectly by writing $\sin 28° = \frac{2}{b}$ $\left(\text{rather than } \sin 28° = \frac{b}{2}\right)$ and solving for b.

- Students who answered **H** incorrectly used the cosine and solved $\cos 28° = \frac{b}{2}$ for b when they should have used the sine $\left(\sin 28° = \frac{b}{2}\right)$.

- Students who answered **J** incorrectly used the cosine and solved $\cos 28° = \frac{2}{b}$ for b, when they should have used the sine $\left(\sin 28° = \frac{b}{2}\right)$.

Multiple Choice: Item 5

- Students who answered **A** may think that the cosine is the ratio of the length of the leg opposite the angle to the length of the hypotenuse.

- Students who answered **B** may not understand that trigonometric ratios are defined for the acute angles of a right triangle.

- Students who answered **D** may think that the tangent is the ratio of the length of the leg opposite the angle to the length of the hypotenuse.

Constructed Response: Item 9

- Students who try to set up a trigonometric ratio without using the Law of Sines or the Law of Cosines may not understand that trigonometric ratios are generally used to find unknown side lengths only in right triangles.

- Students who try to use the Law of Sines may not understand that the Law of Sines does not apply when given SAS information.

- Students who use the Law of Cosines but find an incorrect distance between the landmarks may have made an error in solving the equation $p^2 = 190^2 + 241^2 - 2(190)(241) \cos 78°$ for p.

CHAPTER 8 COMMON CORE ASSESSMENT READINESS

Name ______________________ Class ____________ Date ________

MULTIPLE CHOICE

1. Given that $x°$ is the measure of an acute angle, which of the following is equal to $\sin x°$?
   - A. $\cos x°$
   - B. $\cos(90 - x)°$
   - C. $\sin(90 - x)°$
   - D. $\tan x°$

2. Shauntay is proving the Law of Sines. She draws the figure below.

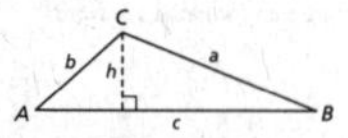

Then she writes $\sin A = \frac{h}{b}$ and $\sin B = \frac{h}{a}$. From this, she concludes that $h = b\sin A$ and $h = a\sin B$. What should she do next?

   - F. Draw an altitude from B to side $\overline{AC}$.
   - G. Add the equations to get $2h = b\sin A + a\sin B$.
   - H. Use the Pythagorean Theorem to write $c^2 + h^2 = a^2$.
   - J. Write $b\sin A = a\sin B$ and then divide both sides by ab.

3. Which is closest to m$\angle S$?

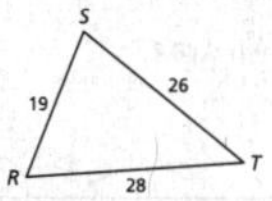

   - A. 41°
   - B. 64°
   - C. 75°
   - D. 81°

4. Connor is building a skateboard ramp with the dimensions shown. Which expression can he use to find the height b of the ramp?

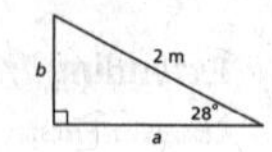

   - F. $2\sin 28°$
   - G. $\frac{2}{\sin 28°}$
   - H. $2\cos 28°$
   - J. $\frac{2}{\cos 28°}$

5. In the right triangles shown below, $\angle M \cong \angle Q$. This leads to the observation that $\triangle MNP \sim \triangle QRS$ by the AA Similarity Criterion. Therefore, corresponding sides are proportional, so $\frac{RS}{NP} = \frac{QR}{MN}$ and algebra shows that $\frac{RS}{QR} = \frac{NP}{MN}$. This last proportion is the basis for defining which of the following?

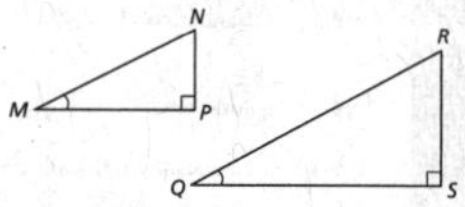

   - A. the cosine of $\angle M$
   - B. the cosine of $\angle P$
   - C. the sine of $\angle M$
   - D. the tangent of $\angle M$

CONSTRUCTED RESPONSE

6. $\triangle ABC$ and $\triangle PQR$ are similar right triangles, with right angles at B and Q. Which of the following represents the ratio of PQ to QR?
   - F. the sine of $\angle C$
   - G. the cosine of $\angle C$
   - H. the tangent of $\angle C$
   - J. the tangent of $\angle A$

7. You paddle a kayak due north at the rate of 2.5 mi/h. The river has a 2 mi/h current that flows due east. You want to find the kayak's actual speed and direction.

   a. In the space below, sketch and label vectors that represent the situation.

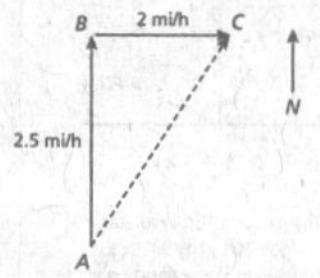

   b. Find the kayak's actual speed and direction.

   Actual speed: ≈ 3.2 mi/h

   Actual direction: 38.7° east of due north

8. To prove the Law of Cosines, you first draw the following figure.

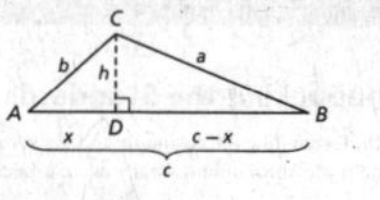

Then you note that $\cos A = \frac{x}{b}$ so $x = b\cos A$ and you note that $x^2 + h^2 = b^2$ by the Pythagorean Theorem. How do you complete the proof that $a^2 = b^2 + c^2 - 2bc\cos A$?

In $\triangle CDB$, $a^2 = (c - x)^2 + h^2$ by the Pythagorean Theorem. Expanding gives $a^2 = c^2 - 2cx + x^2 + h^2$. By substitution, $a^2 = c^2 - 2cx + b^2$ or $a^2 = b^2 + c^2 - 2cx$. So, $a^2 = b^2 + c^2 - 2cb\cos A$ by substitution.

9. A surveyor at point P locates two landmarks, A and B, as shown in the figure. Explain how the surveyor can find the distance between the landmarks to the nearest meter.

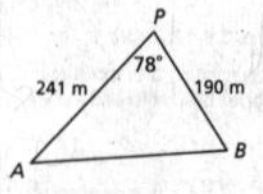

By the Law of Cosines, $p^2 = a^2 + b^2 - 2ab\cos P$, so $p^2 = 190^2 + 241^2 - 2(190)(241)\cos 78°$. Simplifying gives $p^2 = 75{,}140.4$ and $p \approx 274.1$. So, the distance between the landmarks is about 274 m.

Notes

CHAPTER 9

Extending Transformational Geometry

CHAPTER 9

Extending Transformational Geometry

Chapter Focus

A transformation is a function that changes the position, shape, and/or size of a figure. In this unit, you will work with a variety of transformations, but you will focus on transformations that are rigid motions. Rigid motions preserve the size and shape of a figure. As you will see, reflections (flips), translations (slides), and rotations (turns) are all rigid motions. As you work with these transformations, you will learn to draw transformed figures and describe transformations in words and with symbols.

Chapter at a Glance

Lesson		Standards for Mathematical Content
9-1	Reflections	CC.9-12.G.CO.2, CC.9-12.G.CO.4, CC.9-12.G.CO.5
9-2	Translations	CC.9-12.G.CO.2, CC.9-12.G.CO.4, CC.9-12.G.CO.5
9-3	Rotations	CC.9-12.G.CO.2, CC.9-12.G.CO.5
9-4	Compositions of Transformations	CC.9-12.G.CO.5
9-5	Symmetry	CC.9-12.G.CO.3
9-6	Tessellations	CC.9-12.G.CO.5
9-7	Dilations	CC.9-12.G.CO.2
	Performance Tasks	
	Assessment Readiness	

COMMON CORE PROFESSIONAL DEVELOPMENT

CC.9-12.G.CO.2

Transformations can be studied as functions, and as such present an opportunity to connect geometry and algebra. In the case of a transformation function, the inputs (domain) and outputs (range) are points in the plane instead of numbers.

Unpacking the Standards

Understanding the standards and the vocabulary terms in the standards will help you know exactly what you are expected to learn in this chapter.

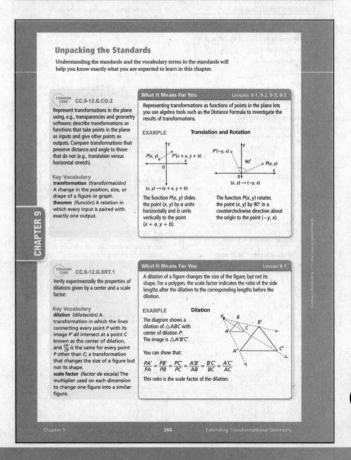

CC.9-12.G.CO.2

Represent transformations in the plane using, e.g., transparencies and geometry software; describe transformations as functions that take points in the plane as inputs and give other points as outputs. Compare transformations that preserve distance and angle to those that do not (e.g., translation versus horizontal stretch).

Key Vocabulary
transformation *(transformación)* A change in the position, size, or shape of a figure or graph.
theorem *(función)* A relation in which every input is paired with exactly one output.

What It Means For You   Lessons 9-1, 9-2, 9-3, 9-7

Representing transformations as functions of points in the plane lets you use algebra tools such as the Distance Formula to investigate the results of transformations.

EXAMPLE   **Translation and Rotation**

$(x, y) \rightarrow (x + a, y + b)$

The function $P(x, y)$ slides the point (x, y) by a units horizontally and b units vertically to the point $(x + a, y + b)$.

$(x, y) \rightarrow (-y, x)$

The function $P(x, y)$ rotates the point (x, y) by 90° in a counterclockwise direction about the origin to the point $(-y, x)$.

CC.9-12.G.SRT.1

Verify experimentally the properties of dilations given by a center and a scale factor:

Key Vocabulary
dilation *(dilatación)* A transformation in which the lines connecting every point P with its image P' all intersect at a point C known as the center of dilation, and $\frac{CP'}{CP}$ is the same for every point P other than C; a transformation that changes the size of a figure but not its shape.
scale factor *(factor de escala)* The multiplier used on each dimension to change one figure into a similar figure.

What It Means For You   Lesson 9-7

A dilation of a figure changes the size of the figure, but not its shape. For a polygon, the scale factor indicates the ratio of the side lengths after the dilation to the corresponding lengths before the dilation.

EXAMPLE   **Dilation**

The diagram shows a dilation of $\triangle ABC$ with center of dilation P. The image is $\triangle A'B'C'$.

You can show that:

$$\frac{PA'}{PA} = \frac{PB'}{PB} = \frac{PC'}{PC} = \frac{A'B'}{AB} = \frac{B'C'}{BC} = \frac{A'C'}{AC}$$

This ratio is the scale factor of the dilation.

Students build on their experiences with rigid motions from earlier grades, using more precise definitions and more formal reasoning. Students should understand that rigid motions are based on geometric concepts. For example, translations move points a specified distance along a line and rotations move objects along a circular arc through a specified angle.

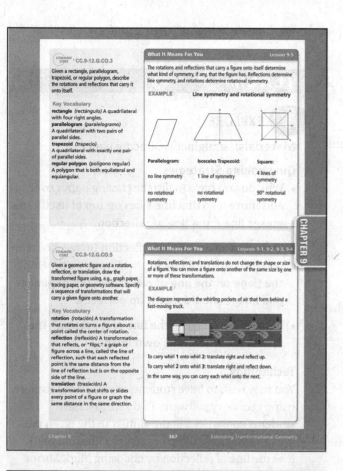

CC.9-12.G.CO.3

Given a rectangle, parallelogram, trapezoid, or regular polygon, describe the rotations and reflections that carry it onto itself.

Key Vocabulary

rectangle *(rectángulo)* A quadrilateral with four right angles.
parallelogram *(paralelogramo)* A quadrilateral with two pairs of parallel sides.
trapezoid *(trapecio)* A quadrilateral with exactly one pair of parallel sides.
regular polygon *(polígono regular)* A polygon that is both equilateral and equiangular.

What It Means For You Lesson 9-5

The rotations and reflections that carry a figure onto itself determine what kind of symmetry, if any, that the figure has. Reflections determine line symmetry, and rotations determine rotational symmetry.

EXAMPLE Line symmetry and rotational symmetry

Parallelogram:	Isosceles Trapezoid:	Square:
no line symmetry	1 line of symmetry	4 lines of symmetry
no rotational symmetry	no rotational symmetry	90° rotational symmetry

CC.9-12.G.CO.5

Given a geometric figure and a rotation, reflection, or translation, draw the transformed figure using, e.g., graph paper, tracing paper, or geometry software. Specify a sequence of transformations that will carry a given figure onto another.

Key Vocabulary

rotation *(rotación)* A transformation that rotates or turns a figure about a point called the center of rotation.
reflection *(reflexión)* A transformation that reflects, or "flips," a graph or figure across a line, called the line of reflection, such that each reflected point is the same distance from the line of reflection but is on the opposite side of the line.
translation *(traslación)* A transformation that shifts or slides every point of a figure or graph the same distance in the same direction.

What It Means For You Lessons 9-1, 9-2, 9-3, 9-4

Rotations, reflections, and translations do not change the shape or size of a figure. You can move a figure onto another of the same size by one or more of these transformations.

EXAMPLE

The diagram represents the whirling pockets of air that form behind a fast-moving truck.

To carry whirl **1** onto whirl **2**: translate right and reflect up.
To carry whirl **2** onto whirl **3**: translate right and reflect down.
In the same way, you can carry each whirl onto the next.

Key Vocabulary

angle of rotation *(ángulo de rotación)* An angle formed by a rotating ray, called the terminal side, and a stationary reference ray, called the initial side.

angle of rotational symmetry *(ángulo de simetría de rotación)* The smallest angle through which a figure with rotational symmetry can be rotated to coincide with itself.

center of dilation *(centro de dilatación)* The intersection of the lines that connect each point of the image with the corresponding point of the preimage.

center of rotation *(centro de rotación)* The point around which a figure is rotated.

component form *(forma de componente)* The form of a vector that lists the vertical and horizontal change from the initial point to the terminal point.

dilation *(dilatación)* A transformation in which the lines connecting every point P with its image P' all intersect at a point C known as the center of dilation, and $\frac{CP'}{CP}$ is the same for every point P other than C; a transformation that changes the size of a figure but not its shape.

line of symmetry *(eje de simetría)* A line that divides a plane figure into two congruent reflected halves.

line symmetry *(simetría axial)* A figure that can be reflected across a line so that the image coincides with the preimage.

reflection *(reflexión)* A transformation that reflects, or "flips," a graph or figure across a line, called the line of reflection, such that each reflected point is the same distance from the line of reflection but is on the opposite side of the line.

rotation *(rotación)* A transformation that rotates or turns a figure about a point called the center of rotation.

scale factor *(factor de escala)* The multiplier used on each dimension to change one figure into a similar figure.

rotational symmetry *(simetría de rotación)* A figure that can be rotated about a point by an angle less than 360° so that the image coincides with the preimage has rotational symmetry.

symmetry *(simetría)* In the transformation of a figure such that the image coincides with the preimage, the image and preimage have symmetry.

tessellation *(teselado)* A repeating pattern of plane figures that completely covers a plane with no gaps or overlaps.

transformation *(transformación)* A change in the position, size, or shape of a figure or graph.

translation *(traslación)* A transformation that shifts or slides every point of a figure or graph the same distance in the same direction.

CHAPTER 9

© Houghton Mifflin Harcourt Publishing Company

9-1

Reflections
Going Deeper

Essential question: *How do you draw the image of a figure under a reflection?*

© Houghton Mifflin Harcourt Publishing Company

COMMON CORE Standards for Mathematical Content

CC.9-12.G.CO.2 ... describe transformations as functions that take points in the plane as inputs and give other points as outputs. ...

CC.9-12.G.CO.4 Develop definitions of ... reflections ... in terms of ... perpendicular lines ... and line segments.

CC.9-12.G.CO.5 Given a geometric figure and a ... reflection, ... draw the transformed figure using, e.g., graph paper, tracing paper, or geometry software.

CC.9-12.G.CO.6 Use geometric descriptions of rigid motions to transform figures and to predict the effect of a given rigid motion on a given figure; ...

Prerequisites

Constructing perpendicular lines

Transformations and rigid motions

Math Background

Reflections may be considered the most basic of the rigid motions because the other two rigid motions, translations and rotations, can be expressed in terms of reflections. In particular, every translation is a composition of reflections across parallel lines. Every rotation is a composition of reflections across intersecting lines.

INTRODUCE

Ask students to describe everyday examples of reflections. Students might mention mirrors or the reflection of a mountain in a lake. Ask students to describe characteristics of these reflections. Be sure students realize that in every case the reflected object is the same size and shape as the original object.

TEACH

1 EXPLORE

Materials: straightedge, tracing paper

Questioning Strategies

- Why do you have to flip the tracing paper over and move it so that line ℓ lies on top of itself? **This makes line ℓ the line of reflection.**

- Once you've drawn the reflection image, how can you use paper folding to check your work? **Fold the page on the line of reflection. The pre-image and image should match up perfectly.**

- What is the image of the line of reflection? **The line of reflection is its own image.**

Technology

You may wish to have students carry out the Explore using geometry software. To do so, first have students construct a figure similar to the given pre-image. Then have them construct a line and mark it as the line of reflection by choosing Mark Mirror from the Transform menu. Finally, have students select the pre-image and choose Reflect from the Transform menu.

MATHEMATICAL PRACTICE **Highlighting the Standards**

Making conjectures is an essential part of mathematics and an important aspect of Standard 3 (Construct viable arguments and critique the reasoning of others). This standard states that students should "reasoning inductively" and the Explore gives students an excellent opportunity to do so. In particular, students should look back at their work and make a conjecture about the reflection image of a point that lies on the line of reflection.

Name _____ Class _____ Date _____

Reflections
Going Deeper

Essential question: *How do you draw the image of a figure under a reflection?*

One type of rigid motion is a reflection.
A *reflection* is a transformation that
moves points by flipping them over
a line called the *line of reflection*.
The figure shows the reflection of
quadrilateral *ABCD* across line ℓ.
Notice that the pre-image and image
are mirror images of each other.

Video Tutor

CC.9-12.G.CO.4

1 EXPLORE   Drawing a Reflection Image

Follow the steps below to draw the reflection image of each figure.

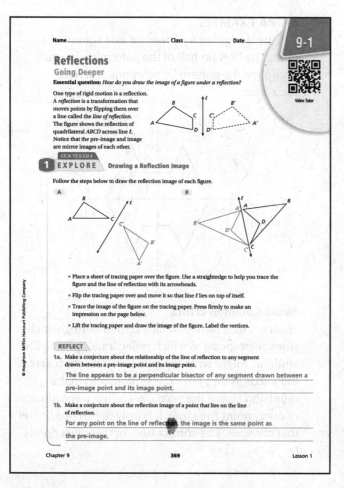

- Place a sheet of tracing paper over the figure. Use a straightedge to help you trace the figure and the line of reflection with its arrowheads.
- Flip the tracing paper over and move it so that line ℓ lies on top of itself.
- Trace the image of the figure on the tracing paper. Press firmly to make an impression on the page below.
- Lift the tracing paper and draw the image of the figure. Label the vertices.

REFLECT

1a. Make a conjecture about the relationship of the line of reflection to any segment drawn between a pre-image point and its image point.

The line appears to be a perpendicular bisector of any segment drawn between a pre-image point and its image point.

1b. Make a conjecture about the reflection image of a point that lies on the line of reflection.

For any point on the line of reflection, the image is the same point as the pre-image.

Chapter 9   369   Lesson 1

© Houghton Mifflin Harcourt Publishing Company

CC.9-12.G.CO.5

2 EXAMPLE   Constructing a Reflection Image

Work directly on the figure below and follow the given steps to construct the image of △*ABC* after a reflection across line *m*.

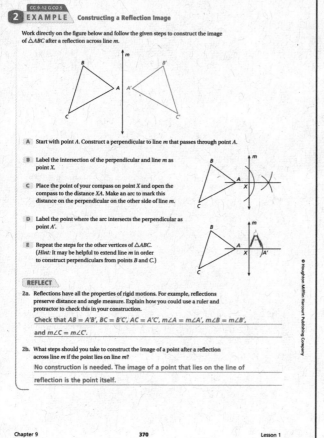

A   Start with point *A*. Construct a perpendicular to line *m* that passes through point *A*.

B   Label the intersection of the perpendicular and line *m* as point *X*.

C   Place the point of your compass on point *X* and open the compass to the distance *XA*. Make an arc to mark this distance on the perpendicular on the other side of line *m*.

D   Label the point where the arc intersects the perpendicular as point *A′*.

E   Repeat the steps for the other vertices of △*ABC*. (*Hint:* It may be helpful to extend line *m* in order to construct perpendiculars from points *B* and *C*.)

REFLECT

2a. Reflections have all the properties of rigid motions. For example, reflections preserve distance and angle measure. Explain how you could use a ruler and protractor to check this in your construction.

Check that $AB = A′B′$, $BC = B′C′$, $AC = A′C′$, $m\angle A = m\angle A′$, $m\angle B = m\angle B′$, and $m\angle C = m\angle C′$.

2b. What steps should you take to construct the image of a point after a reflection across line *m* if the point lies on line *m*?

No construction is needed. The image of a point that lies on the line of reflection is the point itself.

Chapter 9   370   Lesson 1

© Houghton Mifflin Harcourt Publishing Company

---

2 EXAMPLE

Questioning Strategies

- How many perpendiculars to line *m* will you have to construct in order to construct the reflection image of △*ABC*? Why? **Three; you construct one perpendicular for each vertex of the triangle.**

- How can you check that you constructed the image correctly? **Fold the page on line *m* and check that the image and pre-image match up perfectly.**

EXTRA EXAMPLE

Construct the image of △*DEF* after a reflection across line *m*.

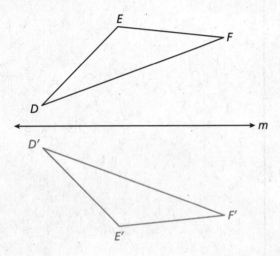

EXTRA EXAMPLE

You are designing a pattern for one square of a quilt. The bottom half of the pattern is shown. Complete the pattern by reflecting it across the *x*-axis.

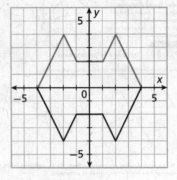

Avoid Common Errors

Students may have difficulty remembering which rules correspond to which reflections. Specifically, students might write the rule for a reflection across the *y*-axis as $(x, y) \rightarrow (x, -y)$. Point out that a reflection across the *y*-axis, keeps the *y*-coordinate of every point the same; it is only the *x*-coordinate that changes. The correct rule for this reflection is $(x, y) \rightarrow (-x, y)$.

3 EXAMPLE

Questioning Strategies

- How will the right half of the logo compare to the left half? **It will be the same size and shape as the left half, but it will be a mirror image of the left half.**

- What does the rule $(x, y) \rightarrow (-x, y)$ mean? **To reflect a point across the *y*-axis, use the opposite of the *x*-coordinate and keep the *y*-coordinate the same.**

The table provides coordinate notation for reflections in a coordinate plane.

Rules for Reflections in a Coordinate Plane	
Reflection across the x-axis	$(x, y) \rightarrow (x, -y)$
Reflection across the y-axis	$(x, y) \rightarrow (-x, y)$
Reflection across the line $y = x$	$(x, y) \rightarrow (y, x)$

CC.9-12.G.CO.2

3 EXAMPLE Drawing a Reflection in a Coordinate Plane

You are designing a logo for a bank. The left half of the logo is shown. You will complete the logo by reflecting this figure across the y-axis.

A In the space below, sketch your prediction of what the completed logo will look like.

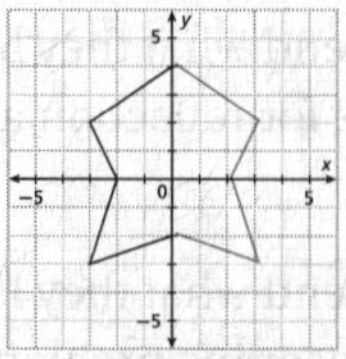

B In the table at right, list the vertices of the left half of the logo. Then use the rule for a reflection across the y-axis to write the vertices of the right half of the logo.

C Plot the vertices of the right half of the logo. Then connect the vertices to complete the logo. Compare the completed logo to your prediction.

Left Half (x, y)	Right Half (−x, y)
(0, 4)	(0, 4)
(−3, 2)	(3, 2)
(−2, 0)	(2, 0)
(−3, −3)	(3, −3)
(0, −2)	(0, −2)

REFLECT

3a. Explain how your prediction compares to the completed logo.

Answers will vary.

3b. How can you use paper folding to check that you completed the logo correctly?

Fold along the line of reflection and check that the two halves lie on top

of each other.

PRACTICE

Use tracing paper to help you draw the reflection image of each figure across line m. Label the vertices of the image using prime notation.

1.

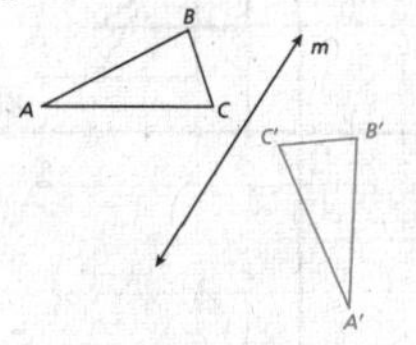

2.

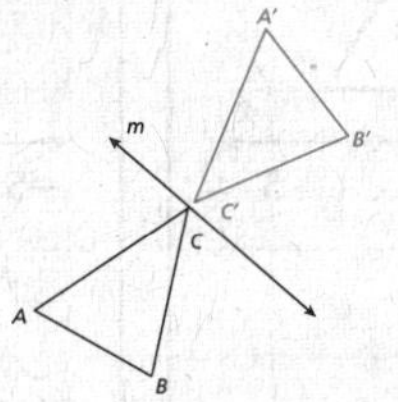

3.

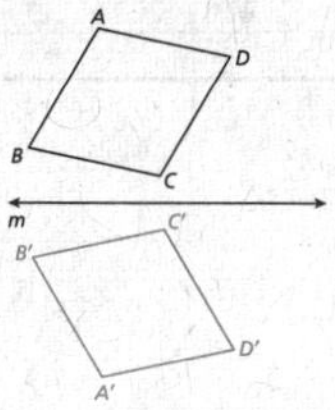

4.

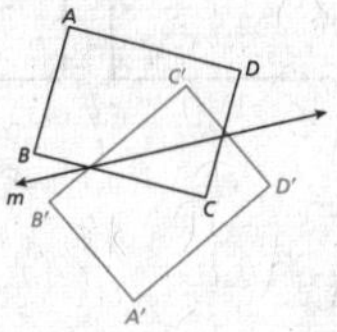

5.

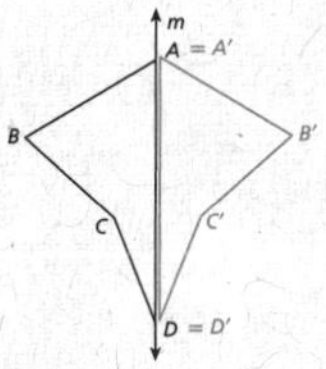

6.

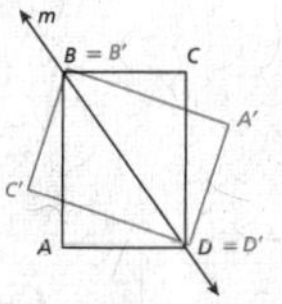

Essential Question

How do you draw the image of a figure under a reflection?

You can draw the image of a figure under a reflection by using tracing paper or by doing a compass-and-straightedge construction.

Summarize

Have students make a graphic organizer that summarizes reflections in a coordinate plane. A sample is shown below.

Where skills are taught	Where skills are practiced
1 EXPLORE	EXS. 1–6
2 EXAMPLE	EXS. 7–8
3 EXAMPLE	EXS. 9–17, 19

Exercise 18: Students extend what they learned in **3** EXAMPLE to find a rule for reflection across the line $y = -x$.

Exercise 20: Students extend what they learned in **3** EXAMPLE to solve a reasoning problem.

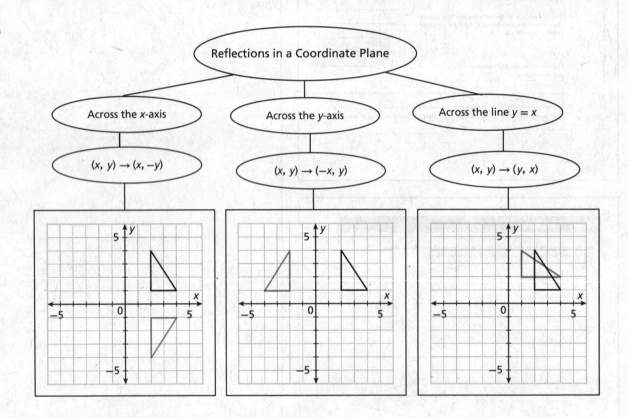

Use a compass and straightedge to construct the reflection image of each figure across line *m*. Label the vertices of the image using prime notation.

7.

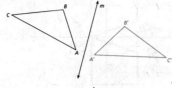

8.

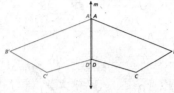

Give the image of each point after a reflection across the given line.

9. (3, 1); *x*-axis
   (3, −1)

10. (−6, −3); *y*-axis
    (6, −3)

11. (0, −2); *y* = *x*
    (−2, 0)

12. (−4, 3); *y*-axis
    (4, 3)

13. (5, 5); *y* = *x*
    (5, 5)

14. (−7, 0); *x*-axis
    (−7, 0)

15. (−1, 5); *y* = *x*
    (5, −1)

16. (10, 6); *x*-axis
    (10, −6)

17. (8, 0); *y*-axis
    (−8, 0)

18. Plot several points on a coordinate plane. Then find their images after a reflection across the line $y = -x$. Use the results to develop a rule for reflection across the line $y = -x$.

   Possible answer: (3, 4) is reflected to (−4, −3), (2, −1) is reflected to (1, −2),

   (5, 0) is reflected to (0, −5), (−7, 7) is reflected to (−7, 7); in general, the

   image of (*x*, *y*) after a reflection across the line $y = -x$ is (−*y*, −*x*).

19. As the first step in designing a logo, you draw the figure shown in the first quadrant of the coordinate plane. Then you reflect the figure across the *x*-axis. You complete the design by reflecting the original figure and its image across the *y*-axis. Draw the completed design.

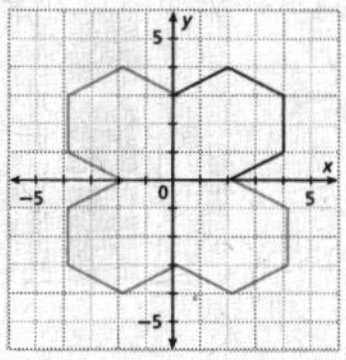

20. When point *P* is reflected across the *y*-axis, its image lies in Quadrant IV. When point *P* is reflected across the line $y = x$, its position does not change. What can you say about the coordinates of point *P*?

   Both coordinates are negative, and the *x*- and

   y-coordinates are equal.

Notes

Assign these pages to help your students practice
and apply important lesson concepts. For
additional exercises, see the Student Edition.

Answers

Additional Practice

1. yes

2. no

3. yes

4. no

5.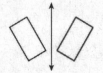

6.

7.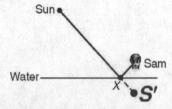

8.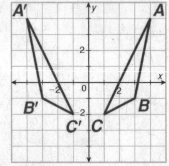

9.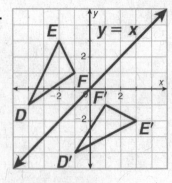

10.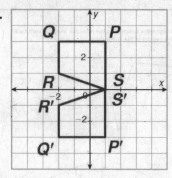

11.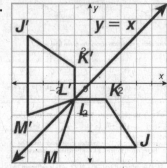

Problem Solving

1. $(-3, 5)$

2.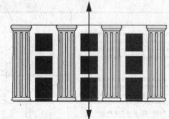

3. $(-6, -729)$

4. B

5. H

6. D

7. J

Additional Practice

Tell whether each transformation appears to be a reflection.

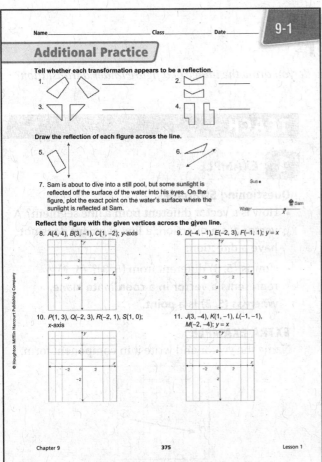

1. _____

2. _____

3. _____

4. _____

Draw the reflection of each figure across the line.

5.

6.

7. Sam is about to dive into a still pool, but some sunlight is reflected off the surface of the water into his eyes. On the figure, plot the exact point on the water's surface where the sunlight is reflected at Sam.

Reflect the figure with the given vertices across the given line.

8. $A(4, 4)$, $B(3, -1)$, $C(1, -2)$; y-axis

9. $D(-4, -1)$, $E(-2, 3)$, $F(-1, 1)$; $y = x$

10. $P(1, 3)$, $Q(-2, 3)$, $R(-2, 1)$, $S(1, 0)$; x-axis

11. $J(3, -4)$, $K(1, -1)$, $L(-1, -1)$, $M(-2, -4)$; $y = x$

© Houghton Mifflin Harcourt Publishing Company

Problem Solving

1. Quadrilateral $JLKM$ has vertices $J(7, 9)$, $K(0, -4)$, $L(2, 2)$, and $M(5, -3)$. If the figure is reflected across the line $y = x$, what are the coordinates of M'?

2. In the drawing, the left side of a structure is shown with its line of reflection. Draw the right side of the structure.

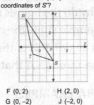

3. The function $y = -3^x$ passes through the point $P(6, -729)$. If the graph is reflected across the y-axis, what are the coordinates of the image of P?

Choose the best answer.

4. A park planner is designing two paths that connect picnic areas E and F to a point on the park road. Which point on the park road will make the total length of the paths as small as possible? (Hint: Use a reflection. What is the shortest distance between two points?)

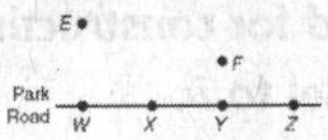

Park Road   W   X   Y   Z

A W C Y
B X D Z

5. $\triangle RST$ is reflected across a line so that T' has coordinates $(1, 3)$. What are the coordinates of S'?

F $(0, 2)$ H $(2, 0)$
G $(0, -2)$ J $(-2, 0)$

6. $\triangle MNP$ with vertices $M(1, 5)$, $N(0, -3)$, and $P(-2, 2)$ is reflected across a line. The coordinates of the reflection image are $M'(7, 5)$, $N'(8, -3)$, and $P'(10, 2)$. Over which line was $\triangle MNP$ reflected?

A $y = 2$
B $x = 2$
C $y = 4$
D $x = 4$

7. Sarah is using a coordinate plane to design a rug. The rug is to have a triangle with vertices at $(8, 13)$, $(2, -13)$, and $(14, -13)$. She wants the rug to have a second triangle that is the reflection of the first triangle across the x-axis. Which is a vertex of the second triangle?

F $(-13, 14)$ H $(-2, -13)$
G $(-14, 13)$ J $(2, 13)$

© Houghton Mifflin Harcourt Publishing Company

Translations
Going Deeper

Essential question: *How do you draw the image of a figure under a translation?*

CC.9-12.G.CO.2 ... describe transformations as functions that take points in the plane as inputs and give other points as outputs. ...

CC.9-12.G.CO.4 Develop definitions of ... translations ... in terms of ... parallel lines ... and line segments.

CC.9-12.G.CO.5 Given a geometric figure and a ... translation, ... draw the transformed figure using, e.g., graph paper, tracing paper, or geometry software.

CC.9-12.G.CO.6 Use geometric descriptions of rigid motions to transform figures and to predict the effect of a given rigid motion on a given figure; ...

Vocabulary

vector
initial point
terminal point
component form
translation

Prerequisites

Constructing parallel lines
Transformations and rigid motions

Math Background

Translations are the second of the three rigid motions that students will study in this course. It is easy to understand a translation informally by thinking of it as a slide in a given direction by a given distance. Providing a mathematical definition of translations requires a bit more groundwork. In fact, it is most efficient to define translations in terms of vectors.

INTRODUCE

Ask students to give everyday examples of slides or translations. If no one suggests it, you might describe an object moving along a straight conveyor belt in a factory. This is an example of a translation because the object slides along a straight path from a starting point to an ending point. Tell the class they will learn more about translations and will see how to define translations in terms of vectors.

TEACH

1 EXAMPLE

Questioning Strategies

• How is a vector different from a line segment? A vector has a direction; a line segment does not have a direction.

• How is $\langle 5, 3 \rangle$ different from $(5, 3)$? $\langle 5, 3 \rangle$ represents a vector in a coordinate plane, whereas $(5, 3)$ is a point.

EXTRA EXAMPLE
Name the vector and write it in component form.

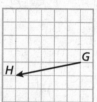

$\overrightarrow{GH}$; $\langle -5, -1 \rangle$

2 EXAMPLE

Questioning Strategies

• Before constructing the translation image, where do you predict the image will lie? Why? It will lie about 5 cm to the right and a bit above the pre-image. This is the distance and direction given by the translation vector.

• What can you say about the length AA'? It is equal to the magnitude of $\vec{v}$.

• Why do the figures that accompany the steps of the example show the construction marks for copying an angle? This is the method for constructing a line through A that is parallel to $\vec{v}$.

EXTRA EXAMPLE
Construct the image of $\triangle DEF$ after a translation along $\vec{v}$.

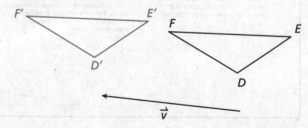

Name _____ Class _____ Date _____

9-2

Translations
Going Deeper

Essential question: *How do you draw the image of a figure under a translation?*

Video Tutor

You have seen that a reflection is one
type of rigid motion. A *translation*
is another type of rigid motion.
A translation slides all points of
a figure the same distance in the
same direction. The figure shows a
translation of a triangle.

It is convenient to describe translations using the language
of vectors. A **vector** is a quantity that has both direction and
magnitude. The **initial point** of a vector is the starting point.
The **terminal point** of a vector is the ending point. The vector
at right may be named $\overline{EF}$ or $\vec{v}$.

A vector can also be named using **component form**, $\langle a, b \rangle$, which
specifies the horizontal change a and the vertical change b from the
initial point to the terminal point. The component form for $\overline{PQ}$ is $(5, 3)$.

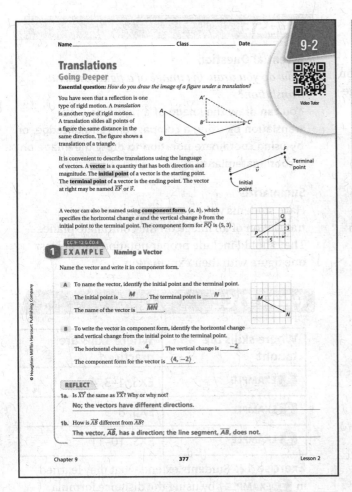

CC.9-12.G.CO.4

1 EXAMPLE Naming a Vector

Name the vector and write it in component form.

A To name the vector, identify the initial point and the terminal point.

The initial point is ___M___. The terminal point is ___N___.

The name of the vector is ___$\overline{MN}$___.

B To write the vector in component form, identify the horizontal change
and vertical change from the initial point to the terminal point.

The horizontal change is ___4___. The vertical change is ___−2___.

The component form for the vector is ___$\langle 4, -2 \rangle$___.

REFLECT

1a. Is $\overline{XY}$ the same as $\overline{YX}$? Why or why not?

No; the vectors have different directions.

1b. How is $\overline{AB}$ different from $\overline{AB}$?

The vector, $\overline{AB}$, has a direction; the line segment, $\overline{AB}$, does not.

Chapter 9   377   Lesson 2

You can use vectors to give a formal definition of *translation*.

A **translation** is a transformation along a vector such that the segment joining a
point and its image has the same length as the vector and is parallel to the vector.

The notation $T_{\vec{v}}(P) = P'$ says that the image of point P after a translation along
vector $\vec{v}$ is P'.

CC.9-12.G.CO.5

2 EXAMPLE Constructing a Translation Image

Work directly on the figure below and follow the given steps to construct the image
of $\triangle ABC$ after a translation along $\vec{v}$.

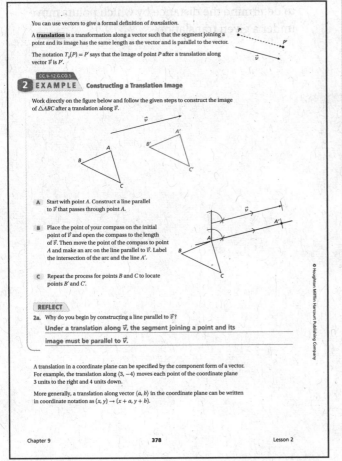

A Start with point A. Construct a line parallel
to $\vec{v}$ that passes through point A.

B Place the point of your compass on the initial
point of $\vec{v}$ and open the compass to the length
of $\vec{v}$. Then move the point of the compass to point
A and make an arc on the line parallel to $\vec{v}$. Label
the intersection of the arc and the line A'.

C Repeat the process for points B and C to locate
points B' and C'.

REFLECT

2a. Why do you begin by constructing a line parallel to $\vec{v}$?

Under a translation along $\vec{v}$, the segment joining a point and its
image must be parallel to $\vec{v}$.

A translation in a coordinate plane can be specified by the component form of a vector.
For example, the translation along $(3, -4)$ moves each point of the coordinate plane
3 units to the right and 4 units down.

More generally, a translation along vector $\langle a, b \rangle$ in the coordinate plane can be written
in coordinate notation as $(x, y) \rightarrow (x + a, y + b)$.

Chapter 9   378   Lesson 2

Questioning Strategies

- Suppose you transform a figure with a translation along $\langle -8, 0 \rangle$. How will the location of the image compare to the location of the pre-image? The image will be 8 units directly to the left of the pre-image.

- How can you write the translation along $\langle -8, 0 \rangle$ in coordinate notation? $(x, y) \rightarrow (x - 8, y)$

EXTRA EXAMPLE

Draw the image of the triangle under a translation along $\langle 5, -3 \rangle$.

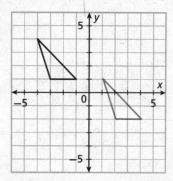

```
MATHEMATICAL    Highlighting
  PRACTICE      the Standards
```

Standard 2 (Reason abstractly and quantitatively) can be addressed in the follow-up discussion to Example 3. In particular, the Reflect questions include some "what-if" scenarios. Such questions present an excellent opportunity for students to stretch their reasoning abilities. You might have students pose their own "what-if" questions related to Example 3. Then have them answer the questions posed by classmates.

CLOSE

Essential Question

How do you draw the image of a figure under a translation?

You can draw the image of a figure under a translation by using a compass and straightedge, or by using coordinate notation to draw the image on a coordinate plane.

Summarize

Have students write a paragraph about the translation of an image on the coordinate plane. They should include proper notation and at least one figure with their explanation.

PRACTICE

Where skills are taught	Where skills are practiced
1 EXAMPLE	EXS. 1–3, 4–7
2 EXAMPLE	EXS. 8–9
3 EXAMPLE	EXS. 10–11

Exercise 12: Students extend what they learned in **3** EXAMPLE by using the distance formula to determine the distance by which points move under a given translation.

CC.9-12.G.CO.2

3 EXAMPLE Drawing a Translation in a Coordinate Plane

Draw the image of the triangle under a translation along $\langle -3, 2 \rangle$.

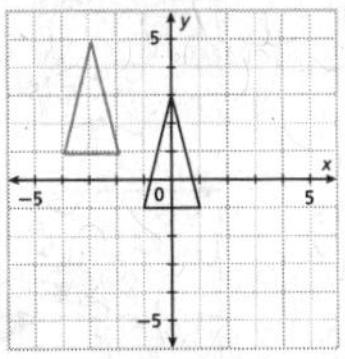

A Before drawing the image, predict the quadrant in which the image will lie.

Possible answer: Quadrant II

B In the table below, list the vertices of the triangle. Then use the rule for the translation to write the vertices of the image.

Pre-Image (x, y)	Image $(x - 3, y + 2)$
(0, 3)	(−3, 5)
(1, −1)	(−2, 1)
(−1, −1)	(−4, 1)

C Plot the vertices of the image. Then connect the vertices to complete the image. Compare the completed image to your prediction.

REFLECT

3a. Give an example of a translation that would move the original triangle into Quadrant IV.

Possible answer: translation along $\langle 2, -5 \rangle$

3b. Suppose you translate the original triangle along $\langle -10, -10 \rangle$ and then reflect the image across the y-axis. In which quadrant would the final image lie? Explain.

Quadrant IV; the translation image lies in Quadrant III. After a reflection across

the y-axis, all points in Quadrant III are mapped to Quadrant IV.

PRACTICE

Name the vector and write it in component form.

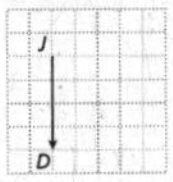

1.

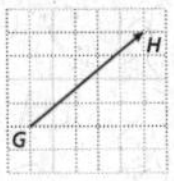

2.

3.

$\overrightarrow{GH}; \langle 5, 4 \rangle$ $\overrightarrow{JD}; \langle 0, -4 \rangle$ $\overrightarrow{VS}; \langle -2, 3 \rangle$

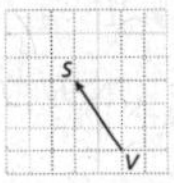

Draw and label a vector with the given name and component form.

4. $\overrightarrow{MP}; \langle 3, -1 \rangle$ **5.** $\overrightarrow{CB}; \langle -3, 0 \rangle$ 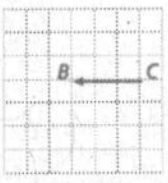   **6.** $\overrightarrow{HK}; \langle -5, 4 \rangle$

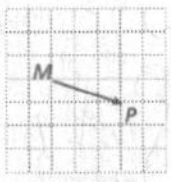

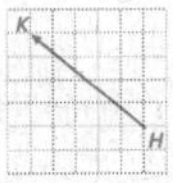

7. A vector has initial point $(-2, 2)$ and terminal point $(2, -1)$. Write the vector in component form. Then find the magnitude of the vector by using the distance formula.

$\langle 4, -3 \rangle; 5$

Use a compass and straightedge to construct the image of each triangle after a translation along $\vec{v}$. Label the vertices of the image.

8. 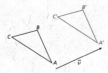   **9.**

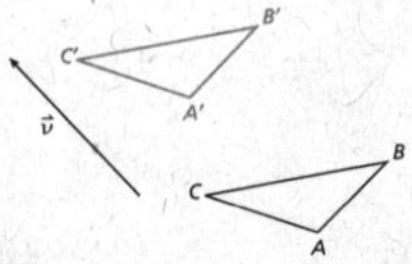

Draw the image of the figure under the given translation.

10. $\langle 3, -2 \rangle$ **11.** $\langle -4, 4 \rangle$

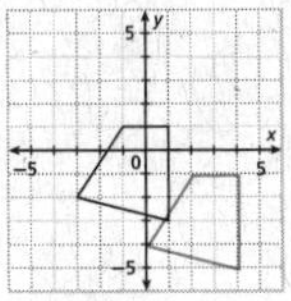

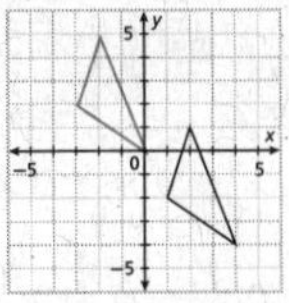

12. a. Use coordinate notation to name the translation that maps $\triangle ABC$ to $\triangle A'B'C'$.

$(x, y) \rightarrow (x - 1, y - 5)$

b. What distance does each point move under this translation?

$\sqrt{26}$ units

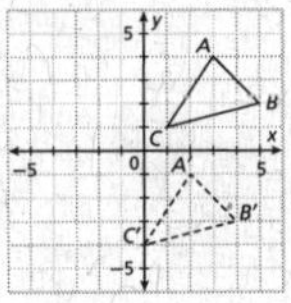

ADDITIONAL PRACTICE AND PROBLEM SOLVING

Assign these pages to help your students practice and apply important lesson concepts. For additional exercises, see the Student Edition.

Answers

Additional Practice

1. yes

2. no

3. no

4. yes

5.

6.

7.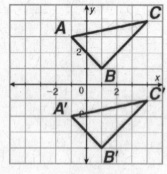

8.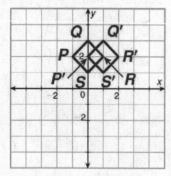

9.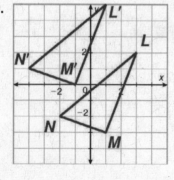

10.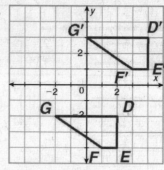

11. $(13, 31)$; $\langle 4, 15 \rangle$

Problem Solving

1. $\langle -4, 6 \rangle$

2. $\langle 3, -9 \rangle$

3. $(11, 8), (15, 9), (17, 5), (13, 4)$

4. $\langle 6, 1 \rangle$

5. C

6. F

7. C

Notes

Name_____ Class_____ Date_____

Additional Practice

Tell whether each transformation appears to be a translation.

1.  _____   2. _____

3.  _____   4. _____

Draw the translation of each figure along the given vector.

5.    6.

Translate the figure with the given vertices along the given vector.

7. $A(-1, 3)$, $B(1, 1)$, $C(4, 4)$; $\langle 0, -5 \rangle$

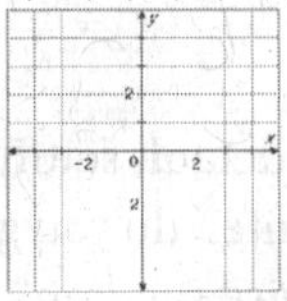

8. $P(-1, 2)$, $Q(0, 3)$, $R(1, 2)$, $S(0, 1)$; $\langle 1, 0 \rangle$

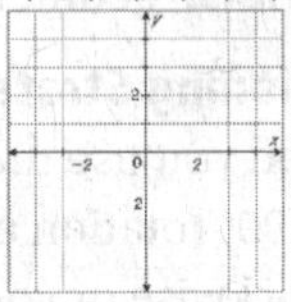

9. $L(3, 2)$, $M(1, -3)$, $N(-2, -2)$; $\langle -2, 3 \rangle$

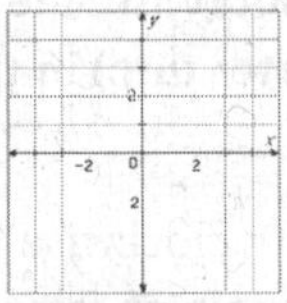

10. $D(2, -2)$, $E(2, -4)$, $F(1, -4)$, $G(-2, -2)$; $\langle 2, 5 \rangle$

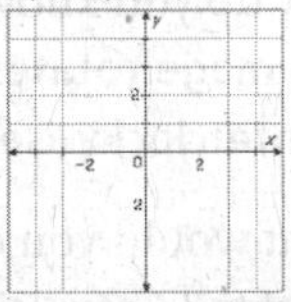

11. A builder is trying to level out some ground with a front-end loader. He picks up some excess dirt at (9, 16) and then maneuvers through the job site along the vectors $\langle -6, 0 \rangle$, $\langle 2, 5 \rangle$, and $\langle 8, 10 \rangle$ to get to the spot to unload the dirt. Find the coordinates of the unloading point. Find a single vector from the loading point to the unloading point.

_____

© Houghton Mifflin Harcourt Publishing Company

Problem Solving

1. A checker player's piece begins at K and, through a series of moves, lands on L. What translation vector represents the path from K to L?

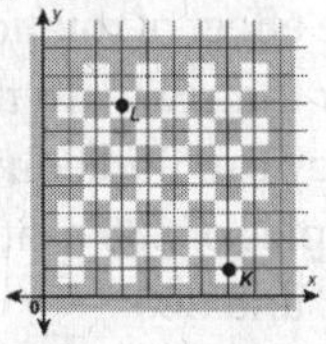

2. The preimage of M' has coordinates $(-6, 5)$. What is the vector that translates $\triangle MNP$ to $\triangle M'N'P'$?

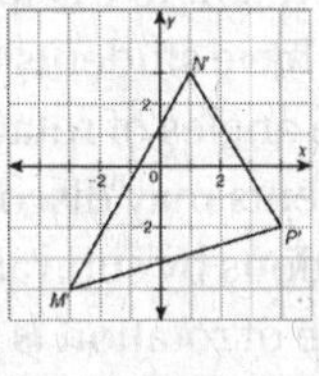

_____

3. In a quilt pattern, a polygon with vertices $(3, -2)$, $(7, -1)$, $(9, -5)$, and $(5, -6)$ is translated repeatedly along the vector $\langle 4, 5 \rangle$. What are the coordinates of the third polygon in the pattern?

_____

4. A group of hikers walks 2 miles east and then 1 mile north. After taking a break, they then hike 4 miles east and set up camp. What vector describes their hike from their starting position to their camp? Let 1 unit represent 1 mile.

_____

Choose the best answer.

5. In a video game, a character at (8, 3) moves three times, as described by the translations shown at right. What is the final position of the character after the three moves?

   A (-8, 3)   C (1, 1)

   B (-7, -2)   D (9, 2)

   Move 1: $\langle 2, 7 \rangle$
   Move 2: $\langle -10, -4 \rangle$
   Move 3: $\langle 1, -5 \rangle$

6. The logo is translated along the vector $\langle 8, 15 \rangle$. What are the coordinates of R'?

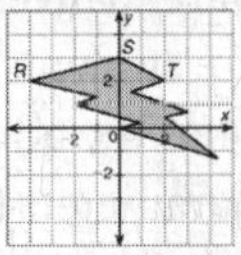

   F (4, 17)   H (15, 18)

   G (12, 17)   J (11, 19)

7. $\triangle DEF$ is translated so that the image of E has coordinates (0, 3). What is the image of F after this translation?

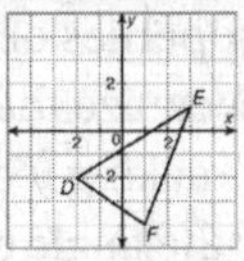

   A (1, -1)   C (-2, -2)

   B (4, -2)   D (-2, 6)

© Houghton Mifflin Harcourt Publishing Company

© Houghton Mifflin Harcourt Publishing Company

9-3

Rotations
Going Deeper

Essential question: *How do you draw the image of a figure under a rotation?*

Standards for Mathematical Content

CC.9-12.G.CO.2 ... describe transformations as functions that take points in the plane as inputs and give other points as outputs. ...

CC.9-12.G.CO.4 Develop definitions of rotations ... in terms of angles, circles, ...

CC.9-12.G.CO.5 Given a geometric figure and a rotation, ... draw the transformed figure using, e.g., graph paper, tracing paper, or geometry software.

CC.9-12.G.CO.6 Use geometric descriptions of rigid motions to transform figures and to predict the effect of a given rigid motion on a given figure; ...

Vocabulary

center of rotation

angle of rotation

rotation

Prerequisites

Transformations and rigid motions

Math Background

Rotations are the last of the three rigid motions that students will study in this course. Rotations are presented last because they are somewhat more difficult to draw than the other rigid motions and because predicting the effect of a rotation may be more difficult for some students than predicting the effect of a reflection or translation. For these reasons, rotations lend themselves well to investigations that use geometry software.

INTRODUCE

Ask students to describe familiar examples of turns or rotations. Students might mention the motion of a DVD in a DVD player, the motion of the wheel of a car, or the motion of a doorknob. Ask students what these motions have in common. Help them see that they all involve moving points around a fixed point.

TEACH

1 EXPLORE

Materials: geometry software

Questioning Strategies

- When you use the software's default setting of a 90° rotation about the center, do you get a clockwise or counterclockwise rotation? How do you know? **Counterclockwise; the pre-image rotates 90° (a quarter turn) in the counterclockwise direction.**

- What would you do to get a 90° clockwise rotation? **Enter 270° for the angle of rotation.**

- Which points, if any, do not move under the rotation? **Point *P***

Technology

If time permits, be sure to have students use the software to experiment with different angles of rotation. In particular, ask students to investigate what happens when the angle of rotation is 360°. Students should find that this rotation moves points back to their starting point; as such, this rotation is equivalent to the identity transformation. You might also have students explore the effect of rotations that have angles of rotation greater than 360°. In this case, students may discover that they can find equivalent rotations by subtracting multiples of 360° until the angle of rotation is between 0° and 360°.

> **MATHEMATICAL PRACTICE** **Highlighting the Standards**
>
> As students work through the Explore, address Standard 5 (Use appropriate tools strategically) by asking students to discuss the pros and cons of using geometry software to investigate properties of rotations. Be sure students recognize that such software has the advantage of making it easy to change parameters (such as the angle of rotation) so that they can observe the effects of the changes.

Name _____ Class _____ Date _____

9-3

Rotations
Going Deeper

Essential question: *How do you draw the image of a figure under a rotation?*

You have seen that reflections and translations are two types of rigid motions. The final rigid motion you will consider is a *rotation*. A rotation turns all points of the plane around a point called the **center of rotation**. The **angle of rotation** tells you the number of degrees through which points rotate around the center of rotation.

The figure shows a 120° counterclockwise rotation around point *P*. When no direction is specified, you can assume the rotation is in the counterclockwise direction.

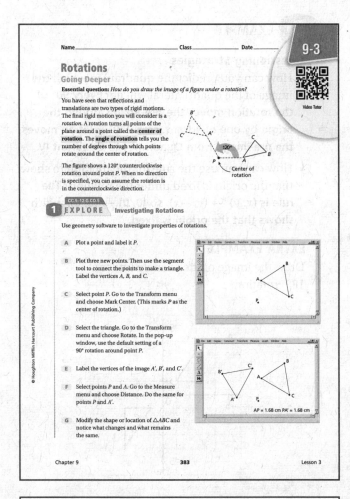

Video Tutor

Center of rotation

CC.9-12.G.CO.5

1 EXPLORE   Investigating Rotations

Use geometry software to investigate properties of rotations.

A   Plot a point and label it *P*.

B   Plot three new points. Then use the segment tool to connect the points to make a triangle. Label the vertices *A*, *B*, and *C*.

C   Select point *P*. Go to the Transform menu and choose Mark Center. (This marks *P* as the center of rotation.)

D   Select the triangle. Go to the Transform menu and choose Rotate. In the pop-up window, use the default setting of a 90° rotation around point *P*.

E   Label the vertices of the image *A′*, *B′*, and *C′*.

F   Select points *P* and *A*. Go to the Measure menu and choose Distance. Do the same for points *P* and *A′*.

G   Modify the shape or location of △*ABC* and notice what changes and what remains the same.

AP = 1.68 cm PA′ = 1.68 cm

Chapter 9   383   Lesson 3

REFLECT

1a.   Make a conjecture about the distance of a point and its image from the center of rotation.

Every point and its image are the same distance from the center of rotation.

1b.   What are the advantages of using geometry software rather than tracing paper or a compass and straightedge to investigate rotations?

Possible answer: Geometry software makes it easy to observe the effect of changing the shape or location of the pre-image.

A **rotation** is a transformation about a point *P* such that (1) every point and its image are the same distance from *P* and (2) all angles with vertex *P* formed by a point and its image have the same measure.

The notation $R_{P,\,m°}(A) = A′$ says that the image of point *A* after a rotation of *m°* about point *P* is *A′*.

CC.9-12.G.CO.5

2 EXAMPLE   Drawing a Rotation Image

Work directly on the figure below and follow the given steps to draw the image of △*ABC* after a 150° rotation about point *P*.

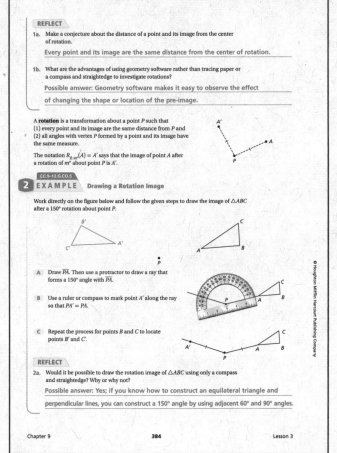

A   Draw $\overline{PA}$. Then use a protractor to draw a ray that forms a 150° angle with $\overline{PA}$.

B   Use a ruler or compass to mark point *A′* along the ray so that *PA′ = PA*.

C   Repeat the process for points *B* and *C* to locate points *B′* and *C′*.

REFLECT

2a.   Would it be possible to draw the rotation image of △*ABC* using only a compass and straightedge? Why or why not?

Possible answer: Yes; if you know how to construct an equilateral triangle and perpendicular lines, you can construct a 150° angle by using adjacent 60° and 90° angles.

Chapter 9   384   Lesson 3

© Houghton Mifflin Harcourt Publishing Company

Questioning Strategies

- What is m∠CPC'? **150°**

- What segment has the same length as $\overline{BP}$? **$\overline{B'P}$**

- How can you use tracing paper to check your construction? **Trace △ABC. Place the point of the pencil on P and rotate the paper 150° counterclockwise. The traced version of △ABC should lie on top of △A'B'C'.**

EXTRA EXAMPLE

Draw the image of △JKL after a 70° rotation about point P.

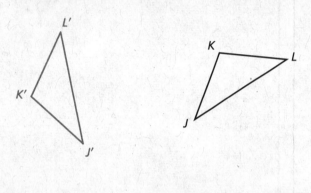

Teaching Strategies

Take a moment to discuss the tools that are used for this construction. Students should realize that they are using a protractor and ruler because they do not have a way to use a compass and straightedge to construct a 150° angle. Although it is theoretically possible to use a compass and straightedge to construct a 150° angle, students do not yet have the necessary background for this. Also, students should be aware that it is generally not possible to construct an angle with an arbitrary given measure. For example, in order to draw the rotation image of a figure under a 13° rotation, a protractor and ruler are the only feasible tools.

Questioning Strategies

- How can you predict the quadrant in which the image of the quadrilateral will lie? **Every 90° of the rotation moves the pre-image around the origin by one quadrant, so a 270° rotation moves the pre-image from Quadrant I to Quadrant IV.**

- How can you use the rule for the rotation to show that the origin is fixed under the rotation? **The rule is $(x, y) \rightarrow (y, -x)$, so $(0, 0) \rightarrow (0, 0)$, which shows that the origin is fixed.**

EXTRA EXAMPLE

Draw the image of the triangle under a 180° rotation.

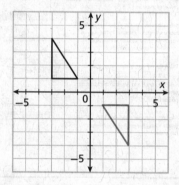

The table provides coordinate notation for rotations in a coordinate plane. You can assume that all rotations in a coordinate plane are rotations about the origin. Also, note that a 270° rotation is equivalent to turning $\frac{3}{4}$ of a complete circle.

Rules for Rotations in a Coordinate Plane	
Rotation of 90°	$(x, y) \rightarrow (-y, x)$
Rotation of 180°	$(x, y) \rightarrow (-x, -y)$
Rotation of 270°	$(x, y) \rightarrow (y, -x)$

CC.9-12.G.CO.2

3 EXAMPLE Drawing a Rotation in a Coordinate Plane

Draw the image of the quadrilateral under a 270° rotation.

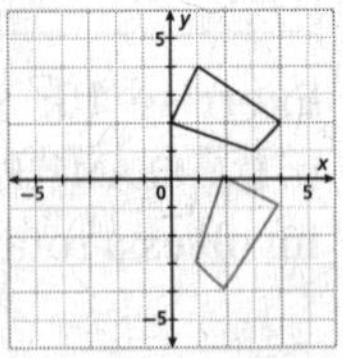

A Before drawing the image, predict the quadrant in which the image will lie.

Possible answer: Quadrant IV

B In the table below, list the vertices of the quadrilateral. Then use the rule for the rotation to write the vertices of the image.

Pre-Image (x, y)	Image $(y, -x)$
(3, 1)	(1, −3)
(4, 2)	(2, −4)
(1, 4)	(4, −1)
(0, 2)	(2, 0)

C Plot the vertices of the image. Then connect the vertices to complete the image. Compare the completed image to your prediction.

REFLECT

3a. What would happen if you rotated the image of the quadrilateral an additional 90° about the origin? Why does this make sense?

The final image would coincide with the original figure. The total amount

of the rotation would be 360°, which is a full circle.

3b. Suppose you rotate the original quadrilateral by 810°. In which quadrant will the image lie? Explain.

Quadrant II; subtracting 720° (2 × 360°) from 810° shows that this rotation is

equivalent to a 90° rotation, which moves the quadrilateral in Quadrant II.

PRACTICE

Use a ruler and protractor to draw the image of each figure after a rotation about point P by the given number of degrees. Label the vertices of the image.

1. 50°

2. 80°

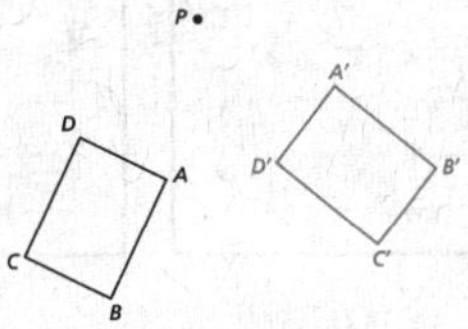

3. 160°

4. a. Use coordinate notation to write a rule for the rotation that maps △ABC to △A'B'C'.

$(x, y) \rightarrow (-y, x)$

b. What is the angle of rotation?

90°

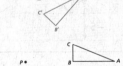

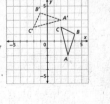

Essential Question

How do you draw the image of a figure under a rotation?

You can draw the image of a figure under a rotation by using geometry software or by using protractor and ruler.

Summarize

Have students make a graphic organizer to summarize what they know about rotations in a coordinate plane. A sample is shown below.

Where skills are taught	Where skills are practiced
2 EXAMPLE	EXS. 1–3
3 EXAMPLE	EXS. 4–9

Exercise 10: Students extend what they learned in 3 EXAMPLE by writing a transformation that involves a rotation followed by a translation.

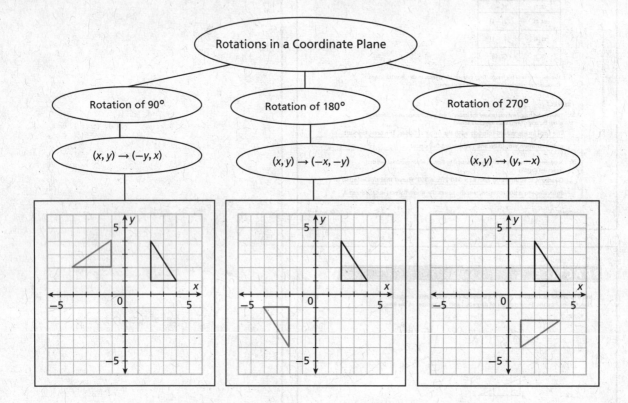

Draw the image of the figure after the given rotation.

5. 180°

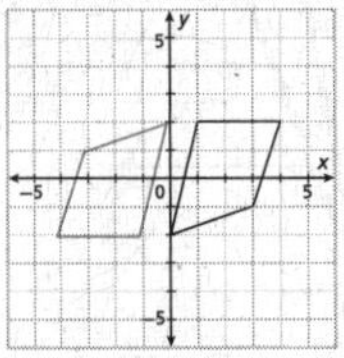

6. 90°

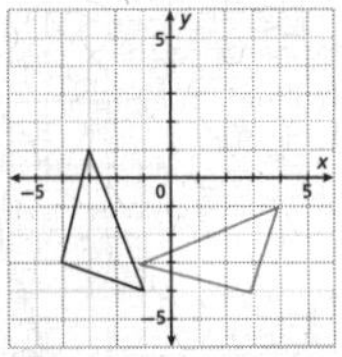

7. 270°

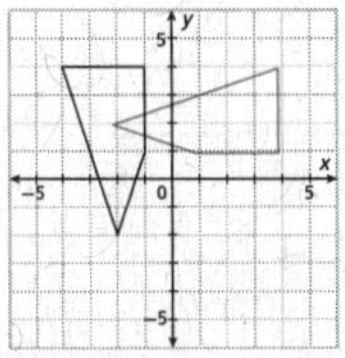

8. 180°

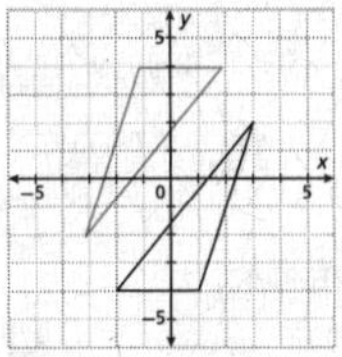

9. a. Reflect △JKL across the x-axis. Then reflect the image across the y-axis. Draw the final image of the triangle and label it △J'K'L'.

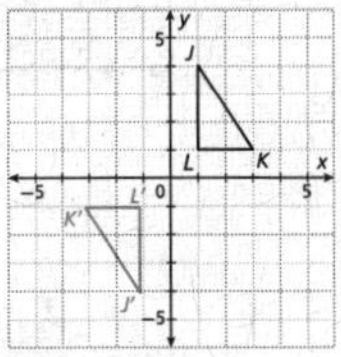

b. Describe a single rotation that maps △JKL to △J'K'L'.

180° rotation about the origin

c. Use coordinate notation to show that your answer to part **b** is correct.

$(x, y) \rightarrow (x, -y) \rightarrow (-x, -y)$ gives the

sequence of reflections; $(x, y) \rightarrow (-x, -y)$

is a 180° rotation.

d. Describe a composition of reflections that maps △J'K'L' back to △JKL.

Possible answer: Reflect across the x-axis. Then reflect the image across the

y-axis. Or, more generally, reflect across any two perpendicular lines that

intersect at (0, 0).

10. Error Analysis A student was asked to use coordinate notation to describe the result of a 180° rotation followed by a translation 3 units to the right and 5 units up. The student wrote this notation: $(x, y) \rightarrow (-[x + 3], -[y + 5])$. Describe and correct the student's error.

The student wrote notation that is correct if the translation is performed first

and the rotation is performed second. The coordinate notation for the correct

order of transformations is $(x, y) \rightarrow (-x + 3, -y + 5)$.

Assign these pages to help your students practice and apply important lesson concepts. For additional exercises, see the Student Edition.

Answers

Additional Practice

1. yes

2. no

3. no

4. no

5.

6.
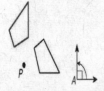

7.
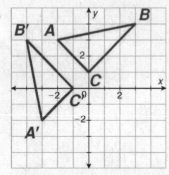

8.
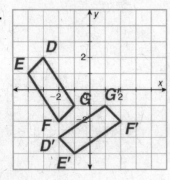

9.
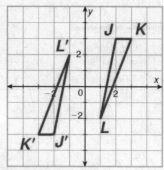

10.
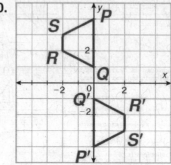

11. (6.5, 3.8)

Problem Solving

1. (−3, 2)

2. (6.6, 20.4)

3.

4. D

5. F

6. C

7. J

Additional Practice

Tell whether each transformation appears to be a rotation.

1.  _____   2. _____

3. 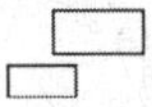 _____   4. _____

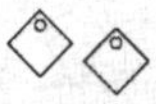

Draw the rotation of each figure about point P by m∠A.

5.    6.

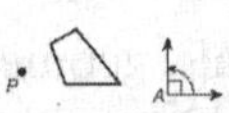

Rotate the figure with the given vertices about the origin using the given angle of rotation.

7. A(–2, 3), B(3, 4), C(0, 1); 90°

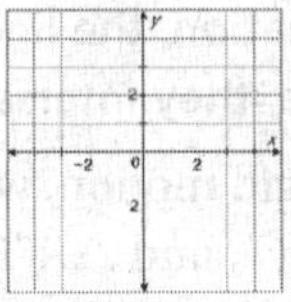

8. D(–3, 2), E(–4, 1), F(–2, –2), G(–1, –1); 90°

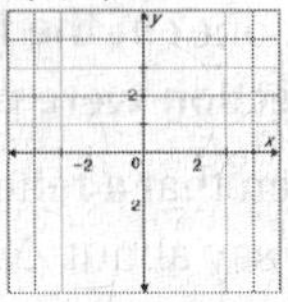

9. J(2, 3), K(3, 3), L(1, –2); 180°

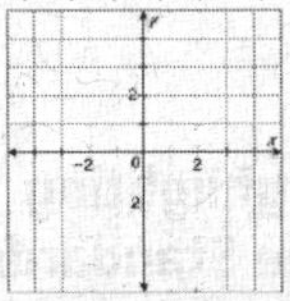

10. P(0, 4), Q(0, 1), R(–2, 2), S(–2, 3); 180°

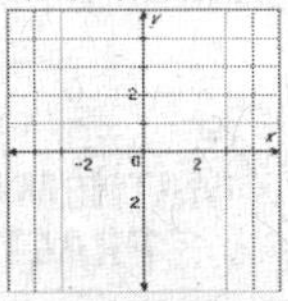

11. The steering wheel on Becky's car has a 15-inch diameter, and its center is at (0, 0). Point X at the top of the wheel has coordinates (0, 7.5). To turn left off her street, Becky must rotate the steering wheel by 300°. Find the coordinates of X when the steering wheel is rotated. Round to the nearest tenth. (*Hint:* How many degrees short of a full rotation is 300°?) _____

Chapter 9   389   Lesson 3

Problem Solving

1. △ABC is rotated about the origin so that A′ has coordinates (–1, –5). What are the coordinates of B′?

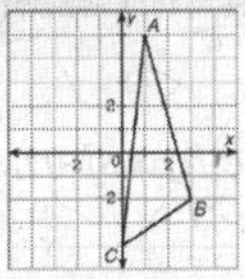

2. A spinning ride at an amusement park is a wheel that has a radius of 21.5 feet and rotates counterclockwise 12 times per minute. A car on the ride starts at position (21.5, 0). What are the coordinates of the car's location after 6 seconds? Round coordinates to the nearest tenth.

_____

3. To make a design, Trent rotates the figure 120° about point P, and then rotates that image 120° about point P. Draw the final design.

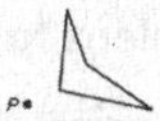

Choose the best answer.

4. Point K has coordinates (6, 8). After a counterclockwise rotation about the origin, the image of point K lies on the y-axis. What are the coordinates of K′?
   A (0, 5)   C (0, 8)
   B (0, 6)   D (0, 10)

5. △NPQ has vertices N(–6, –4), P(–3, 4), and Q(1, 1). If the triangle is rotated 90° counterclockwise about the origin, what are the coordinates of P′?
   F (–4, –3)   H (3, 4)
   G (–4, 3)   J (3, –4)

6. The Top of the World Restaurant in Las Vegas, Nevada, revolves 360° in 1 hour and 20 minutes. A piano that is 38 feet from the center of the restaurant starts at position (38, 0). What are the coordinates of the piano after 15 minutes? Round coordinates to the nearest tenth if necessary
   A (0, 38)
   B (–38, 0)
   C (14.5, 35.1)
   D (35.1, 14.5)

7. The five blades of a ceiling fan form a regular pentagon. Which clockwise rotation about point P maps point B to point D? 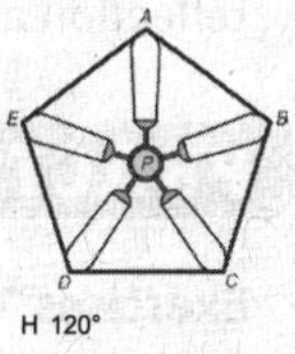
   F 60°   H 120°
   G 72°   J 144°

Chapter 9   390   Lesson 3

Chapter 9   390   Lesson 3

Compositions of Transformations
Going Deeper

Essential question: *How can you use more than one transformation to map one figure onto another?*

© Houghton Mifflin Harcourt Publishing Company

COMMON CORE **Standards for Mathematical Content**

CC.9-12.G.CO.5 Given a geometric figure and a rotation, reflection, or translation, draw the transformed figures using, e.g., graph paper, tracing paper, or geometry software. Specify a sequence of transformations that will carry a given figure onto another.

Prerequisites
Transformations and rigid motions

Math Background
Students have studied reflections, translations, and rotations. These three types of transformations are isometries. An isometry is a transformation that preserves both the size and shape of a figure, so the image is always congruent to the preimage.

INTRODUCE

Remind students of what a reflection is. Draw a line and a point not on the line. Ask students to describe how to find the reflection of the point across the line. Then ask them what would happen if the image of the point were reflected across the line. The reflection would be the original point. Point out that this double reflection is a special case of a more general result that students will investigate in Explore 1.

TEACH

1 EXPLORE

Materials: geometry software
Questioning Strategies
• Is $\triangle A''B''C''$ congruent to $\triangle ABC$? How do you know? A reflection is a rigid motion, so $\triangle A'B'C'$ is congruent to $\triangle ABC$ and $\triangle A''B''C''$ is congruent to $\triangle A'B'C'$. So, $\triangle A''B''C''$ is congruent to $\triangle ABC$ by transitivity.

• If the distance between lines m and n were 0 (so that the lines became the same line), what would happen to the double reflection of $\triangle ABC$? The double reflection would produce the original triangle.

2 EXPLORE

Materials: geometry software
Questioning Strategies
• What makes this investigation different from the first one? In the first investigation, the lines of reflection were parallel. Here, they intersect.

• Given that a reflection is a rigid motion, what can you say about $\triangle ABC$, $\triangle A'B'C'$, and $\triangle A''B''C''$? They are all congruent.

> MATHEMATICAL PRACTICE **Highlighting the Standards**
>
> Explore 1 and Explore 2 provide opportunities to address Standard 5 (Use appropriate tools strategically). By using technology as a tool, students can generate many examples of double reflections. They can use these drawings to make conjectures about the reflections.

CLOSE

Essential Question
How can you use more than one transformation to map one figure onto another?
A composition of two reflections across two parallel lines is equivalent to a translation. A composition of two reflections across two intersecting lines is equivalent to a rotation.

Summarize
Have students write a journal entry in which they list the properties of a double reflection across parallel lines and the properties of a double reflection across intersecting lines.

PRACTICE

Exercises 1 and 2: Students use reasoning to draw two lines of reflection so that a composition of reflections maps a figure onto another figure.

Name_____ Class_____ Date_____

9-4

Video Tutor

Compositions of Transformations
Going Deeper

Essential question: *How can you use more than one transformation to map one figure onto another?*

CC.9-12.G.CO.5

1 EXPLORE Investigating Reflections Across Parallel Lines

Use geometry software, or paper and pencil, to investigate properties of a double reflection across parallel lines.

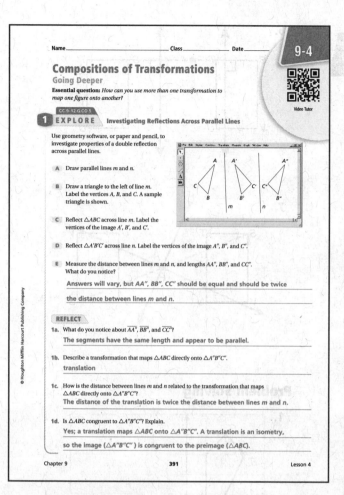

A Draw parallel lines *m* and *n*.

B Draw a triangle to the left of line *m*. Label the vertices *A*, *B*, and *C*. A sample triangle is shown.

C Reflect △*ABC* across line *m*. Label the vertices of the image *A'*, *B'*, and *C'*.

D Reflect △*A'B'C'* across line *n*. Label the vertices of the image *A"*, *B"*, and *C"*.

E Measure the distance between lines *m* and *n*, and lengths *AA"*, *BB"*, and *CC"*. What do you notice?

Answers will vary, but *AA"*, *BB"*, *CC"* should be equal and should be twice

the distance between lines *m* and *n*.

REFLECT

1a. What do you notice about $\overline{AA''}$, $\overline{BB''}$, and $\overline{CC''}$?

The segments have the same length and appear to be parallel.

1b. Describe a transformation that maps △*ABC* directly onto △*A"B"C"*.

translation

1c. How is the distance between lines *m* and *n* related to the transformation that maps △*ABC* directly onto △*A"B"C"*?

The distance of the translation is twice the distance between lines *m* and *n*.

1d. Is △*ABC* congruent to △*A"B"C"*? Explain.

Yes; a translation maps △*ABC* onto △*A"B"C"*. A translation is an isometry,

so the image (△*A"B"C"*) is congruent to the preimage (△*ABC*).

Chapter 9   391   Lesson 4

© Houghton Mifflin Harcourt Publishing Company

CC.9-12.G.CO.5

2 EXPLORE Investigating Reflections Across Intersecting Lines

Use geometry software, or paper and pencil, to investigate properties of a double reflection across intersecting lines.

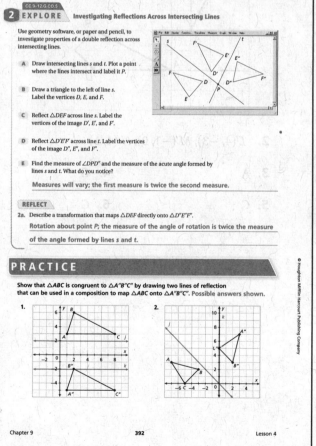

A Draw intersecting lines *s* and *t*. Plot a point where the lines intersect and label it *P*.

B Draw a triangle to the left of line *s*. Label the vertices *D*, *E*, and *F*.

C Reflect △*DEF* across line *s*. Label the vertices of the image *D'*, *E'*, and *F'*.

D Reflect △*D'E'F'* across line *t*. Label the vertices of the image *D"*, *E"*, and *F"*.

E Find the measure of ∠*DPD"* and the measure of the acute angle formed by lines *s* and *t*. What do you notice?

Measures will vary; the first measure is twice the second measure.

REFLECT

2a. Describe a transformation that maps △*DEF* directly onto △*D"E"F"*.

Rotation about point *P*; the measure of the angle of rotation is twice the measure

of the angle formed by lines *s* and *t*.

PRACTICE

Show that △*ABC* is congruent to △*A"B"C"* by drawing two lines of reflection that can be used in a composition to map △*ABC* onto △*A"B"C"*. Possible answers shown.

1.

2.

© Houghton Mifflin Harcourt Publishing Company

Chapter 9   392   Lesson 4

© Houghton Mifflin Harcourt Publishing Company

Assign these pages to help your students practice and apply important lesson concepts. For additional exercises, see the Student Edition.

Answers

Additional Practice

1.

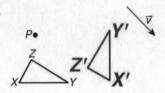

2.

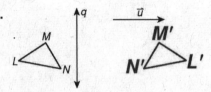

3.

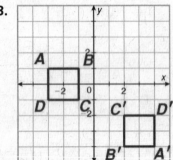

4.

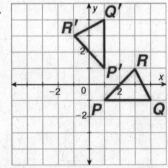

5. The sides of the image will lie on the sides of the preimage, but the position of the vertices will be different. E'' will coincide with F, F'' with G, and G'' with E.

6.

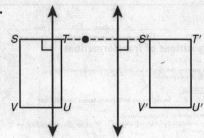

7.

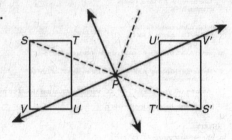

Problem Solving

1.

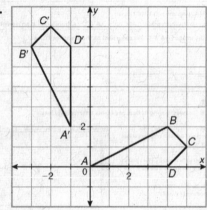

2. $L'(4, -3)$, $M'(-1, 0)$, $N'(4, 1)$

3. A   4. G

5. C   6. G

Additional Practice

Draw the result of each composition of isometries.

1. Rotate △XYZ 90° about point P and then translate it along $\vec{v}$.

2. Reflect △LMN across line q and then translate it along $\vec{u}$.

3. ABCD has vertices A(−3, 1), B(−1, 1), C(−1, −1), and D(−3, −1). Rotate ABCD 180° about the origin and then translate it along the vector ⟨1, −3⟩.

4. △PQR has vertices P(1, −1), Q(4, −1), and R(3, 1). Reflect △PQR across the x-axis and then reflect it across y = x.

5. Ray draws equilateral △EFG. He draws two lines that make a 60° angle through the triangle's center. Ray wants to reflect △EFG across ℓ_1 and then across ℓ_2. Describe what will be the same and what will be different about the image of △E″F″G″ compared to △EFG.

_____

_____

Draw two lines of reflection that produce an equivalent transformation for each figure.

6. translation: STUV → S′T′U′V′

7. rotation with center P: STUV → S′T′U′V′

© Houghton Mifflin Harcourt Publishing Company

Problem Solving

1. A pattern for a new fabric is made by rotating the figure 90° counterclockwise about the origin and then translating along the vector ⟨−1, 2⟩. Draw the resulting figure in the pattern.

2. △LMN is reflected across the line y = x and then reflected across the y-axis. What are the coordinates of the final image of △LMN?

_____

Choose the best answer.

3. △EFG has vertices E(1, 5), F(0, −3), and G(−1, 2). △EFG is translated along the vector ⟨7, 1⟩, and the image is reflected across the x-axis. What are the coordinates of the final image of G?

   A (6, −3)   C (−6, 3)
   B (6, 3)   D (−6, −3)

4. △KLM with vertices K(8, −1), L(−1, −4), and M(2, 3) is rotated 180° about the origin. The image is then translated. The final image of K has coordinates (−2, −3). What is the translation vector?

   F (6, 4)   H ⟨−1, −11⟩
   G ⟨6, −4⟩   J ⟨−10, −2⟩

5. To create a logo for new sweatshirts, a designer reflects the letter T across line h. That image is then reflected across line j. Describe a single transformation that moves the figure from its starting position to its final position.

   A translation
   B rotation of 110°
   C rotation of 220°
   D reflection across vertical line

6. Which composition of transformations maps △QRS into Quadrant III?

   F Translate along the vector ⟨−6, 4⟩ and then reflect across the y-axis.
   G Rotate by 90° about the origin and then reflect across the x-axis.
   H Reflect across the y-axis and then rotate by 180° about the origin.
   J Translate along the vector ⟨1, 2⟩ and then rotate 90° about the origin.

© Houghton Mifflin Harcourt Publishing Company

9-5

Symmetry
Going Deeper

Essential question: *How do you determine whether a figure has line symmetry or rotational symmetry?*

COMMON CORE Standards for Mathematical Content

CC.9-12.G.CO.3 Given a rectangle, parallelogram, trapezoid, or regular polygon, describe the rotations and reflections that carry it onto itself.

Vocabulary

symmetry

line symmetry

line of symmetry

rotational symmetry

angle of rotational symmetry

Prerequisites

Reflections

Rotations

Math Background

Symmetry is a familiar concept from everyday situations. The goal of this lesson is to define symmetry in mathematical terms. Students may be surprised to learn that there are two types of symmetry: line (or reflection) symmetry and rotational symmetry. In fact, it is also possible to define a symmetry based on translations. A pattern has *translation symmetry* if it can be translated along a vector so that the image coincides with the pre-image. The pattern of hexagons shown below has translation symmetry (assuming the pattern continues indefinitely in all directions).

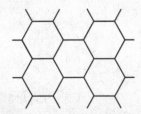

INTRODUCE

Ask students if they can give examples of objects that have symmetry. Students might mention a cat's face, a butterfly's wings, or a valentine heart. Tell students they will learn how to use mathematical language to identify and describe symmetry.

TEACH

1 EXAMPLE

Questioning Strategies

- How could you use a mirror to check a figure for line symmetry? **If you stand the mirror on edge along a line of symmetry, the part of the figure that is visible and its reflection will together form the whole figure.**

- How many lines of symmetry does an equilateral triangle have? What are the lines of symmetry? **Three; they are the three angle bisectors.**

EXTRA EXAMPLE

Determine whether each figure has line symmetry. If so, draw all lines of symmetry.

A.

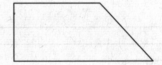

no line symmetry

B.

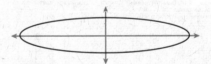

line symmetry

C.

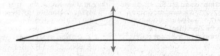

line symmetry

D.

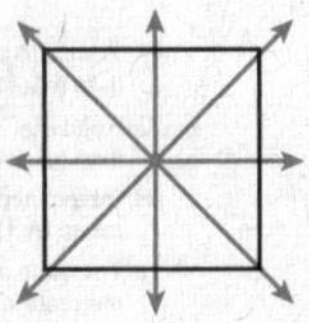

line symmetry

© Houghton Mifflin Harcourt Publishing Company

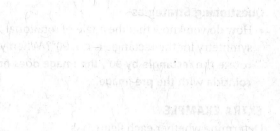

Notes

Name_____ Class_____ Date_____

9-5

Symmetry
Going Deeper

Essential question: *How do you determine whether a figure has line symmetry or rotational symmetry?*

A figure has **symmetry** if there is a rigid motion such that the image of the figure coincides with the pre-image.

A figure has **line symmetry** (or *reflection symmetry*) if the figure can be reflected across a line so that the image coincides with the pre-image. In this case, the line of reflection is called the **line of symmetry**.

Line of symmetry

CC.9-12.G.CO.3
1 EXAMPLE Identifying Line Symmetry

Determine whether each figure has line symmetry. If so, draw all lines of symmetry. (Use the steps given for figure A to help you with the other figures.)

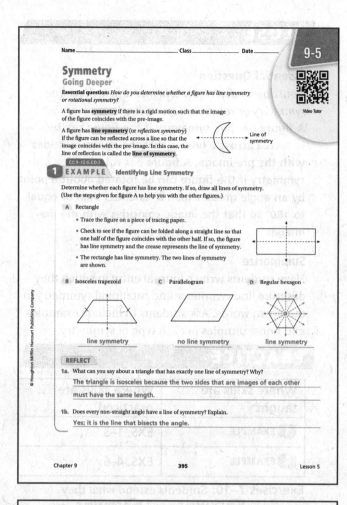

A Rectangle

* Trace the figure on a piece of tracing paper.
* Check to see if the figure can be folded along a straight line so that one half of the figure coincides with the other half. If so, the figure has line symmetry and the crease represents the line of symmetry.
* The rectangle has line symmetry. The two lines of symmetry are shown.

B Isosceles trapezoid   **C** Parallelogram   **D** Regular hexagon

line symmetry   no line symmetry   line symmetry

REFLECT

1a. What can you say about a triangle that has exactly one line of symmetry? Why?

The triangle is isosceles because the two sides that are images of each other must have the same length.

1b. Does every non-straight angle have a line of symmetry? Explain.

Yes; it is the line that bisects the angle.

A figure has **rotational symmetry** if the figure can be rotated about a point by an angle greater than 0° and less than or equal to 180° so that the image coincides with the pre-image. The smallest angle that maps the figure onto itself is the **angle of rotational symmetry**.

Angle of rotational symmetry: 90°

CC.9-12.G.CO.3
2 EXAMPLE Identifying Rotational Symmetry

Determine whether each figure has rotational symmetry. If so, give the angle of rotational symmetry. (Use the steps given for figure A to help you with the other figures.)

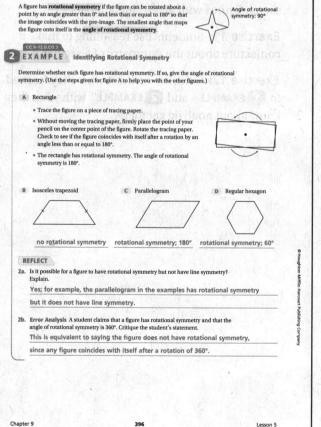

A Rectangle

* Trace the figure on a piece of tracing paper.
* Without moving the tracing paper, firmly place the point of your pencil on the center point of the figure. Rotate the tracing paper. Check to see if the figure coincides with itself after a rotation by an angle less than or equal to 180°.
* The rectangle has rotational symmetry. The angle of rotational symmetry is 180°.

B Isosceles trapezoid   **C** Parallelogram   **D** Regular hexagon

no rotational symmetry   rotational symmetry; 180°   rotational symmetry; 60°

REFLECT

2a. Is it possible for a figure to have rotational symmetry but not have line symmetry? Explain.

Yes; for example, the parallelogram in the examples has rotational symmetry but it does not have line symmetry.

2b. **Error Analysis** A student claims that a figure has rotational symmetry and that the angle of rotational symmetry is 360°. Critique the student's statement.

This is equivalent to saying the figure does not have rotational symmetry, since any figure coincides with itself after a rotation of 360°.

2 EXAMPLE

Questioning Strategies

- How do you know that the angle of rotational symmetry for the rectangle is not 90°? **When you rotate the rectangle by 90°, the image does not coincide with the pre-image.**

EXTRA EXAMPLE

Determine whether each figure has rotational symmetry. If so, give the angle of rotational symmetry.

A.

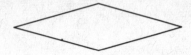

rotational symmetry; 180°

B.

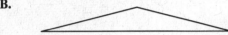

no rotational symmetry

C.

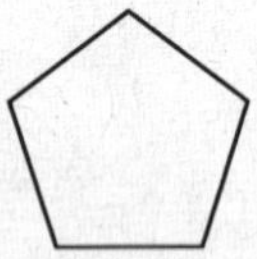

rotational symmetry; 72°

D.

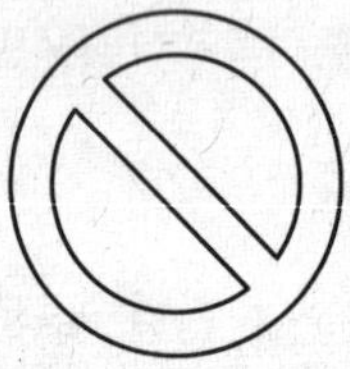

rotational symmetry; 180°

MATHEMATICAL PRACTICE **Highlighting the Standards**

Exercise 11 gives students a chance to use inductive reasoning to make a conjecture. This is an important part of Standard 3 (Construct viable arguments and critique the reasoning of others). Have students describe the process they used to make their conjectures and ask them what they could do to check that their conjectures are correct.

CLOSE

Essential Question

How do you determine whether a figure has line symmetry or rotational symmetry?

A figure has line symmetry if the figure can be reflected across a line so that the image coincides with the pre-image. A figure has rotational symmetry if the figure can be rotated about a point by an angle greater than 0° and less than or equal to 180° so that the image coincides with the pre-image.

Summarize

Have students write a journal entry in which they describe line symmetry and rotational symmetry in their own words. Ask students to include examples and non-examples of each type of symmetry.

PRACTICE

Where skills are taught	Where skills are practiced
1 EXAMPLE	EXS. 1–3
2 EXAMPLE	EXS. 4–6

Exercises 7–10: Students extend what they learned in 1 EXAMPLE and 2 EXAMPLE to sketch figures with given characteristics.

Exercise 11: Students use reasoning to make a conjecture about the symmetry of a regular *n*-gon.

Exercise 12: Students connect what they learned in 1 EXAMPLE and 2 EXAMPLE with what they know about analytic geometry.

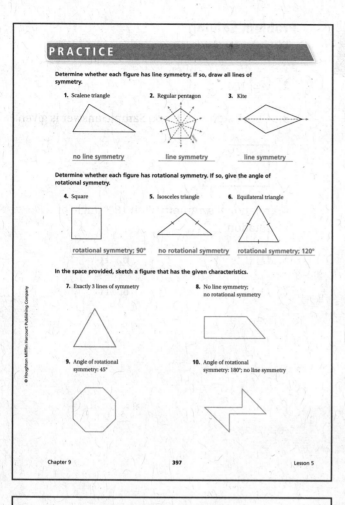

PRACTICE

Determine whether each figure has line symmetry. If so, draw all lines of symmetry.

1. Scalene triangle

no line symmetry

2. Regular pentagon

line symmetry

3. Kite

line symmetry

Determine whether each figure has rotational symmetry. If so, give the angle of rotational symmetry.

4. Square

rotational symmetry; 90°

5. Isosceles triangle

no rotational symmetry

6. Equilateral triangle

rotational symmetry; 120°

In the space provided, sketch a figure that has the given characteristics.

7. Exactly 3 lines of symmetry

8. No line symmetry; no rotational symmetry

9. Angle of rotational symmetry: 45°

10. Angle of rotational symmetry: 180°; no line symmetry

---

11. A *regular n-gon* is a polygon with n sides where all the sides are congruent and all the angles are congruent. For example, when $n = 4$, the regular n-gon is a square. When $n = 5$, the regular n-gon is a regular pentagon.

 a. How many lines of symmetry does a regular n-gon have? ___n___

 b. What is the angle of rotational symmetry for a regular n-gon? ___$\frac{360°}{n}$___

12. A quadrilateral has vertices $A(4, 0)$, $B(0, 2)$, $C(-4, 0)$, and $D(0, -2)$. Describe all the reflections and rotations that map the quadrilateral onto itself.

reflection across the x-axis; reflection across the y-axis; rotation of 180°

about the origin

© Houghton Mifflin Harcourt Publishing Company

Assign these pages to help your students practice and apply important lesson concepts. For additional exercises, see the Student Edition.

Answers

Additional Practice

1. no

2. yes

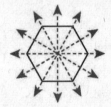

3. yes

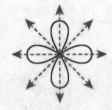

4.

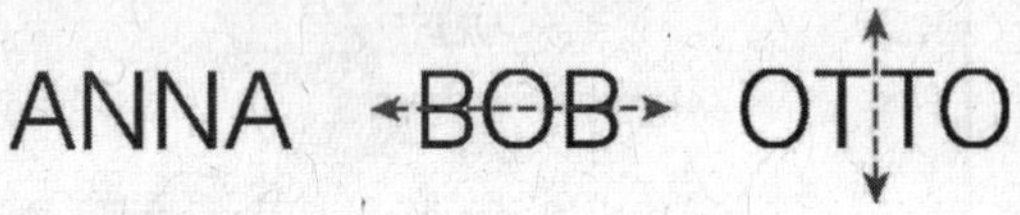

ANNA ◄BOB► OTTO

5. yes; 180°; 2   **6.** no

7. yes; 45°; 8

8. 90°; 4

9–10. Check students' work. Sample answers are given.

9.

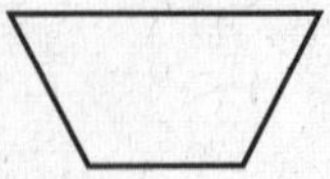

10.

Problem Solving

1. yes

2. yes; 180°

3. Check students' work. Sample answer is given.

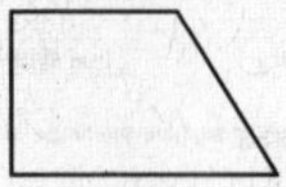

4. rotational symmetry with 180° angle of rotation

5. D   **6.** H

7. D   **8.** H

Name _____ Class _____ Date _____

9-5

Additional Practice

Tell whether each figure has line symmetry. If so, draw all lines of symmetry.

1.

2.

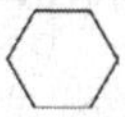

3.

4. Anna, Bob, and Otto write their names in capital letters. Draw all lines of symmetry for each whole name if possible.

ANNA   BOB   OTTO

Tell whether each figure has rotational symmetry. If so, give the angle of rotational symmetry.

5.

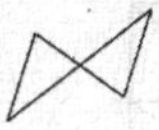

6.

7.

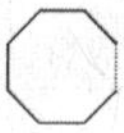

8. This figure shows the Roman symbol for Earth. Draw all lines of symmetry. Give the angle of any rotational symmetry.

In the space provided, sketch a figure that has the given characteristics.

9. Exactly 1 line of symmetry

10. Angle of rotational symmetry: 180°
Exactly 2 lines of symmetry

Chapter 9   399   Lesson 5

Problem Solving

1. Tell whether the window has line symmetry. If so, draw all the lines of symmetry.

_____

2. Tell whether the quilt block design has rotational symmetry. If so, give the angle of rotational symmetry.

3. Draw an example of a trapezoid that has no line symmetry and no rotational symmetry.

4. The figure is a net of an octahedron. Describe the symmetry of the net.

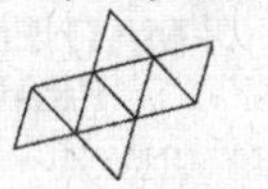

Choose the best answer.

5. Which is a true statement about the figure with vertices Q(−2, −4), R(0, 1), S(8, 1), and T(5, −4)?

A QRST has line symmetry only.
B QRST has rotational symmetry only.
C QRST has both line symmetry and rotational symmetry.
D QRST has neither line symmetry nor rotational symmetry.

7. Which of these figures has exactly three lines of symmetry?

A
B
C
D

6. Suppose you rotate this figure around its center point P by the given angle of rotation. Which angle measure would produce an image that coincides with the original figure?

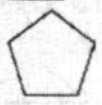

F 45°   H 90°
G 60°   J 120°

8. How many lines of symmetry does a regular pentagon have?

F 0
G 4
H 5
J 10

Tessellations
Connection: Using Transformations

Essential question: *How can you use transformations to describe tessellations?*

© Houghton Mifflin Harcourt Publishing Company

COMMON CORE **Standards for Mathematical Content**

CC.9-12.G.CO.5 Given a geometric figure and a rotation, reflection, or translation, draw the transformed figure using, e.g., graph paper, tracing paper, or geometric software. Specify a sequence of transformations that will carry a given figure onto another.

Prerequisites
Transformations and rigid motions
Compositions of transformations

Math Background
Students have studied reflections, translations, and rotations as well as compositions of these transformations. In this lesson, students will consider how a transformation or a composition of transformations maps a tessellation onto itself.

INTRODUCE

Have students investigate tessellations by creating their own. Begin by dividing the class into groups and having each group draw a quadrilateral on a piece of paper and cut it out. Then assign each group a transformation (or pair of transformations) and challenge the groups to create a tessellation of the quadrilateral using only the assigned transformation(s). Discuss the tessellations as a class.

TEACH

1 EXAMPLE

Questioning Strategies
- In Part A, is there only one possible answer? Explain. No; each of the triangles in the tessellation can be mapped onto more than one other triangle through a translation.
- Is it possible to map one of the triangles onto another triangle so that the image and preimage share a side? If so, describe the transformation(s). Yes; a rotation of one of the triangles about the midpoint of one of its sides, or a reflection of one of the triangles in one of its sides

EXTRA EXAMPLE
Describe the transformations that can map the tessellation onto itself. You can number figures in the tessellation if you need to refer to the figures.

A horizontal translation maps triangle 1 onto triangle 2. A rotation of 180° about the midpoint of the common side maps triangle 1 onto triangle 3.

CLOSE

Essential Question
How can you use transformations to describe tessellations?
Translations, rotations, and reflections can all be used to create tessellations. When describing tessellations, look for translations, rotations, and reflections that map the tessellation onto itself.

Summarize
Have students write a journal entry in which they describe how translations, rotations, and reflections can be used to create a tessellation. They should give examples of each transformation used in a tessellation, possibly the same tessellation.

MATHEMATICAL PRACTICE | **Highlighting the Standards**

Working with tessellations provides an opportunity to address Standard 7 (Look for and make use of structure) as students analyze a tessellation for the transformations used to produce it.

PRACTICE

Where skills are taught	Where skills are practiced
1 EXAMPLE	EXS. 1–3

Exercise 4: Students determine whether a concave quadrilateral can tessellate.

Name_____ Class_____ Date_____

9-6

Video Tutor

Tessellations
Connection: Using Transformations
Essential question: How can you use transformations to describe tessellations?

CC.9-12.G.CO.5

1 EXAMPLE Describing Tessellations

Describe the transformations that can map the tessellation onto itself. (The tessellation is made using congruent triangles, and it continues in all directions.) Possible answers are given.

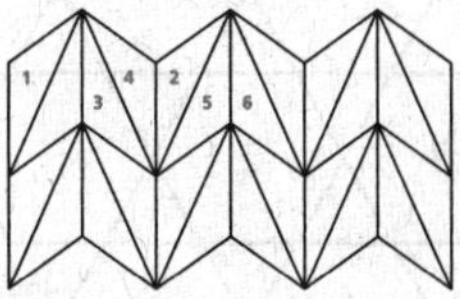

A Look for translations in the tessellation. If there are translations, then number two triangles in the tessellation and complete the statement below.

Triangle __1__ maps onto triangle __2__ by a translation.

B Look for rotations in the tessellation. If there are rotations, then number two triangles in the tessellation and complete the statement below.

Triangle __3__ maps onto triangle __4__ by a rotation of __180°__ about

a midpoint of its longest side.

C Look for reflections in the tessellation. If there are reflections, then number two triangles in the tessellation and complete the statement below.

Triangle __5__ maps onto triangle __6__ by a reflection.

REFLECT

1a. Describe a sequence of transformations that will map triangle 1 onto triangle 2 in part of the tessellation shown at the right.

Possible answer: Rotate triangle 1 180° about

the midpoint of its longest side, then translate

the triangle to the right.

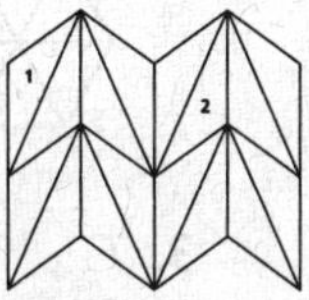

Chapter 9   401   Lesson 6

© Houghton Mifflin Harcourt Publishing Company

PRACTICE

Describe the transformations that can map the tessellation onto itself. (The tessellation is made using congruent figures, and it continues in all directions.) You can number figures in the tessellation if you need to refer to them. Possible answers are given.

1.

A translation maps triangle 1 onto triangle 2. A rotation of 180° about a midpoint of a side maps triangle 3 onto triangle 4.

2.

A translation maps pentagon 1 onto pentagon 2. A reflection maps pentagon 3 onto pentagon 4. A rotation of 90° maps pentagon 5 onto pentagon 6.

3. Describe a sequence of transformations that will map figure 1 onto figure 2 in the tessellation.

Rotate figure 1 180° about the midpoint of one of its sides, then translate that figure until it coincides with figure 2.

4. Determine whether a concave quadrilateral can be used to create a tessellation. Explain your answer, using a drawing to support your answer.

Yes; possible answer: a concave quadrilateral can be rotated 180° about a midpoint of a side. Then the two quadrilaterals can be translated to create a tessellation.

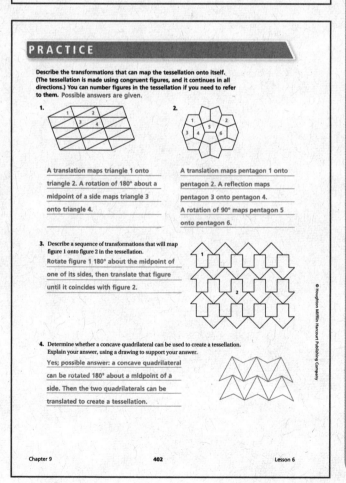

© Houghton Mifflin Harcourt Publishing Company

Chapter 9   402   Lesson 6

© Houghton Mifflin Harcourt Publishing Company

Assign these pages to help your students practice and apply important lesson concepts. For additional exercises, see the Student Edition.

Answers

Additional Practice

1. A translation maps figure 1 onto figure 2. A rotation about the midpoint of the lower side of figure 1 maps it onto figure 3.

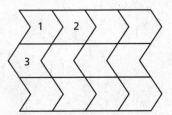

2. Yes; Possible answers: Hexagon 1 can be reflected in the side it shares with hexagon 2 to form hexagon 2. Hexagon 1 can also be rotated about a vertex to form hexagon 2.

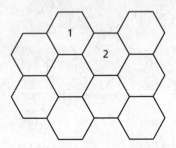

3.

4.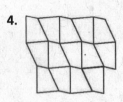

5. no

6. yes

7. no

Problem Solving

1. Possible answer: Draw hexagon 1. Reflect it in one of its sides to form hexagon 2. Translate hexagon 2 to form hexagon 3.

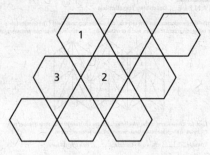

2.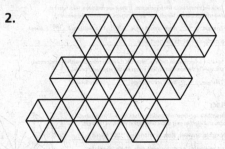

3. C

4. F

Name_____ Class_____ Date_____

9-6

Additional Practice

1. Describe the transformations that can map the tessellation onto itself. (The tessellation is made of congruent figures, and it continues in all directions.) You may number figures in the tessellation if you need to refer to them.

_____
_____
_____

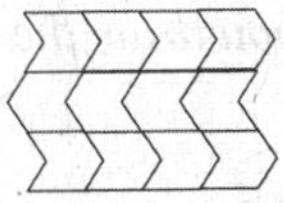

2. The tessellation shown is made from regular hexagons. Your friend says that a tessellation like this one can be made by repeatedly translating a single hexagon. Is there another transformation that can produce the tessellation? Explain. You may number hexagons in the tessellation if you need to refer to them.

_____
_____
_____

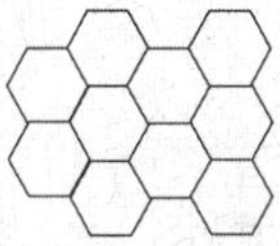

Use the given figure to create a tessellation.

3.

4.

Determine whether the given regular polygon(s) can be used to form a tessellation. If so, draw the tessellation.

5.

6.

7.

Problem Solving

Sue draws a regular hexagon and then uses it to create a tessellating pattern. As shown, the pattern also includes equilateral triangles.

1. Describe a way to make the pattern by performing transformations on the hexagon. You may number hexagons in the pattern if you need to refer to them.

_____
_____
_____

2. Show how you can draw line segments in Sue's pattern to make a pattern of tessellating equilateral triangles.

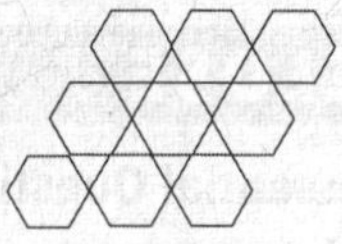

Choose the best answer.

3. In the diagram below, three congruent pentagons form each hexagon. What sequence of transformations could map one of the pentagons onto two other pentagons to form a hexagon?

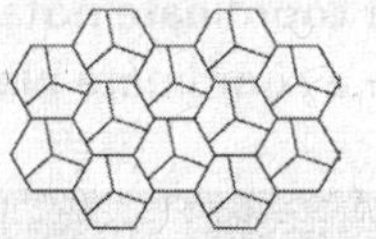

A 60° rotation around a vertex; a reflection

B 120° rotation around a vertex, a reflection

C 60° rotation around a vertex; 60° rotation around the same vertex

D 120° rotation around a vertex; 120° rotation around the same vertex

4. Which is a true statement about figures 1 and 2 in the diagram below?

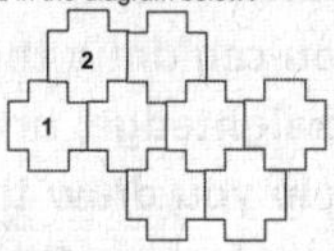

F Figure 1 is mapped onto figure 2 by a translation.

G Figure 1 is mapped onto figure 2 by a rotation.

H Figure 1 is mapped onto figure 2 by a rotation and a translation.

J Figure 1 is mapped onto figure 2 by a reflection.

Dilations
Going Deeper

Essential question: *How do you draw the image of a figure under a dilation?*

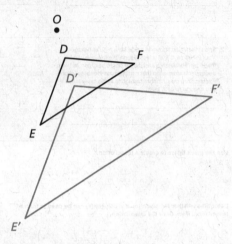

COMMON CORE Standards for Mathematical Content

CC.9-12.G.CO.2 Represent transformations in the plane using, e.g., transparencies and geometry software; ...

Prerequisites

Dilations and similarity

Math Background

In this lesson, students extend their earlier work with dilations by learning how to construct the dilation image of a given figure.

INTRODUCE

Briefly remind students of the definition of *dilation*. Tell students they will be using a compass and straightedge to draw the dilation image of a figure. To that end, you may want to spend a few minutes reviewing the compass-and-straightedge construction for copying a line segment, as the steps for constructing a dilation image are based on that.

TEACH

1 EXAMPLE

Questioning Strategies

- How do you know $OA' = 3OA$? You add two copies of $\overline{OA}$ onto the end of $\overline{OA}$, so the total length is $3OA$.

- What would you do differently if the scale factor of the dilation were 4? I would add one more copy of $\overline{OA}$ onto the end of $\overline{OA}$ to locate A', and repeat for B' and C'.

EXTRA EXAMPLE

Construct the image of $\triangle DEF$ after a dilation with center of dilation O and scale factor 2.

MATHEMATICAL PRACTICE

Highlighting the Standards

This lesson provides an opportunity to discuss Standard 5 (Use appropriate tools strategically). While using a compass and straightedge is reasonable for performing a dilation when the scale factor is a positive whole number, it becomes unreasonable when the scale factor is a positive rational number. In that case, other techniques, such as using coordinates or geometry software, are better.

CLOSE

Essential Question

How do you draw the image of a figure under a dilation?
You can draw the image using a compass and straightedge, or you can use coordinate notation to help you draw the image on a coordinate plane.

PRACTICE

Where skills are taught	Where skills are practiced
1 EXAMPLE	EXS. 1–3

Name_____ Class_____ Date_____

Dilations
Going Deeper

Essential question: *How do you draw the image of a figure under a dilation?*

You have already used geometry software to draw the image of a figure under a dilation. The following example shows how to construct the image using a compass and straightedge.

CC.9-12.G.CO.2

1 EXAMPLE   Constructing a Dilation Image

Work directly on the figure below and follow the given steps to construct the image of $\triangle ABC$ after a dilation with center of dilation O and scale factor 3.

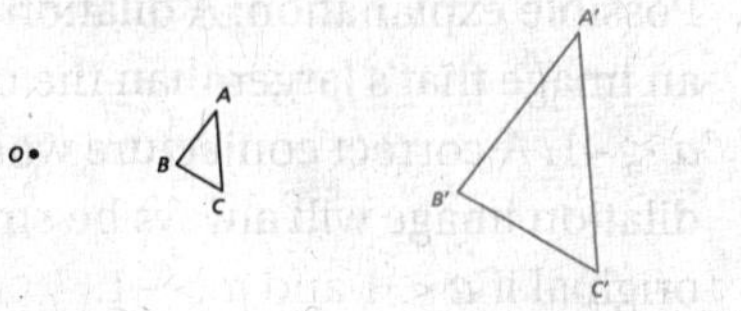

A   Use a straightedge to draw $\overrightarrow{OA}$.

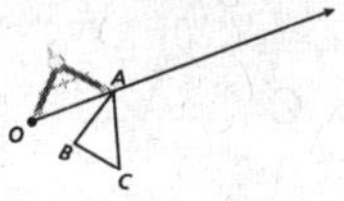

B   Place the point of your compass on point O and open the compass to the distance OA.

C   Without adjusting the compass, place the point of the compass on point A and make an arc that intersects $\overrightarrow{OA}$.

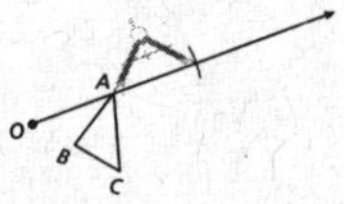

D   Move the compass to the point of intersection of the arc and the ray. Make another arc that intersects $\overrightarrow{OA}$. Label this point of intersection A'.

E   Repeat the steps for the other vertices of $\triangle ABC$.

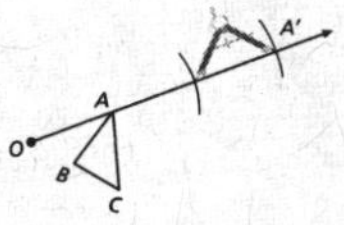

F   Once you have located A', B', and C', use a straightedge to draw $\triangle A'B'C'$.

REFLECT

1a. Explain how you can you use a ruler to check your construction.

Measure the sides of the triangle and its image to check that $OA' = 3OA$, $OB' = 3OB$, and $OC' = 3OC$.

1b. Without using a protractor, how does $m\angle OAB$ compare to $m\angle OA'B'$? Why?

$m\angle OAB = m\angle OA'B'$ since $\overline{AB} \parallel \overline{A'B'}$ and these are corresponding angles.

1c. How can you change the construction to draw the image of $\triangle ABC$ after a dilation with center of dilation O and scale factor $\frac{1}{2}$?

Construct the bisectors of $\overline{OA}$, $\overline{OB}$, and $\overline{OC}$ to find the midpoints of these segments. Use the straightedge to connect the midpoints to form $\triangle A'B'C'$.

PRACTICE

Use a compass and straightedge to construct the image of the figure after a dilation with center O and the given scale factor. Label the vertices of the image.

1. scale factor: 4

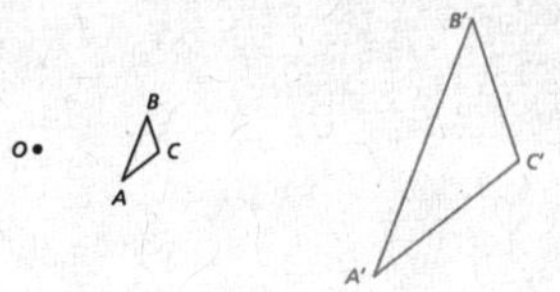

2. scale factor: $\frac{1}{2}$

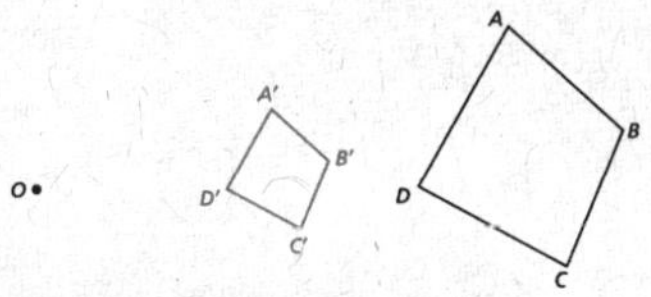

3. $\triangle A'B'C'$ is the image of $\triangle ABC$ under a dilation. Explain how you can use a straightedge to find the center of dilation. Then use your method to draw a dot at the center of dilation.

Draw $\overleftrightarrow{AA'}$ and $\overleftrightarrow{BB'}$. The point where the lines intersect is the center of dilation.

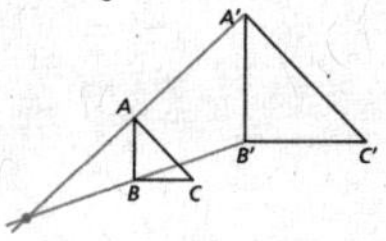

Assign these pages to help your students practice and apply important lesson concepts. For additional exercises, see the Student Edition.

Answers

Additional Practice

1.

2.

3.
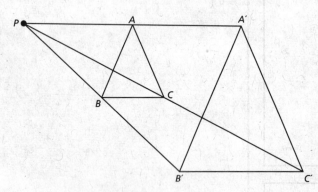

4.
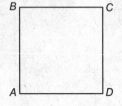

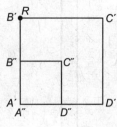

Problem Solving

1. 3 (Accept answers reasonably close to 3)

2. $-\dfrac{1}{2}$

3. a dilation with scale factor $\dfrac{1}{3}$ with center of dilation A

4. Possible explanation: A dilation will produce an image that's larger than the original if $a < -1$. A correct conjecture would say that a dilation image will always be smaller than the original if $a < 1$ and $a > -1$.

5. C   6. G

Additional Practice

Draw the dilation of each figure under the given scale factor with center of dilation P.

1. scale factor: $\frac{1}{2}$

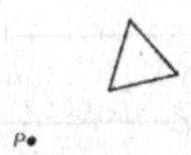

P•

2. scale factor: –2

P•

3. $\triangle A'B'C'$ is the dilation image of $\triangle ABC$ with a center of dilation P and a scale factor of 2. Construct $\triangle ABC$.

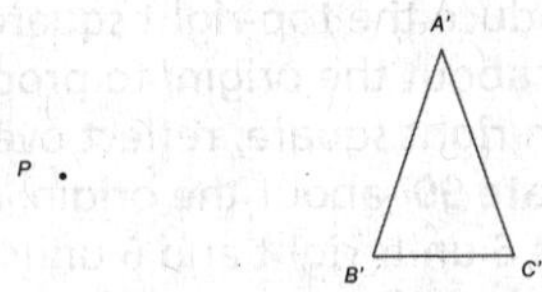

4. Translate square ABCD so that vertex B corresponds with point R.
   Then dilate the square with a scale factor of $\frac{1}{2}$ and center A.

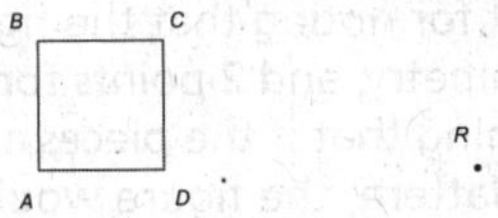

Problem Solving

For Exercises 1 and 2, determine the scale factor that would dilate triangle KLM to triangle K'L'M'.

1.

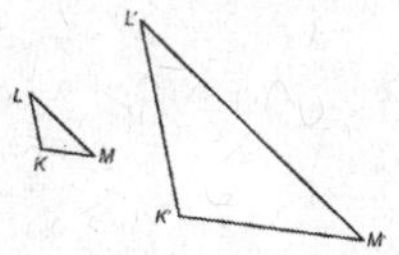

2.

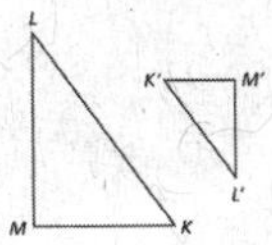

3. Rectangle ABCD is dilated by a scale factor of 3 centered on A. What translation will transform A'B'C'D, the image of the dilation, back to the original figure?

_____

_____

4. Suzette makes a conjecture about dilations. She says that if a dilation has scale factor a, then the dilation image will always be smaller than the original if a < 1. Explain why Suzette's conjecture is incorrect and revise it.

_____

_____

_____

Choose the best answer.

5. Steven is enlarging a photograph by a scale factor of 2.5 and then placing 2-inch matting around the perimeter of the enlarged photograph. If the photograph is 3 inches by 5 inches, what will be the area of the matting?

   A 37.5 in²   C 96 in²

   B 93.75 in²   D 189.75 in²

6. A blueprint for a horse stable shows a reduction of the stable using a scale factor of $\frac{1}{24}$. In the blueprint, a horse stall is shown by the diagram below. What is the actual area of the stall?

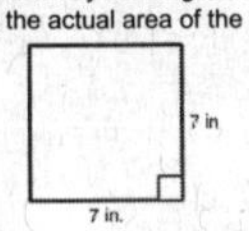

7 in

7 in.

   F 144 ft²   H 576 ft²

   G 196 ft²   J 1176 ft²

This page provides students with the opportunity to apply concepts from the Common Core in real-world problem situations. There are three different levels of performance tasks:

⭐ **Novice:** These are short word problems that require students to apply the math they have learned in straightforward, real-world situations.

⭐⭐ **Apprentice:** These are more involved problems that guide students step-by-step through more complex tasks. These exercises include more complicated reasoning, writing, and open-ended elements.

⭐⭐⭐ **Expert:** These are open-ended, non-routine problems that, instead of stepping the students through, ask them to choose their own methods for solving and justify their answers and reasoning.

Sample answers

1. Possible answer: A series of four reflections—across the x-axis, across the y-axis, across the x-axis again, and finally across the y-axis again—will leave the rectangle where it began.

2. 6.6 inches by 11 inches

3. Scoring Guide:

Task	Possible points
a	1 point for correctly describing how to produce each square from the top-left square (3 points in all): for example: to produce the top-right square, rotate 90° about the origin; to produce the bottom-right square, reflect over the x-axis, rotate 90° about the origin, and translate 6 units right and 6 units down; to produce the bottom-left square, reflect over the y-axis, then translate 6 units left and 6 units down
b	1 point for noting that the figure has no symmetry, and 2 points for correctly explaining that if the pieces all had the same pattern, the figure would have translational symmetry

Total possible points: 6

Name _____ Class _____ Date _____

Performance Tasks

COMMON CORE
CC-9-12.G.CO.2
CC-9-12.G.CO.3
CC-9-12.G.CO.5
CC-9-12.G.CO.6

⭐ **1.** George is playing a computer game where he has to perform one or more transformations on a rectangular shape so that the shape ends up where it started. He rotates the shape 360° about the origin. For an alternative move, describe one or more reflections that will also transform the rectangle so that it ends up where it started.

⭐ **2.** Jillian makes an enlargement of a photograph that was originally 3 inches by 5 inches. She wants the enlargement to be similar to the original. She is using a piece of paper that is 8.5 inches by 11 inches. What are the dimensions of the greatest dilation she can fit onto this paper?

⭐ **3.** The figure at the right shows part of a quilt.

a. Treat the figure as if it were a coordinate plane, with the horizontal line that passes the center representing the *x*-axis from −6 to 6 and the vertical line that passes through the center representing the *y*-axis from −6 to 6. Describe specific transformations you could perform to the top-left square that would create each of the other three squares.

b. Describe any type of symmetry that the figure has. If the individual pieces all had the same pattern, how would the symmetry change?

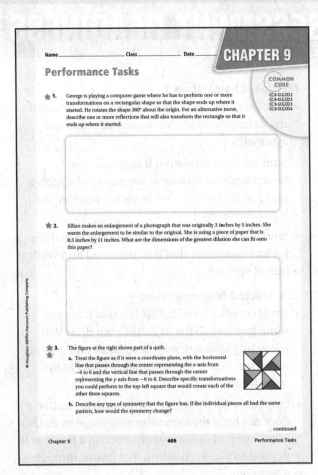

continued

⭐ **4.** Use the figure at the right to answer the questions.

a. Does the figure have line symmetry? If so, sketch the figure with its line(s) of symmetry.

b. Does the figure have rotational symmetry? If so, give the order of the rotational symmetry.

c. How could you change the shading of the figure so that it has *more* symmetries than it does now? Draw a sketch and identify the symmetries that have been added.

d. How could you change the shading of the figure so that it has *fewer* symmetries than it does now? Draw a sketch and identify the symmetries that no longer apply.

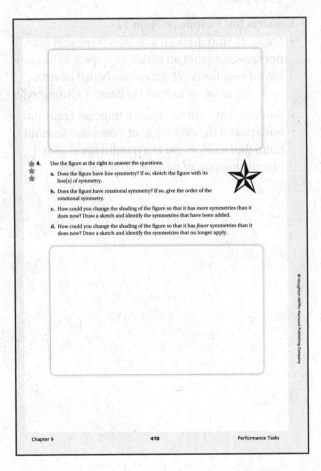

---

4. Scoring Guide:

Task	Possible points
a	1 point for correctly answering that the figure has no line symmetry
b	1 point for correctly answering that the figure has rotational symmetry and for correctly giving the order of 5
c	1 point for a sketch and 1 point for listing the symmetries added, for example: The student draws the star so that the shading is solid, which adds 5 lines of symmetry.
d	1 point for a sketch and 1 point for listing the symmetries that no longer apply, for example: The student draws the star so that only one of the five points is half-shaded, which removes all of the rotational symmetry.

Total possible points: 6

CHAPTER 9 ◌COMMON CORE◌ ASSESSMENT READINESS

◌COMMON CORE◌ CORRELATION

Standard	Items
CC.9-12.G.CO.2	1, 10
CC.9-12.G.CO.3	3, 7, 11, 12
CC.9-12.G.CO.4	4
CC.9-12.G.CO.5	5, 8, 9
CC.9-12.G.CO.6	2, 6, 10
CC.9-12.G.CO.9	13

TEST PREP DOCTOR ⊕

Multiple Choice: Item 1
- Students who answered **A** may not understand the parallel nature of function notation for transformations and function notation for algebraic functions. The letter R in $R_{P, 60°}(G) = G'$ is the name of the function, in the same way that f is the name of the function in the equation $f(x) = y$.
- Students who answered **B** may not understand that the subscripts give the center and angle of rotation.
- Students who answered **C** may be confusing the image and pre-image.

Multiple Choice: Item 3
- Students who answered **A** may have incorrectly drawn radial line segments from the center of the hexagon to the vertices in order to determine the angle of rotational symmetry. There should be six such line segments that are evenly spaced around the center.
- Students who answered **B** may have confused the angle of rotational symmetry with the interior angles of the figure.
- Students who answered **D** may be confusing rotational symmetry with line symmetry.

Multiple Choice: Item 7
- Students who answered **A** may not understand the definition of line symmetry or rotational symmetry.
- Students who answered **B** may not have recognized the rotational symmetry of a regular polygon that is oriented in such a way that no side is horizontal.
- Students who answered **C** may only be looking for line symmetry that is determined by a vertical line of symmetry.

Constructed Response: Item 9
- Students who drew $\triangle A'B'C'$ so that it has the same size and shape as $\triangle ABC$, but drew it in the wrong location, may have had trouble using their compass to mark distances equal to the magnitude of $\vec{v}$.
- Students who drew $\triangle A'B'C'$ in such a way that it does not have the same size and shape as $\triangle ABC$ may have had difficulty constructing a line that is parallel to a given line and that passes through a given point.

Constructed Response: Item 12
- Students who drew an isosceles trapezoid may not recognize that an isosceles trapezoid has one line of symmetry. The trapezoid must be non-isosceles in order to have no lines of symmetry.
- Students who did not draw a trapezoid may not understand the definition of *trapezoid*. Remind them that a trapezoid is a quadrilateral with exactly one pair of parallel opposite sides.

s© Houghton Mifflin Harcourt Publishing Company

sChapter 9

Assessment Readiness

CHAPTER 9 (COMMON CORE) ASSESSMENT READINESS

Name _____ Class _____ Date _____

MULTIPLE CHOICE

1. The function notation $R_{P,60°}(G) = G'$ describes the effect of a rotation. Which point is the image under this rotation?

A. point R C. point G

B. point P **D.** point G'

2. What is the image of the point $(4, -1)$ after a reflection across the line $y = x$?

F. $(-4, 1)$ **H.** $(-1, 4)$

G. $(4, 1)$ J. $(1, -4)$

3. Which of the following figures has an angle of rotational symmetry of 90°?

A.

B.

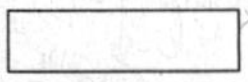

C

D.

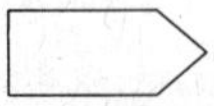

4. Which transformation is defined as a transformation along a vector such that the segment joining a point and its image has the same length as the vector and is parallel to the vector?

F. reflection

G. rigid motion

H. rotation

J. translation

5. Keisha wants to use a compass and straightedge to draw the image of △XYZ after a reflection across line m. What should she do first?

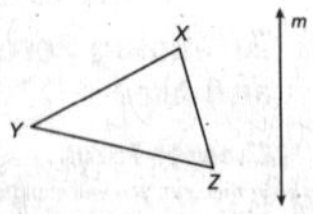

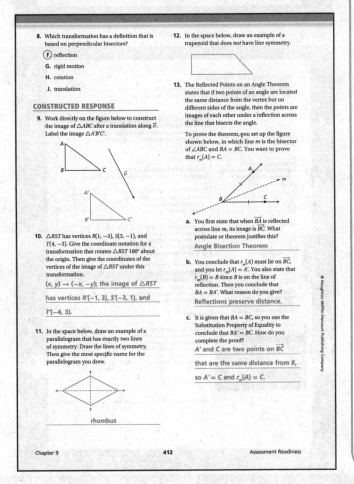

A. Construct a perpendicular to line m that passes through point X.

B. Construct a line parallel to line m that passes through point X.

C. Copy ∠X on the opposite side of line m.

D. Copy $\overline{XZ}$ on the opposite side of line m.

6. You transform a figure on the coordinate plane using the rigid motion $(x, y) \rightarrow (-y, x)$. What effect does this transformation have on the figure?

F. 90° rotation about the origin

G. 180° rotation about the origin

H. reflection across the x-axis

J. reflection across the y-axis

7. Which is the best description of the symmetry of this regular pentagon?

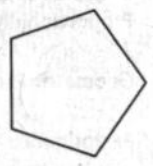

A. has neither line symmetry nor rotational symmetry

B. has line symmetry but not rotational symmetry

C. has rotational symmetry but not line symmetry

D. has both line symmetry and rotational symmetry

Chapter 9   411   Assessment Readiness

---

8. Which transformation has a definition that is based on perpendicular bisectors?

F. reflection

G. rigid motion

H. rotation

J. translation

CONSTRUCTED RESPONSE

9. Work directly on the figure below to construct the image of △ABC after a translation along $\vec{v}$. Label the image △A'B'C'.

10. △RST has vertices $R(1, -3)$, $S(3, -1)$, and $T(4, -3)$. Give the coordinate notation for a transformation that rotates △RST 180° about the origin. Then give the coordinates of the vertices of the image of △RST under this transformation.

$(x, y) \rightarrow (-x, -y)$; the image of △RST has vertices $R'(-1, 3)$, $S'(-3, 1)$, and $T'(-4, 3)$.

11. In the space below, draw an example of a parallelogram that has exactly two lines of symmetry. Draw the lines of symmetry. Then give the most specific name for the parallelogram you drew.

rhombus

12. In the space below, draw an example of a trapezoid that does *not* have line symmetry.

13. The Reflected Points on an Angle Theorem states that if two points of an angle are located the same distance from the vertex but on different sides of the angle, then the points are images of each other under a reflection across the line that bisects the angle.

To prove the theorem, you set up the figure shown below, in which line m is the bisector of ∠ABC and $BA = BC$. You want to prove that $r_m(A) = C$.

a. You first state that when $\overrightarrow{BA}$ is reflected across line m, its image is $\overrightarrow{BC}$. What postulate or theorem justifies this?

Angle Bisection Theorem

b. You conclude that $r_m(A)$ must lie on $\overrightarrow{BC}$, and you let $r_m(A) = A'$. You also state that $r_m(B) = B$ since B is on the line of reflection. Then you conclude that $BA = BA'$. What reason do you give?

Reflections preserve distance.

c. It is given that $BA = BC$, so you use the Substitution Property of Equality to conclude that $BA' = BC$. How do you complete the proof?

A' and C are two points on $\overrightarrow{BC}$ that are the same distance from B, so $A' = C$ and $r_m(A) = C$.

Chapter 9   412   Assessment Readiness

© Houghton Mifflin Harcourt Publishing Company

CHAPTER 10

Extending Perimeter, Circumference, and Area

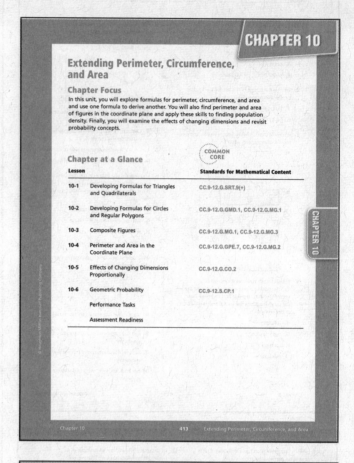

Extending Perimeter, Circumference, and Area

Chapter Focus

In this unit, you will explore formulas for perimeter, circumference, and area and use one formula to derive another. You will also find perimeter and area of figures in the coordinate plane and apply these skills to finding population density. Finally, you will examine the effects of changing dimensions and revisit probability concepts.

Chapter at a Glance

COMMON CORE

Lesson		Standards for Mathematical Content
10-1	Developing Formulas for Triangles and Quadrilaterals	CC.9-12.G.SRT.9(+)
10-2	Developing Formulas for Circles and Regular Polygons	CC.9-12.G.GMD.1, CC.9-12.G.MG.1
10-3	Composite Figures	CC.9-12.G.MG.1, CC.9-12.G.MG.3
10-4	Perimeter and Area in the Coordinate Plane	CC.9-12.G.GPE.7, CC.9-12.G.MG.2
10-5	Effects of Changing Dimensions Proportionally	CC.9-12.G.CO.2
10-6	Geometric Probability	CC.9-12.S.CP.1
	Performance Tasks	
	Assessment Readiness	

Chapter 10   413   Extending Perimeter, Circumference, and Area

---

COMMON CORE PROFESSIONAL DEVELOPMENT

CC.9-12.A.SSE.1*
CC.9-12.G.GMD.1

Geometric formulas are often mathematical statements of a relationship among quantities in the context of a specific shape. Most students have used geometry formulas for areas of triangles and quadrilaterals. In this chapter, students will begin to derive new geometric formulas for new geometric figures, based on the relationships that come from combining figures, dividing a figure in half, or rearranging pieces of it. This creative approach to deriving formulas for shapes developed by halving or rearranging shapes allows students to see how seemingly complex expressions can sometimes simply express a simple change in a known shape.

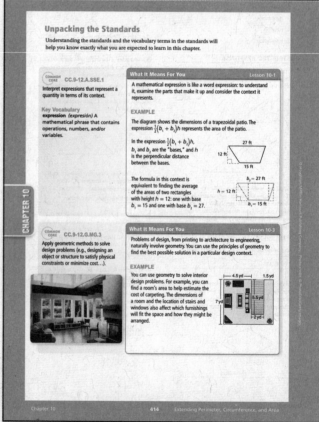

Unpacking the Standards

Understanding the standards and the vocabulary terms in the standards will help you know exactly what you are expected to learn in this chapter.

COMMON CORE **CC.9-12.A.SSE.1**
Interpret expressions that represent a quantity in terms of its context.

Key Vocabulary
expression *(expresión)* A mathematical phrase that contains operations, numbers, and/or variables.

What It Means For You   *Lesson 10-1*

A mathematical expression is like a word expression: to understand it, examine the parts that make it up and consider the context it represents.

EXAMPLE

The diagram shows the dimensions of a trapezoidal patio. The expression $\frac{1}{2}(b_1 + b_2)h$ represents the area of the patio.

In the expression $\frac{1}{2}(b_1 + b_2)h$, b_1 and b_2 are the "bases," and h is the perpendicular distance between the bases.

The formula in this context is equivalent to finding the average of the areas of two rectangles with height $h = 12$: one with base $b_1 = 15$ and one with base $b_2 = 27$.

$b_2 = 27$ ft
$h = 12$ ft
$b_1 = 15$ ft

COMMON CORE **CC.9-12.G.MG.3**
Apply geometric methods to solve design problems (e.g., designing an object or structure to satisfy physical constraints or minimize cost...).

What It Means For You   *Lesson 10-3*

Problems of design, from printing to architecture to engineering, naturally involve geometry. You can use the principles of geometry to find the best possible solution in a particular design context.

EXAMPLE

You can use geometry to solve interior design problems. For example, you can find a room's area to help estimate the cost of carpeting. The dimensions of a room and the location of stairs and windows also affect which furnishings will fit the space and how they might be arranged.

Chapter 10   414   Extending Perimeter, Circumference, and Area

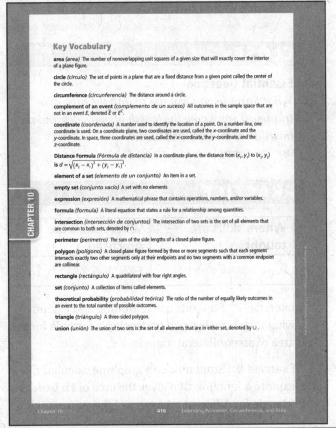

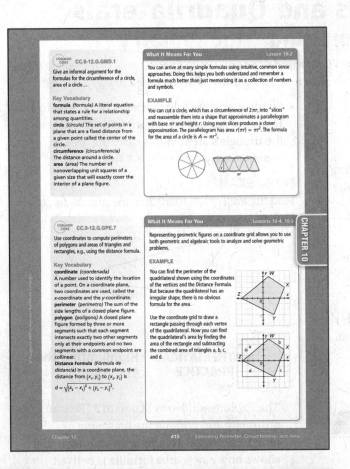

COMMON CORE CC.9-12.G.GMD.1

Give an informal argument for the formulas for the circumference of a circle, area of a circle...

Key Vocabulary
formula *(formula)* A literal equation that states a rule for a relationship among quantities.
circle *(círculo)* The set of points in a plane that are a fixed distance from a given point called the center of the circle.
circumference *(circunferencia)* The distance around a circle.
area *(area)* The number of nonoverlapping unit squares of a given size that will exactly cover the interior of a plane figure.

What It Means For You   Lesson 10-2

You can arrive at many simple formulas using intuitive, common sense approaches. Doing this helps you both understand and remember a formula much better than just memorizing it as a collection of numbers and symbols.

EXAMPLE

You can cut a circle, which has a circumference of $2\pi r$, into "slices" and reassemble them into a shape that approximates a parallelogram with base πr and height r. Using more slices produces a closer approximation. The parallelogram has area $r(\pi r) = \pi r^2$. The formula for the area of a circle is $A = \pi r^2$.

COMMON CORE CC.9-12.G.GPE.7

Use coordinates to compute perimeters of polygons and areas of triangles and rectangles, e.g., using the distance formula.

Key Vocabulary
coordinate *(coordenada)* A number used to identify the location of a point. On a coordinate plane, two coordinates are used, called the x-coordinate and the y-coordinate.
perimeter *(perímetro)* The sum of the side lengths of a closed plane figure.
polygon *(polígono)* A closed plane figure formed by three or more segments such that each segment intersects exactly two other segments only at their endpoints and no two segments with a common endpoint are collinear.
Distance Formula *(Fórmula de distancia)* In a coordinate plane, the distance from (x_1, y_1) to (x_2, y_2) is
$$d = \sqrt{(x_2 - x_1)^2 + (y_2 - y_1)^2}.$$

What It Means For You   Lessons 10-4, 10-5

Representing geometric figures on a coordinate grid allows you to use both geometric and algebraic tools to analyze and solve geometric problems.

EXAMPLE

You can find the perimeter of the quadrilateral shown using the coordinates of the vertices and the Distance Formula. But because the quadrilateral has an irregular shape, there is no obvious formula for the area.

Use the coordinate grid to draw a rectangle passing through each vertex of the quadrilateral. Now you can find the quadrilateral's area by finding the area of the rectangle and subtracting the combined area of triangles a, b, c, and d.

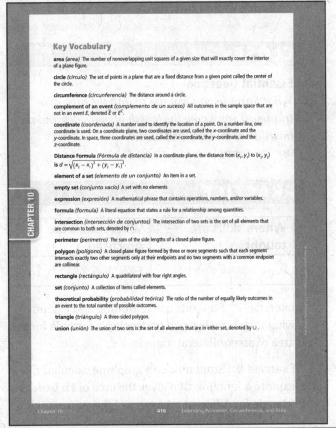

CHAPTER 10

Key Vocabulary

area *(área)* The number of nonoverlapping unit squares of a given size that will exactly cover the interior of a plane figure.

circle *(círculo)* The set of points in a plane that are a fixed distance from a given point called the center of the circle.

circumference *(circunferencia)* The distance around a circle.

complement of an event *(complemento de un suceso)* All outcomes in the sample space that are not in an event E, denoted $\bar{E}$ or E^c.

coordinate *(coordenada)* A number used to identify the location of a point. On a number line, one coordinate is used. On a coordinate plane, two coordinates are used, called the x-coordinate and the y-coordinate. In space, three coordinates are used, called the x-coordinate, the y-coordinate, and the z-coordinate.

Distance Formula *(Fórmula de distancia)* In a coordinate plane, the distance from (x_1, y_1) to (x_2, y_2) is $d = \sqrt{(x_2 - x_1)^2 + (y_2 - y_1)^2}$.

element of a set *(elemento de un conjunto)* An item in a set.

empty set *(conjunto vacío)* A set with no elements.

expression *(expresión)* A mathematical phrase that contains operations, numbers, and/or variables.

formula *(fórmula)* A literal equation that states a rule for a relationship among quantities.

intersection *(intersección de conjuntos)* The intersection of two sets is the set of all elements that are common to both sets, denoted by ∩.

perimeter *(perímetro)* The sum of the side lengths of a closed plane figure.

polygon *(polígono)* A closed plane figure formed by three or more segments such that each segment intersects exactly two other segments only at their endpoints and no two segments with a common endpoint are collinear.

rectangle *(rectángulo)* A quadrilateral with four right angles.

set *(conjunto)* A collection of items called elements.

theoretical probability *(probabilidad teórica)* The ratio of the number of equally likely outcomes in an event to the total number of possible outcomes.

triangle *(triángulo)* A three-sided polygon.

union *(unión)* The union of two sets is the set of all elements that are in either set, denoted by ∪.

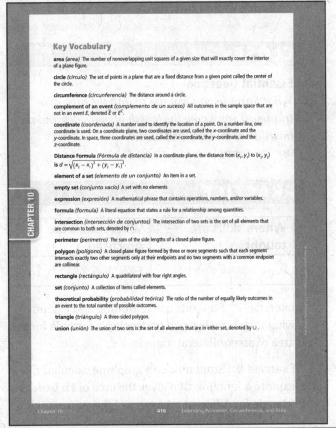

COMMON CORE PROFESSIONAL DEVELOPMENT **CC.9-12.G.GPE.7***

In previous chapters, students learned to apply both algebraic and geometric tools in coordinate proofs to analyze and solve problems. In this chapter, students use coordinate geometry to explore and measure the effects on the perimeter and area when one or more of the dimensions of a figure are changed. Whereas students have applied coordinate geometry to find distances before, in this chapter students learn to devise non-routine solution methods that utilize the relevant algebraic and geometric skills in coordinate proof.

CHAPTER 10

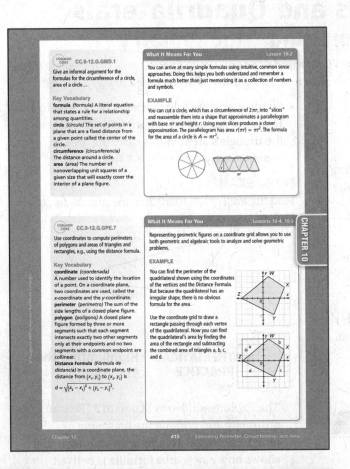

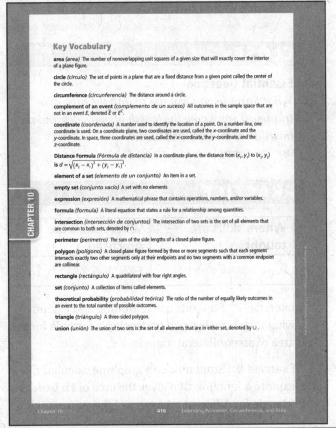

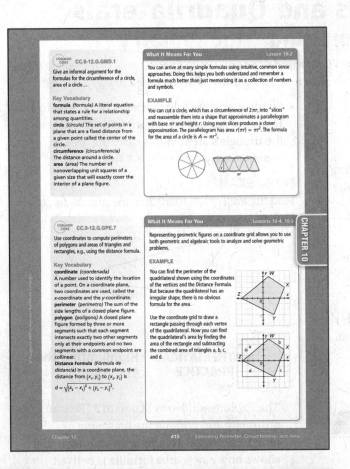

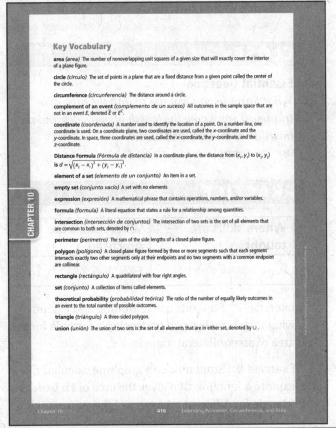

© Houghton Mifflin Harcourt Publishing Company

Chapter 10   415   Extending Perimeter, Circumference, and Area

Chapter 10   416   Extending Perimeter, Circumference, and Area

10-1

Developing Formulas for Triangles and Quadrilaterals
Connection: Using Trigonometry

Essential question: What formula can you use to find the area of a triangle if you know the length of two sides and the measure of an included angle?

COMMON **Standards for**
CORE **Mathematical Content**

CC.9-12.G.SRT.9(+) Derive the formula $A = \frac{1}{2} ab \sin(C)$ for the area of a triangle by drawing an auxiliary line from a vertex perpendicular to the opposite side.

Prerequisites
Trigonometric ratios of any angle with a measure between 0° and 180°

Math Background
The area formula for a triangle, $A = \frac{1}{2} bh$, is used when the triangle's base b and height h are known. In cases where the lengths, a and b, of two sides and the measure of the included angle, $\angle C$, are known, the area formula becomes $A = \frac{1}{2} ab \sin C$.

INTRODUCE

Begin by drawing a triangle and asking what information is needed in order to find the area of the triangle. Students should recall that knowing the length of one side, called the *base*, and the length of the altitude to that side, called the *height*, allows them to use the formula $A = \frac{1}{2} bh$.

TEACH

 EXPLORE

Questioning Strategies
- What formula do you already know for the area of a triangle? $A = \frac{1}{2} bh$

- What do the variables stand for in this formula? b is the length of the triangle's base; h is the triangle's height.

 EXAMPLE

Questioning Strategies
- What units will you use for your answer? How do you know? Square centimeters; the lengths are given in centimeters, so the area should be expressed in square centimeters.

- Suppose you are told that sin 114° is close to 1. How can you use this information to estimate the triangle's area? In this case, the area is approximately $\frac{1}{2} \cdot 13 \cdot 11 \cdot 1 = 71.5$ cm².

EXTRA EXAMPLE
Find the area of the triangle to the nearest tenth. 42.9 m²

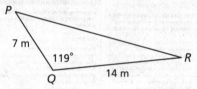

| MATHEMATICAL PRACTICE | Highlighting the Standards |

The Explore addresses Standard 2 (Reason abstractly and critique the reasoning of others). Students complete an argument that shows how a new area formula is derived from a well-known one.

CLOSE

Essential Question
What formula can you use to find the area of a triangle if you know the length of two sides and the measure of an included angle?
Use the formula $A = \frac{1}{2} ab \sin C$.

PRACTICE

Where skills are taught	Where skills are practiced
2 EXAMPLE	EXS. 1–6

Exercise 7: Students use reasoning and extend what they have learned to develop a formula for the area of an equilateral triangle.

Exercise 8: Students use a graphing calculator to explore a function that gives the area of an isosceles triangle for different measures of the vertex angle.

© Houghton Mifflin Harcourt Publishing Company

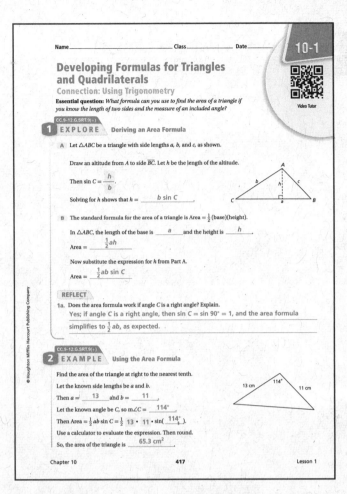

Name_____ Class_____ Date_____

10-1
Video Tutor

Developing Formulas for Triangles and Quadrilaterals
Connection: Using Trigonometry

Essential question: *What formula can you use to find the area of a triangle if you know the length of two sides and the measure of an included angle?*

CC.9-12.G.SRT.9(+)

1 EXPLORE   Deriving an Area Formula

A Let △ABC be a triangle with side lengths *a*, *b*, and *c*, as shown.

Draw an altitude from A to side $\overline{BC}$. Let *h* be the length of the altitude.

Then $\sin C = \dfrac{h}{b}$.

Solving for *h* shows that $h = \underline{\quad b \sin C \quad}$.

B The standard formula for the area of a triangle is Area $= \frac{1}{2}$(base)(height).

In △ABC, the length of the base is ___*a*___ and the height is ___*h*___.

Area $= \underline{\quad \frac{1}{2}ah \quad}$

Now substitute the expression for *h* from Part A.

Area $= \underline{\quad \frac{1}{2}ab \sin C \quad}$

REFLECT

1a. Does the area formula work if angle *C* is a right angle? Explain.

Yes; if angle *C* is a right angle, then $\sin C = \sin 90° = 1$, and the area formula

simplifies to $\frac{1}{2} ab$, as expected.

CC.9-12.G.SRT.9(+)

2 EXAMPLE   Using the Area Formula

Find the area of the triangle at right to the nearest tenth.

Let the known side lengths be *a* and *b*.

Then $a = \underline{\quad 13 \quad}$ and $b = \underline{\quad 11 \quad}$.

Let the known angle be C, so $m\angle C = \underline{\quad 114° \quad}$.

Then Area $= \frac{1}{2}ab \sin C = \frac{1}{2} \cdot \underline{13} \cdot \underline{11} \cdot \sin(\underline{114°})$.

Use a calculator to evaluate the expression. Then round.

So, the area of the triangle is $\underline{\quad 65.3 \text{ cm}^2 \quad}$.

© Houghton Mifflin Harcourt Publishing Company

REFLECT

2a. Suppose you double each of the given side lengths in the triangle but keep the measure of the included angle the same. How does the area change? Explain.

The area is multiplied by 4, because $\frac{1}{2}(2 \cdot 13)(2 \cdot 11) \sin 114° =$

$(2 \cdot 2)\frac{1}{2}(13)(11) \sin 114°$.

PRACTICE

Find the area of each triangle to the nearest tenth.

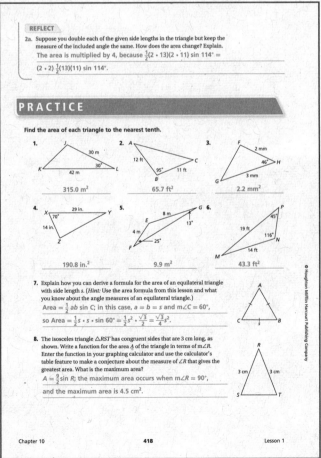

1.   315.0 m²

2.   65.7 ft²

3.   2.2 mm²

4.   190.8 in.²

5.   9.9 m²

6.   43.3 ft²

7. Explain how you can derive a formula for the area of an equilateral triangle with side length *s*. (*Hint:* Use the area formula from this lesson and what you know about the angle measures of an equilateral triangle.)

Area $= \frac{1}{2} ab \sin C$; in this case, $a = b = s$ and $m\angle C = 60°$,

so Area $= \frac{1}{2} s \cdot s \cdot \sin 60° = \frac{1}{2}s^2 \cdot \frac{\sqrt{3}}{2} = \frac{\sqrt{3}}{4}s^2$.

8. The isosceles triangle △RST has congruent sides that are 3 cm long, as shown. Write a function for the area *A* of the triangle in terms of m∠R. Enter the function in your graphing calculator and use the calculator's table feature to make a conjecture about the measure of ∠R that gives the greatest area. What is the maximum area?

$A = \frac{9}{2} \sin R$; the maximum area occurs when $m\angle R = 90°$,

and the maximum area is 4.5 cm².

© Houghton Mifflin Harcourt Publishing Company

Assign these pages to help your students practice
and apply important lesson concepts. For
additional exercises, see the Student Edition.

Answers

Additional Practice

1. 16.0 cm^2

2. 1.0 ft^2

3. 38.5 in.^2

4. 10.2 yd^2

5. 55.2 cm^2

6. 42.1 in.^2

Problem Solving

1. 49.2 in.^2

2. 15.3 cm^2

3. C

4. H

5. D

6. J

Additional Practice

Find the area of each triangle. Round your answers to the nearest tenth. (Figures are not drawn to scale.)

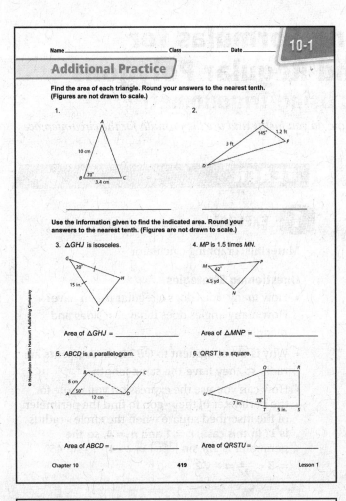

1.

2.

_____

Use the information given to find the indicated area. Round your answers to the nearest tenth. (Figures are not drawn to scale.)

3. △GHJ is isosceles.

4. MP is 1.5 times MN.

Area of △GHJ = _____

Area of △MNP = _____

5. ABCD is a parallelogram.

6. QRST is a square.

Area of ABCD = _____

Area of QRSTU = _____

Problem Solving

Write the correct answer.

1. A piece of glass is in the shape of an isosceles triangle. The congruent sides measure 10 inches, and the base angles measure 40°. To the nearest tenth of a square inch, what is the area of the piece of glass?

2. A triangle has side lengths of 5 cm, 7 cm, and 10 cm. The measure of one of its angles is 118.8°. To the nearest tenth of a square centimeter, what is the area of the triangle? (Hint: 118.8° is the largest of the three angle measures.)

Choose the best answer.

3. An ice cream store makes the sign shown at right, which is a semicircle on top of a triangle. What is the approximate area of the sign? (Figure is not drawn to scale.)

   A 314 in.²
   B 338 in.²
   C 495 in.²
   D 652 in.²

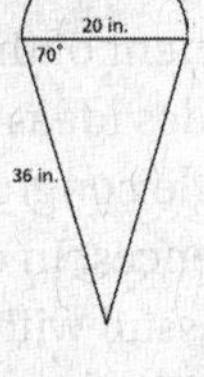

4. A parallelogram has sides of length 30 centimeters and 18 centimeters. One of its angles measures 58°. Which is the best estimate for the area of the parallelogram?

   F 274.8 cm²
   G 286.2 cm²
   H 457.9 cm²
   J 540.0 cm²

5. What is the approximate area of the kite? (Figure is not drawn to scale.)

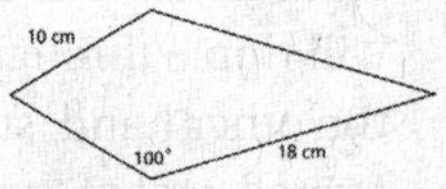

   A 88 cm²
   B 98 cm²
   C 159 cm²
   D 177 cm²

6. A triangle has side lengths of 4 ft, 8 ft, and 9 ft. The smallest angle measures 26.4°. What is the approximate area of the triangle?

   F 6.7 ft²
   G 8.0 ft²
   H 12.3 ft²
   J 16.0 ft²

Notes

Developing Formulas for Circles and Regular Polygons
Connection: Using Trigonometry

Essential question: *How do you justify and use the formula for the circumference of a circle?*

© Houghton Mifflin Harcourt Publishing Company

COMMON CORE Standards for Mathematical Content

CC.9-12.G.GMD.1 Give an informal argument for the formula for the circumference of a circle....

CC.9-12.G.MG.1 Use geometric shapes, their measures, and their properties to describe objects (e.g., modeling a tree trunk or a human torso as a cylinder).*

Prerequisites

Triangle congruence criteria

Trigonometric ratios

Math Background

Students have already seen the formula for the circumference of a circle in earlier grades. In this lesson, they will explore a justification of the formula that is based on an informal limit argument. These types of arguments are of central importance in calculus. Although the term *limit* is not used here, and there is no attempt to give a rigorous explanation of the concept, the underlying idea should be accessible to students at this level, and it offers a preview of the mathematical thinking that students will do in future courses.

INTRODUCE

Begin by reminding students that π is a mathematical constant that is approximately equal to 3.14159. Tell students that π is irrational, which means it cannot be written as $\frac{a}{b}$ for any integers a and b. This also means its decimal form does not terminate and does not repeat. Explain to the class that they will be developing and justifying a formula for the circumference of a circle and that the constant π will play an important role in this investigation. (*Note:* In the Explore, students will need to recognize a sequence of numerical values that approach π.)

TEACH

1 EXPLORE

Materials: graphing calculator

Questioning Strategies

- How many sides does a regular n-gon have? How many angles does it have? **n sides and n angles**

- Why is $\overline{OA}$ congruent to $\overline{OB}$? **Both segments are radii, so they have the same length.**

- How can you use the expression you wrote for the perimeter of the n-gon to find the perimeter of the inscribed square when the circle's radius is 1? **In this case, $r = 1$ and $n = 4$, so the perimeter is $2nr \sin\left(\frac{180°}{n}\right) = 2 \cdot 4 \cdot 1 \cdot \sin 45° = 8 \cdot \frac{\sqrt{2}}{2} = 4\sqrt{2}$**

MATHEMATICAL PRACTICE — Highlighting the Standards

Standard 8 (Look for and express regularity in repeated reasoning) includes the statement that mathematically proficient students "maintain oversight of the process, while attending to details." This skill is essential in navigating the sophisticated argument of the Explore. The argument includes ideas about regular polygons, triangle congruence, trigonometry, and sequences. In order for students to be successful with this, they must continually check that their calculations are correct, since an error at any stage of the argument will ripple through the rest of their work. On the other hand, students must remember the overall goal of the argument so that they do not get lost in the details. Be sure students understand the plan for the argument before they begin the first step.

Name_____ Class_____ Date_____

10-2

Developing Formulas for Circles and Regular Polygons
Connection: Using Trigonometry

Essential question: *How do you justify and use the formula for the circumference of a circle?*

Video Tutor

Circumference of a Circle Formula

The circumference C of a circle with radius r is given by $C = 2\pi r$.

CC.9-12.G.GMD.1

1 EXPLORE   Justifying the Circumference Formula

Plan: To find the circumference of a given circle, consider regular polygons that are inscribed in the circle. As the number of sides of the polygons increases, the perimeter of the polygons gets closer to the circumference of the circle. The first steps of the argument consist of writing an expression for the perimeter of an inscribed n-gon.

Inscribed pentagon   Inscribed hexagon   Inscribed octagon

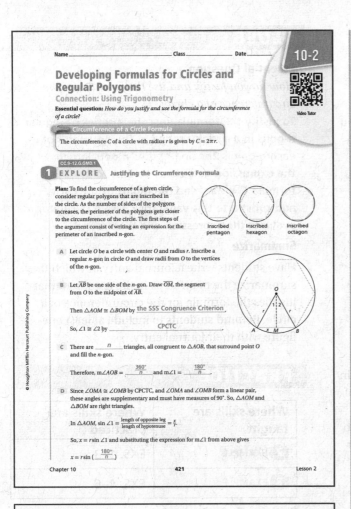

A   Let circle O be a circle with center O and radius r. Inscribe a regular n-gon in circle O and draw radii from O to the vertices of the n-gon.

B   Let $\overline{AB}$ be one side of the n-gon. Draw $\overline{OM}$, the segment from O to the midpoint of $\overline{AB}$.

Then $\triangle AOM \cong \triangle BOM$ by ___the SSS Congruence Criterion___

So, $\angle 1 \cong \angle 2$ by _____CPCTC_____

C   There are _____n_____ triangles, all congruent to $\triangle AOB$, that surround point O and fill the n-gon.

Therefore, $m\angle AOB = \dfrac{360°}{n}$ and $m\angle 1 = \dfrac{180°}{n}$.

D   Since $\angle OMA \cong \angle OMB$ by CPCTC, and $\angle OMA$ and $\angle OMB$ form a linear pair, these angles are supplementary and must have measures of 90°. So, $\triangle AOM$ and $\triangle BOM$ are right triangles.

In $\triangle AOM$, $\sin \angle 1 = \dfrac{\text{length of opposite leg}}{\text{length of hypotenuse}} = \dfrac{x}{r}$.

So, $x = r \sin \angle 1$ and substituting the expression for $m\angle 1$ from above gives

$x = r \sin \left(\dfrac{180°}{n} \right)$

Chapter 10   421   Lesson 2

E   Now express the perimeter of the n-gon in terms of x.

The length of $\overline{AB}$ is $2x$, since ___M is the midpoint of $\overline{AB}$___

This means the perimeter of the n-gon is ___$2nx$___

Substitute the expression for x from Step D.

Then the perimeter is given by the expression ___$2nr \sin\left(\dfrac{180°}{n}\right)$___

F   Your expression for the perimeter of the n-gon should include $n \sin\left(\dfrac{180°}{n}\right)$ as a factor. Use a calculator, as follows, to find out what happens to the value of this expression as n gets larger.

- Enter the expression $x \sin\left(\dfrac{180°}{x}\right)$ as Y_1.
- Go to the Table Setup menu and enter the values shown at right.
- View a table for the function.
- Use the arrow keys to scroll down.

TABLE SETUP
TblStart=3
△Tbl=1
Indpnt: **Auto** Ask
Depend: **Auto** Ask

X	Y1
3	2.5981
4	2.8284
5	2.9389
6	3
7	3.0372
8	3.0615
9	3.0782

X=3

What happens to the value of $n \sin\left(\dfrac{180°}{n}\right)$ as n gets larger?

___The value gets closer to π.___

G   Consider the expression you wrote for the perimeter of the n-gon at the end of Step E. What happens to the value of this expression as n gets larger?

___The expression gets closer to $2\pi r$.___

REFLECT

1a. When n is very large, does the perimeter of the n-gon ever equal the circumference of the circle? Why or why not?

___No; the perimeter gets very close to the circumference, but is always a bit___
___less than the circumference.___

1b. How does the above argument justify the formula $C = 2\pi r$?

___When n is very large, the regular n-gon is virtually indistinguishable from the___
___circle and the expression for the n-gon's perimeter is virtually indistinguishable___
___from $2\pi r$.___

Chapter 10   422   Lesson 2

© Houghton Mifflin Harcourt Publishing Company

Questioning Strategies

- How can you find the radius if you know the diameter? **Divide the diameter by 2.**

- At what point in the solution process should you round? **You should round only as the final step of the solution.**

EXTRA EXAMPLE

Find the circumference of circle Q. Round to the nearest tenth.

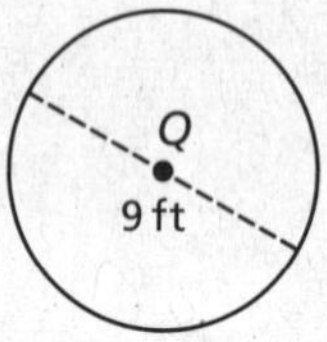

28.3 ft²

Avoid Common Errors

When students are given the diameter of a circle in a figure, they may sometimes make the mistake of using the given diameter as r in the formula $C = 2\pi r$. Remind students to pay close attention to whether they are given the radius or the diameter in a figure.

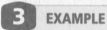
3 **EXAMPLE**

Questioning Strategies

- What assumption do you make in order to use this mathematical model? **You assume that the tree's base is a perfect circle.**

- What units will you use for the diameter? How do you know? **Feet; the circumference is given in feet, so the diameter will also be measured in feet.**

EXTRA EXAMPLE

The Mirny Diamond Mine in eastern Russia is one of the largest open mines in the world. The mine is approximately circular, with a circumference of 3.77 km. What is the approximate diameter of the mine? Round to the nearest tenth of a kilometer.
1.2 km

Essential Question

How do you justify and use the formula for the circumference of a circle?

To justify the formula, inscribe a series of regular n-gons in a circle of radius r. The perimeter of each n-gon is $2nr \sin\left(\frac{180°}{n}\right)$ As n gets larger, the expression gets closer to $2\pi r$. To use the formula $C = 2\pi r$, find the radius of the circle, and substitute this value for r. Use a calculator to evaluate the expression and then round.

Summarize

Have students write a journal entry in which they summarize the main steps in the argument that justifies the formula for the circumference of a circle. Remind students to include at least one figure with their journal entry.

Where skills are taught	Where skills are practiced
2 EXAMPLE	EXS. 1–3
3 EXAMPLE	EXS. 4–6

Exercise 7: Students apply what they have learned to solve a reasoning problem.

PREP FOR CC.9-12.G.MG.1

2 EXAMPLE   Finding the Circumference of a Circle

Find the circumference of circle O. Round to the nearest tenth.

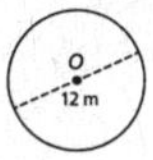

A   Find the radius. The diameter is twice the radius, so $r = $ ___6 m___.

B   Use the formula $C = 2\pi r$.

$C = 2\pi(\underline{\quad 6 \quad})$ Substitute the value for r.

$C \approx \underline{\quad 37.7 \text{ m} \quad}$ Use the π key to evaluate the expression on a calculator. Then round.

REFLECT

2a.   Suppose you multiply the diameter of the circle by a factor k, for some $k > 0$. How does the circumference change? Explain.

The circumference is also multiplied by k, since the new radius is kr and the

new circumference is $2\pi(kr) = k(2\pi r)$.

CC.9-12.G.MG.1

3 EXAMPLE   Solving a Circumference Problem

The General Sherman tree in Sequoia National Park, California, is considered the world's largest tree. The tree is approximately circular at its base, with a circumference of 102.6 feet. What is the approximate diameter of the tree? Round to the nearest foot.

A   Substitute 102.6 for C in the formula for the circumference of a circle.

$102.6 = 2\pi r$ Substitute 102.6 for C in the formula.

$\dfrac{102.6}{2\pi} = r$ Solve for r.

$r \approx \underline{\quad 16.329 \text{ ft} \quad}$ Use a calculator to evaluate the expression.

B   The diameter of a circle is twice the radius.

So, the diameter of the tree is approximately ___33 ft___.

REFLECT

3a.   The maximum distance across the base of the General Sherman tree is 36.5 feet. What explains the difference between this distance and the diameter you calculated above?

The base of the tree is not perfectly circular, so the diameter calculated

above is just an approximation.

© Houghton Mifflin Harcourt Publishing Company

Chapter 10   423   Lesson 2

PRACTICE

Find the circumference of each circle. Round to the nearest tenth.

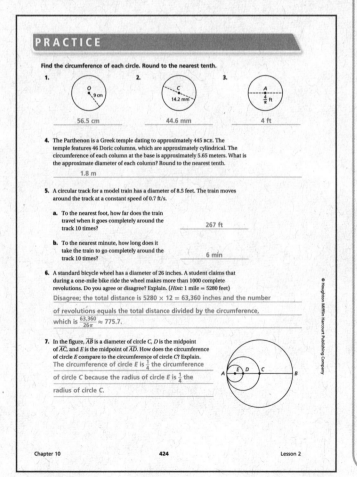

1. O .9 cm
56.5 cm

2. C 14.2 mm
44.6 mm

3. A $\frac{4}{\pi}$ ft
4 ft

4.   The Parthenon is a Greek temple dating to approximately 445 BCE. The temple features 46 Doric columns, which are approximately cylindrical. The circumference of each column at the base is approximately 5.65 meters. What is the approximate diameter of each column? Round to the nearest tenth.

1.8 m

5.   A circular track for a model train has a diameter of 8.5 feet. The train moves around the track at a constant speed of 0.7 ft/s.

a.   To the nearest foot, how far does the train travel when it goes completely around the track 10 times?

267 ft

b.   To the nearest minute, how long does it take the train to go completely around the track 10 times?

6 min

6.   A standard bicycle wheel has a diameter of 26 inches. A student claims that during a one-mile bike ride the wheel makes more than 1000 complete revolutions. Do you agree or disagree? Explain. (Hint: 1 mile = 5280 feet)

Disagree; the total distance is $5280 \times 12 = 63,360$ inches and the number

of revolutions equals the total distance divided by the circumference,

which is $\frac{63,360}{26\pi} \approx 775.7$.

7.   In the figure, $\overline{AB}$ is a diameter of circle C, D is the midpoint of $\overline{AC}$, and E is the midpoint of $\overline{AD}$. How does the circumference of circle E compare to the circumference of circle C? Explain.

The circumference of circle E is $\frac{1}{4}$ the circumference

of circle C because the radius of circle E is $\frac{1}{4}$ the

radius of circle C.

© Houghton Mifflin Harcourt Publishing Company

Chapter 10   424   Lesson 2

ADDITIONAL PRACTICE AND PROBLEM SOLVING

Assign these pages to help your students practice and apply important lesson concepts. For additional exercises, see the Student Edition.

Answers

Additional Practice

1. $C = 50\pi$ m
2. $C = 4a\pi$ in
3. $C = (2x + 2y)\pi$ yd
4. $C = 1200\pi$ mi
5. $r = \pi$ cm
6. $d = (4x + 4)$ km
7. **a.** 37.698 in.

   b. 37.384 in.

   c. No; the approximation is 0.314 inch less than the circumference as calculated in part a.

Problem Solving

1. 3o ft
2. 151 in.
3. A
4. G
5. C
6. H

Name_____ Class_____ Date_____ **10-2**

Additional Practice

Find each measurement. Give your answers in terms of π.

1.
⊙ with 25 m, V

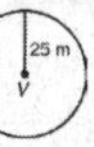

the circumference of ⊙V

_____

2.
⊙ with H, 4a in.

the circumference of ⊙H

_____

3.
⊙ with M, (x + y) yd

the circumference of ⊙M

_____

4.
⊙ with R, 1200 mi

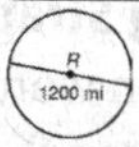

the circumference of ⊙R

_____

5. the radius of ⊙D in which $C = 2\pi^2$ cm _____

6. the diameter of ⊙K in which $C = (4x + 4)\pi$ km _____

7. Daniel is approximating the circumference of a circle by finding the perimeter of an inscribed polygon. The circle has a radius of 6 inches.

a. Find the circumference of the circle using the expression $2\pi r$ with 3.1415 for π.

_____

b. Find the perimeter of an inscribed polygon with 14 sides. Round your answer to the nearest thousandth of an inch.

_____

c. Daniel claims that the perimeter of a 14-sided inscribed polygon is within 0.1 in. of the circumference of the circle as calculated in part a. Is he correct? Explain why or why not.

_____

_____

Problem Solving

Write the correct answer.

1. A circular swimming pool is surrounded by a walkway that is 3 feet wide, as shown below. The circumference of the outer edge of the walkway is 208 feet. What is the radius of the pool to the nearest foot? Use 3.14 for π.

3 ft

2. A wedding cake is made of three circular tiers, as shown below. The cake decorator is going to put one ring of frosting around the circumference of each tier. How many inches of frosting will the cake decorator need? Use 3.14 for π and round to the nearest whole inch.

4 in. / 4 in. / 4 in.

Choose the best answer.

3. The circumference of a circle with a radius of 2 meters is approximated by the perimeter of an inscribed polygon with 10 sides. Which expression gives the described approximation of the circumference?

A $40\sin(18°)$

B $2(2)\pi\sin(18°)$

C $2(2)10\sin\left(\dfrac{180°}{2}\right)$

D $2\pi(10)\sin\left(\dfrac{180°}{10}\right)$

4. An amusement park ride is made up of a large circular frame that holds 50 riders. The circumference of the frame is about 138 feet. What is the diameter of the ride to the nearest foot?

F 22 ft   H 69 ft

G 44 ft   J 138 ft

5. A cyclist travels 50 feet after 7.34 rotations of her bicycle wheels. What is the approximate diameter of the wheels?

A 13 in.   C 26 in.

B 24 in.   D 28 in.

6. A car has a wheel rim with a diameter of 19 inches. The tire itself has a diameter that is 5 inches wider than the rim. What is the approximate circumference of the tire to the nearest whole inch?

F 37 inches

G 42 inches

H 75 inches

J 151 inches

Composite Figures
Going Deeper

Essential question: *How can you find areas of irregular shapes?*

 COMMON CORE Standards for Mathematical Content

CC.9-12.G.MG.1 Use geometric shapes, their measures, and their properties to describe objects ...*

CC.9-12.G.MG.3 Apply geometric methods to solve design problems ...*

Prerequisites
Basic area formulas

Math Background
An important concept that underlies finding areas of composite figures is the following: The area of a region remains the same no matter how it is separated into disjoint regions whose union is the original region. This suggests that the area of a region can be found if it can be separated into simpler shapes such as triangles, rectangles, and so on.

INTRODUCE
Review basic area formulas with students.

TEACH

1 EXAMPLE

Questioning Strategies
• What is the formula for the area of a rectangle? Area = length × width

• The large rectangle is 1000 ft by 800 ft, with an area of 800,000 ft². How can you use this fact to find the area of the parking lot? Subtract the areas of the two buildings from the overall area: 800,000 − 90,000 − 80,000 = 630,000 ft²

EXTRA EXAMPLE
Find the area of the playground shown. Except for the edge whose length is not given, the edges of the playground meet at right angles. 520,000 ft²

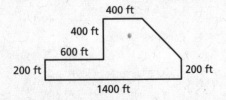
400 ft
400 ft
600 ft
200 ft   200 ft
1400 ft

2 EXAMPLE

Questioning Strategies
• Describe in words the expression you that you write for Step B . The area of the unshaded region is the area of the square minus the area of each of the two quarter circles.

EXTRA EXAMPLE
The rectangular park shown will have the shaded portion, which consists of two semicircles and a rectangle, covered in grass. Find the exact area of the park not covered in grass.

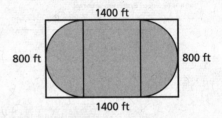
1400 ft
800 ft   800 ft
1400 ft

640,000 − 160,000π ft²

CLOSE

Essential Question
How can you find areas of irregular shapes?
Identify simpler shapes within or around an irregular shape and find the areas of the simpler shapes. If the simpler shapes make up the irregular shape, add the areas. If the simpler shapes are outside the irregular shape, subtract their areas from the area of the overall shape.

Summarize
Have students make up and solve a problem involving areas of irregular shapes.

PRACTICE

Where skills are taught	Where skills are practiced
1 EXAMPLE	EXS. 1, 2, 4
2 EXAMPLE	EXS. 1–4

© Houghton Mifflin Harcourt Publishing Company

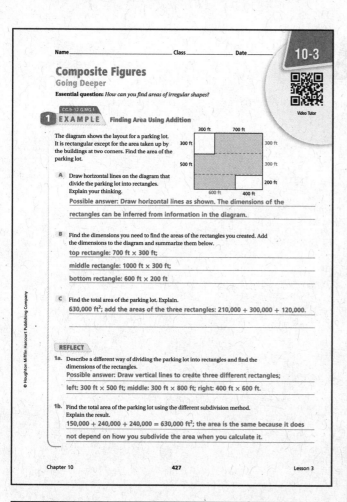

Name_____ Class_____ Date_____

10-3

Composite Figures
Going Deeper

Essential question: *How can you find areas of irregular shapes?*

Video Tutor

CC.9-12.G.MG.1

1 EXAMPLE Finding Area Using Addition

The diagram shows the layout for a parking lot. It is rectangular except for the area taken up by the buildings at two corners. Find the area of the parking lot.

A Draw horizontal lines on the diagram that divide the parking lot into rectangles. Explain your thinking.

Possible answer: Draw horizontal lines as shown. The dimensions of the

rectangles can be inferred from information in the diagram.

B Find the dimensions you need to find the areas of the rectangles you created. Add the dimensions to the diagram and summarize them below.

top rectangle: 700 ft × 300 ft;

middle rectangle: 1000 ft × 300 ft;

bottom rectangle: 600 ft × 200 ft

C Find the total area of the parking lot. Explain.

630,000 ft²; add the areas of the three rectangles: 210,000 + 300,000 + 120,000.

REFLECT

1a. Describe a different way of dividing the parking lot into rectangles and find the dimensions of the rectangles.

Possible answer: Draw vertical lines to create three different rectangles;

left: 300 ft × 500 ft; middle: 300 ft × 800 ft; right: 400 ft × 600 ft.

1b. Find the total area of the parking lot using the different subdivision method. Explain the result.

150,000 + 240,000 + 240,000 = 630,000 ft²; the area is the same because it does

not depend on how you subdivide the area when you calculate it.

Chapter 10   427   Lesson 3

© Houghton Mifflin Harcourt Publishing Company

CC.9-12.G.MG.3

2 EXAMPLE Finding Area Using Subtraction

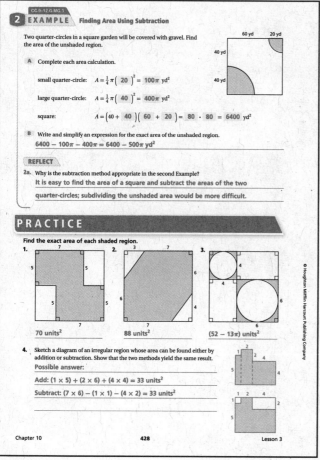

Two quarter-circles in a square garden will be covered with gravel. Find the area of the unshaded region.

A Complete each area calculation.

small quarter-circle: $A = \frac{1}{4}\pi\left(20\right)^2 = 100\pi$ yd²

large quarter-circle: $A = \frac{1}{4}\pi\left(40\right)^2 = 400\pi$ yd²

square: $A = \left(40 + 40\right)\left(60 + 20\right) = 80 \cdot 80 = 6400$ yd²

B Write and simplify an expression for the exact area of the unshaded region.

$6400 - 100\pi - 400\pi = 6400 - 500\pi$ yd²

REFLECT

2a. Why is the subtraction method appropriate in the second Example?

It is easy to find the area of a square and subtract the areas of the two

quarter-circles; subdividing the unshaded area would be more difficult.

PRACTICE

Find the exact area of each shaded region.

1. 70 units²

2. 88 units²

3. (52 − 13π) units²

4. Sketch a diagram of an irregular region whose area can be found either by addition or subtraction. Show that the two methods yield the same result.

Possible answer:

Add: (1 × 5) + (2 × 6) + (4 × 4) = 33 units²

Subtract: (7 × 6) − (1 × 1) − (4 × 2) = 33 units²

Chapter 10   428   Lesson 3

© Houghton Mifflin Harcourt Publishing Company

ADDITIONAL PRACTICE AND PROBLEM SOLVING

Assign these pages to help your students practice and apply important lesson concepts. For additional exercises, see the Student Edition.

Answers

Additional Practice

1. $A = 1080\ \text{ft}^2$
2. $A = 6\ \text{in}^2$
3. $A = 3888\ \text{mm}^2$
4. $A \approx 411.3\ \text{mi}^2$
5. $A = 90\ \text{m}^2$
6. $A \approx 27.5\ \text{yd}^2$
7. $A \approx 448.1\ \text{cm}^2$
8. $A \approx 1342.5\ \text{m}^2$
9. \$241.54
10. $A \approx 10\ \text{cm}^2$
11. $A \approx 7.5\ \text{cm}^2$

Problem Solving

1. $128.6\ \text{cm}^2$
2. \$13.80
3. A
4. G
5. C
6. H

Notes

Name_____ Class_____ Date_____

Additional Practice

Find the shaded area. Round to the nearest tenth if necessary.

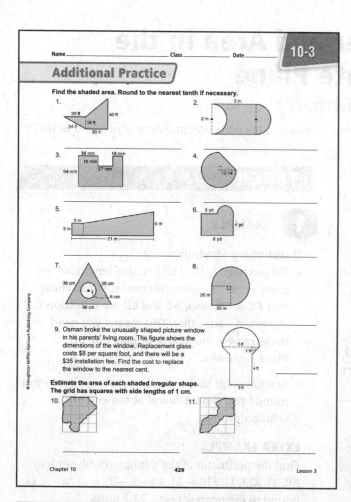

1.
30 ft · 40 ft · 34 ft · 16 ft · 30 ft

2.
3 in. · 2 in.

3.
36 mm · 18 mm · 18 mm · 54 mm · 27 mm

4.
12 mi

5.
3 m · 3 m · 6 m · 21 m

6.
3 yd · 4 yd · 6 yd

7.
36 cm · 35 cm · 6 cm · 36 cm · r

8.
20 m · 20 m

9. Osman broke the unusually shaped picture window in his parents' living room. The figure shows the dimensions of the window. Replacement glass costs $8 per square foot, and there will be a $35 installation fee. Find the cost to replace the window to the nearest cent.

5 ft · 1 ft · 4 ft · 3 ft

Estimate the area of each shaded irregular shape.
The grid has squares with side lengths of 1 cm.

10.

11.

Chapter 10 · 429 · Lesson 3

Problem Solving

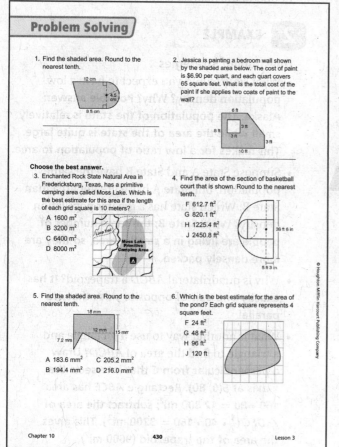

1. Find the shaded area. Round to the nearest tenth.

12 cm · 4.5 cm · 9.5 cm

2. Jessica is painting a bedroom wall shown by the shaded area below. The cost of paint is $6.90 per quart, and each quart covers 65 square feet. What is the total cost of the paint if she applies two coats of paint to the wall?

6 ft · 3 ft · 8 ft · 3 ft · 10 ft

Choose the best answer.

3. Enchanted Rock State Natural Area in Fredericksburg, Texas, has a primitive camping area called Moss Lake. Which is the best estimate for this area if the length of each grid square is 10 meters?

A 1600 m²
B 3200 m²
C 6400 m²
D 8000 m²

Loop Trail · Moss Lake Primitive Camping Area · A

4. Find the area of the section of basketball court that is shown. Round to the nearest tenth.

F 612.7 ft²
G 820.1 ft²
H 1225.4 ft²
J 2450.8 ft²

39 ft 6 in · 5 ft 3 in.

5. Find the shaded area. Round to the nearest tenth.

18 mm · 12 mm · 15 mm · 7.2 mm

A 183.6 mm²   C 205.2 mm²
B 194.4 mm²   D 216.0 mm²

6. Which is the best estimate for the area of the pond? Each grid square represents 4 square feet.

F 24 ft²
G 48 ft²
H 96 ft²
J 120 ft²

Chapter 10 · 430 · Lesson 3

Perimeter and Area in the Coordinate Plane
Extension: Density

Essential question: *How do you find the perimeter and area of polygons in the coordinate plane?*

Standards for Mathematical Content

CC.9-12.G.GPE.7 Use coordinates to compute perimeters of polygons and areas of triangles and rectangles, e.g., using the distance formula.*

CC.9-12.G.MG.1 Use geometric shapes, their measures, and their properties to describe objects (e.g., modeling a tree trunk or a human torso as a cylinder).*

CC.9-12.G.MG.2 Apply concepts of density based on area ... in modeling situations (e.g., persons per square mile, ...).*

Vocabulary
population density

Prerequisites
The distance formula

Math Background
Students have already worked with perimeter and area in middle school and in Algebra 1. This lesson extends these concepts to the coordinate plane. Finding the perimeter of a polygon is an application of the distance formula. Finding the area of a polygon is based on dividing the polygon into simpler shapes for which it is easy to calculate the area, such as rectangles and triangles.

INTRODUCE

Remind students that the perimeter of a figure is the distance around the figure. In the case of a polygon, the perimeter is simply the sum of the lengths of the polygon's sides. You may wish to draw a polygon with vertical and horizontal sides on a coordinate plane and ask students to determine the perimeter. Explain that horizontal and vertical sides are easy to work with. For sides that are not horizontal or vertical, the distance formula is needed.

TEACH

1 EXAMPLE

Questioning Strategies

- Do you need to find all five side lengths or are there some shortcuts you can use? **You know that $BC = CD$ since $\overline{BC}$ and $\overline{CD}$ are reflection images of each other. This means you need to determine the length of only one of those segments.**

- At what point in the solution process should you round? **You should round at the end of the solution process.**

EXTRA EXAMPLE
Find the perimeter of the pentagon with vertices $J(0, 3)$, $K(3, 1)$, $L(0, -3)$, $M(-5, -3)$, and $N(-3, 1)$. Round to the nearest tenth. **21.7 units**

2 EXAMPLE

Questioning Strategies

- What state would you expect to have a low population density? Why? **Possible answer: Alaska. The population of the state is relatively small while the area of the state is quite large. This makes for a low ratio of population to area.**

- Suppose State A and State B have the same population, but State A has a greater area than State B. Which state has a greater population density? Why? **State B; the same number of people are living in a smaller area, so they are more densely packed.**

- Why is quadrilateral $ABCD$ a trapezoid? **It has exactly one pair of opposite sides that are parallel.**

- What is another way to use a rectangle and a triangle to find the area of $ABCD$? **Draw a perpendicular from C that intersects the x-axis at E(0, 80). Rectangle ABCE has area $160 \cdot 80 = 12{,}800$ mi²; subtract the area of $\triangle DEC$ ($\frac{1}{2} \cdot 40 \cdot 160 = 3200$ mi²). This gives the area of the trapezoid (9600 mi²).**

Name_____ Class_____ Date_____

10-4

Perimeter and Area in the Coordinate Plane
Extension: Density

Essential question: *How do you find the perimeter and area of polygons in the coordinate plane?*

Recall that the perimeter of a polygon is the sum of the lengths of the polygon's sides. You can use the distance formula to help you find perimeters of polygons in a coordinate plane.

CC.9-12.G.GPE.7

1 EXAMPLE Finding a Perimeter

Find the perimeter of the pentagon with vertices $A(-4, 2)$, $B(-4, -2)$, $C(0, -3)$, $D(4, -2)$, and $E(2, 3)$. Round to the nearest tenth.

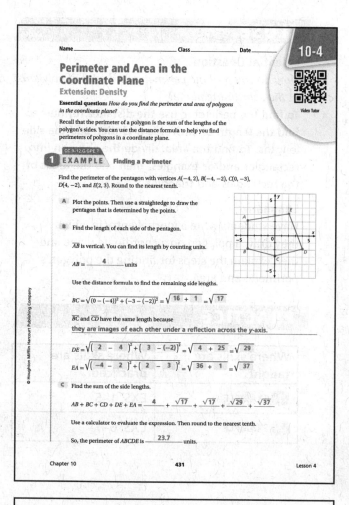

A Plot the points. Then use a straightedge to draw the pentagon that is determined by the points.

B Find the length of each side of the pentagon.

$\overline{AB}$ is vertical. You can find its length by counting units.

$AB = \underline{\quad 4 \quad}$ units

Use the distance formula to find the remaining side lengths.

$BC = \sqrt{(0 - (-4))^2 + (-3 - (-2))^2} = \sqrt{\underline{16} + \underline{1}} = \sqrt{\underline{17}}$

$\overline{BC}$ and $\overline{CD}$ have the same length because
they are images of each other under a reflection across the y-axis.

$DE = \sqrt{(\underline{2} - \underline{4})^2 + (\underline{3} - (-2))^2} = \sqrt{\underline{4} + \underline{25}} = \sqrt{\underline{29}}$

$EA = \sqrt{(\underline{-4} - \underline{2})^2 + (\underline{2} - \underline{3})^2} = \sqrt{\underline{36} + \underline{1}} = \sqrt{\underline{37}}$

C Find the sum of the side lengths.

$AB + BC + CD + DE + EA = \underline{4} + \sqrt{\underline{17}} + \sqrt{\underline{17}} + \sqrt{\underline{29}} + \sqrt{\underline{37}}$

Use a calculator to evaluate the expression. Then round to the nearest tenth.

So, the perimeter of ABCDE is $\underline{23.7}$ units.

© Houghton Mifflin Harcourt Publishing Company

Chapter 10   431   Lesson 4

REFLECT

1a. Explain how you can find the perimeter of a rectangle to check that your answer is reasonable.

The perimeter is approximately equal to the perimeter of the rectangle with
vertices (−4, 2), (−4, −2), (4, −2), and (4, 2). This rectangle has a perimeter
of 24 units, so the answer is reasonable.

The *density* of an object is its mass per unit volume. For example, the density of gold is 19.3 g/cm³. This means each cubic centimeter of gold has a mass of 19.3 grams. You can also define density in other situations that involve area or volume. For example, the **population density** of a region is the population per unit area.

CC.9-12.G.MG.2

2 EXAMPLE Approximating a Population Density

Vermont has a population of 621,760. Its border can be modeled by the trapezoid with vertices $A(0, 0)$, $B(0, 160)$, $C(80, 160)$, and $D(40, 0)$, where each unit of the coordinate plane represents one mile. Find the approximate population density of Vermont. Round to the nearest tenth.

A Plot the points. Then use a straightedge to draw the trapezoid that is determined by the points.

B Find the area of the trapezoid. To do so, draw a perpendicular from D to $\overline{BC}$. This forms a rectangle and a triangle. The area of the trapezoid is the sum of the area of the rectangle and the area of the triangle.

Area of rectangle $= \ell \cdot w = \underline{160} \cdot \underline{40} = \underline{6400}$

Area of triangle $= \frac{1}{2}bh = \frac{1}{2} \cdot \underline{40} \cdot \underline{160} = \underline{3200}$

Area of trapezoid $= \underline{6400} + \underline{3200} = \underline{9600}$ mi²

C Find the population density.

Population density $= \frac{\text{population}}{\text{area}} = \frac{\underline{621,760}}{\underline{9600}} \approx \underline{64.77}$

Round to the nearest tenth.

So, the approximate population density of Vermont is $\underline{64.8}$ persons/mi².

© Houghton Mifflin Harcourt Publishing Company

Chapter 10   432   Lesson 4

EXTRA EXAMPLE

New Hampshire has a population of 1,324,575. Its border can be modeled by the trapezoid with vertices $R(0, 0)$, $S(70, 0)$, $T(70, 190)$, and $U(50, 190)$, where each unit of the coordinate plane represents one mile. Find the approximate population density of New Hampshire. Round to the nearest tenth.

154.9 persons/mi^2

Avoid Common Errors

When calculating a population density, students may be confused about the order in which to form the ratio (i.e., population divided by area, or area divided by population). Tell students that the units of population density provide a clue. Because population density is expressed as persons per square mile, the ratio should be formed by dividing the population (the number of persons) by the area (the number of square miles).

MATHEMATICAL PRACTICE — Highlighting the Standards

To address Standard 4 (Model with mathematics), discuss the modeling process that is used in the example on population density. In particular, ask students what assumptions they must make in order to use this mathematical model. Help students understand that the shape of the state of Vermont, which has some irregular boundaries formed by rivers, is assumed to be a perfect trapezoid. You may want to have students look at a map of the state and find the coordinates of a polygon that approximates the state's border even more closely. Students should see that when developing a mathematical model, there is often a trade-off between a model that is a better "fit" (e.g., a more complex polygon) and one that is easy to work with (e.g., a trapezoid).

CLOSE

Essential Question

How do you find the perimeter and area of polygons in the coordinate plane?

To find the perimeter, use the distance formula to find the length of each side and then add the side lengths. To find the area, divide the polygon into rectangles and/or triangles, then add the areas of the rectangles and triangles.

Summarize

Have students write a journal entry in which they draw a polygon on a coordinate plane and then explain the steps for finding the polygon's perimeter and area.

PRACTICE

Where skills are taught	Where skills are practiced
1 EXAMPLE	EXS. 1–5
2 EXAMPLE	EXS. 6–7

REFLECT

2a. The actual area of Vermont is 9620 mi². Is your approximation of the population density an overestimate or underestimate? Why?

Overestimate; to find the exact population density, you divide by a greater value,

so the population density decreases.

2b. Suppose the population of Vermont doubles in the next century. Would the population density change? If so, how?

Yes; the population density would also double.

PRACTICE

1. Find the side lengths of the triangle with vertices $X(0, 1)$, $Y(5, 4)$, and $Z(2, 6)$. Round to the nearest tenth.

$XY = $ **5.8 units**

$YZ = $ **3.6 units**

$ZX = $ **5.4 units**

2. Find the side lengths of the quadrilateral with vertices $P(2, 5)$, $Q(-3, 0)$, $R(2, -5)$, and $S(6, 0)$. Round to the nearest tenth.

$PQ = $ **7.1 units**

$QR = $ **7.1 units**

$RS = $ **6.4 units**

$SP = $ **6.4 units**

3. Find the perimeter of the hexagon with vertices $A(-5, 1)$, $B(0, 3)$, $C(5, 1)$, $D(4, -2)$, $E(0, -4)$, and $F(-2, -4)$. Round to the nearest tenth.

26.2 units

4. Find the perimeter of the hexagon with vertices $J(0, 5)$, $K(4, 3)$, $L(4, -1)$, $M(0, -4)$, $N(-4, -1)$, and $P(-4, 3)$. Round to the nearest tenth.

26.9 units

5. A plot of land is a pentagon with vertices $Q(-4, 4)$, $R(2, 4)$, $S(4, 1)$, $T(2, -4)$, and $U(-4, -4)$. Each unit of the coordinate grid represents one meter.

a. Fencing costs $24.75 per meter. What is the cost of placing a fence around the plot of land?   **$717.52**

b. Sod costs $1.85 per square meter. What is the cost of covering the plot of land with sod?   **$103.60**

6. Suppose that Colorado has a population of 5,024,748. Its border can be modeled by the rectangle with vertices $A(-190, 0)$, $B(-190, 280)$, $C(190, 280)$, and $D(190, 0)$, where each unit of the coordinate plane represents one mile. Find the approximate population density of Colorado. Round to the nearest tenth.

47.2 persons/mi²

7. For the maximum grain yield, corn should be planted at a density of 38,000 plants per acre. A farmer has a field in the shape of a quadrilateral with vertices $J(0, 0)$, $K(0, 400)$, $L(500, 600)$, and $M(500, 0)$, where each unit of the coordinate plane represents one foot.

a. What is the area of the field in square feet?   **250,000 ft²**

b. What is the area of the field to the nearest hundredth of an acre? (*Hint:* 1 acre equals 43,560 ft².)   **5.74 acres**

c. Approximately how many corn plants should be planted in the field for maximum grain yield? Round to the nearest ten thousand.   **220,000**

Assign these pages to help your students practice
and apply important lesson concepts. For
additional exercises, see the Student Edition.

Answers

Additional Practice

1. 16.5 units

2. 17.9 units

3.

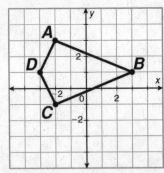

kite; $P \approx 15.2$ units; $A = 12$ units^2

4.

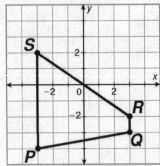

trapezoid; $P \approx 20.3$ units; $A = 21$ units^2

5.

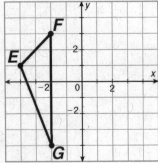

scalene triangle; $P \approx 15.2$ units; $A = 7$ units^2

6.

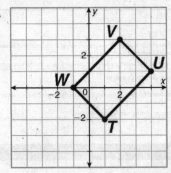

rectangle; $P \approx 14.1$ units; $A = 12$ units^2

Problem Solving

1. $P \approx 22.8$ units; $A = 28$ units^2

2. $P \approx 12.1$ units; $A = 4$ units^2

3. $A = 31.5$ units^2

4. 1432 yards

5. C   **6.** F

7. D

© Houghton Mifflin Harcourt Publishing Company

Notes

Additional Practice

Find the perimeter of the figure shown. Round to the nearest tenth of a unit.

1.

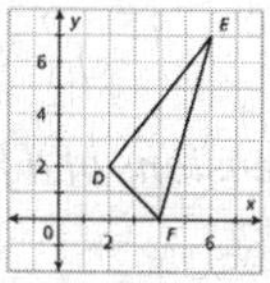

2.

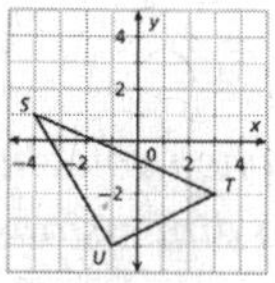

Draw and classify each polygon with the given vertices. Find the perimeter and area of the polygon. Round to the nearest tenth if necessary.

3. $A(-2, 3)$, $B(3, 1)$, $C(-2, -1)$, $D(-3, 1)$

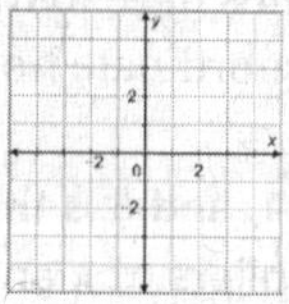

4. $P(-3, -4)$, $Q(3, -3)$, $R(3, -2)$, $S(-3, 2)$

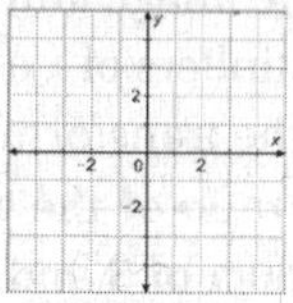

5. $E(-4, 1)$, $F(-2, 3)$, $G(-2, -4)$

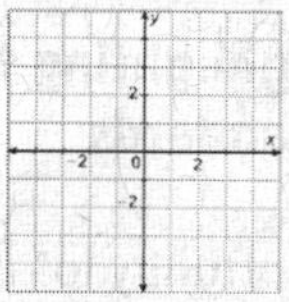

6. $T(1, -2)$, $U(4, 1)$, $V(2, 3)$, $W(-1, 0)$

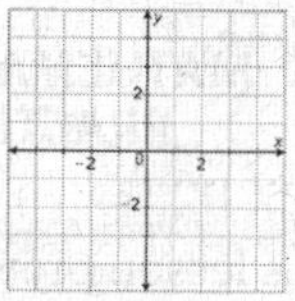

_____

_____

Problem Solving

1. Find the perimeter and area of a polygon with vertices $A(-3, -2)$, $B(2, 4)$, $C(5, 2)$, and $D(0, -4)$. Round to the nearest tenth.

2. What are the perimeter and area of the triangle that is formed when the lines below are graphed in the coordinate plane? Round to the nearest tenth.

   $y = 2x$, $y = 4$, and $y = x + 4$

3. Find the area of polygon $HJKL$ with vertices $H(-3, 3)$, $J(2, 1)$, $K(4, -4)$, and $L(-3, -3)$.

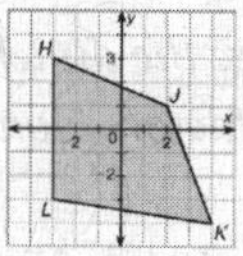

4. A children's zoo has a train that runs around the perimeter of the zoo. It is approximately rectangular in shape, passing through points $(-100, 300)$, $(200, 200)$, $(-100, -100)$, and $(200, -200)$, where each unit represents 1 yard. How long is the train track to the nearest whole yard?

Choose the best answer.

5. A graph showing the top view of a circular fountain has its center at $(4, 6)$. The circle representing the fountain passes through $(2, 1)$. What is the area of the space covered by the fountain?

   A $\sqrt{29}\,\pi$

   B $2\sqrt{29}\,\pi$

   C 29π

   D 58π

6. Trapezoid $QRST$ with vertices $Q(1, 5)$ and $R(9, 5)$ has an area of 12 square units. Which are possible locations for vertices S and T?

   F $S(6, 7)$ and $T(2, 7)$

   G $S(4, 7)$ and $T(2, 7)$

   H $S(6, 8)$ and $T(3, 8)$

   J $S(6, 1)$ and $T(3, 1)$

7. A square has one vertex located at $(-5, 0)$ and has an area of 16 square units. Which of the following could be another vertex of the square?

   A $(-1, 1)$

   B $(-1, \sqrt{5})$

   C $(-2, \sqrt{6})$

   D $(-2, \sqrt{7})$

Effects of Changing Dimensions Proportionally
Extension: Stretching with Different Scale Factors

Essential question: *What happens when you change the dimensions of a figure using different scale factors along two dimensions?*

© Houghton Mifflin Harcourt Publishing Company

COMMON CORE Standards for Mathematical Content

CC.9-12.G.CO.2 Represent transformations in the plane... Compare transformations that preserve distance and angle to those that do not (e.g., translation versus horizontal stretch).

Prerequisites

Coordinate notation for transformations

Basic area formulas

Math Background

The transformation below is a dilation centered at the origin in the coordinate plane.

$$P(x, y) \rightarrow P'(ax, ay) \text{ where } a > 0$$

If O represents the origin, then $OP' = a(OP)$. Angle measurements are preserved but distance is scaled, or multiplied, by a factor of a. The ratio of the area of the image to that of the preimage is a^2.

If $P(x, y) \rightarrow P'(ax, by)$ and $a \neq b$, then scaling will not be uniform and angle measurements may not be preserved. A transformation of this kind is sometimes called a non-uniform scaling.

INTRODUCE

Point out to students that the Explore involves the coordinate plane. Make sure students know how to find the distance between two points.

TEACH

1 EXPLORE

Questioning Strategies

- What line segments are the diagonals of kite *ABCD*? How long are they?
  $\overline{AC}$ and $\overline{BD}$; $AC = 5$ and $BD = 4$

- What line segments are the diagonals of kite *A'B'C'D'*? How long are they?
  $\overline{A'C'}$ and $\overline{B'D'}$; $A'C' = 15$ and $B'D' = 8$

- What relationship does the ratio of the areas of the image and preimage kites have to the multipliers of *x* and *y* in the coordinate notation for the transformation?
  The ratio of the areas is 6 to 1, and 6 is the product of 3 and 2, the multipliers of *x* and *y* in the coordinate notation.

MATHEMATICAL PRACTICE — Highlighting the Standards

This lesson provides an opportunity to address Standard 3 (Construct viable arguments and critique the reasoning of others). By investigating what happens to various figures under the transformation $(x, y) \rightarrow (ax, by)$, students are able to reason inductively about the effect of the transformation on angle measure and area.

CLOSE

Essential Question

What happens when you change the dimensions of a figure using different scale factors along two dimensions?

For the transformation $(x, y) \rightarrow (ax, by)$ where $a > 0$ and $b > 0$, the area of the image is the area of the preimage multiplied by a factor of *ab*.

Summarize

Have students explain how to find the area of the image of a polygon under the transformation $(x, y) \rightarrow (ax, by)$.

PRACTICE

Where skills are taught	Where skills are practiced
 EXPLORE	EXS. 1–4

Name _____ Class _____ Date _____ **10-5**

Effects of Changing Dimensions Proportionally

Extension: Stretching with Different Scale Factors

Video Tutor

Essential question: *What happens when you change the dimensions of a figure using different scale factors along two dimensions?*

The transformation $(x, y) \rightarrow (ax, ay)$ can be called a *uniform scaling*.
Transformations such as $(x, y) \rightarrow (ax, y)$, $(x, y) \rightarrow (x, by)$, and $(x, y) \rightarrow (ax, by)$ have different effects.

CC.9-12.G.CO.2

1 EXPLORE Experimenting with Non-Uniform Scaling

A, B, C, and D are vertices of a kite. Consider the transformation with the rule $(x, y) \rightarrow (3x, 2y)$.

A Complete the table of coordinates.

Preimage (x, y)	A(0, 2)	B(2, 4)	C(5, 2)	D(2, 0)
Image (3x, 2y)	A'(0, 4)	B'(6, 8)	C'(15, 4)	D'(6, 0)

B Kite *ABCD* is shown on the graph below. Draw *A'B'C'D'*.

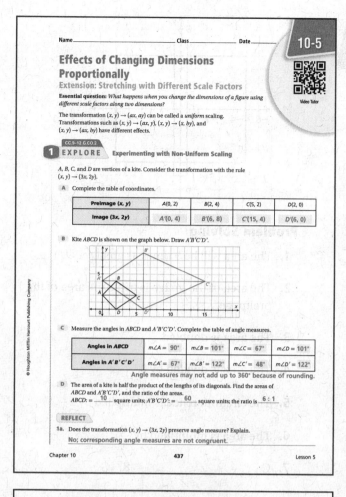

C Measure the angles in *ABCD* and *A'B'C'D'*. Complete the table of angle measures.

Angles in *ABCD*	$m\angle A = 90°$	$m\angle B = 101°$	$m\angle C = 67°$	$m\angle D = 101°$
Angles in *A'B'C'D'*	$m\angle A' = 67°$	$m\angle B' = 122°$	$m\angle C' = 48°$	$m\angle D' = 122°$

Angle measures may not add up to 360° because of rounding.

D The area of a kite is half the product of the lengths of its diagonals. Find the areas of *ABCD* and *A'B'C'D'*, and the ratio of the areas.
ABCD: = __10__ square units; *A'B'C'D'*: = __60__ square units; the ratio is __6 : 1__.

REFLECT

1a. Does the transformation $(x, y) \rightarrow (3x, 2y)$ preserve angle measure? Explain.

No; corresponding angle measures are not congruent.

1b. Write a conjecture about how the transformation $(x, y) \rightarrow (ax, by)$ affects area when *a* and *b* are positive numbers.

Possible conjecture: The transformation $(x, y) \rightarrow (ax, by)$ causes the area of a figure

to be multiplied by the product *ab*.

1c. Is your conjecture compatible with what you know about how the transformation $(x, y) \rightarrow (ax, ay)$ affects area? Explain.

Yes; if the two scale factors are both *a*, their product is a^2. When all dimensions of

a figure are multiplied by *a*, the area changes by a factor of a^2.

PRACTICE

Draw the image of the given figure under the transformation. Find the areas of the figures, and calculate the ratio of the image area to the preimage area.

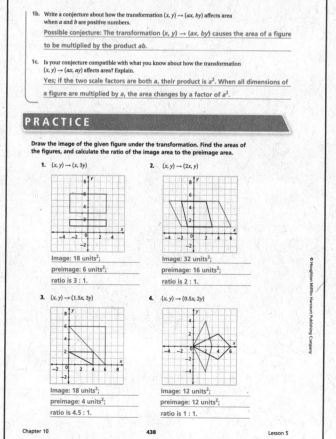

1. $(x, y) \rightarrow (x, 3y)$

Image: 18 units²;

preimage: 6 units²;

ratio is 3 : 1.

2. $(x, y) \rightarrow (2x, y)$

Image: 32 units²;

preimage: 16 units²;

ratio is 2 : 1.

3. $(x, y) \rightarrow (1.5x, 3y)$

Image: 18 units²;

preimage: 4 units²;

ratio is 4.5 : 1.

4. $(x, y) \rightarrow (0.5x, 2y)$

Image: 12 units²;

preimage: 12 units²;

ratio is 1 : 1.

Assign these pages to help your students practice and apply important lesson concepts. For additional exercises, see the Student Edition.

Answers

Additional Practice

1.

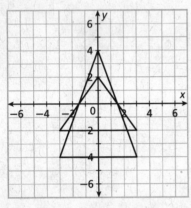

2.

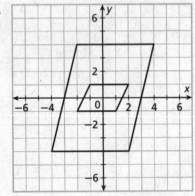

3.

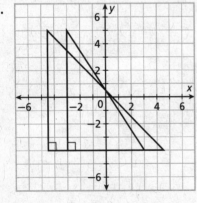

4.

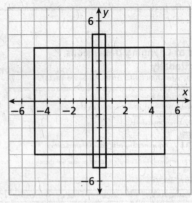

Problem Solving

1. The area will be 9 times as great.

2. The area of the image is triple the area of the preimage.

3. The area is doubled.

4. The area is divided by 2.

5. The circumference is multiplied by $1\frac{1}{2}$.

6. The area is multiplied by $\frac{9}{4}$.

7. C   8. G

10-5

Additional Practice

Draw the image of the given figure under the indicated transformation.
Find the area of each figure, and calculate the ratio of the image area
to the preimage area.

1. $(x,y) \rightarrow (x, 2y)$

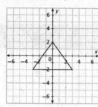

2. $(x,y) \rightarrow (0.5x, 0.25y)$

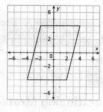

_____

_____

3. $(x,y) \rightarrow \left(\frac{3}{2}x, y\right)$

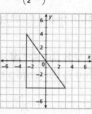

4. $(x,y) \rightarrow \left(\frac{1}{12}x, 1\frac{1}{4}y\right)$

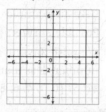

_____

_____

Problem Solving

1. Mara has a photograph 5 inches by 7 inches. She wants to enlarge the photo so that the length and width are each tripled. Describe how the area of the photo will change.

2. A rectangle has vertices (–1, 3), (4, 3), (4, 1), and (–1, 1). If the transformation $(x, y) \rightarrow (3x, y)$ is applied to the rectangle, how does the area of the preimage compare to the image?

3. A triangle has vertices $N(3, 5)$, $P(7, 2)$, and $Q(3, 1)$. Point P is moved to be twice as far from $\overline{NQ}$ as in the original triangle. Describe the effect on the area.

4. The length of each base of a trapezoid is divided by 2. How does the area change?

_____

Use the information below for Exercises 5 and 6.

Steven's dog is on a chain 6 feet long with one end of the chain attached to the ground as shown in the diagram. Steven replaces the chain with one that is $1\frac{1}{2}$ times as long.

5. Describe how the circumference of the circle determined by the chain is changed.

6. Describe how the area of the circle determined by the chain is changed.

_____

_____

Choose the best answer.

7. In kite $RSTU$, $RT = 2.5$ centimeters and $SU = 4.3$ centimeters. Both diagonals of the kite are doubled. What happens to the area of the kite?

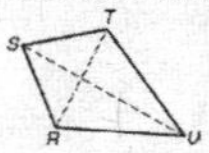

A The area is doubled.
B The area is tripled.
C The area is 4 times as great.
D The area is 8 times as great.

8. The side length of the regular hexagon is divided by 3. Which is a true statement?

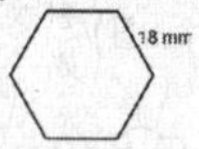

F The perimeter is divided by 9, and the area is divided by 3.
G The perimeter is divided by 3, and the area is divided by 9.
H The perimeter and area are both divided by 3.
J The perimeter and area are both divided by 9.

10-6 Geometric Probability
Connection: Set Theory

Essential question: *How can you use set theory to help you calculate theoretical probabilities?*

© Houghton Mifflin Harcourt Publishing Company

COMMON CORE Standards for Mathematical Content

CC.9-12.S.CP.1 Describe events as subsets of a sample space (the set of outcomes) using characteristics (or categories) of the outcomes, or as unions, intersections, or complements of other events ("or," "and," "not").*

Vocabulary

set

element

empty set

universal set

subset

intersection

union

complement

theoretical probability

Prerequisites

None

Math Background

Students are likely to be familiar with basic probability concepts, and they may have seen set notation and terminology in earlier grades. However, they may not have explored the connections between these ideas. In this lesson, students use set theory to build a definition of the theoretical probability of an event. The notation of set theory will also be useful in later lessons when students consider the probability of compound events.

INTRODUCE

Define *set*. Ask students to give examples of sets from everyday life. Students might mention the set of all states of the United States or the set of all teachers at school. Be sure students understand that a set may be specified in different ways. For the purposes of this unit, most sets can be specified by a written description (for example, the set of all odd numbers less than 8) or by a list that shows all elements of the set (for example, {1, 3, 5, 7}).

TEACH

1 ENGAGE

Questioning Strategies

- If S is the set of prime numbers less than 10 and T is the set of even numbers less than 10, what is $S \cup T$? What is $S \cap T$? $S \cup T = \{2, 3, 4, 5, 6, 7, 8\}$; $S \cap T = \{2\}$

- Give an example of a set that is a subset of set S. **Possible answer: {2, 3}**

- Suppose the universal set U is the set of whole numbers less than 10. What is the complement of set S? **{0, 1, 4, 6, 8, 9}**

2 EXAMPLE

Questioning Strategies

- When you roll a number cube, what are the possible outcomes? **1, 2, 3, 4, 5, 6**

- How does $P(A)$ compare with $P(B)$? Why does this make sense? $P(A) = P(B) = \frac{1}{2}$; **both events are equally likely, and this makes sense since both events contain 3 outcomes.**

- Is it possible for the probability of an event to be 0? If so, give an example. **Yes; the probability of rolling a 7 is 0.**

EXTRA EXAMPLE

You spin a spinner with 8 equal sections that are numbered 1 through 8. Event A is the spinner landing on an odd number. Event B is the spinner landing on 8. Calculate each of the following probabilities.

A. $P(A)$ $\frac{1}{2}$

B. $P(A \cup B)$ $\frac{5}{8}$

C. $P(A \cap B)$ 0

D. $P(A^c)$ $\frac{1}{2}$

Name_____ Class_____ Date_____

10-6

Video Tutor

Geometric Probability
Connection: Set Theory

Essential question: *How can you use set theory to help you calculate theoretical probabilities?*

CC.9-12.S.CP.1

1 ENGAGE   Introducing the Vocabulary of Sets

You will see that set theory is useful in calculating probabilities. A **set** is a well-defined collection of distinct objects. Each object in a set is called an **element** of the set. A set may be specified by writing its elements in braces. For example, the set S of prime numbers less than 10 may be written as $S = \{2, 3, 5, 7\}$.

The number of elements in a set S may be written as $n(S)$. For the set S of prime numbers less than 10, $n(S) = 4$.

The set with no elements is the **empty set** and is denoted by ø or { }. The set of all elements under consideration is the **universal set** and is denoted by U. The following terms describe how sets are related to each other.

Term	Notation	Venn Diagram
Set A is a **subset** of set B if every element of A is also an element of B.	$A \subset B$	
The **intersection** of sets A and B is the set of all elements that are in both A and B.	$A \cap B$	
The **union** of sets A and B is the set of all elements that are in A or B.	$A \cup B$	
The **complement** of set A is the set of all elements in the universal set U that are not in A.	A^c	

REFLECT

1a. For any set A, what is $A \cap$ ø? Explain.

$A \cap$ ø $=$ ø since $A \cap$ ø is the intersection of A and ø and there are no elements in both A and ø.

Chapter 10   441   Lesson 6

Recall that a *probability experiment* is an activity involving chance. Each repetition of the experiment is a *trial* and each possible result is an *outcome*. The *sample space* of an experiment is the set of all possible outcomes. An *event* is a set of outcomes.

When all outcomes of an experiment are equally likely, the **theoretical probability** that an event A will occur is given by $P(A) = \frac{n(A)}{n(S)}$, where S is the sample space.

CC.9-12.S.CP.1

2 EXAMPLE   Calculating Theoretical Probabilities

You roll a number cube. Event A is rolling an even number. Event B is rolling a prime number. Calculate each of the following probabilities.

A $P(A)$ **B** $P(A \cup B)$ **C** $P(A \cap B)$ **D** $P(A^c)$

A $P(A)$ is the probability of rolling an even number. To calculate $P(A)$, first identify the sample space S.

$S = $ ___{1, 2, 3, 4, 5, 6}___ , so $n(S) = $ __6__ .

$A = $ ___{2, 4, 6}___ , so $n(A) = $ __3__ .

So, $P(A) = \frac{n(A)}{n(S)} = \frac{3}{6} = \frac{1}{2}$.

B $P(A \cup B)$ is the probability of rolling an even number *or* a prime number.

$A \cup B = $ ___{2, 3, 4, 5, 6}___ , so $n(A \cup B) = $ __5__ .

So, $P(A \cup B) = \frac{n(A \cup B)}{n(S)} = \frac{5}{6}$.

C $P(A \cap B)$ is the probability of rolling an even number *and* a prime number.

$A \cap B = $ ___{2}___ , so $n(A \cap B) = $ __1__ .

So, $P(A \cap B) = \frac{n(A \cap B)}{n(S)} = \frac{1}{6}$.

D $P(A^c)$ is the probability of rolling a number that is *not* even.

$A^c = $ ___{1, 3, 5}___ , so $n(A^c) = $ __3__ .

So, $P(A^c) = \frac{n(A^c)}{n(S)} = \frac{3}{6} = \frac{1}{2}$.

REFLECT

2a. Explain what $P(S)$ represents and then calculate this probability. Do you think this result is true in general? Explain.

$P(S)$ is the probability of rolling any number in the sample space (1, 2, 3, 4, 5, or 6).

$P(S) = 1$. This is true in general since $P(S) = \frac{n(S)}{n(S)} = 1$.

Chapter 10   442   Lesson 6

© Houghton Mifflin Harcourt Publishing Company

Questioning Strategies

- **What is the sample space in this problem?** It is all possible pairs of numbers that you can roll on two number cubes.

- **Aside from the table shown on the student page, what is another way you could find all outcomes in the sample space?** Make a tree diagram or an organized list.

- **Based on your results, how likely is it that you will not roll doubles? Explain.** It is quite likely that you will not roll doubles, since the probability of this event is close to 1.

EXTRA EXAMPLE

You roll a blue number cube and white number cube at the same time. What is the probability that the sum of the numbers that you roll is not 2? $\frac{35}{36}$

Avoid Common Errors

Some students may state that the sample space for this experiment consists of 21 outcomes because they may not distinguish between outcomes like 3-5 and 5-3. Point out to students that the number cubes have different colors, so the outcome 3-5 means rolling a 3 on the blue cube and a 5 on the white cube, whereas 5-3 means rolling a 5 on the blue cube and a 3 on the white cube. This should help students understand that the sample space actually consists of 36 distinct outcomes.

MATHEMATICAL PRACTICE **Highlighting the Standards**

To address Standard 2 (Reason abstractly and quantitatively), be sure to ask students to move back and forth between the decontextualized calculations that are involved in solving a probability problem and the contextualized interpretation of the results. That is, when students calculate that an event has a probability of 0.9, be sure they understand what this means in the context of the original problem. In particular, students should realize that an event with such a probability is very likely to occur.

CLOSE

Essential Question

How can you use set theory to help you calculate theoretical probabilities? You can use the number of elements in a set to define theoretical probability: the theoretical probability that an event A will occur is given by $P(A) = \frac{n(A)}{n(S)}$, where S is the sample space.

Summarize

Have students write a journal entry in which they write and solve their own probability problems. Remind students to use set notation in their solutions to the problems.

PRACTICE

Where skills are taught	Where skills are practiced
2 EXAMPLE	EXS. 1–7
3 EXAMPLE	EXS. 8–9

Exercise 10: Students use reasoning to critique another student's work.

You may have noticed in the example that $P(A) + P(A^c) = 1$. To see why this is true in general, note that an event and its complement represent all outcomes in the sample space, so $n(A) + n(A^c) = n(S)$.

$$P(A) + P(A^c) = \frac{n(A)}{n(S)} + \frac{n(A^c)}{n(S)} \qquad \text{Definition of theoretical probability}$$

$$= \frac{n(A) + n(A^c)}{n(S)} \qquad \text{Add.}$$

$$= \frac{n(S)}{n(S)} = 1 \qquad n(A) + n(A^c) = n(S)$$

You can write this relationship as $P(A) = 1 - P(A^c)$ and use it to help you find probabilities when it is more convenient to calculate the probability of the complement of an event.

Probabilities of an Event and Its Complement

The probability of an event and the probability of its complement have a sum of 1. So, the probability of an event is one minus the probability of its complement. Also, the probability of the complement of an event is one minus the probability of the event.

$$P(A) + P(A^c) = 1$$

$$P(A) = 1 - P(A^c)$$

$$P(A^c) = 1 - P(A)$$

CC.9-12.S.CP.1

3 EXAMPLE Using the Complement of an Event

You roll a blue number cube and white number cube at the same time. What is the probability that you do not roll doubles?

A   Let A be the event that you do not roll doubles. Then A^c is the event that you do roll doubles.

Complete the table at right to show all outcomes in the sample space.

Circle the outcomes in A^c (rolling doubles).

B   Find the probability of rolling doubles.

$$P(A^c) = \frac{n(A^c)}{n(S)} = \frac{6}{36} = \frac{1}{6}$$

		White Number Cube				
Blue Number Cube		**1**	**2**	**3**	**4**	**5**	**6**
1	1-1	1-2	1-3	1-4	1-5	1-6
2	2-1	2-2	2-3	2-4	2-5	2-6
3	3-1	3-2	3-3	3-4	3-5	3-6
4	4-1	4-2	4-3	4-4	4-5	4-6
5	5-1	5-2	5-3	5-4	5-5	5-6
6	6-1	6-2	6-3	6-4	6-5	6-6

C   Find the probability that you do not roll doubles.

$$P(A) = 1 - P(A^c) = 1 - \frac{1}{6} = \frac{5}{6}$$

REFLECT

3a.   Describe a different way you could have calculated the probability that you do not roll doubles.

Use the table to count the number of outcomes in event A. Since $n(A) = 30$,

$$P(A) = \frac{n(A)}{n(S)} = \frac{30}{36} = \frac{5}{6}.$$

PRACTICE

You have a set of 10 cards numbered 1 to 10. You choose a card at random. Event A is choosing a number less than 7. Event B is choosing an odd number. Calculate each of the following probabilities.

1. $P(A)$

$\frac{3}{5}$

2. $P(B)$

$\frac{1}{2}$

3. $P(A \cup B)$

$\frac{4}{5}$

4. $P(A \cap B)$

$\frac{3}{10}$

5. $P(A^c)$

$\frac{2}{5}$

6. $P(B^c)$

$\frac{1}{2}$

7.   A bag contains 5 red marbles and 10 blue marbles. You choose a marble without looking. Event A is choosing a red marble. Event B is choosing a blue marble. What is $P(A \cap B)$? Explain.

0; $A \cap B = \varnothing$ since a marble cannot be both red and blue.

8.   A standard deck of cards has 13 cards (2, 3, 4, 5, 6, 7, 8, 9, 10, jack, queen, king, ace) in each of 4 suits (hearts, clubs, diamonds, spades). You choose a card from a deck at random. What is the probability that you do not choose an ace? Explain.

$\frac{12}{13}$; there are 4 aces in the 52-card deck, so $P(\text{ace}) = \frac{4}{52} = \frac{1}{13}$.

This means $P(\text{not ace}) = 1 - \frac{1}{13} = \frac{12}{13}$.

9.   You choose a card from a standard deck of cards at random. What is the probability that you do not choose a club? Explain.

$\frac{3}{4}$; there are 13 clubs in the 52-card deck, so $P(\text{club}) = \frac{13}{52} = \frac{1}{4}$.

This means $P(\text{not club}) = 1 - \frac{1}{4} = \frac{3}{4}$.

10.   **Error Analysis**   A bag contains white tiles, black tiles, and gray tiles. $P(W)$, the probability of choosing a tile at random and choosing a white tile, is $\frac{1}{4}$. A student claims that the probability of choosing a black tile, $P(B)$, is $\frac{3}{4}$ since $P(B) = 1 - P(W) = 1 - \frac{1}{4} = \frac{3}{4}$. Do you agree? Explain.

No; choosing a black tile is not the complement of choosing a white tile since the bag also contains gray tiles. It is not possible to calculate $P(B)$ from the given information.

Assign these pages to help your students practice
and apply important lesson concepts. For
additional exercises, see the Student Edition.

Answers

Additional Practice

1. $\{2, 3, 5, 7, 11, 13, 17, 19\}$

2. $\{2, 3, 4, 5, 6, 7, 8, 10, 11, 13, 17, 19\}$

3. $\{2\}$

4. $\dfrac{5}{26}$

5. $\dfrac{3}{13}$

6. $\dfrac{9}{26}$

7. $\dfrac{1}{13}$

8. $\dfrac{21}{26}$

9. $\dfrac{10}{13}$

10. 0.7

11. $\dfrac{3}{4}$

12. $\dfrac{5}{6}$

13. $\dfrac{1}{2}$

14. Check students' work. Possible answer:
$A = \{1, 3, 5\}$ and $B = \{1, 3\}$.

Problem Solving

1. $\dfrac{17}{20}$

2. $\dfrac{7}{10}$

3. $\{1, 2\}$

4. $\dfrac{35}{36}$

5. B

6. H

7. C

8. G

10-6

Notes

Additional Practice

Set A = {2, 4, 6, 8, 10} and Set B is the set of all prime numbers less
than 20. List the elements in each of the following sets.

1. B

2. $A \cup B$

3. $A \cap B$

A bag contains 26 tiles, one for each letter of the alphabet. Event A is
drawing a tile with a vowel on it. Event B is drawing a tile with the
letter A, B, C, D, E, or F on it. Calculate each of the following
probabilities.

4. $P(A)$

5. $P(B)$

6. $P(A \cup B)$

7. $P(A \cap B)$

8. $P(A^C)$

9. $P(B^C)$

Find the probability of A^C for each of the following situations.

10. $P(A) = 0.3$

11. $P(A) = \frac{1}{4}$

12. A number cube with sides numbered 1–6 is rolled. A is rolling a 5.

13. A number cube with sides numbered 1–6 is rolled. A is rolling an
even number.

14. Give an example of two sets A and B, for which A and $A \cup B$ both
contain the exact same elements. Both sets should contain at least two
elements, and the sets should not be the same.

Problem Solving

Write the correct answer.

1. The universal set U is the set of all
integers from 1 through 20. You select
one element of U at random. Event A is
choosing 2, 6, or 18. What is $P(A^C)$?

2. A bag contains a total of 10 marbles.
Four of the marbles are black, and 3
of the marbles are white. If Event A is
drawing a black marble and Event B
is drawing a white marble, what is
$P(A \cup B)$?

3. Set C = {–2, –1, 0, 1, 2} and Set D is the
set of all positive integers. What elements
are in the set $C \cap D$?

4. You roll two six-sided number cubes at
the same time. Event A is rolling a 1 on
both cubes. What is $P(A^C)$?

Select the best answer.

5. A spinner has four sections of equal size.
The sections are painted blue, red, green,
and yellow. Event A is spinning a yellow,
and Event B is spinning a red. What is
$P(A \cup B)$?

   A $\frac{1}{4}$ C $\frac{3}{4}$

   B $\frac{1}{2}$ D 1

6. What is $P(B^C)$ for the situation described
in Exercise 5?

   F $\frac{1}{4}$ H $\frac{3}{4}$

   G $\frac{1}{2}$ J 1

7. Set J = {$-\pi$, $\sqrt{2}$, 0, 1} and Set Q is the
set of all rational numbers. Which set
represents $J \cap Q$?

   A $\varnothing$

   B {0}

   C {0, 1}

   D Q

8. If you have two sets, A and B, and A and
$A \cap B$ have the exact same elements,
which statement must be true?

   F B is the null set.

   G Every element in A is also in B.

   H Every element in B is also in A.

   J $A \cup B$ is the null set.

This page provides students with the opportunity to apply concepts from the Common Core in real-world problem situations. There are three different levels of performance tasks:

⭐ Novice: These are short word problems that require students to apply the math they have learned in straightforward, real-world situations.

⭐⭐ Apprentice: These are more involved problems that guide students step-by-step through more complex tasks. These exercises include more complicated reasoning, writing, and open-ended elements.

⭐⭐⭐ Expert: These are open-ended, non-routine problems that, instead of stepping the students through, ask them to choose their own methods for solving and justify their answers and reasoning.

Sample answers

1. 24,025 ft²; Since two additional sides are necessary to divide the paddock as described, each side of the paddock is $\frac{930}{6} = 155$ ft, so the area is 155^2 ft².

2a. 27 in.

b. 45 snips; The circumference is $2\pi \cdot 27$ in., so the number of snips is $2\pi \cdot 27 \div 3.8$.

3. Scoring Guide:

Task	Possible points
a	1 point for the area of 48,000 ft², and 1 point for appropriate work.
b	1 point for the area of 2400 ft², and 1 point for appropriate work.
c	1 point for the probability of 95%, and 1 point for a suitable explanation, for example: The probability of its landing in the pond is $\frac{2400}{48,000} = 0.05$, so the probability of its *not* landing in the pond is $1 - 0.05 = 0.95$.

Total possible points: 6

CHAPTER 10

Performance Tasks

COMMON CORE
CC.9-12.G.MG.3
CC.9-12.S.CP.1

★ 1. A horse owner is designing a square enclosure that requires 930 feet of fence to build. In addition to the outer perimeter, the enclosure has interior fencing that divides it into 4 congruent squares. What is the total area of the paddock? Justify your answer.

★ 2. Shari is cutting a circular tablecloth from a rectangular piece of material that is 54 inches wide and 59 inches long.

   a. What is the radius of the largest circle she can cut?

   b. Her scissors cut 3.8 inches per snip. How many snips will she make to cut out the entire circle? Round to the nearest whole number.

★★ 3. A landscape architect is designing a small park in the shape of an isosceles trapezoid. It has a triangular pond, △KJM. Points E, F, G, and H are midpoints of the segments they lie on, and L is the midpoint of both $\overline{KM}$ and $\overline{GH}$. GH = 300 ft, CD = 420 ft, and EF = 160 ft.

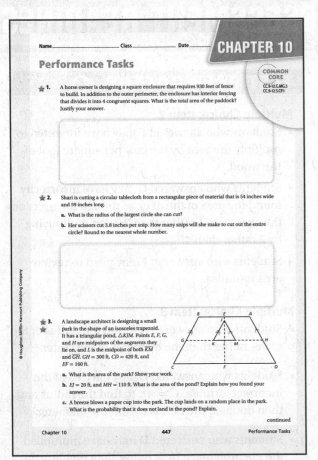

   a. What is the area of the park? Show your work.

   b. EJ = 20 ft, and MH = 110 ft. What is the area of the pond? Explain how you found your answer.

   c. A breeze blows a paper cup into the park. The cup lands on a random place in the park. What is the probability that it does not land in the pond? Explain.

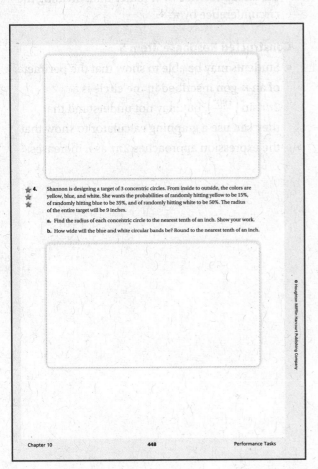

continued

★★★★ 4. Shannon is designing a target of 3 concentric circles. From inside to outside, the colors are yellow, blue, and white. She wants the probabilities of randomly hitting yellow to be 15%, of randomly hitting blue to be 35%, and of randomly hitting white to be 50%. The radius of the entire target will be 9 inches.

   a. Find the radius of each concentric circle to the nearest tenth of an inch. Show your work.

   b. How wide will the blue and white circular bands be? Round to the nearest tenth of an inch.

4. Scoring Guide:

Task	Possible points
a	1 point for each correct radius: yellow is 3.5 in., blue is 6.4 in., and white is 9 in.; and 1 point for showing appropriate work
b	1 point for correctly finding the width of the white band to be about 2.6 in., and 1 point for finding the width of the blue band to be about 2.9 in.

Total possible points: 6

COMMON CORE CORRELATION

Standard	Items
CC.9-12.G.CO.2	1
CC.9-12.G.SRT.9(+)	6
CC.9-12.G.GPE.7*	4, 7
CC.9-12.G.GMD.1	5
CC.9-12.G.MG.1*	2, 3
CC.9-12.G.MG.2*	7

TEST PREP DOCTOR ⊕

Multiple Choice: Item 2

- Students who answered **F** may have forgotten to multiply the area by the cost per square foot of the wood.

- Students who answered **G** may have incorrectly found the area of the deck as though the units on the axes were 1 rather than 2, then multiplying by 2 rather than 4.

- Students who answered **J** may need to review area formulas.

Multiple Choice: Item 3

- Students who answered **A** found the radius of the crater rather than the diameter of the crater.

- Students who answered **C** may have used the incorrect formula, $C = \pi r$, to find the radius and then doubled the radius to find the diameter.

- Students who answered **D** may have multiplied the circumference by π rather than dividing the circumference by π.

Constructed Response: Item 5

- Students may be able to show that the perimeter of an n-gon inscribed in the circle is $2nr \sin\left(\frac{180°}{n}\right)$, but may not understand that they can use a graphing calculator to show that the expression approaches $2\pi r$ as n increases.

Name _____ Class _____ Date _____

MULTIPLE CHOICE

1. A transformation has the rule $(x, y) \to$ $(-3x, -3y)$. Which of the following statements about the transformation is accurate?

(A.) The transformation preserves angle measures but not distances.

B. The transformation preserves distances but not angle measures.

C. The transformation preserves neither angle measures nor distances.

D. The transformation preserves both angle measures and distances.

2. A homeowner wants to make a new deck for the backyard. Redwood costs $8 per square foot. The units on the graph are in feet. How much will it cost for the wood to create the deck shown?

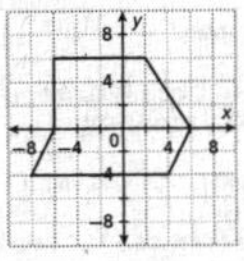

F. $108

G. $432

(H.) $864

J. $960

3. Meteor Crater, near Flagstaff, Arizona, is an approximately circular crater, with a circumference of 2.32 miles. What is the diameter of the crater to the nearest hundredth of a mile?

A. 0.37 mi

(B.) 0.74 mi

C. 1.48 mi

D. 7.29 mi

4. The figure shows a polygonal fence for part of a garden. Each unit of the coordinate plane represents one meter. What is the length of the fence to the nearest tenth of a meter?

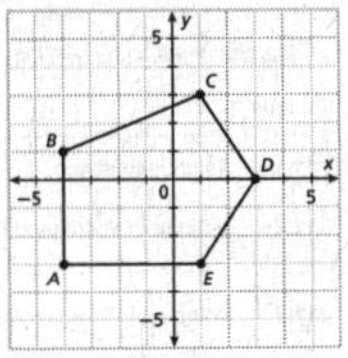

F. 16.1 m

G. 18.0 m

(H.) 21.6 m

J. 31.0 m

CONSTRUCTED RESPONSE

5. In order to justify the formula for the circumference of a circle, you inscribe a regular n-gon in a circle of radius r, as shown in the figure.

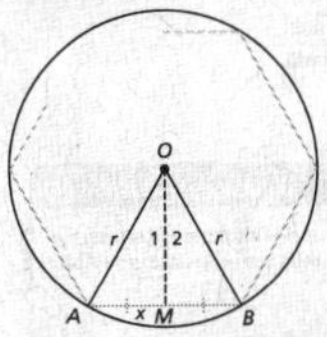

You show that $\triangle AOM \cong \triangle BOM$ and conclude that $\angle 1 \cong \angle 2$ by CPCTC. Then you state that $m\angle AOB = \frac{360°}{n}$ and $m\angle 1 = \frac{180°}{n}$. Describe the main steps for finishing the justification of the circumference formula.

Show that $x = r \sin\left(\frac{180°}{n}\right)$, so that the

perimeter of n-gon is $2nr \sin\left(\frac{180°}{n}\right)$.

Use the table feature of a graphing

calculator to show that this expression

gets closer to $2\pi r$ as n gets larger.

6. You are using the figure below to derive a formula for the area of a triangle that involves the sine ratio.

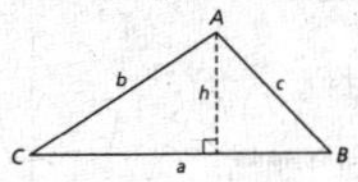

First you note that $\sin C = \frac{h}{b}$ and, therefore, $h = b \sin C$. How do you complete the derivation of the formula?

The area of the triangle is Area $= \frac{1}{2}ah$.

So, by substitution, Area $= \frac{1}{2}ab \sin C$.

7. The border of Utah can be modeled by the polygon with vertices $A(0, 0)$, $B(0, 350)$, $C(160, 350)$, $D(160, 280)$, $E(270, 280)$, and $F(270, 0)$. Each unit on the coordinate plane represents 1 mile.

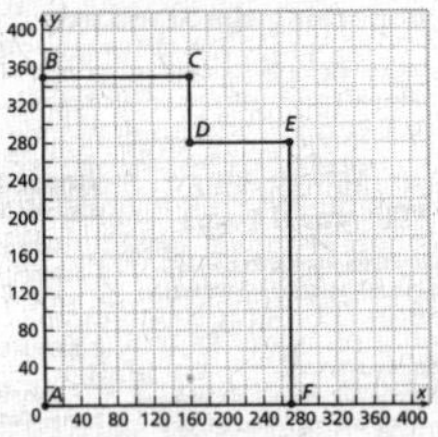

a. What is the approximate area of the state?

86,800 mi²

b. The population of Utah is 2,784,572. Explain how to find the state's population density. Round to the nearest tenth.

To find population density, find the

ratio of population to area.

Population density $= \frac{2,784,572}{86,800} \approx 32.1$

persons per square mile.

© Houghton Mifflin Harcourt Publishing Company

CHAPTER 11

Spatial Reasoning

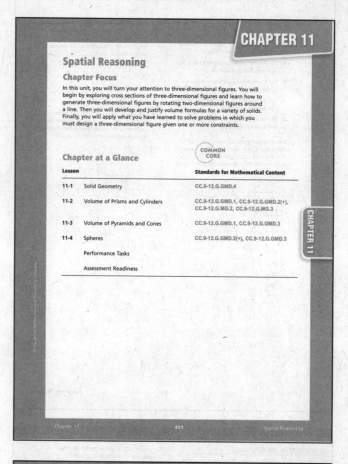

Spatial Reasoning

CHAPTER 11

Spatial Reasoning

Chapter Focus

In this unit, you will turn your attention to three-dimensional figures. You will begin by exploring cross sections of three-dimensional figures and learn how to generate three-dimensional figures by rotating two-dimensional figures around a line. Then you will develop and justify volume formulas for a variety of solids. Finally, you will apply what you have learned to solve problems in which you must design a three-dimensional figure given one or more constraints.

Chapter at a Glance

COMMON CORE

Lesson		Standards for Mathematical Content
11-1	Solid Geometry	CC.9-12.G.GMD.4
11-2	Volume of Prisms and Cylinders	CC.9-12.G.GMD.1, CC.9-12.G.GMD.2(+), CC.9-12.G.MG.2, CC.9-12.G.MG.3
11-3	Volume of Pyramids and Cones	CC.9-12.G.GMD.1, CC.9-12.G.GMD.3
11-4	Spheres	CC.9-12.G.GMD.2(+), CC.9-12.G.GMD.3
	Performance Tasks	
	Assessment Readiness	

Chapter 11   451   Spatial Reasoning

COMMON CORE PROFESSIONAL DEVELOPMENT   **CC.9-12.G.GMD.3***

Students use a generalized formula for volume, $V = Bh$, to develop formulas for volume of other three-dimensional figures, including prisms, cylinders, cones, pyramids, and spheres. Developing formulas for volume extends students' previous knowledge of area and perimeter of polygons into three dimensions. Problems that students solve in this chapter combine inductive and deductive reasoning skills with algebra skills, as students adapt algebraic expressions in volume formulas to match specific shapes.

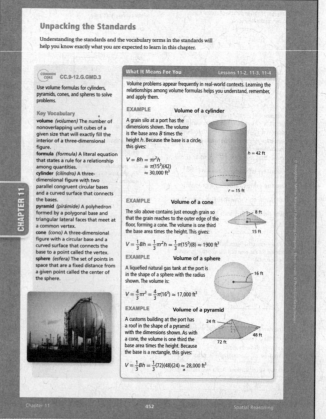

Unpacking the Standards

Understanding the standards and the vocabulary terms in the standards will help you know exactly what you are expected to learn in this chapter.

COMMON CORE   **CC.9-12.G.GMD.3**

Use volume formulas for cylinders, pyramids, cones, and spheres to solve problems.

Key Vocabulary

volume *(volumen)* The number of nonoverlapping unit cubes of a given size that will exactly fill the interior of a three-dimensional figure.

formula *(formula)* A literal equation that states a rule for a relationship among quantities.

cylinder *(cilindro)* A three-dimensional figure with two parallel congruent circular bases and a curved surface that connects the bases.

pyramid *(pirámide)* A polyhedron formed by a polygonal base and triangular lateral faces that meet at a common vertex.

cone *(cono)* A three-dimensional figure with a circular base and a curved surface that connects the base to a point called the vertex.

sphere *(esfera)* The set of points in space that are a fixed distance from a given point called the center of the sphere.

What It Means For You   Lessons 11-2, 11-3, 11-4

Volume problems appear frequently in real-world contexts. Learning the relationships among volume formulas helps you understand, remember, and apply them.

EXAMPLE   **Volume of a cylinder**

A grain silo at a port has the dimensions shown. The volume is the base area B times the height h. Because the base is a circle, this gives:

$$V = Bh = \pi r^2 h$$
$$= \pi (15^2)(42)$$
$$\approx 30,000 \text{ ft}^3$$

$h = 42$ ft

$r = 15$ ft

EXAMPLE   **Volume of a cone**

The silo above contains just enough grain so that the grain reaches to the outer edge of the floor, forming a cone. The volume is one third the base area times the height. This gives:

$$V = \frac{1}{3}Bh = \frac{1}{3}\pi r^2 h = \frac{1}{3}\pi (15^2)(8) \approx 1900 \text{ ft}^3$$

8 ft

15 ft

EXAMPLE   **Volume of a sphere**

A liquefied natural gas tank at the port is in the shape of a sphere with the radius shown. The volume is:

$$V = \frac{4}{3}\pi r^3 = \frac{4}{3}\pi (16^3) \approx 17,000 \text{ ft}^3$$

16 ft

EXAMPLE   **Volume of a pyramid**

A customs building at the port has a roof in the shape of a pyramid with the dimensions shown. As with a cone, the volume is one third the base area times the height. Because the base is a rectangle, this gives:

$$V = \frac{1}{3}Bh = \frac{1}{3}(72)(48)(24) \approx 28,000 \text{ ft}^3$$

24 ft

48 ft

72 ft

Chapter 11   452   Spatial Reasoning

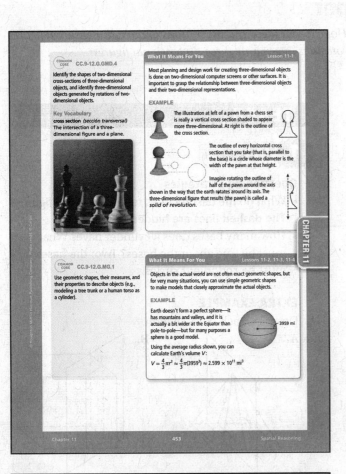

COMMON CORE CC.9-12.G.GMD.4

Identify the shapes of two-dimensional cross-sections of three-dimensional objects, and identify three-dimensional objects generated by rotations of two-dimensional objects.

Key Vocabulary

cross section *(sección transversal)* The intersection of a three-dimensional figure and a plane.

What It Means For You — Lesson 11-1

Most planning and design work for creating three-dimensional objects is done on two-dimensional computer screens or other surfaces. It is important to grasp the relationship between three-dimensional objects and their two-dimensional representations.

EXAMPLE

The illustration at left of a pawn from a chess set is really a vertical cross section shaded to appear more three-dimensional. At right is the outline of the cross section.

The outline of every horizontal cross section that you take (that is, parallel to the base) is a circle whose diameter is the width of the pawn at that height.

Imagine rotating the outline of half of the pawn around the axis shown in the way that the earth rotates around its axis. The three-dimensional figure that results (the pawn) is called a *solid of revolution*.

COMMON CORE CC.9-12.G.MG.1

Use geometric shapes, their measures, and their properties to describe objects (e.g., modeling a tree trunk or a human torso as a cylinder).

What It Means For You — Lessons 11-2, 11-3, 11-4

Objects in the actual world are not often exact geometric shapes, but for very many situations, you can use simple geometric shapes to make models that closely approximate the actual objects.

EXAMPLE

Earth doesn't form a perfect sphere—it has mountains and valleys, and it is actually a bit wider at the Equator than pole-to-pole—but for many purposes a sphere is a good model.

3959 mi

Using the average radius shown, you can calculate Earth's volume V:

$$V = \frac{4}{3}\pi r^3 \approx \frac{4}{3}\pi(3959)^3 \approx 2.599 \times 10^{11} \text{ mi}^3$$

Chapter 11 — 453 — Spatial Reasoning

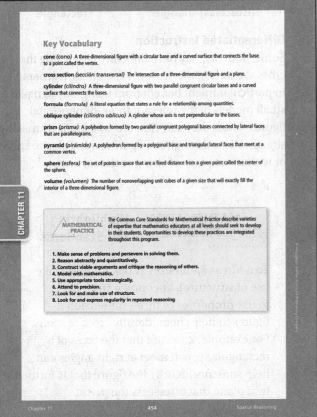

Key Vocabulary

cone *(cono)* A three-dimensional figure with a circular base and a curved surface that connects the base to a point called the vertex.

cross section *(sección transversal)* The intersection of a three-dimensional figure and a plane.

cylinder *(cilindro)* A three-dimensional figure with two parallel congruent circular bases and a curved surface that connects the bases.

formula *(fórmula)* A literal equation that states a rule for a relationship among quantities.

oblique cylinder *(cilindro oblicuo)* A cylinder whose axis is not perpendicular to the bases.

prism *(prisma)* A polyhedron formed by two parallel congruent polygonal bases connected by lateral faces that are parallelograms.

pyramid *(pirámide)* A polyhedron formed by a polygonal base and triangular lateral faces that meet at a common vertex.

sphere *(esfera)* The set of points in space that are a fixed distance from a given point called the center of the sphere.

volume *(volumen)* The number of nonoverlapping unit cubes of a given size that will exactly fill the interior of a three-dimensional figure.

MATHEMATICAL PRACTICE

The Common Core Standards for Mathematical Practice describe varieties of expertise that mathematics educators at all levels should seek to develop in their students. Opportunities to develop these practices are integrated throughout this program.

1. Make sense of problems and persevere in solving them.
2. Reason abstractly and quantitatively.
3. Construct viable arguments and critique the reasoning of others.
4. Model with mathematics.
5. Use appropriate tools strategically.
6. Attend to precision.
7. Look for and make use of structure.
8. Look for and express regularity in repeated reasoning

Chapter 11 — 454 — Spatial Reasoning

© Houghton Mifflin Harcourt Publishing Company

CHAPTER 11

CC.9-12.G.MG.1*

The three-dimensional shapes discussed in this chapter are used to model the shapes in the real world. Students show that they are able to take adequate information about a three- dimensional figure, and use the basic formula $V = Bh$ to find out what information is missing. In this chapter, students will practice using mathematical modeling by using geometric models to solve problems in real-world scenarios.

CHAPTER 11

Solid Geometry
Going Deeper

Essential question: *How do you identify cross sections of three-dimensional figures and how do you use rotations to generate three-dimensional figures?*

© Houghton Mifflin Harcourt Publishing Company

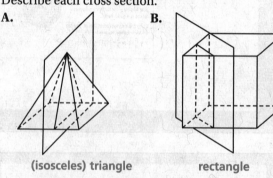

COMMON CORE Standards for Mathematical Content

CC.9-12.G.GMD.4 Identify the shapes of two-dimensional cross-sections of three-dimensional objects, and identify three-dimensional objects generated by rotations of two-dimensional objects.

Vocabulary
cross section

Prerequisites
Rotations

Math Background
Until now, students have worked primarily with two-dimensional figures in this course. The focus now shifts to three-dimensional figures. Students have already explored three-dimensional figures in earlier grades, especially in the context of volume problems, but this unit offers an approach that is likely to be more deductive in nature than what students have seen before. Specifically, students will learn how to justify the essential volume formulas. This first lesson of the unit gives students experience in visualizing three-dimensional figures. It can also serve as an opportunity to review key vocabulary associated with such figures.

INTRODUCE

Remind students of some of the vocabulary related to three-dimensional figures. You may wish to sketch on the board figures like the ones below and work with students to label the parts of the figures.

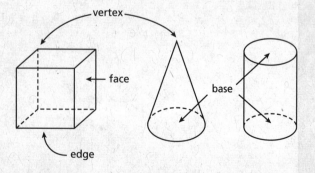

TEACH

1 EXAMPLE

Questioning Strategies
• What do the dashed lines represent in the figures? **The dashed lines are hidden lines.**
• How many bases does a cylinder have? What must be true about the bases? **Two; the bases must be congruent circles.**

EXTRA EXAMPLE
Describe each cross section.

A.   **B.**

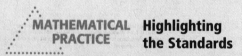

(isosceles) triangle   rectangle

Differentiated Instruction
Some students may have difficulty visualizing the cross sections in this lesson. Kinesthetic learners in particular might benefit from using clay to make small models of the relevant three-dimensional figures. Then, they can view cross sections by making straight slices through the figures with a plastic knife or with a taut piece of string or dental floss.

MATHEMATICAL PRACTICE   Highlighting the Standards

To address Standard 7 (Look for and make use of structure), encourage students to use properties of three-dimensional figures to help them identify cross sections. For example, knowing that the faces of a rectangular prism meet at right angles can help students identify the figure that is formed by a plane that intersects the prism.

Name_____ Class_____ Date_____

Solid Geometry
Going Deeper

11-1

Video Tutor

Essential question: *How do you identify cross sections of three-dimensional figures and how do you use rotations to generate three-dimensional figures?*

Recall that an *intersection* is the set of all points that two or more figures have in common. A **cross section** is the intersection of a three-dimensional figure and a plane.

CC.9-12.G.GMD.4

1 EXAMPLE Identifying Cross Sections of a Cylinder

Describe each cross section of a cylinder.

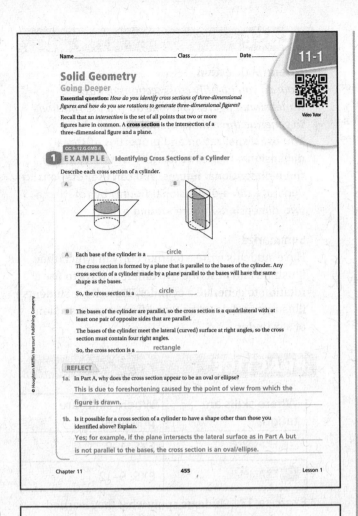

A   Each base of the cylinder is a ___circle___

The cross section is formed by a plane that is parallel to the bases of the cylinder. Any cross section of a cylinder made by a plane parallel to the bases will have the same shape as the bases.

So, the cross section is a ___circle___

B   The bases of the cylinder are parallel, so the cross section is a quadrilateral with at least one pair of opposite sides that are parallel.

The bases of the cylinder meet the lateral (curved) surface at right angles, so the cross section must contain four right angles.

So, the cross section is a ___rectangle___

REFLECT

1a. In Part A, why does the cross section appear to be an oval or ellipse?

This is due to foreshortening caused by the point of view from which the

figure is drawn.

1b. Is it possible for a cross section of a cylinder to have a shape other than those you identified above? Explain.

Yes; for example, if the plane intersects the lateral surface as in Part A but

is not parallel to the bases, the cross section is an oval/ellipse.

© Houghton Mifflin Harcourt Publishing Company

You have learned how to perform transformations in a plane. Transformations may also be carried out in three-dimensional space. In particular, you can rotate a two-dimensional figure around a line to generate a three-dimensional figure.

CC.9-12.G.GMD.4

2 EXAMPLE Generating Three-Dimensional Figures

Sketch and describe the figure that is generated by each rotation in three-dimensional space.

A   Rotate a right triangle around a line that contains one of its legs.

- Draw a right triangle and draw a line that contains one of its legs, as shown at right.
- To model the rotation of the triangle around the line, trace and cut out the triangle. Then tape the triangle to a piece of string so that one leg of the triangle is attached to the string. Hold both ends of the string and twirl it between your fingers to see the three-dimensional figure generated by the rotation. Sketch the figure at right.

Sketch of Two-Dimensional Figure and Line of Rotation	Sketch of Three-Dimensional Figure Generated by the Rotation

So, the figure that is generated by the rotation is a ___cone___

B   Rotate a rectangle around a line that contains one of its sides.

- Draw a rectangle and draw a line that contains one of its sides, as shown at right.
- To model the rotation of the rectangle around the line, trace and cut out the rectangle. Then tape the rectangle to a piece of string so that one side of the rectangle is attached to the string. Hold both ends of the string and twirl it between your fingers to see the three-dimensional figure generated by the rotation. Sketch the figure at right.

Sketch of Two-Dimensional Figure and Line of Rotation	Sketch of Three-Dimensional Figure Generated by the Rotation

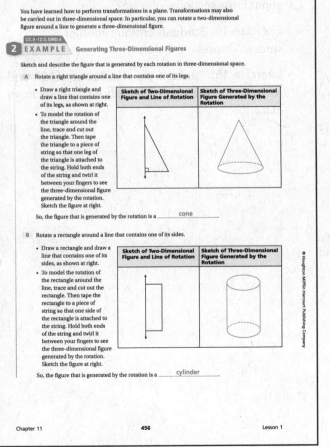

So, the figure that is generated by the rotation is a ___cylinder___

© Houghton Mifflin Harcourt Publishing Company

Questioning Strategies

- How do you think a rotation around a line in space is similar to a rotation around a point in a plane? All points in space move around the line in such a way that their distance from the line is unchanged; points on the line of rotation are fixed.

- In part A, what part of the cone is formed by the hypotenuse of the triangle? Explain. As the hypotenuse is rotated around the line, it forms the lateral (curved) surface of the cone.

EXTRA EXAMPLE

Sketch and describe the figure that is generated by each rotation in three-dimensional space.

A. Rotate a rectangle around one of the rectangle's lines of symmetry.

cylinder

B. Rotate a circle around a line containing the circle's diameter.

sphere

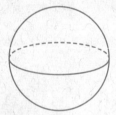

Differentiated Instruction

Challenge students by asking them to describe the three-dimensional figures that are formed by rotating figures in a coordinate plane. For example, you might have students describe the figure formed by rotating the part of the line $y = -x + 2$ that lies in quadrant I around the x-axis. Students should find that the figure is a cone with radius 2 and height 2.

CLOSE

Essential Question

How do you identify cross sections of three-dimensional figures and how do you use rotations to generate three-dimensional figures?
You use visualization and properties of three-dimensional figures to identify cross sections of three-dimensional figures. You can use rotations to generate three-dimensional figures by rotating a two-dimensional figure around a line.

Summarize

Have students write a journal entry in which they illustrate and describe two different ways to use a rotation to generate a cylinder. Then, have students illustrate and describe two different cross sections of a cylinder.

PRACTICE

Where skills are taught	Where skills are practiced
1 EXAMPLE	EXS. 1–8
2 EXAMPLE	EXS. 9–12

Exercise 13: Students apply what they learned about cross sections.

Exercise 14: Students critique another student's work.

Exercise 15: Students use visualization skills and reasoning to solve a problem about cross sections of a cube.

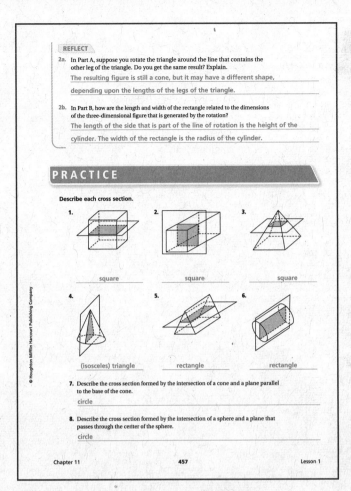

REFLECT

2a. In Part A, suppose you rotate the triangle around the line that contains the other leg of the triangle. Do you get the same result? Explain.

The resulting figure is still a cone, but it may have a different shape,

depending upon the lengths of the legs of the triangle.

2b. In Part B, how are the length and width of the rectangle related to the dimensions of the three-dimensional figure that is generated by the rotation?

The length of the side that is part of the line of rotation is the height of the

cylinder. The width of the rectangle is the radius of the cylinder.

PRACTICE

Describe each cross section.

1.

square

2.

square

3.

square

4.

(isosceles) triangle

5.

rectangle

6.

rectangle

7. Describe the cross section formed by the intersection of a cone and a plane parallel to the base of the cone.

circle

8. Describe the cross section formed by the intersection of a sphere and a plane that passes through the center of the sphere.

circle

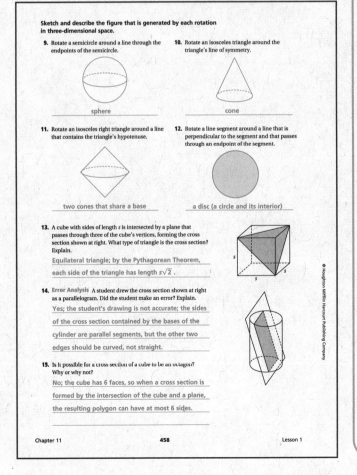

Sketch and describe the figure that is generated by each rotation in three-dimensional space.

9. Rotate a semicircle around a line through the endpoints of the semicircle.

sphere

10. Rotate an isosceles triangle around the triangle's line of symmetry.

cone

11. Rotate an isosceles right triangle around a line that contains the triangle's hypotenuse.

two cones that share a base

12. Rotate a line segment around a line that is perpendicular to the segment and that passes through an endpoint of the segment.

a disc (a circle and its interior)

13. A cube with sides of length s is intersected by a plane that passes through three of the cube's vertices, forming the cross section shown at right. What type of triangle is the cross section? Explain.

Equilateral triangle; by the Pythagorean Theorem,

each side of the triangle has length $s\sqrt{2}$.

14. **Error Analysis** A student drew the cross section shown at right as a parallelogram. Did the student make an error? Explain.

Yes; the student's drawing is not accurate; the sides

of the cross section contained by the bases of the

cylinder are parallel segments, but the other two

edges should be curved, not straight.

15. Is it possible for a cross section of a cube to be an octagon? Why or why not?

No; the cube has 6 faces, so when a cross section is

formed by the intersection of the cube and a plane,

the resulting polygon can have at most 6 sides.

ADDITIONAL PRACTICE AND PROBLEM SOLVING

Assign these pages to help your students practice and apply important lesson concepts. For additional exercises, see the Student Edition.

Answers

Additional Practice

1. hexagon
2. circle
3. circle
4. rectangle
5. Possible answer: If a cross section intersects a solid parallel to a base, then the cross section has the same shape as the base.
6.
7.

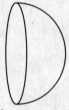

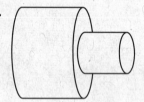

Problem Solving

1. rectangle
2. trapezoid
3. C
4. F
5. D
6. J

Name_____ Class_____ Date_____

Additional Practice

Describe each cross section.

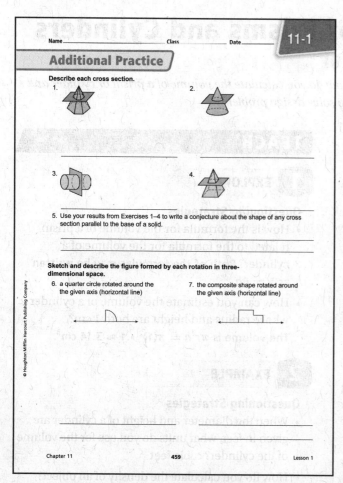

1.

2.

_____

3.

4.

_____

5. Use your results from Exercises 1–4 to write a conjecture about the shape of any cross section parallel to the base of a solid.

_____

Sketch and describe the figure formed by each rotation in three-dimensional space.

6. a quarter circle rotated around the the given axis (horizontal line)

7. the composite shape rotated around the given axis (horizontal line)

Problem Solving

1. A slice of cheese is cut from the cylinder-shaped cheese as shown. Describe the cross section.

_____

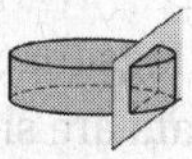

2. A square pyramid is intersected by a plane as shown. Describe the cross section.

_____

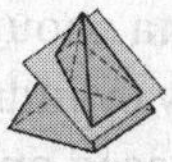

3. Which of the following does NOT have a cross section in the shape of a circle?

A sphere

B cylinder

C pyramid

D cone

4. Which of the following could be rotated through three-dimensional space to form a cone?

F right triangle

G parallelogram

H semicircle

J trapezoid

5. Which of the following could NOT be a cross section of a rectangular prism with square bases?

A rectangle

B line segment

C square

D two points

6. Which of the following could be rotated through three-dimensional space to form a cylinder?

F semicircle

G trapezoid

H equilateral triangle

J square

Volume of Prisms and Cylinders
Going Deeper

Essential question: *How do you calculate the volume of a prism or cylinder and use volume formulas to solve design problems?*

Standards for Mathematical Content

CC.9-12.G.GMD.1 Give an informal argument for the formula for the ... volume of a cylinder ....

CC.9-12.G.GMD.2(+) Give an informal argument using Cavalieri's principle for the formulas for the volume of ... other solid figures.

CC.9-12.G.GMD.3 Use volume formulas for cylinders ... to solve problems.*

CC.9-12.G.MG.1 Use geometric shapes, their measures, and their properties to describe objects (e.g., modeling a tree trunk or a human torso as a cylinder).*

CC.9-12.G.MG.2 Apply concepts of density based on area and volume in modeling situations (e.g., persons per square mile, BTUs per cubic foot).*

CC.9-12.G.MG.3 Apply geometric methods to solve design problems (e.g., designing an object or structure to satisfy physical constraints or minimize cost ...).*

Vocabulary
oblique cylinder

Prerequisites
Visualizing three-dimensional figures

Math Background
This lesson introduces Cavalieri's principle, which is named after the Italian mathematician Bonaventura Cavalieri (1598–1647). The principle, which is taken here as a postulate, is one of the most useful ideas in geometry because it allows volume formulas to be extended from simple solids to more complex solids.

INTRODUCE

Begin by briefly reviewing the definitions of *prism* and *cylinder*. Be sure that students can identify the bases of a given prism or cylinder.

TEACH

1 EXPLORE

Questioning Strategies
- How is the formula for the volume of a prism related to the formula for the volume of a cylinder? **Both of the formulas may be written as $V = Bh$.**
- How can you estimate the volume of a cylinder whose radius and height are both 1 cm? **The volume is $\pi r^2 h \doteq \pi(1)^2 \cdot 1 \approx 3.14 \text{ cm}^3$.**

2 EXAMPLE

Questioning Strategies
- When the diameter and height of a cylinder are given in feet, what units do you use for the volume of the cylinder? **cubic feet**
- How do you calculate the density of an object? **Divide the weight or mass by the volume.**
- What are some possible units of density? **kg/m^3, lb/ft^3, g/cm^3, etc.**

EXTRA EXAMPLE
You gather data about two wood logs that are approximately cylindrical. The data are shown in the table. Based on your data, which wood is denser, larch or cypress?

Type of Wood	Larch	Cypress
Diameter (m)	1	0.5
Height (m)	2	3
Mass (kg)	926.8	300.4

Larch ($\approx 590 \text{ kg/m}^3$) is denser than cypress ($\approx 510 \text{ kg/m}^3$).

Name_____ Class_____ Date_____

11-2

Video Tutor

Volume of Prisms and Cylinders
Going Deeper

Essential question: *How do you calculate the volume of a prism or cylinder and use volume formulas to solve design problems?*

Recall that the *volume* of a three-dimensional figure is the number of nonoverlapping cubic units contained in the interior of the figure. For example, the prism at right has a volume of 8 cubic centimeters. You can use this idea to develop volume formulas.

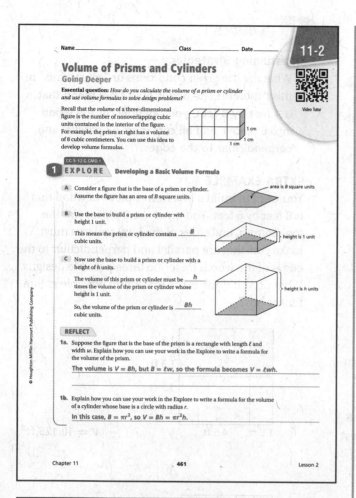

1 cm
1 cm
1 cm

CC.9-12.G.GMD.1

1 EXPLORE Developing a Basic Volume Formula

A Consider a figure that is the base of a prism or cylinder. Assume the figure has an area of *B* square units.

area is *B* square units

B Use the base to build a prism or cylinder with height 1 unit.

This means the prism or cylinder contains ___*B*___ cubic units.

height is 1 unit

C Now use the base to build a prism or cylinder with a height of *h* units.

The volume of this prism or cylinder must be ___*h*___ times the volume of the prism or cylinder whose height is 1 unit.

So, the volume of the prism or cylinder is ___*Bh*___ cubic units.

height is *h* units

REFLECT

1a. Suppose the figure that is the base of the prism is a rectangle with length ℓ and width *w*. Explain how you can use your work in the Explore to write a formula for the volume of the prism.

The volume is $V = Bh$, but $B = \ell w$, so the formula becomes $V = \ell wh$.

1b. Explain how you can use your work in the Explore to write a formula for the volume of a cylinder whose base is a circle with radius *r*.

In this case, $B = \pi r^2$, so $V = Bh = \pi r^2 h$.

Chapter 11   461   Lesson 2

Volume of a Cylinder

The volume *V* of a cylinder with base area *B* and height *h* is given by $V = Bh$ (or $V = \pi r^2 h$, where *r* is the radius of the base).

CC.9-12.G.MG.2

2 EXAMPLE Comparing Densities

You gather data about two wood logs that are approximately cylindrical. Based on the data in the table, which wood is denser, Douglas fir or American redwood?

Type of Wood	Diameter (ft)	Height (ft)	Weight (lb)
Douglas fir	1	6	155.5
American redwood	3	4	791.7

A Find the volume of the Douglas fir log.

$V = \pi r^2 h$

$V = \pi(\underline{0.5})^2 \cdot \underline{6}$ Substitute 0.5 for *r* and 6 for *h*.

$V \approx \underline{4.7}$ ft³   Use a calculator. Round to the nearest tenth.

B Find the volume of the American redwood log.

$V = \pi r^2 h$

$V = \pi(\underline{1.5})^2 \cdot \underline{4}$ Substitute 1.5 for *r* and 4 for *h*.

$V \approx \underline{28.3}$ ft³   Use a calculator. Round to the nearest tenth.

C Calculate and compare densities.

The density of the wood is the ___weight___ per ___unit volume___

Density of Douglas fir = $\dfrac{155.5}{4.7} \approx \underline{33}$ lb/ft³   Round to the nearest unit.

Density of American redwood = $\dfrac{791.7}{28.3} \approx \underline{28}$ lb/ft³   Round to the nearest unit.

So, ___Douglas fir___ is denser than ___American redwood___

REFLECT

2a. Explain in your own words what your results tell you about the two types of wood.

Possible answer: Given blocks of wood with identical dimensions, a block of

Douglas fir is heavier than a block of American redwood.

Chapter 11   462   Lesson 2

Teaching Strategies

Kinesthetic learners can use a stack of pennies to understand Cavalieri's principle. Have students arrange the pennies to form a right cylinder and ask them to estimate the volume. Then, have students push the stack to form an oblique cylinder. Students should see that the volume of the stack does not change. This is supported by Cavalieri's principle because the cross-sectional area at each level (i.e., the area of the face of a penny) is unchanged.

3 EXAMPLE

Questioning Strategies

- How is an oblique cylinder similar to a right cylinder? **The bases are circles. The bases are connected by a curved lateral surface. The same volume formula works for both types of cylinders.**

- How is an oblique cylinder different from a right cylinder? **In an oblique cylinder, the axis is not perpendicular to the bases.**

- When you solve $r^2 = 64$, how do you know $r = 8$ rather than -8? **The radius is a length, so it must be nonnegative.**

EXTRA EXAMPLE
The height of the cylinder shown here is half the diameter. What is the volume of the cylinder? Round to the nearest tenth.

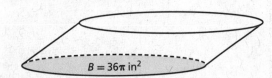

$B = 36\pi$ in^2

678.6 in.^{3}

> ⟍ **MATHEMATICAL PRACTICE** **Highlighting the Standards**
>
> This lesson offers several opportunities to address Standard 6 (Attend to precision) as students work with units of measure. The lesson includes linear measures, areas, volumes, and densities. Encourage students to look over their work to make sure they have specified appropriate units for each of these measures wherever they occur.

4 EXAMPLE

Questioning Strategies

- What are the given conditions or "constraints" in this problem? **The box is built from wood that is 4 feet by 8 feet, you can only cut the wood into 6 pieces, and all cuts must be parallel and perpendicular to the edges.**

EXTRA EXAMPLE
You want to build a box from a piece of wood that is 6 feet by 6 feet. You must use 6 pieces (for the top, bottom, and sides of the box) and you must make cuts that are parallel and perpendicular to the edges of the wood. Describe three possible designs. What do you think is the maximum possible volume for the box?

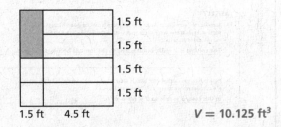

$V = 10.125$ ft^3

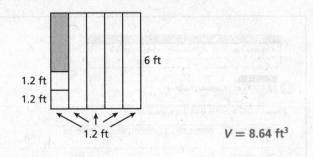

$V = 8.64$ ft^3

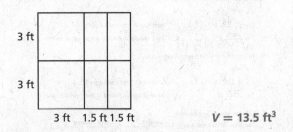

$V = 13.5$ ft^3

Based on these designs, the maximum possible volume appears to be 13.5 ft^3.

The axis of a cylinder is the segment whose endpoints are the centers of the bases. A right cylinder is a cylinder whose axis is perpendicular to the bases. An **oblique cylinder** is a cylinder whose axis is not perpendicular to the bases. Cavalieri's principle makes it possible to extend the formula for the volume of a cylinder to oblique cylinders.

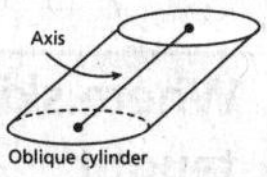

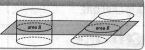

Cavalieri's Principle

If two solids have the same height and the same cross-sectional area at every level, then the two solids have the same volume.

area B area B

You can think of any oblique cylinder as a right cylinder that has been "pushed over" so that the cross sections at every level have equal areas. By Cavalieri's principle, the volume of an oblique cylinder is equal to the volume of the associated right cylinder. This means the formula $V = Bh = \pi r^2 h$ works for any cylinder.

CC.9-12.G.GMD.2(+)

3 EXAMPLE Finding the Volume of an Oblique Cylinder

The height of the cylinder shown here is twice the radius. What is the volume of the cylinder? Round to the nearest tenth.

$B = 64\pi$ cm²

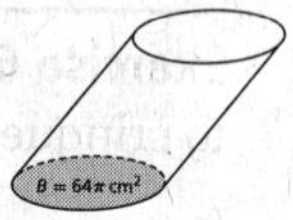

A Find the height of the cylinder. To do so, first find the radius of the cylinder.

Use the fact that the area of the base B is 64π cm².

$\pi r^2 = 64\pi$ The base is a circle, so $B = \pi r^2$.

$r^2 = \underline{64}$ Divide both sides by π.

$r = \underline{8}$ cm   Take the square root of both sides.

Since the height is twice the radius, the height is $\underline{16}$ cm.

B Find the volume of the cylinder.

$V = Bh$ The volume V of any cylinder is $V = Bh$.

$V = \underline{64\pi} \cdot \underline{16}$ Substitute.

$V \approx \underline{3217.0}$ cm³   Use a calulator. Round to the nearest tenth.

REFLECT

3a. A rectangular prism has the same height as the oblique cylinder in the example. The cross-sectional area at every level of the prism is 64π cm². Can you use Cavalieri's principle to make a conclusion about the volume of the prism? Why or why not?

Yes; since the heights are equal and the cross-sectional areas at every

level are equal, the prism has the same volume as the cylinder.

© Houghton Mifflin Harcourt Publishing Company

Chapter 11   463   Lesson 2

CC.9-12.G.MG.3

4 EXAMPLE Designing a Box with Maximum Volume

You want to build a storage box from a piece of plywood that is 4 feet by 8 feet. You must use 6 pieces (for the top, bottom, and sides of the box) and you must make cuts that are parallel and perpendicular to the edges of the plywood. Describe three possible designs. What do you think is the maximum possible volume for the box?

A Consider Design 1 at right. The top, bottom, front, and back of the box are congruent rectangles. The ends are squares. The gray piece is waste.

Design 1

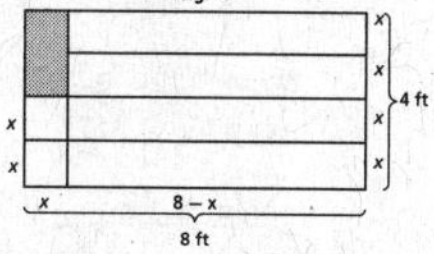

From the figure, $4x = \underline{4}$, so $x = \underline{1}$ ft

and $8 - x = \underline{7}$ ft.

$V = \underline{7} \cdot \underline{1} \cdot \underline{1} = \underline{7}$ ft³

B Consider Design 2 at right. The top, bottom, front, and back of the box are congruent rectangles. The ends are squares. The gray piece is waste.

Design 2

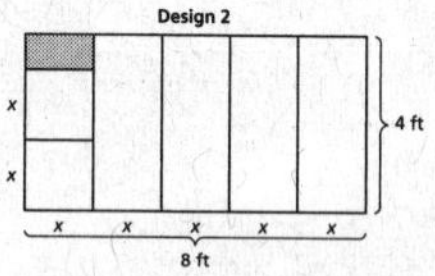

From the figure, $5x = \underline{8}$, so $x = \underline{1.6}$ ft.

$V = \underline{4} \cdot \underline{1.6} \cdot \underline{1.6} = \underline{10.24}$ ft³

C Consider Design 3 at right. The top, bottom, front, and back of the box are congruent rectangles. The ends are squares. There is no waste.

Design 3

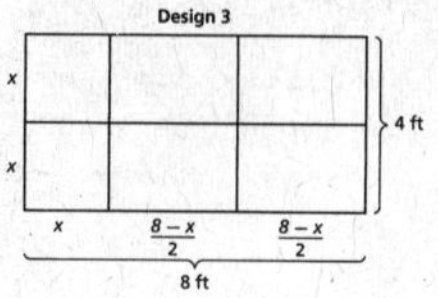

From the figure, $2x = \underline{4}$, so $x = \underline{2}$ ft

and $\frac{8-x}{2} = \underline{3}$ ft.

$V = \underline{3} \cdot \underline{2} \cdot \underline{2} = \underline{12}$ ft³

D Based on these designs, the maximum possible volume appears to be $\underline{12}$ ft³.

REFLECT

4a. Is it possible to make a box all of whose sides are not squares? If so, give the dimensions of the box and find its volume.

Yes; possible answer: a box with dimensions 2 ft, $\frac{4}{3}$ ft, and 4 ft can be made with

no waste. Its volume is about 10.66 ft³.

4b. Is it possible to say what the maximum volume of the box is based on your work above? Why or why not?

No; although 12 ft³ is the greatest volume among the three designs,

there might be a design that results in a greater volume.

© Houghton Mifflin Harcourt Publishing Company

© Houghton Mifflin Harcourt Publishing Company

Chapter 11   464   Lesson 2

Essential Question

How do you calculate the volume of a prism or cylinder and use volume formulas to solve design problems? You calculate the volume, V, of a prism and the volume, V, of a right or oblique cylinder using the same formula, $V = Bh$, where B is the area of the base and h is the height. You can solve design problems by using given information to draw a diagram that meets the given requirements.

Summarize

Have students write a journal entry in which they write a problem that requires finding the volume of a cylinder. Remind students to include a complete solution for the problem.

Where skills are taught	Where skills are practiced
1 EXPLORE	EXS. 1–3
2 EXAMPLE	EX. 4
3 EXAMPLE	EX. 5
4 EXAMPLE	EXS. 7–9

Exercise 6: Students apply what they have learned to critique another student's reasoning.

© Houghton Mifflin Harcourt Publishing Company

PRACTICE

Find the volume of each prism or cylinder. Round to the nearest tenth.

1.

5.6 mm
3.5 mm
8.4 mm

164.6 mm³

2.

0.9 ft
1.6 ft

4.1 ft³

3.

3.1 m
7.6 m

_229.4 m³_

4. You gather data about two wood logs that are approximately cylindrical. The data are shown in the table. Based on your data, which wood is denser, aspen or juniper? Explain.

Type of Wood	Diameter (ft)	Height (ft)	Weight (lb)
Aspen	1.5	3	137.8
Juniper	2	5	549.8

Juniper; its density is approximately 35 lb/ft³, compared to a density of
approximately 26 lb/ft³ for aspen.

5. A vase in the shape of an oblique cylinder has the dimensions shown at right. How many liters of water does the vase hold? Round to the nearest tenth. (*Hint:* 1 liter = 1000 cm³)

17 cm
14 cm

1.5 liters

6. Error Analysis A student claims that the cylinder and cone at right have the same volume by Cavalieri's principle. Explain the student's error.

$h = 4$ cm
$B = 13$ cm²
$B = 13$ cm²

Cavalieri's principle does not apply; the cross-
sectional areas are not the same at every level.

7. You have 500 cm³ of clay and want to make a sculpture in the shape of a cylinder. You want the height of the cylinder to be 3 times the cylinder's radius and you want to use all the clay. What radius and height should the sculpture have?

$r \approx 3.76$ cm; $h \approx 11.27$ cm

© Houghton Mifflin Harcourt Publishing Company

Chapter 11   465   Lesson 2

---

8. You want to build a box in the shape of a rectangular prism. The box must have a volume of 420 in.³ As shown in the figure, the ends of the box must be squares. In order to minimize the cost, you want to use the least possible amount of material. Follow these steps to determine the dimensions you should use for the box.

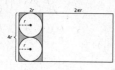

x
x
ℓ

a. Let the ends of the box be x in. by x in. and let the length of the box be ℓ in. The amount of material M needed to make the box is its surface area. Write an expression for M by adding the areas of the six faces.

$M = 2x^2 + 4x\ell$

b. Write an equation for the volume of the box and then solve it for ℓ.

$x^2\ell = 420; \ell = \frac{420}{x^2}$

c. Substitute the expression for ℓ in the expression for M from part (a).

$M = 2x^2 + \frac{1680}{x}$

d. To find the value of x that minimizes M, enter the expression for M as Y_1 in your calculator. Graph the function in a suitable viewing window. Go to the Calc menu and choose **3: minimum** to find the value of x that minimizes M. Use your equation from part (b) to find the corresponding value of ℓ. What dimensions should you use for the box?

The box should be a cube where each side has length ≈ 7.49 in.

9. You have a flexible piece of sheet metal that measures 4 feet by 8 feet. You want to build a cylinder by cutting out two circles for the bases and a rectangular piece that can be bent to form the lateral surface.

$2r$
$2\pi r$
r
r
$4r$

a. Let r be the radius of the cylinder. From the figure, there are two constraints on r: $4r \le 4$ (based on the width of the metal) and $2r + 2\pi r \le 8$ (based on the length of the metal). What is the greatest value of r that satisfies both constraints?

$r = \frac{4}{1 + \pi} \approx 0.966$

b. What is the approximate volume of the cylinder with this radius?

11.7 ft³

© Houghton Mifflin Harcourt Publishing Company

© Houghton Mifflin Harcourt Publishing Company

Chapter 11   466   Lesson 2

Notes

ADDITIONAL PRACTICE AND PROBLEM SOLVING

Assign these pages to help your students practice and apply important lesson concepts. For additional exercises, see the Student Edition.

Answers

Additional Practice

1. $V = 42 \text{ mi}^3$

2. $V \approx 7242.6 \text{ mm}^3$

3. $V \approx 0.4 \text{ m}^3$

4. $V = 32\pi \text{ yd}^3$; $V \approx 100.5 \text{ yd}^3$

5. $V = 13.5\pi \text{ km}^3$; $V \approx 42.4 \text{ km}^3$

6. $V = 810\pi \text{ ft}^3$; $V \approx 2544.7 \text{ ft}^3$

7. $V \approx 278.3 \text{ cm}^3$

8. The volume is divided by 8.

9. The volume is divided by 125.

10. $V \approx 109.9 \text{ ft}^3$
11. $V \approx 166.3 \text{ cm}^3$

Problem Solving

1. about 23.50 cups
2. about 25 gal
3. B
4. J
5. C
6. F

Name_____ Class_____ Date_____

11-2

Additional Practice

Find the volume of each prism. Round to the nearest tenth if necessary.

1.
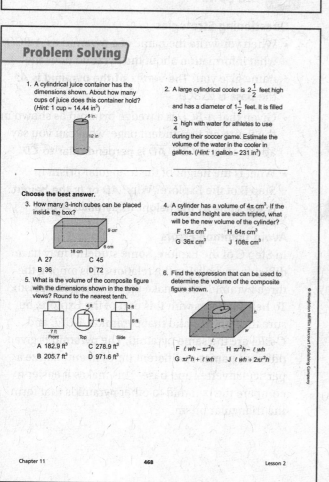

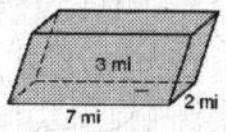

3 mi

7 mi — 2 mi

the oblique rectangular prism

2.

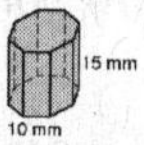

15 mm

10 mm

the regular octagonal prism

_____   _____

3. a cube with edge length 0.75 m

_____

Find the volume of each cylinder. Give your answers both in terms of π and rounded to the nearest tenth.

4.

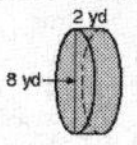

2 yd

8 yd

5.

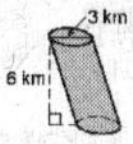

3 km

6 km

_____   _____

6. a cylinder with base circumference 18π ft and height 10 ft

_____

7. CDs have the dimensions shown in the figure. Each CD is 1 mm thick. Find the volume in cubic centimeters of a stack of 25 CDs. Round to the nearest tenth.

0.75 cm

5.25 cm

_____

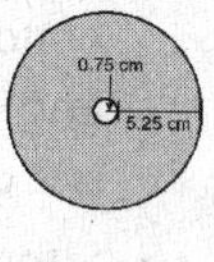

Describe the effect of each change on the volume of the given figure.

8.

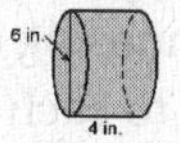

6 in.

4 in.

The dimensions are halved.

9.

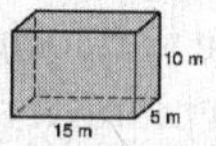

10 m

5 m

15 m

The dimensions are divided by 5.

_____   _____

Find the volume of each composite figure. Round to the nearest tenth.

10.

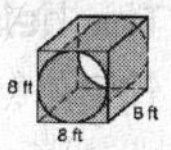

8 ft

8 ft — 5 ft

11.

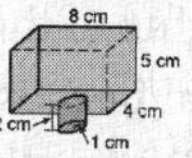

8 cm

5 cm

2 cm — 4 cm

1 cm

_____   _____

Problem Solving

1. A cylindrical juice container has the dimensions shown. About how many cups of juice does this container hold? (*Hint:* 1 cup ≈ 14.44 in³)

6 in.

12 in.

_____

2. A large cylindrical cooler is $2\frac{1}{2}$ feet high and has a diameter of $1\frac{1}{2}$ feet. It is filled $\frac{3}{4}$ high with water for athletes to use during their soccer game. Estimate the volume of the water in the cooler in gallons. (*Hint:* 1 gallon ≈ 231 in³)

_____

Choose the best answer.

3. How many 3-inch cubes can be placed inside the box?

9 cm

6 cm

18 cm

A 27   C 45

B 36   D 72

4. A cylinder has a volume of 4π cm³. If the radius and height are each tripled, what will be the new volume of the cylinder?

F 12π cm³   H 64π cm³

G 36π cm³   J 108π cm³

5. What is the volume of the composite figure with the dimensions shown in the three views? Round to the nearest tenth.

4 ft

4 ft

3 ft

6 ft

7 ft

Front   Top   Side

A 182.9 ft³   C 278.9 ft³

B 205.7 ft³   D 971.6 ft³

6. Find the expression that can be used to determine the volume of the composite figure shown.

h

ℓ

w

F $\ell wh - \pi r^2 h$ H $\pi r^2 h - \ell wh$

G $\pi r^2 h + \ell wh$ J $\ell wh + 2\pi r^2 h$

Volume of Pyramids and Cones
Going Deeper

Essential question: *How do you calculate the volume of a pyramid or cone and use volume formulas to solve problems??*

© Houghton Mifflin Harcourt Publishing Company

⬡ **COMMON CORE** **Standards for Mathematical Content**

CC.9-12.G.GMD.1 Give an informal argument for the formula for the ... volume of a ... pyramid and cone. Use dissection arguments ....

CC.9-12.G.GMD.3 Use volume formulas for ... pyramids, cones ... to solve problems.*

Prerequisites
Volume of prisms and cylinders

Math Background
In this lesson, students develop and use a formula for the volume of a pyramid. Students will first explore a key postulate about pyramids (pyramids that have equal base areas and equal heights have equal volumes). Then, students will find a volume formula for a "wedge pyramid." Finally, students will use an informal dissection argument to divide any pyramid into wedge pyramids.

The approach to finding a formula for the volume of a cone in this lesson is very similar to the approach to finding a formula for the circumference of a circle. In this lesson, students inscribe a sequence of pyramids in a given cone and use similar reasoning to show that the volume, V, of the cone is given by $V = \frac{1}{3}Bh$, where B is the base area and h is the cone's height.

INTRODUCE

Remind students of the definition of *pyramid* and the associated vocabulary (lateral face, vertex, base). Review the definition of *cone* and how the terms *vertex* and *base* are applied to cones. You may also want to review how to sketch the two solids.

TEACH

1 EXPLORE

Questioning Strategies
- Suppose $b = 4$ cm and $h = 1$ cm. What can you conclude about the triangles formed in Steps A and B of the Explore? **The area of the triangles is 2 cm².**
- Suppose you form a pyramid by choosing a point in plane R and connecting it to each vertex of the polygon. Then, you form a different pyramid in this way. What can you say about the heights of the pyramids? Why? **The heights are equal because in each case the height is the perpendicular distance between the plane of the base and plane R.**

2 EXPLORE

Questioning Strategies
- When you write the name of a pyramid as A-BCD, what information about the pyramid does the name give you? **The vertex of the pyramid is A; the base is $\triangle BCD$.**
- Given that A-BCD is a wedge pyramid as shown in the figure on the student page, what can you say about $\overline{AD}$ and $\overline{CD}$? **$\overline{AD}$ is perpendicular to $\overline{CD}$.**
- What is the height of the triangular prism in Step B of the Explore? Why? **AD or h; the height is the same as the height of pyramid A-BCD.**

Avoid Common Errors
In Step C of the Explore, some students may have difficulty visualizing the relationships among the three pyramids that make up the triangular prism. To help students with this part of the Explore, be sure they understand that pyramids A-CFE and C-EFA are the same pyramid. The pyramid is given different names at different times to emphasize a particular vertex and base. This makes it easier to compare the pyramid to other pyramids that form the triangular prism.

Name_____ Class_____ Date_____

11-3

Volume of Pyramids and Cones
Going Deeper

Essential question: *How do you calculate the volume of a pyramid or cone and use volume formulas to solve problems?*

Recall that a *pyramid* is a polyhedron formed by a polygonal base and triangular lateral faces that meet at a common point, called the vertex of the pyramid. The goal of this lesson is to develop a formula for volume of a pyramid.

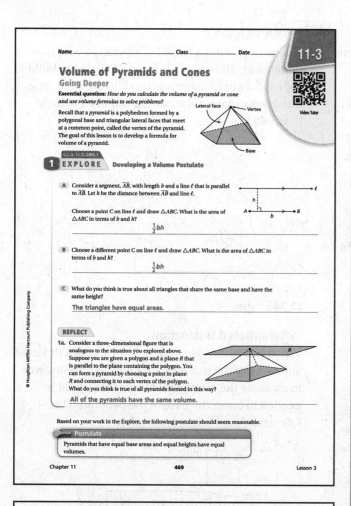

CC.9-12.G.GMD.1
1 EXPLORE   Developing a Volume Postulate

A Consider a segment, $\overline{AB}$, with length b and a line ℓ that is parallel to $\overline{AB}$. Let h be the distance between $\overline{AB}$ and line ℓ.

Choose a point C on line ℓ and draw $\triangle ABC$. What is the area of $\triangle ABC$ in terms of b and h?

$$\tfrac{1}{2}bh$$

B Choose a different point C on line ℓ and draw $\triangle ABC$. What is the area of $\triangle ABC$ in terms of b and h?

$$\tfrac{1}{2}bh$$

C What do you think is true about all triangles that share the same base and have the same height?

The triangles have equal areas.

REFLECT

1a. Consider a three-dimensional figure that is analogous to the situation you explored above. Suppose you are given a polygon and a plane R that is parallel to the plane containing the polygon. You can form a pyramid by choosing a point in plane R and connecting it to each vertex of the polygon. What do you think is true of all pyramids formed in this way?

All of the pyramids have the same volume.

Based on your work in the Explore, the following postulate should seem reasonable.

> **Postulate**
> Pyramids that have equal base areas and equal heights have equal volumes.

Chapter 11   469   Lesson 3

In order to find a formula for the volume of any pyramid, you will first find a formula for the volume of a "wedge pyramid." A wedge pyramid is one in which the base is a triangle and a perpendicular segment from the pyramid's vertex to the base intersects the base at a vertex of the triangle. Pyramid A-BCD is a wedge pyramid.

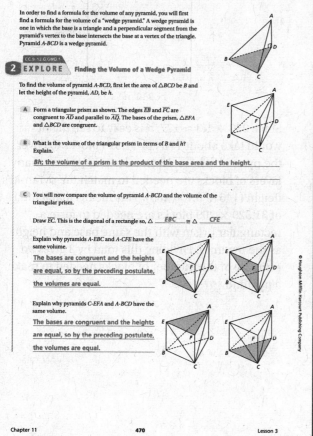

CC.9-12.G.GMD.1
2 EXPLORE   Finding the Volume of a Wedge Pyramid

To find the volume of pyramid A-BCD, first let the area of $\triangle BCD$ be B and let the height of the pyramid, AD, be h.

A Form a triangular prism as shown. The edges $\overline{EB}$ and $\overline{FC}$ are congruent to $\overline{AD}$ and parallel to $\overline{AQ}$. The bases of the prism, $\triangle EFA$ and $\triangle BCD$ are congruent.

B What is the volume of the triangular prism in terms of B and h? Explain.

Bh; the volume of a prism is the product of the base area and the height.

C You will now compare the volume of pyramid A-BCD and the volume of the triangular prism.

Draw $\overline{EC}$. This is the diagonal of a rectangle so, $\triangle \underline{\quad EBC \quad} \cong \triangle \underline{\quad CFE \quad}$

Explain why pyramids A-EBC and A-CFE have the same volume.

The bases are congruent and the heights are equal, so by the preceding postulate, the volumes are equal.

Explain why pyramids C-EFA and A-BCD have the same volume.

The bases are congruent and the heights are equal, so by the preceding postulate, the volumes are equal.

Chapter 11   470   Lesson 3

© Houghton Mifflin Harcourt Publishing Company

Teaching Strategies

If time permits, a hands-on activity can help students develop the formula for the volume of a pyramid from an inductive-reasoning perspective. Have students make nets for a square-based pyramid and a square-based prism that has the same height as the pyramid. Then, have students cut out, fold, and tape the nets to form the three-dimensional figures. Students can model the volume of the pyramid by filling it with uncooked rice, sand, or another granular material. Ask students to pour the rice from the pyramid into the prism as many times as necessary to see how the volumes of the figures are related. Students will discover that it takes three batches of rice from the pyramid to fill the prism. That is, the volume of the pyramid is one-third the volume of the associated prism.

3 EXAMPLE

Questioning Strategies

- What are the main steps you will use to solve this problem? **First, find the volume of the pyramid. Then, find the volume of an average block. Then, divide the volume of the pyramid by the volume of an average block to estimate the number of blocks in the pyramid.**

- What units should you use for the volume of the pyramid? Why? **Use cubic meters since the lengths are given in meters.**

- The Great Pyramid has internal passageways and internal chambers. What might this tell you about your estimate of the number of blocks used to build the pyramid? Why? **The estimate may be an overestimate since fewer blocks would be needed.**

EXTRA EXAMPLE

You want to build a model of a pyramid with the dimensions shown in the figure. You plan to build the model out of cubes whose sides are 3 cm long. About how many cubes would you need to build the model?

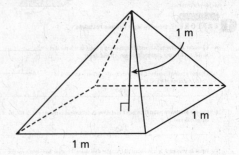

12,346 cubes

Differentiated Instruction

Visual learners might benefit from seeing a different approach to the example. Begin by asking students to estimate the number of blocks that would be needed to cover the base of the pyramid. The following figure might be helpful.

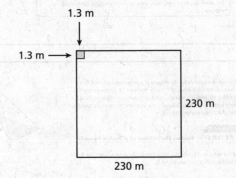

Since $230 \div 1.3 \approx 177$, it is easy to see that it would take about 177^2, or 31,329 blocks to cover the pyramid's base. Next, ask students how many layers of blocks are needed to match the pyramid's height ($146 \div 0.7 \approx 209$). This means that a total of $31{,}329 \times 209$ blocks are needed to form a rectangular prism with the same base and height as the pyramid. Dividing this total by 3 gives an estimate of the number of blocks needed to make a pyramid.

D You have shown that the three pyramids that form the triangular prism all have the same volume. Compare the volume of pyramid *A-BCD* and the volume of the triangular prism.

The volume of pyramid *A-BCD* is one-third the volume of the triangular prism.

E Write the volume of pyramid *A-BCD* in terms of *B* and *h*.

The volume of pyramid *A-BCD* is $\frac{1}{3}Bh$.

REFLECT

2a. Explain how you know that the three pyramids that form that triangular prism all have the same volume.

Pyramids *A-EBC* and *A-CFE* have the same volume and pyramids *C-EFA* and *A-BCD* have the same volume. But *A-CFE* and *C-EFA* are two names for the same pyramid, so by the Transitive Property of Equality, the pyramids all have the same volume.

In the Explore, you showed that the volume of any "wedge pyramid" is one-third the product of the base area and the height. Now consider a general pyramid. As shown in the figure, the pyramid can be partitioned into nonoverlapping wedge pyramids by drawing a perpendicular from the vertex to the base.

The volume *V* of the given pyramid is the sum of the volumes of the wedge pyramids.

That is, $V = \frac{1}{3}B_1h + \frac{1}{3}B_2h + \frac{1}{3}B_3h + \frac{1}{3}B_4h$.

Using the distributive property, this may be rewritten as $V = \frac{1}{3}h(B_1 + B_2 + B_3 + B_4)$.

Notice that $B_1 + B_2 + B_3 + B_4 = B$, where *B* is the base area of the given pyramid.

So, $V = \frac{1}{3}Bh$.

The above argument provides an informal justification for the following result.

> **Volume of a Pyramid**
>
> The volume *V* of a pyramid with base area *B* and height *h* is given by
> $V = \frac{1}{3}Bh$.

CC.9-12.G.GMD.3

3 EXAMPLE   Solving a Volume Problem

The Great Pyramid in Giza, Egypt, is approximately a square pyramid with the dimensions shown. The pyramid is composed of stone blocks that are rectangular prisms. An average block has dimensions 1.3 m by 1.3 m by 0.7 m. Approximately how many stone blocks were used to build the pyramid? Round to the nearest hundred thousand.

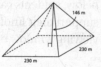

A Find the volume of the pyramid.

The area of the base *B* is the area of a square with sides of length 230 m.

So, $B = $ **52,900 m²**

The volume *V* of the pyramid is $\frac{1}{3}Bh = \frac{1}{3} \cdot$ **52,900** $\cdot$ **146**

So, $V = $ **2,574,466.$\overline{6}$ m³**

B Find the volume of an average block.

The volume of a rectangular prism is given by the formula $V = \ell wh$

So, the volume *W* of an average block is **1.183 m³**

C Find the approximate number of stone blocks in the pyramid.

To estimate the number of blocks in the pyramid, divide **V** by **W**

So, the approximate number of blocks is **2,200,000**

REFLECT

3a. What aspects of the model in this problem may lead to inaccuracies in your estimate?

Possible answer: The given dimensions of the pyramid and the blocks are approximations; the blocks form not a true pyramid but rather a pyramid consisting of many layers or "steps."

3b. Suppose you are told that the average height of a stone block is 0.69 m rather than 0.7 m. Would this increase or decrease your estimate of the total number of blocks in the pyramid? Explain.

Increase; this change would decrease *W*, so $\frac{V}{W}$ would increase.

Notes

MATHEMATICAL PRACTICE — Highlighting the Standards

The process used in this lesson to develop the formula for the volume of a pyramid offers a connection to Standard 1 (Make sense of problems and persevere in solving them). The standard discusses "looking for entry points" and planning a "solution pathway." Explain to students that mathematicians use these strategies not only when solving specific problems but also when making generalizations and writing proofs.

For example, to find an entry point for developing the formula for the volume of a pyramid, a mathematician might start by asking what is already known. In this case, we already know the formula for the volume of a prism and cylinder. This suggests that it may be useful to somehow connect pyramids to prisms. Some initial efforts in this direction might show that it is awkward to relate a general pyramid to a prism but that a "wedge pyramid" can be related to a prism, as shown in the Explore.

This solution pathway illustrates how a new problem (finding the formula for the volume of a pyramid) may sometimes be related to a simpler problem that has already been solved (finding the formula for the volume of a prism). Encourage students to identify additional examples of this type of thinking as they continue to explore volume formulas.

Questioning Strategies

- To develop a formula for the volume of a cone, why does it make sense to work with inscribed pyramids? **We already have a formula for the volume of a pyramid.**

- In general, what happens as the number of sides of the base of the inscribed pyramid gets larger? **The pyramid becomes a better fit for the cone; that is, the volume of the pyramid gets closer to the volume of the cone.**

- How is the area of the base of the pyramid related to the area of $\triangle AOB$? Why? **The area of the base of the pyramid is n times the area of $\triangle AOB$ since the base is composed of n triangles, all congruent to $\triangle AOB$.**

Teaching Strategies

In the Explore, students use their calculator's table feature to find out what happens to the expression

$$n \sin\left(\frac{180°}{n}\right) \cos\left(\frac{180°}{n}\right)$$

as n gets larger. You may also wish to have students investigate this question through graphing. Specifically, once students have entered the expression as Y_1, they can view the graph of the function and use the TRACE feature to see that as n gets larger, the y-values get closer to π. As shown below, students can also graph the function $Y_2 = \pi$ to support their findings. (The graph shown here has a viewing window of $3 \leq x \leq 20$ and $0 \leq y \leq 5$.)

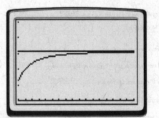

Recall that a *cone* is a three-dimensional figure with a circular base and a curved lateral surface that connects the base to a point called the vertex. You can use the formula for the volume of a pyramid to develop a formula for the volume of a cone.

Vertex
Lateral surface
Base

4 EXPLORE CC.9-12.G.GMD.1 **Developing a Volume Formula**

Plan: To find the volume of a given cone, consider pyramids with regular polygonal bases that are inscribed in the cone. As the number of sides of the polygonal bases increases, the volume of the pyramid gets closer to the volume of the cone. The first steps of the argument consist of writing an expression for the volume of an inscribed pyramid.

Base of inscribed pyramid has 3 sides.   Base of inscribed pyramid has 4 sides.   Base of inscribed pyramid has 5 sides.

A Let O be the center of the cone's base and let r be the radius of the cone. Let h be the height of the cone. Inscribe a pyramid whose base is a regular n-gon in the cone. Draw radii from O to the vertices of the n-gon.

B Let $\overline{AB}$ be one side of the n-gon. Draw $\overline{OM}$, the segment from O to the midpoint of $\overline{AB}$.

Then $\triangle AOM \cong \triangle BOM$ by <u>the SSS Congruence Criterion</u>

So, $\angle 1 \cong \angle 2$ by <u>CPCTC</u>

C There are <u>n</u> triangles, all congruent to $\triangle AOB$, that surround point O and fill the n-gon.

Therefore, $m\angle AOB = \dfrac{360°}{n}$ and $m\angle 1 = \dfrac{180°}{n}$.

D Since $\angle OMA \cong \angle OMB$ by CPCTC, and $\angle OMA$ and $\angle OMB$ form a linear pair, these angles are supplementary and must have measures of 90°. So, $\triangle AOM$ and $\triangle BOM$ are right triangles.

In $\triangle AOM$, $\sin \angle 1 = \dfrac{x}{r}$, so $x = r \sin \angle 1$.

Substituting the expression for $m\angle 1$ from above gives $x = r \sin \left(\dfrac{180°}{n} \right)$.

© Houghton Mifflin Harcourt Publishing Company

E In $\triangle AOM$, $\cos \angle 1 = \dfrac{y}{r}$, so $y = r \cos \angle 1$.

Substituting the expression for $m\angle 1$ from above gives $y = r \cos \left(\dfrac{180°}{n} \right)$.

F To write an expression for the area of the base of the pyramid, first write an expression for the area of $\triangle AOB$.

$\text{Area}(\triangle AOB) = \frac{1}{2} \cdot \text{base} \cdot \text{height} = \frac{1}{2} \cdot 2x \cdot y = xy$

Substituting the expressions for x and y from above gives the following.

$\text{Area}(\triangle AOB) = \underline{r \sin \left(\frac{180°}{n} \right) r \cos \left(\frac{180°}{n} \right)}$

The base of the pyramid is composed of n triangles that are congruent to $\triangle AOB$, so the area of the base of the pyramid is given by the following.

$\text{Area (base of pyramid)} = \underline{nr \sin \left(\frac{180°}{n} \right) r \cos \left(\frac{180°}{n} \right)}$

The volume of the pyramid is $\frac{1}{3} \cdot \text{base} \cdot \text{height}$, which may be written as

$\text{Volume (pyramid)} = \underline{\frac{1}{3} r^2 hn \sin \left(\frac{180°}{n} \right) \cos \left(\frac{180°}{n} \right)}$

G Your expression for the pyramid's volume should include the expression

$n \sin \left(\dfrac{180°}{n} \right) \cos \left(\dfrac{180°}{n} \right)$

as a factor. Use a calculator, as follows, to find out what happens to the value of this expression as n gets larger and larger.

* Enter the expression $x \sin \left(\dfrac{180}{x} \right) \cos \left(\dfrac{180}{x} \right)$ as Y_1.

* Go to the Table Setup menu and enter the values shown at right.

* View a table for the function.

* Use the arrow keys to scroll down.

What happens to the value of $n \sin \left(\frac{180°}{n} \right) \cos \left(\frac{180°}{n} \right)$ as n gets larger?
The value gets closer to π.

H Consider the expression you wrote for the volume of the inscribed pyramid at the end of Step F. What happens to the value of this expression as n gets larger?
The expression gets closer to $\frac{1}{3} \pi r^2 h$.

© Houghton Mifflin Harcourt Publishing Company

Questioning Strategies

- Can you find the volume of the cone using only the given dimensions? Why or why not? **No; the formula requires the height of the cone, which is not given.**

- Once you know the volume of the cone, what do you need to do? How can you do this? **Convert the volume to fluid ounces using the fact that 1 in.^{3} is approximately 0.554 fl oz. (That is, multiply the volume in cubic inches by the factor 0.554 to convert to fluid ounces.)**

- Does the paper cone hold a cup of water? Why or why not? **No; a cup is 8 fl oz, but the volume of the cone is only 5.8 fl oz.**

EXTRA EXAMPLE

A conical paper cup has the dimensions shown. How many liters of liquid does the cup hold? Round to the nearest tenth. (*Hint:* 1 cm^3 ≈ 0.001 L)

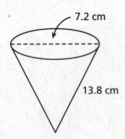

7.2 cm

13.8 cm

0.2 L

MATHEMATICAL PRACTICE | **Highlighting the Standards**

To address Standard 1 (Make sense of problems and persevere in solving them), ask students whether their answer to the example seems reasonable. Help students recognize that a volume of 5.8 fl oz is a bit less than a cup (8 fl oz) and that this is a sensible volume for a cone with the given dimensions. Also, ask students to give examples of answers that might have raised a red flag and prompted them to double check their calculations.

Essential Question

How do you calculate the volume of a pyramid or cone and use volume formulas to solve problems? The volume, V, of a pyramid with base area B and height h is given by $V = \frac{1}{3}Bh$. The volume, V, of a cone with base area B and height h is given by $V = \frac{1}{3}Bh$ (or $V = \frac{1}{3}\pi r^2 h$, where r is the radius of the base).

Summarize

Have students write a journal entry in which they summarize the main steps in developing the formula for the volume of a cone. Encourage students to include figures to illustrate the steps.

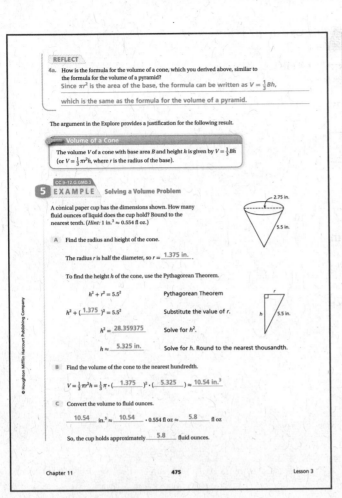

REFLECT

4a. How is the formula for the volume of a cone, which you derived above, similar to the formula for the volume of a pyramid?

Since πr^2 is the area of the base, the formula can be written as $V = \frac{1}{3}Bh$,

which is the same as the formula for the volume of a pyramid.

The argument in the Explore provides a justification for the following result.

> **Volume of a Cone**
>
> The volume V of a cone with base area B and height h is given by $V = \frac{1}{3}Bh$
> (or $V = \frac{1}{3}\pi r^2 h$, where r is the radius of the base).

CC.9-12.G.GMD.3

5 EXAMPLE Solving a Volume Problem

A conical paper cup has the dimensions shown. How many fluid ounces of liquid does the cup hold? Round to the nearest tenth. (*Hint:* 1 in.^{3} ≈ 0.554 fl oz.)

2.75 in.

5.5 in.

A Find the radius and height of the cone.

The radius r is half the diameter, so $r = \underline{1.375}$ in.

To find the height h of the cone, use the Pythagorean Theorem.

$h^2 + r^2 = 5.5^2$ Pythagorean Theorem

$h^2 + (\underline{1.375})^2 = 5.5^2$ Substitute the value of r.

$h^2 = \underline{28.359375}$ Solve for h^2.

$h \approx \underline{5.325}$ in.   Solve for h. Round to the nearest thousandth.

r

h 5.5 in.

B Find the volume of the cone to the nearest hundredth.

$V = \frac{1}{3}\pi r^2 h = \frac{1}{3}\pi \cdot (\underline{1.375})^2 \cdot (\underline{5.325}) \approx \underline{10.54}$ in.^{3}

C Convert the volume to fluid ounces.

$\underline{10.54}$ in.^{3} ≈ $\underline{10.54}$ · 0.554 fl oz ≈ $\underline{5.8}$ fl oz

So, the cup holds approximately $\underline{5.8}$ fluid ounces.

© Houghton Mifflin Harcourt Publishing Company

REFLECT

5a. A cylindrical cup has the same diameter and height as the conical cup. How can you find the number of fluid ounces that the cylindrical cup holds?

Multiply the conical cup's volume in fluid ounces by 3.

5b. Suppose the height of the conical paper cup is doubled, but the base radius is not changed. How would the volume of the cup change?

The volume of the cup would double if the height doubled.

5c. Suppose the height of the conical paper cup is not changed, but the base radius is doubled. How would the volume of the cup change?

The volume would quadruple, because the radius is squared in the formula.

PRACTICE

Find the volume of each pyramid. Round to the nearest tenth.

1. 4.9 cm, h, 4.1 cm, 6.2 cm

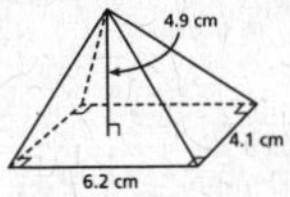

   $\underline{41.5 \text{ cm}^3}$

2. 7 ft, h, 7 ft

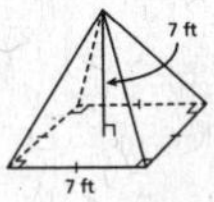

   $\underline{114.3 \text{ ft}^3}$

3. 8.1 mm, 15.2 mm, 12.5 mm, h

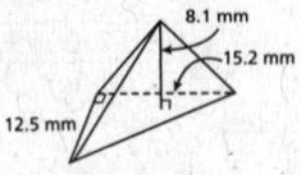

   $\underline{256.5 \text{ mm}^3}$

4. As shown in the figure, polyhedron *ABCDEFGH* is a cube and *P* is any point on face *EFGH*. Compare the volume of pyramid *P-ABCD* and the volume of the cube.

   The volume of *P-ABCD* is $\frac{1}{3}$ the volume of the cube.

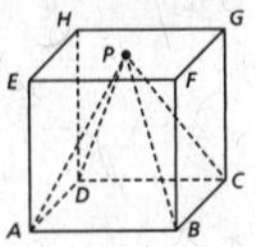

   (figure: cube labeled H, G, E, P, F, A, D, B, C)

5. A storage container for grain is in the shape of a square pyramid with the dimensions shown.

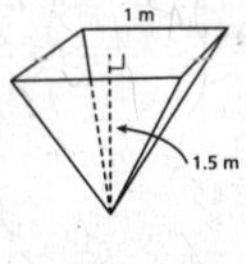

   a. What is the volume of the container in cubic centimeters?

   $\underline{500,000 \text{ cm}^3}$

   b. Grain leaks from the container at a rate of 4 cm^3 per second. Assuming the container starts completely full, about how many hours does it take until the container is empty?

   approximately 34.7 hours

   (figure: pyramid, 1 m, 1.5 m)

© Houghton Mifflin Harcourt Publishing Company

© Houghton Mifflin Harcourt Publishing Company

PRACTICE

Where skills are taught	Where skills are practiced
3 EXAMPLE	EXS. 1–3, 5
5 EXAMPLE	EXS. 8–11

Exercise 4: Students use visualization and reasoning to compare the volumes of solids.

Exercises 6 and 7: Students extend what they learned by solving problems that require ideas from earlier lessons or algebra skills.

Exercise 12: Students compare the volume of a cone and the volume of a pyramid.

Exercise 13: Students use reasoning to compare the volume a solid consisting of a cylinder with a cone removed and the volume of the original cylinder.

© Houghton Mifflin Harcourt Publishing Company

6. A piece of pure silver in the shape of a rectangular pyramid with the dimensions shown at right has a mass of 19.7 grams.

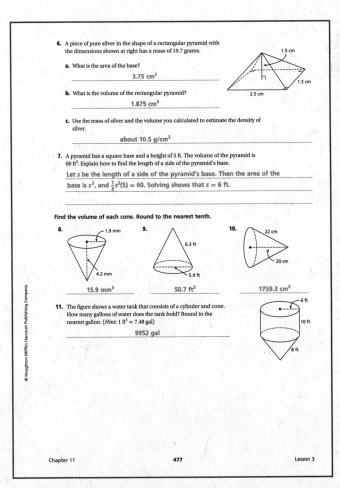

    a. What is the area of the base?

                3.75 cm²

    b. What is the volume of the rectangular pyramid?

                1.875 cm³

    c. Use the mass of silver and the volume you calculated to estimate the density of silver.

                about 10.5 g/cm³

7. A pyramid has a square base and a height of 5 ft. The volume of the pyramid is 60 ft³. Explain how to find the length of a side of the pyramid's base.

    Let s be the length of a side of the pyramid's base. Then the area of the base is s^2, and $\frac{1}{3}s^2(5) = 60$. Solving shows that $s = 6$ ft.

Find the volume of each cone. Round to the nearest tenth.

8.

    15.9 mm³

9.

    50.7 ft³

10.

    1759.3 cm³

11. The figure shows a water tank that consists of a cylinder and cone. How many gallons of water does the tank hold? Round to the nearest gallon. (*Hint:* 1 ft³ ≈ 7.48 gal)

    9952 gal

---

12. Popcorn is available in two cups: a square pyramid or a cone, as shown. The price of each cup of popcorn is the same. Which cup is the better deal? Explain.

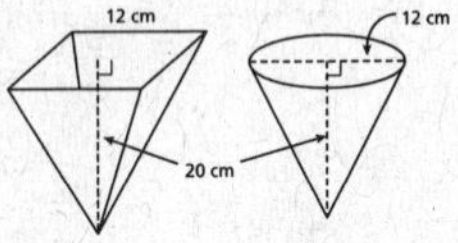

    The pyramid is the better deal because you get a greater volume of popcorn (960 cm³ versus 754 cm³) for the same price.

13. A sculptor removes a cone from a cylindrical block of wood so that the vertex of the cone is the center of the cylinder's base, as shown. Explain how the volume of the remaining solid compares with the volume of the original cylindrical block of wood.

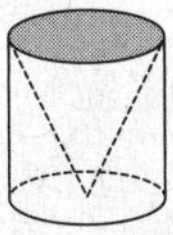

    The solid has $\frac{2}{3}$ the volume of the cylinder since the cone that is removed has $\frac{1}{3}$ the volume of the cylinder.

Notes

ADDITIONAL PRACTICE AND PROBLEM SOLVING

Assign these pages to help your students practice and apply important lesson concepts. For additional exercises, see the Student Edition.

Answers

Additional Practice

1. $V \approx 3934.2\ mm^3$
2. $V = 56\ yd^3$
3. $4{,}013{,}140\ ft^3$
4. $V = 80\pi\ cm^3$; $V \approx 251.3\ cm^3$
5. $V = 25{,}088\pi\ mi^3$; $V \approx 78{,}816.3\ mi^3$
6. $V = 4.5\pi\ m^3$; $V \approx 14.1\ m^3$
7. The volume of the cone is one-third the volume of the cylinder.
8. The volume is multiplied by $\frac{8}{27}$.
9. The volume is multiplied by 27.
10. $V \approx 21.4\ ft^3$
11. $V \approx 123.7\ mm^3$

Problem Solving

1. $V \approx 940.0\ m^3$
2. $V = 50.75\pi\ cm^3$
3. $V \approx 210.8\ cm^3$
4. $V = 98\pi\ in^3$
5. A
6. G
7. A

Name_____ Class_____ Date_____   **11-3**

Additional Practice

Find the volume of each pyramid. Round to the nearest tenth if necessary.

1. 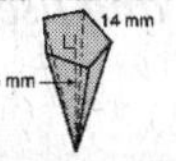
14 mm
35 mm

the regular pentagonal pyramid

2. 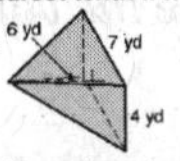
6 yd   7 yd
4 yd

the rectangular right pyramid

3. Giza in Egypt is the site of the three great Egyptian pyramids. Each pyramid has a square base. The largest pyramid was built for Khufu. When first built, it had base edges of 754 feet and a height of 481 feet. Over the centuries, some of the stone eroded away and some was taken for newer buildings. Khufu's pyramid today has base edges of 745 feet and a height of 471 feet. To the nearest cubic foot, find the difference between the original and current volumes of the pyramid.

_____

Find the volume of each cone. Give your answers both in terms of π and rounded to the nearest tenth.

4. 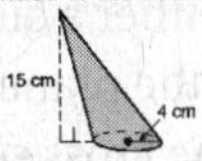
15 cm
4 cm

5. 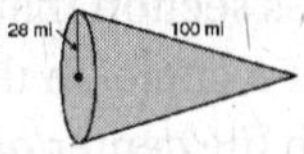
28 mi   100 mi

6. a cone with base circumference 6π m and a height equal to half the radius

_____

7. Compare the volume of a cone and the volume of a cylinder with equal height and base area.

_____

Describe the effect of each change on the volume of the given figure.

8. 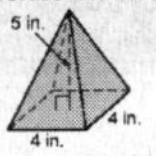
5 in.
4 in.   4 in.

The dimensions are multiplied by $\frac{2}{3}$.

9. 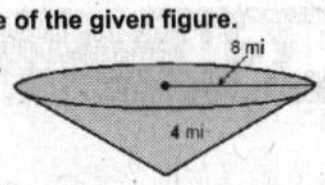
8 mi
4 mi

The dimensions are tripled.

_____

Find the volume of each composite figure. Round to the nearest tenth.

10. 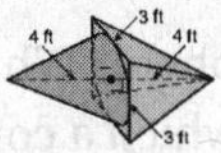
4 ft   3 ft   4 ft
3 ft

11. 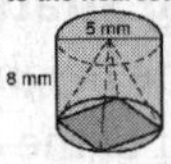
5 mm
8 mm

© Houghton Mifflin Harcourt Publishing Company

Problem Solving

1. A regular square pyramid has a base area of 196 meters and a lateral area of 448 square meters. What is the volume of the pyramid? Round your answer to the nearest tenth.

_____

2. A paper cone for serving roasted almonds has a volume of 406π cubic centimeters. A smaller cone has half the radius and half the height of the first cone. What is the volume of the smaller cone? Give your answer in terms of π.

_____

3. The hexagonal base in the pyramid is a regular polygon. What is the volume of the pyramid if its height is 9 centimeters? Round to the nearest tenth.

5.2 cm

_____

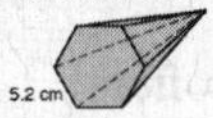

4. Find the volume of the shaded solid in the figure shown. Give your answer in terms of π.

9 in.   3 in.
6 in.   5 in.

_____

Choose the best answer.

5. The diameter of the cone equals the width of the cube, and the figures have the same height. Find the expression that can be used to determine the volume of the composite figure.

A $4(4)(4) - \frac{1}{3}\pi(2^2)(4)$

B $4(4)(4) + \frac{1}{3}\pi(2^2)(4)$

C $4(4)(4) - \pi(2^2)(4)$

D $4(4)(4) + \frac{1}{3}\pi(2^2)$

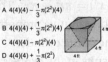
4 ft
4 ft
4 ft

6. Approximately how many fluid ounces of water can the paper cup hold? (*Hint:* 1 fl oz ≈ 1.805 in³)

2 in.
5 in.

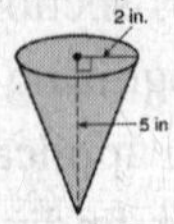

F 10.9 fl oz   H 32.7 fl oz
G 11.6 fl oz   J 36.3 fl oz

7. The Step Pyramid of Djoser in Lower Egypt was the first pyramid in the history of architecture. Its original height was 204 feet, and it had a rectangular base measuring 411 feet by 358 feet. Which is the best estimate for the volume of the pyramid in cubic yards?

A 370,570 yd³   C 3,335,128 yd³
B 1,111,709 yd³   D 10,005,384 yd³

© Houghton Mifflin Harcourt Publishing Company

© Houghton Mifflin Harcourt Publishing Company

Spheres
Going Deeper

Essential question: *How do you calculate the volume of a sphere and use the volume formula to solve problems?*

COMMON CORE **Standards for Mathematical Content**

CC.9-12.G.GMD.2(+) Give an informal argument using Cavalieri's principle for the formula for the volume of a sphere ....

CC.9-12.G.GMD.3 Use volume formulas for ... spheres to solve problems.*

CC.9-12.G.MG.2 Apply concepts of density based on area and volume in modeling situations (e.g., ... BTUs per cubic foot).*

Prerequisites
Volume of cylinders and cones

Math Background
The steps used in this lesson to develop a formula for the volume of a sphere offer a surprising application of Cavalieri's principle. It is surprising because the argument is based on showing that two seemingly unrelated solids have the same volume. The solids—a hemisphere and a cylinder from which a cone has been removed—are shown to have the same cross-sectional area at every level and therefore must have the same volume.

The formula for the volume, V, of a sphere with radius r is $V = \frac{4}{3}\pi r^3$. A bit of algebra shows that the volume of a sphere is equal to $\frac{2}{3}$ the volume of its circumscribed cylinder. This result, which has been known since ancient times, was of such importance to the Greek mathematician Archimedes that he requested that a drawing of a sphere and cylinder be placed on his tomb.

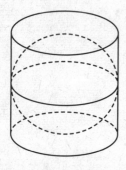

INTRODUCE

Review the definition of *sphere* and discuss the related terms *hemisphere* and *great circle*. Explain to students that when a plane intersects a sphere, the cross section that is formed is either a single point or a circle. In the case where the plane passes through the center of the sphere, the cross section is a great circle. Tell students that a great circle is sometimes called an equator.

TEACH

1 EXPLORE

Questioning Strategies
- What is the height of the hemisphere? What is the height of the cylinder from which a cone has been removed? **Both have height r.**
- What do you need to show to use Cavalieri's principle? **Show that the figures have the same cross-sectional area at every level.**
- What does Cavalieri's principle allow you to conclude? **The two figures have the same volume.**

MATHEMATICAL PRACTICE **Highlighting the Standards**

The argument in the Explore offers opportunities to focus on Standard 7 (Look for and make use of structure). For example, showing that the two figures have equal cross-sectional areas at every level requires recognizing that $\pi(r^2 - x^2) = \pi r^2 - \pi x^2$. This is an application of the distributive property. Later, finding the volume of the cylinder with a cone removed results in the expression $\pi r^2 h - \frac{1}{3}\pi r^2 h$. Students should be able to view this as a difference of two expressions. However, they should also be able to see that it has the form $a - \frac{1}{3}a$, which makes it possible to combine like terms.

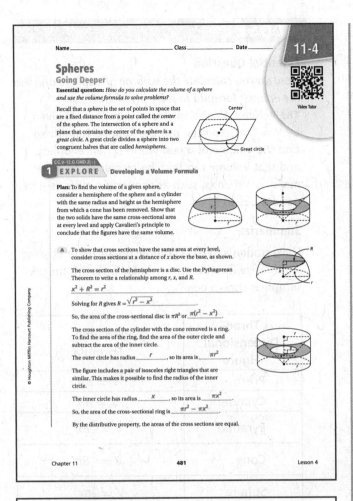

Name _____ Class _____ Date _____

11-4

Video Tutor

Spheres
Going Deeper

Essential question: *How do you calculate the volume of a sphere and use the volume formula to solve problems?*

Recall that a *sphere* is the set of points in space that are a fixed distance from a point called the *center* of the sphere. The intersection of a sphere and a plane that contains the center of the sphere is a *great circle*. A great circle divides a sphere into two congruent halves that are called *hemispheres*.

Center

Great circle

CC.9-12.G.GMD.2(+)

1 EXPLORE Developing a Volume Formula

Plan: To find the volume of a given sphere, consider a hemisphere of the sphere and a cylinder with the same radius and height as the hemisphere from which a cone has been removed. Show that the two solids have the same cross-sectional area at every level and apply Cavalieri's principle to conclude that the figures have the same volume.

A To show that cross sections have the same area at every level, consider cross sections at a distance of x above the base, as shown.

The cross section of the hemisphere is a disc. Use the Pythagorean Theorem to write a relationship among r, x, and R.

$$x^2 + R^2 = r^2$$

Solving for R gives $R = \underline{\sqrt{r^2 - x^2}}$.

So, the area of the cross-sectional disc is πR^2 or $\underline{\pi(r^2 - x^2)}$.

The cross section of the cylinder with the cone removed is a ring. To find the area of the ring, find the area of the outer circle and subtract the area of the inner circle.

The outer circle has radius $\underline{r}$, so its area is $\underline{\pi r^2}$.

The figure includes a pair of isosceles right triangles that are similar. This makes it possible to find the radius of the inner circle.

The inner circle has radius $\underline{x}$, so its area is $\underline{\pi x^2}$.

So, the area of the cross-sectional ring is $\underline{\pi r^2 - \pi x^2}$.

By the distributive property, the areas of the cross sections are equal.

Chapter 11   481   Lesson 4

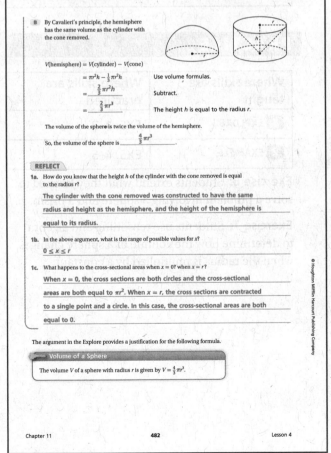

B By Cavalieri's principle, the hemisphere has the same volume as the cylinder with the cone removed.

$V(\text{hemisphere}) = V(\text{cylinder}) - V(\text{cone})$

$= \pi r^2 h - \frac{1}{3}\pi r^2 h$ Use volume formulas.

$= \underline{\frac{2}{3}\pi r^2 h}$ Subtract.

$= \underline{\frac{2}{3}\pi r^3}$ The height h is equal to the radius r.

The volume of the sphere is twice the volume of the hemisphere.

So, the volume of the sphere is $\underline{\frac{4}{3}\pi r^3}$.

REFLECT

1a. How do you know that the height h of the cylinder with the cone removed is equal to the radius r?

The cylinder with the cone removed was constructed to have the same

radius and height as the hemisphere, and the height of the hemisphere is

equal to its radius.

1b. In the above argument, what is the range of possible values for x?

$0 \le x \le r$

1c. What happens to the cross-sectional areas when $x = 0$? when $x = r$?

When $x = 0$, the cross sections are both circles and the cross-sectional

areas are both equal to πr^2. When $x = r$, the cross sections are contracted

to a single point and a circle. In this case, the cross-sectional areas are both

equal to 0.

The argument in the Explore provides a justification for the following formula.

Volume of a Sphere

The volume V of a sphere with radius r is given by $V = \frac{4}{3}\pi r^3$.

Chapter 11   482   Lesson 4

2 EXAMPLE

Questioning Strategies

- The gas tank provides 275,321 BTU. How can you interpret this measurement? **This is the amount of energy required to increase the temperature of 275,321 pounds of water by one degree Fahrenheit.**

- What dimension or dimensions do you need to know to find the volume of the sphere? **You need to know the radius.**

EXTRA EXAMPLE

A spherical gas tank has the dimensions shown. When filled with propane, it provides 4506.2 BTU. How many BTUs does one cubic foot of propane yield? Round to the nearest BTU.

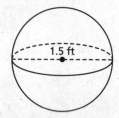

1.5 ft

2550 BTU

Avoid Common Errors

Students may not be sure whether they need to divide 275,321 by $\frac{256}{3}\pi$ or vice versa. Explain that 275,321 BTU corresponds to a volume of $\frac{256}{3}\pi$ ft^3 of natural gas. This may be written as follows.

$$275{,}321 \text{ BTU} \leftrightarrow \frac{256}{3}\pi \text{ ft}^3$$

You are interested in the number of BTUs that correspond to 1 ft^3 of natural gas. You can get 1 ft^3 on the right side of the correspondence by dividing both sides by $\frac{256}{3}\pi$. That is, divide 275,321 by $\frac{256}{3}\pi$.

CLOSE

Essential Question

How do you calculate the volume of a sphere and use the volume formula to solve problems?

The volume, *V*, of a sphere with radius *r* is given by $V = \frac{4}{3}\pi r^3$. You can use the volume formula to find the volume of a real-world spherical object, and that volume can then be converted to other more useful units, such as converting cubic feet of natural gas to BTUs.

Summarize

Have students make a graphic organizer or chart to summarize the volume formulas from this unit. A sample is shown below.

Three-Dimensional Figure	Volume Formula
Prism	$V = Bh$
Cylinder	$V = Bh$
Pyramid	$V = \frac{1}{3}Bh$
Cone	$V = \frac{1}{3}Bh$
Sphere	$V = \frac{4}{3}\pi r^3$

PRACTICE

Where skills are taught	Where skills are practiced
1 EXPLORE	EXS. 1–3
2 EXAMPLE	EXS. 4–5

Exercise 6: Students extend what they learned to solve a problem involving a sphere and a prism.

Exercise 7: Students use reasoning and algebra to determine how the volume of a sphere changes when the radius is multiplied by a constant.

A British thermal unit (BTU) is a unit of energy. It is approximately the amount of energy needed to increase the temperature of one pound of water by one degree Fahrenheit. As you will see in the following example, the energy content of a fuel may be measured in BTUs per unit of volume.

CC.9-12.G.GMD.3

2 EXAMPLE Solving a Volume Problem

A spherical gas tank has the dimensions shown. When filled with natural gas, it provides 275,321 BTU. How many BTUs does one cubic foot of natural gas yield? Round to the nearest BTU.

8 ft

A. Find the volume of the sphere.

The diameter is 8 feet, so the radius r is ___4 ft.___

$V = \frac{4}{3}\pi r^3$ Use the volume formula for a sphere.

$V = \frac{4}{3}\pi(4)^3$ Substitute for r.

$V = \frac{256}{3}\pi \text{ ft}^3$ Simplify. Leave the answer in terms of π.

B. Find the number of BTUs contained in one cubic foot of natural gas.

Since there are 275,321 BTU in $\frac{256}{3}\pi$ ft³ of natural gas, divide

___275,321___ by $\frac{256}{3}\pi$ to find the number of BTUs in 1 ft³.

Use a calculator to divide. Round to the nearest whole number.

So, one cubic foot of natural gas yields about ___1027___ BTU.

REFLECT

2a. How many pounds of water can be heated from 59°F to 60°F by one cubic foot of natural gas? Explain.

1027 pounds; each BTU of natural gas can increase the temperature of one pound of water by one degree Fahrenheit.

2b. How many pounds of water can be heated from 70°F to 83°F by one cubic foot of natural gas? Explain.

79 pounds; for each pound of water, it takes 13 BTU of natural gas to increase the temperature by 13°F, and 1027 ÷ 13 = 79.

© Houghton Mifflin Harcourt Publishing Company

PRACTICE

Find the volume of each sphere. Round to the nearest tenth.

1. 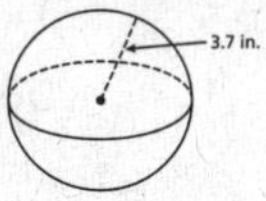
3.7 in.
___212.2 in³___

2. 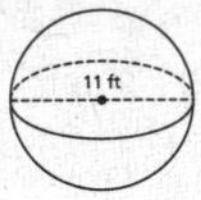
11 ft
___696.9 ft³___

3. 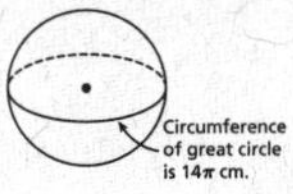
Circumference of great circle is 14π cm.
___1436.8 cm³___

4. One gallon of propane yields approximately 91,500 BTU. About how many BTUs does the spherical storage tank at right provide? Round to the nearest million BTUs. (*Hint:* 1 ft³ ≈ 7.48 gal)

5 ft

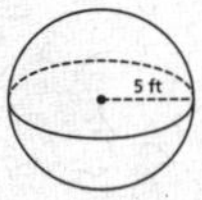

___358,000,000 BTU___

5. **Error Analysis** A student solved the following problem as shown below. Explain the student's error and give the correct answer to the problem.

A spherical gasoline tank has a radius of 0.5 ft. When filled, the tank provides 446,483 BTU. How many BTUs does one gallon of gasoline yield? Round to the nearest thousand BTUs and use the fact that 1 ft³ ≈ 7.48 gal.

> The volume of the tank is $\frac{4}{3}\pi r^3 = \frac{4}{3}\pi(0.5)^3$ ft³. Multiplying by 7.48 shows that this is approximately 3.92 gal. So the number of BTUs in one gallon of gasoline is approximately 446,483 × 3.92 ≈ 1,750,000 BTU.

The student should have divided the total number of BTUs by 3.92; the correct answer is 114,000 BTU.

6. The aquarium shown at right is a rectangular prism that is filled with water. You drop a spherical ball with a diameter of 6 inches into the aquarium. The ball sinks, causing water to spill from the tank. How much water is left in the tank? Express your answer to the nearest cubic inch and nearest gallon. (*Hint:* 1 in.³ ≈ 0.00433 gal)

12 in.
12 in.
20 in.

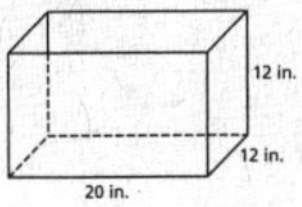

___2767 in.³; 12 gal___

7. How does the volume of a sphere change when you multiply its radius by a factor k, where $k > 0$? Explain.

The volume is multiplied by k^3, since the new volume is

$\frac{4}{3}\pi(kr)^3 = \frac{4}{3}\pi k^3 r^3 = k^3 \cdot \frac{4}{3}\pi r^3$, which is k^3 times the

original volume.

© Houghton Mifflin Harcourt Publishing Company

© Houghton Mifflin Harcourt Publishing Company

Assign these pages to help your students practice and apply important lesson concepts. For additional exercises, see the Student Edition.

Answers

Additional Practice

1. $V = 3888\pi \text{ mm}^3$

2. $V = \dfrac{8788\pi}{3} \text{ ft}^3 = 2929\dfrac{1}{3} \text{ ft}^3$

3. $d = 10\text{m}$

4. $V = \dfrac{250\pi}{3} \text{ cm}^3; \; V = \dfrac{32\pi}{9} \text{ cm}^3$

5. $\dfrac{5{,}324\pi}{3} \text{ in}^3$

6. $\dfrac{128\pi}{3} \text{ yd}^3$

7. The volume is divided by 64.

8. The volume is multiplied by $\dfrac{8}{125}$.

9. $V \approx 234.8 \text{ in}^3$

Problem Solving

1. 6 in

2. 347.3 in^3

3. about 3.5 times

4. D

5. F

6. B

7. J

Name_____ Class_____ Date_____ 11-4

Additional Practice

Find each measurement. Give your answers in terms of π.

1.

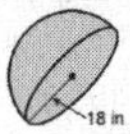

18 in

the volume of the hemisphere

_____

2.

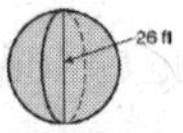

26 ft

the volume of the sphere

_____

3. the diameter of a sphere with volume $\frac{500\pi}{3}$ m³

_____

4. The figure shows a grapefruit half. The radius to the outside of the rind is 5 cm. The radius to the inside of the rind is 4 cm. The edible part of the grapefruit is divided into 12 equal sections. Find the volume of the half grapefruit and the volume of one edible section. Give your answers in terms of π.

_____

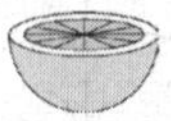

Find each measurement. Give your answers in terms of π.

5.

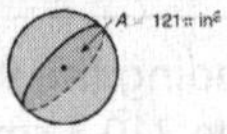

A = 121π in²

the volume of the sphere

_____

6.

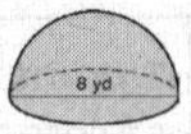

8 yd

the volume of the closed hemisphere

_____

Describe the effect of each change on the volume of the figure.

7.

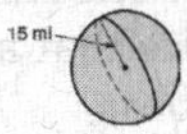

15 ml

The dimensions are divided by 4.

_____

8.

36 m

The dimensions are multiplied by $\frac{2}{5}$.

_____

9. Find the volume of the hemisphere with the prism-shaped space removed. Round to the nearest tenth.

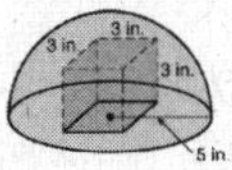

3 in. 3 in.
3 in.
5 in.

_____

Chapter 11   485   Lesson 4

Problem Solving

1. A globe has a volume of 288π in³. What is the radius of the globe? Give your answer in terms of π.

_____

2. Eight bocce balls are in a box 18 inches long, 9 inches wide, and 4.5 inches deep. If each ball has a diameter of 4.5 inches, what is the volume of the space around the balls? Round to the nearest tenth.

4.5 in
9 in.
18 in.

_____

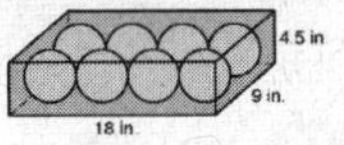

3. Ganymede, one of Jupiter's moons, is the largest moon in the solar system. Approximately how many times as great as the volume of Earth's moon is the volume of Ganymede?

_____

Moon	Diameter
Earth's moon	2160 mi
Ganymede	3280 mi

Choose the best answer.

4. What is the volume of a sphere with a great circle that has an area of 225π cm²?

A 300π cm³   C 2500π cm³
B 900π cm³   D 4500π cm³

5. A hemisphere has a volume of 972π cm³. If the radius is multiplied by $\frac{1}{3}$, what will be the volume of the new hemisphere?

F 36π cm³   H 162π cm³
G 108π cm³   J 324π cm³

6. Which expression represents the volume of the composite figure formed by the hemisphere and cone?

6 mm   25 mm

A 52π mm³   C 276π mm³
B 156π mm³   D 288π mm³

7. Which best represents the volume of the composite figure?

3 in.
10 in.
6 in.

F 129π in³   H 201π in³
G 138π in³   J 396π in³

Chapter 11   486   Lesson 4

This page provides students with the opportunity to apply concepts from the Common Core in real-world problem situations. There are three different levels of performance tasks:

⭐ Novice: These are short word problems that require students to apply the math they have learned in straightforward, real-world situations.

⭐⭐ Apprentice: These are more involved problems that guide students step-by-step through more complex tasks. These exercises include more complicated reasoning, writing, and open-ended elements.

⭐⭐⭐ Expert: These are open-ended, non-routine problems that, instead of stepping the students through, ask them to choose their own methods for solving and justify their answers and reasoning.

Sample answers

1. 21.6 cm by 27.9 cm, 21.6 cm by 26.1 cm, and 27.9 cm by 26.1 cm

2a. 13 storage containers; The volume of the cooking pot is $\pi \cdot 6^2 \cdot 13$, or 468π in.^{3}. The volume of each storage container is $\pi \cdot 3^2 \cdot 4$, or 36π in.^{3}. The number of containers needed is $(468\pi) \div (36\pi)$.

b. 7.5 servings; One storage container holds 36π in.^{3}, so divide: $36\pi \div 15$.

3. Scoring Guide:

Task	Possible points
a	1 point for correctly finding the radius to be 3.5 cm, and 1 point for a correct explanation, for example: The length of the box, 14 cm, is twice the diameter of one shaker.
b	1 point for correctly finding the volume of shredded paper to be 210.3 cm^3, and 3 points for showing work that involves calculating the volume of one shaker and then subtracting twice that amount from the volume of the box

Total possible points: 6

Name _____ Class _____ Date _____

CHAPTER 11

Performance Tasks

COMMON CORE
CC-9-12.G.GMD.3
CC-9-12.G.GMD.4
CC-9-12.G.MG.1
CC-9-12.G.MG.3

★ **1.** Rectangular sheets of paper are in a sealed box that is 21.6 centimeters by 27.9 centimeters by 26.1 centimeters. What are the three largest possible sizes for the paper? Assume that all of the sheets are the same size and that the box is full.

★ **2.** A caterer is making soup in a cylindrical pot that has a 12-inch diameter and can be filled to a depth of 13 inches. The caterer has cylindrical storage containers for the soup that have 6-inch diameters and can be filled to a depth of 4 inches.

   a. How many storage containers does the caterer need for a full pot of soup? Explain.

   b. One serving of soup is about 15 cubic inches. To the nearest tenth of a serving, about how many servings of soup does one storage container hold? How do you know?

★ **3.** Two congruent, cylindrical salt-and-pepper shakers fit snugly beside one another inside a rectangular prism box, as shown at right. The box is 7 centimeters wide, 14 centimeters long, and 10 centimeters high, and the shakers are upright. The shakers are the same height as the box.

   a. Find the radius of one shaker. Justify your answer.

   b. After the shakers are put into the box, the remaining empty space is filled with shredded paper. What volume of shredded paper will be included in the box? Round your answer to the nearest cubic centimeter and show your work.

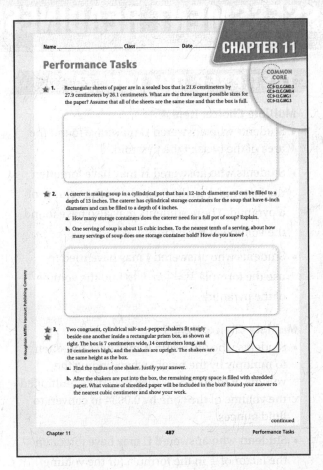

continued

★★ **4.** A carpenter has a wooden cone with a slant height of 16 inches and a base diameter of 12 inches. The vertex of the cone is directly above the center of its base. The carpenter measures halfway down the slant height and makes a cut parallel to the base. The carpenter now has a truncated cone and a cone half the height of the original.

   a. The carpenter expected the two parts to weigh about the same, but they don't. Which is heavier? Explain your reasoning.

   b. Find the ratio of the weight of the small cone to that of the truncated cone. Do not round any quantities until you get to your final answer. Show your work.

---

4. Scoring Guide:

Task	Possible points
a	1 point for correctly stating that the truncated cone is heavier, and 2 points for an appropriate explanation, for example: The volume of the small cone is about 69.9 in.^{3}, and the volume of the truncated cone is $559.2 - 69.9 = 489.1$ in.^{3}. Assuming that the wood has the same density throughout, the truncated cone will be heavier because it has more volume.
b	3 points for correctly stating the ratio as $1 : 7$ and 2 points for showing correct work: The vertical cross section of the full cone is an isosceles triangle, so the height of the cone is the third side of a right triangle with a hypotenuse of 16 in. and one leg, which is the radius, of 6 in. By the Pythagorean Theorem, the height is $\sqrt{220}$. The volume of the full cone is $\frac{1}{3}\pi \cdot 6^2 \cdot \sqrt{220} = 12\pi\sqrt{220}$. The radius of the small cone is 3 and its height is $\frac{\sqrt{220}}{2}$, so the volume of the small cone is $\frac{1}{3}\pi \cdot 3^2 \cdot \frac{\sqrt{220}}{2} = 1.5\pi\sqrt{220}$. The volume of the truncated cone is the volume of the full cone minus the volume of the small cone: $12\pi\sqrt{220} - 1.5\pi\sqrt{220} = 10.5\pi\sqrt{220}$. The ratio is $\frac{1.5\pi\sqrt{220}}{10.5\pi\sqrt{220}} = \frac{1}{7}$.

Total possible points: 6

COMMON CORE CORRELATION

Standard	Items
CC.9-12.G.GMD.1	7
CC.9-12.G.GMD.2(+)	9
CC.9-12.G.GMD.3*	3, 4, 5, 6, 8
CC.9-12.G.GMD.4	1, 2
CC.9-12.G.MG.1*	3
CC.9-12.G.MG.2*	3, 8
CC.9-12.G.MG.3*	6

TEST PREP DOCTOR ⊕

Multiple Choice: Item 4
- Students who answered **G** may have found the area of the base of the pyramid.
- Students who answered **H** may have forgotten the factor of $\frac{1}{3}$ in the formula for the volume of a pyramid. These students may also have found the volume of the cube.
- Students who answered **J** may have tried to use the formula $V = \frac{1}{3}\pi r^2 h$ to find the volume of the pyramid.

Multiple Choice: Item 5
- Students who answered **A** may have forgotten to multiply by the height when finding the volume of the cone, or they may have multiplied the volume of the cone by 0.0034 to convert to fluid ounces.
- Students who answered **C** may have forgotten the factor of $\frac{1}{3}$ in the formula for the volume of a cone.
- Students who answered **D** may have used 8 cm as the radius of the cone rather than 4 cm.

Constructed Response: Item 8
- Students who answered 10,595 BTU may have used an incorrect formula for the volume of a sphere ($V = \frac{4}{3}\pi r^2$ rather than $V = \frac{4}{3}\pi r^3$).
- Students who answered 4347 BTU may have forgotten the factor of $\frac{4}{3}$ in the formula for the volume of a sphere.
- Students who answered 67,405,417 BTU may have multiplied the volume of the sphere by 468,766 BTU rather than divided 468,766 BTU by the volume of the sphere.

CHAPTER 11 COMMON CORE ASSESSMENT READINESS

Name _____ Class _____ Date _____

MULTIPLE CHOICE

1. The figure shows a rectangular prism that is intersected by a plane parallel to a face of the prism. Which is the most precise description of the cross section?

A. parallelogram C. trapezoid
B. rectangle D. triangle

2. In the figure, $\overline{BA} \cong \overline{BC}$. You rotate $\angle ABC$ around a line that bisects the angle. What figure is generated by this rotation in three-dimensional space?

F. cone H. pyramid
G. cylinder J. sphere

3. A wood log is approximately cylindrical with the dimensions shown below. The log weighs 206.8 pounds. What is the density of the wood, to the nearest whole number?

1.5 ft
4.5 ft

A. 7 lb/ft³ C. 20 lb/ft³
B. 8 lb/ft³ **D.** 26 lb/ft³

4. A wire frame in the shape of the cube is used to support a pyramid-shaped basket, as shown. The vertex of the pyramid lies in the same plane as a face of the cube. To the nearest tenth, what is the volume of the pyramid-shaped basket?

1.3 ft

F. 0.7 ft³ H. 2.2 ft³
G. 1.7 ft³ J. 2.3 ft³

5. A food manufacturer sells yogurt in cone-shaped cups with the dimensions shown. To the nearest tenth, how many fluid ounces of yogurt does the cup hold? (*Hint:* 1 cm³ ≈ 0.034 fl oz)

8 cm
10 cm

A. 0.6 fl oz C. 17.1 fl oz
B. 5.7 fl oz D. 22.8 fl oz

6. You want to design a cylindrical container for oatmeal that has a volume of 90 in.³ You also want the height of the container to be 3.5 times the radius. To the nearest tenth, what should the radius of the container be?

F. 2.0 in. H. 3.0 in.
G. 2.9 in. J. 3.1 in.

© Houghton Mifflin Harcourt Publishing Company

CONSTRUCTED RESPONSE

7. In order to develop and justify the formula for the volume of a cone, you begin with a given cone that has radius r and height h. You consider pyramids with regular polygonal bases that are inscribed in the cone.

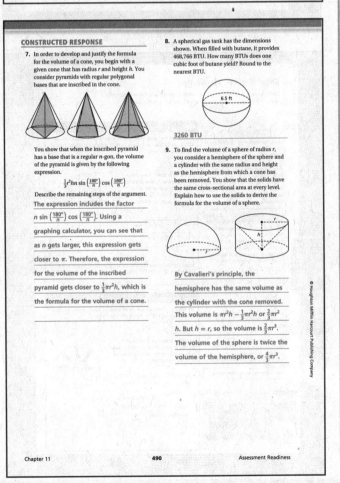

You show that when the inscribed pyramid has a base that is a regular n-gon, the volume of the pyramid is given by the following expression.

$$\frac{1}{3}r^2 hn \sin\left(\frac{180°}{n}\right)\cos\left(\frac{180°}{n}\right)$$

Describe the remaining steps of the argument.

The expression includes the factor

$n \sin\left(\frac{180°}{n}\right)\cos\left(\frac{180°}{n}\right)$. Using a

graphing calculator, you can see that

as n gets larger, this expression gets

closer to π. Therefore, the expression

for the volume of the inscribed

pyramid gets closer to $\frac{1}{3}\pi r^2 h$, which is

the formula for the volume of a cone.

8. A spherical gas tank has the dimensions shown. When filled with butane, it provides 468,766 BTU. How many BTUs does one cubic foot of butane yield? Round to the nearest BTU.

6.5 ft

3260 BTU

9. To find the volume of a sphere of radius r, you consider a hemisphere of the sphere and a cylinder with the same radius and height as the hemisphere from which a cone has been removed. You show that the solids have the same cross-sectional area at every level. Explain how to use the solids to derive the formula for the volume of a sphere.

By Cavalieri's principle, the

hemisphere has the same volume as

the cylinder with the cone removed.

This volume is $\pi r^2 h - \frac{1}{3}\pi r^2 h$ or $\frac{2}{3}\pi r^2$

h. But $h = r$, so the volume is $\frac{2}{3}\pi r^3$.

The volume of the sphere is twice the

volume of the hemisphere, or $\frac{4}{3}\pi r^3$.

© Houghton Mifflin Harcourt Publishing Company

CHAPTER 12

Circles

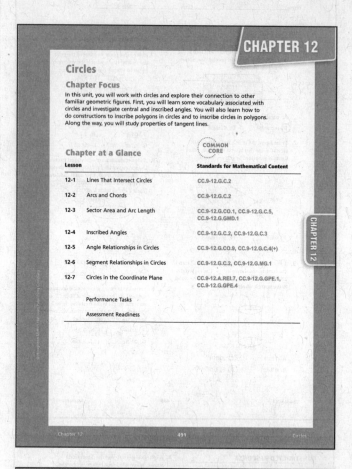

Circles

Chapter Focus

In this unit, you will work with circles and explore their connection to other familiar geometric figures. First, you will learn some vocabulary associated with circles and investigate central and inscribed angles. You will also learn how to do constructions to inscribe polygons in circles and to inscribe circles in polygons. Along the way, you will study properties of tangent lines.

Chapter at a Glance

Lesson		COMMON CORE Standards for Mathematical Content
12-1	Lines That Intersect Circles	CC.9-12.G.C.2
12-2	Arcs and Chords	CC.9-12.G.C.2
12-3	Sector Area and Arc Length	CC.9-12.G.CO.1, CC.9-12.G.C.5, CC.9-12.G.GMD.1
12-4	Inscribed Angles	CC.9-12.G.C.2, CC.9-12.G.C.3
12-5	Angle Relationships in Circles	CC.9-12.G.CO.9, CC.9-12.G.C.4(+)
12-6	Segment Relationships in Circles	CC.9-12.G.C.2, CC.9-12.G.MG.1
12-7	Circles in the Coordinate Plane	CC.9-12.A.REI.7, CC.9-12.G.GPE.1, CC.9-12.G.GPE.4
	Performance Tasks	
	Assessment Readiness	

Chapter 12   491   Circles

COMMON CORE PROFESSIONAL DEVELOPMENT CC.9-12.G.C.2

Students learned to identify tangents, secants, chords, radii, diameters, circumference, and arcs in the middle grades. In this chapter, students learn properties and measures of these geometric figures in relation to circles, and apply relationships among them to solving problems. Geometry software is a powerful dynamic tool that allows students to investigate and quantify geometric phenomena in order to make conjectures.

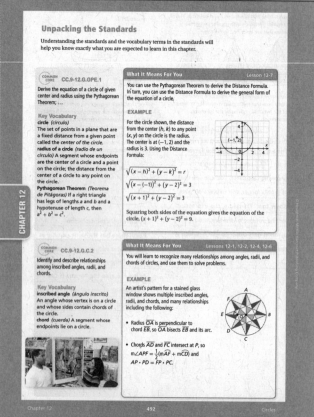

Unpacking the Standards

Understanding the standards and the vocabulary terms in the standards will help you know exactly what you are expected to learn in this chapter.

COMMON CORE CC.9-12.G.GPE.1

Derive the equation of a circle of given center and radius using the Pythagorean Theorem; ...

Key Vocabulary
circle (*círculo*)
The set of points in a plane that are a fixed distance from a given point called the *center of the circle*.
radius of a circle (*radio de un círculo*) A segment whose endpoints are the center of a circle and a point on the circle; the distance from the center of a circle to any point on the circle.
Pythagorean Theorem (*Teorema de Pitágoras*) If a right triangle has legs of lengths a and b and a hypotenuse of length c, then $a^2 + b^2 = c^2$.

What It Means For You   Lesson 12-7

You can use the Pythagorean Theorem to derive the Distance Formula. In turn, you can use the Distance Formula to derive the general form of the equation of a circle.

EXAMPLE

For the circle shown, the distance from the center (h, k) to any point (x, y) on the circle is the radius. The center is at $(-1, 2)$ and the radius is 3. Using the Distance Formula:

$$\sqrt{(x-h)^2 + (y-k)^2} = r$$
$$\sqrt{(x-(-1))^2 + (y-2)^2} = 3$$
$$\sqrt{(x+1)^2 + (y-2)^2} = 3$$

Squaring both sides of the equation gives the equation of the circle, $(x+1)^2 + (y-2)^2 = 9$.

COMMON CORE CC.9-12.G.C.2

Identify and describe relationships among inscribed angles, radii, and chords.

Key Vocabulary
inscribed angle (*ángulo inscrito*) An angle whose vertex is on a circle and whose sides contain chords of the circle.
chord (*cuerda*) A segment whose endpoints lie on a circle.

What It Means For You   Lessons 12-1, 12-2, 12-4, 12-6

You will learn to recognize many relationships among angles, radii, and chords of circles, and use them to solve problems.

EXAMPLE

An artist's pattern for a stained glass window shows multiple inscribed angles, radii, and chords, and many relationships including the following:

- Radius $\overline{OA}$ is perpendicular to chord $\overline{EB}$, so $\overline{OA}$ bisects $\overline{EB}$ and its arc.

- Chords $\overline{AD}$ and $\overline{FC}$ intersect at P, so $m\angle APF = \frac{1}{2}(m\widehat{AF} + m\widehat{CD})$ and $AP \cdot PD = FP \cdot PC$.

Chapter 12   492   Circles

Students saw many applications of proportions in every course since the middle grades. In this course, students review the concept of similarity transformations and formalize them as a basis for the definition of similar figures. In this chapter, students again see the application of similarity and proportion with arc measurement. Students derive a formula for the length of an arc based on the proportional relationship in a given circle between the measure of a central angle and the length of the arc that it intercepts. The constant of proportionality is the radian measure of the angle.

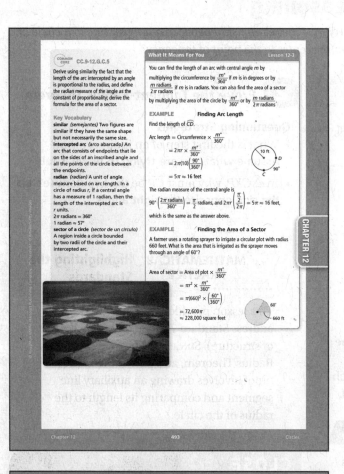

COMMON CORE CC.9-12.G.C.5

Derive using similarity the fact that the length of the arc intercepted by an angle is proportional to the radius, and define the radian measure of the angle as the constant of proportionality; derive the formula for the area of a sector.

Key Vocabulary

similar *(semejantes)* Two figures are similar if they have the same shape but not necessarily the same size.

intercepted arc *(arco abarcado)* An arc that consists of endpoints that lie on the sides of an inscribed angle and all the points of the circle between the endpoints.

radian *(radian)* A unit of angle measure based on arc length. In a circle of radius r, if a central angle has a measure of 1 radian, then the length of the intercepted arc is r units.

2π radians = 360°

1 radian ≈ 57°

sector of a circle *(sector de un círculo)* A region inside a circle bounded by two radii of the circle and their intercepted arc.

What It Means For You   Lesson 12-3

You can find the length of an arc with central angle m by multiplying the circumference by $\frac{m°}{360°}$ if m is in degrees or by $\frac{m \text{ radians}}{2\pi \text{ radians}}$ if m is in radians. You can also find the area of a sector by multiplying the area of the circle by $\frac{m°}{360°}$ or by $\frac{m \text{ radians}}{2\pi \text{ radians}}$.

EXAMPLE   **Finding Arc Length**

Find the length of $\overset{\frown}{CD}$.

Arc length = Circumference × $\frac{m°}{360°}$

$= 2\pi \times \frac{m°}{360°}$

$= 2\pi(10)\left(\frac{90°}{360°}\right)$

$= 5\pi ≈ 16$ feet

The radian measure of the central angle is

$90°\left(\frac{2\pi \text{ radians}}{360°}\right) = \frac{\pi}{2}$ radians, and $2\pi r\left(\frac{\frac{\pi}{2}}{2\pi}\right) = 5\pi ≈ 16$ feet, which is the same as the answer above.

EXAMPLE   **Finding the Area of a Sector**

A farmer uses a rotating sprayer to irrigate a circular plot with radius 660 feet. What is the area that is irrigated as the sprayer moves through an angle of 60°?

Area of sector = Area of plot × $\frac{m°}{360°}$

$= \pi r^2 \times \frac{m°}{360°}$

$= \pi(660)^2 \times \left(\frac{60°}{360°}\right)$

$= 72,600\pi$

$≈ 228,000$ square feet

Chapter 12   493   Circles

Key Vocabulary

arc *(arco)* An unbroken part of a circle consisting of two points on the circle, called the endpoints, and all the points on the circle between them.

arc length *(longitud de arco)* The distance along an arc measured in linear units.

central angle of a circle *(ángulo central de un círculo)* An angle whose vertex is the center of a circle.

chord *(cuerda)* A segment whose endpoints lie on a circle.

circle *(círculo)* The set of points in a plane that are a fixed distance from a given point called the center of the circle.

concentric circles *(círculos concéntricos)* Coplanar circles with the same center.

inscribed angle *(ángulo inscrito)* An angle whose vertex is on a circle and whose sides contain chords of the circle.

intercepted arc *(arco abarcado)* An arc that consists of endpoints that lie on the sides of an inscribed angle and all the points of the circle between the endpoints.

major arc *(arco mayor)* An arc of a circle whose points are on or in the exterior of a central angle.

minor arc *(arco menor)* An arc of a circle whose points are on or in the interior of a central angle.

point of tangency *(punto de tangencia)* The point of intersection of a circle or sphere with a tangent line or plane.

Pythagorean Theorem *(Teorema de Pitágoras)* If a right triangle has legs of lengths a and b and a hypotenuse of length c, then $a^2 + b^2 = c^2$.

radian *(radian)* A unit of angle measure based on arc length. In a circle of radius r, if a central angle has a measure of 1 radian, then the length of the intercepted arc is r units.

2π radians = 360°   1 radian ≈ 57°

radius of a circle *(radio de un círculo)* A segment whose endpoints are the center of a circle and a point on the circle; the distance from the center of a circle to any point on the circle.

secant of a circle *(secante de un círculo)* A line that intersects a circle at two points.

sector of a circle *(sector de un círculo)* A region inside a circle bounded by two radii of the circle and their intercepted arc.

semicircle *(semicírculo)* An arc of a circle whose endpoints lie on a diameter

similar *(semejantes)* Two figures are similar if they have the same shape but not necessarily the same size.

tangent of a circle *(tangente de un círculo)* A line that is in the same plane as a circle and intersects the circle at exactly one point.

Chapter 12   494   Circles

Lines That Intersect Circles
Focus on Reasoning

Essential question: *What is the relationship between a tangent line to a circle and the radius drawn from the center to the point of tangency?*

COMMON CORE Standards for Mathematical Content

CC.9-12.G.C.2 Identify and describe relationships among inscribed angles, radii, and chords.

Vocabulary
tangent
point of tangency
circumscribed angle

Prerequisites
Central angles and inscribed angles

Math Background
In this Focus on Reasoning lesson, students investigate the relationship between a tangent line to a circle and the radius to the point of tangency. As in all Focus on Reasoning lessons, the approach is inductive at first, followed by a deductive proof.

INTRODUCE

Define *tangent*. Tell students that the term comes from a Latin word, *tangere*, which means "to touch." Then, draw sketches to help students see that for every point on a circle, there is one and only one tangent to the circle at that point.

TEACH

1 Investigate tangents and radii.

Materials: compass, straightedge, protractor
Questioning Strategies
• What must be true about the line you draw through point *P* for it to be a tangent? The line should intersect the circle at no other point.
• Suppose $\overline{AB}$ is a diameter and you draw tangents through points *A* and *B*. What do you think would be true about the two tangent lines? The tangent lines would be parallel.

2 Prove the Tangent-Radius Theorem.

Questioning Strategies
• What is the first step of an indirect proof? Assume what you are trying to prove is false.
• In $\triangle CXP$, why must $\overline{CP}$ be the hypotenuse? It is the side opposite the right angle.

MATHEMATICAL PRACTICE Highlighting the Standards

This lesson provides an opportunity to address Standard 7 (Look for and make use of structure). Students prove the Tangent-Radius Theorem, and part of the indirect proof involves drawing an auxiliary line segment and comparing its length to the radius of the circle.

CLOSE

Essential Question
What is the relationship between a tangent line to a circle and the radius drawn from the center to the point of tangency?
If a line is tangent to a circle, then it is perpendicular to the radius drawn to the point of tangency.

Summarize
Have students summarize the properties of a line tangent to a circle, including the theorems they have just learned.

Name _____ Class _____ Date _____

12-1

Lines That Intersect Circles
Focus on Reasoning

COMMON CORE

CC.9-12.G.C.2

Essential question: *What is the relationship between a tangent line to a circle and the radius drawn from the center to the point of tangency?*

A **tangent** is a line in the same plane as a circle that intersects the circle in exactly one point. The point where a tangent and a circle intersect is the **point of tangency**. In the figure, lines *m* is a tangent to circle *C*, and point *P* is the point of tangency.

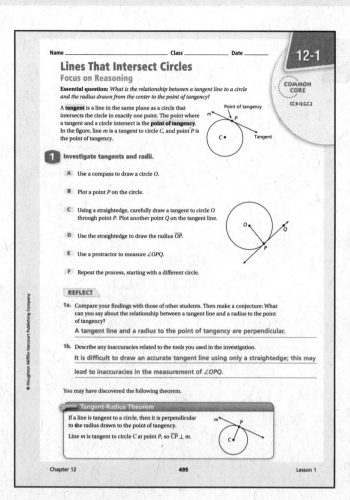

1 **Investigate tangents and radii.**

A   Use a compass to draw a circle *O*.

B   Plot a point *P* on the circle.

C   Using a straightedge, carefully draw a tangent to circle *O* through point *P*. Plot another point *Q* on the tangent line.

D   Use the straightedge to draw the radius $\overline{OP}$.

E   Use a protractor to measure ∠*OPQ*.

F   Repeat the process, starting with a different circle.

> **REFLECT**

1a. Compare your findings with those of other students. Then make a conjecture: What can you say about the relationship between a tangent line and a radius to the point of tangency?

A tangent line and a radius to the point of tangency are perpendicular.

1b. Describe any inaccuracies related to the tools you used in the investigation.

It is difficult to draw an accurate tangent line using only a straightedge; this may

lead to inaccuracies in the measurement of ∠OPQ.

You may have discovered the following theorem.

> **Tangent-Radius Theorem**
> If a line is tangent to a circle, then it is perpendicular to the radius drawn to the point of tangency.
> Line *m* is tangent to circle *C* at point *P*, so $\overline{CP} \perp m$.

---

2 **Prove the Tangent-Radius Theorem.**

Given: Line *m* is tangent to circle *C* at point *P*.

Prove: $\overline{CP} \perp m$

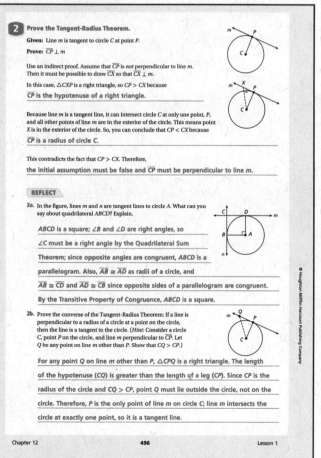

Use an indirect proof. Assume that $\overline{CP}$ is *not* perpendicular to line *m*. Then it must be possible to draw $\overline{CX}$ so that $\overline{CX} \perp m$.

In this case, △*CXP* is a right triangle, so *CP* > *CX* because

$\overline{CP}$ is the hypotenuse of a right triangle.

Because line *m* is a tangent line, it can intersect circle *C* at only one point, *P*, and all other points of line *m* are in the exterior of the circle. This means point *X* is in the exterior of the circle. So, you can conclude that *CP* < *CX* because

$\overline{CP}$ is a radius of circle *C*.

This contradicts the fact that *CP* > *CX*. Therefore,

the initial assumption must be false and $\overline{CP}$ must be perpendicular to line *m*.

> **REFLECT**

2a. In the figure, lines *m* and *n* are tangent lines to circle *A*. What can you say about quadrilateral *ABCD*? Explain.

ABCD is a square; ∠B and ∠D are right angles, so

∠C must be a right angle by the Quadrilateral Sum

Theorem; since opposite angles are congruent, ABCD is a

parallelogram. Also, $\overline{AB} \cong \overline{AD}$ as radii of a circle, and

$\overline{AB} \cong \overline{CD}$ and $\overline{AD} \cong \overline{CB}$ since opposite sides of a parallelogram are congruent.

By the Transitive Property of Congruence, ABCD is a square.

2b. Prove the converse of the Tangent-Radius Theorem: If a line is perpendicular to a radius of a circle at a point on the circle, then the line is a tangent to the circle. (*Hint:* Consider a circle *C*, point *P* on the circle, and line *m* perpendicular to $\overline{CP}$. Let *Q* be any point on line *m* other than *P*. Show that *CQ* > *CP*.)

For any point Q on line m other than P, △CPQ is a right triangle. The length

of the hypotenuse (CQ) is greater than the length of a leg (CP). Since CP is the

radius of the circle and CQ > CP, point Q must lie outside the circle, not on the

circle. Therefore, P is the only point of line m on circle C; line m intersects the

circle at exactly one point, so it is a tangent line.

ADDITIONAL PRACTICE AND PROBLEM SOLVING

Assign these pages to help your students practice and apply important lesson concepts. For additional exercises, see the Student Edition.

Answers

Additional Practice

1. 90°; OTBU is a square.

2. It is a square.

3. They are squares.

4. It is a square. Possible answer: Because quadrilaterals OTBU, OUCV, OVDW, and ATOW are all squares, all their angles are congruent right angles. So, ABCD has four right angles. Also, OTBU, OUCV, OVDW, and ATOW are congruent squares because the side length of each is the radius of circle O. Because each side length of ABCD is the sum of two side lengths of congruent squares, the side lengths of ABCD are congruent.

5. Tangent-radius theorem

Problem Solving

1. A line segment tangent to a circle is perpendicular to a radius of the circle, so it is also perpendicular to a diameter. Each diameter in the window therefore has two tangent line segments perpendicular to it.

2. Agree; The diameter is perpendicular to the tangent segments drawn through its endpoints. So, the same-side interior angles formed by the tangent segments and the line containing the diameter measure 90° and are supplementary. When same-side interior angles formed by two lines intersected by a transversal are supplementary, the lines (and segments that are part of those lines) must be parallel.

3. B

4. H

Name _____ Class _____ Date _____

12-1

Additional Practice

In the diagram, $\overline{AB}$, $\overline{BC}$, $\overline{CD}$, and $\overline{DA}$ are tangent to circle O at their midpoints. Use the diagram for Exercises 1–4. For some exercises, you will need to draw on the diagram.

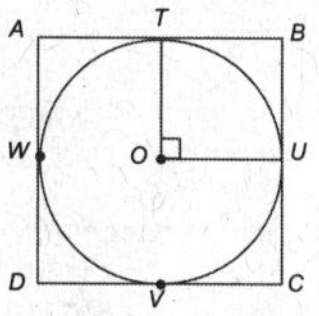

1. What is the measure of $\angle B$? What can you conclude about quadrilateral OTBU?

   _____

   _____

2. Use a straightedge to draw a radius to point V. What can you conclude about quadrilateral OUCV?

   _____

3. Use a straightedge to draw a radius to a point W. What can you conclude about quadrilaterals WOVD and ATOW?

   _____

4. Based on your answers to Exercises 1–3, what can you conclude about quadrilateral ABCD? Justify your answer.

   _____

   _____

   _____

   _____

   _____

   _____

5. Suppose a line is tangent to a circle. What theorem can you use to prove that the line is perpendicular to a diameter drawn to the point of tangency?

   _____

   _____

Problem Solving

1. In the stained glass window shown, six segments are tangent to a circle. Three diameters divide the circle into six panes. Explain how you know that any one of the diameters shown is perpendicular to two of the tangent segments shown.

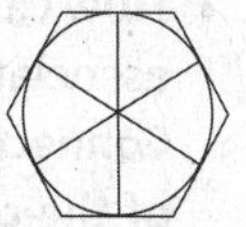

   _____

   _____

   _____

2. Annie constructed a circle and its diameter. She drew a line tangent to the circle at one endpoint of the diameter. Then she drew a line tangent to the circle at the other endpoint of the diameter She claims the two tangent lines are parallel. Do you agree? Why or why not?

   _____

   _____

   _____

Choose the best answer.

3. Maria drew a design for a company logo. Her design is based on the diagram shown at the right. In the diagram, $\overline{KM}$ is tangent to circle J and to circle L at point N. Point N is the midpoint of $\overline{KM}$ and $\overline{JL}$. If JL = 4 cm, what is the area of quadrilateral JKLM?

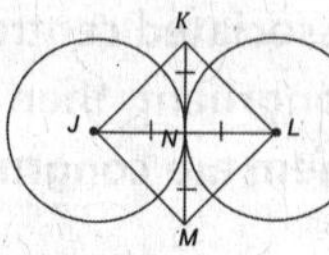

   A 2 cm^2 C 4 cm^2

   B 8 cm^2 D 16 cm^2

4. Paul also drew a design for a company logo. His design is based on the diagram shown at the right. In the diagram, $\overline{BD}$ is tangent to a half circle with radius AD at point D. If AD = BD = x centimeters, and $\overline{DC}$ is three times as long as $\overline{AD}$, which expression represents the area of $\triangle ABC$?

   F 0.5x^2 cm^2 H 2x^2 cm^2

   G 1.5x^2 cm^2 J 3x^2 cm^2

Arcs and Chords
Going Deeper

Essential question: *How are arcs and chords of circles associated with central angles?*

COMMON CORE **Standards for Mathematical Content**

CC.9-12.G.C.2 Identify and describe relationships among inscribed angles, radii, and chords.

Vocabulary

chord
central angle
inscribed angle
arc

minor arc
major arc
semicircle

Prerequisites

Basic terms and constructions

Math Background

This lesson introduces key vocabulary relating to circles and the idea of the measure of an arc. Note that the measure of an arc is connected to the measure of its central angle. The connection between central angles and arcs may be seen as the foundation for much of students' future work with circles.

INTRODUCE

Ask a volunteer to remind the class of the definition of a circle. Then, have students brainstorm facts about circles that they already know. Students might mention the relationship between the diameter of a circle and the radius.

TEACH

1   ENGAGE

Questioning Strategies

- How can you tell whether an arc is a minor arc or a major arc? A minor arc is less than a semicircle; a major arc is more than a semicircle.
- What does the prefix *semi-* mean in the word *semicircle*? half

⚠ MATHEMATICAL PRACTICE   Highlighting the Standards

You can address Standard 7 (Look for and make use of structure) as you discuss the Arc Addition Postulate. The standard states that "Mathematically proficient students look closely to discern a pattern or structure." Point out that there are underlying patterns and structures in the properties and postulates that they study in this course. For example, students may note the similarities among the Segment Addition Postulate, the Angle Addition Postulate, and the Arc Addition Postulate.

2   EXPLORE

Materials: compass, straightedge, protractor

Questioning Strategies

- How can you measure the central angle associated with a chord?
  Connect the endpoints of the chord to the center of the circle and use a protractor to measure the angle formed by those two segments.

CLOSE

Essential Question

How are arcs and chords of circles associated with central angles?
The measure of an arc is the measure of its associated central angle. If two chords are congruent, then the central angles associated with them are congruent.

Summarize

Have students write a journal entry in which they summarize the main vocabulary and concepts from this lesson.

Name_____ Class_____ Date_____

12-2

Video Tutor

Arcs and Chords
Going Deeper

Essential question: *How are arcs and chords of circles associated with central angles?*

CC.9-12.G.C.2

1 ENGAGE · **Introducing Angles and Arcs**

In order to begin working with circles, it is helpful to introduce some vocabulary.

A **chord** is a segment whose endpoints lie on a circle. A **central angle** is an angle whose vertex is the center of a circle. An **inscribed angle** is an angle whose vertex lies on a circle and whose sides contain chords of the circle.

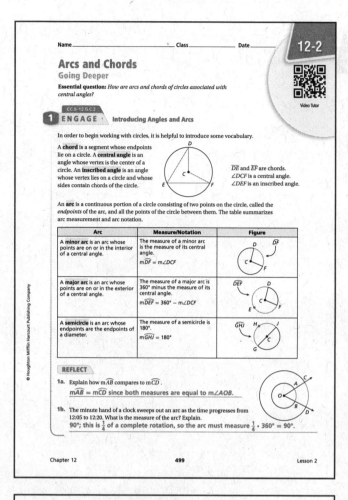

$\overline{DE}$ and $\overline{EF}$ are chords.
$\angle DCF$ is a central angle.
$\angle DEF$ is an inscribed angle.

An **arc** is a continuous portion of a circle consisting of two points on the circle, called the *endpoints* of the arc, and all the points of the circle between them. The table summarizes arc measurement and arc notation.

Arc	Measure/Notation	Figure
A **minor arc** is an arc whose points are on or in the interior of a central angle.	The measure of a minor arc is the measure of its central angle. $m\widehat{DF} = m\angle DCF$	
A **major arc** is an arc whose points are on or in the exterior of a central angle.	The measure of a major arc is 360° minus the measure of its central angle. $m\widehat{DEF} = 360° - m\angle DCF$	
A **semicircle** is an arc whose endpoints are the endpoints of a diameter.	The measure of a semicircle is 180°. $m\widehat{GHJ} = 180°$	

REFLECT

1a. Explain how $m\widehat{AB}$ compares to $m\widehat{CD}$.

$m\widehat{AB} = m\widehat{CD}$ since both measures are equal to $m\angle AOB$.

1b. The minute hand of a clock sweeps out an arc as the time progresses from 12:05 to 12:20. What is the measure of the arc? Explain.

90°; this is $\frac{1}{4}$ of a complete rotation, so the arc must measure $\frac{1}{4} \cdot 360° = 90°$.

Chapter 12   499   Lesson 2

Two arcs of a circle are *adjacent arcs* if they share an endpoint. The following postulate states that you can add the measures of adjacent arcs.

> **Arc Addition Postulate**
>
> The measure of an arc formed by two adjacent arcs is the sum of the measures of the two arcs.
>
> $m\widehat{ABC} = m\widehat{AB} + m\widehat{BC}$

CC.9-12.G.C.2

2 EXPLORE · **Investigating Congruent Chords in a Circle**

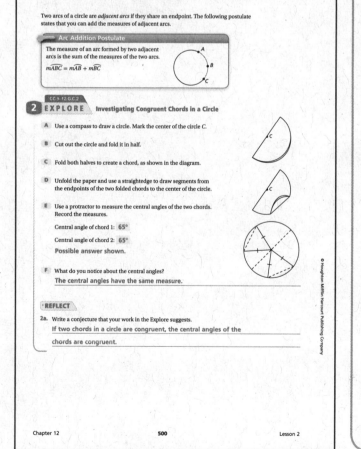

A Use a compass to draw a circle. Mark the center of the circle *C*.

B Cut out the circle and fold it in half.

C Fold both halves to create a chord, as shown in the diagram.

D Unfold the paper and use a straightedge to draw segments from the endpoints of the two folded chords to the center of the circle.

E Use a protractor to measure the central angles of the two chords. Record the measures.

Central angle of chord 1: **65°**

Central angle of chord 2: **65°**

Possible answer shown.

F What do you notice about the central angles?

The central angles have the same measure.

REFLECT

2a. Write a conjecture that your work in the Explore suggests.

If two chords in a circle are congruent, the central angles of the chords are congruent.

Chapter 12   500   Lesson 2

ADDITIONAL PRACTICE AND PROBLEM SOLVING

Assign these pages to help your students practice and apply important lesson concepts. For additional exercises, see the Student Edition.

Answers

Additional Practice

1. 45°	**2.** 30°
3. 105°	**4.** 45°
5. 45°	**6.** 135°
7. 125°; 227°	**8.** 67°; 203°
9. 102°	**10.** 49 cm

Problem Solving

1. 180°	**2.** 72°
3. 154.8°	**4.** 115.2°
5. C	**6.** H
7. D	

12-2

Additional Practice

Use the figure to find each of the following measurements. A is the center of the circle.

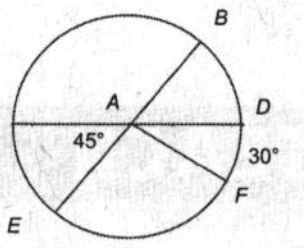

1. m$\widehat{CE}$ _____

2. m∠DAF _____

3. m$\widehat{EF}$ _____

4. m$\widehat{BD}$ _____

5. m∠BAD _____

6. m$\widehat{EFD}$ _____

Find each measure.

7.

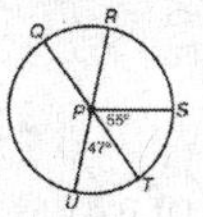

m$\widehat{QS}$ _____

m$\widehat{RQT}$ _____

8.

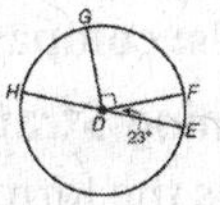

m$\widehat{HG}$ _____

m$\widehat{FEH}$ _____

9.

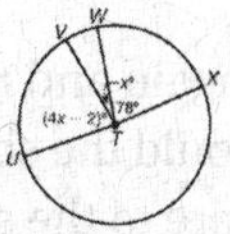

Find m∠UTW. _____

10.

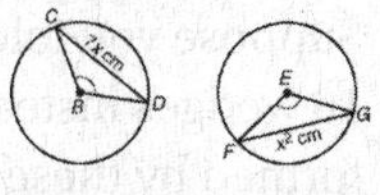

⊙L ≅ ⊙E, and ∠CBD ≅ ∠FEG.

Find FG. _____

Problem Solving

1. Circle D has center (–2, –7) and radius 7. What is the measure, in degrees, of the major arc that passes through points H(–2, 0), J(5, –7), and K(–9, –7)?

_____

2. A circle graph is composed of sectors with central angles that measure 3x°, 3x°, 4x°, and 5x°. What is the measure, in degrees, of the smallest minor arcs?

_____

Use the following information for Exercises 3 and 4.

The circle graph shows the results of a survey in which teens were asked what says the most about them at school. Find each of the following.

Teens Surveyed

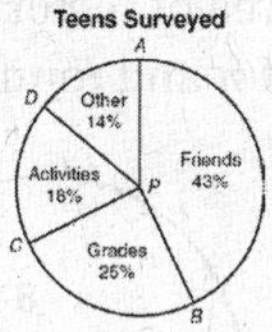

Other 14%
Friends 43%
Activities 18%
Grades 25%

3. m$\widehat{AB}$

_____

4. m∠APC

_____

Use the table for Exercises 5–7. Choose the best answer.

5. Students were asked to name their favorite cafeteria food. The results of the survey are shown in the table. In a circle graph showing these results, which is closest to the measure of the central angle for the section representing chicken tenders?

A 21°   C 83°
B 75°   D 270°

Favorite Lunch	Number of Students
Pizza	108
Chicken tenders	75
Taco salad	90
Other	54

6. Which is the closest measure of the arc for the sector in the circle graph representing taco salad?

F 59°   H 100°
G 90°   J 180°

7. If the sectors for pizza and chicken tenders are adjacent in the circle graph, which is the closest measure for the arc that spans both sectors?

A 100°   C 183°
B 166°   D 201°

Notes

Sector Area and Arc Length
Going Deeper

Essential question: *How do you find the area of a sector of a circle, and how do you calculate arc length in a circle?*

© Houghton Mifflin Harcourt Publishing Company

COMMON CORE Standards for Mathematical Content

CC.9-12.G.CO.1 Know ... the undefined notion of ... distance around a circular arc.

CC.9-12.G.C.5 Derive using similarity the fact that the length of the arc intercepted by an angle is proportional to the radius, and define the radian measure of the angle as the constant of proportionality; derive the formula for the area of a sector.

CC.9-12.G.GMD.1 Give an informal argument for the formula for the ... area of a circle, ...

Vocabulary

sector

arc length

radian measure

Prerequisites

Central angles and inscribed angles

Circumference

Math Background

In this lesson, students will find the area of a sector by considering the fraction of a full circle that is represented by a given circle. Then, students will use a similar process to find arc lengths by considering the fraction of a full circle that is represented by a given arc. Be sure to point out to students that proportional reasoning is used in both cases.

INTRODUCE

Explain to students that the problem of finding the area of a circle has interested mathematicians since ancient times. In fact, Euclid's *Elements* (circa 300 BCE) contains a statement that is equivalent to the formula $A = \pi r^2$. Tell students that there are many ways to derive the formula for the area of a circle and that they will use a method that incorporates some ideas that they may study more deeply in a future calculus course.

TEACH

1 EXPLORE

Materials: compass, scissors

Questioning Strategies

- What is the formula for the area of a parallelogram? **$A = bh$, where b is the base and h is the height.**

- Suppose you folded the circle again and made 16 wedges instead of 8. How would the shape formed by these wedges compare to the shape formed in the Explore? **The shape would be an even closer approximation to a parallelogram.**

2 EXAMPLE

Questioning Strategies

- How does the area of sector *AOB* compare to the area of the complete circle? **The area of the sector is one-third of the area of the circle.**

- What are appropriate units for the area of the sector? Why? **Square millimeters; the radius is given in millimeters and areas are always expressed in square units.**

EXTRA EXAMPLE

Find the area of sector *GOH*. Express your answer in terms of π and rounded to the nearest tenth.

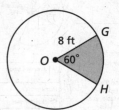

$\frac{32}{3}\pi$ ft^2; 33.5 ft^2

Name _____ Class _____ Date _____

12-3

Sector Area and Arc Length
Going Deeper

Essential question: *How do you find the area of a sector of a circle, and how do you calculate arc length in a circle?*

CC.9-12.G.GMD.1

Video Tutor

1 EXPLORE Developing a Formula for the Area of a Circle

A   Use a compass to draw a large circle on a sheet of paper. Cut out the circle.

B   Fold the circle in half. Then fold the resulting semicircle in half.
Then fold the resulting quarter-circle in half.

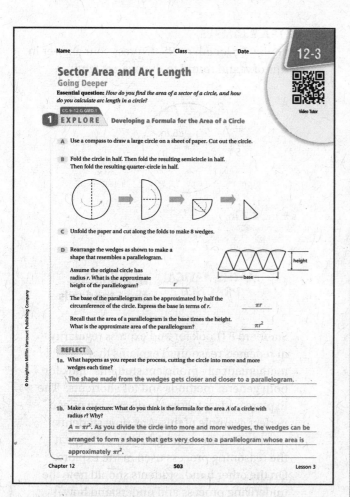

C   Unfold the paper and cut along the folds to make 8 wedges.

D   Rearrange the wedges as shown to make a
shape that resembles a parallelogram.

Assume the original circle has
radius *r*. What is the approximate
height of the parallelogram?   *r*

The base of the parallelogram can be approximated by half the
circumference of the circle. Express the base in terms of *r*. πr

Recall that the area of a parallelogram is the base times the height.
What is the approximate area of the parallelogram? πr^2

REFLECT

1a. What happens as you repeat the process, cutting the circle into more and more
wedges each time?

The shape made from the wedges gets closer and closer to a parallelogram.

1b. Make a conjecture: What do you think is the formula for the area *A* of a circle with
radius *r*? Why?

$A = \pi r^2$. As you divide the circle into more and more wedges, the wedges can be

arranged to form a shape that gets very close to a parallelogram whose area is

approximately πr^2.

Chapter 12   503   Lesson 3

Area of a Circle

The area *A* of a circle with radius *r* is given by $A = \pi r^2$.

A **sector** of a circle is a region bounded by two radii and their intercepted
arc. A sector is named by the endpoints of the arc and the center of the circle.
For example, the figure shows sector *POQ*.

In the same way that you used proportional reasoning to find the length
of an arc, you can use proportional reasoning to find the area of a sector.

CC.9-12.G.C.5

2 EXAMPLE Finding the Area of a Sector

Find the area of sector *AOB*. Express your answer in terms of π and rounded
to the nearest tenth.

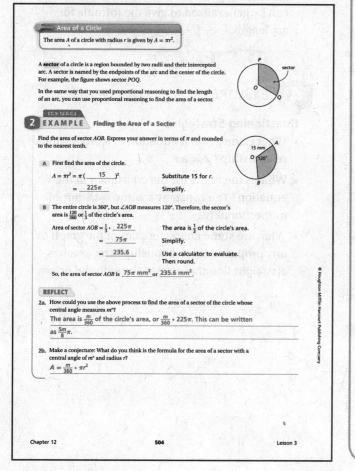

A   First find the area of the circle.

$A = \pi r^2 = \pi (\underline{\quad 15 \quad })^2$ Substitute 15 for *r*.

$= \underline{\quad 225\pi \quad }$ Simplify.

B   The entire circle is 360°, but ∠*AOB* measures 120°. Therefore, the sector's
area is $\frac{120}{360}$ or $\frac{1}{3}$ of the circle's area.

Area of sector $AOB = \frac{1}{3} \cdot \underline{\quad 225\pi \quad }$ The area is $\frac{1}{3}$ of the circle's area.

$= \underline{\quad 75\pi \quad }$ Simplify.

$= \underline{\quad 235.6 \quad }$ Use a calculator to evaluate.
Then round.

So, the area of sector *AOB* is $\underline{\ 75\pi\ }$ mm² or $\underline{\ 235.6\ }$ mm².

REFLECT

2a. How could you use the above process to find the area of a sector of the circle whose
central angle measures *m*°?

The area is $\frac{m}{360}$ of the circle's area, or $\frac{m}{360} \cdot 225\pi$. This can be written

as $\frac{5m}{8}\pi$.

2b. Make a conjecture: What do you think is the formula for the area of a sector with a
central angle of *m*° and radius *r*?

$A = \frac{m}{360} \cdot \pi r^2$

Chapter 12   504   Lesson 3

Differentiated Instruction

You may want to challenge students by having them derive the area formula for a circle by using a sequence of inscribed regular polygons. In this case, the area of an inscribed n-gon is given by the expression $n \cdot r \sin \left(\frac{180°}{n}\right) \cdot r \cos \left(\frac{180°}{n}\right)$. Students can use the table feature of their calculator to show that as n gets larger, the expression $n \sin \left(\frac{180°}{n}\right) \cdot \cos \left(\frac{180°}{n}\right) \cdot$ gets closer to π. Thus, the expression for the area gets closer to πr^2.

 MATHEMATICAL PRACTICE **Highlighting the Standards**

Standard 6 (Attend to precision) states that mathematically proficient students are "careful about specifying units of measure." In this lesson, students should check their answers to make sure areas are always expressed in terms of square units, such as square inches or square meters.

Avoid Common Errors

If students are getting answers that are different from those in the text, check that they are using the π key on their calculator and then rounding as the final step of the solution. Students who enter 3.14 as an approximation of π will often get different results from students who use the π key and then round.

3 EXAMPLE

Questioning Strategies

• What does the 60° mark mean next to the arc? It means the arc measures 60°; the central angle whose sides pass through A and B measures 60°.

• What units should you use for the arc length? Why? Centimeters; the radius is given in centimeters, so the circumference and arc length will also be measured in centimeters.

Find the arc length of $\overset{\frown}{RS}$. Express your answer in terms of π and round to the nearest tenth.

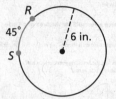

$\frac{3}{2}\pi$ in.; 4.7 in.

MATHEMATICAL PRACTICE **Highlighting the Standards**

Standard 8 (Look for and express regularity in repeated reasoning) explains that mathematically proficient students "look for both general methods and for shortcuts." The Explore and its follow-up discussion offer a perfect example of this. Any time students need to find an arc length, they can repeat the reasoning process used in the Explore. On the other hand, students should note the underlying process and understand how it can be generalized to give the formula for arc length.

4 EXPLORE

Questioning Strategies

• What is the general equation of a proportional relationship? $y = ax$

• What is the name for the constant a in the equation? The constant a is the constant of proportionality.

• What are some characteristics of the graph of any proportional relationship? The graph is a straight line that passes through the origin.

The proportional reasoning process you used in the example can be generalized. Given a sector with a central angle of $m°$ and radius r, the area of the entire circle is πr^2 and the area of the sector is $\frac{m}{360}$ times the circle's area. This gives the following formula.

Area of a Sector

The area A of a sector of a circle with a central angle of $m°$ and radius r is given by $A = \frac{m}{360} \cdot \pi r^2$.

Arc length is understood to be the distance along a circular arc measured in linear units (such as feet or centimeters). You can use proportional reasoning to find arc lengths.

CC.9-12.G.C.0.1

3 EXAMPLE Finding Arc Length

Find the arc length of $\overset{\frown}{AB}$. Express your answer in terms of π and rounded to the nearest tenth.

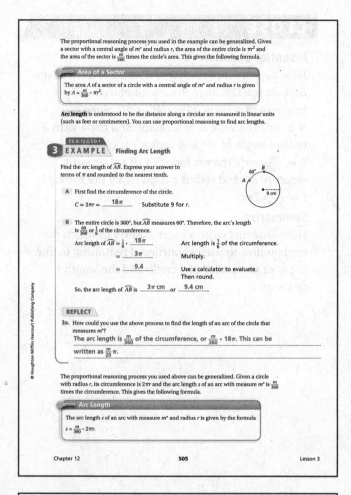

A First find the circumference of the circle.

$C = 2\pi r = \underline{\quad 18\pi \quad}$ Substitute 9 for r.

B The entire circle is 360°, but $\overset{\frown}{AB}$ measures 60°. Therefore, the arc's length is $\frac{60}{360}$ or $\frac{1}{6}$ of the circumference.

Arc length of $\overset{\frown}{AB} = \frac{1}{6} \cdot \underline{\quad 18\pi \quad}$ Arc length is $\frac{1}{6}$ of the circumference.

$= \underline{\quad 3\pi \quad}$ Multiply.

$= \underline{\quad 9.4 \quad}$ Use a calculator to evaluate. Then round.

So, the arc length of $\overset{\frown}{AB}$ is $\underline{\quad 3\pi \text{ cm} \quad}$ or $\underline{\quad 9.4 \text{ cm} \quad}$.

REFLECT

3a. How could you use the above process to find the length of an arc of the circle that measures $m°$?

The arc length is $\frac{m}{360}$ of the circumference, or $\frac{m}{360} \cdot 18\pi$. This can be written as $\frac{m}{20}\pi$.

The proportional reasoning process you used above can be generalized. Given a circle with radius r, its circumference is $2\pi r$ and the arc length s of an arc with measure $m°$ is $\frac{m}{360}$ times the circumference. This gives the following formula.

Arc Length

The arc length s of an arc with measure $m°$ and radius r is given by the formula $s = \frac{m}{360} \cdot 2\pi r$.

© Houghton Mifflin Harcourt Publishing Company

CC.9-12.G.C.5

4 EXPLORE Investigating Arc Lengths in Concentric Circles

Consider a set of concentric circles with center O and radius 1, 2, 3, and so on. The central angle shown in the figure is a right angle and it cuts off arcs that measure 90°.

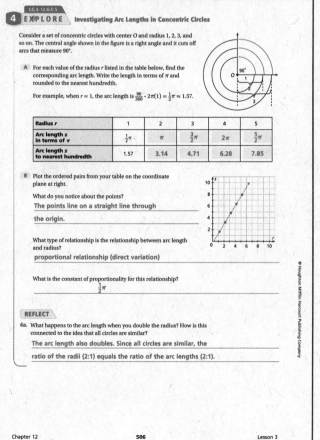

A For each value of the radius r listed in the table below, find the corresponding arc length. Write the length in terms of π and rounded to the nearest hundredth.

For example, when $r = 1$, the arc length is $\frac{90}{360} \cdot 2\pi(1) = \frac{1}{2}\pi \approx 1.57$.

Radius r	1	2	3	4	5
Arc length s in terms of π	$\frac{1}{2}\pi$	π	$\frac{3}{2}\pi$	2π	$\frac{5}{2}\pi$
Arc length s to nearest hundredth	1.57	3.14	4.71	6.28	7.85

B Plot the ordered pairs from your table on the coordinate plane at right.

What do you notice about the points?

The points line on a straight line through the origin.

What type of relationship is the relationship between arc length and radius?

proportional relationship (direct variation)

What is the constant of proportionality for this relationship?

$\frac{1}{2}\pi$

REFLECT

4a. What happens to the arc length when you double the radius? How is this connected to the idea that all circles are similar?

The arc length also doubles. Since all circles are similar, the ratio of the radii (2:1) equals the ratio of the arc lengths (2:1).

© Houghton Mifflin Harcourt Publishing Company

Questioning Strategies

- How do you convert an angle's degree measure to radian measure? Substitute the angle's degree measure for m in the expression $\frac{m}{360} \cdot 2\pi$.

- You know that 360° is the degree measure that corresponds to a full circle. What radian measure corresponds to a full circle? 2π

- What degree measure and what radian measure correspond to a semi-circle? 180°; π

EXTRA EXAMPLE

Convert each angle measure to radian measure.

A. 18° $\frac{\pi}{10}$ radians

B. 20° $\frac{\pi}{9}$ radians

CLOSE

Essential Question

How do you find the area of a sector of a circle, and how do you calculate arc length in a circle?

The area of a circle with radius r is given by $A = \pi r^2$. The area A of a sector of a circle with a central angle of $m°$ and radius r is given by $A = \frac{m}{360} \cdot \pi r^2$. The arc length s of an arc with measure $m°$ and radius r is given by the formula $s = \frac{m}{360} \cdot 2\pi r$.

Summarize

Have students write a journal entry in which they explain how to use proportional reasoning to find the area of a sector of a circle and the length of an arc.

© Houghton Mifflin Harcourt Publishing Company

As you discovered in the Explore, when the central angle is fixed at $m°$, the length of the arc cut off by the central angle is proportional to (or varies directly with) the radius. In fact, you can see that the formula for arc length is a proportional relationship when m is fixed.

$$s = \frac{m}{360} \cdot 2\pi r$$
constant of proportionality

The constant of proportionality for the proportional relationship is $\frac{m}{360} \cdot 2\pi$. This constant of proportionality is defined to be the **radian measure** of the angle.

CC.9-12.G.C.5

5 EXAMPLE Converting to Radian Measure

Convert each angle measure to radian measure.

A 180°   B 60°

A To convert 180° to radian measure, let $m = 180$ in the expression $\frac{m}{360} \cdot 2\pi$.

$180° = \dfrac{180}{360} \cdot 2\pi$ radians   Substitute 180 for m.

$\quad\quad = \underline{\quad \pi \quad}$ radians   Simplify.

B To convert 60° to radian measure, let $m = 60$ in the expression $\frac{m}{360} \cdot 2\pi$.

$60° = \dfrac{60}{360} \cdot 2\pi$ radians   Substitute 60 for m.

$\quad\quad = \underline{\dfrac{\pi}{3}}$ radians   Simplify.

REFLECT

5a. Explain why the radian measure for an angle of $m°$ is sometimes defined as the length of the arc cut off on a circle of radius 1 by a central angle of $m°$.

By the arc length formula, the length of the arc cut off on a circle of

radius 1 by a central angle of $m°$ is $\frac{m}{360} \cdot 2\pi(1)$, and this is the radian

measure of the angle.

5b. Explain how to find the degree measure of an angle whose radian measure is $\frac{\pi}{4}$.

Solve $\frac{\pi}{4} = \frac{m}{360} \cdot 2\pi$. Dividing both sides by π and simplifying gives $\frac{1}{4} = \frac{m}{180}$

and multiplying both sides by 180 shows that $m = 45$, so the angle

measures 45°.

PRACTICE

Find the area of sector *AOB*. Express your answer in terms of π and rounded to the nearest tenth.

1.

63π cm^2

197.9 cm^2

2.

2π ft^2

6.3 ft^2

3.

$\dfrac{\pi}{9}$ mm^2

0.3 mm^2

4.

44π m^2

138.2 m^2

5.

100π in^2

314.2 in^2

6.

$\dfrac{320}{3}\pi$ cm^2

335.1 cm^2

7. The area of sector *AOB* is $\frac{9}{2}\pi$ m^2. Explain how to find m$\angle AOB$.

Let m$\angle AOB = m°$, then $\frac{m}{360} \cdot \pi(6)^2 = \frac{9}{2}\pi$. Solving for m shows

that m$\angle AOB = 45°$.

8. **Error Analysis** A student claims that when you double the radius of a sector while keeping the measure of the central angle constant, you double the area of the sector. Do you agree or disagree? Explain.

Disagree; the original area is $\frac{m}{360} \cdot \pi r^2$ and the new area is $\frac{m}{360} \cdot \pi(2r)^2$ or

$4 \cdot \frac{m}{360} \cdot \pi r^2$, so the area becomes 4 times greater.

Where skills are taught	Where skills are practiced
2 EXAMPLE	EXS. 1–6
3 EXAMPLE	EXS. 9–14
5 EXAMPLE	EX. 17

Exercise 7: Students extend what they learned to find the measure of a central angle when given the area of a sector.

Exercise 8: Students use reasoning to critique a claim made by another student.

Exercise 15: Students apply what they learned to solve a real-world problem.

Exercise 16: Students critique the work of another student.

Exercise 18: Students use proportional reasoning to find the measure of 1 radian in degrees.

Find the arc length of $\overset{\frown}{AB}$. Express your answer in terms of π and rounded to the nearest tenth.

9.

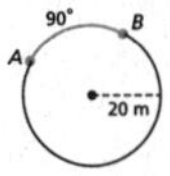

10π m

31.4 m

10.

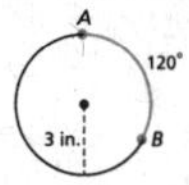

2π in.

6.3 in.

11.

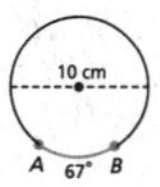

$\frac{67}{36}\pi$ cm

5.8 cm

12.

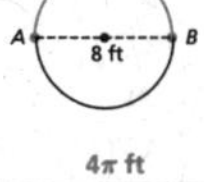

4π ft

12.6 ft

13.

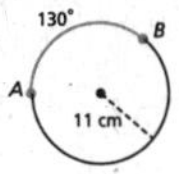

$\frac{143}{18}\pi$ cm

25.0 cm

14.

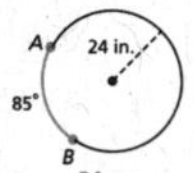

$\frac{34}{3}\pi$ in.

35.6 in.

15. The minute hand of a clock is 4 inches long. To the nearest tenth of an inch, how far does the tip of the minute hand travel as the time progresses from 12:00 to 12:25?

10.5 in.

16. Error Analysis A student was asked to find the arc length of $\overset{\frown}{PQ}$. The student's work is shown below. Explain the student's error and give the correct arc length.

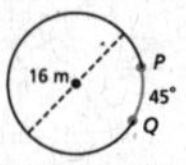

The entire circumference is $2\pi \cdot 16 = 32\pi$ and 45° is $\frac{1}{8}$ of the circle, so the arc length is $\frac{1}{8} \cdot 32\pi = 4\pi$ m.

The student used the diameter instead of the radius in the circumference

formula. The correct arc length is 2π m.

17. It is convenient to know the radian measure for benchmark angles such as 0°, 30°, 45°, and so on. Complete the table by finding the radian measure for each of the given benchmark angles.

Benchmark Angles									
Degree Measure	0°	30°	45°	60°	90°	120°	135°	150°	180°
Radian Measure	0	$\frac{\pi}{6}$	$\frac{\pi}{4}$	$\frac{\pi}{3}$	$\frac{\pi}{2}$	$\frac{2\pi}{3}$	$\frac{3\pi}{4}$	$\frac{5\pi}{6}$	π

18. Explain how to convert a radian measure into degrees. Then use your method to find what 1 radian is in degrees. Round to the nearest tenth of a degree.

The conversion factor from degrees to radians is $\frac{2\pi}{360}$, so the conversion factor

from radians to degrees is $\frac{360}{2\pi}$; so, 1 radian $= \frac{360}{2\pi}$ degrees, or

about 57.3 degrees.

Assign these pages to help your students practice and apply important lesson concepts. For additional exercises, see the Student Edition.

Answers

Additional Practice

1. sector BAC 126 π mm^2; 395.84 mm^2

2. sector UTV 30 π in^2; 94.25 in^2

3. sector KJL π ft^2; 3.14 ft^2

4. sector FEG 100π m^2; 314.16 m^2

5. 4.54 in^2 6. 63.36 km^2

7. 245.44 yd^2 8. 0.79 cm^2

9. 16.76 mi^2 10. π ft; 3.14 ft

11. 14π m; 43.98 m 12. $\frac{\pi}{2}$ mi; 1.57 mi

13. 10π mm; 31.42 mm

Problem Solving

1. 366.5 cm^2 2. 9 ft

3. 42.4 in.^{2}; possible explanation: There are 12 equal sectors formed by each pair of numbers on the clock face. The hands at two o'clock span two of those sectors, so I found the area of the clock face and then multiplied it by $\frac{2}{12} = \frac{1}{6}$.

4. D   5. H

6. A   7. H

Name_____ Class_____ Date_____

12-3

Additional Practice

Find the area of each sector. Give your answer in terms of π and rounded to the nearest hundredth.

1.

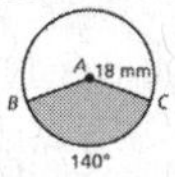

sector BAC _____

2.

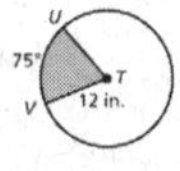

sector UTV _____

3.

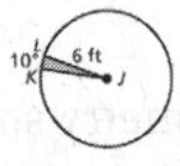

sector KJL _____

4.

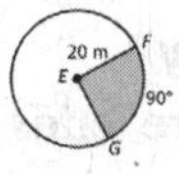

sector FEG _____

5. The speedometer needle in Ignacio's car is 2 inches long. The needle sweeps out a 130° sector during acceleration from 0 to 60 mi/h. Find the area of this sector. Round to the nearest hundredth. _____

Find the area of each shaded sector to the nearest hundredth.

6.

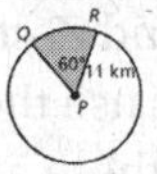

7.

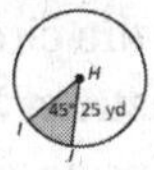

8.

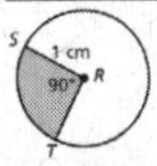

9.

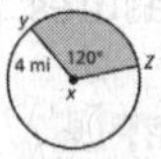

Find each arc length. Give your answer in terms of π and rounded to the nearest hundredth.

10.

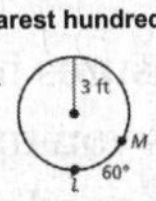

11.

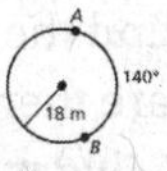

12. an arc with measure 45° in a circle with radius 2 mi _____
13. an arc with measure 120° in a circle with radius 15 mm _____

© Houghton Mifflin Harcourt Publishing Company

Problem Solving

1. A circle with a radius of 20 centimeters has a sector that has an arc measure of 105°. What is the area of the sector? Round to the nearest tenth.

_____

2. A sector whose central angle measures 72° has an area of 16.2π square feet. What is the radius of the circle?

_____

3. A circular wall clock has a diameter of 18 inches. If the hour and minute hand were extended to reach to the edge of the clock, what would be the area of the smaller of the two sectors formed by the hands at 2 o'clock? Round your answer to the nearest tenth of a square inch, and explain how you found your answer.

_____

_____

Choose the best answer.

4. The circular shelves in diagram are each 28 inches in diameter. The "cut-out" portion of each shelf is 90°. Approximately how much shelf paper is needed to cover both shelves?

   A 154 in²
   B 308 in²
   C 462 in²
   D 924 in²

5. Find the area of the shaded region. Round to the nearest tenth.

   F 8.2 in²   H 71.4 in²
   G 19.6 in²   J 78.5 in²

6. A semicircular garden with a diameter of 6 feet is to have 2 inches of mulch spread over it. To the nearest tenth, what is the volume of mulch that is needed?

   A 2.4 ft³   C 14.1 ft³
   B 4.8 ft³   D 20.3 ft³

7. A round cheesecake 12 inches in diameter and 3 inches high is cut into 8 equal-sized pieces. If five pieces have been taken, what is the approximate volume of the cheesecake that remains?

   F 42.4 in³   H 127.2 in³
   G 70.7 in³   J 212.1 in³

© Houghton Mifflin Harcourt Publishing Company

Inscribed Angles
Going Deeper

Essential question: *What is the relationship between central angles and inscribed angles in a circle?*

COMMON CORE Standards for Mathematical Content

CC.9-12.G.C.2 Identify and describe relationships among inscribed angles, radii, and chords.

CC.9-12.G.C.3 ... prove properties of angles for a quadrilateral inscribed in a circle.

Prerequisites
Inscribed and central angles

Math Background
Because a circle can be circumscribed around a triangle, students may think that a circle can be circumscribed around any quadrilateral. The situation for quadrilaterals, however, is more complex. A circle can be circumscribed around a quadrilateral if and only if the opposite angles of the quadrilateral are supplementary.

INTRODUCE

Draw a circle on the board and draw a central angle and an inscribed angle that intercept the same arc. Ask students to identify the inscribed angle and the central angle, and discuss whether or not the two angles have the same measure. Then, use a protractor to measure the angles and compare them.

TEACH

1 EXPLORE

Materials: compass, straightedge, protractor

Questioning Strategies
• Is it possible for multiple inscribed angles to have the same associated central angle? yes
• What is true about the inscribed angles in this case? They all have the same measure.

Technology
The **Explore** lends itself well to geometry software. Have students construct a circle with center C and then have them plot three points, X, Y, and Z on the circle. Student can construct $\angle XYZ$ and $\angle XCZ$. By selecting the circle and points X and Z, students can also construct $\widehat{XZ}$. Have students use the Measure menu to find and compare these angle and arc measures.

2 EXAMPLE

Questioning Strategies
• Can you find the four required measures in any order, or are there certain measures you must find first? Find m$\widehat{BC}$ or m$\angle ABC$ (you need m$\widehat{BC}$ in order to find m$\widehat{BD}$).

EXTRA EXAMPLE
Find m$\widehat{FG}$, m$\widehat{FGH}$, m$\angle HJF$, and m$\angle JFG$.

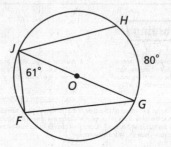

m$\widehat{FG}$ = 122°; m$\widehat{FGH}$ = 202°; m$\angle HJF$ = 101°; m$\angle JFG$ = 90°

Teaching Strategies
Whenever students solve a problem like the one in the example, encourage them to do a "consistency check" as the final step. To do so, students should label the figure with all of the measures they found and make sure that the sum of the angle measures in any triangle is 180°, that the sum of any arc measures that make a full circle is 360°, and that the measure of any inscribed angle is half the measure of its intercepted arc.

Name_____ Class_____ Date_____

12-4

Video Tutor

Inscribed Angles
Going Deeper

Essential question: *What is the relationship between central angles and inscribed angles in a circle?*

CC.9-12.G.C.2

1 EXPLORE Investigating Central Angles and Inscribed Angles

A Use a compass to draw a circle. Label the center *C*.

B Use a straightedge to draw an inscribed angle, ∠*XYZ*.

C Use the straightedge to draw the central angle, ∠*XCZ*.

D Use a protractor to measure the inscribed angle and the central angle. Use the measure of the central angle to determine the measure of the intercepted arc.

E Repeat the process four more times. Be sure to draw a variety of inscribed angles (acute, right, obtuse, passing through the center, etc.). Record your results in the table.
Possible measures shown.

	Circle 1	Circle 2	Circle 3	Circle 4	Circle 5
Measure of Inscribed Angle	26°	35°	90°	102°	120°
Measure of Intercepted Arc	52°	70°	180°	204°	240°

REFLECT

1a. Compare your work with that of other students. Then make a conjecture: What is the relationship between the measure of an inscribed angle and the measure of its intercepted arc?
The measure of an inscribed angle is half the measure of its intercepted arc.

1b. Suppose an inscribed angle, ∠*XYZ*, measures *x*°. If ∠*XYZ* is acute, what is the measure of its associated central angle, ∠*XCZ*? What if ∠*XYZ* is obtuse?
If ∠*XYZ* is acute, m∠*XCZ* = (2*x*)°; if ∠*XYZ* is obtuse, m∠*XCZ* = (360 − 2*x*)°.

1c. Draw a triangle inscribed in a circle so that the center of the circle lies in the interior of the triangle. Then draw the central angle associated with each inscribed angle of the triangle. What is the sum of the measures of the inscribed angles? What is the sum of the measures of the central angles?
The sum of the measures of the inscribed angles is 180°. The sum of the measures of the central angles is 360°.

Chapter 12   513   Lesson 4

You may have discovered the following relationship between an inscribed angle and its intercepted arc.

Inscribed Angle Theorem

The measure of an inscribed angle is half the measure of its intercepted arc.

$m\angle ADB = \frac{1}{2}m\widehat{AB}$

CC.9-12.G.C.2

2 EXAMPLE Finding Arc and Angle Measures

Find m$\widehat{BC}$, m$\widehat{BD}$, m∠*DAB*, and m∠*ABC*.

A Find m$\widehat{BC}$.

$m\angle BAC = \frac{1}{2}m\widehat{BC}$ Inscribed Angle Theorem

$2m\angle BAC = m\widehat{BC}$ Multiply both sides by 2.

$2 \cdot \underline{31°} = m\widehat{BC}$ Substitute.

$\underline{62°} = m\widehat{BC}$ Multiply.

B By the Arc Addition Postulate, m$\widehat{BD}$ = m$\widehat{BC}$ + m$\widehat{CD}$ = $\underline{62°}$ + 88° = $\underline{150°}$.

C By the Inscribed Angle Theorem, m∠*DAB* = $\frac{1}{2}$m$\widehat{BD}$ = $\frac{1}{2} \cdot \underline{150°}$ = $\underline{75°}$.

D To find m∠*ABC*, note that $\widehat{ADC}$ is a $\underline{semicircle}$.
Therefore, m$\widehat{ADC}$ = $\underline{180°}$, and m∠*ABC* = $\frac{1}{2}$m$\widehat{ADC}$ = $\frac{1}{2} \cdot \underline{180°}$ = $\underline{90°}$.

REFLECT

2a. Is it possible to find m$\widehat{DAB}$? If so, how? If not, why not?
Yes; m$\widehat{DAB}$ = 360° − m$\widehat{BD}$ = 360° − 150° = 210°.

2b. Show two different methods to find m$\widehat{AB}$.
Method 1: $\overline{AC}$ is a diameter, so m$\widehat{AB}$ + m$\widehat{BC}$ = 180°, and m$\widehat{BC}$ = 62°,
so m$\widehat{AB}$ = 180° − 62° = 118°.

Method 2: By the Triangle Sum Theorem, m∠*BAC* + m∠*ABC* + m∠*BCA* = 180°;
31° + 90° + m∠*BCA* = 180°, so m∠*BCA* = 59°. By the Inscribed Angle Theorem,
m$\widehat{AB}$ = 2m∠*BCA* = 2(59°) = 118°.

2c. Consider ∠*ABC* and make a conjecture: What do you think must be true about any inscribed angle that contains endpoints of a diameter? Why?
The angle must be a right angle because the diameter determines a semicircle with measure 180° and the inscribed angle must have half this measure.

Chapter 12   514   Lesson 4

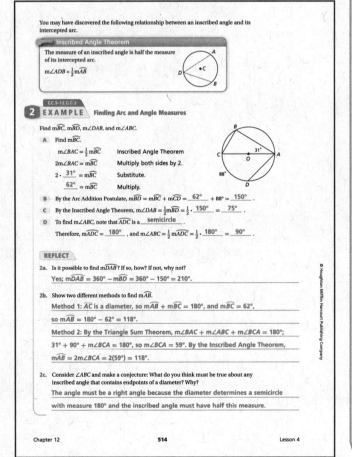

Questioning Strategies

- How do you prove that two angles are supplementary? **Show that the sum of their measures is 180°.**

- What can you say about two arcs that together form a complete circle? **The sum of the measures of the arcs is 360°.**

MATHEMATICAL PRACTICE **Highlighting the Standards**

To address Standard 5 (Use appropriate tools strategically), ask students why geometry software is a good tool for investigating inscribed quadrilaterals. Students should recognize that geometry software makes it easy to change the shape of the quadrilateral and see if relationships among the angles still hold as the shape changes.

CLOSE

Essential Question

What is the relationship between central angles and inscribed angles in a circle?

The measure of an inscribed angle is half the measure of its intercepted arc. The measure of the arc is equal to the measure of its central angle (for minor arcs) or 360° minus the measure of its central angle (for major arcs).

Summarize

Have students write a journal entry in which they summarize the main vocabulary and theorems from this lesson. Encourage students to include figures to illustrate the vocabulary and theorems.

PRACTICE

Where skills are taught	Where skills are practiced
2 EXAMPLE	EXS. 1–12

Exercise 13: Students prove a theorem about inscribed angles.

Exercise 14: Students use what they learned in this lesson to solve a real-world problem.

The following theorem describes a key relationship between inscribed angles and diameters.

Theorem

The endpoints of a diameter lie on an inscribed angle if and only if the inscribed angle is a right angle.

Another theorem that relies on the Inscribed Angle Theorem in its proof is shown below. It is a theorem about the measures of the angles in any quadrilateral that is inscribed in a circle.

Inscribed Quadrilateral Theorem

If a quadrilateral is inscribed in a circle, then its opposite angles are supplementary.

The converse of the Inscribed Quadrilateral Theorem is also true. Taken together, the theorem and its converse tell you that a quadrilateral can be inscribed in a circle *if and only if* its opposite angles are supplementary.

CC.9-12.G.C.3

3 PROOF   **Inscribed Quadrilateral Theorem**

Given: Quadrilateral *ABCD* is inscribed in circle *O*.

Prove: $\angle A$ and $\angle C$ are supplementary;
$\angle B$ and $\angle D$ are supplementary.

A $\overset{\frown}{BCD}$ and $\overset{\frown}{DAB}$ make a complete circle. Therefore,

$m\overset{\frown}{BCD} + m\overset{\frown}{DAB} = \underline{\quad 360° \quad}$.

B $\angle A$ is an inscribed angle and its intercepted arc is $\overset{\frown}{BCD}$; $\angle C$ is an inscribed angle and its intercepted arc is $\overset{\frown}{DAB}$. By the Inscribed Angle Theorem,

$m\angle A = \underline{\frac{1}{2}m\overset{\frown}{BCD}}$ and $m\angle C = \underline{\frac{1}{2}m\overset{\frown}{DAB}}$.

C   So, $m\angle A + m\angle C = \underline{\frac{1}{2}m\overset{\frown}{BCD} + \frac{1}{2}m\overset{\frown}{DAB}}$ Substitution

$= \underline{\frac{1}{2}(m\overset{\frown}{BCD} + m\overset{\frown}{DAB})}$ Distributive Property

$= \underline{\frac{1}{2}(360°)}$ Substitution

$= \underline{\quad 180° \quad}$ Simplify.

This shows that $\angle A$ and $\angle C$ are supplementary. Similar reasoning shows that $\angle B$ and $\angle D$ are supplementary.

© Houghton Mifflin Harcourt Publishing Company

REFLECT

3a. What must be true about a parallelogram that is inscribed in a circle? Explain.

It is a rectangle. Opposite angles of a parallelogram are congruent, but they must also be supplementary, so they measure 90°.

3b. What must be true about a rhombus that is inscribed in a circle? Explain.

It is a square. A rhombus is a parallelogram, so if it is inscribed in a circle, it must be a rectangle. A rhombus has four congruent sides. So, if it is a rectangle with four congruent sides, it must be a square.

PRACTICE

Use the figure to find each of the following.

1. $m\overset{\frown}{BA}$ 96°   2. $m\angle BOA$ 96°

3. $m\overset{\frown}{AE}$ 84°   4. $m\angle AOE$ 84°

5. $m\overset{\frown}{BAE}$ 180°   6. $m\angle BDE$ 90°

7. $m\angle DBE$ 20°   8. $m\overset{\frown}{DE}$ 40°

9. $m\overset{\frown}{DB}$ 140°   10. $m\overset{\frown}{ABD}$ 236°

11. $m\angle EDA$ 42°   12. $m\angle OAD$ 28°

13. Prove that if two inscribed angles of a circle intercept the same arc, then the angles are congruent.

Given: $\angle ABC$ and $\angle ADC$ intercept $\overset{\frown}{AC}$.

Prove: $\angle ABC \cong \angle ADC$

By the Inscribed Angle Theorem, $m\angle ABC = \frac{1}{2}m\overset{\frown}{AC}$ and $m\angle ADC = \frac{1}{2}m\overset{\frown}{AC}$. By substitution, $m\angle ABC = m\angle ADC$, so $\angle ABC \cong \angle ADC$.

14. A carpenter's square is a tool that is used to draw right angles. Suppose you are building a toy car and you have a small circle of wood that will serve as a wheel. Explain how you can use the carpenter's square to find the center of the circle.

Use the tool to draw an inscribed right angle. The sides of the angle intersect the circle at the endpoints of a diameter. Draw the diameter. Repeat the process to draw a different diameter. The point of intersection of the two diameters is the center of the circle.

ADDITIONAL PRACTICE AND PROBLEM SOLVING

Assign these pages to help your students practice and apply important lesson concepts. For additional exercises, see the Student Edition.

Answers

Additional Practice

1. 33°; 192°

2. 9°; 78°

3. 130°; 138°

4. 10°; 90.5°

5. 73°

6. 48°

7. 13

8. 6

9. 77°

10. 71°; 109°; 109°; 71°

11. 90°; 90°; 90°; 90°

12. 68°; 95°; 112°; 85°

13. 59°; 73°; 121°; 107°

Problem Solving

1. 160°

2. 112°; 52°; 68°; 128°

3. C

4. G

5. B

6. G

Name _____ Class _____ Date _____ **12-4**

Additional Practice

Find each measure.

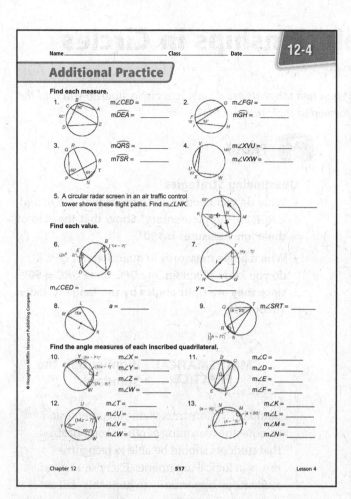

1. m∠CED = _____
   mDEA = _____

2. m∠FGI = _____
   mGH = _____

3. mQRS = _____
   mTSR = _____

4. m∠XVU = _____
   m∠VXW = _____

5. A circular radar screen in an air traffic control tower shows these flight paths. Find m∠LNK. _____

Find each value.

6. m∠CED = _____

7. y = _____

8. a = _____

9. m∠SRT = _____

Find the angle measures of each inscribed quadrilateral.

10. m∠X = _____
    m∠Y = _____
    m∠Z = _____
    m∠W = _____

11. m∠C = _____
    m∠D = _____
    m∠E = _____
    m∠F = _____

12. m∠T = _____
    m∠U = _____
    m∠V = _____
    m∠W = _____

13. m∠K = _____
    m∠L = _____
    m∠M = _____
    m∠N = _____

© Houghton Mifflin Harcourt Publishing Company

Problem Solving

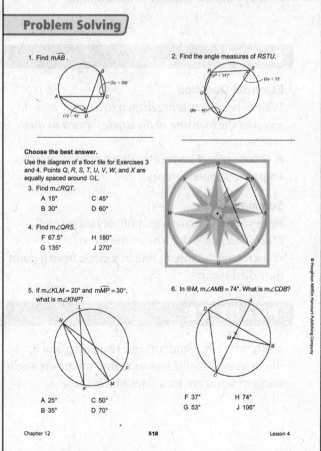

1. Find mAB. _____

2. Find the angle measures of RSTU. _____

Choose the best answer.

Use the diagram of a floor tile for Exercises 3 and 4. Points Q, R, S, T, U, V, W, and X are equally spaced around ⊙L.

3. Find m∠RQT.
   A 15°   C 45°
   B 30°   D 60°

4. Find m∠QRS.
   F 67.5°   H 180°
   G 135°   J 270°

5. If m∠KLM = 20° and mMP = 30°, what is m∠KNP?
   A 25°   C 50°
   B 35°   D 70°

6. In ⊙M, m∠AMB = 74°. What is m∠CDB?
   F 37°   H 74°
   G 53°   J 106°

© Houghton Mifflin Harcourt Publishing Company

Angle Relationships in Circles
Going Deeper

Essential question: *When two tangents are drawn to a circle, how do you find the measure of the angle formed at their intersection?*

© Houghton Mifflin Harcourt Publishing Company

COMMON CORE Standards for Mathematical Content

CC.9-12.G.CO.9 Prove theorems about lines and angles.

CC.9-12.G.C.4(+) Construct a tangent line from a point outside a given circle to the circle.

Vocabulary
circumscribed angle

Prerequisites
Central angles and inscribed angles

Math Background
Students learn to construct a tangent to a circle from a given point outside the circle. The justification for this construction depends upon the Converse of the Tangent-Radius Theorem. Students also prove the Circumscribed Angle Theorem, which depends upon the Tangent-Radius Theorem and the Quadrilateral Sum Theorem.

INTRODUCE

Review the definition of a tangent to a circle and remind students that the tangent is perpendicular to the radius of the circle that contains the point of tangency.

TEACH

1 EXPLORE

Questioning Strategies
- How do you construct the midpoint of $\overline{CP}$? **Construct the perpendicular bisector of the segment by drawing arcs with the same radius from each endpoint. The line through the points of intersection of the arcs is the perpendicular bisector.**
- What type of angle is ∠*CXP*? Why? **It is a right angle because it is an inscribed angle in circle *M* and the endpoints of diameter $\overline{CP}$ lie on the angle.**

2 PROOF

Questioning Strategies
- What do you need to do to prove that ∠*PQR* and ∠*PCR* are supplementary? **Show that the sum of the angle measures is 180°.**
- Which angle measures in quadrilateral *QPCR* do you know? Explain. **m∠*QPC* = m∠*QRC* = 90° since they are right angles by the Tangent-Radius Theorem.**

MATHEMATICAL PRACTICE **Highlighting the Standards**

Standard 3 (Construct viable arguments and critique the reasoning of others) emphasizes that students should be able to recognize errors in logical arguments. Exercise 11 gives students an opportunity to hone this skill as they evaluate another student's work.

CLOSE

Essential Question
When two tangents are drawn to a circle, how do you find the measure of the angle formed at their intersection?
A circumscribed angle and its associated central angle are supplementary.

Summarize
Have students make a graphic organizer or illustrated guide that shows the steps for constructing a tangent line to a circle from a point outside the circle.

PRACTICE

Exercises 1–8: Students use reasoning and apply the theorems of this lesson to find unknown angle measures and arc measures in a figure.

Name _____ Class _____ Date _____

12-5

Angle Relationships in Circles
Going Deeper

Essential question: When two tangents are drawn to a circle, how do you find the measure of the angle formed at their intersection?

Video Tutor

CC.9-12.G.C.4(+)

1 EXPLORE Constructing Tangents to a Circle

Construct a tangent line from point P to circle C.

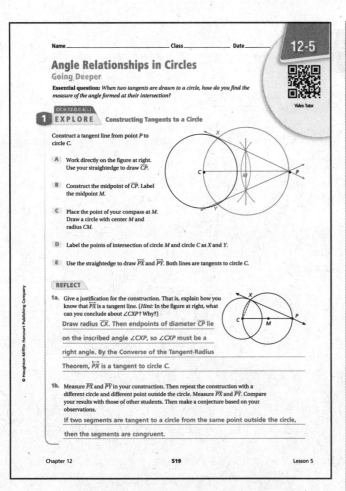

A Work directly on the figure at right. Use your straightedge to draw $\overline{CP}$.

B Construct the midpoint of $\overline{CP}$. Label the midpoint M.

C Place the point of your compass at M. Draw a circle with center M and radius CM.

D Label the points of intersection of circle M and circle C as X and Y.

E Use the straightedge to draw $\overrightarrow{PX}$ and $\overrightarrow{PY}$. Both lines are tangents to circle C.

REFLECT

1a. Give a justification for the construction. That is, explain how you know that $\overrightarrow{PX}$ is a tangent line. (*Hint:* In the figure at right, what can you conclude about $\angle CXP$? Why?)

Draw radius $\overline{CX}$. Then endpoints of diameter $\overline{CP}$ lie

on the inscribed angle $\angle CXP$, so $\angle CXP$ must be a

right angle. By the Converse of the Tangent-Radius

Theorem, $\overrightarrow{PX}$ is a tangent to circle C.

1b. Measure $\overrightarrow{PX}$ and $\overrightarrow{PY}$ in your construction. Then repeat the construction with a different circle and different point outside the circle. Measure $\overrightarrow{PX}$ and $\overrightarrow{PY}$. Compare your results with those of other students. Then make a conjecture based on your observations.

If two segments are tangent to a circle from the same point outside the circle,

then the segments are congruent.

Chapter 12   519   Lesson 5

As you discovered in the above construction, given any point outside a circle, you can draw two tangent lines to the circle. The two tangent lines form a *circumscribed angle*.

A **circumscribed angle** is an angle formed by two tangents to a circle. In the figure, $\overrightarrow{QP}$ and $\overrightarrow{QR}$ are tangents to circle C, so $\angle PQR$ is a circumscribed angle.

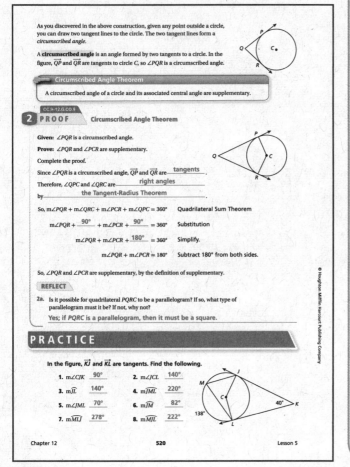

Circumscribed Angle Theorem

A circumscribed angle of a circle and its associated central angle are supplementary.

CC.9-12.G.CO.9

2 PROOF Circumscribed Angle Theorem

Given: $\angle PQR$ is a circumscribed angle.

Prove: $\angle PQR$ and $\angle PCR$ are supplementary.

Complete the proof.

Since $\angle PQR$ is a circumscribed angle, $\overrightarrow{QP}$ and $\overrightarrow{QR}$ are ____tangents____ .

Therefore, $\angle QPC$ and $\angle QRC$ are ____right angles____

by ____the Tangent-Radius Theorem____ .

So, $m\angle PQR + m\angle QRC + m\angle PCR + m\angle QPC = 360°$ Quadrilateral Sum Theorem

$m\angle PQR + \underline{90°} + m\angle PCR + \underline{90°} = 360°$ Substitution

$m\angle PQR + m\angle PCR + \underline{180°} = 360°$ Simplify.

$m\angle PQR + m\angle PCR = 180°$ Subtract 180° from both sides.

So, $\angle PQR$ and $\angle PCR$ are supplementary, by the definition of supplementary.

REFLECT

2a. Is it possible for quadrilateral $PQRC$ to be a parallelogram? If so, what type of parallelogram must it be? If not, why not?

Yes; if $PQRC$ is a parallelogram, then it must be a square.

PRACTICE

In the figure, $\overleftrightarrow{KJ}$ and $\overleftrightarrow{KL}$ are tangents. Find the following.

1. $m\angle CJK$ ___90°___   **2.** $m\angle JCL$ ___140°___

3. $m\widehat{JL}$ ___140°___   **4.** $m\widehat{JML}$ ___220°___

5. $m\angle JML$ ___70°___   **6.** $m\angle M$ ___82°___

7. $m\widehat{MLJ}$ ___278°___   **8.** $m\widehat{MJL}$ ___222°___

Chapter 12   520   Lesson 5

© Houghton Mifflin Harcourt Publishing Company

ADDITIONAL PRACTICE AND PROBLEM SOLVING

Assign these pages to help your students practice and apply important lesson concepts. For additional exercises, see the Student Edition.

Answers

Additional Practice

1. 64
2. 97
3. 155°
4. 105°
5. 50°
6. 130°
7. 36°
8. 108°
9. 36°
10. 144°
11. 72°
12. 144°
13. 112°

Problem Solving

1. 60
2. 110.8°
3. 162.6°
4. A
5. J

Additional Practice

Find the value of *x*.

1.

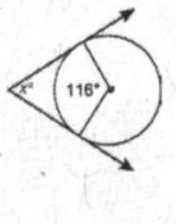

116°

2.

x°   83°

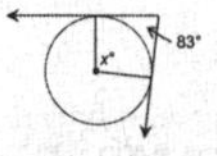

In the figure, $\overline{AB}$, $\overline{BC}$, and $\overline{AC}$ are tangent to circle *O* at the points labeled *X*, *Y*, and *Z*. Find the following.

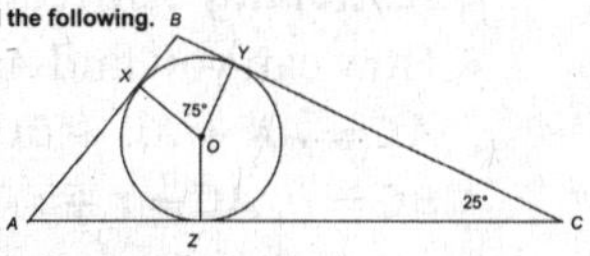

3. m∠YOZ _____

4. m∠XBY _____

5. m∠XAZ _____

6. m∠XOZ _____

75°, 25°

In the figure, the sides of △EFG are tangent to circle *M* at the points labeled *P*, *Q*, and *R*. The angle measures of △EFG are in the ratio 1 : 3 : 1. Find each of the following.

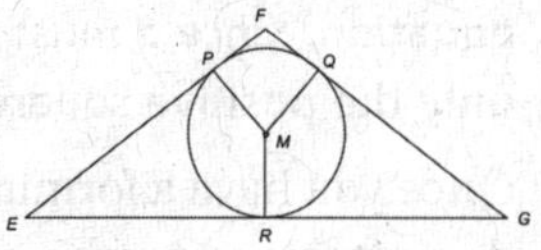

7. m∠E _____

8. m∠F _____

9. m∠G _____

10. m∠PMR _____

11. m∠PMQ _____

12. m∠QMR _____

13. The two lines in the diagram are tangent to the circle. Find the measure of ∠1.

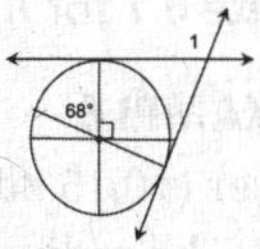

_____

68°, 1

Problem Solving

1. The figure shows a spinning wheel. The large wheel is turned by hand or with a foot trundle. A belt attaches to a small bobbin that turns very quickly. The bobbin twists raw materials into thread, twine, or yarn. Each pair of spokes forms the sides of a 30° central angle. Find the value of *x*.

_____

For Exercises 2 and 3, use the diagrams.

2. A polar orbiting satellite is about 850 kilometers above Earth. About 69.2 arc degrees of the planet are visible to a camera in the satellite. What is m∠P?

_____

3. A geostationary satellite is about 35,800 kilometers above Earth. How many arc degrees of the planet are visible to a camera in the satellite?

_____

69.2°, 17.4°

Polar Orbiting Satellite

Geostationary Satellite

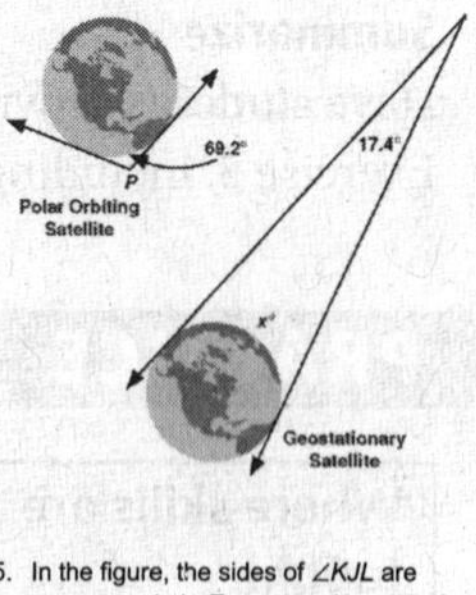

Choose the best answer.

4. Andy drew circle *Q* and then drew a circumscribed angle *X* with sides tangent to circle *Q* at points *Y* and *Z*. He also drew segments *QY* and *QZ*. Which statement about Andy's diagram is *not* true?

   A Quadrilateral *XYQZ* cannot be a square.

   B m∠XYQ = m∠XZQ

   C m∠YQZ + m∠YXZ = 180°

   D m∠QYX + m∠QZX = 180°

5. In the figure, the sides of ∠KJL are tangent to circle *T* at points *K* and *L*. If the ratio of m∠KJL to m∠KTL is 1 : 5, what is m∠KTL?

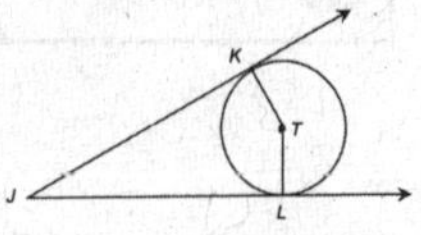

   F 30°   H 120°

   G 60°   J 150°

Segment Relationships in Circles
Extension: Distance to the Horizon

Essential question: *How can you estimate the distance to the horizon using results about segments related to circles?*

COMMON CORE Standards for Mathematical Content

CC.9-12.G.C.2 Identify and describe relationships among inscribed angles, radii, and chords.

CC.9-12.G.MG.1 Use geometric shapes, their measures, and their properties to describe objects...*

Prerequisites

Angle relationships in circles

Math Background

In this lesson, students will learn how to apply a theorem about segment lengths of a secant and tangent to the real world problem of finding the distance to the horizon.

INTRODUCE

Review the concepts of tangents and secants and theorems related to the measures of angles inscribed in a circle. Also review the concept of similar triangles and proportions that can be obtained from similarity.

TEACH

1 PROOF

Questioning Strategies

• What figures do $\overline{AD}$ and $\overline{BD}$ create? **They create two triangles, $\triangle CAD$ and $\triangle CDB$.**

• What arc do $\angle CDB$ and $\angle CAD$ intercept? **$\overgroup{BD}$**

• What triangles can you show are similar? **$\triangle CAD$ and $\triangle CDB$**

• What proportion can help you finish the proof? **a proportion involving the ratios of the lengths AC, BC, and DC**

MATHEMATICAL PRACTICE

Highlighting the Standards

The proof in this lesson provides an opportunity to address Mathematical Practices Standard 3 (Construct viable arguments and critique the reasoning of others).

2 EXAMPLE

Questioning Strategies

• How can you find AC? Explain.
$AC = AX + XB + BC$. Since $AX = r$, $XB = r$, and $BC = h$, $AC = r + r + h$, or $2r + h$.

• In Step B, how can you solve the equation for d? **Take the square root of each side of the equation. Since d must be nonnegative, consider only the positive square root.**

• Once you have a formula for d, what should you do next to answer the question? **Substitute 0.1 for h and 6378.1 for r.**

EXTRA EXAMPLE

An observer is 0.15 kilometer above the surface of Earth at C. The radius of Earth, r, is about 6378.1 kilometers. What is the distance to the horizon from the observer? Round to the nearest tenth of a kilometer. **43.7 kilometers**

CLOSE

Essential Question

How can you estimate the distance to the horizon using results about segments related to circles?
You can apply the Secant-Tangent Product theorem to find a formula for the distance to the horizon.

Summarize

Have students provide a worked-out solution to Exercise 5, including art.

PRACTICE

Where skills are taught	Where skills are practiced
2 EXAMPLE	EXS. 1–5

12-6

Video Tutor

Name _____ Class _____ Date _____

Segment Relationships in Circles
Extension: Distance to the Horizon

Essential question: *How can you estimate the distance to the horizon using results about segments related to circles?*

The following theorem provides a relationship between the length of a secant and the length of a tangent.

> **Secant-Tangent Product Theorem**
>
> If a secant and a tangent intersect in the exterior of a circle, then the product of the lengths of the secant segment and its external segment equals the length of the tangent segment squared.
>
> Secant $\overline{AC}$ and tangent $\overline{DC}$ intersect at C.
> $$AC \cdot BC = DC^2$$

CC.9-12.G.C.2

1 PROOF Secant-Tangent Product Theorem

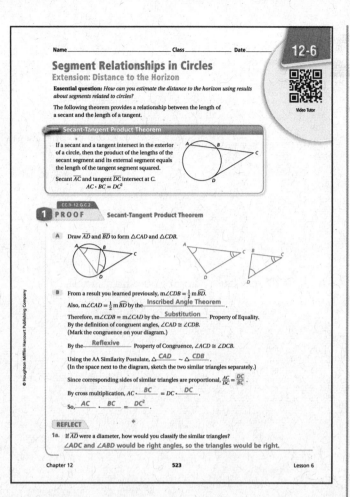

A Draw $\overline{AD}$ and $\overline{BD}$ to form $\triangle CAD$ and $\triangle CDB$.

B From a result you learned previously, $m\angle CDB = \frac{1}{2}\,m\,\widehat{BD}$.

Also, $m\angle CAD = \frac{1}{2}\,m\,\widehat{BD}$ by the __Inscribed Angle Theorem__ .

Therefore, $m\angle CDB = m\angle CAD$ by the __Substitution__ Property of Equality.
By the definition of congruent angles, $\angle CAD \cong \angle CDB$.
(Mark the congruence on your diagram.)

By the __Reflexive__ Property of Congruence, $\angle ACD \cong \angle DCB$.

Using the AA Similarity Postulate, $\triangle$__CAD__ ~ $\triangle$__CDB__ .
(In the space next to the diagram, sketch the two similar triangles separately.)

Since corresponding sides of similar triangles are proportional, $\frac{AC}{DC} = \frac{DC}{BC}$.

By cross multiplication, $AC \cdot$__BC__ $= DC \cdot$__DC__ .

So, __AC__ · __BC__ $=$ __DC^2__ .

REFLECT

1a. If $\overline{AD}$ were a diameter, how would you classify the similar triangles?
$\angle ADC$ and $\angle ABD$ would be right angles, so the triangles would be right.

Chapter 12   523   Lesson 6

CC.9-12.G.MG.1

2 EXAMPLE Approximating the Distance to the Horizon

An observer is 0.1 kilometer above the surface of Earth at C. The radius of Earth, r, is about 6378.1 kilometers. What is the distance to the horizon from the observer?

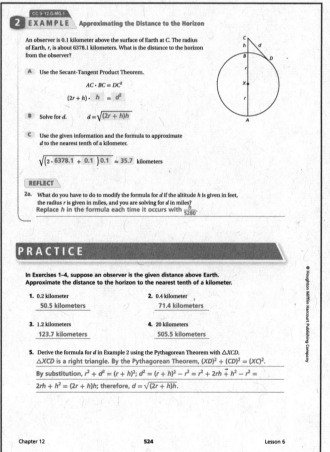

A Use the Secant-Tangent Product Theorem.

$$AC \cdot BC = DC^2$$
$$(2r + h) \cdot \; h \; = \; d^2$$

B Solve for d. $d = \sqrt{(2r + h)h}$

C Use the given information and the formula to approximate d to the nearest tenth of a kilometer.

$$\sqrt{\left(2 \cdot 6378.1 + 0.1\right)0.1} \approx 35.7 \text{ kilometers}$$

REFLECT

2a. What do you have to do to modify the formula for d if the altitude h is given in feet, the radius r is given in miles, and you are solving for d in miles?
Replace h in the formula each time it occurs with $\frac{h}{5280}$.

PRACTICE

In Exercises 1–4, suppose an observer is the given distance above Earth. Approximate the distance to the horizon to the nearest tenth of a kilometer.

1. 0.2 kilometer
   50.5 kilometers

2. 0.4 kilometer
   71.4 kilometers

3. 1.2 kilometers
   123.7 kilometers

4. 20 kilometers
   505.5 kilometers

5. Derive the formula for d in Example 2 using the Pythagorean Theorem with $\triangle XCD$.
$\triangle XCD$ is a right triangle. By the Pythagorean Theorem, $(XD)^2 + (CD)^2 = (XC)^2$.

By substitution, $r^2 + d^2 = (r + h)^2$; $d^2 = (r + h)^2 - r^2 = r^2 + 2rh + h^2 - r^2 =$

$2rh + h^2 = (2r + h)h$; therefore, $d = \sqrt{(2r + h)h}$.

Chapter 12   524   Lesson 6

© Houghton Mifflin Harcourt Publishing Company

ADDITIONAL PRACTICE AND PROBLEM SOLVING

Assign these pages to help your students practice and apply important lesson concepts. For additional exercises, see the Student Edition.

Answers

Additional Practice

1. $x = 6$
2. $x = 1.5$
3. $y = 10$
4. $z = 78$
5. $y^2 = 2x^2$
6.

x	y	$\frac{y}{x}$
1	1.4	1.4
2	2.8	1.4
3	4.2	1.4

The ratios are all the same.

Problem Solving

1. 21,450 km
2. 25,595 km
3. 30,723 km
4. 35,815 km
5. 37 in.
6. B
7. J

Name________________________ Class________________ Date____________

12-6

Additional Practice

Find the value of the variable.

1. 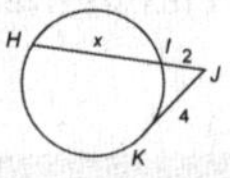

____

2. 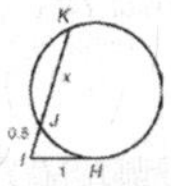

____

3. 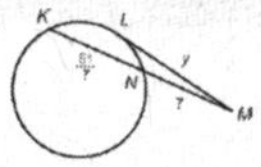

____

4. 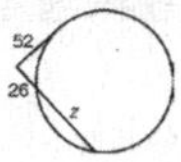

____

In the figure shown, $\overline{QP}$ is tangent to circle *N* at *Q*, and *MP* = 2 • *MO*.

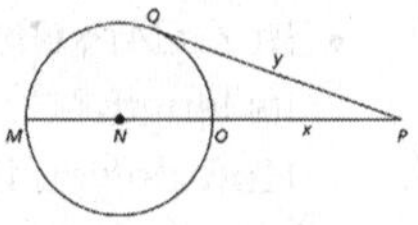

5. Let *x* = *OP* and *y* = *QP*. Write an equation relating *x* and *y*.

____

6. Use your equation to find the value of *y* for the given value of *x*. Round to the nearest tenth. Then find the ratio $\frac{x}{y}$. What do you notice about the ratios?

x	*y*	$\frac{x}{y}$
1		
2		
3		

____

Problem Solving

A satellite is *h* kilometers above the surface of Earth at point *S*. Given that Earth's radius is about 6378.1 kilometers, approximate the distance to the horizon to the nearest tenth of a kilometer.

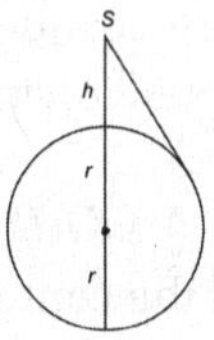

1. *h* = 16,000 km _______________
2. *h* = 20,000 km _______________
3. *h* = 25,000 km _______________
4. *h* = 30,000 km _______________
5. A wall hanging is made of a circular piece of wood 24 inches in diameter. Angela wants to use wire to hang the wall hanging from a nail at point *N*. The wire will be tangent to the circle and attached at points *P* and *Q*. What is the total length of wire needed if the distance from the top of the circle (point *R*) to the nail is 10 inches? Round to the nearest inch.

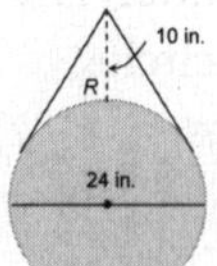

____

Choose the best answer.

6. A jet is cruising at point *P* at an altitude of 6 miles. Given that Earth's radius is about 4000 mi, find the approximate distance from the jet to the horizon.

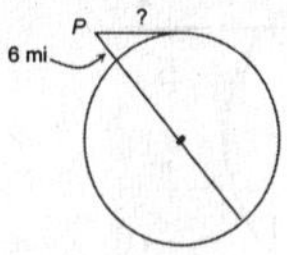

A 155 mi
B 219 mi
C 4006 mi
D 8006 mi

7. In the diagram, the ratio of *AB* to *BC* is 5 : 4. What is the length of $\overline{AC}$?

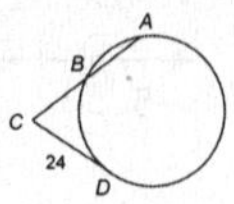

F 9
G 16
H 20
J 36

Notes

Circles in the Coordinate Plane
Connection: Completing the Square

Essential question: *How can you write and use equations of circles in the coordinate plane?*

© Houghton Mifflin Harcourt Publishing Company

COMMON CORE Standards for Mathematical Content

CC.9-12.A.REI.7 Solve a simple system consisting of a linear equation and a quadratic equation in two variables algebraically and graphically.

CC.9-12.G.GPE.1 Derive the equation of a circle of given center and radius using the Pythagorean Theorem; complete the square to find the center and radius of a circle given by an equation.

CC.9-12.G.GPE.4 Use coordinates to prove simple geometric theorems algebraically.

Prerequisites
Completing the square

Math Background
In later courses, students may study the equations of the four major conic sections: circles, ellipses, hyperbolas, and parabolas. In this unit, students get a preview of these ideas by using the Pythagorean Theorem and the distance formula to derive equations for circles and parabolas. Students connect the geometric definition of a circle (the set of points that are a fixed distance from a given point) with the algebraic representation of it (the equation of a circle with center (h, k) and radius r is $(x - h)^2 + (y - k)^2 = r^2$).

INTRODUCE

Remind students of the definition of a circle. Then, ask students to draw a circle that has center $(3, -1)$ and radius 2 on a coordinate plane. Be sure students understand that they should plot the center first and then count 2 units up from the center, 2 units down from the center, 2 units left from the center, and 2 units right from the center to plot four points that lie on the circle. Then, students can use a compass to help draw the rest of the circle.

TEACH

1 EXPLORE

Questioning Strategies
- In $\triangle CAP$, which side is the hypotenuse? What is its length? $\overline{CP}$; r
- How do you find the length of a horizontal segment like $\overline{CA}$? Take the absolute value of the difference of the x-coordinates.
- Why do you take the absolute value? Distance cannot be negative.

2 EXAMPLE

Questioning Strategies
- What three values do you need to find? the x- and y-coordinates of the center, and the length of the radius
- How do you complete the square? Add half the coefficient of the x-term squared and add half the coefficient of the y-term squared. Add the same quantities to the other side of the equation. Now, the equation will contain two perfect squares, one involving the variable x and one involving the variable y.

EXTRA EXAMPLE
Find the center and radius of the circle whose equation is $x^2 - 2x + y^2 + 4y = 4$. Then, graph the circle.
center: $(1, -2)$; radius: 3

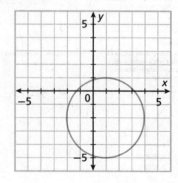

Name_____ Class_____ Date_____

12-7

Circles in the Coordinate Plane
Connection: Completing the Square

Essential question: *How can you write and use equations of circles in the coordinate plane?*

Recall that a circle is the set of all points in a plane that are a fixed distance from a given point. Now you will investigate circles in a coordinate plane.

Video Tutor

CC.9-12.G.GPE.1

1 EXPLORE Deriving the Equation of a Circle

Consider the circle in a coordinate plane that has its center at $C(h, k)$ and that has radius r.

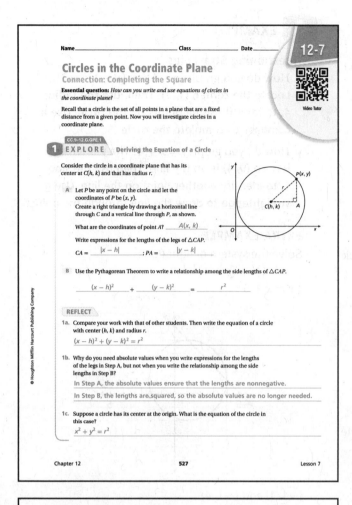

A Let P be any point on the circle and let the coordinates of P be (x, y).

Create a right triangle by drawing a horizontal line through C and a vertical line through P, as shown.

What are the coordinates of point A? ___$A(x, k)$___

Write expressions for the lengths of the legs of $\triangle CAP$.

$CA = $ ___$|x - h|$___ ; $PA = $ ___$|y - k|$___

B Use the Pythagorean Theorem to write a relationship among the side lengths of $\triangle CAP$.

___$(x - h)^2$___ + ___$(y - k)^2$___ = ___r^2___

REFLECT

1a. Compare your work with that of other students. Then write the equation of a circle with center (h, k) and radius r.

$(x - h)^2 + (y - k)^2 = r^2$

1b. Why do you need absolute values when you write expressions for the lengths of the legs in Step A, but not when you write the relationship among the side lengths in Step B?

In Step A, the absolute values ensure that the lengths are nonnegative.

In Step B, the lengths are squared, so the absolute values are no longer needed.

1c. Suppose a circle has its center at the origin. What is the equation of the circle in this case?

$x^2 + y^2 = r^2$

© Houghton Mifflin Harcourt Publishing Company

Equation of a Circle

The equation of a circle with center (h, k) and radius r is $(x - h)^2 + (y - k)^2 = r^2$.

CC.9-12.G.GPE.1

2 EXAMPLE Finding the Center and Radius of a Circle

Find the center and radius of the circle whose equation is $x^2 - 4x + y^2 + 2y = 4$.
Then graph the circle.

A Complete the square to write the equation in the form $(x - h)^2 + (y - k)^2 = r^2$.

$x^2 - 4x + \boxed{} + y^2 + 2y + \boxed{} = 4 + \boxed{}$ Set up to complete the square.

$x^2 - 4x + \left(\frac{-4}{2}\right)^2 + y^2 + 2y + \left(\frac{2}{2}\right)^2 = 4 + \left(\frac{-4}{2}\right)^2 + \left(\frac{2}{2}\right)^2$ Add $\left(\frac{-4}{2}\right)^2$ and $\left(\frac{2}{2}\right)^2$ to both sides.

$x^2 - 4x + \underline{4} + y^2 + 2y + \underline{1} = 4 + \underline{5}$ Simplify.

$(x - \underline{2})^2 + (y + \underline{1})^2 = \underline{9}$ Factor.

B Identify h, k, and r to determine the center and radius.

$h = \underline{2}$ $k = \underline{-1}$ $r = \underline{3}$

So, the center is ($\underline{2}$, $\underline{-1}$) and the radius is $\underline{3}$.

C Graph the circle.

• Locate the center of the circle.
• Place the point of your compass at the center.
• Open the compass to the radius.
• Use the compass to draw the circle.

REFLECT

2a. How can you check your graph by testing specific points from the graph in the original equation? Give an example.

Check that points on the graph satisfy the equation. For example, (2, 2) is on the

graph and this point satisfies the equation: $2^2 - 4 \cdot 2 + 2^2 + 2 \cdot 2 = 4$.

2b. Suppose you translate the circle by the translation $(x, y) \rightarrow (x + 4, y - 1)$.
What is the equation of the image of the circle? Explain.

The equation is $(x - 6)^2 + (y + 2)^2 = 9$, because the center is translated to $(6, -2)$

and the radius does not change.

© Houghton Mifflin Harcourt Publishing Company

Avoid Common Errors

Some students may say that the circle with equation $(x - 2)^2 + (y + 1)^2 = 9$ has center $(-2, 1)$. It may help these students to rewrite the equation as $(x - 2)^2 + (y - (-1))^2 = 9$ and compare this to the general equation, $(x - h)^2 + (y - k)^2 = r^2$, which has center (h, k). This may help them see that the correct center is $(2, -1)$.

3 EXAMPLE

Questioning Strategies

- What steps can you use to write this proof?
  First, write the equation of the circle. Then, check to see whether the given point is a solution of the equation. If so, the point lies on the circle.

- How do you determine the radius of the circle?
  Count units on the coordinate grid, moving horizontally or vertically from the center to the circle.

EXTRA EXAMPLE

Prove or disprove that the point $(3, 4)$ lies on the circle that is centered at the origin and contains the point $(-5, 0)$.
The radius of the circle is 5. The equation of the circle is $x^2 + y^2 = 25$. Substituting the x- and y-coordinates of the given point into the left side of the equation gives $3^2 + 4^2$. Since this is equal to 25, the point is a solution of the equation, so it lies on the circle.

MATHEMATICAL PRACTICE — Highlighting the Standards

This lesson offers an opportunity to address Standard 6 (Attend to precision). In particular, the standard discusses the need for students to "calculate accurately and efficiently." This skill is of vital importance when students complete the square to find the center and radius of a circle. It is easy to make errors when completing the square. For instance, some students may add quantities to one side of the equation and forget to add them to the other side. Remind students to work slowly and carefully and write neatly, whenever they complete the square. Then have students check work for accuracy.

4 EXAMPLE

Questioning Strategies

- How do you graph $(x - 1)^2 + (y - 1)^2 = 16$?
  Locate the center, (1, 1). Then, use the radius, 4, to identify some points on the circle. Use a compass to complete the circle.

- How do you graph $y = x + 4$? **The y-intercept is 4, so (0, 4) is on the line. Then use the slope, 1, to identify another point on the line. Use a straightedge to draw the line through the points.**

EXTRA EXAMPLE

Solve the system of equations.
$$\begin{cases} (x + 1)^2 + (y - 1)^2 = 9 \\ y = x + 5 \end{cases}$$

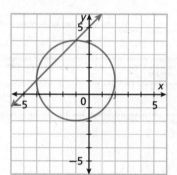

$(-4, 1)$ and $(-1, 4)$

MATHEMATICAL PRACTICE — Highlighting the Standards

Standard 1 (Make sense of problems and persevere in solving them) emphasizes that students should continually ask themselves, "Does this make sense?" To that end, when students solve a system by graphing, remind them that they must check their answers to make sure they are solutions of each equation in the ordered pair.

3 EXAMPLE CC.9-12.G.GPE.4 **Writing a Coordinate Proof**

Prove or disprove that the point $(1, \sqrt{15})$ lies on the circle that is centered at the origin and contains the point $(0, 4)$.

A Plot a point at the origin and at $(0, 4)$. Use these to help you draw the circle centered at the origin that contains $(0, 4)$.

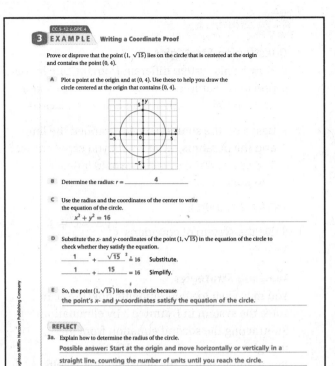

B Determine the radius: $r = \underline{\quad 4 \quad}$

C Use the radius and the coordinates of the center to write the equation of the circle.

$\underline{x^2 + y^2 = 16}$

D Substitute the x- and y-coordinates of the point $(1, \sqrt{15})$ in the equation of the circle to check whether they satisfy the equation.

$\underline{\quad 1 \quad}^2 + \underline{\quad \sqrt{15} \quad}^2 \stackrel{?}{=} 16$ Substitute.

$\underline{\quad 1 \quad} + \underline{\quad 15 \quad} = 16$ Simplify.

E So, the point $(1, \sqrt{15})$ lies on the circle because

the point's x- and y-coordinates satisfy the equation of the circle.

REFLECT

3a. Explain how to determine the radius of the circle.

Possible answer: Start at the origin and move horizontally or vertically in a

straight line, counting the number of units until you reach the circle.

3b. Name another point with noninteger coordinates that lies on the circle. Explain.

Possible answer: $(3, \sqrt{7})$, because $3^2 + (\sqrt{7})^2 = 16$.

3c. Explain how you can prove that the point $(2, \sqrt{5})$ does *not* lie on the circle.

The point's x- and y-coordinates do not satisfy the equation of the circle:

$2^2 + (\sqrt{5})^2 \neq 16$.

Chapter 12   **529**   Lesson 7

Recall that you can solve a system of two equations in two unknowns by graphing both equations and finding the point(s) of intersection of the graphs. You can also solve a system using the algebraic methods of substitution or elimination. In the next Examples, you will see how these techniques may be used with systems that include a quadratic equation.

4 EXAMPLE CC.9-12.A.REI.7 **Solving a System by Graphing**

Solve the system of equations. $\begin{cases} (x-1)^2 + (y-1)^2 = 16 \\ y = x + 4 \end{cases}$

A The equation $(x-1)^2 + (y-1)^2 = 16$ represents a circle with center $\underline{(1, 1)}$ and radius $\underline{4}$.

The equation $y = x + 4$ represents a line with slope $\underline{1}$ and y-intercept $\underline{4}$.

B Graph the equations on the coordinate plane below.

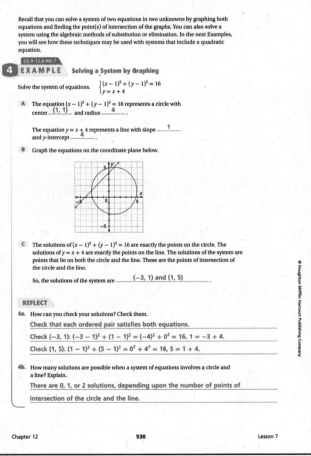

C The solutions of $(x-1)^2 + (y-1)^2 = 16$ are exactly the points on the circle. The solutions of $y = x + 4$ are exactly the points on the line. The solutions of the system are points that lie on both the circle and the line. These are the points of intersection of the circle and the line.

So, the solutions of the system are $\underline{(-3, 1) \text{ and } (1, 5)}$.

REFLECT

4a. How can you check your solutions? Check them.

Check that each ordered pair satisfies both equations.

Check $(-3, 1)$: $(-3 - 1)^2 + (1 - 1)^2 = (-4)^2 + 0^2 = 16$, $1 = -3 + 4$.

Check $(1, 5)$: $(1 - 1)^2 + (5 - 1)^2 = 0^2 + 4^2 = 16$, $5 = 1 + 4$.

4b. How many solutions are possible when a system of equations involves a circle and a line? Explain.

There are 0, 1, or 2 solutions, depending upon the number of points of

intersection of the circle and the line.

Chapter 12   **530**   Lesson 7

© Houghton Mifflin Harcourt Publishing Company

Notes

Chapter 12   **530**   Lesson 7

Questioning Strategies

- What does it mean to solve a system by substitution? You solve one equation for one variable. Then, you substitute the resulting expression in the other equation to get a new equation in one variable. Solving this equation gives the value of x or y. Substituting this value back into one of the original equations gives the value of the other variable.

EXTRA EXAMPLE
Solve the system of equations.

$$\begin{cases} x^2 + y^2 = 20 \\ y = 3x \end{cases}$$

$(\sqrt{2}, 3\sqrt{2})$ and $(-\sqrt{2}, -3\sqrt{2})$

Questioning Strategies

- How is this system different from the one in the previous example? This system involves a line and a parabola rather than a line and a circle.

- Based on the solution, if you graphed the line and the parabola, what would you expect to see? The line and the parabola would intersect at one point, (4, 13).

EXTRA EXAMPLE
Solve the system of equations. $\begin{cases} y = -x^2 + 1 \\ y = 2x + 2 \end{cases}$
$(-1, 0)$

Teaching Strategies
You may wish to show students how they can solve the system in Example 3 by elimination. Subtracting the second equation from the first gives $0 = x^2 - 3 - 8x + 19$. Note that this is equivalent to the equation that results from substitution.

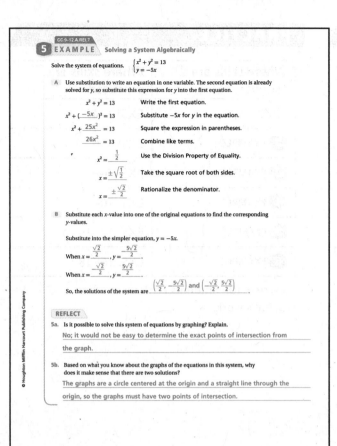

5 EXAMPLE Solving a System Algebraically

Solve the system of equations. $\begin{cases} x^2 + y^2 = 13 \\ y = -5x \end{cases}$

A Use substitution to write an equation in one variable. The second equation is already solved for y, so substitute this expression for y into the first equation.

$x^2 + y^2 = 13$	Write the first equation.
$x^2 + (\underline{-5x})^2 = 13$	Substitute $-5x$ for y in the equation.
$x^2 + \underline{25x^2} = 13$	Square the expression in parentheses.
$\underline{26x^2} = 13$	Combine like terms.
$x^2 = \underline{\frac{1}{2}}$	Use the Division Property of Equality.
$x = \underline{\pm\sqrt{\frac{1}{2}}}$	Take the square root of both sides.
$x = \underline{\pm\frac{\sqrt{2}}{2}}$	Rationalize the denominator.

B Substitute each x-value into one of the original equations to find the corresponding y-values.

Substitute into the simpler equation, $y = -5x$.

When $x = \frac{\sqrt{2}}{2}$, $y = \underline{-\frac{5\sqrt{2}}{2}}$.

When $x = \underline{-\frac{\sqrt{2}}{2}}$, $y = \underline{\frac{5\sqrt{2}}{2}}$.

So, the solutions of the system are $\underline{\left(\frac{\sqrt{2}}{2}, -\frac{5\sqrt{2}}{2}\right)}$ and $\underline{\left(-\frac{\sqrt{2}}{2}, \frac{5\sqrt{2}}{2}\right)}$.

REFLECT

5a. Is it possible to solve this system of equations by graphing? Explain.

No; it would not be easy to determine the exact points of intersection from the graph.

5b. Based on what you know about the graphs of the equations in this system, why does it make sense that there are two solutions?

The graphs are a circle centered at the origin and a straight line through the origin, so the graphs must have two points of intersection.

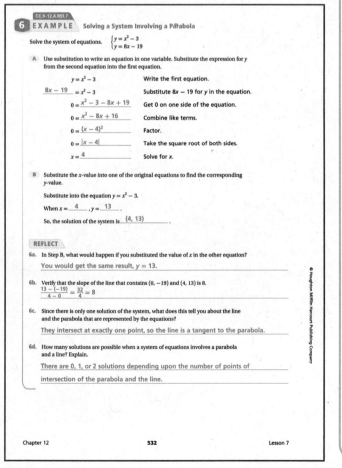

6 EXAMPLE Solving a System Involving a Parabola

Solve the system of equations. $\begin{cases} y = x^2 - 3 \\ y = 8x - 19 \end{cases}$

A Use substitution to write an equation in one variable. Substitute the expression for y from the second equation into the first equation.

$y = x^2 - 3$	Write the first equation.
$\underline{8x - 19} = x^2 - 3$	Substitute $8x - 19$ for y in the equation.
$0 = x^2 - 3 - 8x + 19$	Get 0 on one side of the equation.
$0 = \underline{x^2 - 8x + 16}$	Combine like terms.
$0 = \underline{(x-4)^2}$	Factor.
$0 = \underline{|x-4|}$	Take the square root of both sides.
$x = \underline{4}$	Solve for x.

B Substitute the x-value into one of the original equations to find the corresponding y-value.

Substitute into the equation $y = x^2 - 3$.

When $x = \underline{4}$, $y = \underline{13}$.

So, the solution of the system is $\underline{(4, 13)}$.

REFLECT

6a. In Step B, what would happen if you substituted the value of x in the other equation?

You would get the same result, $y = 13$.

6b. Verify that the slope of the line that contains $(0, -19)$ and $(4, 13)$ is 8.

$\frac{13 - (-19)}{4 - 0} = \frac{32}{4} = 8$

6c. Since there is only one solution of the system, what does this tell you about the line and the parabola that are represented by the equations?

They intersect at exactly one point, so the line is a tangent to the parabola.

6d. How many solutions are possible when a system of equations involves a parabola and a line? Explain.

There are 0, 1, or 2 solutions depending upon the number of points of intersection of the parabola and the line.

Essential Question

How can you write and use equations of circles in the coordinate plane?

The equation of a circle with center (h, k) and radius r is $(x - h)^2 + (y - k)^2 = r^2$. Equations of circles can be used to find whether points lie on a circle and to solve some systems of equations.

Summarize

Have students write a journal entry in which they explain how to solve a system of equations consisting of a linear equation in two variables and a quadratic equation in two variables.

Where skills are taught	Where skills are practiced
1 EXPLORE	EXS. 1–4
2 EXAMPLE	EXS. 5–6
3 EXAMPLE	EXS. 7–9
4 EXAMPLE	EXS. 10–12
5 EXAMPLE	EXS. 13–15
6 EXAMPLE	EXS. 16–18

Exercise 19: Students critique another student's work.

PRACTICE

Write the equation of the circle with the given center and radius.

1. center: (0, 2); radius: 5
   $$x^2 + (y - 2)^2 = 25$$

2. center: (−1, 3); radius 8
   $$(x + 1)^2 + (y - 3)^2 = 64$$

3. center: (−4, −5); radius: $\sqrt{2}$
   $$(x + 4)^2 + (y + 5)^2 = 2$$

4. center: (9, 0); radius $\sqrt{3}$
   $$(x - 9)^2 + y^2 = 3$$

Find the center and radius of the circle with the given equation. Then graph the circle.

5. $x^2 - 2x + y^2 = 15$
   center: (1, 0); radius: 4

6. $x^2 + 4x + y^2 - 6y = -9$
   center: (−2, 3); radius: 2

7. Prove or disprove that the point $(1, \sqrt{3})$ lies on the circle that is centered at the origin and contains the point (0, 2).

   The radius of the circle is 2, so its equation is $x^2 + y^2 = 4$. The point $(1, \sqrt{3})$

   does lie on the circle, because its x- and y-coordinates satisfy the equation:

   $1^2 + (\sqrt{3})^2 = 1 + 3 = 4.$

8. Prove or disprove that the point $(2, \sqrt{3})$ lies on the circle that is centered at the origin and contains the point (−3, 0).

   The radius of the circle is 3, so its equation is $x^2 + y^2 = 9$. The point $(2, \sqrt{3})$

   does not lie on the circle, because its x- and y-coordinates do not satisfy the

   equation: $2^2 + (\sqrt{3})^2 \neq 9.$

9. Prove or disprove that the circle with equation $x^2 - 4x + y^2 = -3$ intersects the y-axis.

   Points on the y-axis have x-coordinate 0. Substituting $x = 0$ in the equation gives

   $y^2 = -3$. This equation has no real solutions, so there are no points of the

   form (0, y) on the circle. Therefore, the circle does not intersect the y-axis.

Solve each system of equations by graphing.

10. $\begin{cases} (x - 2)^2 + y^2 = 4 \\ y = -x \end{cases}$

11. $\begin{cases} (x + 1)^2 + (y - 1)^2 = 9 \\ y = x - 1 \end{cases}$

12. $\begin{cases} y = x^2 - 1 \\ y = -x + 1 \end{cases}$

(0, 0); (2, −2)   (−1, −2); (2, 1)   (−2, 3); (1, 0)

Solve each system of equations algebraically.

13. $\begin{cases} x^2 + y^2 = 10 \\ y = -3x \end{cases}$
    (1, −3); (−1, 3)

14. $\begin{cases} x^2 + y^2 = 25 \\ y = 7x \end{cases}$
    $\left(\frac{\sqrt{2}}{2}, \frac{7\sqrt{2}}{2}\right); \left(-\frac{\sqrt{2}}{2}, -\frac{7\sqrt{2}}{2}\right)$

15. $\begin{cases} x^2 + y^2 = 13 \\ y = -8x \end{cases}$
    $\left(\frac{\sqrt{5}}{5}, -\frac{8\sqrt{5}}{5}\right); \left(-\frac{\sqrt{5}}{5}, \frac{8\sqrt{5}}{5}\right)$

16. $\begin{cases} y = x^2 \\ y = -x + 2 \end{cases}$
    (−2, 4); (1, 1)

17. $\begin{cases} y = x^2 + 2 \\ y = 4 \end{cases}$
    $(-\sqrt{2}, 4); (\sqrt{2}, 4)$

18. $\begin{cases} y = -x^2 + 2 \\ y = x - 4 \end{cases}$
    (−3, −7); (2, −2)

19. **Error Analysis** A student was asked to solve the system $\begin{cases} x^2 + y^2 = 9 \\ y = x \end{cases}$

    The student's solution is shown below. Critique the student's work.
    If there is an error, give the correct solution.

    > The graph of $x^2 + y^2 = 9$ is a circle centered at the origin with radius 3. The graph of $y = x$ is a straight line through the origin. The graphs intersect at (2, 2) and (−2, −2), so these are the solutions.

    It is not possible to identify the points of intersection accurately from the graph.

    The actual points of intersection are $\left(\frac{3\sqrt{2}}{2}, \frac{3\sqrt{2}}{2}\right)$ and $\left(-\frac{3\sqrt{2}}{2}, -\frac{3\sqrt{2}}{2}\right)$.

Assign these pages to help your students practice and apply important lesson concepts. For additional exercises, see the Student Edition.

Answers

Additional Practice

1. $x^2 + (y + 2)^2 = 40$

2. $(x + 1)^2 + (y - 3)^2 = 4$; $(-1, 3)$; $r = 2$

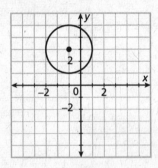

3. $(x + 2)^2 + (y + 3)^2 = 4$; $(-2, -3)$; $r = 2$

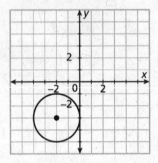

4. $(x - 1)^2 + (y - 1)^2 = 16$; $(1, 1)$; $r = 4$

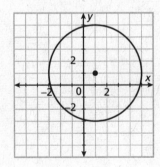

5. $x^2 + (y + 3)^2 = 1$; $(0, -3)$; $r = 1$

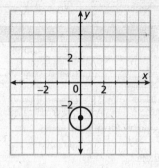

6. $(0, -1)$ and $(3, 2)$

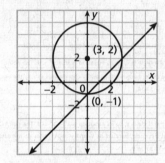

7. $(5, 0)$ and $(0, -5)$

8. $(-1, -1)$ and $(2, -4)$

9. $(2, -10)$

Problem Solving

1. The radius of the circle is 5, so its equation is $x^2 + y^2 = 25$. The line $y = 6$ does not intersect the circle because all points on this line have a y-coordinate of 6, and there are no points $(x, 6)$ that satisfy the equation $x^2 + y^2 = 25$.

2. yes

3. 6 miles

4. B

5. H

6. D

7. F

Additional Practice

1. Write an equation of a circle with center $B(0, -2)$ that passes through $(-6, 0)$. _____

Complete the square to rewrite the given equation in the form $(x - h)^2 + (y - k)^2 = r^2$. Identify the center and radius of the circle. Then graph the circle.

2. $x^2 + 2x + y^2 - 6y = -6$ _____

3. $x^2 + 4x + y^2 + 6y = -9$ _____

4. $x^2 - 2x + y^2 - 2y = 14$ _____

5. $x^2 + y^2 + 6y = -8$ _____

6. Solve the system of equations by graphing.

$$\begin{cases} x^2 + (y - 2)^2 = 9 \\ y = x - 1 \end{cases}$$

Solve each system of equations algebraically.

7. $\begin{cases} x^2 + y^2 = 25 \\ x - y = 5 \end{cases}$

8. $\begin{cases} y = -x^2 \\ y = -x - 2 \end{cases}$

9. $\begin{cases} (x - 2)^2 + y^2 = 100 \\ y = -10 \end{cases}$

Problem Solving

1. Prove or disprove that the circle that is centered at the origin and contains the point $(-4, -3)$ intersects the line $x = 6$.

_____

_____

_____

Crater Lake in Oregon is roughly circular. Suppose that $A(-4, 1)$ and $B(-2, -3)$ represent points on the circular shoreline of the lake. The center of the lake is at $(1, 1)$.

2. Does the point $C(5, -2)$ lie on the shoreline of the lake?

_____

3. Each unit of the coordinate plane represents $\frac{3}{5}$ mile. Find the diameter of Crater Lake.

_____

Choose the best answer.

4. An English knot garden has hedges planted to form geometric shapes. A blueprint of a knot garden contains three circular hedges as described in the table. Flowers are to be planted in the space that is within all three circles. Which is a point that could be planted with flowers?

   A (7, 1)   C (0, 5)
   B (5, 1)   D (0, 0)

Circular Hedge	Center	Radius
A	(3, 2)	3 ft
B	(7, 2)	4 ft
C	(5, -1)	3 ft

5. An amusement park ride consists of a circular ring that holds 50 riders. Suppose the center of the ride is at the origin and that one of the riders on the circular ring is at (16, 15.1). If one unit on the coordinate plane equals 1 foot, which is a close approximation of the distance the rider travels during one complete revolution of the circle?

   F 22 ft   H 138 ft
   G 44 ft   J 1521 ft

6. Which of these circles intersects the circle that has center (0, 6) and radius 1?

   A $(x - 5)^2 + (y + 3)^2 = 4$
   B $(x - 4)^2 + (y - 3)^2 = 9$
   C $(x + 5)^2 + (y + 1)^2 = 16$
   D $(x + 1)^2 + (y - 4)^2 = 4$

7. The center of a circle is (9, 2), and the radius of the circle is 5 units. Which is a point on the circle?

   F (4, 2)   H (9, 4)
   G (14, 0)   J (9, -5)

This page provides students with the opportunity to apply concepts from the Common Core in real-world problem situations. There are three different levels of performance tasks:

⭐ **Novice:** These are short word problems that require students to apply the math they have learned in straightforward, real-world situations.

⭐⭐ **Apprentice:** These are more involved problems that guide students step-by-step through more complex tasks. These exercises include more complicated reasoning, writing, and open-ended elements.

⭐⭐⭐ **Expert:** These are open-ended, non-routine problems that, instead of stepping the students through, ask them to choose their own methods for solving and justify their answers and reasoning.

Sample answers

1. 33.9 in.; The diagonal of the table is the diameter of the circle, which is 48 in. Therefore, each side of the square table must be $\frac{48}{\sqrt{2}} \approx 33.9$ in.

2. 16.7 in.

3. Scoring Guide:

Task	Possible points
a	1 point for correctly finding the equation of the circle to be $(x - 10)^2 + (y - 10)^2 = 100$
b	1 point for giving the side length of 17.32 units, and 1 point for appropriate work
c	1 point each for vertices (5, 18.66) and (5, 1.34), and 1 point for showing appropriate work, which should involve using half the side length to find the y-coordinates of the two final vertices and then substituting one of those into the equation for the circle to find the x-coordinate of both points.

Total possible points: 6

© Houghton Mifflin Harcourt Publishing Company

Performance Tasks

CHAPTER 12

COMMON CORE
CC.9-12.G.SRT.8
CC.9-12.G.C.2
CC.9-12.G.GPE.1

⭐ **1.** A circular table has a diameter of 48 inches. A carpenter is remaking it into a square table. To the nearest tenth of an inch, what is the greatest possible side length of the square table? Explain.

⭐ **2.** A moving company needs to replace a circular glass mirror that it broke during a move. The dimensions of a piece of the broken mirror are shown in the figure. What was the diameter of the original mirror? Round your answer to the nearest tenth of an inch.

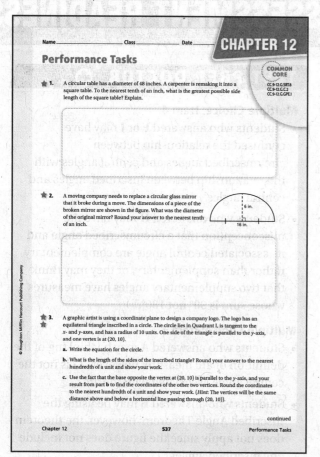

6 in.

16 in.

⭐⭐ **3.** A graphic artist is using a coordinate plane to design a company logo. The logo has an equilateral triangle inscribed in a circle. The circle lies in Quadrant I, is tangent to the x- and y-axes, and has a radius of 10 units. One side of the triangle is parallel to the y-axis, and one vertex is at (20, 10).

a. Write the equation for the circle.

b. What is the length of the sides of the inscribed triangle? Round your answer to the nearest hundredth of a unit and show your work.

c. Use the fact that the base opposite the vertex at (20, 10) is parallel to the y-axis, and your result from part **b** to find the coordinates of the other two vertices. Round the coordinates to the nearest hundredth of a unit and show your work. (*Hint*: The vertices will be the same distance above and below a horizontal line passing through (20, 10)).

continued

⭐⭐⭐ **4.** An artist is using a coordinate plane to plan a string design for a wall. The artist plans to hammer a nail at each vertex of a regular hexagon. Then the artist will use string to connect the vertices to make the hexagon shape. The artist starts with a circle centered at the origin and places the first vertex at (8, 0).

a. Where are the other vertices? Write coordinates in radical form, if necessary.

b. Not considering knots, what is the minimum amount of string the artist needs to outline the hexagon and connect all the diagonals? Round to the nearest tenth.

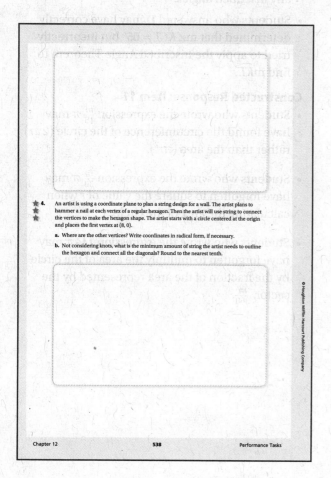

4. Scoring Guide:

Task	Possible points
a	5 points for correctly finding the coordinates to be $(4, -4\sqrt{3})$, $(-4, -4\sqrt{3})$, $(-8, 0)$, $(-4, 4\sqrt{3})$, and $(4, 4\sqrt{3})$ or the decimal equivalents
b	1 point for correctly finding the total length of the string to be 48 units

Total possible points: 6

© Houghton Mifflin Harcourt Publishing Company

COMMON CORE CORRELATION

Standard	Items
CC.9-12.A.REI.7	3
CC.9-12.G.CO.1	12
CC.9-12.G.C.2	4, 5, 7, 9
CC.9-12.G.C.3	13
CC.9-12.G.C.4(+)	8
CC.9-12.G.C.5	6, 11, 12
CC.9-12.G.GPE.1	1, 2
CC.9-12.G.GPE.4	10

TEST PREP DOCTOR +

Multiple Choice: Item 4

- Students who answered **F** or **J** may have confused the relationship between circumscribed angles and central angles with the relationship between inscribed angles and central angles.

- Students who answered **H** may have the misconception that a circumscribed angle and its associated central angle are complementary rather than supplementary, or they may think that two supplementary angles have measures whose sum is 90° not 180°.

Multiple Choice: Item 7

- Students who answered **A** may be thinking of the definition of arc measure; however, $\angle J$ is not the central angle associated with the arc.

- Students who answered **B** may be using the Inscribed Angle Theorem; however, the theorem does not apply since the figure does not include any inscribed angles.

- Students who answered **D** may have correctly determined that $m\angle KCJ = 65°$ but incorrectly tried to apply the Inscribed Angle Theorem to find $m\overset{\frown}{KL}$.

Constructed Response: Item 11

- Students who wrote the expression $\frac{m}{15}\pi$ may have found the circumference of the circle ($2\pi r$) rather than the area (πr^2).

- Students who wrote the expression $\frac{m}{30}\pi$ may have forgotten to square the value of r when calculating the area of the circle.

- Students who wrote the expression 144π may have forgotten to multiply the area of the circle by the fraction of the area represented by the sector, $\frac{m}{360}$.

Name _____ Class _____ Date _____

MULTIPLE CHOICE

1. What is the center of the circle whose equation is $x^2 - 6x + y^2 + 6y = -9$?

A. (3, −3)
B. (3, 3)
C. (−3, 3)
D. (−3, −3)

2. What is the equation of the circle with center (4, −5) and radius 4?

F. $(x + 4)^2 + (y - 5)^2 = 4$
G. $(x - 4)^2 + (y + 5)^2 = 4$
H. $(x + 4)^2 + (y - 5)^2 = 16$
J. $(x - 4)^2 + (y + 5)^2 = 16$

3. The ordered pair (x, y) is a solution of this system of equations.

$$\begin{cases} x^2 + y^2 = 10 \\ y = 7x \end{cases}$$

Which of the following could be the value of x?

A. $\frac{\sqrt{2}}{2}$
B. $\frac{\sqrt{5}}{5}$
C. $\frac{\sqrt{5}}{2}$
D. $\frac{\sqrt{10}}{7}$

4. $\overline{PR}$ and $\overline{QR}$ are tangents to circle C. Which expression represents $m\angle C$?

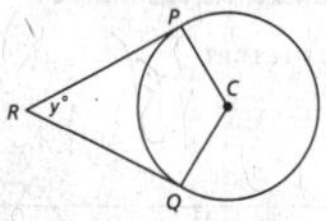

F. $(2y)°$
G. $(180 - y)°$
H. $(90 - y)°$
J. $\left(\frac{1}{2}y\right)°$

5. In circle O, $\angle ABC$ is an inscribed angle and $\overline{AC}$ is a diameter. Which of the following must be true?

A. $\angle ABC$ is an acute angle.
B. $\angle ABC$ is a right angle.
C. $\overline{AB}$ is a radius.
D. $\overline{AC} \perp \overline{BC}$

6. What is the radian measure of the angle whose degree measure is 20°?

F. $\frac{\pi}{20}$
G. $\frac{\pi}{18}$
H. $\frac{\pi}{9}$
J. $\frac{2\pi}{9}$

7. $\overline{JK}$ is a tangent to circle C. What is $m\widehat{KL}$?

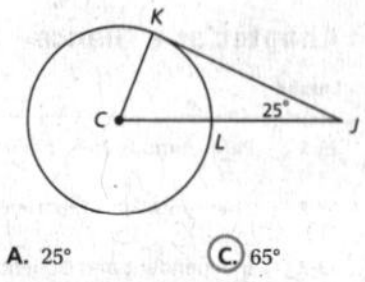

A. 25°
B. 50°
C. 65°
D. 130°

8. Noah is constructing a tangent from P to circle C. The figure shows what he has done so far. What should he do next?

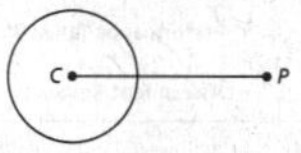

F. Construct a perpendicular at point P.
G. Construct a perpendicular at point C.
H. Construct a circle whose center is at the intersection of $\overline{CP}$ and circle C.
J. Construct the midpoint of $\overline{CP}$.

9. What is $m\angle GCJ$?

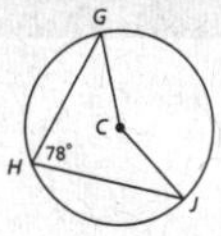

A. 39°
B. 78°
C. 102°
D. 156°

CONSTRUCTED RESPONSE

10. Prove or disprove that the point $(2, \sqrt{5})$ lies on the circle that is centered at the origin and contains the point $(0, -3)$.

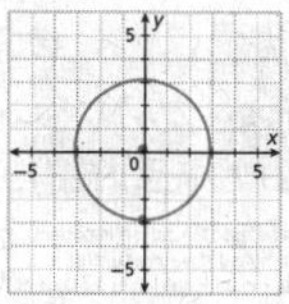

The radius of the circle is 3, so the equation of the circle is $x^2 + y^2 = 9$.

Substituting the x- and y-coordinates of the given point into the equation shows that $(2, \sqrt{5})$ is a solution of the equation: $2^2 + (\sqrt{5})^2 = 4 + 5 = 9$. This means the point lies on the circle.

11. Write an expression in terms of m that you can use to find the area of sector AOB.

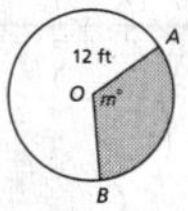

$\frac{2m}{5}\pi$

12. Using the figure below, Andrea discovers that the length of the arc intercepted by the 60° angle is proportional to the radius. What is the constant of proportionality for the relationship? Show your reasoning.

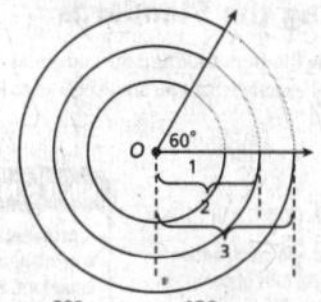

$\frac{\pi}{3} \cdot \frac{60°}{360°} \cdot 2\pi = \frac{120\pi}{360} = \frac{\pi}{3}$

13. Quadrilateral $WXYZ$ is inscribed in circle O. Complete the following proof to show that opposite angles are supplementary.

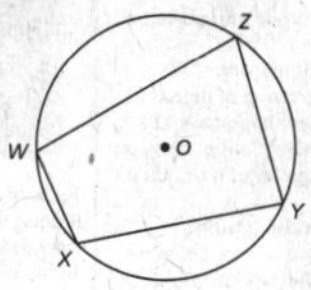

a. $\widehat{YZW}$ and $\widehat{WXY}$ make a complete circle. Therefore, $m\widehat{YZW} + m\widehat{WXY} =$ __360°__.

b. By the Inscribed Angle Theorem,

$m\angle X = \frac{1}{2}m\widehat{YZW}$ and $m\angle Z = \frac{1}{2}m\widehat{WXY}$.

c. Complete the proof by showing that the sum of $m\angle X$ and $m\angle Z$ is 180°.

$m\angle X + m\angle Z = \frac{1}{2}m\widehat{YZW} + \frac{1}{2}m\widehat{WXY}$

$\qquad\qquad = \frac{1}{2}\left(m\widehat{YZW} + m\widehat{WXY}\right)$

$\qquad\qquad = \frac{1}{2} \cdot 360°$

$\qquad\qquad = 180°$

Similar reasoning can be used to show angles W and Y are supplementary.

CHAPTER 13

Probability

COMMON CORE PROFESSIONAL DEVELOPMENT **CC.9-12.S.CP.9(+)***

In previous courses, students listed the elements of a sample space using tables, organized lists, and diagrams, and found probability using the ratio of the number of favorable events to total number of possible events. In this chapter, students take a more sophisticated approach to probability by identifying patterns used to develop formulas. These include permutations and combinations formulas, as well as formulas for conditional probability, probability of mutually exclusive and overlapping events, and the Addition Rule.

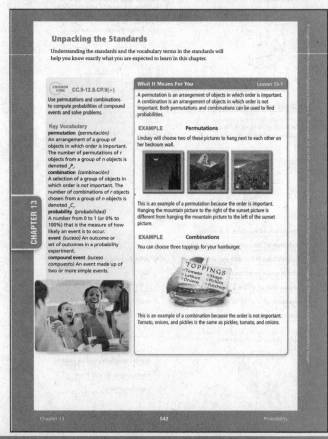

Probability

Chapter Focus

Probability theory is the branch of mathematics concerned with situations involving chance. You will learn how to use set theory to help you calculate basic probabilities and will investigate the role of permutations and combinations in probability. You will also learn how to determine the probability of mutually exclusive events, overlapping events, independent events, and dependent events. Along the way, you will perform simulations and learn how to use probability to make and analyze decisions.

CHAPTER 13

COMMON CORE

Chapter at a Glance

Lesson		Standards for Mathematical Content
13-1	Permutations and Combinations	CC.9-12.S.CP.9(+)
13-2	Theoretical and Experimental Probability	CC.9-12.S.MD.6(+)
13-3	Independent and Dependent Events	CC.9-12.S.CP.2, CC.9-12.S.CP.3, CC.9-12.S.CP.4, CC.9-12.S.CP.8(+)
13-4	Two-Way Tables	CC.9-12.S.CP.3, CC.9-12.S.CP.6
13-5	Compound Events	CC.9-12.S.CP.7
	Performance Tasks	
	Assessment Readiness	

Chapter 13   541   Probability

Unpacking the Standards

Understanding the standards and the vocabulary terms in the standards will help you know exactly what you are expected to learn in this chapter.

COMMON CORE **CC.9-12.S.CP.9(+)**

Use permutations and combinations to compute probabilities of compound events and solve problems.

Key Vocabulary

permutation *(permutación)* An arrangement of a group of objects in which order is important. The number of permutations of r objects from a group of n objects is denoted $_nP_r$.

combination *(combinación)* A selection of a group of objects in which order is *not* important. The number of combinations of r objects chosen from a group of n objects is denoted $_nC_r$.

probability *(probabilidad)* A number from 0 to 1 (or 0% to 100%) that is the measure of how likely an event is to occur.

event *(suceso)* An outcome or set of outcomes in a probability experiment.

compound event *(suceso compuesto)* An event made up of two or more simple events.

What It Means For You Lesson 13-1

A permutation is an arrangement of objects in which order is important. A combination is an arrangement of objects in which order is not important. Both permutations and combinations can be used to find probabilities.

EXAMPLE **Permutations**

Lindsey will choose two of these pictures to hang next to each other on her bedroom wall.

This is an example of a permutation because the order is important. Hanging the mountain picture to the right of the sunset picture is different from hanging the mountain picture to the left of the sunset picture.

EXAMPLE **Combinations**

You can choose three toppings for your hamburger.

TOPPINGS
Tomato Mayo
Lettuce Pickle
Onions Ketchup

This is an example of a combination because the order is not important. Tomato, onions, and pickles is the same as pickles, tomato, and onions.

Chapter 13   542   Probability

COMMON CORE CC.9-12.S.CP.1

Describe events as subsets of a sample space (the set of outcomes) using characteristics (or categories) of the outcomes, or as unions, intersections, or complements of other events ("or," "and," "not").

Key Vocabulary

sample space *(espacio muestral)* The set of all possible outcomes of a probability experiment.
outcome *(resultado)* A possible result of a probability experiment.
union *(unión)* The union of two sets is the set of all elements that are in either set, denoted by $\cup$.
intersection *(intersección de conjuntos)* The intersection of two sets is the set of all elements that are common to both sets, denoted by $\cap$.
complement of an event *(complemento de un suceso)* All outcomes in the sample space that are not in an event *E*, denoted $\bar{E}$ or E^c.

What It Means For You Lesson 13-5

To calculate the probability of a particular event, you may need to find the sample space, which is the set of all possible outcomes. You may also need to determine which outcome(s) in the sample space make up the event.

EXAMPLE **Sample Spaces**

The sample space for rolling two standard number cubes is shown. The circled outcomes make up the event "rolling a sum of 10."

COMMON CORE CC.9-12.S.CP.4

Construct and interpret two-way frequency tables of data when two categories are associated with each object being classified. Use the two-way table as a sample space to decide if events are independent and to approximate conditional probabilities.

Key Vocabulary

frequency table *(tabla de frecuencia)* A table that lists the number of times, or frequency, that each data value occurs.
independent events *(sucesos independientes)* Events for which the occurrence or non-occurrence of one event does not affect the probability of the other event.
conditional probability *(probabilidad condicional)* The probability of event *B*, given that event *A* has already occurred or is certain to occur, denoted $P(B|A)$.

What It Means For You Lessons 13-3, 13-4

A two-way table organizes data about two variables. A two-way frequency table can be very helpful when finding probabilities.

EXAMPLE **Finding Conditional Probability**

		Owns a cat		
		Yes	No	Total
Owns a dog	Yes	0.15	0.24	0.39
	No	0.18	0.43	0.61
	Total	0.33	0.67	1

This two-way frequency table describes data collected by a sociologist who surveyed 100 randomly selected people about their pets. You can use this table to answer the question, "If a person in this survey has a dog, what is the probability that he or she also has a cat?"

CHAPTER 13

Key Vocabulary

combination *(combinación)* A selection of a group of objects in which order is *not* important. The number of combinations of *r* objects chosen from a group of *n* objects is denoted ${}_nC_r$.

complement of an event *(complemento de un suceso)* All outcomes in the sample space that are not in an event *E*, denoted $\bar{E}$ or E^C.

compound event *(suceso compuesto)* An event made up of two or more simple events.

conditional probability *(probabilidad condicional)* The probability of event *B*, given that event *A* has already occurred or is certain to occur, denoted $P(B|A)$.

convenience sample *(muestra de conveniencia)* A sample based on members of the population that are readily available.

dependent events *(sucesos dependientes)* Events for which the occurrence or non-occurrence of one event affects the probability of the other event.

event *(suceso)* An outcome or set of outcomes in a probability experiment.

factorial *(factorial)* If *n* is a positive integer, then *n* factorial, written $n!$, is $n \bullet (n-1) \bullet (n-2) \bullet \ldots \bullet 2 \bullet 1$. The factorial of 0 is defined to be 1.

frequency table *(tabla de frecuencia)* A table that lists the number of times, or frequency, that each data value occurs.

independent events *(sucesos independientes)* Events for which the occurrence or non-occurrence of one event does not affect the probability of the other event.

intersection *(intersección de conjuntos)* The intersection of two sets is the set of all elements that are common to both sets, denoted by $\cap$.

mutually exclusive events *(sucesos mutuamente excluyentes)* Two events are mutually exclusive if they cannot both occur in the same trial of an experiment.

outcome *(resultado)* A possible result of a probability experiment.

permutation *(permutación)* An arrangement of a group of objects in which order is important. The number of permutations of *r* objects from a group of *n* objects is denoted ${}_nP_r$.

probability *(probabilidad)* A number from 0 to 1 (or 0% to 100%) that is the measure of how likely an event is to occur.

random sample *(muestra aleatoria)* A sample selected from a population so that each member of the population has an equal chance of being selected.

sample space *(espacio muestral)* The set of all possible outcomes of a probability experiment.

union *(unión)* The union of two sets is the set of all elements that are in either set, denoted by $\cup$.

CHAPTER 13

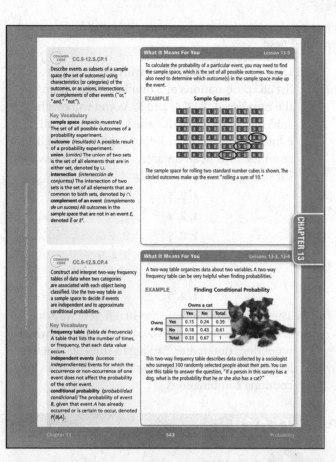

COMMON CORE PROFESSIONAL DEVELOPMENT

CC.9-12.S.CP.4*

Students have studied relationships in bivariate data by plotting ordered pairs in a coordinate plane to create a scatter plot. In a two-way table, the variables are categorical and quantities are frequencies. In this chapter, students will use two-way tables to organize data categorized by two variables. Students can use two-way tables to calculate or to approximate conditional probability, and to develop a formula for conditional probability.

CHAPTER 13

Permutations and Combinations
Going Deeper

Essential question: *What are permutations and combinations and how can you use them to calculate probabilities?*

© Houghton Mifflin Harcourt Publishing Company

COMMON CORE Standards for Mathematical Content

CC.9-12.S.CP.9(+) Use permutations and combinations to compute probabilities of compound events and solve problems.*

Vocabulary
permutation
factorial
combination

Prerequisites
Probability and set theory

Math Background
A compound event is an event that consists of more than one outcome. To find the probability of a compound event, find the ratio of the number of outcomes in the event to the number of outcomes in the sample space. Counting the number of outcomes in the event and in the sample space can often be the most challenging part of calculating a probability. Permutations and combinations are two tools for counting outcomes.

INTRODUCE

Define *permutation*. Work with students to list all permutations of the numbers 1, 2, and 3. You may want to construct a tree diagram as shown below. The diagram shows that there are 6 different permutations of the numbers.

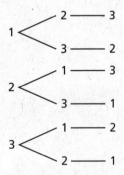

Define *combination*. Work with students to list all combinations of 3 numbers taken from the numbers 1, 2, 3, 4, and 5. As you work with students, emphasize that the key to finding all combinations while avoiding duplicates is to list the combinations in an organized way. The following list shows one way to do this:

1, 2, 3	2, 3, 4
1, 2, 4	2, 3, 5
1, 2, 5	2, 4, 5
1, 3, 4	3, 4, 5
1, 3, 5	
1, 4, 5	

The list shows that there are 10 different ways to choose 3 numbers from the set of 5 numbers when order does not matter. Explain to students that this lesson will introduce more efficient techniques for counting combinations.

TEACH

1 EXAMPLE

Questioning Strategies
- Suppose the club needs to choose only a president. In how many different ways can the position be filled in this case? **7**
- Suppose the club needs to choose only a president and a vice-president. In how many different ways can the positions be filled in this case? Why? **42; once you choose a president, you have 6 remaining candidates for vice-president.**
- Why is this situation an example of a permutation? **The order in which you fill the positions is important.**

EXTRA EXAMPLE
There are 6 different flavors of frozen yogurt. A cafeteria offers 1 flavor per day. The manager of the cafeteria wants to choose 4 different flavors to serve on Monday, Tuesday, Wednesday, and Thursday. In how many different ways can the manager choose the flavors and assign them to days of the week? **360**

Name_____ Class_____ Date_____

13-1

Permutations and Combinations
Going Deeper

Essential question: *What are permutations and combinations and how can you use them to calculate probabilities?*

A **permutation** is a selection of a group of objects in which order is important. For example, there are 6 permutations of the letters A, B, and C.

ABC	ACB
BAC	BCA
CAB	CBA

Video Tutor

1 EXAMPLE Finding Permutations
CC.9-12.S.CP.9(+)

The members of a club want to choose a president, a vice-president, and a treasurer. Seven members of the club are eligible to fill these positions. In how many different ways can the positions be filled?

A Consider the number of ways each position can be filled.

There are ____7____ different ways the position of president can be filled.

Once the president has been chosen, there are ____6____ different ways the position of vice-president can be filled.

Once the president and vice-president have been chosen, there are ____5____ different ways the position of treasurer can be filled.

B Multiply to find the total number of different ways the positions can be filled.

| President | Vice-President | Treasurer |

___7___ × ___6___ × ___5___ = ___210___ permutations

So, there are ___210___ different ways that the positions can be filled.

REFLECT

1a. Suppose the club members also want to choose a secretary from the group of 7 eligible members. In how many different ways can the four positions (president, vice-president, treasurer, secretary) be filled? Explain.

840; there are 7 × 6 × 5 × 4 = 840 permutations

1b. Suppose 8 members of the club are eligible to fill the original three positions (president, vice-president, treasurer). In how many different ways can the positions be filled? Explain.

336; there are 8 × 7 × 6 = 336 permutations

Chapter 13   545   Lesson 1

© Houghton Mifflin Harcourt Publishing Company

The process you used in the example can be generalized to give a formula for permutations. To do so, it is helpful to use factorials. For a positive integer n, n **factorial**, written $n!$, is defined as follows.

$$n! = n \cdot (n-1) \cdot (n-2) \cdot \ldots \cdot 3 \cdot 2 \cdot 1$$

That is, $n!$ is the product of n and all the positive integers less than n. Note that $0!$ is defined to be 1.

In the example, the number of permutations of 7 objects taken 3 at a time is

$$7 \cdot 6 \cdot 5 = \frac{7 \cdot 6 \cdot 5 \cdot \cancel{4} \cdot \cancel{3} \cdot \cancel{2} \cdot \cancel{1}}{\cancel{4} \cdot \cancel{3} \cdot \cancel{2} \cdot \cancel{1}} = \frac{7!}{4!} = \frac{7!}{(7-3)!}.$$

This can be generalized as follows.

> **Permutations**
>
> The number of permutations of n objects taken r at a time is given by
> $$_nP_r = \frac{n!}{(n-r)!}.$$

Recall that the probability of an event is equal to the number of outcomes that result in the event, divided by the number of all possible outcomes.

2 EXAMPLE Using Permutations to Calculate a Probability
CC.9-12.S.CP.9(+)

Every student at your school is assigned a four-digit code, such as 6953, to access the computer system. In each code, no digit is repeated. What is the probability that you are assigned a code with the digits 1, 2, 3, and 4 in any order?

A Let S be the sample space. Find $n(S)$.

The sample space consists of all permutations of 4 digits taken from the 10 digits 0 through 9.

$$n(S) = {}_{10}P_4 = \frac{10!}{(10-4)!} = \frac{10!}{6!} = \frac{10 \cdot 9 \cdot 8 \cdot 7 \cdot \cancel{6} \cdot \cancel{5} \cdot \cancel{4} \cdot \cancel{3} \cdot \cancel{2} \cdot \cancel{1}}{\cancel{6} \cdot \cancel{5} \cdot \cancel{4} \cdot \cancel{3} \cdot \cancel{2} \cdot \cancel{1}} = \boxed{5040}$$

B Let A be the event that your code has the digits 1, 2, 3, and 4. Find $n(A)$.

The event consists of all permutations of 4 digits chosen from the 4 digits 1 through 4.

$$n(A) = {}_4P_4 = \frac{4!}{(4-4)!} = \frac{4!}{0!} = \frac{4 \cdot 3 \cdot 2 \cdot 1}{1} = \boxed{24}$$

C Find $P(A)$.

$$P(A) = \frac{n(A)}{n(S)} = \frac{24}{5040} = \frac{1}{210}$$

So, the probability that your code has the digits 1, 2, 3, and 4 is $\frac{1}{210}$.

© Houghton Mifflin Harcourt Publishing Company

Chapter 13   546   Lesson 1

Highlighting the Standards

The process of developing a formula for permutations is a good opportunity to address Standard 8 (Look for and express regularity in repeated reasoning). Have students calculate the number of permutations in various situations "by hand"; that is, by reasoning about the situation and using multiplication, as in the first example. Then ask students what patterns they notice. A common element of every solution should be the product of a string of descending, consecutive integers. Once students have been introduced to factorial notation, the formula for the number of permutations of n objects taken r at a time should seem natural.

Technology

You may want to have students use their calculators to check their work. In fact, graphing calculators have a built-in function that calculates permutations. For example, to find $_{10}P_4$, first enter 10. Then press MATH and use the arrow keys to choose the PRB menu. Select **2:nPr** and press ENTER. Now enter 4 and then press ENTER to see that $_{10}P_4 = 5040$.

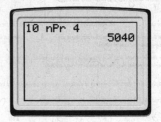

```
10 nPr 4
              5040
```

2 EXAMPLE

Questioning Strategies

- What are some examples of four-digit codes in the sample space? **Possible answers: 7421, 9605, 7534**

- Is the code 4878 in the sample space? Why or why not? **No; no digit may be repeated in a code.**

- What are some examples of four-digit codes in event A? **Possible answers: 1234, 2314, 4231**

- Is the code 4215 in event A? Why or why not? **No; codes in event A consist of the digits 1, 2, 3, and 4 in any order.**

EXTRA EXAMPLE

To buy concert tickets at a Web site, you must first type a random code consisting of 5 letters, such as JQBKN. (This prevents computer programs from purchasing the tickets.) In each code, no letter is repeated. When you buy concert tickets at the Web site, what is the probability that your code will consist of the letters A, E, I, O, and U in any order? $\frac{1}{65,780}$

3 EXAMPLE

Questioning Strategies

- Give some examples of possible combinations. **Possible answers: beets-potatoes-carrots, beets-salad-rice, broccoli-salad-carrots, etc.**

- Once you find the number of ways to choose 3 side dishes when order does matter, why do you then divide by $_3P_3$? **When order matters, each side dish is counted $_3P_3 = 6$ times, so you must divide by 6 to count each combination just once.**

EXTRA EXAMPLE

A winner on a game show gets to choose 4 prize boxes from a set of 10 prize boxes. In how many different ways can the contestant choose 4 prize boxes? **210**

Teaching Strategies

You may wish to show students a different way of solving the problem in the first example. There are 8 choices for the first side dish, 7 choices for the second side dish, and 6 choices for the third side dish. This is $8 \times 7 \times 6 = 336$ possibilities. However, each combination is counted $3! = 6$ times, so the number of combinations is $336 \div 6 = 56$.

REFLECT

2a. What is the probability that you are assigned the code 1234? Explain.

$\frac{1}{5040}$; in this case $n(A) = 1$, so $P(A) = \frac{n(A)}{n(S)} = \frac{1}{5040}$.

A **combination** is a grouping of objects in which order does not matter. For example, when you choose 3 letters from the letters A, B, C, and D, there are 4 different combinations.

ABC   ABD   ACD   BCD

PREP FOR CC.9–12.S.CP.9(+)

3 EXAMPLE   Finding Combinations

A restaurant offers 8 side dishes. When you order an entree, you can choose 3 of the side dishes. In how many ways can you choose 3 side dishes?

Side Dishes	
Beets	Rice
Potatoes	Broccoli
Carrots	Cole slaw
Salad	Apple sauce

A First find the number of ways to choose 3 sides dishes when order does matter. This is the number of permutations of 8 objects taken 3 at a time.

$_8P_3 = \frac{8!}{(8-3)!} = \frac{8!}{5!} = \frac{8 \cdot 7 \cdot 6 \cdot \cancel{5} \cdot \cancel{4} \cdot \cancel{3} \cdot \cancel{2} \cdot \cancel{1}}{\cancel{5} \cdot \cancel{4} \cdot \cancel{3} \cdot \cancel{2} \cdot \cancel{1}} = \underline{336}$

B In this problem, order does not matter, since choosing beets, carrots, and rice is the same as choosing rice, beets, and carrots.

Divide the result from Step A by $_3P_3$, which is the number of ways the 3 side dishes can be ordered.

$_3P_3 = \frac{3!}{(3-3)!} = \frac{3!}{0!} = \underline{6}$

So, the number of ways you can choose 3 side dishes is $\frac{336}{6} = \underline{56}$.

REFLECT

3a. Suppose the restaurant offers a special on Mondays that allows you to choose 4 side dishes. In how many ways can you choose the side dishes?

    70

3b. In general, are there more ways or fewer ways to select objects when order does not matter? Why?

Fewer; when order does not matter, multiple selections are counted as the same combination.

The process you used in the example can be generalized to give a formula for combinations. In order to find $_8C_3$, the number of combinations of 8 objects taken 3 at a time, you first found the number of permutations of 8 objects taken 3 at a time, then you divided by 3! That is,

$$_8C_3 = \frac{8!}{(8-3)!} \div 3! \text{ or } \frac{8!}{3!(8-3)!}.$$

This can be generalized as follows.

> **Combinations**
>
> The number of combinations of n objects taken r at a time is given by
>
> $_nC_r = \frac{n!}{r!(n-r)!}.$

CC.9–12.S.CP.9(+)

4 EXAMPLE   Using Combinations to Calculate a Probability

There are 5 boys and 6 girls in a school play. The director randomly chooses 3 of the students to meet with a costume designer. What is the probability that the director chooses all boys?

A Let S be the sample space. Find $n(S)$.

The sample space consists of all combinations of 3 students taken from the group of 11 students.

$n(S) = {}_{11}C_3 = \frac{11!}{3!(11-3)!} = \frac{11!}{3! \cdot 8!} = \frac{11 \cdot 10 \cdot 9 \cdot \cancel{8} \cdot \cancel{7} \cdot \cancel{6} \cdot \cancel{5} \cdot \cancel{4} \cdot \cancel{3} \cdot \cancel{2} \cdot \cancel{1}}{3 \cdot 2 \cdot 1 \cdot \cancel{8} \cdot \cancel{7} \cdot \cancel{6} \cdot \cancel{5} \cdot \cancel{4} \cdot \cancel{3} \cdot \cancel{2} \cdot \cancel{1}} = \underline{165}$

B Let A be the event that the director chooses all boys. Find $n(A)$.

Suppose the 11 students are $B_1, B_2, B_3, B_4, B_5, G_1, G_2, G_3, G_4, G_5, G_6$, where the Bs represent boys and the Gs represent girls.

The combinations in event A are combinations like $B_2B_4B_5$ and $B_1B_3B_4$. That is, event A consists of all combinations of 3 boys taken from the set of 5 boys.

So, $n(A) = {}_5C_3 = \frac{5!}{3!(5-3)!} = \frac{5!}{3! \cdot 2!} = \frac{5 \cdot 4 \cdot \cancel{3} \cdot \cancel{2} \cdot \cancel{1}}{\cancel{3} \cdot \cancel{2} \cdot \cancel{1} \cdot 2 \cdot 1} = \underline{10}$

C Find $P(A)$.

$P(A) = \frac{n(A)}{n(S)} = \frac{10}{165} = \underline{\frac{2}{33}}$

So, the probability that the director chooses all boys is $\underline{\frac{2}{33}}$.

Highlighting the Standards

To address Standard 7 (Look for and make use of structure) ask students to explain how the formula for the number of combinations of n objects taken r at a time is related to the formula for the number of permutations of n objects taken r at a time. Students should see that the number of permutations divided by $r!$ is equal to the number of combinations.

4 EXAMPLE

Questioning Strategies

- Does this problem involve permutations or combinations? Why? Combinations; the order in which the students are chosen does not matter.

- Based on your answer, is the director likely to choose all boys? Explain. No; this is not likely, since the probability is only $\frac{2}{33}$.

EXTRA EXAMPLE

A box contains 4 bottles of orange juice and 5 bottles of grapefruit juice. You randomly choose 3 of the bottles to serve at a school breakfast. What is the probability that you choose 3 bottles of grapefruit juice? $\frac{5}{42}$

Teaching Strategies

You might want to revisit the example once students have learned about the probability of dependent events. At that point, students will have another way to solve the problem. Specifically, the probability of choosing 3 boys is the probability that the first student is a boy times the probability that the second student is a boy given that the first student was a boy times the probability that the third student is a boy given that the first two students were boys. This probability is $\frac{5}{11} \cdot \frac{4}{10} \cdot \frac{3}{9} = \frac{2}{33}$.

CLOSE

Essential Question

What are permutations and combinations and how can you use them to calculate probabilities?

A permutation is a selection of a group of objects in which order is important. You can use permutations to find the number of outcomes in a sample space and/or the number of outcomes in an event.

A combination is a grouping of objects in which order does not matter. You can use combinations to find the number of outcomes in a sample space and/or the number of outcomes in an event.

Summarize

Have students make graphic organizers to summarize what they know about permutations and combinations. Samples are shown.

Definition	Example
A permutation is a selection of a group of objects in which order is important.	Permutations of A, B, and C: ABC ACB BAC BCA CAB CBA

Permutations

Formula	Factorials
$_nP_r = \dfrac{n!}{(n-r)!}$	n factorial ($n!$) is the product of n and all the positive integers less than n. 0! is 1.

Definition	Example
A combination is a grouping of objects in which order does not matter.	Combinations of 2 letters from A, B, C, and D: AB AC AD BC BD CD

Combinations

Formula	Factorials
$_nC_r = \dfrac{n!}{r!(n-r)!}$	n factorial ($n!$) is the product of n and all the positive integers less than n. 0! is 1.

PRACTICE

Where skills are taught	Where skills are practiced
1 EXAMPLE	EXS. 1–4
2 EXAMPLE	EXS. 5–6
3 EXAMPLE	EXS. 8–9
4 EXAMPLE	EXS. 10–13

Exercise 7: Students apply what they learned to critique another student's work.

Exercises 14–15: Students use reasoning to state a generalization about combinations.

REFLECT

4a. Is the director more likely to choose all boys or all girls? Why?

All girls; $_6C_3 = 20$, so $P(\text{all girls}) = \frac{20}{165} = \frac{4}{33}$, which is greater than the

probability of choosing all boys, $\frac{2}{33}$.

PRACTICE

1. An MP3 player has a playlist with 12 songs. You select the shuffle option for the playlist. In how many different orders can the songs be played?

479,001,600

2. There are 10 runners in a race. Medals are awarded for 1st, 2nd, and 3rd place. In how many different ways can the medals be awarded?

720

3. There are 9 players on a baseball team. In how many different ways can the coach choose players for first base, second base, third base, and shortstop?

3024

4. You have 15 photographs of your school. In how many different ways can you arrange 6 of them in a line for the cover of the school yearbook?

3,603,600

5. A bag contains 9 tiles, each with a different number from 1 to 9. You choose a tile, put it aside, choose a second tile, put it aside, and then choose a third tile. What is the probability that you choose tiles with the numbers 1, 2, and 3 in that order?

$\frac{1}{362,880}$

6. There are 11 students on a committee. To decide which 3 of these students will attend a conference, 3 names are chosen at random by pulling names one at a time from a hat. What is the probability that Sarah, Jamal, and Mai are chosen in any order?

$\frac{1}{165}$

7. **Error Analysis** A student solved the problem at right. The student's work is shown. Did the student make an error? If so, explain the error and provide the correct answer.

The student made an error; $n(A)$

should be 1 since the tiles must

appear in the order B-E-A-D. The

correct probability is $\frac{1}{360}$.

A bag contains 6 tiles with the letters A, B, C, D, E, and F. You choose 4 tiles one at a time without looking and line up the tiles as you choose them. What is the probability that your tiles spell BEAD?

Let S be the sample space and let A be the event that the tiles spell BEAD.

$n(S) = {}_6P_4 = \frac{6!}{(6-4)!} = \frac{6!}{2!} = 360$

$n(A) = {}_4P_4 = \frac{4!}{(4-4)!} = \frac{4!}{0!} = 4! = 24$

So, $P(A) = \frac{n(A)}{n(S)} = \frac{24}{360} = \frac{1}{15}$.

8. A cat has a litter of 6 kittens. You plan to adopt 2 of the kittens. In how many ways can you choose 2 of the kittens from the litter?

15

9. An amusement park has 11 roller coasters. In how many ways can you choose 4 of the roller coasters to ride during your visit to the park?

330

10. A school has 5 Spanish teachers and 4 French teachers. The school's principal randomly chooses 2 of the teachers to attend a conference. What is the probability that the principal chooses 2 Spanish teachers?

$\frac{5}{18}$

11. There are 6 fiction books and 8 nonfiction books on a reading list. Your teacher randomly assigns you 4 books to read over the summer. What is the probability that you are assigned all nonfiction books?

$\frac{10}{143}$

12. A bag contains 26 tiles, each with a different letter of the alphabet written on it. You choose 3 tiles from the bag without looking. What is the probability that you choose the tiles containing the letters A, B, and C?

$\frac{1}{2600}$

13. You are randomly assigned a password consisting of 6 different characters chosen from the digits 0 to 9 and the letters A to Z. As a percent, what is the probability that you are assigned a password consisting of only letters?

$\approx 11.8\%$

14. Calculate $_{10}C_6$ and $_{10}C_4$.

a. What do you notice about these values? Explain why this makes sense.

$_{10}C_6 = _{10}C_4 = 210$; it makes sense that these values are equal because every

combination of 6 objects that are selected has a corresponding combination

of 4 objects that are not selected.

b. Use your observations to help you state a generalization about combinations.

In general, $_nC_r = {}_nC_{n-r}$.

15. Use the formula for combinations to make a generalization about $_nC_n$. Explain why this makes sense.

Using the formula for combinations and the fact that $0! = 1$, $_nC_n = \frac{n!}{n!(n-n)!} =$

$\frac{n!}{n!(0!)} = \frac{n!}{n!} = 1$; this makes sense because there is only 1 combination of n objects

taken n at a time.

Assign these pages to help your students practice
and apply important lesson concepts. For
additional exercises, see the Student Edition.

Answers

Additional Practice

1. 8 T-shirts   2. 24 packages

3. 720   4. 720

5. 60,360   6. 90 ways

7. 2184 ways   8. 120

9. 3   10. 336

11. a. 91 ways

    b. 462 ways

    c. 2300 ways

Problem Solving

1. a. $12 \times 11 \times 10 = 1320$

    b. Permutation; possible answer: the order of
the 3 numbers matters.

2. a. 720 codes

    b. 5040 codes

    c. 151,200 codes

3. a. 78 ways

    b. Combination; possible answer: the order
in which she chooses the locks does not
matter.

4. Because order matters, *combination locks*
represent permutations.

5. C   6. J

13-1

Additional Practice

Use the Fundamental Counting Principle.

1. The soccer team is silk-screening T-shirts. They have 4 different colors of T-shirts and 2 different colors of ink. How many different T-shirts can be made using one ink color on a T-shirt? _____

2. A travel agent is offering a vacation package. Participants choose the type of tour, a meal plan, and a hotel class from the table below.

Tour	Meal	Hotel
Walking	Restaurant	4-Star
Boat	Picnic	3-Star
Bicycle		2-Star
		1-Star

How many different vacation packages are offered? _____

Evaluate.

3. $\dfrac{3!6!}{3!}$

4. $\dfrac{10!}{7!}$

5. $\dfrac{9!-6!}{(9-6)!}$

_____ _____ _____

Solve.

6. In how many ways can the debate team choose a president and a secretary if there are 10 people on the team? _____

7. A teacher is passing out first-, second-, and third-place prizes for the best student actor in a production of *Hamlet*. If there are 14 students in the class, in how many different ways can the awards be presented? _____

Evaluate.

8. $_5P_4$

9. $_3C_2$

10. $_8P_3$

_____ _____ _____

Solve.

11. Mrs. Marshall has 11 boys and 14 girls in her kindergarten class this year.

   a. In how many ways can she select 2 girls to pass out a snack? _____

   b. In how many ways can she select 5 boys to pass out new books? _____

   c. In how many ways can she select 3 students to carry papers to the office? _____

Problem Solving

Rosalie is looking at locks. The label *combination lock* confuses her. She wonders about the number of possible permutations or combinations a lock can have.

1. She looks at one circular lock with 12 positions. To open it she turns the dial clockwise to a first position, then counterclockwise to a second position, then clockwise to a third position

   a. Write an expression for the number of 3-position codes that are possible, if no position is repeated.

   b. Explain how this represents a combination or a permutation.

2. Rosalie looks at cable locks. Each position can be set from 0 to 9. How many different codes are possible for each lock if no digits are repeated in each code?

   a. a 3-digit cable lock

   b. a 4-digit cable lock

   c. a 6-digit cable lock

3. Rosalie needs 2 cable locks, but there are 13 types of locks to choose from.

   a. In how many ways can she choose 2 different locks?

   b. Explain how this represents a permutation or a combination.

4. Explain why you think Rosalie might be confused by the label *combination lock*.

Rosalie wants to lock her bicycle near the library. There are 7 slots still open in the bike rack. Choose the letter for the best answer.

5. Rosalie arrives at the same time as 2 other cyclists. In how many ways can they arrange their bikes in the open slots?

   A 7   C 210

   B 35   D 343

6. Suppose Rosalie arrived just ahead of the 2 other cyclists and selected a slot. In how many ways can the others arrange their bikes in the open slots?

   F 2   H 24

   G 15   J 30

Theoretical and Experimental Probability
Connection: Sampling

Essential question: *How can you use probabilities to help you make fair decisions?*

COMMON CORE **Standards for Mathematical Content**

CC.9-12.S.MD.6(+) Use probabilities to make fair decisions (e.g., drawing by lots, using a random number generator).*

Prerequisites
Probability and set theory

Math Background
Standards CC.9-12.S.MD.6(+) and CC.9-12.S.MD.7(+) are concerned with using probability to make and analyze decisions. In this lesson, students work with a single overarching investigation to explore the connections among random samples, convenience samples, fairness, and probability.

INTRODUCE

Begin by reviewing random samples and convenience samples. To do so, ask students how you could choose 5 students from the class using a random sample. Students might suggest putting the names of all students in a hat and choosing 5 names without looking. Ask students what makes the sample a random sample and be sure students understand that a key characteristic of a random sample is that each member of the population has an equal probability of being chosen.

Next, ask students how you might choose 5 students from the class using a convenience sample. Students might suggest choosing the first 5 students in the first row of desks or the 5 students who sit closest to the teacher. Be sure students understand that a key characteristic of a convenience sample is that the members of the sample are easy to choose.

Explain to students that they will now explore connections among random samples, convenience samples, and probability and learn how these ideas can help them make fair decisions.

TEACH

1 ENGAGE

Questioning Strategies
- Look at the square in the center of the 5-by-5 grid on the student page. What information is contained in this square? The resident is resident number 13. This resident prefers that the money be used for a senior center. There is a 20% chance that the resident is at the movie theater when the survey is conducted.
- Which resident is most likely to be at the movie theater when the survey is conducted? Why? Resident number 25; his or her probability of being at the movie theater is 90%, which is greater than every other resident's probability.

2 EXPLORE

Materials: calculator

Questioning Strategies
- When you use your calculator and choose the random integer function, why do you enter "(1,25)" after the name of the function? This ensures that the random integer is greater than or equal to 1 and less than or equal to 25.
- Does every student in your class get the same result for the percent of residents who favor the teen center? Why or why not? No; the results are based on a random sample that is chosen through a random-number generator. Each student is likely to get a different set of numbers and a different percent of residents who favor the teen center.

© Houghton Mifflin Harcourt Publishing Company

Name_____ Class_____ Date_____

13-2

Theoretical and Experimental Probability
Connection: Sampling
Essential question: *How can you use probabilities to help you make fair decisions?*

Video Tutor

CC.9-12.S.MD.6(+)

1 ENGAGE Introducing a Decision-Making Problem

A small town has 25 residents. The state has given the town money that must be used for something that benefits the community. The town's mayor has decided that the money will be used to build a teen center or a senior center.

In order to make a decision about the type of community center to build, the mayor plans to survey a subset of town residents. There are two survey methods: a random sample and a convenience sample. The convenience sample will be conducted by surveying town residents at a local movie theater.

In the table below, each resident of the town is identified by a number from 1 to 25. The table shows each resident's preference: T for the teen center, S for the senior center. The table also gives the probability that each resident is at the movie theater when the convenience-sample survey is conducted.

1	2	3	4	5
S	S	T	S	T
0.2	0.3	0.8	0.1	0.8
6	7	8	9	10
T	S	T	S	S
0.7	0.2	0.8	0.1	0.3
11	12	13	14	15
S	T	S	S	S
0.1	0.7	0.2	0.2	0.4
16	17	18	19	20
T	S	S	S	T
0.6	0.7	0.1	0.1	0.6
21	22	23	24	25
S	S	S	S	T
0.3	0.2	0.3	0.1	0.9

REFLECT

1a. Based on the data in the table, what percent of all residents favor the teen center? the senior center?

Teen center: 32%; senior center: 68%

1b. If it were possible for the mayor to survey every resident, what decision do you think the mayor would make? Why?

Senior center; this is the choice of more than $\frac{2}{3}$ of the town's residents.

© Houghton Mifflin Harcourt Publishing Company

Chapter 13   553   Lesson 2

CC.9-12.S.MD.6(+)

2 EXPLORE Using a Random Sample

Suppose the mayor of the town is not able to survey every resident, so the mayor decides to survey a random sample of 10 residents.

A You can use your calculator to simulate the process of choosing and surveying a random sample of residents.

- Go to the MATH menu.
- Use the right arrow key to access the PRB menu.
- Use the down arrow key to select **5:randInt(**.
- Use "randInt(1,25)" as shown at the right.
- Each time you press Enter, the calculator will return a random integer from 1 to 25.

randInt(1,25)
           13

Generate 10 random integers in this way. For each integer, note the corresponding preference (T or S) of that resident of the town. (If a number is selected more than once, ignore the duplicates and choose a new number. This ensures that no resident is surveyed more than once.) Record your results in the table. **Sample results are shown.**

Resident Number	13	4	19	17	24	6	23	11	3	16
Preference (T or S)	S	S	S	S	S	T	S	S	T	T

B Based on the random sample, what percent of residents favor the teen center? the senior center?

Sample answer: Teen center: 30%; senior center: 70%

REFLECT

2a. What is the probability that any resident is chosen to be part of the random sample? Explain.

$\frac{1}{25}$; there are 25 possible outcomes of the random-number generator and all are equally likely.

2b. What decision do you think the mayor would make based on the random sample? Why?

Senior center; this appears to be the choice of a majority of residents.

2c. Compare your results with those of other students. In general, how well do the results of the random sample predict the preferences of the town as a whole?

The random sample closely matches the preferences of the town as a whole.

© Houghton Mifflin Harcourt Publishing Company

Chapter 13   554   Lesson 2

Highlighting the Standards

To address Standard 5 (Use appropriate tools strategically), ask students about the advantages and disadvantages of using a calculator to generate random numbers. For example, students might suggest that the calculator is easy to use and can be counted on to return numbers that are truly random. On the other hand, the calculator may repeat numbers. This inconvenience would not arise if students generated the random numbers by choosing numbered slips of paper from a bag without replacing the slips of paper after they are chosen.

3 EXPLORE

Materials: small slips of paper, bag

Questioning Strategies

- How do you represent Resident 13 in this simulation? Why? There should be 2 slips of paper with the number 13 since this resident has a 0.2 probability of being at the movie theater.

- Which resident is represented by the greatest number of slips of paper? Why does this make sense? Resident 25; this resident has the greatest probability of being at the theater, so he or she should have the greatest chance of being picked for the survey.

- Which sampling method does a better job of representing the wishes of the town as a whole? Why? The random sample; since every resident has an equal probability of being chosen for the sample, this method does a better job of representing the wishes of the town as a whole.

Avoid Common Errors

Some students may replace a slip of paper in the bag once it has been chosen. Remind students that once someone has been selected for the survey, he or she should not be surveyed again. For this reason, once a slip of paper is chosen, it should be put aside and any future draws of that resident's number should be ignored.

CLOSE

Essential Question

How can you use probabilities to help you make fair decisions? You can use probabilities to help you choose a random sample from a population. The results of surveying a random sample are likely to be representative of the population as a whole.

Summarize

Have students write a journal entry in which they summarize the main steps of this investigation. Ask them to include a discussion of how probability helped them conduct the random sample and the convenience sample.

© Houghton Mifflin Harcourt Publishing Company

3 EXPLORE Using a Convenience Sample

CC.9–12.S.MD.6(+)

The mayor of the town decides to use a convenience sample by surveying the first 10 residents of the town to leave a local movie theater.

A You can use slips of paper to simulate the process of choosing and surveying this convenience sample.

- For each resident, prepare 1 to 10 small slips of paper with the resident's number on them. The number of slips of paper is determined by the probability that the resident is at the movie theater when the survey is conducted. For example, Resident 1 has a 0.2 probability of being at the theater, so prepare 2 slips of paper with the number 1; Resident 2 has a 0.3 probability of being at the theater, so prepare 3 slips of paper with the number 2; and so on.
- Place all of the slips of paper in a bag and mix them well.
- Choose slips of paper one at a time without looking.

Choose 10 residents in this way. For each resident, note the corresponding preference (T or S) using the table on the first page of the lesson. (If a resident is selected more than once, ignore the duplicates and choose a new number from the bag. This ensures that no resident is surveyed more than once.) Record your results in the table.

Sample results are shown.

Resident Number	8	5	14	25	12	7	20	9	23	16
Preference (T or S)	T	T	S	T	T	S	T	S	S	T

B Based on the convenience sample, what percent of residents favor the teen center? the senior center?

Sample answer: Teen center: 60%; senior center: 40%

REFLECT

3a. Why do some residents of the town have more slips of paper representing them than other residents? How does this connect to the way the convenience sample is conducted?

Residents who have a greater probability of being at the movie theater when the survey is conducted have more slips of paper representing them. This simulates the fact that they are more likely to be chosen for the convenience sample.

© Houghton Mifflin Harcourt Publishing Company

3b. What decision do you think the mayor would make based on the convenience sample? Why?

Teen center; this appears to be the choice of a majority of residents.

3c. Compare your results with those of other students. In general, how well do the results of the convenience sample predict the preferences of the town as a whole?

The convenience sample does not do a good job of predicting the preferences of the town as a whole.

3d. Which sampling method is more likely to lead to fair decision-making? Explain.

The random sample gives results that are more likely to be representative of the whole population, so it is more likely to lead to fair decisions.

3e. What factors might explain why the results of the convenience sample are different from the results of the random sample?

There may be a greater proportion of young people at the movie theater than in the general population and young people might be more likely to favor building a teen center.

3f. When you conduct the random-sample simulation is it possible that you might choose 10 residents who all favor the senior center? Is this result possible when you conduct the convenience-sample simulation? In which simulation do you think this result is more likely?

This result is possible (but unlikely) in both simulations. It is more likely to happen in the random-sample simulation, since the convenience-sample simulation is weighted toward residents who prefer the teen center.

3g. What are some limitations or drawbacks of the simulations?

The convenience-sample simulation depends on knowing the probability that each resident is at the movie theater; the simulation method would be impractical to carry out with a larger population.

3h. In a town of 25 residents, it is likely that the mayor could actually survey all the residents, instead of using a random sample or convenience sample. What are some reasons that sampling might be used in situations involving populations that are much larger than 25?

It may be difficult to survey all members of a population; it may be too expensive, too time-consuming, or too impractical to attempt to reach every member of a very large population.

© Houghton Mifflin Harcourt Publishing Company

© Houghton Mifflin Harcourt Publishing Company

Assign these pages to help your students practice and apply important lesson concepts. For additional exercises, see the Student Edition.

Answers

Additional Practice

1. Check students' work.

2. $\frac{1}{3}$

3. Check student's work.

4. 70%; check students' comparisons.

5. The teacher could randomly choose 3 students from each class as a sample, for a total of 9 students, which is 10% of 90.

Problem Solving

1. 90%

2. No; the employee only surveyed people in his neighborhood, so those residents had a higher probability of being chosen.

3. A convenience sample; the city employee only surveyed people that live nearby him in the suburbs.

4. Possible answer: No, this sample is probably not representative. People in the suburbs might be more likely to support road repair in their neighborhood than bike lanes downtown.

5. A

6. G

Additional Practice

The table represents a class of 30 students. Each student was asked if he or she would prefer having a written report (R) or an oral presentation (O) for the final. Use the table for Exercises 1–4.

1 R	2 R	3 O	4 R	5 O
6 R	7 R	8 R	9 O	10 R
11 O	12 O	13 R	14 R	15 R
16 R	17 O	18 R	19 R	20 R
21 R	22 R	23 O	24 R	25 R
26 O	27 R	28 O	29 R	30 R

1. Use a calculator or slips of paper to choose 10 random numbers from 1 to 30. Circle the 10 numbers you generate.

2. What is the probability of any given student being chosen for your sample?

_____

3. According to your sample, what percent of the class would prefer to have a written report as the final?

_____

4. What percent of the class would prefer to have a written report if you take into account *all* of the students? How does this compare to what you found in your sample?

_____

_____

5. Another teacher wants to survey his classes with the same question. He has three classes of 90 students each. Explain a way he could collect responses from a random sample of 10% of his students. The sample should have equal representation for each of the three classes.

_____

_____

_____

Problem Solving

The council of a city of 200,000 people is deciding on one of two improvement projects. The two proposed projects are (1) creating bike lanes in the downtown area and (2) repairing a road that passes through the suburbs. An employee of the city takes a survey of 50 people near his house in the suburbs. Of those surveyed, 45 people said they would prefer the road repair. Use this information for Exercises 1–4.

1. According to the survey, what percent of the city residents prefer the road repair project?

_____

2. The city employee calculates that every city resident had a $\frac{50}{200,000} = \frac{1}{4,000}$ probability of being chosen for his survey. Do you agree? Explain why or why not.

_____

_____

3. Is the sample a random sample or a convenience sample? Explain your reasoning.

_____

_____

4. Do you think it's likely that the sample represents the population as a whole? Explain why or why not.

_____

_____

Select the best answer.

5. A survey asks a question of 30 people out of a total of 3,000 visiting a mall in one day. If the sample is random, what is the probability of any given person being surveyed?

    A 1%   C 10%

    B 3%   D 30%

6. A survey finds that 65% of town residents support leash laws. If that number was found by taking a sample of 40 residents, how many people in the sample support leash laws?

    F 12   H 40

    G 26   J 6

Independent and Dependent Events
Going Deeper

Essential question: *How do you find the probability of independent and dependent events?*

© Houghton Mifflin Harcourt Publishing Company

COMMON CORE Standards for Mathematical Content

CC.9-12.S.CP.2 Understand that two events *A* and *B* are independent if the probability of *A* and *B* occurring together is the product of their probabilities, and use this characterization to determine if they are independent.*

CC.9-12.S.CP.3 ... interpret independence of *A* and *B* as saying that the conditional probability of *A* given *B* is the same as the probability of *A*, and the conditional probability of *B* given *A* is the same as the probability of *B*.*

CC.9-12.S.CP.4 Construct and interpret two-way frequency tables of data when two categories are associated with each object being classified. Use the two-way table as a sample space to decide if events are independent ....*

CC.9-12.S.CP.5 Recognize and explain the concept of ... independence in everyday language and everyday situations.*

CC.9-12.S.CP.8(+) Apply the general Multiplication Rule in a uniform probability model, $P(A \text{ and } B) = P(A) P(B \mid A) = P(B) P(A \mid B)$, and interpret the answer in terms of the model.*

Vocabulary
independent events
dependent events

Prerequisites
Probability and set theory
Conditional probability
Independent events

Math Background
In the first part of this lesson, students learn two different ways to identify independent events. For two events *A* and *B*, if $P(A) = P(A \mid B)$, then the events are independent. Also, if $P(A \text{ and } B) = P(A) \cdot P(B)$, then the events are independent.

Then, students use what they have learned about conditional probability to develop the Multiplication Rule. This rule can be used to find the probability of dependent events.

INTRODUCE

Define *independent events*. Ask students to suggest examples of independent events. Be sure to discuss examples from everyday life, such as the event that it is cloudy tomorrow and the event that there is a math test tomorrow. The events are independent since the occurrence of one event does not affect the occurrence of the other.

Define *dependent events*. To illustrate the difference between independent events and dependent events, discuss two different ways of choosing two colored marbles from a bag: 1) with replacement and 2) without replacement.

When you choose with replacement, you select the first marble, note its color, and put the marble back in the bag before choosing the second marble. In this case, the two selections are independent events. The sample space for the two events is the same.

When you choose without replacement, you select the first marble, put it aside, and then choose the second marble. In this case, the two selections are dependent events because the marble you choose first changes the sample space for your second selection.

TEACH

1 EXAMPLE

Questioning Strategies
- What percent of all flights are late? Where do you find this information? 10%; look at the bottom row of the table.
- What percent of all domestic flights are late? Where do you find this information? 10%; look at the "Domestic Flight" row of the table.
- What percent of all international flights are late? Where do you find this information? 10%; Look at the "International Flight" row of the table.

continued

Name_____ Class_____ Date_____

13-3

Independent and Dependent Events
Going Deeper

Essential question: *How do you find the probability of independent and dependent events?*

Two events are **independent events** if the occurrence of one event does not affect the occurrence of the other event. For example, rolling a 1 on a number cube and choosing an ace at random from a deck of cards are independent events.

If two events A and B are independent events, then the fact that event B has occurred does not affect the probability of event A. In other words, for independent events A and B, $P(A) = P(A \mid B)$. You can use this as a criterion to determine whether two events are independent.

CC.9-12.S.CP.4

1 EXAMPLE Determining If Events are Independent

An airport employee collects data on 180 random flights that arrive at the airport. The data is shown in the two-way table. Is a late arrival independent of the flight being an international flight? Why or why not?

	Late Arrival	On Time	TOTAL
Domestic Flight	12	108	120
International Flight	6	54	60
TOTAL	18	162	180

A Let event A be the event that a flight arrives late. Let event B be the event that a flight is an international flight.

To find $P(A)$, first note that there is a total of ___180___ flights.

Of these flights, there is a total of ___18___ late flights.

So, $P(A) = \dfrac{18}{180} = \underline{\ 10\% \ }$

To find $P(A \mid B)$, first note that there is a total of ___60___ international flights.

Of these flights, there is a total of ___6___ late flights.

So, $P(A \mid B) = \dfrac{6}{60} = \underline{\ 10\% \ }$

B Compare $P(A)$ and $P(A \mid B)$.

So, a late arrival is independent of the flight being an international flight because

$P(A) = P(A \mid B)$, which means that events A and B are independent events.

REFLECT

1a. In the example, you compared $P(A)$ and $P(A \mid B)$. Suppose you compare $P(B)$ and $P(B \mid A)$. What do you find? What does this tell you?

$P(B) = P(B \mid A) = 33.3\%$; this also shows A and B are independent events.

Chapter 13   559   Lesson 3

You can use a tree diagram to help you understand the formula for the probability of independent events. For example, consider tossing a coin two times. The outcome of one toss does not affect the outcome of the other toss, so the events are independent.

The tree diagram shows that the probability of the coin landing heads up on both tosses is $\frac{1}{4}$ because this is 1 of 4 equally-likely outcomes at the end of Toss 2. This probability is simply the product of the probabilities of the coin landing heads up on each individual toss: $\frac{1}{2} \cdot \frac{1}{2} = \frac{1}{4}$.

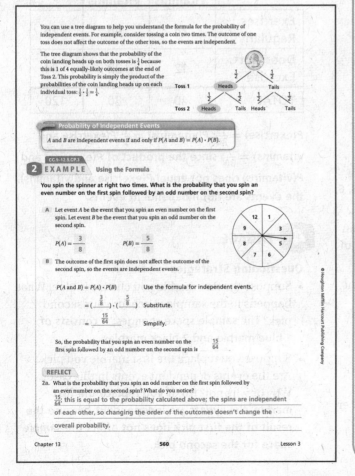

Probability of Independent Events

A and B are independent events if and only if $P(A \text{ and } B) = P(A) \cdot P(B)$.

CC.9-12.S.CP.3

2 EXAMPLE Using the Formula

You spin the spinner at right two times. What is the probability that you spin an even number on the first spin followed by an odd number on the second spin?

A Let event A be the event that you spin an even number on the first spin. Let event B be the event that you spin an odd number on the second spin.

$P(A) = \dfrac{3}{8}$ $P(B) = \dfrac{5}{8}$

B The outcome of the first spin does not affect the outcome of the second spin, so the events are independent events.

$P(A \text{ and } B) = P(A) \cdot P(B)$ Use the formula for independent events.

$= \left(\dfrac{3}{8} \right) \cdot \left(\dfrac{5}{8} \right)$ Substitute.

$= \dfrac{15}{64}$ Simplify.

So, the probability that you spin an even number on the first spin followed by an odd number on the second spin is $\dfrac{15}{64}$.

REFLECT

2a. What is the probability that you spin an odd number on the first spin followed by an even number on the second spin? What do you notice?

$\frac{15}{64}$; this is equal to the probability calculated above; the spins are independent of each other, so changing the order of the outcomes doesn't change the overall probability.

Chapter 13   560   Lesson 3

© Houghton Mifflin Harcourt Publishing Company

1 EXAMPLE   continued

EXTRA EXAMPLE

A doctor collects data on 120 randomly-chosen patients. The data are shown in the two-way table. Is taking vitamins independent of exercising regularly? Why or why not?

	Takes Vitamins	No Vitamins	TOTAL
Exercises Regularly	28	48	76
Does Not Exercise	12	32	44
TOTAL	40	80	120

No; the events are not independent because P(exercise) does not equal P(exercise|vitamins).

```
MATHEMATICAL    Highlighting the
  PRACTICE        Standards
```

Standard 6 (Attend to precision) states that mathematically proficient students "try to use clear definitions in discussion with others." Have students communicate their results from this lesson orally and in writing. Ask them to check that they are using terms correctly. In particular, be sure students understand that the word *independent* has a specific meaning in probability theory that may be different from its meaning in everyday conversation.

---

2 EXAMPLE

Questioning Strategies

• What is the sample space for each spin? {1, 3, 5, 6, 7, 8, 9, 12}

• On any given spin, are you more likely to spin an even number or an odd number? Why? Odd; 5 of the 8 numbers on the spinner are odd.

• Why are the events in this problem independent events? The outcome of the first spin does not affect the outcome of the second spin.

EXTRA EXAMPLE

A number cube has the numbers 3, 5, 6, 8, 10, and 12 on its faces. You roll the number cube twice. What is the probability that you roll an odd number on both rolls? $\frac{1}{9}$

Avoid Common Errors

Students sometimes confuse independent events and mutually exclusive events. This may lead students to add the probabilities of event A and event B in the second example. If students do add the probabilities, they will find that $P(A) + P(B) = 1$, which would mean that $A \cap B$ is a certainty. This result, which does not make sense in the context of the problem, should alert students that they may have made an error.

3 EXAMPLE

Questioning Strategies

• Which column or row of the table do you look at to calculate $P(A)$? the bottom row of the table

• Which column or row of the table do you look at to calculate $P(B)$? the right- most column of the table

EXTRA EXAMPLE

The two-way table shows the data from the first extra example. Show that a patient taking vitamins and a patient exercising regularly are not independent events.

	Takes Vitamins	No Vitamins	TOTAL
Exercises Regularly	28	48	76
Does Not Exercise	12	32	44
TOTAL	40	80	120

P(exercise) $= \frac{19}{30}$; P(vitamins) $= \frac{1}{3}$; P(exercise and vitamins) $= \frac{7}{30}$; since the product of P(exercise) and P(vitamins) does not equal P(exercise and vitamins), the events are not independent events.

4 ENGAGE

Questioning Strategies

• Suppose the first marble you choose is blue. What happens to the sample space for your second pick? The sample space changes; it consists of 1 blue marble and 2 black marbles.

• Suppose you replace the first marble you pick. Are the events dependent events in this case? Why or why not? No; if you replace the first marble, the events are independent because the result of the first pick does not affect the sample space for the second pick.

The formula for the probability of independent events gives you another way to determine whether two events are independent. That is, two events A and B are independent events if $P(A \text{ and } B) = P(A) \cdot P(B)$.

CC.9-12.S.CP.2

3 EXAMPLE Showing that Events are Independent

The two-way table shows the data from the first example. Show that a flight arriving on time and a flight being a domestic flight are independent events.

	Late Arrival	On Time	TOTAL
Domestic Flight	12	108	120
International Flight	6	54	60
TOTAL	18	162	180

A Let event A be the event that a flight arrives on time. Let event B be the event that a flight is a domestic flight.

To find $P(A)$, $P(B)$, and $P(A \text{ and } B)$ note that there is a total of —180— flights.

There is a total of —162— on-time flights.

So, $P(A) = \dfrac{162}{180} = \dfrac{9}{10}$.

There is a total of —120— domestic flights.

So, $P(B) = \dfrac{120}{180} = \dfrac{2}{3}$.

There is a total of —108— on-time domestic flights.

So, $P(A \text{ and } B) = \dfrac{108}{180} = \dfrac{3}{5}$.

B Compare $P(A \text{ and } B)$ and $P(A) \cdot P(B)$.

$P(A) \cdot P(B) = (\dfrac{9}{10}) \cdot (\dfrac{2}{3}) = \dfrac{3}{5}$

So, the events are independent events because

$P(A \text{ and } B) = P(A) \cdot P(B)$.

REFLECT

3a. Describe a different way you can show that a flight arriving on time and a flight being a domestic flight are independent events.

Let events A and B be as in the example and show that $P(A) = P(A \mid B)$.

CC.9-12.S.CP.8(+)

4 ENGAGE Introducing Dependent Events

Two events are **dependent events** if the occurrence of one event affects the occurrence of the other event.

Suppose you have a bag containing 2 blue marbles and 2 black marbles. You choose a marble without looking, put it aside, and then choose a second marble. Consider the following events.

Event A: The first marble you choose is blue.

Event B: The second marble you choose is black.

Events A and B are dependent events, because the marble you choose for your first pick changes the sample space for your second pick. That is, the occurrence of event A affects the probability of event B.

Recall that you developed the following formula for conditional probability.

$$P(B \mid A) = \frac{P(A \text{ and } B)}{P(A)}$$

Multiplying both sides by $P(A)$ results in $P(A) \cdot P(B \mid A) = P(A \text{ and } B)$. This is known as the Multiplication Rule.

Multiplication Rule

$P(A \text{ and } B) = P(A) \cdot P(B \mid A)$, where $P(B \mid A)$ is the conditional probability of event B, given that event A has occurred.

You can use the Multiplication Rule to find the probability of dependent or independent events. Note that when A and B are independent events, $P(B \mid A) = P(B)$ and the rule may be rewritten as $P(A \text{ and } B) = P(A) \cdot P(B)$, which is the rule for independent events.

REFLECT

4a. How can you write the Multiplication Rule in a different way by starting with the formula for the conditional probability $P(A \mid B)$ and multiplying both sides of that equation by $P(B)$?

$P(A \mid B) = \dfrac{P(A \text{ and } B)}{P(B)}$; multiplying both sides by $P(B)$ results in

$P(A \text{ and } B) = P(B) \cdot P(A \mid B)$.

CC.9-12.S.CP.8(+)

5 EXAMPLE Finding the Probability of Dependent Events

There are 5 tiles with the letters A, B, C, D, and E in a bag. You choose a tile without looking, put it aside, and then choose another tile. Find the probability that you choose a consonant followed by a vowel.

A Let event A be the event that the first tile is a consonant.

Let event B be the event that the second tile is a vowel.

Find $P(A)$ and $P(B \mid A)$.

$P(A) = \dfrac{3}{5}$ Of the 5 tiles, 3 are consonants.

© Houghton Mifflin Harcourt Publishing Company

Notes

5 EXAMPLE

Questioning Strategies

- Why are these events dependent events? **The tile you choose first changes the sample space for your second pick. That is, the occurrence of event *A* affects the probability of event *B*.**

- How many consonants and vowels are in the bag? **3 consonants, 2 vowels**

EXTRA EXAMPLE

You choose a marble at random from the bag shown here. You put the marble aside and then choose another marble. Find the probability that you choose a gray marble followed by a blue marble. $\frac{4}{15}$

Teaching Strategies

The student page shows two different ways to determine the probability: 1) by using the formula for the Multiplication Rule and 2) by making a tree diagram. Students can also determine the probability by thinking about permutations. The number of outcomes in the sample space is $_5P_2 = 20$. The number of favorable outcomes (that is, outcomes consisting of a consonant followed by a vowel) is $3 \cdot 2 = 6$, since there are 3 consonants and 2 vowels in the bag. Thus, the required probability is $\frac{6}{20}$, or $\frac{3}{10}$.

© Houghton Mifflin Harcourt Publishing Company

Standard 1 (Make sense of problems and persevere in solving them) discusses the need for students to plan a "solution pathway" when they are confronted with a new problem. The material in this lesson can serve as an illustration to students that a single problem may have many correct solution pathways. Students can find probabilities by using a formula, by making a tree diagram, or by using permutations.

CLOSE

Essential Question

How do you find the probability of independent and dependent events? **Use the Multiplication Rule: $P(A \text{ and } B) = P(A) \cdot P(B \mid A)$, where $P(B \mid A)$ is the conditional probability of event *B*, given that event *A* has occurred.**
For independent events, $P(B \mid A) = P(B)$

Summarize

Have students write a journal entry in which they explain what is meant by independent events and give an example of how to determine whether two events are independent.

PRACTICE

Where skills are taught	Where skills are practiced
1 EXAMPLE	EX. 1
3 EXAMPLE	EX. 2
5 EXAMPLE	EX. 3–6

$$P(B \mid A) = \frac{2}{4} = \frac{1}{2}$$ Of the 4 remaining tiles, 2 are vowels.

B Use the Multiplication Rule.

$$P(A \text{ and } B) = P(A) \cdot P(B \mid A)$$ Use the Multiplication Rule.

$$= \left(\frac{3}{5}\right) \cdot \left(\frac{1}{2}\right)$$ Substitute.

$$= \frac{3}{10}$$ Multiply.

So, the probability that you choose a consonant followed by a vowel is $\frac{3}{10}$.

REFLECT

5a. Complete the tree diagram below. Then explain how you can use it to check your answer.

1st tile   A   B   C   D   E

2nd tile B C D E A C D E A B D E A B C E A B C D

The tree diagram has 20 "branches" and 6 of these (circled) correspond to a

consonant followed by a vowel; so, the probability of a consonant followed

by a vowel is $\frac{6}{20} = \frac{3}{10}$.

5b. What does your answer tell you about the likelihood of choosing a consonant followed by a vowel?

The outcome is unlikely (it will theoretically occur 30% of the time).

PRACTICE

1. A farmer wants to know if an insecticide is effective in preventing small insects called aphids from living on tomato plants. The farmer checks 80 plants. The data is shown in the two-way table. Is having aphids independent of being sprayed with the insecticide? Why or why not?

	Has Aphids	No Aphids	TOTAL
Was sprayed with insecticide	12	40	52
Was not sprayed with insecticide	14	14	28
TOTAL	26	54	80

No; $P(\text{aphids}) = \frac{26}{80} = 32.5\%$ and $P(\text{aphids} \mid \text{insecticide}) = \frac{12}{52} \approx 23\%$; since these

probabilities are not equal, the events are not independent.

2. A student wants to know if right-handed people are more or less likely to play a musical instrument than left-handed people. The student collects data from 250 people, as shown in the two-way table. Show that being right handed and playing a musical instrument are independent events.

	Right Handed	Left Handed	TOTAL
Plays a musical instrument	44	6	50
Does not play a musical instrument	176	24	200
TOTAL	220	30	250

$P(\text{right}) = \frac{220}{250} = \frac{22}{25}$; $P(\text{plays}) = \frac{50}{250} = \frac{1}{5}$; $P(\text{right and plays}) = \frac{44}{250} = \frac{22}{125}$;

since $P(\text{right}) \cdot P(\text{plays}) = P(\text{right and plays})$, the events are independent.

3. A basket contains 6 bottles of apple juice and 8 bottles of grape juice. You choose a bottle without looking, put it aside, and then choose another bottle. What is the probability that you choose a bottle of apple juice followed by a bottle of grape juice?

$$\frac{6}{14} \cdot \frac{8}{13} = \frac{24}{91}$$

4. You have a set of ten cards that are numbered 1 through 10. You shuffle the cards and choose a card at random. You put the card aside and choose another card. What is the probability that you choose an even number followed by an odd number?

$$\frac{5}{10} \cdot \frac{5}{9} = \frac{5}{18}$$

5. There are 12 boys and 14 girls in Ms. Garcia's class. She chooses a student at random to solve a geometry problem at the board. Then she chooses another student at random to check the first student's work. Is she more likely to choose a boy followed by a girl, a girl followed by a boy, or are these both equally likely? Explain.

Equally likely; the probability of a boy followed by a girl is $\frac{12}{26} \cdot \frac{14}{25} = \frac{84}{325}$;

the probability of a girl followed by a boy is $\frac{14}{26} \cdot \frac{12}{25} = \frac{84}{325}$.

6. A bag contains 4 blue marbles and 4 red marbles. You choose a marble without looking, put it aside, and then choose another marble. Is there a greater than or less than 50% chance that you choose two marbles with different colors? Explain.

Greater than 50%; the probability of choosing blue then red is $\frac{4}{8} \cdot \frac{4}{7}$; the

probability of choosing red then blue is $\frac{4}{8} \cdot \frac{4}{7}$; the sum of these probabilities

is $\frac{4}{7}$, which is greater than 50%.

© Houghton Mifflin Harcourt Publishing Company

Assign these pages to help your students practice
and apply important lesson concepts. For
additional exercises, see the Student Edition.

Answers

Additional Practice

1. $\frac{3}{50}$ 2. $\frac{1}{9}$

3. **a.** The events are dependent because
$P(\text{sum} \geq 6)$ is different when it is known
that a black 3 occurred.

 b. $\frac{1}{9}$

4. **a.** The events are dependent because
$P(\text{sum} = 8)$ is different when it is known
that the white cube shows an even number.

 b. $\frac{1}{12}$

5. 0.52 6. 0.09

7. 0.12

8. Independent; $\frac{15}{121}$

9. Dependent; $\frac{3}{43}$

Problem Solving

1. **a.** $P(10) = \frac{135}{440}$

 b. $P(Tr|10) = \frac{6}{135}$

 c. $P(10 \text{ and } Tr) = \frac{6}{440} \approx 0.014$

2. **a.** $P(12) = \frac{85}{440}$

 b. $P(Tr \text{ or } Te \mid 12)\ \frac{7+12}{85} = \frac{19}{85}$

 c. $P(12 \text{ and } (Tr \text{ or } Te)) = \frac{19}{85} \cdot \frac{85}{440} \approx 0.043$

3. **a.** $\frac{19}{440}$ **b.** $\frac{6}{439}$ **c.** $\frac{19}{440} \cdot \frac{6}{439} \approx 0.0006$

 d. Dependent; possible answer: the second
student is one of the remaining 439
students.

4. D 5. F

Additional Practice

Find each probability.

1. A bag contains 5 red, 3 green, 4 blue, and 8 yellow marbles. Find the probability of randomly selecting a green marble, and then a yellow marble if the first marble is replaced. _____

2. A sock drawer contains 5 rolled-up pairs of each color of socks, white, green, and blue. What is the probability of randomly selecting a pair of blue socks, replacing it, and then randomly selecting a pair of white socks? _____

Two 1–6 number cubes are rolled—one is black and one is white.

3. The sum of the rolls is greater than or equal to 6 and the black cube shows a 3.

   a. Explain why the events are dependent.

   _____

   _____

   b. Find the probability. _____

4. The white cube shows an even number, and the sum is 8.

   a. Explain why the events are dependent.

   _____

   b. Find the probability. _____

The table below shows numbers of registered voters by age in the United States in 2004 based on the census. Find each probability in decimal form.

Age	Registered Voters (in thousands)	Not Registered to Vote (in thousands)
18–24	14,334	13,474
25–44	49,371	32,763
45–64	51,659	19,355
65 and over	26,706	8,033

5. A randomly selected person is registered to vote, given that the person is between the ages of 18 and 24. _____

6. A randomly selected person is between the ages of 45 and 64 and is not registered to vote. _____

7. A randomly selected person is registered to vote and is at least 65 years old. _____

A bag contains 12 blue cubes, 12 red cubes, and 20 green cubes. Determine whether the events are independent or dependent, and find each probability.

8. A green cube and then a blue cube are chosen at random with replacement. _____

9. Two blue cubes are chosen at random without replacement. _____

Problem Solving

The table shows student participation in different sports at a high school. Suppose a student is selected at random.

Sports Participation by Grade				
	Track	Volleyball	Basketball	Tennis	No Sport
Grade 9	12	18	15	9	66
Grade 10	6	20	12	2	95
Grade 11	15	11	8	5	61
Grade 12	7	6	10	12	50

1. What is the probability that a student is in grade 10 and runs track?

   a. Find the probability that a student is in grade 10, $P(10)$. _____

   b. Find the probability that a student runs track, given that the student is in grade 10, $P(Tr \mid 10)$. _____

   c. Find $P(10$ and $Tr) = P(10) \cdot P(Tr \mid 10)$. _____

2. What is the probability that a student is in grade 12 and runs track or plays tennis?

   a. Find the probability that a student is in grade 12, $P(12)$. _____

   b. Find the probability that a student runs track or plays tennis, given that the student is in grade 12, $P(Tr$ or $Te \mid 12)$. _____

   c. Find $P(12$ or $(Tr$ or $Te))$. _____

3. During a fire drill, the students are waiting in the parking lot. What is the probability that one student is in grade 12 and runs track or plays tennis, and the student standing next to her is in grade 10 and runs track?

   a. Find the probability for the first student. _____

   b. Find the probability for the second student. _____

   c. Find the probability for the event occurring. _____

   d. Are these events independent or dependent? Explain.

Samantha is 1 of 17 students in a class of 85 who have decided to pursue a business degree. Each week, a student in the class is randomly selected to tutor younger students. Choose the letter for the best answer.

4. What is the probability of drawing a business student one week, replacing the name, and drawing the same name the next week?

   A 3.4   C 0.04

   B 0.2   D 0.002

5. What is the probability of drawing Samantha's name one week, not replacing her name, and drawing the name of another business student the next week?

   F $\frac{1}{85} \cdot \frac{16}{84}$ H $\frac{17}{85} \cdot \frac{16}{84}$

   G $\frac{1}{85} \cdot \frac{17}{84}$ J $\frac{17}{85} \cdot \frac{17}{84}$

Two-Way Tables
Going Deeper

Essential question: *How do you calculate a conditional probability?*

© Houghton Mifflin Harcourt Publishing Company

Standards for Mathematical Content

CC.9-12.S.CP.3 Understand the conditional probability of *A* given *B* as *P*(*A* and *B*)/*P*(*B*) ... .*

CC.9-12.S.CP.4 Construct and interpret two-way frequency tables of data when two categories are associated with each object being classified. Use the two-way table ... to approximate conditional probabilities.*

CC.9-12.S.CP.5 Recognize and explain the concept of conditional probability ... in everyday language and everyday situations.*

CC.9-12.S.CP.6 Find the conditional probability of *A* given *B* as the fraction of *B*'s outcomes that also belong to *A*, and interpret the answer in terms of the model.*

Vocabulary

conditional probability

Prerequisites

Probability and Set Theory

Math Background

In this lesson students will be given opportunities to work with two-way tables, which can be used to make sense of a wide range of probability and statistics problems. These tables are used to develop a formula for calculating conditional probability. This formula is given by

$$P(B \mid A) = \frac{P(A \cap B)}{P(A)}.$$

INTRODUCE

Define *conditional probability*. Give students a simple example. For instance, when you roll a number cube, the probability that you roll a 6 is $\frac{1}{6}$. The conditional probability that you roll a 6 given that you roll a number greater than 4 is $\frac{1}{2}$ since this condition effectively restricts the sample space to {5, 6}.

TEACH

1 EXAMPLE

Questioning Strategies

• What percent of the participants in the study were given the medicine? **60%**

• How many participants in the study did not get a headache? **73**

• Was a participant who got a headache more likely to have taken the medicine or not? **The participant was more likely to have not taken the medicine.**

EXTRA EXAMPLE

The manager of a produce stand wants to find out whether there is a connection between people who buy fresh vegetables and people who buy eggs. The manager collects data on 200 randomly chosen shoppers, as shown in the two-way table.

	Bought Vegetables	No Vegetables	TOTAL
Eggs	56	20	76
No Eggs	49	75	124
TOTAL	105	95	200

A. To the nearest percent, what is the probability that a shopper who bought eggs also bought vegetables? **74%**

B. To the nearest percent, what is the probability that a shopper who bought vegetables also bought eggs? **53%**

Name_____ Class_____ Date_____

Two-Way Tables
Going Deeper

Essential question: *How do you calculate a conditional probability?*

The probability that event *B* occurs given that event *A* has already occurred is called the **conditional probability** of *B* given *A* and is written $P(B \mid A)$.

CC.9-12.S.CP.6

1 EXAMPLE   Finding Conditional Probabilities

One hundred people who frequently get migraine headaches were chosen to participate in a study of a new anti-headache medicine. Some of the participants were given the medicine; others were not. After one week, the participants were asked if they got a headache during the week. The two-way table summarizes the results.

	Took Medicine	No Medicine	TOTAL
Headache	12	15	27
No Headache	48	25	73
TOTAL	60	40	100

A To the nearest percent, what is the probability that a participant who took the medicine did not get a headache?

Let event *A* be the event that a participant took the medicine. Let event *B* be the event that a participant did not get a headache.

To find the probability that a participant who took the medicine did not get a headache, you must find $P(B \mid A)$. You are only concerned with participants who took the medicine, so look at the data in the "Took Medicine" column.

There were ___60___ participants who took the medicine.

Of these participants, ___48___ participants did not get a headache.

So, $P(B \mid A) = \dfrac{48}{60} = $ ___80%___ .

B To the nearest percent, what is the probability that a participant who did not get a headache took the medicine?

To find the probability that a participant who did not get a headache took the medicine, you must find $P(A \mid B)$. You are only concerned with participants who did not get a headache, so look at the data in the "No headache" row.

There were ___73___ participants who did not get a headache.

Of these participants, ___48___ participants took the medicine.

So, $P(A \mid B) = \dfrac{48}{73} \approx $ ___66%___ .

© Houghton Mifflin Harcourt Publishing Company

REFLECT

1a. In general, do you think $P(B \mid A) = P(A \mid B)$? Why or why not?

No; these conditional probabilities are not equal in the example.

1b. How can you use set notation to represent the event that a participant took the medicine and did not get a headache? Is the probability that a participant took the medicine and did not get a headache equal to either of the conditional probabilities you calculated in the example?

This is represented by $A \cap B$; $P(A \cap B) = \frac{48}{100} = 48\%$; this probability is not

equal to $P(B \mid A)$ or $P(A \mid B)$.

CC.9-12.S.CP.3

2 EXPLORE   Developing a Formula for Conditional Probability

You can generalize your work from the previous example to develop a formula for finding conditional probabilities.

A Recall how you calculated $P(B \mid A)$, the probability that a participant who took the medicine did not get a headache.

You found that $P(B \mid A) = \frac{48}{60}$.

Use the table shown here to help you write this quotient in terms of events *A* and *B*.

		Event A		
		Took Medicine	No Medicine	TOTAL
Event B	Headache	12	15	27
	No Headache	$48 = n(A \cap B)$	25	$73 = n(B)$
	TOTAL	$60 = n(A)$	40	100

$P(B \mid A) = \dfrac{n(A \cap B)}{n(A)}$

B Now divide the numerator and denominator of the quotient by $n(S)$, the number of outcomes in the sample space. This converts the counts to probabilities.

$P(B \mid A) = \dfrac{n(A \cap B)\big/ n(S)}{n(A)\big/ n(S)} = \dfrac{P(A \cap B)}{P(A)}$

REFLECT

2a. Write a formula for $P(A \mid B)$ in terms of $n(A \cap B)$ and $n(B)$.

$P(A \mid B) = \dfrac{n(A \cap B)}{n(B)}$

2b. Write a formula for $P(A \mid B)$ in terms of $P(A \cap B)$ and $P(B)$.

$P(A \mid B) = \dfrac{P(A \cap B)}{P(B)}$

© Houghton Mifflin Harcourt Publishing Company

Highlighting the Standards

Standard 4 (Model with mathematics) includes the statement that mathematically proficient students are able to map relationships among important quantities using tools like two-way tables. Furthermore, "they can analyze those relationships mathematically to draw conclusions." This lesson offers many opportunities for such analyses. After the first example, ask students what conclusions they can draw about the effectiveness of the headache medicine. The data in the two-way table and the conditional probabilities indicate that the medicine is at least somewhat effective in preventing headaches.

2 EXPLORE

- What does $A \cap B$ represent? participants who took the medicine and did not get a headache

- How many participants are in $A \cap B$? How do you know? 48; this is the number in the cell corresponding to "Took Medicine" and "No Headache."

- What is $n(S)$? Why? 100;100 people participated in the study.

Teaching Strategies

English language learners may have difficulty with conditional probability because so much depends upon understanding that "What is the probability that a participant who took the medicine did not get a headache?" and "What is the probability that a participant who did not get a headache took the medicine?" are different questions. When working with such statements, you may want to prompt students to underline the words that correspond to the event that is assumed to have already occurred.

3 EXAMPLE

Questioning Strategies

- In this situation, which event can be considered to have already occurred? the event that the card is red

- What are the red cards in a deck of cards? The red cards are the 13 hearts and the 13 diamonds.

EXTRA EXAMPLE

In a standard deck of playing cards, find the probability that a face card is a king. $\frac{1}{3}$

CLOSE

Essential Question

How do you calculate a conditional probability?
You can calculate a conditional probability from a two-way table. You can also use the formula $P(B \mid A) = \frac{P(A \cap B)}{P(A)}$.

Summarize

Have students write a journal entry in which they explain conditional probability in their own words. Also, ask students to give an example of how to use the formula for conditional probability.

PRACTICE

Where skills are taught	Where skills are practiced
1 EXAMPLE	EXS. 1–2
3 EXAMPLE	EXS. 3–9

You may have discovered the following formula for conditional probability.

Conditional Probability

The conditional probability of B given A (the probability that event B occurs given that event A occurs) is given by the following formula:

$$P(B \mid A) = \frac{P(A \cap B)}{P(A)}$$

3 EXAMPLE CC.9-12.S.CP.3   Using the Conditional Probability Formula

In a standard deck of playing cards, find the probability that a red card is a queen.

A   Let event Q be the event that a card is a queen. Let event R be the event that a card is red. You are asked to find $P(Q \mid R)$. First find $P(R \cap Q)$ and $P(R)$.

$R \cap Q$ represents cards that are both red and a queen; that is, red queens.

There are ___2___ red queens in the deck of 52 cards, so $P(R \cap Q) = \frac{2}{52}$.

There are ___26___ red cards in the deck, so $P(R) = \frac{26}{52}$.

B   Use the formula for conditional probability.

$$P(Q \mid R) = \frac{P(Q \cap R)}{P(R)} = \frac{\frac{2}{52}}{\frac{26}{52}}$$ Substitute probabilities from above.

$$= \frac{2}{26}$$ Multiply numerator and denominator by 52.

$$= \frac{1}{13}$$ Simplify.

So, the probability that a red card is a queen is $\frac{1}{13}$.

REFLECT

3a. How can you interpret the probability you calculated above?

If you choose a red card at random, it is very unlikely that it will be a queen

(it will be a queen about 8% of the time).

3b. Is the probability that a red card is a queen equal to the probability that a queen is red? Explain.

No; $P(R \mid Q) = \frac{1}{2}$, whereas $P(Q \mid R) = \frac{1}{13}$.

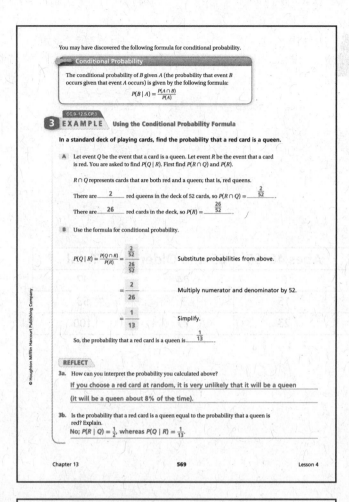

PRACTICE

1. In order to study the connection between the amount of sleep a student gets and his or her school performance, data was collected about 120 students. The two-way table shows the number of students who passed and failed an exam and the number of students who got more or less than 6 hours of sleep the night before.

	Passed Exam	Failed Exam	TOTAL
Less than 6 hours of sleep	12	10	22
More than 6 hours of sleep	90	8	98
TOTAL	102	18	120

a. To the nearest percent, what is the probability that a student who failed the exam got less than 6 hours of sleep? **56%**

b. To the nearest percent, what is the probability that a student who got less than 6 hours of sleep failed the exam? **45%**

c. To the nearest percent, what is the probability that a student got less than 6 hours of sleep and failed the exam? **8%**

2. A botanist studied the effect of a new fertilizer by choosing 100 orchids and giving 70% of these plants the fertilizer. Of the plants that got the fertilizer, 40% produced flowers within a month. Of the plants that did not get the fertilizer, 10% produced flowers within a month. Find each probability to the nearest percent. (Hint: Construct a two-way table.)

a. Find the probability that a plant that produced flowers got the fertilizer. **90%**

b. Find the probability that a plant that got the fertilizer produced flowers. **40%**

3. At a school fair, a box contains 24 yellow balls and 76 red balls. One-fourth of the balls of each color are labeled "Win a prize." Find each probability as a percent.

a. Find the probability that a ball labeled "Win a prize" is yellow. **24%**

b. Find the probability that a ball labeled "Win a prize" is red. **76%**

c. Find the probability that a ball is labeled "Win a prize" and is red. **19%**

d. Find the probability that a yellow ball is labeled "Win a prize." **25%**

In Exercises 4–9, consider a standard deck of playing cards and the following events: A: the card is an ace; B: the card is black; C: the card is a club. Find each probability as a fraction.

4. $P(A \mid B)$ $\frac{1}{13}$

5. $P(B \mid A)$ $\frac{1}{2}$

6. $P(A \mid C)$ $\frac{1}{13}$

7. $P(C \mid A)$ $\frac{1}{4}$

8. $P(B \mid C)$ 1

9. $P(C \mid B)$ $\frac{1}{2}$

Notes

ADDITIONAL PRACTICE AND PROBLEM SOLVING

Assign these pages to help your students practice and apply important lesson concepts. For additional exercises, see the Student Edition.

Answers

Additional Practice

1.

	Ages 10–20	Ages 21–45	Ages 46–65	65 and Older	Total
Yes	13	2	8	24	47
No	25	10	15	3	53
Total	38	12	23	27	100

a. 17%

b. 51%

2. **a.** 0.45

b. 0.70

Problem Solving

1. **a.** 79%

b. 79%

2. **a.** 0.81

b. 0.27

3. D

4. J

Additional Practice

1. The table shows the results of a customer satisfaction survey of 100 randomly selected shoppers at the mall who were asked if they would shop at an earlier time if the mall opened earlier. Complete the table below and use it to answer parts **a** and **b**.

	Ages 10–20	Ages 21–45	Ages 46–65	Ages Over 65
Yes	13	2	8	24
No	25	10	15	3

	Ages 10–20	Ages 21–45	Ages 46–65	Ages Over 65	Total
Yes					
No					
Total					

a. To the nearest whole percent, what is the probability that a shopper who is in the age range 21 to 45 said that he or she would shop earlier?

_____

b. To the nearest whole percent, what is the probability that a shopper who would shop earlier is in the age range 65 and older?

_____

2. Jerrod collected data on 100 randomly selected students, and summarized the results in a table.

		Owns an MP3 player	
		Yes	No
Owns a	Yes	28	12
Smart phone	No	34	26

a. If you are given that a student owns an MP3 player, what is the probability that the student also owns a smart phone? Round your answer to the nearest hundredth.

_____

b. If you are given that a student owns a smart phone, what is the probability that the student also owns an MP3 player? Round your answer to the nearest hundredth.

_____

Problem Solving

1. The table shows the number of students who would drive to school if the school provided parking spaces. Complete the table below and use it to answer parts **a** and **b**.

	Lowerclassmates	Upperclassmates
Always	32	122
Sometimes	58	44
Never	24	120

a. To the nearest whole percent, what is the probability that a student who said "always" is an upperclassmate?

_____

b. To the nearest whole percent, what is the probability that a lowerclassmate said "always" or "sometimes"?

_____

2. Gerry collected data and did a table of marginal relative frequencies on the number of students who participate in chorus and the number who participate in band.

		Chorus	
		Yes	No
Band	Yes	38	29
	No	9	24

a. If you are given that a student is in chorus, what is the probability that the student also is in band? Round your answer to the nearest hundredth.

_____

b. If you are given that a student is not in band, what is the probability that the student is in chorus? Round your answer to the nearest hundredth.

_____

Use the table in Exercise 2 to answer Exercises 3 and 4. Select the best answer.

3. What is the probability if a student is not in chorus, then that student is in band?
   A 0.29   B 0.38
   C 0.43   D 0.55

4. What is the probability that if a student is not in band then the student is not in chorus?
   F 0.09   G 0.33
   H 0.44   J 0.73

Compound Events
Going Deeper

Essential question: *How do you find the probability of mutually exclusive events and overlapping events?*

 **Standards for Mathematical Content**

CC.9-12.S.CP.7 Apply the Addition Rule, $P(A \text{ or } B) = P(A) + P(B) - P(A \text{ and } B)$, and interpret the answer in terms of the model.*

Vocabulary
mutually exclusive events

overlapping events

Prerequisites
Probability and Set Theory

Math Background
Mutually exclusive events have no outcomes in common. Thus, mutually exclusive events cannot both occur on the same trial of an experiment. Overlapping or inclusive events have one or more outcomes in common. For overlapping events A and B, $P(A \text{ or } B) = P(A) + P(B) - P(A \text{ and } B)$. In the case that A and B are mutually exclusive events, $P(A \text{ and } B) = 0$, so the rule takes on the simpler form $P(A \text{ or } B) = P(A) + P(B)$.

INTRODUCE

Define *mutually exclusive events*. Give students an example of mutually exclusive events. For example, when you roll a standard number cube, rolling a number less than 3 and rolling a 6 are mutually exclusive events because the events have no outcomes in common. Ask students to give additional examples of mutually exclusive events based on rolling a number cube.

TEACH

 **EXAMPLE**

Questioning Strategies
• Why are events A and B mutually exclusive events? They have no outcomes in common.

• How is this reflected in the Venn diagram? The ovals representing the events do not intersect.

EXTRA EXAMPLE
You choose a card at random from a standard deck of playing cards. What is the probability that you choose a queen or the 7 of diamonds? $\frac{5}{52}$

2 **EXAMPLE**

Questioning Strategies
• Why are events A and B overlapping? They have some outcomes in common.

• How is this reflected in the Venn diagram? The ovals representing the events intersect.

• If A and B are overlapping events, what can you say about $A \cap B$? $A \cap B$ is not the empty set.

EXTRA EXAMPLE
You have a set of 20 cards that are numbered 1–20. You shuffle the cards and choose one at random. What is the probability that you choose an even number or a number greater than 15? $\frac{3}{5}$

MATHEMATICAL PRACTICE | **Highlighting the Standards**

According to Standard 1 (Make sense of problems and persevere in solving them), mathematically proficient students continually ask themselves, "Does this make sense?" This lesson provides an especially good opportunity for this type of reflective thinking. Whenever students calculate a probability they should ask themselves whether the probability seems reasonable. For instance, in the second example, students find that the probability, of rolling an even number or a number greater than 7 on a dodecahedral number cube is $\frac{2}{3}$. This seems reasonable since more than half of the outcomes in the sample space are in at least one of these events.

Name_____ Class_____ Date_____

13-5

Video Tutor

Compound Events
Going Deeper

Essential question: *How do you find the probability of mutually exclusive events and overlapping events?*

Two events are **mutually exclusive events** if the events cannot both occur in the same trial of an experiment. For example, when you toss a coin, the coin landing heads up and the coin landing tails up are mutually exclusive events.

CC.9-12.S.CP.7

1 EXAMPLE Finding the Probability of Mutually Exclusive Events

A dodecahedral number cube has 12 sides numbered 1 through 12. What is the probability that you roll the cube and the result is an even number or a 7?

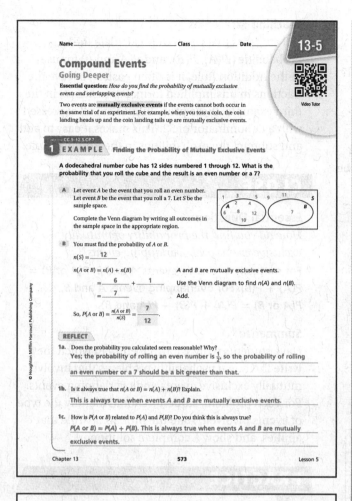

A Let event A be the event that you roll an even number. Let event B be the event that you roll a 7. Let S be the sample space.

Complete the Venn diagram by writing all outcomes in the sample space in the appropriate region.

B You must find the probability of A or B.

$n(S) = $ __12__

$n(A \text{ or } B) = n(A) + n(B)$ A and B are mutually exclusive events.

$= $ __6__ $+$ __1__   Use the Venn diagram to find $n(A)$ and $n(B)$.

$= $ __7__   Add.

So, $P(A \text{ or } B) = \frac{n(A \text{ or } B)}{n(S)} = $ __7__ / __12__.

REFLECT

1a. Does the probability you calculated seem reasonable? Why?

Yes; the probability of rolling an even number is $\frac{1}{2}$, so the probability of rolling

an even number or a 7 should be a bit greater than that.

1b. Is it always true that $n(A \text{ or } B) = n(A) + n(B)$? Explain.

This is always true when events A and B are mutually exclusive events.

1c. How is $P(A \text{ or } B)$ related to $P(A)$ and $P(B)$? Do you think this is always true?

$P(A \text{ or } B) = P(A) + P(B)$. This is always true when events A and B are mutually

exclusive events.

Chapter 13   573   Lesson 5

© Houghton Mifflin Harcourt Publishing Company

The process you used in the example can be generalized to give a formula for the probability of mutually exclusive events.

Mutually Exclusive Events

If A and B are mutually exclusive events, then $P(A \text{ or } B) = P(A) + P(B)$.

Two events are **overlapping events** (or *inclusive events*) if they have one or more outcomes in common.

CC.9-12.S.CP.7

2 EXAMPLE Finding the Probability of Overlapping Events

What is the probability that you roll a dodecahedral number cube and the result is an even number or a number greater than 7?

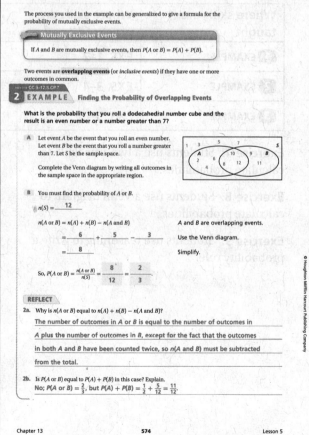

A Let event A be the event that you roll an even number. Let event B be the event that you roll a number greater than 7. Let S be the sample space.

Complete the Venn diagram by writing all outcomes in the sample space in the appropriate region.

B You must find the probability of A or B.

$n(S) = $ __12__

$n(A \text{ or } B) = n(A) + n(B) - n(A \text{ and } B)$ A and B are overlapping events.

$= $ __6__ $+$ __5__ $-$ __3__   Use the Venn diagram.

$= $ __8__   Simplify.

So, $P(A \text{ or } B) = \frac{n(A \text{ or } B)}{n(S)} = $ __8__ / __12__ $= $ __2__ / __3__.

REFLECT

2a. Why is $n(A \text{ or } B)$ equal to $n(A) + n(B) - n(A \text{ and } B)$?

The number of outcomes in A or B is equal to the number of outcomes in

A plus the number of outcomes in B, except for the fact that the outcomes

in both A and B have been counted twice, so $n(A \text{ and } B)$ must be subtracted

from the total.

2b. Is $P(A \text{ or } B)$ equal to $P(A) + P(B)$ in this case? Explain.

No; $P(A \text{ or } B) = \frac{2}{3}$, but $P(A) + P(B) = \frac{1}{2} + \frac{5}{12} = \frac{11}{12}$.

Chapter 13   574   Lesson 5

© Houghton Mifflin Harcourt Publishing Company

Questioning Strategies

- How are the cards in a standard deck organized? There are 13 cards (ace, 2, 3, 4, 5, 6, 7, 8, 9, 10, jack, queen, king), each in 4 suits (hearts, clubs, diamonds, spades), for a total of 52 cards.

- What card or cards does $A \cap B$ represent? Why? $A \cap B$ is the king of hearts since the card must be both a king and a heart.

EXTRA EXAMPLE

You have a set of 26 cards with the letters A through Z. You shuffle the cards and choose one at random. What is the probability that you choose a card with a consonant or a letter in the word PROBABILITY? $\frac{12}{13}$

Differentiated Instruction

Some students may find it easier to solve the problem in the third example by making a chart that shows all of the cards in a deck of cards and then highlighting the cards in events A and B.

A ♥	A ♣	A ♦	A ♠
2 ♥	2 ♣	2 ♦	2 ♠
3 ♥	3 ♣	3 ♦	3 ♠
4 ♥	4 ♣	4 ♦	4 ♠
5 ♥	5 ♣	5 ♦	5 ♠
6 ♥	6 ♣	6 ♦	6 ♠
7 ♥	7 ♣	7 ♦	7 ♠
8 ♥	8 ♣	8 ♦	8 ♠
9 ♥	9 ♣	9 ♦	9 ♠
10 ♥	10 ♣	10 ♦	10 ♠
J ♥	J ♣	J ♦	J ♠
Q ♥	Q ♣	Q ♦	Q ♠
K ♥	K ♣	K ♦	K ♠

Teaching Strategies

Tell students that when they calculate the probabilities $P(A)$, $P(B)$, and $P(A \text{ and } B)$ for use in the Addition Rule, it is often easiest to leave the fractions in unsimplified form. For instance, in the third example, these probabilities are all expressed with a denominator of 52. This makes it easy to add and subtract the probabilities in the Addition Rule.

CLOSE

Essential Question

How do you find the probability of mutually exclusive events and overlapping events?
For mutually exclusive events A and B, $P(A \text{ or } B) = P(A) + P(B)$. For overlapping events A and B, $P(A \text{ or } B) = P(A) + P(B) - P(A \text{ and } B)$.

Summarize

Have students write a journal entry in which they write their own probability problems that involve mutually exclusive events and overlapping events. For each problem, students should identify the type of events involved, state the probability rule that applies, and show a complete solution.

PRACTICE

Where skills are taught	Where skills are practiced
1 EXAMPLE	EXS. 1–2
2 EXAMPLE	EXS. 3–4
3 EXAMPLE	EXS. 5–6

Exercise 7: Students use a two-way table to calculate probabilities.

Exercise 8: Students use a Venn diagram to calculate probabilities.

Exercise 9: Students use reasoning to write a probability rule.

In the previous example you saw that for overlapping events A and B, $n(A \cup B) = n(A) + n(B) - n(A \cap B)$. You can convert these counts to probabilities by dividing each term by $n(S)$ as shown below.

$$\frac{n(A \cup B)}{n(S)} = \frac{n(A)}{n(S)} + \frac{n(B)}{n(S)} - \frac{n(A \cap B)}{n(S)}$$

Rewriting each term as a probability results in the following rule.

Addition Rule

$$P(A \text{ or } B) = P(A) + P(B) - P(A \text{ and } B)$$

Notice that when A and B are mutually exclusive events, $P(A \text{ and } B) = 0$, and the rule becomes the simpler rule for mutually exclusive events on the previous page.

CC.9-12.S.CP.7

3 EXAMPLE Using the Addition Rule

You shuffle a standard deck of playing cards and choose a card at random. What is the probability that you choose a king or a heart?

A Let event A be the event that you choose a king. Let event B be the event that you choose a heart. Let S be the sample space.

There are 52 cards in the deck, so $n(S) = \underline{52}$.

There are 4 kings in the deck, so $n(A) = \underline{4}$ and $P(A) = \underline{\frac{4}{52}}$.

There are 13 hearts in the deck, so $n(B) = \underline{13}$ and $P(B) = \underline{\frac{13}{52}}$.

There is one king of hearts in the deck, so $P(A \text{ and } B) = \underline{\frac{1}{52}}$.

B Use the Addition Rule.

$$P(A \text{ or } B) = P(A) + P(B) - P(A \text{ and } B)$$

$$= \underline{\frac{4}{52}} + \underline{\frac{13}{52}} - \underline{\frac{1}{52}} \qquad \text{Substitute.}$$

$$= \underline{\frac{16}{52}} \text{ or } \underline{\frac{4}{13}} \qquad \text{Simplify.}$$

So, the probability of choosing a king or a heart is $\underline{\frac{4}{13}}$.

REFLECT

3a. What does the answer tell you about the likelihood of choosing a king or a heart from the deck?

The probability is about 31%, so the outcome is not very likely (it will occur about 31% of the time).

© Houghton Mifflin Harcourt Publishing Company

PRACTICE

1. A bag contains 3 blue marbles, 5 red marbles, and 4 green marbles. You choose a marble without looking. What is the probability that you choose a red marble or a green marble?
$\frac{3}{4}$

2. An icosahedral number cube has 20 sides numbered 1 through 20. What is the probability that you roll the cube and the result is a number that is less than 4 or greater than 11?
$\frac{3}{5}$

3. A bag contains 26 tiles, each with a different letter of the alphabet written on it. You choose a tile without looking. What is the probability that you choose a vowel or a letter in the word GEOMETRY?
$\frac{5}{13}$

4. You roll two number cubes at the same time. Each cube has sides numbered 1 through 6. What is the probability that the sum of the numbers rolled is even or greater than 9?
$\frac{5}{9}$

5. You shuffle a standard deck of playing cards and choose a card at random. What is the probability that you choose a face card (jack, queen, or king) or a club?
$\frac{11}{26}$

6. You have a set of 25 cards numbered 1 through 25. You shuffle the cards and choose a card at random. What is the probability that you choose a multiple of 3 or a multiple of 4?
$\frac{12}{25}$

7. The two-way table provides data on the students at a high school. You randomly choose a student at the school. Find each probability.

	Freshman	Sophomore	Junior	Senior	TOTAL
Boy	98	104	100	94	396
Girl	102	106	96	108	412
TOTAL	200	210	196	202	808

a. The student is a senior. $\frac{1}{4}$

b. The student is a girl. $\frac{103}{202}$

c. The student is a senior and a girl. $\frac{27}{202}$

d. The student is a senior or a girl. $\frac{253}{404}$

8. A survey of the 1108 employees at a software company finds that 621 employees take a bus to work and 445 employees take a train to work. Some employees take both a bus and a train, and 312 employees take only a train. To the nearest percent, what is the probability that a randomly-chosen employee takes a bus or a train to work? (*Hint:* Make a Venn diagram.)
84%

9. Suppose A and B are complementary events. Explain how you can rewrite the Addition Rule in a simpler form for this case.
Because $P(A \text{ and } B) = 0$ for complementary events, $P(A \text{ or } B) = P(A) + P(B) = 1$.

© Houghton Mifflin Harcourt Publishing Company

ADDITIONAL PRACTICE AND PROBLEM SOLVING

Assign these pages to help your students practice and apply important lesson concepts. For additional exercises, see the Student Edition.

Answers

Additional Practice

1. These events are mutually exclusive because each can contains only one type of vegetable.

2. $\frac{13}{40}$ 3. $\frac{1}{3}$

4. $\frac{5}{6}$ 5. $\frac{2}{3}$

6. $\frac{7}{8}$ 7. $\frac{29}{40}$

8. $\frac{4}{5}$ 9. $\frac{67}{110}$ or 0.61

10. 0.81

Problem Solving

1. **a.** The total number of male students; 44

    b. The total number of students in favor of the change; 54

    c. $54 - 20 = 34$

    e. $\frac{44}{100} + \frac{54}{100} - \frac{34}{100} = \frac{64}{100} = 0.64$

2. **a.** $100 - 44 = 56$

    b. $100 - 54 = 46$

    c. The number of females who are opposed to the change; 36

    d. $\frac{56}{100} + \frac{46}{100} - \frac{36}{100} = \frac{66}{100} = 0.66$

3. $\frac{27}{100} + \frac{54}{100} - \frac{18}{100} = \frac{63}{100} = 0.63$

4. C   5. J

© Houghton Mifflin Harcourt Publishing Company

13-5

Additional Practice

A can of vegetables with no label has a $\frac{1}{8}$ chance of being green beans and a $\frac{1}{5}$ chance of being corn.

1. Explain why the events "green beans" or "corn" are mutually exclusive.

_____

_____

2. What is the probability that an unlabeled can of vegetables is either green beans or corn? _____

Ben rolls a 1–6 number cube. Find each probability.

3. Ben rolls a 3 or a 4. _____

4. Ben rolls a number greater than 2 or an even number. _____

5. Ben rolls a prime number or an odd number. _____

Of the 400 doctors who attended a conference, 240 practiced family medicine and 130 were from countries outside the United States. One-third of the family medicine practitioners were not from the United States.

6. What is the probability that a doctor practices family medicine or is from the United States? _____

7. What is the probability that a doctor practices family medicine or is not from the United States? _____

8. What is the probability that a doctor does not practice family medicine or is from the United States? _____

Use the data to fill in the Venn diagram. Then solve.

9. Of the 220 people who came into the Italian deli on Friday, 104 bought pizza and 82 used a credit card. Half of the people who bought pizza used a credit card. What is the probability that a customer bought pizza or used a credit card?

Bought Pizza   Used credit card

Solve.

10. There are 6 people in a gardening club. Each gardener orders seeds from a list of 11 different types of seeds available. What is the probability that 2 gardeners will order the same type of seeds? _____

Problem Solving

Of 100 students surveyed, 44 are male and 54 are in favor of a change to a 9-period, 4-day school week. Of those in favor, 20 are female. One student is picked at random from those surveyed.

1. What is the probability that the student is male or favors the change? Use the Venn diagram.

   a. What is represented by the total of $A + B$?

   _____

   b. What is represented by the total of $B + C$?

   _____

   School Week Survey

   A B C

   Male Students   In Favor of the Change

   c. How many of those in favor of the change are male?

   d. Find the values for A, B, and C and label the diagram.

   e. Write and evaluate an expression for the probability that the student is male or favors the change. _____

2. What is the probability that the student is female or opposes the change?

   a. How many students are female? _____

   b. How many students oppose the change? _____

   c. If you draw a Venn diagram to show females and those opposed to the change, what is the meaning and value of the overlapping area?

   _____

   d. Write and evaluate an expression for the probability that the student is female or opposes the change. _____

3. Of the students surveyed, 27 plan to start their own businesses. Of those, 18 are in favor of the change to the school week. Write and evaluate an expression for the probability that a student selected at random plans to start his or her own business or favors the change.

   _____

Sean asks each student to cast a vote for the type of class he or she would prefer. Of the students, 55% voted for online classes, 30% voted for projects, and 15% voted for following the textbook. Choose the letter for the best answer.

4. Which description best describes Sean's experiment?

   A Simple events

   B Compound events

   C Mutually exclusive events

   D Inclusive events

5. What is the probability that a randomly selected student voted for online classes or projects?

   F $\frac{33}{200}$ H $\frac{1}{4}$

   G $\frac{7}{10}$ J $\frac{17}{20}$

© Houghton Mifflin Harcourt Publishing Company

This page provides students with the opportunity to apply concepts from the Common Core in real-world problem situations. There are three different levels of performance tasks:

⭐ **Novice:** These are short word problems that require students to apply the math they have learned in straightforward, real-world situations.

⭐⭐ **Apprentice:** These are more involved problems that guide students step-by-step through more complex tasks. These exercises include more complicated reasoning, writing, and open-ended elements.

⭐⭐⭐ **Expert:** These are open-ended, non-routine problems that, instead of stepping the students through, ask them to choose their own methods for solving and justify their answers and reasoning.

Sample answers

1. $\frac{1}{6}$; no, P(Sam moves back to the beginning) $=$ $\frac{1}{3}$, and $\frac{1}{6} + \frac{1}{3} \neq 1$.

2   40% or 0.4

3. Scoring Guide:

Task	Possible points
a	1 point for the correct answer no, and 1 point for a correct explanation, for example: Since Mel must choose a different tea than Alice, the events are not independent.
b	2 points for a correct Venn diagram: 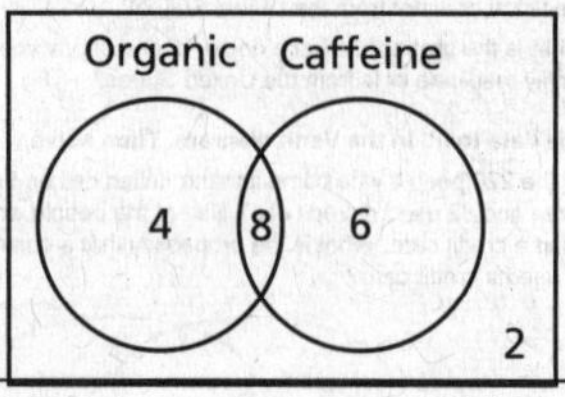
c	2 points for the correct answer: $\frac{4}{7} \approx 0.571$

Total possible points: 6

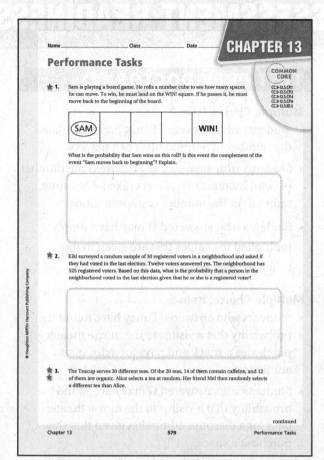

Name_____ Class_____ Date_____

CHAPTER 13

COMMON
CORE
CC-9-12.S.CP.1
CC-9-12.S.CP.2
CC-9-12.S.CP.2
CC-9-12.S.CP.6
CC-9-12.S.ID.5

Performance Tasks

★ 1. Sam is playing a board game. He rolls a number cube to see how many spaces he can move. To win, he must land on the WIN! square. If he passes it, he must move back to the beginning of the board.

SAM				WIN!

What is the probability that Sam wins on this roll? Is this event the complement of the event "Sam moves back to beginning"? Explain.

★ 2. Kiki surveyed a random sample of 30 registered voters in a neighborhood and asked if they had voted in the last election. Twelve voters answered yes. The neighborhood has 525 registered voters. Based on this data, what is the probability that a person in the neighborhood voted in the last election given that he or she is a registered voter?

★ 3. The Teacup serves 20 different teas. Of the 20 teas, 14 of them contain caffeine, and 12 ★ of them are organic. Alice selects a tea at random. Her friend Mel then randomly selects a different tea than Alice.

continued

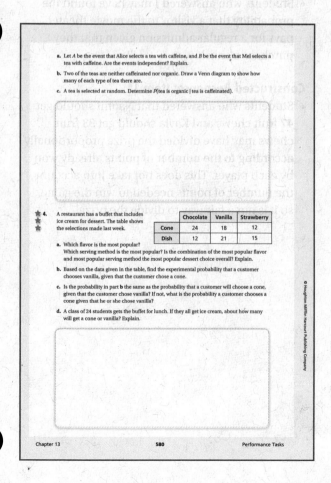

a. Let A be the event that Alice selects a tea with caffeine, and B be the event that Mel selects a tea with caffeine. Are the events independent? Explain.

b. Two of the teas are neither caffeinated nor organic. Draw a Venn diagram to show how many of each type of tea there are.

c. A tea is selected at random. Determine P(tea is organic | tea is caffeinated).

★ 4. A restaurant has a buffet that includes
★ ice cream for dessert. The table shows
★ the selections made last week.

	Chocolate	Vanilla	Strawberry
Cone	24	18	12
Dish	12	21	15

a. Which flavor is the most popular? Which serving method is the most popular? Is the combination of the most popular flavor and most popular serving method the most popular dessert choice overall? Explain.

b. Based on the data given in the table, find the experimental probability that a customer chooses vanilla, given that the customer chose a cone.

c. Is the probability in part b the same as the probability that a customer will choose a cone, given that the customer chose vanilla? If not, what is the probability a customer chooses a cone given that he or she chose vanilla?

d. A class of 24 students gets the buffet for lunch. If they all get ice cream, about how many will get a cone or vanilla? Explain.

---

4. Scoring Guide:

Task	Possible points
a	1 point total for the correct answers *vanilla* and *cone*, and 1 point for correctly noting that the most popular dessert choice is a chocolate cone, not a vanilla cone
b	1 point for the correct answer, $\frac{1}{3}$
c	1 point total for the correct answer *no* and the correct probability, $\frac{6}{13}$
d	1 point for the correct answer of about 18 students, and 1 point for correctly explaining that 75 of 102 or about 73.5% of customers chose either a cone or vanilla, so 73.5% of 24 students, which is $17.64 \approx 18$ students, will get a cone or vanilla.

Total possible points: 6

Standard	Items
CC.9-12.S.CP.1*	1
CC.9-12.S.CP.2*	8
CC.9-12.S.CP.3*	9
CC.9-12.S.CP.4*	5
CC.9-12.S.CP.5*	5
CC.9-12.S.CP.6*	6
CC.9-12.S.CP.7*	4
CC.9-12.S.CP.8(+)*	7
CC.9-12.S.CP.9(+)*	2, 3
CC.9-12.S.MD.6(+)*	11
CC.9-12.S.MD.7(+)*	10

TEST PREP DOCTOR ⊕

Multiple Choice: Item 2
- Students who answered **F** may have calculated the number of permutations of 4 players.
- Students who answered **G** calculated the number of combinations of 9 players taken 4 at a time, rather than the number of permutations.
- Students who answered **H** may have simply multiplied the values that are given in the problem ($9 \cdot 4 \cdot 5 = 180$).

Multiple Choice: Item 6
- Students who answered **F** may have found the probability that a visitor to the movie theater purchases a snack and pays for a discount admission.
- Students who answered **G** may have found the probability that a visitor to the movie theater pays for a discount admission given that they purchase a snack.
- Students who answered **J** may have found the probability that a visitor to the movie theater pays for a regular admission given that they purchase a snack.

Constructed Response: Item 11
- Students who answered that Naomi should get 47 fruit chews and Kayla should get 33 fruit chews may have divided the prize proportionally according to the number of points already won by each player. This does not take into account the number of points needed to win the game, so it is not a fair way to divide the prize.

Name _____ Class _____ Date _____

MULTIPLE CHOICE

1. You spin a spinner with 10 equal sections that are numbered 1 through 10. Event A is rolling an odd number. Event B is rolling a number greater than 5. What is $P(A \cap B)$?

    A. $\frac{1}{8}$

    C. $\frac{1}{2}$

    B. $\frac{1}{5}$

    D. $\frac{4}{5}$

2. There are 9 players on a basketball team. For a team photo, 4 of the players are seated on a row of chairs and 5 players stand behind them. In how many different ways can 4 players be arranged on the row of chairs?

    F. 24

    H. 180

    G. 126

    J. 3024

3. There are 5 peaches and 4 nectarines in a bowl. You randomly choose 2 pieces of fruit to pack in your lunch. What is the probability that you choose 2 peaches?

    A. $\frac{5}{36}$

    C. $\frac{2}{5}$

    B. $\frac{5}{18}$

    D. $\frac{5}{9}$

4. You shuffle the cards shown below and choose one at random. What is the probability that you choose a gray card or an even number?

1	2	4	5	7	9
10	11	13	16	18	19

    F. $\frac{1}{10}$

    H. $\frac{5}{6}$

    G. $\frac{35}{144}$

    J. 1

The two-way table provides data about 240 randomly chosen people who visit a movie theater. Use the table for Items 5 and 6.

	Discount Admission	Regular Admission	TOTAL
Purchases a snack	24	72	96
Purchases no snack	36	108	144
TOTAL	60	180	240

5. Consider the following events.

    Event A: Pays for a regular admission.
    Event B: Purchases a snack.

    Which is the best description of the two events?

    A. complementary events

    B. dependent events

    C. independent events

    D. mutually exclusive events

6. What is the probability that a visitor to the movie theater purchases a snack given that the visitor pays for a discount admission?

    F. 0.1

    H. 0.4

    G. 0.25

    J. 0.75

7. A bag contains 8 yellow marbles and 4 blue marbles. You choose a marble, put it aside, and then choose another marble. What is the probability that you choose two yellow marbles?

    A. $\frac{7}{18}$

    C. $\frac{4}{9}$

    B. $\frac{14}{33}$

    D. $\frac{2}{3}$

8. Events A and B are independent events. Which of the following must be true?

    F. $P(A \text{ and } B) = P(A) \cdot P(B)$

    G. $P(A \text{ and } B) = P(A) + P(B)$

    H. $P(A) = P(B)$

    J. $P(B|A) = P(A|B)$

9. Which expression can you use to calculate the conditional probability of event A given that event B has occurred?

    A. $P(A) + P(B) - P(A \text{ and } B)$

    B. $P(B) \cdot P(A|B)$

    C. $\frac{P(A \text{ and } B)}{P(B)}$

    D. $\frac{P(A)}{P(B)}$

CONSTRUCTED RESPONSE

10. It is known that 1% of all mice in a laboratory have a genetic mutation. A test for the mutation correctly identifies mice that have the mutation 98% of the time. The test correctly identifies mice that do not have the mutation 96% of the time. A lab assistant tests a mouse and finds that the mouse tests positive for the mutation. The lab assistant decides that the mouse must have the mutation. Is this a good decision? Explain.

    No; there is only a 19.8% probability that a mouse that tests positive for the mutation actually has the mutation.

11. Two students, Naomi and Kayla, play a game using the rules shown below. The winner of the game gets a box of 80 fruit chews.

Game Rules
• One student repeatedly tosses a coin.
• When the coin lands heads up, Naomi gets a point.
• When the coin lands tails up, Kayla gets a point.
• The first student to reach 8 points wins the game and gets the fruit chews.

    The game gets interrupted when Naomi has 7 points and Kayla has 5 points. How should the 80 fruit chews be divided between the students given that the game was interrupted at this moment? Explain why your answer provides a fair way to divide the fruit chews.

    Naomi should get $\frac{7}{8}$ of the fruit chews (i.e., 70 fruit chews) and Kayla should get $\frac{1}{8}$ of the fruit chews (i.e., 10 fruit chews). The game would end in at most three additional coin tosses. There are 8 possible outcomes of these tosses: 7 result in a win for Naomi, while 1 results in a win for Kayla.

Correlation of *Explorations in Core Math* to the Common Core State Standards

Standards	Algebra 1	Geometry	Algebra 2
Number and Quantity			
The Real Number System			
CC.9-12.N.RN.1 Explain how the definition of the meaning of rational exponents follows from extending the properties of integer exponents to those values, allowing for a notation for radicals in terms of rational exponents.	Lessons 6-1, 6-2		Lesson 5-6
CC.9-12.N.RN.2 Rewrite expressions involving radicals and rational exponents using the properties of exponents.	Lesson 6-2		Lesson 5-6
CC.9-12.N.RN.3 Explain why the sum or product of two rational numbers is rational; that the sum of a rational number and an irrational number is irrational; and that the product of a nonzero rational number and an irrational number is irrational.	Lesson 6-2		
Quantities			
CC.9-12.N.Q.1 Use units as a way to understand problems and to guide the solution of multi-step problems; choose and interpret units consistently in formulas; choose and interpret the scale and the origin in graphs and data displays.*	Lessons 1-8, 1-9, 3-2, 4-1, 4-9		Lessons 2-8, 10-1
CC.9-12.N.Q.2 Define appropriate quantities for the purpose of descriptive modeling.*	Lessons 4-9, 5-6		
CC.9-12.N.Q.3 Choose a level of accuracy appropriate to limitations on measurement when reporting quantities.*	Lesson 1-10		
The Complex Number System			
CC.9-12.N.CN.1 Know there is a complex number i such that $i^2 = -1$, and every complex number has the form $a + bi$ with a and b real.			Lesson 2-5
CC.9-12.N.CN.2 Use the relation $i^2 = -1$ and the commutative, associative, and distributive properties to add, subtract, and multiply complex numbers.			Lesson 2-9
CC.9-12.N.CN.3(+) Find the conjugate of a complex number; use conjugates to find moduli and quotients of complex numbers.			Lesson 2-9

(+) Advanced   * = Also a Modeling Standard

Explorations in Core Math Geometry   **C1**   Common Core Correlations

Standards	Algebra 1	Geometry	Algebra 2
CC.9-12.N.CN.7 Solve quadratic equations with real coefficients that have complex solutions.			Lesson 2-6
CC.9-12.N.CN.9(+) Know the Fundamental Theorem of Algebra; show that it is true for quadratic polynomials.			Lesson 3-6
Algebra			
Seeing Structure in Expressions			
CC.9-12.A.SSE.1 Interpret expressions that represent a quantity in terms of its context.* a. Interpret parts of an expression, such as terms, factors, and coefficients. b. Interpret complicated expressions by viewing one or more of their parts as a single entity.	Lessons 1-1, 1-8, 6-3, 7-1, 7-2, 7-6		Lessons 2-8, 3-9, 9-5, 12-6
CC.9-12.A.SSE.2 Use the structure of an expression to identify ways to rewrite it.	Lessons 6-5, 6-6, 7-2, 7-3, 7-4, 7-5, 7-6		Lessons 3-6, 12-6
CC.9-12.A.SSE.3 Choose and produce an equivalent form of an expression to reveal and explain properties of the quantity represented by the expression. a. Factor a quadratic expression to reveal the zeros of the function it defines. b. Complete the square in a quadratic expression to reveal the maximum or minimum value of the function it defines. c. Use the properties of exponents to transform expressions for exponential functions.	Lessons 8-3, 8-6, 8-8		Lessons 4-5, 6-1, 6-7
CC.9-12.A.SSE.4 Derive the formula for the sum of a finite geometric series (when the common ratio is not 1), and use the formula to solve problems.			Lessons 9-4, 9-5
Arithmetic with Polynomials and Rational Expressions			
CC.9-12.A.APR.1 Understand that polynomials form a system analogous to the integers, namely, they are closed under the operations of addition, subtraction, and multiplication; add, subtract, and multiply polynomials.	Lessons 6-4, 6-5		Lessons 3-1, 3-2
CC.9-12.A.APR.2 Know and apply the Remainder Theorem: For a polynomial $p(x)$ and a number a, the remainder on division by $x - a$ is $p(a)$, so $p(a) = 0$ if and only if $(x - a)$ is a factor of $p(x)$.			Lessons 3-3, 3-4, 3-6
CC.9-12.A.APR.3 Identify zeros of polynomials when suitable factorizations are available, and use the zeros to construct a rough graph of the function defined by the polynomial.			Lesson 3-5
CC.9-12.A.APR.4 Prove polynomial identities and use them to describe numerical relationships.			Lesson 3-2

(+) Advanced   * = Also a Modeling Standard

Standards	Algebra 1	Geometry	Algebra 2
CC.9-12.A.APR.5(+) Know and apply the Binomial Theorem for the expansion of $(x + y)^n$ in powers of x and y for a positive integer n, where x and y are any numbers, with coefficients determined for example by Pascal's Triangle. (The Binomial Theorem can be proved by mathematical induction or by a combinatorial argument.)			Lesson 3-2
CC.9-12.A.APR.6 Rewrite simple rational expressions in different forms; write $a(x)/b(x)$ in the form $q(x) + r(x)/b(x)$, where $a(x)$, $b(x)$, $q(x)$, and $r(x)$ are polynomials with the degree of $r(x)$ less than the degree of $b(x)$, using inspection, long division, or, for the more complicated examples, a computer algebra system.			Lesson 5-4
CC.9-12.A.APR.7(+) Understand that rational expressions form a system analogous to the rational numbers, closed under addition, subtraction, multiplication, and division by a nonzero rational expression; add, subtract, multiply, and divide rational expressions.			Lessons 5-2, 5-3
Creating Equations			
CC.9-12.A.CED.1 Create equations and inequalities in one variable and use them to solve problems.*	Lessons 1-9, 2-1, 8-6, 8-7	**Lesson 1-4**	Lessons 2-7, 3-9, 5-5
CC.9-12.A.CED.2 Create equations in two or more variables to represent relationships between quantities; graph equations on coordinate axes with labels and scales.*	Lessons 1-7, 3-3, 3-4, 4-5, 4-6, 4-9, 4-10, 8-1, 8-2, 8-4, 8-5, 8-10, 9-2, 9-4		Lessons 2-8, 3-9, 4-8, 6-1, 6-3, 6-6, 6-7, 11-6
CC.9-12.A.CED.3 Represent constraints by equations or inequalities, and by systems of equations and/or inequalities, and interpret solutions as viable or nonviable options in a modeling context.*	Lessons 4-9, 5-6		Lessons 2-8, 3-9, 9-5
CC.9-12.A.CED.4 Rearrange formulas to highlight a quantity of interest, using the same reasoning as in solving equations.*	Lesson 1-6	**Lesson 1-5**	Lessons 4-8, 10-1
Reasoning with Equations and Inequalities			
CC.9-12.A.REI.1. Explain each step in solving a simple equation as following from the equality of numbers asserted at the previous step, starting from the assumption that the original equation has a solution. Construct a viable argument to justify a solution method.	Lessons 1-2, 1-3, 1-4, 1-5, 1-7, 9-4		
CC.9-12.A.REI.2 Solve simple rational and radical equations in one variable, and give examples showing how extraneous solutions may arise.			Lessons 5-5, 5-8
CC.9-12.A.REI.3 Solve linear equations and inequalities in one variable, including equations with coefficients represented by letters.	Lessons 1-2, 1-6, 2-2, 2-3, 2-4, 2-5, 2-6, 2-7		

(+) Advanced   * = Also a Modeling Standard

Standards	Algebra 1	Geometry	Algebra 2
CC.9-12.A.REI.4 Solve quadratic equations in one variable. **a.** Use the method of completing the square to transform any quadratic equation in x into an equation of the form $(x - p)^2 = q$ that has the same solutions. Derive the quadratic formula from this form. **b.** Solve quadratic equations by inspection (e.g., for $x^2 = 49$), taking square roots, completing the square, the quadratic formula and factoring, as appropriate to the initial form of the equation. Recognize when the quadratic formula gives complex solutions and write them as $a \pm bi$ for real numbers a and b.	Lessons 8-6, 8-7, 8-8, 8-9		Lesson 2-6
CC.9-12.A.REI.5 Prove that, given a system of two equations in two variables, replacing one equation by the sum of that equation and a multiple of the other produces a system with the same solutions.	Lesson 5-3		
CC.9-12.A.REI.6 Solve systems of linear equations exactly and approximately (e.g., with graphs), focusing on pairs of linear equations in two variables.	Lessons 5-1, 5-2, 5-3, 5-4, 5-6		
CC.9-12.A.REI.7 Solve a simple system consisting of a linear equation and a quadratic equation in two variables algebraically and graphically.	Lesson 8-10	**Lesson 12-7**	Lesson 12-7
CC.9-12.A.REI.10 Understand that the graph of an equation in two variables is the set of all its solutions plotted in the coordinate plane, often forming a curve (which could be a line).	Lesson 4-2		
CC.9-12.A.REI.11 Explain why the x-coordinates of the points where the graphs of the equations $y = f(x)$ and $y = g(x)$ intersect are the solutions of the equation $f(x) = g(x)$; find the solutions approximately, e.g., using technology to graph the functions, make tables of values, or find successive approximations. Include cases where $f(x)$ and/or $g(x)$ are linear, polynomial, rational, absolute value, exponential, and logarithmic functions.*	Lessons 1-7, 4-6, 8-5, 9-4		Lesson 4-5
CC.9-12.A.REI.12 Graph the solutions to a linear inequality in two variables as a half-plane (excluding the boundary in the case of a strict inequality), and graph the solution set to a system of linear inequalities in two variables as the intersection of the corresponding half-planes.	Lesson 5-5		
Functions			
Interpreting Functions			
CC.9-12.F.IF.1 Understand that a function from one set (called the domain) to another set (called the range) assigns to each element of the domain exactly one element of the range. If f is a function and x is an element of its domain, then $f(x)$ denotes the output of f corresponding to the input x. The graph of f is the graph of the equation $y = f(x)$.	Lessons 3-2, 4-1, 9-3		Lesson 10-3

(+) Advanced   * = Also a Modeling Standard

Explorations in Core Math Geometry

Common Core Correlations

© Houghton Mifflin Harcourt Publishing Company

Standards	Algebra 1	Geometry	Algebra 2
CC.9-12.F.IF.2 Use function notation, evaluate functions for inputs in their domains, and interpret statements that use function notation in terms of a context.	Lessons 3-2, 3-3, 3-4, 3-6, 4-1, 4-5, 4-10, 8-1, 8-2, 8-4, 9-2		Lessons 3-5, 4-4, 4-6, 4-8, 6-3, 6-6, 6-7, 9-1, 11-6
CC.9-12.F.IF.3 Recognize that sequences are functions, sometimes defined recursively, whose domain is a subset of the integers.	Lessons 3-6, 4-1		Lesson 9-1
CC.9-12.F.IF.4 For a function that models a relationship between two quantities, interpret key features of graphs and tables in terms of the quantities, and sketch graphs showing key features given a verbal description of the relationship.*	Lessons 3-1, 3-4, 4-3, 4-5, 4-6, 4-10, 8-1, 8-4		Lessons 2-8, 3-9, 4-8, 6-3, 6-7, 11-6
CC.9-12.F.IF.5 Relate the domain of a function to its graph and, where applicable, to the quantitative relationship it describes.*	Lessons 3-2, 3-4, 4-1, 8-1, 8-2, 9-3		Lessons 1-1, 6-3
CC.9-12.F.IF.6 Calculate and interpret the average rate of change of a function (presented symbolically or as a table) over a specified interval. Estimate the rate of change from a graph.*	Lessons 4-3, 4-4		Lesson 2-8
CC.9-12.F.IF.7 Graph functions expressed symbolically and show key features of the graph, by hand in simple cases and using technology for more complicated cases.* **a.** Graph linear and quadratic functions and show intercepts, maxima, and minima. **b.** Graph square root, cube root, and piecewise-defined functions, including step functions and absolute value functions. **c.** Graph polynomial functions, identifying zeros when suitable factorizations are available, and showing end behavior. **d.** (+) Graph rational functions, identifying zeros and asymptotes when suitable factorizations are available, and showing end behavior. **e.** Graph exponential and logarithmic functions, showing intercepts and end behavior, and trigonometric functions, showing period, midline, and amplitude.	Lessons 3-4, 4-1, 4-5, 4-6, 4-10, 8-1, 8-2, 8-3, 8-4, 9-2, 9-3		Lessons 2-1, 2-2, 2-8, 3-5, 3-7, 4-1, 4-2, 4-3, 4-6, 5-1, 5-4, 6-3, 6-7, 11-1, 11-2, 11-6
CC.9-12.F.IF.8 Write a function defined by an expression in different but equivalent forms to reveal and explain different properties of the function. **a.** Use the process of factoring and completing the square in a quadratic function to show zeros, extreme values, and symmetry of the graph, and interpret these in terms of a context. **b.** Use the properties of exponents to interpret expressions for exponential functions.	Lessons 4-7, 8-3, 8-6		Lessons 2-3, 2-4, 6-1, 6-7
CC.9-12.F.IF.9 Compare properties of two functions each represented in a different way (algebraically, graphically, numerically in tables, or by verbal descriptions).	Lesson 4-1		Lesson 6-2

(+) Advanced   * = Also a Modeling Standard

Standards	Algebra 1	Geometry	Algebra 2
Building Functions			
CC.9-12.F.BF.1 Write a function that describes a relationship between two quantities.* **a.** Determine an explicit expression, a recursive process, or steps for calculation from a context. **b.** Combine standard function types using arithmetic operations. **c.** (+) Compose functions.	Lessons 3-3, 3-4, 4-5, 4-10, 6-4, 8-1, 8-2, 8-4, 9-1		Lessons 3-1, 3-9, 4-8, 5-1, 5-2, 5-3, 5-4, 6-1, 6-3, 6-5, 6-7, 9-1, 9-2, 11-6
CC.9-12.F.BF.2 Write arithmetic and geometric sequences both recursively and with an explicit formula, use them to model situations, and translate between the two forms.*	Lesson 3-6		Lessons 9-3, 9-4
CC.9-12.F.BF.3 Identify the effect on the graph of replacing $f(x)$ by $f(x) + k$, $kf(x)$, $f(kx)$, and $f(x + k)$ for specific values of k (both positive and negative); find the value of k given the graphs. Experiment with cases and illustrate an explanation of the effects on the graph using technology.	Lessons 4-5, 4-10, 8-1, 8-2, 8-4, 9-2		Lessons 1-1, 1-2, 1-3, 2-1, 3-7, 3-8, 4-6, 4-7, 5-1, 5-7, 6-4, 11-2
CC.9-12.F.BF.4 Find inverse functions. **a.** Solve an equation of the form $f(x) = c$ for a simple function f that has an inverse and write an expression for the inverse. **b.** (+) Verify by composition that one function is the inverse of another. **c.** (+) Read values of an inverse function from a graph or a table, given that the function has an inverse. **d.** (+) Produce an invertible function from a non-invertible function by restricting the domain.	Lesson 3-3		Lessons 4-2, 6-6, 6-7
CC.9-12.F.BF.5(+) Understand the inverse relationship between exponents and logarithms and use this relationship to solve problems involving logarithms and exponents.			Lessons 4-3, 4-4, 4-5
Linear, Quadratic, and Exponential Models			
CC.9-12.F.LE.1 Distinguish between situations that can be modeled with linear functions and with exponential functions.* **a.** Prove that linear functions grow by equal differences over equal intervals, and that exponential functions grow by equal factors over equal intervals. **b.** Recognize situations in which one quantity changes at a constant rate per unit interval relative to another. **c.** Recognize situations in which a quantity grows or decays by a constant percent rate per unit interval relative to another.	Lessons 9-3, 9-5		
CC.9-12.F.LE.2 Construct linear and exponential functions, including arithmetic and geometric sequences, given a graph, a description of a relationship, or two input-output pairs (include reading these from a table).*	Lessons 3-3, 3-6, 4-6, 4-7, 9-1, 9-2, 9-3, 9-4		Lessons 9-3, 9-4

(+) Advanced   * = Also a Modeling Standard

© Houghton Mifflin Harcourt Publishing Company

Standards	Algebra 1	Geometry	Algebra 2
CC.9-12.F.LE.3 Observe using graphs and tables that a quantity increasing exponentially eventually exceeds a quantity increasing linearly, quadratically, or (more generally) as a polynomial function.*	Lesson 9-5		Lessons 4-1, 6-1
CC.9-12.F.LE.4 For exponential models, express as a logarithm the solution to $ab^{ct} = d$ where a, c, and d are numbers and the base b is 2, 10, or e; evaluate the logarithm using technology.*			Lesson 4-5
CC.9-12.F.LE.5 Interpret the parameters in a linear or exponential function in terms of a context.*	Lessons 3-3, 4-8, 4-10, 9-3, 9-4		Lesson 4-6
Trigonometric Functions			
CC.9-12.F.TF.1 Understand radian measure of an angle as the length of the arc on the unit circle subtended by the angle.			Lesson 10-2
CC.9-12.F.TF.2 Explain how the unit circle in the coordinate plane enables the extension of trigonometric functions to all real numbers, interpreted as radian measures of angles traversed counterclockwise around the unit circle.			Lesson 10-3
CC.9-12.F.TF.3(+) Use special triangles to determine geometrically the values of sine, cosine, tangent for $\pi/3$, $\pi/4$ and $\pi/6$, and use the unit circle to express the values of sine, cosines, and tangent for x, $\pi + x$, and $2\pi - x$ in terms of their values for x, where x is any real number.			Lesson 10-3
CC.9-12.F.TF.4(+) Use the unit circle to explain symmetry (odd and even) and periodicity of trigonometric functions.			Lesson 11-1
CC.9-12.F.TF.5 Choose trigonometric functions to model periodic phenomena with specified amplitude, frequency, and midline.*			Lesson 11-6
CC.9-12.F.TF.6(+) Understand that restricting a trigonometric function to a domain on which it is always increasing or always decreasing allows its inverse to be constructed.			Lesson 10-4
CC.9-12.F.TF.7(+) Use inverse functions to solve trigonometric equations that arise in modeling contexts; evaluate the solutions using technology, and interpret them in terms of the context.*			Lesson 10-4
CC.9-12.F.TF.8 Prove the Pythagorean identity $\sin^2(\theta) + \cos^2(\theta) = 1$ and use it to calculate trigonometric ratios.			Lesson 11-3
CC.9-12.F.TF.9(+) Prove the addition and subtraction formulas for sine, cosine, and tangent and use them to solve problems.			Lesson 11-4, 11-5

(+) Advanced   * = Also a Modeling Standard

Standards	Algebra 1	Geometry	Algebra 2
Geometry			
Congruence			
CC.9-12.G.CO.1 Know precise definitions of angle, circle, perpendicular line, parallel line, and line segment, based on the undefined notions of point, line, distance along a line, and distance around a circular arc.		Lessons 1-1, 1-4, 12-3	
CC.9-12.G.CO.2 Represent transformations in the plane using, e.g., transparencies and geometry software; describe transformations as functions that take points in the plane as inputs and give other points as outputs. Compare transformations that preserve distance and angle to those that do not (e.g., translation versus horizontal stretch).		Lessons 1-7, 7-2, 7-6, 9-1, 9-2, 9-3, 9-7, 10-5	
CC.9-12.G.CO.3 Given a rectangle, parallelogram, trapezoid, or regular polygon, describe the rotations and reflections that carry it onto itself.		Lesson 9-5	
CC.9-12.G.CO.4 Develop definitions of rotations, reflections, and translations in terms of angles, circles, perpendicular lines, parallel lines, and line segments.		Lessons 9-1, 9-2	
CC.9-12.G.CO.5 Given a geometric figure and a rotation, reflection, or translation, draw the transformed figure using, e.g., graph paper, tracing paper, or geometry software. Specify a sequence of transformations that will carry a given figure onto another.		Lessons 1-7, 4-1, 9-1, 9-2, 9-3, 9-4, 9-6	
CC.9-12.G.CO.6 Use geometric descriptions of rigid motions to transform figures and to predict the effect of a given rigid motion on a given figure; given two figures, use the definition of congruence in terms of rigid motions to decide if they are congruent.		Lessons 4-1, 9-1, 9-2, 9-3	
CC.9-12.G.CO.7 Use the definition of congruence in terms of rigid motions to show that two triangles are congruent if and only if corresponding pairs of sides and corresponding pairs of angles are congruent.		Lessons 4-4, 4-5	
CC.9-12.G.CO.8 Explain how the criteria for triangle congruence (ASA, SAS, and SSS) follow from the definition of congruence in terms of rigid motions.		Lessons 4-5, 4-6	
CC.9-12.G.CO.9 Prove geometric theorems about lines and angles.		Lessons 1-4, 2-6, 2-7, 3-2, 3-4, 4-5, 6-6, 12-5	
CC.9-12.G.CO.10 Prove theorems about triangles.		Lessons 4-3, 4-6, 4-9, 5-3, 5-4, 5-5, 5-6	
CC.9-12.G.CO.11 Prove theorems about parallelograms.		Lessons 6-2, 6-3, 6-4	
CC.9-12.G.CO.12 Make formal geometric constructions with a variety of tools and methods (compass and straightedge, string, reflective devices, paper folding, dynamic geometry software, etc.).		Lessons 1-2, 1-3, 3-3, 3-4	

(+) Advanced   * = Also a Modeling Standard

Standards	Algebra 1	Geometry	Algebra 2
CC.9-12.G.CO.13 Construct an equilateral triangle, a square, and a regular hexagon inscribed in a circle.		Lesson 6-1	
Similarity, Right Triangles, and Trigonometry			
CC.9-12.G.SRT.1 Verify experimentally the properties of dilations given by a center and a scale factor: **a.** A dilation takes a line not passing through the center of the dilation to a parallel line, and leaves a line passing through the center unchanged. **b.** The dilation of a line segment is longer or shorter in the ratio given by the scale factor.		Lesson 7-2	
CC.9-12.G.SRT.2 Given two figures, use the definition of similarity in terms of similarity transformations to decide if they are similar; explain using similarity transformations the meaning of similarity for triangles as the equality of all corresponding angles and the proportionality of all corresponding pairs of sides.		Lessons 7-2, 7-3	
CC.9-12.G.SRT.3 Use the properties of similarity transformations to establish the AA criterion for two triangles to be similar.		Lesson 7-3	
CC.9-12.G.SRT.4 Prove theorems about triangles.		Lessons 7-4, 8-1	
CC.9-12.G.SRT.5 Use congruence and similarity criteria for triangles to solve problems and prove relationships in geometric figures.		Lessons 4-5, 4-6, 6-2, 6-3, 6-4, 7-4, 7-5	
CC.9-12.G.SRT.6 Understand that by similarity, side ratios in right triangles are properties of the angles in the triangle, leading to definitions of trigonometric ratios for acute angles.		Lessons 5-8, 8-2	
CC.9-12.G.SRT.7 Explain and use the relationship between the sine and cosine of complementary angles.		Lesson 8-2	
CC.9-12.G.SRT.8 Use trigonometric ratios and the Pythagorean Theorem to solve right triangles in applied problems.		Lessons 5-7, 5-8, 8-2, 8-3, 8-4	
CC.9-12.G.SRT.9(+) Derive the formula $A = 1/2\ ab \sin(C)$ for the area of a triangle by drawing an auxiliary line from a vertex perpendicular to the opposite side.		Lesson 10-1	
CC.9-12.G.SRT.10(+) Prove the Laws of Sines and Cosines and use them to solve problems.		Lesson 8-5	Lessons 10-5, 10-6
CC.9-12.G.SRT.11(+) Understand and apply the Law of Sines and the Law of Cosines to find unknown measurements in right and non-right triangles (e.g., surveying problems, resultant forces).		Lessons 8-5, 8-6	Lessons 10-5, 10-6
Circles			
CC.9-12.G.C.1 Prove that all circles are similar.		Lesson 7-2	

(+) Advanced   * = Also a Modeling Standard

Explorations in Core Math Geometry

Common Core Correlations

© Houghton Mifflin Harcourt Publishing Company

Standards	Algebra 1	Geometry	Algebra 2
CC.9-12.G.C.2 Identify and describe relationships among inscribed angles, radii, and chords.		**Lessons 12-1, 12-2, 12-4, 12-6**	
CC.9-12.G.C.3 Construct the inscribed and circumscribed circles of a triangle, and prove properties of angles for a quadrilateral inscribed in a circle.		**Lessons 5-2, 12-4**	
CC.9-12.G.C.4(+) Construct a tangent line from a point outside a given circle to the circle.		**Lesson 12-5**	
CC.9-12.G.C.5 Derive using similarity the fact that the length of the arc intercepted by an angle is proportional to the radius, and define the radian measure of the angle as the constant of proportionality; derive the formula for the area of a sector.		**Lesson 12-3**	Lesson 10-1
Expressing Geometric Properties with Equations			
CC.9-12.G.GPE.1 Derive the equation of a circle of given center and radius using the Pythagorean Theorem; complete the square to find the center and radius of a circle given by an equation.		**Lesson 12-7**	Lesson 12-2
CC.9-12.G.GPE.2 Derive the equation of a parabola given a focus and directrix.		**Lesson 5-1**	Lesson 12-5
CC.9-12.G.GPE.3(+) Derive the equations of ellipses and hyperbolas given the foci, using the fact that the sum or difference of distances from the foci is constant.			Lessons 12-3, 12-4
CC.9-12.G.GPE.4 Use coordinates to prove simple geometric theorems algebraically.		**Lessons 1-6, 4-2, 4-8, 5-3, 5-4, 6-5, 12-7**	Lesson 12-1
CC.9-12.G.GPE.5 Prove the slope criteria for parallel and perpendicular lines and use them to solve geometric problems (e.g., find the equation of line parallel or perpendicular to a given line that passes through a given point).		**Lessons 3-5, 3-6, 4-7**	
CC.9-12.G.GPE.6 Find the point on a directed line segment between two given points that partitions the segment in a given ratio.		**Lesson 1-6**	
CC.9-12.G.GPE.7 Use coordinates to compute perimeters of polygons and areas of triangles and rectangles, e.g., using the distance formula.*		**Lessons 4-2, 10-4**	
Geometric Measurement and Dimension			
CC.9-12.G.GMD.1 Give an informal argument for the formulas for the circumference of a circle, area of a circle, volume of a cylinder, pyramid, and cone.		**Lessons 10-2, 11-2, 11-3, 12-3**	
CC.9-12.G.GMD.2(+) Give an informal argument using Cavalieri's principle for the formulas for the volume of a sphere and other solid figures.		**Lessons 11-2, 11-4**	
CC.9-12.G.GMD.3 Use volume formulas for cylinders, pyramids, cones, and spheres to solve problems.*		**Lessons 11-2, 11-3, 11-4**	

(+) Advanced   * = Also a Modeling Standard

© Houghton Mifflin Harcourt Publishing Company

Standards	Algebra 1	Geometry	Algebra 2
CC.9-12.G.GMD.4 Identify the shapes of two-dimensional cross-sections of three-dimensional objects, and identify three-dimensional objects generated by rotations of two-dimensional objects.		Lesson 11-1	
Modeling with Geometry			
CC.9-12.G.MG.1 Use geometric shapes, their measures, and their properties to describe objects (e.g., modeling a tree trunk or a human torso as a cylinder).*		Lessons 10-2, 10-3, 12-6	
CC.9-12.G.MG.2 Apply concepts of density based on area and volume in modeling situations (e.g., persons per square mile, BTUs per cubic foot).*		Lessons 10-4, 11-2	
CC.9-12.G.MG.3 Apply geometric methods to solve design problems (e.g., designing an object or structure to satisfy physical constraints or minimize cost; working with typographic grid systems based on ratios).*		Lessons 7-5, 10-3, 11-2	
Statistics and Probability			
Interpreting Categorical and Quantitative Data			
CC.9-12.S.ID.1 Represent data with plots on the real number line (dot plots, histograms, and box plots).*	Lessons 10-2, 10-3, 10-4		Lesson 8-1
CC.9-12.S.ID.2 Use statistics appropriate to the shape of the data distribution to compare center (median, mean) and spread (interquartile range, standard deviation) of two or more different data sets.*	Lessons 10-2, 10-3, 10-4		
CC.9-12.S.ID.3 Interpret differences in shape, center, and spread in the context of the data sets, accounting for possible effects of extreme data points (outliers).*	Lesson 10-4		Lesson 8-1
CC.9-12.S.ID.4 Use the mean and standard deviation of a data set to fit it to a normal distribution and to estimate population percentages. Recognize that there are data sets for which such a procedure is not appropriate. Use calculators, spreadsheets, and tables to estimate areas under the normal curve.*			Lesson 8-8
CC.9-12.S.ID.5 Summarize categorical data for two categories in two-way frequency tables. Interpret relative frequencies in the context of the data (including joint, marginal, and conditional relative frequencies). Recognize possible associations and trends in the data.*	Lesson 10-5		

(+) Advanced   * = Also a Modeling Standard

© Houghton Mifflin Harcourt Publishing Company

Explorations in Core Math Geometry   **C11**   Common Core Correlations

Standards	Algebra 1	Geometry	Algebra 2
CC.9-12.S.ID.6 Represent data on two quantitative variables on a scatter plot, and describe how the variables are related.* **a.** Fit a function to the data; use functions fitted to data to solve problems in the context of the data. **b.** Informally assess the fit of a function by plotting and analyzing residuals. **c.** Fit a linear function for a scatter plot that suggests a linear association.	Lessons 3-5, 4-8, 9-4		Lessons 1-4, 6-1, 6-7
CC.9-12.S.ID.7 Interpret the slope (rate of change) and the intercept (constant term) of a linear model in the context of the data.*	Lessons 3-5, 4-8		
CC.9-12.S.ID.8 Compute (using technology) and interpret the correlation coefficient of a linear fit.*	Lesson 3-5		
CC.9-12.S.ID.9 Distinguish between correlation and causation.*	Lesson 3-5		
Making Inferences and Justifying Conclusions			
CC.9-12.S.IC.1 Understand statistics as a process for making inferences about population parameters based on a random sample from that population.*			Lesson 8-2
CC.9-12.S.IC.2 Decide if a specified model is consistent with results from a given data-generating process, e.g., using simulation.*			Lesson 8-6
CC.9-12.S.IC.3 Recognize the purposes of and differences among sample surveys, experiments, and observational studies; explain how randomization relates to each.*			Lesson 8-3
CC.9-12.S.IC.4 Use data from a sample survey to estimate a population mean or proportion; develop a margin of error through the use of simulation models for random sampling.*			Lesson 8-5
CC.9-12.S.IC.5 Use data from a randomized experiment to compare two treatments; use simulations to decide if differences between parameters are significant.*			Lesson 8-4
CC.9-12.S.IC.6 Evaluate reports based on data.*			Lesson 8-3
Conditional Probability and the Rules of Probability			
CC.9-12.S.CP.1 Describe events as subsets of a sample space (the set of outcomes) using characteristics (or categories) of the outcomes, or as unions, intersections, or complements of other events ("or," "and," "not").*	Lessons 10-5, 10-6	**Lesson 10-6**	
CC.9-12.S.CP.2 Understand that two events A and B are independent if the probability of A and B occurring together is the product of their probabilities, and use this characterization to determine if they are independent.*	Lesson 10-7	**Lesson 13-3**	Lesson 7-3

(+) Advanced   * = Also a Modeling Standard

© Houghton Mifflin Harcourt Publishing Company

Standards	Algebra 1	Geometry	Algebra 2
CC.9-12.S.CP.3 Understand the conditional probability of A given B as P(A and B)/P(B), and interpret independence of A and B as saying that the conditional probability of A given B is the same as the probability of A, and the conditional probability of B given A is the same as the probability of B.*	Lesson 10-7	**Lessons 13-3, 13-4**	Lessons 7-3, 7-4
CC.9-12.S.CP.4 Construct and interpret two-way frequency tables of data when two categories are associated with each object being classified. Use the two-way table as a sample space to decide if events are independent and to approximate conditional probabilities.*		**Lesson 13-3**	Lesson 7-3
CC.9-12.S.CP.5 Recognize and explain the concepts of conditional probability and independence in everyday language and everyday situations.*		**Lessons 13-3, 13-4**	Lessons 7-3, 7-4
CC.9-12.S.CP.6 Find the conditional probability of A given B as the fraction of B's outcomes that also belong to A, and interpret the answer in terms of the model.*		**Lesson 13-4**	Lesson 7-4
CC.9-12.S.CP.7 Apply the Addition Rule, P(A or B) = P(A) + P(B) − P(A and B), and interpret the answer in terms of the model.*		**Lesson 13-5**	Lesson 7-5
CC.9-12.S.CP.8(+) Apply the general Multiplication Rule in a uniform probability model, P(A and B) = P(A)P(B|A) = P(B)P(A|B), and interpret the answer in terms of the model.*	Lesson 10-7	**Lesson 13-3**	Lesson 7-3
CC.9-12.S.CP.9(+) Use permutations and combinations to compute probabilities of compound events and solve problems.*		**Lesson 13-1**	Lesson 7-1
Using Probability to Make Decisions			
CC.9-12.S.MD.3(+) Develop a probability distribution for a random variable defined for a sample space in which theoretical probabilities can be calculated; find the expected value.*			Lesson 8-6
CC.9-12.S.MD.5(+) Develop a probability distribution for a random variable defined for a sample space in which probabilities are assigned empirically; find the expected value.*			Lesson 8-6
CC.9-12.S.MD.6(+) Use probabilities to make fair decisions (e.g., drawing by lots, using a random number generator).*		**Lesson 13-2**	Lesson 7-2
CC.9-12.S.MD.7(+) Analyze decisions and strategies using probability concepts (e.g., product testing, medical testing, pulling a hockey goalie at the end of a game).*			Lesson 8-8

(+) Advanced   * = Also a Modeling Standard